A WESLEYAN THEOLOGY OF HOLY LIVING FOR THE TWENTY-FIRST CENTURY:

The Pursuit of Perfection Across Twenty Centuries

Volume Two

Vic Reasoner

W0008232

Fundamental
Wesleyan
Publishers

2120 Culverson Ave
Evansville, IN 47714-4811

© 2012 Victor Paul Reasoner
ISBN 978-0-9761003-2-4

Library of Congress Control Number:
2011940557

Dedicated to
Beverly Nora Brush Reasoner,
my wife since December 23, 1976.
Although she knows I am not perfect, she loves me anyway.
οὐχ ὅτι ἤδη τετελείωμαι

CONTENTS

CHAPTER 6
CHRISTIAN PERFECTION and METHODISM

Major Influences on Methodism

John Wesley did not create a new doctrine of holiness. From the time of the early Church to Wesley's day the doctrine of Christian perfection was perpetuated. This is what Wesley meant by defining Methodism as "the true *old Christianity.*" After describing an obedient, ethical, loving faith, Wesley exclaimed "This is true, primitive Christianity."[1] Thus, Wesley emphasized an ethical primitivism. Donald Dayton concluded that "Wesley was not primarily interested in the recovery of lost gifts of the Spirit of apostolic or patristic Christianity, but rather more of norms of behavior and conduct."[2] Claude Thompson wrote that Methodism was a recovery of Christian *koinonia* which sought to reaffirm the basic Christian ethic, not as legalism, but as a new life. Methodism also sought to restore primitive Christian doctrines.[3]

Wesley was aware of the early Church Fathers. He reprinted extracts from Clement, Ignatius, and Polycarp in *The Christian Library*. For the most part these early writers advocated perfection, but were not specific concerning how one attains it. They were more devotional than theological. In general the early Church Fathers emphasized a perfection based upon the grace of God joined with the faith of man which produced these three aspects of perfection in this life: the two great commands to love God and our neighbor, freedom from sin (but not necessarily sinlessness), and conformity to the image and likeness of God.[4]

George Peck concluded that the doctrine of evangelical perfection did not originate with Wesley. While not every facet of the Wesleyan emphasis is found in the early Church Fathers, the foundational elements can be culled from the writings of the best theologians in all ages since the apostles.[5] Yet John

---

[1]Wesley, *Journal*, 16 September 1739; *Works*, 10:85.

[2]Dayton, *Theological Roots of Pentecostalism*, 42; 45.

[3]Thompson, "Witness of American Methodism," 184-190.

[4]Bounds, *Doctrine of Christian Perfection*, 143-169.

[5]Peck, *Christian Perfection*, 66.

McClintock declared,

> We are the only church in history, from the apostles' time until now, that has put forward as its very elemental thought — the great central pervading idea of the whole Book of God from the beginning to the end — the holiness of the human soul, heart, mind and will. Go through all the confessions of all the churches, and you will find this in no other.[6]

Pope explained that while the Methodist doctrine was simply the doctrine of former ages, one element, formerly indistinct, was cleared up. Methodism emphasized "entire sanctification of the believer a provision of the new covenant directly administered by the Holy Spirit to faith. . . . The Methodist doctrine is the only one that has consistently and boldly maintained the possibility of the destruction of the carnal mind, or the inbred sin of our fallen nature. . . . The combination of the two elements, the negative annihilation of the principle of sin and the positive effusion of perfect love, is, it may be said, peculiar to Methodist theology as such."[7]

James Arminius wrote that the regenerate could not perfectly keep God's precepts without the grace of Christ. "But while I never asserted that a believer could perfectly keep the precepts of Christ in this life, I never denied it, but always left it as a matter to be decided." Arminius concluded by an appeal to the writings of Augustine in which he concluded that "it is possible for a man to live in this world without sin." According to Arminius, Augustine also said, "Let Pelagius confess, *that it is possible for man to be without sin*, in no other way than *by the grace of Christ*, and we will be at peace with each other."[8] Arminius also wrote

> This sanctification is not completed in a single moment; but sin, from whose dominion we have been delivered through the cross and death of Christ, is weakened more and more by daily losses, and the inner man is day by day renewed more and more, while we carry about with us in our bodies the death of Christ, and the outward man is perishing.

---

[6]This address, from the first president of Drew Theological Seminary, was delivered 25 January, 1866. Cited by Curtis, *Christian Faith*, 372.

[7]Pope, *Compendium*, 3:88, 97.

[8]Arminius, *Works*, 1:672-684. Augustine seemed both to affirm and deny this conclusion at different stages of his writings. See pp. 365-367. This statement comes from Augustine's *Retractions* ["On Nature and Grace," 2.42, chapter 11 "Grace Subtly Acknowledged by Pelagius"], written later in his life.

Then he raised a question for discussion, "Does the death of the body bring the perfection and completion of sanctification — and how is this effect produced?"[9] Here Arminius is questioning the Calvinistic doctrine of sanctification in the article of death: "If sanctification is a gracious work, how can the enemy death complete it?"[10]

Pope concluded that while the early Arminians wrote much on Christian perfection, they did not lay down any firm principles on this subject. Their statements, however, contain the germ of the doctrine which Methodism developed.[11] George Peck also recognized the views of Arminius on Christian perfection were in a state of development. Episcopius and Limborch built upon this foundation by contenting for a perfection which is according to the requirements of the gospel and the covenant of grace and not according to law and works. Yet these men were not as specific or consistent in their teaching as Wesley.[12]

---

[9]Arminius, *Works*, 2:409-410.

[10]Bangs, *Arminius*, 346.

[11]Pope, *Compendium*, 3:84. However, Flew wrote that he did not find justification for Pope's assumption that Wesley's doctrine of perfection was indebted to the Arminian divines [*Idea of Perfection*, vii].

[12]Peck, *Christian Perfection*, 143-146. Rather than claim that since God is sovereign he may diminish his requirements and prescribe a law mixed with some grace and indulgence, it would be better to maintain that grace enables us to keep his law and that he imputes perfection where our motive is pure love. The issue goes back to a proper view of the atonement. A governmental view, as developed by the Remonstrants, does not understand that divine law must be satisfied. See the discussion in Reasoner, *Romans Commentary*, 141-154.

George Peck sought to shield Methodist teaching from the Presbyterian accusation that it was a legal perfectionism of works. This controversy was initiated by the perfectionistic teachings from Oberlin College. Peck also sought to clarify the differences between Oberlin and Methodist teaching [Cooley, *Possibilities of Grace*, 1-2]. On the issue of legal or evangelical perfection, Peck cited from Wesley's *Plain Account* questions 1-9 [Peck, *Christian Perfection*, 219-225]. Basically, Wesley taught that faith is the condition for salvation, not obedience to the law. The law is not abolished, but faith is imputed for righteousness and love is the fulfillment of the law. George Peck declared that "perfect obedience to the moral law is impracticable during the present probationary state" and that "the Christian perfection attainable, does not imply perfect obedience to the moral law." Yet his denial of the possibility of legal perfection does not mean that God has changed his law, but that he imputes salvation on the basis of faith and he imputes perfection on the basis of faith and love. Thus Peck declared that Wesleyans believe the moral law has been superseded by the law of faith only "as the condition of human acceptance" [*Christian Perfection*, 221; 242; 244]. Peck complained that Wesleyans were unfairly accused of lowering the standard of

Simon Episcopius, educated under Arminius, drew up a confession of faith which was signed by the Remonstrants. Sanctification was defined in this document.

> Sanctification in special manner so called (for otherwise sometimes in the Sacred Scripture it is taken for Regeneration also or Conversion, or effectual Calling (of which before) or finally for any Spiritual cleansing whatever, although it be only outward) is certain, more perfect, and which continually grows and increaseth, separation of the Sons or Children of God from this impure or unclean World, being partly a more plentiful and fuller enlightening of true Believers, and such as out of Faith diligently perform and do their duty in the knowledge of the Will of God (which even God oftentimes is wont to effect and work in many and admirable manners) partly a more effectual and through extimulation or engaging of them unto a constant hatred of Sin, and study of Holiness & true Godliness, and a confirmation of them in this zeal or earnest affection: so that the Will of a Man that is a true Believer is made more prone and inclined, yea more cheerful unto virtue every day than other: And these obstacles or hindrances, which otherwise he is wont to meet with in his study of piety and virtue, he either suffereth them not to be laid in his way, or being laid he diligently and carefully removes them, and courageously and cheerfully overcomes them.[13]

While the subject of Christian perfection is not explicitly addressed, at the Synod of Dort Gomarus charged the Remonstrants with holding several other grievous heresies, besides the errors of the five articles. Among those additional "heresies" was "the perfection of man in this life." Episcopius concluded

> Whether a man, assisted by divine grace, can keep all the commands of God, even to a perfect fulfillment, that is, using the word love in a general manner for keeping the commandments, whether he can love as much as he ought to love according to the requirement of the gospel, or according to the covenant of grace?

---

holiness required by God's holy law [p. 237]. Thus, Calvinists tend to reject Christian perfection by characterizing it as legal perfection. Peck answers that objection without advocating antinomianism.

[13]Episcopius, *Declaration of the Ministers*, 211-212.

I, indeed, have no doubt on this point.[14]

Another Remonstrant, Philipp van Limborch (1633-1712) stated that there is a "perfection in being correspondent to the provisions and terms of the divine covenant. It is not sinless or an absolutely perfect obedience, but such as consists in a sincere love of piety, absolutely excluding every habit of sin."[15] Limborch rejected the opinion of Pelagius that a man might by his own strength fulfill the whole law of God. Limborch then considered three opinions regarding the possibility of keeping the commandments of our Savior. The first opinion was that a man may, by the grace of God, arrive at such a degree of perfection as not to be tempted to sin. This way is too narrow and defines a perfection which is only available in the other world. A second opinion was that a man may not keep the commandments of God, even though he be assisted by the grace of God. This way is too broad and puts off to the next world a perfection which we may obtain here. Limborch then advocated a middle opinion, that a man may, by the assistance of God's grace, keep the precepts commanded. He rejected the first opinion as absurd and recognized the real debate was between the second and third options.[16]

It was left to Wesley to develop this point, although he did not develop it in a vacuum.[17] In his introduction to *A Plain Account of Christian Perfection* Wesley stated that Jeremy Taylor, Thomas à Kempis, and William Law had been the most helpful.

Wesley also incorporated the Calvinistic/Lutheran emphasis on faith, not merit, and the concept of social holiness. Wesley carried the emphasis of Martin Luther on justification on to sanctification. Wesley declared, "Who has wrote more ably than Martin Luther on justification by faith alone? And who was more ignorant of the doctrine of sanctification, or more confused in his conceptions of it?"[18] Thus, Wesley synthesized five major streams of Christian thought: Roman Catholic, Eastern Orthodox, Anglican, Calvinistic, and Lutheran.

---

[14]Peck, *Christian Perfection*, 129; 134; Pope, *Compendium*, 3:84.

[15]Limborch, *Institutiones Theologiae Christianae* (1686); Quoted by Wiley, *Christian Theology*, 2:454. See also the discussion of Pope, *Compendium*, 3:84.

[16]Peck, *Christian Perfection*, 136-143.

[17]Gaddis concluded that Methodist perfectionism was a cross between the corporate type of mystical perfection found in Pietism and the humanistic type of perfection inherent in Arminianism [*Christian Perfection in America*, 160]. This analysis is inadequate, but Gaddis was working from the five types of perfection cited on p. 290 of this book.

[18]Wesley, "On God's Vineyard,"Sermon #107, 1.5.

Kempis, a Roman Catholic monk of the fourteenth century, wrote *The Imitation of Christ*. Wesley found the same emphasis upon "inward religion, the religion of the heart" as he had found in Taylor.

> In the year 1726, I met with Kempis's "Christian's Pattern." The nature and extent of inward religion, the religion of the heart, now appeared to me in a stronger light than ever it had done before. I saw, that giving even all my life to God (supposing it possible to do this, and go no farther) would profit me nothing, unless I gave my heart, yea, all my heart, to him. I saw, that "simplicity of intention, and purity of affection," one design in all we speak or do, and one desire ruling all our tempers, are indeed "the wings of the soul," without which she can never ascend to the mount of God.[19]

Wesley also drew from the Roman Catholic mystics. Cell said that Wesleyan theology was a synthesis of the Protestant ethic of grace with the Catholic ethic of holiness.[20] Yet Colin Williams objected that the Catholic goal of perfection sees man as enabled by grace to rise up the ladder of merit. "This Catholic view of holiness cannot be molded onto the Protestant view of grace. In the Protestant view grace is the free gift of God, and man can never merit his salvation. . . . If it is true that Wesley accepted the Catholic ethic of holiness, it must also be true that he accepted the Catholic and abandoned the Protestant view of grace. . . . Wesley's view is one of sanctification by faith alone." Thus, Wesley built his doctrine of Christian perfection on the basis of justification by faith, not on the basis of faith and works.[21] Wesley denied that his teaching is what the Roman church of his day taught.

> The perfection I teach is perfect love; loving God with all the heart; receiving Christ as Prophet, Priest, and King to reign alone over all our thoughts, words, and actions. The Papists neither teach nor believe this: Give even the devil his due. They teach, there is no perfection here which is not consistent with venial sins; and among venial sins they commonly reckon simple

---

[19]Wesley, *Works*, 11:366-367; see also *Journal*, 14 May 1765.

[20]Cell, *Rediscovery of John Wesley*, 361.

[21]Williams, *John Wesley's Theology Today*, 174-175.

fornication.[22]

Wesley, of course, rejected the Catholic emphasis on the priesthood, but could appreciate the holiness ethic of the mystics within the Roman tradition. Their devotion rose above the corruption of the institution. In his sermon "On God's Vineyard," Wesley recommends Catholic writers Francis de Sales and Juan de Castaniza as having written "strongly and scripturally on sanctification." But he goes on the say that they were unacquainted with the nature of justification because of the Council of Trent which confused sanctification and justification. Thus, the Roman Catholic emphasis was upon self-discipline, appropriating the means of grace provided by the church, until one reached the point of loving God with his whole heart and his neighbor as himself. When this point was attained, then God could justify. Wesley approved of the goal, but not the method.[23] Robert Tuttle concluded that as Wesley approached his conversion at Aldersgate he turned away from mysticism. However, the doctrine of Christian perfection was the area where Wesley retained the mystics goal of "pure distinterested love attainable in this life, resignation, the continual practice of the presence of God; that is, praying without ceasing and in everything giving thanks."[24] Wesley explained,

> In 1729, two young men, reading the Bible, saw they could not be saved without holiness, followed after it, and incited other so to do. In 1737 they saw holiness comes by faith. They saw likewise, that men are justified before they are sanctified; but still holiness was their point. God then thrust them out, utterly against their will, to raise a holy people.[25]

---

[22]Wesley, *Works*, 12:239.

[23]However, this order of salvation, that a life of holy endeavor preceded justification, was expressed in "The Circumcision of the Heart," Sermon #17. It was written in 1733, five years before his conversion. He wrote that he had begun to study this doctrine around 1729 and after weighing this for some years he openly declared his sentiments before Oxford University on January 1, 1733 in the sermon on the Circumcision of the Heart [*Letter* to William Dodd, 5 Feb 1756].

After his Aldersgate experience, he added to ¶ 1.7 in 1748, "that I 'have an advocate with the Father', that 'Jesus Christ the righteous is' *my* Lord, and 'the propitiation for *my* sins.' I know he 'hath loved *me*, and given himself for *me*'. He 'hath reconciled *me*, even *me* to God'; and I 'have redemption through his blood, even the forgiveness of sins'.

[24]Tuttle, *Mysticism in the Wesleyan Tradition*, 147-150.

[25]Wesley, *Works*, 8:300.

Wesley's purpose for Methodism was to "reform the nation, particularly the Church; and to spread scriptural holiness over the land."[26] Concerning Christian perfection, Wesley declared that "this doctrine is the grand depositum which God has lodged with the people called Methodists; and for the sake of propagating this chiefly He appeared to raise us up."[27]

Albert Outler labeled Wesley a conjunctive theologian.[28] Outler concluded that Wesley represented a third alternative to Protestantism and Catholicism, "a Protestant doctrine of original sin minus most of the other elements in classical Protestant soteriology, *plus* a catholic doctrine of perfection *without* its full panoply of priesthood and priestcraft."[29]

The Eastern Influence

Wesley also incorporated from the Eastern Orthodox tradition the dynamic of perfecting grace. Writers from the Eastern Orthodox tradition included Basil and his brother Gregory of Nyssa, Chrysostom, and Macarius the Egyptian. The significance of these writers was their emphasis upon perfection as a process rather than a state. They emphasized perfecting grace, not a perfected state. Perfection meant becoming that which God intended us to be. However, Heitzenrater has demonstrated that Wesley's reliance on Eastern Orthodox theology was not as great as has sometimes been claimed.[30]

Gregory defined Christianity as an imitation of the divine nature of the incarnate Son. He defined perfection as a life in accordance with virtue. By virtue Gregory meant purity and freedom from every passion and every evil. Gregory specified nine areas in which Christ had dominion and in which the Christian is to imitate Christ: justice, wisdom and power, truth, goodness, life, salvation, incorruptibility, permanence, lack of change.[31] Gregory taught this perfection began at baptism and was sustained by the sacrament of communion. He concluded that we should never stop growing towards what is better and never place any limit on perfection. For Gregory the recovery of purity begins with the release from marriage and restoration to the original state of man in Paradise. He

[26]Wesley, *Works*, 8:299.

[27]Wesley, *Letter* to Robert Carr Brackenbury, 15 September 1790.

[28]Outler, "Beyond Pietism," 13.

[29]Outler, *Theology in the Wesleyan Spirit*, 33.

[30]Heitzenrater, "John Wesley's Reading,"25-32. T.A. Noble also cautions against overemphasizing Eastern influence in Wesley's theology in "East and West in the Theology of John Wesley." According to Ted Campbell there are 201 references in Wesley's writings to the early church Fathers. Some are direct quotes, while others are passing references. Half are allusions to something written by the author. They are listed in Appendix 2 [*Christian Antiquity*, 125-134].

[31]Callahan, *Saint Gregory of Nyssa*, 84.

saw virginity as perfection.[32] Unlike Gregory, Wesley put grace prior to works in relation to holiness.[33]

In the Thomas Jackson edition of Wesley's sermons, "On the Holy Spirit," Sermon #141 was actually written by John Gambold, an Eastern patristics scholar. It emphasizes participation in the divine Spirit through regeneration.[34]

The Anglican Influence

Within Anglicanism there also developed a pietistic emphasis which saw holiness as the cultivation of virtue. Thomas Aquinas had emphasized the three theological virtues of faith, hope, and love which can only be imparted supernaturally. These virtues are to be integrated with and expressed through the four cardinal virtues of prudence, temperance, justice, and fortitude. Thus, there is no holiness without moral righteousness and conscientious behavior which is grounded in character.[35] Later Anglicans Jeremy Taylor and William Law emphasized purity of intention, the imitation of Christ, and love to God and our neighbor.[36]

Wesley borrowed from his own Anglican tradition. He felt his own church was "nearer the scriptural plan" than any other European church.[37] But Gaddis pointed out, "It was the devotional, not the creedal side of Anglicanism, which contributed to Wesleyan perfectionism."[38] Robert Gell was rector of St. Mary Aldermanbury in London and chaplain to the archbishop of Canterbury. He had a reputation for teaching "perfectionism." In a sermon he argued that he who has hope of communion with God, purifies himself, as God is pure (1 John 3:3). According to Gell, John anticipated three objections:

1. That it was possible to have communion with God, yet lack holiness. John answers this in 1 John 1:5-7.
2. They already had communion with God because they had no sin. John answers this in 1 John 1: 8-10.

32Callahan, *Saint Gregory of Nyssa*, 44-48.

33Merritt, "'Dialogue' Within a Tradition," 105.

34Wesley, *Works*, 7:508-520.

35Packer, *Rediscovering Holiness*, 102.

36These writers will be revisited in the section discussing the primary contemporary influences upon Wesley, pp. 442-445.

37Wesley, Letter to Sir Harry Trelawny, Aug 1780.

38Gaddis, *Christian Perfection in America*, 111.

3. They cannot choose holiness because sin is a necessity. John answers this in 1 John 2:1-3.

1 John 1:8, therefore, is part of the second objection. John addresses the supposition that some believe they had no sin and therefore are deceived. John defines his terms in 1 John 3:4, where he declares that sin is the transgression of the law. Gell commented that whatever is spoken, done or desired against the law of God is sin. However, Gell observed that expositors do not agree as to whether John, in 1:8, is referring to original sin only or actual sin. Some also attempt to distinguish between venial sin and mortal sin. Aquinas felt that John was referring not only to the sin, but also the guilt and punishment of sin. Augustine thought that the Apostle meant the concupiscence which Paul described in Romans 7:13-17.

Gell dismissed the possibility that John could be referring to original sin because in Romans 6:19 Paul charges the Romans with yielding to sin. Therefore, the subject of 1 John 1:8 has no one to blame for his sin but himself.

Gell argued that the "we" in 1:8 refers explicitly to the "little children" in 2:1. It does not refer to the apostles themselves. While the apostles and most eminent saints of God *have* sinned, according to Romans 3:23, yet the fact that they are now saints infers that they are no longer living sinful lives.

Gell, then refers to the three dispensations of the Father, Son, and Spirit.[39] The law testified against man. Until John the Baptist, Scripture taught forgiveness through repentance. Then the Father disciplined the Son and we are to look to Christ who has suffered for our sins. But we cannot say that we have no sin until the Spirit be poured from on high; until we are born from the dead.

Gell interpreted "children" in 1 John 2:12-14 to refer to those under the dispensation of the Father. In this state, they know forgiveness. But they are then brought to the Son, through whom they overcome the evil one. Finally, they reach spiritual maturity in the dispensation of the Spirit that is without sin.

Gell declared, "Such an estate is possible and attainable through the *grace of God*, and his Holy *Spirit*, that *men may be without sin*." He argued that we may be partakers of the divine nature (2 Peter 1:4). Therefore, Gell concluded

---

[39]While we cannot determine the influence which Gell's doctrine of dispensations may have had on Fletcher, at the least Fletcher felt Gell's position substantiated his own. See Fletcher, "Essay on the Doctrine of the New Birth,"43 where Fletcher called him (though excised) "a judicious Divine." Fletcher wrote that in his judgment, the testimony of Dr. Gell to the dispensations of the Spirit exceeds all previous writers in glory, not only because he stood up with boldness for the much neglected dispensation of the Spirit, but wisely distinguished it from that of the Father and the Son. Then Fletcher copied four paragraphs from Gell. What Fletcher copied was from Gell, *Essay of the Last Translation*, 789.

that it was wrong to apply the statement of 1:8 to all Christians when John was referring to those under the dispensation of the Father.

The Pharisees were deceived when they attempted to justify themselves through legalism. Those who believe, but do not continue to obey, holding to the false position, once a saint and always a saint, are also deceived. Those who rely on good will instead of deed are deceived as well. Yet it is possible for all sin to be subdued. John and the other apostles had attained such a state and they were not deceived.

While it is often argued that all the apostles were taught by the Lord Jesus to pray for the forgiveness of their sins, Gell argued that they were taught this prayer while they were spiritual children who had not yet received the Holy Ghost. After they received the Spirit, we do not read that any one of them used it.

Gell also appealed to a treatise which made the same argument by William Parker, *A Revindication set forth by William Parker, in behalfe of Dr. Drayton deceased, and of himself of the possibility of a total mortification of sin in this life; And of the Saints perfect obedience to the Law of God, to be the Orthodox Protestant Doctrine* (1658).

In 1657 John Tendring had written *A Vindication of the Orthodoxe Protestant Doctrine Against the Innovations of Dr. Drayton and Mr. Parker, Domestique Chaplain to the Right Honourable the E. of Pembroke, in the Following Positions*. This condemnation of their view occasioned the *Revindication*.[40] By this time Drayton was deceased.[41] While Parker argued for the possibility of total mortification of sin in this life, he rejected the doctrine of original sin. According to Parker, we are all created holy by God and we create our own sinfulness.

Whether or not Gell has interpreted Scripture correctly at all points may be debated, but historically we have a few authors a hundred years before Wesley who were arguing for holy living. Gell closed his sermon with a catalog, which ran eight pages, in which he listed all the Scriptures, including the Apocrypha, which he felt proved the possibility of having no sin (in the sense of 1 John 3:4) and living a perfect life according to the will of God.[42] Outler described Gell's

---

[40]Gell, "Some Saints not without Sin for a season," Sermon #20 in *Essay of the Last Translation*, 785-805. These sermons were an appendix to his book evaluating the King James translation.

[41]However, in 1656 Thomas Drayton had published *The Proviso Or Condition of the Promises, the Strait, But the Straight-Way That Leadeth Unto Happiness Being the Substance of Two Sermons Preached at Wilton, March the First, 1656, Upon 2 Cor. 7.1.*

[42]Outler, *Wesley BE Works*, 1:84-85.

sermon on the possibility of Christian perfection in terms of "pure intention."[43] Wesley had read Gell as early as 1741. Again in 1777, Wesley read Gell, calling him "mighty in the Scriptures and well acquainted with the work of God in the soul."[44] Charles Wesley also referred to Gell in his preface to the *Short Hymns on Select Passages of the Holy Scriptures* (1762).

Among the Church of England the non-jurors such as William Law and Thomas Ken taught a respect for the early Church.[45] They are often classified with the Caroline divines such as Jeremy Taylor.[46]

Flew asserted that "of all the earlier writers whom Wesley studied William Law was incomparably the most influential."[47] William Law (1686-1761), a non-juror and mystic, wrote *Christian Perfection* and *A Serious Call to a Devout and Holy Life.* Wesley wrote that after moving to Lincoln College at Oxford,

> A year or two after, Mr. Law's "Christian Perfection" and "Serious Call" were put into my hands. These convinced me, more than ever, of the absolute impossibility of being half a Christian; and I determined, through his grace, (the absolute necessity of which I was deeply sensible of,) to be all-devoted to God, to give him all my soul, my body, and my substance. Will any considerate man say, that this is carrying matters too far? or that anything less is due to Him who has given himself for us, than to give him ourselves, all we hence, and all we are?[48]

---

[43]Outler, "John Wesley: Folk Theologian,"122-123.

[44]Wesley, *Journal*, 17 April 1777.

[45]Ken advocated "the faith professed by the whole church before the disunion of East and West." Ken is still known for writing the Doxology, "Praise God, from Whom All Blessings Flow." The non-jurist position refused to swear allegiance to William, Prince of Orange as the lawful king after James II was expelled in 1688 because of papal tendencies. Those who upheld the validity of King James II were also known as Jacobites. John and Susanna Wesley were Jacobites; Samuel Wesley did not hold this position.

[46]"Caroline divines" were Anglican preachers and theologians in the seventeenth century, under Charles I and Charles II, who rediscovered the Greek fathers and were calling for reform, advocating catholicity separate from Rome or Orthodoxy.

[47]Flew, *Idea of Perfection*, 314.

[48]Wesley, *Works*, 11:367; see also *Journal,* 14 May 1765.

Baker wrote, "At that time God's law meant more to Wesley than his grace."[49] John Wesley experienced a moral awakening by reading Law, but he found Law's ethical ideal impossible to attain. The Wesleys later parted company with Law on the grounds that he had failed to point them to the Lamb of God and the power of the Gospel.[50] Concerning Law's *Serious Call*, Flew wrote, "There is not a word about present power to conquer here on earth."[51]

Wesley wrote, "Although I was much offended at many parts of both, yet they convinced me more than ever of the exceeding height and breadth and depth of the law of God. The light flowed in so mightily upon my soul that everything appeared in a new view.[52] Yet Wesley claimed that Methodism owed its origin to the Holy Scriptures and only indirectly to William Law.[53] Later Wesley wrote in *A Plain Account of Christian Perfection* that Law's writings "convinced me more than ever of the absolute impossibility of being half a Christian; and I determined, through his grace (the absolute necessity of which I was deeply sensible of), to be all devoted to God, to give him all my soul, my body, and my substance."[54]

Law emphasized a life of devotion above theology. He emphasized the imitation of Christ, the renunciation of the world, and resignation to the will of God. Yet in a letter to Law, Wesley asked why he never encouraged faith. "How will you answer it to our common Lord that you never gave me this advice?" Wesley concluded that Law himself did not have saving faith.[55] Following Wesley's Aldergate experience his references to Law are relatively few and

---

[49]*Baker, Heart of True Spirituality*, 1:13.

[50]Wesley, *Letter*, 20 May 1738. See "An Extract of a Letter to the Reverend Mr. Law," 6 January, 1756, Wesley's *Works*, 9:466-509. Wesley began the letter, "In matters of religion I regard no writings but the inspired. Tauler, Behmen, and a whole army of Mystic authors, are with me nothing to St. Paul. In every point I appeal 'to the law and the testimony,' and value no authority but this." Wesley called Law a mystic who denied justification by faith [*Journal*, 30 November, 1767; see also *Letter* to Lady Huntington, 14 September, 1772]. In his letter to Law, Wesley said Law did not appear to know what the term justification even meant [*Works*, 9:487]. See also Lindström, *Wesley and Sanctification*, 56.

[51]Flew, *Idea of Perfection*, 301. Flew added that Law held to an asceticism which did not grasp the concept of ordinary life as a genuine Christian vocation and that his ideal of Christian perfection was too individualistic [pp. 301-303].

[52]Wesley, *Journal*, 24 May, 1738, ¶ 5.

[53]Wesley, "On God's Vineyard," Sermon #107, 1.2.

[54]Wesley, *Works*, 11:367.

[55]Wesley, *Letter*, 14 May 1738.

Wesley rarely recommended him.[56] In a letter to Law, Wesley concluded that Law denied God's omnipotence and justice. Law denied the Scriptural doctrine of justification by faith and misunderstood the new birth, teaching that Christ is naturally present in every man. Law taught stillness as a means of grace and denied the reality of hell.[57] Wesley's last journal entry mentioning Law was 27 July 1749. Wesley was again concerned with Law's subjective understanding of the atonement as an example, but not a propitiation, and felt that Law had given up the very essence of Christianity.

Charles Wesley wrote, "I told him, he was my schoolmaster to bring me to Christ; but the reason why I did not come sooner to Him, was, my seeking to be sanctified before I was justified."[58]

Anglican Bishop Jeremy Taylor wrote *Rules and Exercises of Holy Living and Dying*.[59] *The Rule and Exercises of Holy Living* was published in 1650. It contained practical instruction, but did not begin with anything about a change of heart, conversion, or even repentance.

The Rule and Exercises of Holy Dying was published in 1651. George Worley described Taylor's work

> In the solemn preparation for death, in the quiet prayerfulness of the sick chamber, in the funeral vault, the grave watered with tears and sprinkled with violet, he is quite at home, and give a free rein to his poetic imagination under the inspiration of his awful theme. [60]

From these books Wesley learned the necessity of a life completely dedicated to God and that life must be characterized by a purity of motive. Taylor wrote that "perfection cannot be less than an entire piety, a holiness perfect in its parts, wanting nothing material, allowing no vicious habit, permitting no vile action, but contending towards the greatest excellency, a charitable heart . . . to be pure and pleasing to God in Jesus Christ."[61] Wesley's *A Plain Account of Christian Perfection* opened with this testimony,

---

[56]Tyson, "John Wesley and William Law," 63-73.

[57]Wesley, *Letter*, 6 January 1756.

[58]Charles Wesley, *Journal*, 10 August 1739.

[59]Wesley included this in his *Christian Library*, 16:5-210 and 9:135-297 [2nd ed].

[60]Worley, *Jeremy Taylor*, 147.

[61]*Works of Jeremy Taylor*, 2:437.

> In the year 1725, being in the twenty-third year of my age, I met with Bishop Taylor's "Rule and Exercises of Holy Living and Dying." In reading several parts of this book, I was exceedingly affected; that part in particular which relates to purity of intention. Instantly I resolved to dedicate all my life to God, all my thoughts, and words, and actions; being thoroughly convinced, there was no medium; but that every part of my life (not some only) must either be a sacrifice to God, or myself, that is, in effect, to the devil.[62]

Eight years before his conversion, Wesley was reading Jeremy Taylor and wrote to his mother, quoting Taylor enthusiastically,

> As we hate sin, and grow in grace, and arrive at the state of holiness, which is also a state of repentance and imperfection, but yet of sincerity of heart and diligent endeavor, in the same degree we are to judge concerning the forgiveness of sins. For indeed that is the evangelical forgiveness, and it signifies our pardon, because it effects it; or rather, it is in the nature of the things, so that we are to inquire into no hidden records. Forgiveness of sins is not a secret sentence, a word, or a record. But it is a state of change and effected upon us; and upon ourselves we are to look for it, to read it and understand it.[63]

In this statement Taylor avoids both the Catholic position of pardon without assurance and the Reformed position of imputed righteousness. At this time Wesley had no comprehension of saving faith, but he was clear regarding the goal of holiness. Wesley was impressed with Taylor's emphasis on intention.[64]

Lindström explained that these three writers, Kempis, Law, and Taylor, contributed the concepts of purity of intention, the imitation of Christ, and love to God and our neighbor.[65] Thus, Wesley synthesized the sacramental, evangelical, and mystical. Although he appreciated the place of tradition, reason, and experience, his ultimate authority was the Word of God.

---

[62]Wesley, *Works*, 11:366. See also the opening sentence in the preface to his *Journal* (1735); *Journal*, 14 May 1765 and his letter to John Newton, *Journal*, 14 May 1765.

[63]Wesley, *Letter*, 28 February 1730.

[64]Wesley, *Journal*, 14 May 1765.

[65]Lindström, *Wesley and Sanctification*, 129.

Wesley declared, "My ground is the Bible. Yea, I am a Bible-bigot."[66] He was a "man of one book."[67] If you claim to have a better way, Wesley demanded, "Show me it is so by plain proof of Scripture."[68] His sermons constantly appealed to the Scriptures — the law and the testimony. He described the Bible as the one, "the only standard of truth."[69]

Perkins concluded that Methodism was the prime example of a movement which believed that they can attain perfection through obedience to the Word of God. Methodism has endeavored to retain and to realize the teaching of perfection, while at the same time accepting whole-heartedly the Reformed contention that it must not be separated from the ordinary life of men. When there was a conflict of authorities, the decision rested with the Word. If the Roman Catholic feels that he has the sanction of the Church, he can always find some text to justify it. If the Methodist believes that he has the sanction of the Bible, he is confident that it will work out within the Church. The distinction, however, it between an infallible Church or an infallible Bible.[70]

Perkins categorized the Methodist teaching as based on the Word. He concluded that Methodist experience was always based on Scripture and all progress was by faith, not on a path or ladder of works.[71] Wesley applied Luther's doctrine of *sola fide* to entire sanctification.[72]

In 1756 Wesley wrote,

> When I began to make the Scriptures my study (about seven-and-twenty years ago), I began to see that Christians are called to *love God with all* their *heart* and to *serve Him with all* their

---

[66]Wesley, *Journal*, 2 June 1766.

[67]1746 Preface to his sermons, *BE Works*, 1:105.

[68]Preface to sermons, *BE Works*, 1:107.

[69]Wesley, *Works*, 11:367.

[70]Frank Baker also made the observation that Wesley was one with the Reformers in his tendency to substitute an infallible Book for an infallible Church ["John Wesley's Churchmanship," 270].

[71]Perkins, *Evangelical Perfection*, 205-211. Across church history Perkins identified other ways perfection was sought: through obedience to the law, the way of self-surrender, the way of mystical union, and the way of knowledge. While they may have an element of truth, they tend to degenerate into legalism, mysticism, or gnosticism. The Methodist emphasis on faith based on the Word kept Methodism balanced until it departed from their faith in the Word.

[72]Cell, *Rediscovery of John Wesley*, 347.

> *strength;* which is precisely what I apprehend to be meant by the scriptural term Perfection. After weighing this for some years . . . I published my coolest and latest thoughts in the sermon on that subject. I therein build on no authority, ancient or modern, but the Scripture. If this supports any doctrine it will stand; if not, the sooner it falls the better. Neither the doctrine in question nor any other is anything to me, unless it be the doctrine of Christ and His Apostles. If, therefore, you will please to point out to me any passages in that sermon which are either contrary to Scripture or not supported by it, and to show that they are not, I shall be full as willing to oppose as ever I was to defend them. I search for truth, plain Bible truth, without any regard to the praise or dispraise of men. If you will assist me in this search, more especially by showing me where I have mistaken my way, it will be gratefully acknowledged.[73]

Wesley's tract, *A Plain Account of Christian Perfection* contains 195 scripture quotations, 23 from the Old Testament and 172 from the New Testament.[74] For Wesley, the Scripture was his ultimate authority. When Wesley called himself a "man of one book," this was what he meant.[75] Adherence to the Word of God will keep us from danger and extremism. Obedience to the Word will keep us from sin and will drive us to seek holiness.

On January 25, 1738 Wesley described his spiritual journey, based on Ephesians 4:14.

> For many years have I been tossed about by various winds of doctrine. I asked long ago, What must I do to be saved? The Scriptures answered, 'Keep the commandments. Believe, hope, love; follow after these tempers till thou hast fully attained, that is, till death, by all those outward works and means which God hath appointed, by walking as Christ walked.'
>
> I was early warned against laying, as the Papists do, too much stress either on outward works or on a faith without works, which, as it does not include, so it will never lead to, true hope or charity. Nor am I sensible that to this hour I have laid too much stress on either, having from the very beginning valued both faith, the means of grace, and good works, not on their own

[73]Wesley, *Letter* to William Dodd, 5 Feb 1756.

[74]Sangster, *Path to Perfection*, 36.

[75]"Let me be *homo unius libri*."["Preface" to Wesley's Sermons, ¶ 5].

account, but as believing God, who had appointed them, would by them bring me in due time to the mind that was in Christ.
But before God's time was come I fell among some Lutheran and Calvinist authors, whose confused and indigested accounts magnified faith to such an amazing size that it quite hid all the rest of the commandments. I did not then see that this was the natural effect of their overgrown fear of popery, being so terrified with the cry of 'merit and good works' that they plunged at once into the other extreme. In this labyrinth I was utterly lost, not being able to find out what the error was, not yet to reconcile this uncouth hypothesis either with Scripture of common sense.
The English writers, such as Bishop Beveridge, Bishop Taylor, and Mr. Nelson,[76] a little relieved me from these well-meaning, wrong-headed Germans. Their accounts of Christianity I could easily see to be, in the main, consistent both with reason and Scripture. Only when they interpreted Scripture in different ways I was often much at a loss. And again there was one thing much insisted on in Scripture — the unity of the Church — which none of them I thought clearly explained, or strongly inculcated.
But it was not long before Providence brought me to those who showed me a sure rule for interpreting Scripture, viz, [the ancient consensus: what has been believed by all, everywhere, always].[77] At the same time they sufficiently insisted upon a due regard to the One Church at all times and in all places. Nor was it long before I bent the bow too far the other way: (1) by making antiquity a co-ordinate (rather than subordinate) rule with Scripture; (2) by admitting several doubtful writings as undoubted evidences of antiquity; (3) by extending antiquity too far, even to the middle or end of the fourth century; (4) by believing more practices to have been universal in the ancient Church than ever were so; (5) by not considering that the decrees of one provincial synod could bind only that province, and the decrees of a general synod only those provinces whose representatives met therein; (6) by not considering that most of

---

[76]Here Wesley referred to William Beveridge, who advocated the restoration of primitive piety, Jeremy Taylor, and Robert Nelson, a non-juring layman.

[77]*Consensus veterum* — quod ab omnibus, quod ubique, quod semper creditum. Here Wesley is quoting Vincent of Lérins from the first half of the fifth century.

those decrees were adapted to particular times and occasions, and consequently when those occasions ceased, must cease to bind even those provinces.

These considerations insensibly stole upon me as I grew acquainted with the mystic writers, whose noble descriptions of union with God and internal religion made everything else appear mean, flat, and insipid. But in truth they made good works appear so too; yea, and faith itself, and what not? These gave me an entirely new view of religion, nothing like any I had had before. But alas! It was nothing like that religion which Christ and his apostles lived and taught. I had a plenary dispensation from all the commands of God. The form ran thus: 'Love is all; all the commands beside are only means of love; you must choose those which you feel are means to you, and use them as long as they are so.' Thus were all the bands burst at once. And though I could never fully come into this, nor contentedly omit what God enjoined, yet, I know not how, I fluctuated between obedience and disobedience: I had no heart, no vigour, not zeal in obeying; continually doubting whether I was right or wrong, and never out of perplexities and entanglements. Nor can I at this hour give a distinct account how or when I came a little back toward the right way. Only my present sense is this: all the other enemies of Christianity are triflers; the mystics are the most dangerous of all its enemies. That stab in the vitals, and its most serious professors are most likely to fall by them. May I praise him who hath snatched me out of this fire likewise, by warning all others that it is set on fire of hell.[78]

11. The Wesleyan Synthesis

John Wesley (1703-1791)

Wesley synthesized earlier teaching on Christian perfection and entire sanctification. The primary sources for Wesley's views on Christian perfection are his:

[78]These six paragraphs which were not published in Wesley's *Journal*, but were first printed in Whitehead's *Life of John Wesley* (1793-1796) and included in the Wesley, *BE Works*, 18:212-213.

"The Circumcision of the Heart," Sermon #17 (1733)[79]
Preface to *Hymns and Sacred Poems* (1741)
A Brief History of the Principles of Methodism (1740)
"Christian Perfection" Sermon # 40 (1741)
The Character of a Methodist (1742)
An Earnest Appeal to Men of Reason and Religion (1742)
A Further Appeal to Men of Reason and Religion (1744)
Conference Minutes of 1744-1747; 1758
Thoughts on Christian Perfection (1760)
Farther Thoughts on Christian Perfection (1761)
Cautions and Directions Given to the Greatest Professors in the Methodist Societies (1762)
"The Scripture Way of Salvation" Sermon #43 (1765)
A Plain Account of Christian Perfection (1765)
Brief Thoughts on Christian Perfection (1767)
"The End of Christ's Coming," Sermon #62 (1781)
"On Perfection" Sermon #76 (1784)

Wesley insisted that Christian perfection was a gift for all believers, not simply a few choice saints. And he developed ways through which all could proclaim, teach, and practice holiness of heart and life.

This phrase "heart and life" implies that the two realms are connected. Our hearts are changed within by grace so that we act holy outwardly in life. While the entire Christian tradition believes in holiness of heart, Wesley had to deal with three major questions:

- Is this purity imputed or it is imparted?

---

[79]The New Testament does not specifically equate spiritual circumcision with Christian perfection (see ftnt #49). Nor does Wesley in this sermon. It was written in 1733, five years before his conversion. He wrote that he had begun to study this doctrine around 1729 and after weighing this for some years he openly declared his sentiments before Oxford University on January 1, 1733 in the sermon on the Circumcision of the Heart [*Letter* to William Dodd, 5 Feb 1756].

After his Aldersgate experience, he added to ¶ 1.7 in 1748, which reflected a more biblical order of salvation, acknowledging that justification comes before Christian perfection. On May 14, 1765, Wesley wrote to John Newton that this sermon "contains all that I now teach concerning salvation from all sin, and loving God with an undivided heart." But while it contains his doctrine of Christian perfection, it is broader and does not equate circumcision with perfection. In it Wesley declares that circumcision of the heart is "the distinguishing mark of a true follower of Christ, of one who is in a state of acceptance with God" and that it is the habitual disposition of the soul which Scripture terms "holiness." But "holiness" must not be here restricted to the "second blessing."

- Is this purity a gift of grace of the product of pious effort?
- Is this purity to be fully realized in this life?[80]

George Peck declared that the Wesleyan emphasis "simply asserts *the attainableness, in the present life, of a state of holiness truly denominated* CHRISTIAN PERFECTION."[81] Thus, Methodism emphasized entire sanctification as the birth right of every child of God, not simply the right of a paltry few.[82] According to Sangster, Wesley's idea of perfection was "indwelling love, banishing all conscious sin, received by faith in an instant, and maintained from moment to moment by humble dependence of God."[83]

In his minutes of conversations, Wesley recorded the response to a question regarding what should be done to revive the work of God where it had decayed. Part of the answer was that the Methodists should strongly and explicitly exhort all believers to "go on to perfection," which was possible in this life.

> That we may "all speak the same thing," I ask, once for all, Shall we defend this Perfection, or give it up? You'll agree to defend it, meaning thereby, (as we did from the beginning,) salvation from all sin, by the love of God and man filling our heart. The Papists say, "This cannot be attained, till we have been refined by the fire of purgatory." The Calvinists say, "Nay, it will be attained as soon as the soul and body part." The old Methodists say, "It may be attained before we die: A moment after is too late." Is it so or not? You are all agreed, we may be saved from all sin before death. The substance then is settled; but, as to the circumstance, is the change gradual or instantaneous? It is both the one and the other. From the moment we are justified, there may be a gradual sanctification, a growing in grace, a daily advance in the knowledge and love of God. And if sin cease before death, there must, in the nature of the thing, be an instantaneous change; there must be a last moment wherein it does exist, and a first moment wherein it does not.
> "But should we in preaching insist both on one and the other?" Certainly we must insist on the gradual change; and that

[80]Bassett, *Holiness Teaching*, 31; 36.

[81]Peck, *Christian Perfection*, 41.

[82]Gaddis, *Christian Perfection in America*, 141.

[83]Sangster, *Path to Perfection*, 91.

> earnestly and continually. And are there not reasons why we should insist on the instantaneous also? If there be such a blessed change before death, should we not encourage all believers to expect it? and the rather, because constant experience shows, the more earnestly they expect this, the more swiftly and steadily does the gradual work of God go on in their soul; the more watchful they are against all sin, the more careful to grow in grace, the more zealous of good works, and the more punctual in their attendance on all the ordinances of God. Whereas, just the contrary effects are observed whenever this expectation ceases. They are "saved by hope" by this hope of a total change, with a gradually increasing salvation. Destroy this hope, and that salvation stands still, or, rather, decreases daily. Therefore whoever would advance the gradual change in believers should strongly insist on the instantaneous.[84]

W. B. Pope summarized four contributions Wesley made to our understanding of Christian holiness.[85]

1. Wesley connected law and love. The law of God produces an ethical holiness (Rom 7:12), but a misplaced emphasis leads to legalism. With legalism religion becomes primarily a set of rules and regulations. The basis of assurance is then self-righteousness.

Holiness must never be separated from a love for God. Wesley cautioned that if we were seeking anything other than more love we are "looking wide of the mark, you are getting out of the royal way."[86] Pope wrote, "Methodist doctrine boldly declares that the righteousness of the law is fulfilled in believers, that is the righteousness of the new law of faith; and that as faith is reckoned for righteousness, so faith working by love is reckoned for perfection."[87]

However, love can lead to antinomianism as expressed in the phrase, "No law but love." Wesley taught a perfect love that expresses itself through obedience to God's law and an ethical behavior toward our neighbor. According to Dunning, a cursory look at categories of language reveals "that Wesley used almost exclusively ethical terminology" in describing the work of the Holy

---

[84]Wesley, *Works*, 8:328-329. Q 56

[85]Pope, *Compendium*, 3:96-99.

[86]Wesley, *Works*, 11:430.

[87]Pope, *Compendium*, 3:96-97.

Spirit.[88] David McKenna observed that Reform theologians tends to legalize holiness, Roman Catholics sacramentalize it, and Charismatics emotionalize it. Yet the Wesleyan emphasis brings together obedience, sacrament and emotion.[89]

2. No theological position is more optimistic about deliverance from sin than is Wesley's. Boland wrote, "The only controversy among the Churches is in regard to the time, the place, and the means by which the work is done. Methodism stands alone among all the Churches, in preaching *a present salvation from all sin, by faith in the blood of the Lamb, and the possibility of such a one 'abiding in Christ and sinning not.*'"[90] This effusion of love results in a destruction of sin. Wesley believed that we could be so full of the love of God that there was no room for sin. As we trust and obey, our love for God expels sin.

3. Wesley blended the divine and human components. While we must wait upon God to do the work, we do not wait passively, but attend to all the means of grace. Sanctification is made possible by God's grace, yet we must exercise a present-tense obedient faith. Sam Powell explained that Christian perfection, for Wesley, was not something given to us in the way that a letter is received in the mail. Rather it is formed with us as we put to death the deeds of the body by the practice of Christian disciplines.[91] According to Wesley, the primitive church commonly said, "The soul and the body make a man; the spirit

---

[88]Dunning, *Grace, Faith, and Holiness*, 470.

[89]McKenna, *What a Time to be Wesleyan!* 96.

[90]Boland, *Problem of Methodism*, pp. 25-26. Yet Boland held that this state of grace was realized in regeneration [see the discussion on pp. 415-416]. I could accept Boland's statement as descriptive of regeneration if he had omitted "all" from "a present salvation from all sin." While regeneration is victory over all outward sin, the inward sin nature remains. James Rogers testified concerning his justification, "Though I was happy in a sense of acceptance, and had power also over inward and outward sin, yet the fountain of corruption was not dried up; that I had yet a degree of the carnal mind, which is enmity against God" [Telford, *Wesley's Veterans*, 7:142].

[91]Powell, *Embodied Holiness*, 14. Leclerc objected to the way the term "spiritual disciplines" is substituted for "means of grace." It implies that there is no discipline required in the means of grace. But "means of grace" also implies that more than discipline is involved. "Participating in the means of grace serves to remind us that all we do, all we are, and all we become is only possible through the grace of God within us through the presence of the Holy Spirit" [*Discovering Christian Holiness*, 263-264].

and discipline make a Christian."[92]

4. Wesley's emphasis was marked by reasonableness and moderation. Wesley interviewed thousands of Methodists concerning their experience, had a sharp sense of logic, and a grasp of tradition. He said, "If I were convinced that none in England had attained what has been so clearly and strongly preached . . . I should be clearly convinced that we had all mistaken the meaning of those scriptures."[93] Yet he felt that he could boldly preach Christian perfection because he had seen five hundred witnesses of it.[94] Wesley declared,

> This perfection cannot be a delusion, unless the Bible be a delusion too — I mean, "loving God with all our heart, and our neighbor as ourselves." I pin down all its opposers to this definition of it. No evasion! No shifting of the question! Where is the delusion of this? Either *you* received *this love* or you did not. If you did, dare you call it a delusion?[95]

While the doctrine of Christian perfection has a biblical basis, Wesley believed that if he had interpreted the Scripture properly it would be corroborated by tradition, reason, and experience. This is sometimes referred to as the Wesleyan quadrilateral. At its worst, this statement by Wesley that without examples he would conclude he had been mistaken could be interpreted as a humanistic, subjective theology. At its best, it reflects a pastoral theology in which Wesley's attempts to formulate a scriptural position were tempered by thousands of personal interviews. While Wesley did not believe the scriptures could err, he was humble enough to concede that his interpretation of the scriptures could be mistaken and therefore he made modifications. Staples

---

[92]Wesley, "The Late Work of God in North America," Sermon #113, 1.7; "Causes of the Inefficacy of Christianity," Sermon #122, § 7.

[93]Wesley, *Works*, 11:390. Wesley also declared that if it could be demonstrated that none had ever attained Christian perfection, he would preach it no more [*Works*, 11:405]. On the other hand Clarke declared, "And suppose no one could be found in all the churches of Christ whose heart was purified from all unrighteousness, and loved God and man with all his regenerated powers, yet the doctrine of Christian perfection would still be true" ["Apostolical Preaching," Sermon #38, *Works*, 7:292].

[94]Wesley, *Letter* to Charles Wesley, 9 July 1766.

[95]Wesley, *Journal*, 27 August 1768 records a letter to Lawrence Coughlan who thought holiness consisted in a flow of joy. Wesley wrote that it was love: the love of God and our neighbor; the image of God stamped on the heart; the life of God in the soul of man, the mind that was in Christ, enabling us to walk as Christ also walked.

concluded that for Wesley the substance, or the "what" of holiness, was based on Scripture, but the structure, or the "how" and "when" of holiness, was based on experience.[96]

Pope declared that the most eminent component of Methodist doctrine is its unfaltering assertion of the believer's privilege to be delivered from indwelling sin in the present life. The one element in the Methodist doctrine which may be called distinctive is the article that the work of the Spirit in sanctifying believers from sin is to be complete in this state of probation. This is the hope it sees set before us in the Gospel and therefore, it presses this upon the pursuit and attainment of all who are in Christ. The suppression and destruction of indwelling sin is the one point where its aim is beyond the general aim.

A long chain of ecclesiastical testimonies bear witness that a high doctrine of Christian perfection has been taught in all ages, and in many communities, coming in some instances within a hair's breadth of this, but shrinking back from the last expression of the truth. The best of the ascetics and mystics of ancient and modern times both taught and exemplified a high standard of purification from sin, inner illumination, and supernatural union with God, but whether from misconceived humility or lack of the highest triumph of faith, they invariably reserved the secret residue of evil as necessary to human discipline. This last fetter Methodism will not reserve. Its doctrine pursues the alien and the enemy into its most interior stronghold, and destroys it there, so that the temple of God in the human spirit shall not only be emptied of sin, but swept from every trace that it had been there, and garnished with all the graces of the divine image.

Methodism reads and fearlessly interprets all those clauses in the charter of grace which speak of the destruction of the body of sin, of putting off the old man, of crucifying the flesh unto death, of an entire sanctification of man's whole nature, of a preservation in faultlessness, of a perfect love casting out fear, of being purified as Christ is pure, and of the love of God perfected in the human soul. Redemption from the flesh spiritually understood, is not made synonymous or simultaneous with redemption from the flesh physically interpreted. No sin can pass the threshold of life to be purged through the intermediate fires of discipline and there is no provision in heaven for the destruction of evil. Death itself cannot take the office of the atoning blood and the purifying Spirit. Therefore, it follows that the final stroke must be in the present life. The atonement is not more certainly a finished work than the application of it by the Holy Spirit. There must be a sacred moment of final deliverance from what God sees as sin in the soul. This is Christian perfection — a word when used, is always guarded by its necessary adjectives of Christian, evangelical, and relative.

Methodism began to announce this high and most sacred possibility of the Christian life very early. It has continued the testimony until now, altogether

[96]Staples, "Sanctification and Selfhood," 6.

apart from the vouchers of living witnesses. Its principle has been that God's Word must be true and his standard the right one, however the lives of the saints may halt behind it.

Some forms of the doctrine assert what cannot be maintained by the warrant of the Bible. The "second blessing" is sometimes confounded with the first, as if an entire consecration to God, which is only the perfect beginning were an entire sanctification from all sin. The effusion of divine love in the soul is sometimes mistaken for that "perfected love" of which it is only the earnest. First John gives the most explicit assurance that there is set before the aspiration of the saint a perfected and finished operation of divine love, the triumph of which is the extinction of sin and fear. But it is observable, that before the last testimony to live in man as perfected, we have three testimonies to the gradual operation of the love of God in us, which carry it into the three deportments of the covenant of grace.

First is that of law. "Whoso keepeth his word, in him verily is the love of God perfected" (1 John 2:5). Perfected love is the fulfilling of the righteousness of the law and its triumph is bound up with our habitual obedience in all things.

Second is that of sonship. "If we love one another, God dwelleth in us, and his love is perfected in us" (1 John 4:12). Universal, boundless, self-sacrificing charity is the condition as well as the goal of perfected love.

Third is that of consecration. "He that dwelleth in love, dwelleth in God, and God in him. Herein in our love made perfect" (1 John 4:16-17). Abstraction from all created desire and supreme union with God is also both the condition and the crown of perfected love.

Not withstanding every drawback, it still remains that the testimony borne for a century to the highest privileges of the Christian covenant is the glory of Methodist theology. It has stimulated the religious life of countless multitudes. It has kept before the eyes of the people formed by it the one supreme thought, that Christianity is a religion which has only one goal, whether in the Church or in the individual — the destruction of sin. And we believe the day is coming when the Church of God upon earth will have given to it an enlarged heart to receive this doctrine in all its depth and fullness.[97]

Philip Watson summarized the message of the Wesleys with this simple formula:

All men need to be saved.
All men can be saved.

---

[97]The previous nine paragraphs have been drawn, with only minor editing from William Burt Pope, "Methodist Doctrine," in Clark, *Wesley Memorial Volume*, 183-187.

All men can know they are saved.
All men can be saved to the uttermost.[98]

B. B. Warfield declared, "It was John Wesley who infected the modern Protestant world with this notion of 'entire instantaneous sanctification.'"[99] Yet, as we shall see, Wesley also emphasized the progressive element of sanctification.

When Wesley was 75 years old, he disclosed in his *Journal* that his doctrine of Christian perfection had not changed in over forty years.[100] His first tract on the subject, "The Character of a Methodist," was written in 1739. In 1756 he wrote that he began to study the Scripture some twenty-seven years earlier (1729) and at that time began to see the doctrine of Christian perfection.[101] Thus his sermon "The Circumcision of the Heart" was written in 1733. In 1760 he declared that constant communion with God the Father and Son fills the heart with humble love. "Now this is what I always did and do now mean by 'perfection.'"[102] In 1778 he confided that he doubted he could write a better sermon on "The Circumcision of the Heart" than he had done forty-five years earlier.[103]

In *A Plain Account of Christian Perfection*, written in 1777, he said that he had not added one point that he had not held 38 years earlier in "The Character of a Methodist." In fact, he said that he began this pursuit of Christian perfection in 1725.[104] The title page for *A Plain Account of Christian Perfection* gives the dates 1725-1777. Although Wesley did not die until 1791, his editor, Thomas Jackson, added these words, "It is not to be understood, that Mr. Wesley's sentiments concerning Christian Perfection were in any measure changed after the year 1777."[105]

---

[98]Watson, *Message of the Wesleys*, 35.

[99]*Studies in Perfectionism*, 2:562; 463; Yet Cattell noted that Warfield does not critique the theology of Wesley, but simply assumes him to be in error ["Keswick and Wesleyan," 267]. Leo Cox also noted that Warfield made no analysis of Wesley's own writings [*Perfectionism*, 104].

[100]Wesley, *Journal*, 1 Sept, 1778. See also Cary, "Did Wesley Change?" 73-80.

[101]Wesley, *Letter* to William Dodd, 5 Feb 1756.

[102]Wesley, *Journal*, 6 March 1760.

[103]Wesley, *Journal*, 1 September 1778.

[104]Wesley, *Works*, 11: 373, § 10

[105]Wesley, *Works*, 11:366. Turner thought that toward the end of his life Wesley placed greater stress on the instantaneous aspect [*Vision Which Transforms*, 259; 255]. Peters documents that Wesley reversed himself in 1761 regarding whether

Thus, the evolution of Wesley's doctrine has been greatly exaggerated. Just as higher criticism has attempted to theorize how the biblical text might have evolved, so contemporary Wesley scholars often distinguish between the "early Wesley" (1733-1738), the "middle Wesley" (1738-1765), and the "late Wesley" (1765-1791). The result in either biblical studies or Wesleyan studies is that there is no definitive statement.[106] The result in biblical studies is a purely human document created and edited to uphold the authority of the church. The result in Wesleyan studies is that Wesley has become" the undefined banner."[107] Some Wesley scholars deny that there is any such thing as a "historical Wesley." They delight in pointing out contradictions in Wesley and deny that he had a single consistent view of anything, whether the subject be what a Christian is or the witness of the Spirit. Such an approach provides a flexible Wesley who can be linked to whatever fad or movement is popular with the scholar. Thus, the "mature" Wesley is reconstructed to fit the agenda of the scholar.

While Wesley did fine-tune his theology, he actually tends to be

---

or not Christian perfection may be lost [*Christian Perfection*, 47]. Yet the doctrine of Christian perfection itself remained essentially unchanged.

[106]For example see Abraham, "The End of Wesleyan Theology," 7-25 in which he champions the death of Wesleyan theology. See also Graves, "Wesley's Variations in Belief, 192-211. Yet while Graves argued that Wesley "varied largely in his belief respecting both the distinctive doctrines and the sectarian peculiarities of the Church he founded; the church itself, for more than a century, has been historically uniform in her beliefs, and in their doctrinal statements." I do not think it can be demonstrated that there was large variations in Wesley's theology. In his dissertation Claude Thompson devoted six pages to a summary statement, "How far did Wesley change his view?" Thompson concludes that over time Wesley backed away from more ambitious claims concerning what Christian perfection would accomplish. Wesley's most significant change was concerning the possibility of losing this experience. Yet Wesley did not modify his teaching on the subject of perfection in the direction of less insistence upon it. If anything, Thompson wrote, he urged it even more strongly. Yet Thompson wrote that Tyerman concluded that Wesley quietly let Christian perfection drop [see pp. 475; 483 of this book]. Having checked Tyerman's *Life and Times of Wesley*, I do not see that he is arriving at that conclusion ["Witness of American Methodism," 40-45]. It was the conclusion of Tillett, however, that Wesley let his insistence upon instantaneous sanctification quietly drop [*Personal Salvation*, 528].

[107]Francis Schaeffer made the same observation about the word *Jesus* as a "contentless banner." He described theologians who use familiar words but redefine them to serve their agenda. "It is humanism with a religious banner called 'Jesus' to which they can give any content they wish." He concluded, "We have come to this fearsome place where the word *Jesus* has become the enemy of the Person Jesus, and the enemy of what Jesus taught" ["Jesus the Undefined Banner" in *Escape from Reason* in *Works*, 1:258-259]. See also Reasoner, "Wesley: the Undefined Banner."

remarkably consistent and logical in his overall theology over the years. The fact that he may approach the same subject in different ways under different circumstances does not necessarily constitute a contradiction. Consequently some interpretations in Wesley studies are better than others because they have a more adequate grasp of the body of literature Wesley wrote. And some interpretations may be rejected because they are not consistent with Wesley overarching emphases. Therefore the position that Wesley was inconsistent with himself is useful only to those postmodern scholars who try to cut and paste Wesley to fit their agenda and can thus dismiss any objection that their finished product does not actually reflect what Wesley taught. This treatment of Wesley by certain scholars mirrors their treatment of Scripture.

For Wesley, the goal was Christlikeness. He emphasized an ethical holiness, not an emotional fullness. Of his fifty-two standard sermons, thirteen were based on Christ's ethical teaching in the Sermon on the Mount.

Three weeks after Wesley's conversion he went to Germany to observe the Moravian model.[108] He analyzed their model at Herrnhut and returned to England eager to try out this new found technique. He approved of their emphasis on "ecclesiolae in ecclesia."[109] Within a few weeks he organized bands. Although he eventually began to have some serious doubts about their doctrines, he acknowledged a debt of gratitude to them. He disliked the domination by Zinzendorf, their antinomianism and doctrine of stillness, as well as a tendency toward mysticism. He was concerned by their lack of emphasis on the means of grace, such as communion and baptism.[110]

While George Whitefield is generally regarded as the better preacher, he conceded "my brother Wesley acted wisely. The souls that were awakened under his ministry he joined in class, and thus preserved the fruits of his labours. This

---

[108]Wesley, *Journal*, 11-14 August 1738.

[109]Literally, "little churches within the church." The society meetings were carefully scheduled to avoid conflict with any of the services of the Church of England.

[110]Wesley, *Letter* to Charles Wesley, 21 April 1741; see also Henderson, *Wesley's Class Meeting*, p. 64. *Stillness* corresponds to passivity and quietism. Philipp Molther, a Moravian minister, held that the way to find faith was to be "still." Those who desired the blessing were to give up the public means of grace. They were not even to pray or to read the Scriptures, nor to attempt to do any good works. As practiced by the Moravians, stillness also disregarded the sacraments. See Wesley's debate with Molther in *Journal*, 31 December 1739 and Wesley's debate with Zinzendorf 3 Sept 1741 in which Zinzendorf denied any growth in grace. By 1745 Zinzendorf declared that he and his people had no connection with the Wesleys..

I neglected, and my people are a rope of sand."[111] Wesley recorded this observation:

> And when we have made some impressions on their hearts, if we look not after them, they will soon die away. But as great as this labor of private instruction is, it is absolutely necessary. For, after all our preaching, many of our people are almost as ignorant as if they had never heard the gospel. I speak as plain as I can, yet I frequently meet with those who have been my hearers many years, who know not whether Christ be God or man. And how few are there that know the nature of repentance, faith, and holiness! Most of them have a sort of confidence that God will save them, while the world has their hearts. I have found by experience, that one of these has learned more from one hour's close discourse, than from ten years' public preaching. And undoubtedly this private application is implied in those solemn words of the Apostle: "I charge thee, before God and the Lord Jesus Christ, who shall judge the quick and dead at his appearing, preach the word, be instant in season, out of season; reprove, rebuke, exhort, with all longsuffering."[112]

Wesley recognized the importance of organizing a Methodist society. He wrote,

> I am more and more convinced, that the devil himself desires nothing more than this, that the people of any place should be half-awakened, and then left to themselves to fall asleep again. Therefore I determine, by the grace of God, not to strike one stroke in any place where I cannot follow the blow.[113]

In his journal he recorded that he preached to a couple hundred people, "many of whom seemed full of good desires. But as there is no society, I expect

---

[111]Jackson, *Centenary*, 69. See Wesley's comment in "The Late Work of God in North America," Sermon #113, 1.7, "But those who were more or less affected by Mr. Whitefield's preaching had no discipline at all. They had no shadow of discipline; nothing of the kind. They were formed into no societies. They had no Christian connection with each other, nor were ever taught to watch over each others' souls."

[112]Wesley, "Minutes of Several Conversations," *Works*, 8:303.

[113]Wesley, *Journal*, 13 March 1743.

no deep or lasting work."[114] He said that to preach like an apostle, but to fail to organize and train the new converts is to give birth to children and then turn them over to the devil. Commenting on a preaching point he observed

> I was more convinced than ever, that the preaching like an Apostle, without joining together those that are awakened, and training them up in the ways of God, is only begetting children for the murderer. How much preaching has there been for these twenty years all over Pembrokeshire! But no regular societies, no discipline, no order or connection; and the consequence is, that nine in ten of the once-awakened are now faster asleep than ever.[115]

The Methodist societies were divided into classes, bands, and select societies to promote spiritual growth. All that was necessary to participate was a desire to "flee the wrath to come." Most conversions took place in the small groups or alone as a result of the discipleship.[116]

The class meeting worked on behavioral change. They were in effect house churches. The band provided for close conversation, where a person could bare his feelings. They were segregated by age, sex, and marital status and were restricted to those who had the assurance of salvation.[117]

The highest level was the select society, for those pressing after perfection. Wesley explained, "They had no need of being encumbered with many rules, having the best rule of all in their hearts. No peculiar directions were therefore given to them," except a commitment to confidentiality, submission, and voluntary contribution. "Everyone here has an equal liberty of speaking, there being none greater or less than another. I could say freely to these, when they were met together, 'Ye may all prophesy one by one' (taking that word in its lower sense), 'that all may learn and all may be comforted.'"[118]

The way to perfection for Wesley was through the means of grace. Wesley wrote in *A Plain Account of Christian Perfection*, "Never omit meeting

---

[114]Wesley, *Journal*, 27 August 1763.

[115]Wesley, *Journal*, 25 August 1763.

[116]Albin, "Early Methodist Spirituality," 278. See also Stafford, "Finding God in Small Groups," 42-44.

[117]Wesley, *BE Works*, 9:77-79; 267. The rules of the band societies were drawn up 25 December 1738. Wesley defined "bands" as "little companies."

[118]"A Plain Account of the People Called Methodists,"8.4; *BE Works*, 9:270. See also Watson, *Early Methodist Class Meeting*, 120.

your Class of Band; never absent yourself from any public meeting. These are the very sinews of our Society; and whatever weakens or tends to weaken our regard for these, or our exactness in attending them, strikes at the very root of our community."[119] We have disconnected Wesley's means and his end.

Kevin Watson wrote that Wesleyan doctrine taught entire sanctification was important for growth in holiness and Wesleyan discipline held the importance of accountability for growth in holiness.[120] Although Wesley was accused of reviving "popery" or the Roman Catholic confessional, he simply cited James 5:16 as justification.[121]

Wesley defined Christian perfection as "loving God with all our heart and serving Him with all of our strength. Nor did I ever say or mean any *more* by perfection than *thus* loving and serving God."[122] Wesley's emphasis on perfection of intention and love were not unique. What was different was his understanding of the work of the Holy Spirit in the entire salvation process, beginning with prevenient grace and then through all the sequence of salvation. Wilber Dayton observed that Wesley did not even limit the work of the Spirit to believers. "Grace before salvation (prevenient grace) and even good thoughts and deeds of unsaved persons were all a part of the work of the Holy Spirit."[123]

While later holiness writers seemed to restrict the Holy Spirit to His work in sanctification, A. Skevington Wood stated that "Wesley did not hesitate to ascribe every item in the experience of redemption to the action of the Holy Ghost."[124] Wesley declared, "I assert that till a man 'receives the Holy Ghost,' he is without God in the world."[125]

It is through the agency of the Holy Spirit that man is given prevenient grace, convicted of sin, enabled to repent and believe. The merits of Christ are applied in justification, the believer is regenerated, and the child of God is assured of adoption. For Wesley, Christian perfection is another benefit of Christ's death

---

[119]Wesley, *Works*, 11:433; Q 37.

[120]Watson, "Form and Power," 166-172. Yet Stephen Gibson conceded that the conservative holiness movement has sorely neglected discipleship and spiritual accountability [*Held by Conviction*, 79-80]. I am afraid that they found it much easier to name-it-and-claim-it than to seek-it-and-live-it.

[121]Wesley, "A Plain Account of the People Called Methodists," 6.2; *BE Works*, 9:267; see also "Rules of the Band Societies," 9:77.

[122]Wesley, *Letter* to William Dodd, 12 March 1756.

[123]Dayton, "Entire Sanctification," 1:526.

[124]Wood, *Burning Heart*, 240.

[125]Wesley, *Works*, 8:106.

and is a part of the Spirit's continuing work in the believer.

Along with the writer of Hebrews, Wesley understood that New Testament experience was better than the religious experience described in the Old Testament.[126] He felt the "wide difference there is between the Jewish and the Christian dispensation was important to notice."[127] He asked:

> Has there not been a larger measure of the Holy Spirit given under the Gospel, than under the Jewish dispensation? If not, in what sense was the Spirit not given before Christ was glorified? (John 7:39).[128]

Russ Frazier wrote that Wesley used the term "covenant" to denote the continuity of salvation history, but used the term "dispensation" to describe the progression of God's administration. Thus, neither Wesley, nor Fletcher, can be linked to the discontinuity of modern dispensationalism nor to the attempt by Calvinism to define New Testament Christianity in terms of Old Testament standards.[129] Even though the saints of the Old Testament sometimes fell into sin, Wesley argued:

> The privileges of Christians are in no wise to be measured by what the Old Testament records concerning those who were under the Jewish dispensation; seeing the fulness of time is now come; the Holy Ghost is now given.[130]

Since the Holy Spirit has come, Wesley believed that he would enable the Christian to live as John wrote, "He that is born of God sinneth not."[131] Rob Staples explained:

> "Conversion," to Wesley, meant evangelical conversion—having the "faith of a son" and not merely the "faith of a servant." The pre-Pentecost disciples, though "unconverted" and not Christians in the true sense, were nevertheless "justified" under the old

---

[126]Wesley, *Explanatory Notes*, 583.

[127]Wesley, "Christian Perfection," Sermon #40, 2.11.

[128]Wesley, *Works*, 11:408.

[129]Frazier, "Wesley's Covenantal and Dispensational View," 51-52.

[130]Wesley, "Christian Perfection, Sermon #40, 2.13; see also *Works*, 11:325.

[131]Wesley, "Christian Perfection," Sermon #40, 2.13-20.

covenant.[132]

In his comments on Jeremiah 31:33, Wesley again compared the law and the gospel saying, "neither was the regenerating grace of God so common under the time of the law, as it hath been under the gospel."[133] Because of Wesley's understanding of the Holy Spirit as the One who regenerates, he concluded that "the Apostles themselves had not the proper Christian faith till after the day of Pentecost."[134] Staples concluded that "Wesley consistently refused to see the pre-Calvary disciples as examples of born again Christians."[135] This explains why Kenneth Grider concluded:

> He did not associate Pentecost with the second work of grace (entire sanctification), but rather with justification. . . . In Wesley's *Explanatory Notes,* on Acts chapters 2, 8, 10, 11 and 19, where the Spirit baptism is reported by Luke, one will not find any indication whatever that he sees the Spirit baptism as associated with entire sanctification.[136]

According to Grider, Wesley "did not associate Pentecost with the second work of grace (entire sanctification), but rather with justification."[137] Wesley did not equate Christian perfection with the baptism of the Spirit at any state of his theological development — covering a span of over fifty years. Rather he taught that the new birth is accomplished by receiving or being baptized with the Holy Spirit. In "The First Fruits of the Spirit," Wesley spoke of the justified believer who has not yet been cleansed from inward sin as "filled with the Holy Ghost."[138] In his comments on Acts 1:5, Wesley taught that all true believers are baptized with the Holy Ghost.[139] According to him, Romans 8:9 teaches that if any man does not have the Spirit of Christ "he is not a member of Christ; not a Christian;

132Staples, "The Current Debate," 3.

133Wesley, *Explanatory Notes*, 3:2209.

134Wesley, *Works*, 8:287; 291.

135Staples, "The Current Debate," 3-4.

136Grider, *Entire Sanctification*, 58-59.

137Grider, *Entire Sanctification*, p. 58. Quanstrom made a similar statement [*Century of Holiness Theology*, 131].

138Wesley, *Works*, 5:89; 91.

139Wesley, *Notes*, 275.

not in a state of salvation."[140] Wesley also taught that water baptism should follow Spirit baptism in his comments on Acts10:47.[141]

This same emphasis continued in Wesley's sermons. He preached a sermon titled "Scriptural Christianity" based on Acts 4:31. At the outset, Wesley noted that the same expression, filled with the Holy Ghost, also occurs in Acts 2. However, Wesley opted to choose his text from Acts 4 because there was no account of any miraculous signs or extraordinary gifts. Wesley emphasized the fruit of the Spirit, rather than the gifts of the Spirit. However, in his conclusion his standard of Christianity was to be filled with the Spirit.[142] Herbert McGonigle wrote: "Throughout the sermon Wesley gives not the least hint that he thought this fullness of the Spirit something subsequent to justification by faith; indeed he made it very plain that anyone who was not so filled with the Spirit was not a Christian."[143]

Oden summarized Wesley, "It is typical for the life of the believer to be filled with the Holy Spirit. That is scriptural Christianity in all ages. . . . What happened at Pentecost does not happen only occasionally, but ordinarily and normatively within the faithful community of the baptized. . . . It is thus characteristic for ordinary believers to be 'filled with the Holy Spirit.'"[144]

In *A Farther Appeal to Men of Reason and Religion,* Wesley used several scriptures relating to the Holy Spirit, including Acts 2, which were in the Anglican homily for Whitsunday. He again emphasized the Spirit in salvation:

> And therefore every man, in order to believe unto salvation, must receive the Holy Ghost. This is essentially necessary to every Christian, not in order to his working miracles, but in order to faith, peace, joy, and love—the ordinary fruits of the Spirit.[145]

---

[140]Wesley, *Notes*, 381.

[141]Wesley, *Notes*, 305. Francis Martin observed that Luke did not seem to have considered there being any fixed order [*Acts* in *ACCS*, 5:139].

[142]Wesley, "Scriptural Christianity," Sermon #4, ¶1-4; 4.6.

[143]McGonigle, "Pneumatological Nomenclature," 61. Arnett summarized the sermon by saying, "Wesley expressed the view that every Christian should be Spirit-filled, and the intimation is that anyone who is not Spirit-filled is not a Christian" ["Role of the Holy Spirit," 23]. However, Laurence Wood misrepresents this sermon as highlighting "the personal responsibility of each believer to be made perfect in love" [*Meaning of Pentecost*, 350].

[144]Oden, *Wesley's Scriptural Christianity*, 222.

[145]Wesley, *BE Works*, 11:108.

In the same tract, Wesley returned to this same theme stating that "every true Christian now receives the Holy Ghost, as the Paraclete or Comforter promised by our Lord. . . . I assert that 'till a man 'receives the Holy Ghost' he is without God in the world."[146]

In his sermon "Of the Church," Wesley referred to that baptism of the Holy Ghost which the apostles received at the day of Pentecost, "and which in a lower degree is given to all believers."[147]

Daniel Steele, one of the leading scholars of the American holiness movement at the turn of the twentieth century, stated he had counted twenty-six terms Wesley used to refer to Christian perfection, but "the baptism of (or with) the Spirit" and "the fullness of the Spirit" were not phrases Wesley used

> probably because there is an emotional fullness of a temporary nature, not going down to the very roots of the moral nature. Nor did he use "receiving the Holy Ghost," because "in the sense of entire sanctification" the phrase is not scriptural and not quite proper; for they all received the Holy Ghost when they were justified.[148]

Randy Maddox concluded that for Wesley "the 'baptism' of the Spirit's renewed Presence comes at the beginning of our Christian life, and provides the indispensable empowerment for our growth in holiness all along the Way of Salvation — including the potential attainment of Christian Perfection."[149]

Modern holiness scholars have either tried to reconcile Wesley with what the holiness movement now teaches or they have been forced to admit a shift in emphasis. Timothy Smith tried to argue that since Fletcher equated the baptism of the Spirit with Christian perfection in his "Last Check to Antinomianism" and that since Wesley approved of what Fletcher wrote, that Wesley, too, believed entire sanctification was by Spirit baptism.[150]

In the following issue of the *Wesleyan Theological Journal*, however, Smith was taken to task by Grider. Although Grider himself equates entire sanctification and the baptism of the Spirit, he is not convinced that Wesley made the connection. He implies that Smith avoided the plain statements of Wesley that would not harmonize with his conclusion and he concludes that Smith is

---

[146]Wesley, *Works*, 11:168; 170.

[147]Wesley, Sermon #74, 1.12.

[148]*Steele's Answers*, 130.

[149]Maddox, *Responsible Grace*, p. 177.

[150]Smith, "How John Fletcher Became," 68-87.

mistaken.[151]

In the opinion of Donald Dayton, "Smith relies on more general references to the work of the Holy Spirit and a more general use of 'Pentecostal imagery'" but Smith "fails to establish that the instances to which he points are as characteristic of Wesley as he implies."[152] Later in *A Wesleyan-Holiness Theology* Grider declared, "John Wesley taught that the baptism with the Holy Spirit occurs at the time of our justification."[153]

George Allen Turner recognized there was a shift in emphasis:

> John and Charles said or wrote little about the baptism in the Holy Spirit. This emphasis is relatively recent. It is not easy to find Wesleyan writers devoting much space to it or associating it with entire sanctification and evangelical perfection.[154]

Mildred Wynkoop explained that Wesley wanted to avoid fanaticism by using precisely the Biblical language. She wrote:

> Among the very many terms he used for entire sanctification, never did he call it the baptism of the Holy Spirit or any like term because of the danger of seeking the Holy Spirit for some accompanying gift or emotion instead of seeking Christ and His will.[155]

Leo Cox offered this evaluation:

> Apparently Wesley feared that using the term receiving the Holy Ghost exclusively for the second experience would lessen its meaning for regeneration. Never did Wesley want to lower the content of regeneration to make room for entire sanctification.[156]

Even Timothy L. Smith admitted,

---

[151]Grider, "Evaluation of Timothy Smith's Interpretation of Wesley," *Wesleyan Theological Journal* 15:2 (Fall 1980): 64-69.

[152]Dayton, *Theological Roots of Pentecostalism*, 57.

[153]Grider, *Wesleyan-Holiness Theology*, 426.

[154]Turner, *Vision Which Transforms*, 149.

[155]Wynkoop, *Foundations*, 112.

[156]Cox, *Perfection*, 132.

> Wesley did not adopt Fletcher's doctrine that Pentecost was the moment when the apostles received the experience of perfect love, though after about 1741 he always equated the fullness of the Spirit with that experience. He had long thought Pentecost displayed the whole work of the hallowing Spirit in regeneration as well as entire sanctification.[157]

Donald Bloesch explained, "Wesley carefully refrained from calling the experience of the second blessing the baptism of the Holy Spirit. . . . Wesley regarded the baptism of the Holy Spirit as incorporation into the body of Christ through repentance and faith."[158]

Kenneth Collins concluded that Wesley rejected the restriction of the phrase "receiving the Holy Ghost" to the experience of Christian perfection. Wesley used the phrase "filled with the Holy Ghost" in an interchangeable way: sometimes in terms of the new birth and at other times in terms of entire sanctification. Nor did he link the phrase "baptized with the Holy Ghost" with Christian perfection.[159]

Wesley argued that the Lord's Supper was a converting *and* confirming ordinance. Wesley pointed out that when the Lord's Supper was instituted, "Our Lord commanded those very men who were then *unconverted*, who had *not* yet 'received the Holy Ghost', who (in the full sense of the word) were not *believers*,"to 'do this in remembrance of him'.[160]

Yet Laurence Wood began his attempt to link Pentecost with Christian perfection in early Methodism with this quote from Wesley: "This is that religion which our Lord has established upon earth, ever since the descent of the Holy Ghost on the day of Pentecost . . . Love enthroned in the heart [=entire sanctification]."[161] The unedited quote, however, reveals a different interpretation:

> This is that religion which our Lord has established upon earth, ever since the descent of the Holy Ghost on the day of Pentecost. This is the entire, connected system of Christianity: and thus the several parts of it rise one above another, from that lowest point, 'the assembling ourselves together', to the highest, love

---

[157]Smith, *Nazarenes and the Wesleyan Mission*, 11.

[158]Bloesch, *Holy Spirit*, 127.

[159]Collins, *Theology of John Wesley*, 137-138.

[160]Wesley, *BE Works*, 19:158; see also 9:112.

[161]Wood, *Meaning of Pentecost*, 1.

enthroned in the heart.[162]

Thus, Wesley viewed Pentecost as the inauguration of the entire system of Christianity. Wesley believed that the Holy Spirit in the heart of the believer would lead him on unto perfection. This is not the perfection of God or of angels or of a sinless Adam, but a perfection of love. Wesley preached, "This is the sum of Christian perfection: it is all comprised in that one word, love."[163] Wesley was pessimistic about man's nature, but optimistic about God's grace.[164]

Wesley stated that "*sinless perfection* is a phrase I never use, lest I should seem to contradict myself."[165] He declared, "None feel their need of Christ like these; none so entirely depend upon him."[166] "The best of men still need Christ, in his priestly office, to atone for their omissions, their shortcomings (as some not improperly speak), their mistakes in judgment and practice, and their defects of various kinds. For these are all deviations from the perfect law, and consequently need an atonement."[167] Leo Cox explained,

> Wesley believed that one fact about the sin problem is settled when the sinner is regenerated. The one born of God does not commit sin. The youngest and weakest child of God is finished with this kind of sin. As long as he possesses this living faith, he does not willfully transgress a known law of God. . . . Nor do the sins of the sanctified mean that sinfulness which remains in the believer after justification, but which is purged in the experience of entire sanctification. The "sin in believers" for Wesley was very real and needed the cleansing Blood. This kind

---

[162]Wesley, "On Zeal," Sermon # 92, 2.6.

[163]Wesley, "On Perfection," Sermon #76, 1.4.

[164]Rupp, *Principalities and Powers*, 90. Williams, *Wesley's Theology Today*, 190.

[165]Wesley, *Works*, 11:396. "'Absolute or infallible perfection?' I never contended for it. Sinless perfection? I do not contend for this, seeing it is not scriptural" [*Letter* to Mrs. Maitland, 12 May 1763]. Flew explained, "He must mean that the actual adjective 'sinless' is never used in the New Testament to qualify perfection" [*Idea of Perfection*, 325]. Yet he also wrote, "I do not contend for the term *sinless*, though I do not object against it" [Wesley, *Works*, 11:446].

[166]Wesley, *Works*, 11:395.

[167]Wesley, *Works*, 11:396. Of the two doctrines, the atonement of Christ and Christian perfection, Wesley said he "would sooner give up perfection. But we need not give up either one or the other"[*Works*, 11:418].

of sin is present in the initially sanctified but it no longer remains in the entirely sanctified. . . . But Wesley saw a third kind of sin which he variously called "sins" of ignorance, or "sins" of infirmity, or mistakes. These sins are consistent with perfect love and are experienced constantly by the entirely sanctified. From these sins no saint is ever delivered in this life.[168]

Wesley also warned that Christian perfection may be lost. Wesley came to see the experience of Christian perfection as a relationship that could always be either improved or forfeited. Thus, he did not view it as a static state. Steven Harper came to the same conclusion. "The fact that Wesley allows this possibility among believers (yes, even among those who are sanctified), demonstrates his central conviction that perseverance is not held on the basis of God's election, but on the continuance of faith in those who have been saved."[169]

---

[168]Cox, *Perfection*, 168; see Wesley, "Christian Perfection," Sermon #40, 1.9.

[169]Harper, "A Wesleyan Arminian View," 244. Pope seems to say that theoretically Christian perfection may be lost, but it is not probable [*Compendium*, 3:59].

In April of 2003 I talked with Norm Geisler, who was in the process of writing his four-volume systematic theology. While he is not Wesleyan, he wanted to dialogue with someone who would present the Wesleyan position. He asked me if one who was perfected could lose his salvation. I later submitted to him a four-page reply. Geisler discussed the Wesleyan view of sanctification in his *Systematic Theology* [3:238-240]. It is here that he addresses the question of whether one who was perfected could lose his salvation. Geisler wrote,

> Wesley does not explain how one can be in a sinless state (which he repeatedly said was possible) and yet still commit a sin so serious as to lose his salvation (which he believed could happen). In his Journal (August 1743), Wesley wrote: "I cannot believe . . . that there is a state attainable in this life, from which a man cannot finally fall" (in WJW, 1.427). But if one had attained a state where sin was no longer possible, how could he commit any sin by which he would lose salvation?

I had written to Geisler that the experience of Christian perfection was a relationship that could always be either improved or forfeited. Thus, Wesley did not view it as a static state. I had also quoted Steven Harper (cited above). Yet none of this material was used. My own feeling is that Geisler tended to build up and tear down his own straw man which he labeled "Wesleyan Perfectionism." Burwash explained that the perfect Christian is still within the moral limits of probation, otherwise he may still fail and fall away. "If this were not so, Christian perfection would end probation, and the life of perfect holiness would move forward automatically." Yet we must always

John L. Peters had a page summarizing Wesley's position that Christian perfection may be lost. In his *Journal* 24 August, 1743, Wesley had stated he was inclined to believe, "That there is a state attainable in this life, from which a man cannot finally fall." Peters points out that later Wesley had changed his mind. "I cannot perceive any state mentioned in Scripture from which we may not (in a measure, at least) fall."[170]

Wesley preached, "It is a common thing for those who are thus sanctified, to believe they cannot fall; to suppose *themselves* 'pillars in the temple of God, that shall go out no more.' Nevertheless, we have seen some of the strongest of them, after a time, moved from their steadfastness. Sometimes suddenly, but oftener by slow degrees, they have yielded to temptation; and pride, or anger, or foolish desires have again sprung up in their hearts. Nay, sometimes they have utterly lost the life of God, and sin hath regained dominion over them."[171] Wesley wrote to Jane Hilton,

> I rejoice to hear that you stand fast in the liberty wherewith Christ hath made you free; and the more, because, although many taste of that heavenly gift, deliverance from inbred sin, yet so few, so exceeding few, retain it one year; hardly one in ten; nay, one in thirty. Many hundreds in London were made partakers of it, within sixteen or eighteen months: But I doubt whether twenty of them are now as holy and as happy as they were. And hence, others had doubted whether God *intended that*

---

watch and pray [*Manual of Christian Theology*, 2:321].

Appendix Five in Geisler's *Systematic Theology* was entitled "Wesleyan Perfectionism" [3:574-587]. I do not feel he had a clear understanding of the subject. My greatest disappointment is that he evaluated Wesleyan teaching in light of Warfield's *Studies in Perfectionism*. And yet Warfield had very little to say about Wesley. Warfield's critique was directed mainly towards later Keswick authors. Geisler and I discussed this point and that is why he initially wanted input from a more Wesleyan perspective. Yet in the end, Warfield's concerns with Keswick perfectionism were used to indict Wesleyan Perfectionism. I felt that Warfield went after the mutations within the American holiness movement more than after Wesley's teaching. At one point Warfield even declared, "John Wesley is undeniably right when he says that holiness is the substance of salvation" [*Perfectionism*, 1:108]. Geisler did address the flaws in Warfield's critique of Wesleyan perfectionism in his *Systematic Theology*, 3:585-587. However, Geisler ends the section with his own misunderstanding of Wesleyan perfectionism.

[170]Peters, *Christian Perfection*, 47. Wesley's second citation is from a letter to Elizabeth Hardy, 26 December, 1761.

[171]Wesley, "A Call to Backsliders," Sermon # 86, 2.3 (5).

salvation to be enjoyed long. That many *have* it for a season, that they allow; but are not satisfied that any *retain* it always. Shall not you, for one? You will, if you watch and pray, and continue hanging upon Him.[172]

Two months later he wrote her,

Two things are certain: The one, that it is possible to lose even the pure love of God; the other, that it is not necessary, it is not unavoidable; it may be lost, but it may be kept. Accordingly, we have some, in every part of the kingdom, who have never been moved from their steadfastness. And from this moment you need never be moved: His grace is sufficient for you. But you must continue to grow, if you continue to stand; for no one can stand still. And is it not your Lord's will concerning you, that you should daily receive a fresh increase of love? And see that you labor so much the more, to comfort the feeble-minded, to support the weak, to confirm the wavering, and recover them that are out of the way.[173]

Wesley also wrote to Elizabeth Bennis,

Some years since, I was inclined to think that none who had once enjoyed and then lost the pure love of God must ever look to enjoy it again till they were just stepping into eternity. But experience has taught us better things: We have at present numerous instances of those who had cast away that unspeakable blessing, and now enjoy it in a larger measure than ever. And why should not this be your case? Because you are unworthy? So were they. Because you have been an unfaithful steward? So had they been also; yet God healed them freely: And so he will you, only do not reason against him. Look for nothing in yourself but sin and unworthiness. Forget yourself.[174]

Wesley wrote to Adam Clarke,

To retain the grace of God, is much more than to gain it: Hardly

[172]Wesley, *Letter* to Jane Hilton, 15 March, 1770.

[173]Wesley, *Letter* to Jane Hilton, 8 May, 1770.

[174]Wesley, *Letter* to Elizabeth Bennis, 30 May, 1769.

> one in three does this. And this should be strongly and explicitly urged on all who have tasted of perfect love. If we can prove that any of our Local Preachers or Leaders, either directly or indirectly, speak against it, let him be a Local Preacher or Leader no longer. I doubt whether he should continue in the society; because he that could speak thus in our congregations cannot be an honest man. . . .Last week I had an excellent letter from Mrs. Pawson, (a glorious witness of full salvation,) showing how impossible it is to retain pure love without growing therein.[175]

In *A Plain Account of Christian Perfection*, Wesley wrote,

> Q. 29. Can those who are perfect grow in grace?
> A. Undoubtedly they can; and that not only while they are in the body, but to all eternity.
> Q. 30. Can they fall from it?
> A. I am well assured they can; matter of fact puts this beyond dispute. Formerly we thought, one saved from sin could not fall; now we know the contrary. We are surrounded with instances of those who lately experienced all that I mean by perfection. They had both the fruit of the Spirit, and the witness; but they have now lost both. Neither does any one stand by virtue of anything that is implied in the nature of the state. There is no such height or strength of holiness as it is impossible to fall from. If there be any that cannot fall, this wholly depends on the promise of God.
> Q. 31. Can those who fall from this state recover it?
> A. Why not? We have many instances of this also. Nay, it is an exceeding common thing for persons to lose it more than once, before they are established therein.[176]

Wesley's emphasis was always on the fruit of the Spirit and the purging that produces more fruit (John 15:2). "By perfection I mean the humble, gentle, patient love of God and man ruling all the tempers, words, and actions, the whole

---

[175]Wesley, *Letter* to Adam Clarke, 26 November, 1790. See also Wesley's *Journal*, "Twenty years this society was a pattern to all the country for seriousness and deep devotion. I think seventeen of them were perfected in love; but only three of them remain, and most of the rest are either removed, or grown cold and dead" [17 June, 1790].

[176]Wesley, *Works*, 11:426-427.

heart and the whole life."[177] He was not charismatic in his emphasis on spiritual gifts.[178] In 1739, Wesley went with some friends "to try the spirits" of one known as a "French prophet." She evidently did not speak in other tongues, but spoke mostly in Scripture words. Some of Wesley's friends believed that "she spoke by the Spirit of God," but Wesley stated no opinion at that time.[179]

Five months later, Wesley called on one who had been hindered in his pursuit of holiness by these French prophets. Wesley, then, warned his people against them declaring that all such phenomena must be tested against the Word of God.[180] Almost a half century later, Wesley remembered the "extravagance" of these prophets and saw it as the work of Satan. He believed such fanaticism brought the "real work into contempt." However, Wesley cautioned that whenever fanaticism is reproved, the reprover must himself show a right spirit.[181] Wesley was wise in delaying his judgment until he had seen the fruit of their teaching. However, Howard Snyder saw this "openness to the gifts of the Spirit" as evidence that Wesley was charismatic.[182]

Around 1762 a Methodist preacher named Thomas Maxfield began preaching Christian perfection in a fanatical way. In writing to him, Wesley stated his objection to such practices as several singing, speaking, or praying at once, expressions in prayer that were too bold and bordered on irreverence, and screaming so that the words were unintelligible. Wesley also objected to his practice of telling seekers they would be justified or sanctified just then and affirming them when they were not. Maxfield taught angelic perfection, human infallibility, and depreciated justification by denying that a justified individual was a temple of the Holy Ghost. He also claimed to have the gift of discernment.[183]

Wesley wrote Maxfield, "I dislike your directly or indirectly depreciating justification; saying, a justified person is not in Christ, is not born of God, is not

---

[177]Wesley, *Letters* to Charles Wesley, September 1762; 27 January 1767.

[178]Dayton, *Theological Roots of Pentecostalism*, 42; 45; Schmidt, *John Wesley*, 2:2:22.

[179]Wesley, *Journal*, 28 January, 1739. This woman was named in Wesley's diary as Mary Plewit. She belonged to a sect of French Huguenots.

[180]Wesley, *Journal*, 22 June, 1739.

[181]Wesley, *Journal*, 3 April, 1786.

[182]Snyder and Runyan, *Divided Flame*, 57. Writing as a Wesleyan, Rob Staples declared that we believe in spiritual gifts. "Thus we, too, are charismatics. But we are charismatics *who do not speak in unknown tongues*" ["A Rose is a Rose," 25]. See also Wesley's comments in his *Journal*, 25 November 1759.

[183]Wesley, *Journal*, 2 November 1762; 24 November 1762.

a new creature, has not a new heart, is not sanctified, not a temple of the Holy Ghost; or that he cannot please God, or cannot grow in grace."[184]

Another Methodist preacher, George Bell claimed he heard a voice telling him he was "all holiness to the Lord" and he said he would never die.[185] Bell also predicted the world would end on February 28, 1763.[186] In a letter, Wesley said Bell and his followers "were led to value these extraordinary gifts more than the ordinary grace of God; and I could not convince them that a grain of humble love was better than all these gifts put together."[187] Fletcher concluded, "Bell asserted that his 'Perfection' rendered him infallible, above temptation, and superior to the instructions of all persons who were not perfect."[188]

Wesley finally dismissed Bell from the Methodist society. Maxfield separated from Wesley and formed an independent work. Because of this confusion John wrote to Charles asking, "Shall we go on in asserting perfection against all the world? Or shall we quietly let it drop?"[189] However, this seems to have been a rhetorical question intending to sound out Charles. As late as 1790

---

[184]Wesley, *Journal*, 29 October 1762. Mudge introduced this letter by saying that in his day John Wesley had to rebuke this very error that made the baptism with the Holy Ghost a synonym for entire sanctification [*Growth in Holiness*, 256]. See also the warning against depreciating justification in order to exalt the state of full sanctification, in the minutes of some Methodist conversations. "When we are going to speak of entire sanctification, let us first describe the blessings of a justified state, as strongly as possible" [Wesley, *Works*, 8:298]. As soon as any man believes, he is a new creature, sanctified, pure in heart. Christ dwells therein and he is a temple of the Holy Ghost [Wesley, *Works*, 8:291].

[185]Wesley, *Works*, 10:411. Apparently Bell and his followers professed to have become so holy that they were beyond temptation. Thus, they claimed a third work which lifted their minds above the reach of evil thoughts. Wesley's sermon "On Sin in Believers" was designed to refute this teaching. For other examples of holiness fanaticism resulting in the claim that the sanctified would not die, see p. 690.

[186]Wesley, *Works*, 8:350; see also *Journal* 28 February 1763. After Bell's prophesy failed, he not only gave up the office of prophet, but abandoned all pretense of religion, went into politics, and died an infidel [Boland, *Problem of Methodism*, 95].

[187]Wesley, *Works*, 12:481; see Collins, *John Wesley: Theological Journey*, 203-204.

[188]Wesley, *Letter* to Lady Huntingdon, 9 May 1763; see also his letter to Charles Wesley, 22 Nov 1762 in *Works*, 4:317-318.

[189]Wesley, *Letter*, 14 June 1768. John again ask Charles this question in a letter, 25 March 1772. See also Tyerman, *Life and Times of Wesley*, 2:434; 460.

John advised Clarke to dismiss any leader who spoke against perfect love.[190]

Charles Wesley (1707-1788)

The Methodists learned their theology not only from the sermons of John, but from the hymns of Charles. Charles wrote over nine thousand hymns.[191] Most of these hymns were "censored" by John and, as finally published, reflected his viewpoint as well.[192] But Crichton Mitchell stated, "It is well known that the Wesley brothers had their differences as to the true nature of Christian perfection."[193] According to Timothy Smith, the brothers did not disagree in their understanding of Christian perfection before 1760.[194] However, as early as 1749, John recognized that Charles was going his own way when he reacted to the publication of *Hymns and Sacred Poems*, "As I did not see these before they were published, there were some things in them which I did not approve of."[195]

Charles professed Christian perfection in September of 1740. He recorded in his *Journal*

> I was greatly assisted in the evening to preach the Christian perfection, that is, utter dominion over sin; constant peace, and love, and joy in the Holy Ghost; the full assurance of faith, righteousness, and true holiness. I see more and more into the height of our privileges, and that God will give them to me.

Two days later he testified, "At the sacrament I received power to believe sin shall not have dominion over me."[196]

Yet in December 1740 Charles preached on the "necessity of our being bruised and broken *before* the Comforter would abide in us for ever."[197] Tyson concluded that Charles extended the metaphors of suffering and sanctification

---

[190]Wesley, *Letter*, 26 November 1790.

[191]Tyson, *Charles Wesley on Sanctification*, 47.

[192]Sangster, *Path to Perfection*, 57.

[193]Mitchell, *The Wesley Century*, 260.

[194]Smith, "Holy Spirit in the Hymns of the Wesleys," 2:1014.

[195]Wesley, *Works*, 11:391; Tyson, *Charles Wesley on Sanctification*, 261.

[196]*Journal of Charles Wesley*, 1:250; 26/28 September 1740.

[197]*Journal of Charles Wesley*, 1:264; 22 December 1740.

beyond their biblical basis.[198]

Charles was also prone to self depreciation and tended to set his expectations too high.[199] When Charles had written of the entirely sanctified, "All the struggle then is o'er," and "I wrestle not now," John declared, "These are two of my brother's expressions, which I do not subscribe to."[200] In his great hymn, "Love Divine" he originally wrote, "Take away our power of sinning," but John Fletcher felt this was too strong. Fletcher asked, "Can God take away the power of sinning without taking away our power of free obedience?"[201] Therefore, he suggested, "Take away the love of sinning."[202]

At times Charles expressed a morbid view of life. He was influenced throughout his life by the mystical writers and John felt "he never quite got the 'poison' out of his system."[203] Martin Groves analyzed the spirituality of Charles Wesley, asking whether he was best understood as a mystical or ascetic theologian. Groves concluded that he was both. His asceticism is the disciplined exercise of the desire for God. His mysticism is the account he gives of the goal of that desire, the place where the self is lost in God.[204]

There is not complete harmony of thought in the hymns of Charles. He tended to be more mystical and less precise than was John. Charles believed in the "dark night of the soul."[205] He described the sinner praying for repentance

To feel the clouds that round me roll,
The night that hangs upon my soul:
The darkness of my carnal mind.

---

[198]*Charles Wesley on Sanctification*, 267-268.

[199]Wiseman, *Charles Wesley*, 162; Tyson, *Charles Wesley on Sanctification*, 260-261. See also Peck, *Sketches from the Saddlebag*, 188-189. According to Robert M. Fraser, Charles Wesley fits the description of having Cyclothymic Disorder. This is similar to, but less severe than Bipolar Disorder [*Strains in the Understandings of Christian Perfection*, 97; 463-466].

[200]Failing, "Developments in Holiness Theology," 12.

[201]Cited by Sangster, *Path to Perfection*, 63.

[202]Hogue, "Hymns That Are Immortal,"42. John omitted the second verse in the 1780 *Collection* [*BE Works*, 7:17], but it eventually was included with the line "take away our bent to sinning."

[203]Wiseman, *Charles Wesley*, 157.

[204]Groves, "Charles Wesley's Spirituality," 446-463.

[205]Wiseman, *Charles Wesley*, 157.

My will perverse, my passions blind.[206]

In his *Hymns and Sacred Poems* (1749) Charles began to assert that entire sanctification took place at the article of death. He maintained this emphasis through the rest of his life. Charles also tended to view Christian perfection in absolute terms of sinlessness. Charles longed for an impossible perfection and John warned him, "There is *no such perfection* here as *you* describe — at least, I never met an instance of it; and I doubt I ever shall. Therefore, I still think to set perfection so *high* is effectually to renounce it."[207] Such an emphasis would naturally result in a more progressive view of sanctification.

As early as 1749 Charles was prone to describe Christian perfection as a process of growth and maturation. He did not completely depart from John's point of view, but there was a shift in emphasis.[208] Thomas Jackson wrote that around 1762 Charles began to hold that Christian perfection was a much higher attainment that either he or his brother had previously regarded it. It is not obtained by a present act of faith, but as the result of severe discipline, which included affliction, temptation, long continued labor, and persevering faith through spiritual darkness.[209] Luke Wiseman said that Charles came to think of sanctification as

> a gradual work wrought out through discipline, and not finally achieved until death. He never, indeed, gave up the conviction of his early ministry that the state of entire sanctification is attained by simple faith and therefore might conceivably be realized long before death—a view which John consistently held. But as time went on he realized more vividly the exceeding sinfulness of sin, and its deep penetration into human nature. In the buffetings of life he learned to know himself better and to discern the subtle workings of the old man in actions which seemed to be good. So his natural caution led him to hesitate to declare that he had gained perfection's height.[210]

---

[206]Wesley, *BE Works*, 7:202-203.

[207]Wesley, *Letter*, 9 July 1977.

[208]Tyson, *Charles Wesley on Sanctification*, 171; see Tyson's summary on p. 309.

[209]Jackson, *Life of Charles Wesley*, 2:210.

[210]*Charles Wesley*, 167-168.

J. A. Wood also felt the fanaticism of Bell and Maxfield in 1762 caused Charles to react against the doctrine of instantaneous sanctification.[211] Charles wrote some hymns during this period which contained criticism of fanatics who professed perfection.[212] He felt they were ambition, impatient, schismatic, deceived, and proud. While they claimed instantaneous perfection, according to Charles they were believers whose race had just begun. He compared them to the seed in Matthew 13:20-21 which sprang up in an instant, but was shallow. Charles wrote,

That work of faith the novice blind
Would fain, on fancy's horse, leap o'er,
A short way to Sion find.[213]

Timothy Smith has attempted to establish a connection between the themes of entire sanctification and Pentecost within the hymns.[214] Although the Wesleys did publish thirty-two hymns for Whitsunday, they refer to the general ministry of the Holy Spirit and not to Christian perfection in particular. Charles was converted on Whitsunday and he considered justification, as well as sanctification, from that vantage point. According to John Tyson, the main thrust of these hymns was a connection between the ascended Christ and the presence of the Spirit. The imagery of Pentecost was not the center of Charles' understand of sanctification. Instead his grasp of sanctification was built on the foundation of Christ.[215]

In the hymnal, *A Collection of Hymns for the Use of People Called Methodists,* there is a section "For Believers Seeking for Full Redemption." According to Ken Bible these hymns are "overwhelmingly Christocentric" and "one of the most striking aspects of the Wesleys' holiness hymns is their lack of

---

[211]Wood, *Christian Perfection*, 53. Yet see Rack, "Charles Wesley and Early Methodism," 51 which seems to connect the Bell and Maxfield excesses to the more pessimistic views of Charles. See also Eby, "Images of Perfection," 188. Wood refers to the fanaticism of "Maxwell," but apparently he meant "Maxfield." See also Dallimore, *George Whitefield*, 2:461.

[212]Tyson, *Charles Wesley on Sanctification*, 286-290.

[213]Eby, "Images of Perfection," 188-194; Charles Wesley, *Short Hymns*, 2:323.

[214]Smith, "Holy Spirit in the Hymns of the Wesleys," 1011-1031; see also Smith, *Pentecost Hymns of John and Charles Wesley*. While these hymns were written for liturgical use at Pentecost Sunday and while they speak of the Holy Spirit, including his sanctifying work, they do not speak of pentecostal sanctification.

[215]Tyson, *Charles Wesley on Sanctification*, 194-196.

emphasis on the Spirit."[216] Bible concluded that "a careful examination of their hymns casts grave doubts on any direct connection between Pentecost and full redemption in their thought."[217]

McGonigle reached a similar conclusion, "In these hymns there is little mention of the Spirit's work; it is the Saviour, the righteous Lord, and the gracious Father, who are called upon to cast out sin and perfect the seeker in holiness. . . . Undoubtedly Charles Wesley taught that the Holy Spirit entered the believer's heart when he was born again; yet he prays the Spirit will come again and complete the work begun."[218] Turner also concluded, "Repeatedly, Charles Wesley in his hymns calls on the Lord for instant and complete deliverance from sin, but he seldom invokes the Spirit as the sanctifier."[219]

It is amusing that R. L. Brandt, in an article entitled "Tongues Are Good for You," would say, "Charles Wesley wrote, 'O for a thousand tongues to sing my great Redeemer's praise.' We wonder if he discovered the gift of tongues by which this could be possible."[220] No, but Charles did declare, "He breaks the power of cancelled sin, He sets the prisoner free."

Incredibly, J. Rodman Williams also described this hymn as an intense yearning for multiple tongues as a means of declaring what had been deeply experienced.[221] Actually Charles Wesley yearned for a thousand *people* to join him in worship.

Charles was not only a poet, but he was also an able preacher. His sermon, "Awake, Thou That Sleepest" is included in John Wesley's Standard Sermons, In the sermon Charles asked, "Hast thou received the Holy Ghost? If thou hast not, thou art not yet a Christian."[222]In his journal, Charles recorded the account of his conversion under the heading "The Day of Pentecost."[223]

Early in his ministry, Charles anticipated an outpouring of the Spirit in revival. He told John, "Your day of Pentecost is not fully come. But I doubt not

---

[216]Bible, "Wesleys' Hymns," 82. "There is little or not Pentecostal content in the full redemption hymns, especially in the Scripture backgrounds used and in Holy Spirit material" [p. 86].

[217]Bible, "Wesleys' Hymns," 86.

[218]McGonigle, "Pneumatological Nomenclature," 67-68.

[219]Turner, "Baptism of the Holy Spirit," 71.

[220]Brandt, "Tongues Are Good for You," 35.

[221]Williams, *Renewal Theology*, 2:227; 232.

[222]Wesley, *Works*, 5:30; Newport, *Sermons of Charles Wesley*, Sermon #8, 211-224.

[223]*Journal of Charles Wesley*, 1:90.

it will, and you will then hear of persons sanctified as frequently as you do now of persons justified." In light of his clear statements to the contrary, this statement should not be interpreted as Charles equating Pentecost and entire sanctification. Instead it was a comparison of the revival in the British Isles with the day of Pentecost. Twenty years later John felt that he had lived to see such a revival and said, "That many of these did not retain the gift of God, is no proof that it was not given them. That many of them do retain it at this day is matter of praise and thanksgiving."[224]

John Tyson wrote that Charles Wesley was fond of calling Christian perfection "the grand impossibility, yet he anticipated a real restoration of inner purity through "the omnipotence of grace." Christian perfection was not an empty ideal, but rather the logical fulfillment of the gospel of love.

Love our real holiness,
Love our spotless character,
Love is liberty and peace,
Pardon, and perfection here.

This perfectionist language was not based on moral achievement; it was the language of inner renewal.[225] The foundation of his theology was the concept of recapitulation. Like Irenaeus, Charles began his theology of redemption with the need to recreate the righteousness of Adam through the restoration of the image of God. Charles saw justification and sanctification together as two moments in God's strategy to counteract the effects of the Fall. Charles was attracted to the emphasis of the Eastern church on Christian perfection through love, devotional piety, and a healthy reliance upon the Word, the Spirit, and the sacraments.[226]

In 1762, Charles published *Short Hymns on Select Passages of Scripture* in two volumes. While he continued to believe Christian perfection was possible in this life, there was a difference in emphasis. He continued to see Christian perfection as a process of growth and maturity, moving away from an "instantaneous blessing." Charles wrote,

Yet till thy time is fully come,
I dare not hastily presume
To snatch the perfect grace,

---

[224]John Wesley, *Journal*, 28 October 1762.

[225]Tyson, *Charles Wesley on Sanctification*, 164-166. Tyson quoted from Osborne, *Poetical Works of John and Charles Wesley*, 7:346, #50.

[226]Tyson, *Charles Wesley on Sanctification*, 60-61.

But humbly patient to the end,
And praying at Thy feet attend,
Till Thou unveil Thy face.

Yet John added his editorial comment to the second line, "I dare say 'NOW is the accepted time.'"[227] When Charles wrote that the conquest of sin was not a sudden stroke of grace, but by "degrees insensible," John added "both suddenly and gradually."[228]

According to John Tyson three specific questions framed the controversy between the Wesley brothers:

- Was Charles setting the doctrine of Perfection "too high"?
- Is Christian Perfection an instantaneous blessing or is it received gradually over the course of an entire life?
- Did it occur "in the article of death" or before?

Tyson concluded that Charles's *Short Hymns* show that he took the opposite point of view from that of his brother on all three questions.[229]

John also wrote to Dorothy Furley warning her of "high-strained perfection" which led to "a thousand nervous disorders." He warned that to set the doctrine too high had the effect of driving it out of the world. He concluded by warning, "Take care you are not hurt by anything in the *Short Hymns* contrary to the doctrine you have long received."[230]

In 1766, John wrote encouraging Charles to "press the instantaneous blessing."[231] The next year John wrote to Charles that he believed perfection was wrought in an instant. He explained, "But I believe in a gradual work both preceding and following that instant." Then he asked his brother, "Do we agree or differ here?"[232] Jackson added, "What answer Mr. Charles Wesley returned to

---

[227]Gunter, *The Limits of "Love Divine,"* 221.

[228]Wesley, *BE Works*, 7:16.

[229]Tyson, "This One Thing Needful," 190.

[230]Wesley, *Letter* 15 September 1762.

[231]Wesley, *Letter*, 27 June 1766. This statement should not be lifted out of context as though it represents John Wesley's complete thought concerning Christian perfection. John accepted progressive sanctification, but since Charles repudiated the instantaneous blessing John was trying to maintain balance by emphasizing the instantaneous aspect. Tyson explained that John was trying "to shame his younger brother into a more moderate stance" [*Charles Wesley on Sanctification*, 294].

[232]Wesley, *Letter*, 27 January 1767.

this candid and sensible letter, we have no means of ascertaining."[233]

The next month John accused Charles, "Therefore, *you* are altered in your sentiments. And, unless we come to an explanation, we shall inevitably contradict each other."[234] A year later John wrote to Charles that he was at his wit's end with regard to Christian Perfection.[235] A month later John realized they still had not come to a consensus. "Shall we go on in asserting perfection against all the world? Or shall we quietly let it drop? We really must do one or the other; and, I apprehend, the sooner, the better."[236]

There is no reason to believe they ever came to any agreement on this point. Therefore, it is inconsistent to appeal to Charles as supporting the doctrine of pentecostal sanctification, which emphasizes sanctification as instantaneous.

John Fletcher (1729-1785)

Voltaire was once asked by a skeptic friend if he had ever met anyone like Jesus Christ. After a lapse into silence, Voltaire answered seriously, "I once met Fletcher of Madeley."[237] Fletcher testified that he had been cleansed from all sin. On August 24, 1781 Fletcher testified , "I received this blessing four or five times before; but I lost it by not observing the order of God; who has told us, 'With the heart man believeth unto righteousness, and with the mouth confession is made unto salvation.' But the enemy offered his bait under various colors, to keep me from a public declaration of what my Lord had wrought."[238]

Yet it is also asserted that Fletcher modified the Methodist doctrine of Christian perfection. For twenty-five years Fletcher, an ordained Anglican

---

[233]Jackson, *Life of Charles Wesley*, 2:210.

[234]Wesley, *Letter*, 12 February 1767.

[235]Wesley, *Letter*, 14 May 1768.

[236]Wesley, *Letter*, 14 June 1768.

[237]Abbey and Overton, *English Church in the Eighteenth Century*, 2:113; see also Sangster, *Path to Perfection*, 32; *Pure in Heart*, 60.

[238]Tyerman, *Wesley's Designated Successor*, 492-493; also recorded in *Experience of Hester Ann Rogers*, 82-83. See the evaluation of Peters, *Christian Perfection*, 215-217.

Hester Ann prayed for a baptism with the Holy Ghost to make her clean [*Experience*, 30]. Fraser wrote that Fletcher's theology was spread by Hester Ann Rogers, who did not emphasize his dispensational theology nor the idea of multiple baptisms, but "developed a folk-theology about the baptism of the Spirit that was far more understandable to lay readers" [*Strains in the Understandings of Christian Perfection*, 389].

clergyman, pastored in Madeley, Shropshire, England. He is most famous for his defense of Wesley in his five *Checks to Antinomianism.* It was Wesley's intention for Fletcher to succeed him as the leader of the Methodist societies, but Fletcher died first.

Fletcher taught that there were three dispensations or stages of spiritual growth. The dispensation of the Father refers to those who believe in God as Creator, but have no knowledge of the revelation of God through Jesus Christ. Fletcher put Cornelius in this class.[239]

The dispensation of the Son describes those who know about Christ and believe that he is the Messiah, but have never personally been born again. They were justified, but not regenerated. Fletcher placed the disciples before Pentecost in this class.[240] Paul also was in this state three days and nights before he was born again.[241]

The dispensation of the Spirit begins with receiving the Spirit of Christ in the new birth. Christian perfection, according to Fletcher, is for those who have already entered this third dispensation. There was a perfection possible under each dispensation, but the standard of perfection was not the same. For the lowest class it would be "to fear God and work righteousness." For those who have the Scriptures, the standard would be to keep the law. But Fletcher declared that "the least perfect of all perfect Christians, is more perfect than the most perfect Jew."[242]

In his "Essay on Truth," Fletcher expanded upon "this great salvation from sin" by showing that under the Jewish dispensation even the holiest sometimes committed sin. But he warned that we "cannot measure the privilege of real Christians by those formerly given to the Jews."[243] The least person in the kingdom of God has greater privilege than John the Baptist. The new birth produces victory over sin (1 John 3:9). Robert Lyon concluded that the "new birth meant a radical break with sin."[244]

Fletcher said at Pentecost Christ set up his kingdom in the hearts of the

---

[239]Fletcher, *Works*, 1:275.

[240]Fletcher, *Works*, 3:151.

[241]Fletcher, *Works*, 4:118.

[242]Fletcher, *Works*, 2:523-525. Laurence Wood misrepresents the dispensation of the Son as regeneration and the dispensation of the Spirit as sanctification [*Pentecostal Grace*, 179-198; *Truly Ourselves, Truly the Spirit's*, 22-26]. See Steele, *Love Enthroned*, 98-110 for the traditional Methodist interpretation.

[243]Fletcher, *Works*, 1:589.

[244]Lyon, "Baptism and Spirit-Baptism," 23.

apostles.[245] Christ opened the dispensation of the Spirit at Pentecost.[246] If the new birth is entrance into this kingdom,[247] Christian perfection is the privilege of the Christian dispensation in its fullness.[248] Fletcher defined Christian perfection:

> We give the name of "Christian perfection" to that maturity of grace and holiness which established adult believers attain under the Christian dispensation: and thus we distinguish that maturity of grace, both from the ripeness of *grace*, which belongs to the dispensation of *the Jews below us*; and from the ripeness of *glory*, which belongs to *departed saints above us*. Hence it appears, that by "Christian perfection" we mean nothing but the cluster and maturity of the graces which compose the Christian character in the Church militant.[249]

Fletcher taught that the new birth was accomplished through the baptism of the Spirit. Although that was not the position of George Turner, he did admit this is what Fletcher taught.[250] In "A Sermon on the New Birth," Fletcher declared, "if the Holy Spirit have [sic] not descended upon you . . . purifying your heart by faith; your baptism has not saved you."[251]

In explaining the difference between the reformation of a Pharisee and the regeneration of a Christian, Fletcher taught that "nothing less can effect the second than a baptism of the Holy Ghost."[252] Later in the same sermon he stated, "Yes, you shall be baptized by the Holy Ghost for the remission of sins, and justified freely by faith."[253] Fletcher described the Gospel, not only as repentance, but remission of sins, and the gift of the Holy Ghost."[254] Referring to the outpouring of the Spirit in Acts 2 and 10, Fletcher explained:

---

[245]Fletcher, *Works*, 1:590.

[246]Fletcher, *Works*, 1:593.

[247]Fletcher, *Works*, 1:586.

[248]Fletcher, *Works*, 1:589.

[249]Fletcher, *Works*, 2:492.

[250]Turner, "Doctrine of Sanctification," 96.

[251]Fletcher, *Works*, 4:109.

[252]Fletcher, *Works*, 4:112.

[253]Fletcher, *Works*, 4:115.

[254]Fletcher, *Works*, 4:258.

> That they should be baptized with the Holy Ghost and spiritual fire, was not extraordinary, since it is the common blessing which can alone make a man a Christian, or conform him in the faith: but that the sound of a rushing wind should be heard, and luminous appearances seen resting upon them, that they should have been enabled to speak the wonderful works of God in other tongues, were uncommon circumstances attending their spiritual baptism.[255]

Fletcher continued by distinguishing between that which is normal and that which is extraordinary.

> When the same prejudiced persons are told that they must be "born of the Spirit, and receive the Holy Ghost," as well as Cornelius and his servants, overlooking the ordinary baptism of the Spirit, they pitch upon the extraordinary circumstance of the gift of tongues, imparted for a season, to remove the prejudices of the Jews, and to draw the attention of the Gentiles; and think, with a sneer, and a charge of enthusiasm, to overturn the apostolic saying, "If any man hath not the Spirit of Christ, he is none of his. Be not deceived, sir, by these persons. Acknowledge, that so sure as you want the regenerating knowledge of Christ, you want the manifestation of his Spirit, without which he can never be known savingly.[256]

Of Paul's reception of the Spirit in Acts 9, Fletcher wrote that God "gave peace to his guilty conscience, scattered all his fears, and gave him the Spirit of adoption by revealing Jesus in his heart. . . . Then was he a Christian; then was he born again."[257]

It is important to understand that Fletcher used the concept of Pentecost in a metaphoric, not literal, sense. Joseph Benson explained,

> He expected a Pentecost, not literally, but figuratively speaking. Did he expect cloven or distinct tongues of fire to rest upon him, or the gift of tongues, or that of prophecy, so called or of

---

[255]Fletcher, *Works*, 4:287. He also explained that "at the day of Pentecost [the 120] were filled with power, boldness, and zeal, which are graces common to all believers" [*Works*, 4:28].

[256]Fletcher, *Works*, 4:288.

[257]Fletcher, *Works*, 4:119.

healing? Did he expect to be enabled to raise the dead with a word or a touch? By no means: he looked for nothing of this kind. He expected only those ordinary operations and graces of the Spirit in a full and mature state which the holy Scriptures declare to be essential to the character of a true and perfect Christian.[258]

He wrote in *Appeal to Matter of Fact and Common Sense* about the gift of faith. He advised the seeker to knock "with the earnestness of the importunate widow, til the door of faith open," but he cautioned the seeker not to stop at the threshold of Christianity. "Go on 'from faith to faith' till thy 'day of Pentecost is fully come' till thou art 'endued with power from on high, baptized with the Holy Ghost and with fire.'"[259] This advice comes under the heading, "An Address to Earnest Seekers for Salvation."

However, Fletcher sometimes described the new birth in much broader terms. In "A Sermon on the New Birth," he described initial sanctification, progressive sanctification, and entire sanctification. After describing entire sanctification, Fletcher declared, "This is the highest point of the sanctification of a believer, and consequently his regeneration is complete."[260] Thus, Fletcher taught a progressive regeneration. Wesley recognized that regeneration is "an expression taken also in divers senses," but he explicitly separated the new birth from sanctification.[261]

Fletcher understood that the new creation is not complete until the believer has reached entire sanctification. Fletcher concluded this sermon on the new birth by exhorting seekers, "Yes, you shall be baptized by the Holy Ghost for the remission of sins, and justified freely by faith."[262]

---

[258]Benson, *Life of Fléchère*, 11th ed, 392. This biography was first published in 1804. The second edition was printed in 1805. Note that this statement by Benson was added as an appendix to later editions of his biography. It is not contained in the second edition, reprinted by Allegheny Publications in 1984. See Reasoner, "Joseph Benson Describes John Fletcher," 5-7.

[259]Fletcher, *Works*, 3:356.

[260]Fletcher, *Works*, 4:113-114; 267. Apparently Mary Fletcher, his wife, did not agree with this terminology preferring to preserve "the birth of the Spirit" as a designation for all justified believers [Wood, "Rediscovery of Pentecost," 25].

[261]Wesley, "Christian Perfection," Sermon #40, 2.2; "The New Birth," Sermon #45, 4.3. William H. Shontz pointed out that regeneration was often synonymous with sanctification in the Anglical divines ["Anglican Influence," 44].

[262]Fletcher, *Works*, 4:115. The fact is acknowledged by Wood, *Pentecostal Grace*, 191.

While Fletcher clearly equated regeneration with the baptism of the Spirit, yet his concept of regeneration seems to encompass more than the initial moment of salvation. Thus, Spirit baptism is not only part of conversion-initiation, but part of progressive regeneration. Yet he did not link the birth of the Spirit inextricably to entire sanctification. In a survey of four major positions on Spirit baptism, W. T. Purkiser called this "a holistic view."[263]

In his letters on the "Spiritual Manifestation of the Son of God," Fletcher referred to the day of Pentecost. He said, "That they should be baptized with the Holy Ghost and spiritual fire, was not extraordinary, since it is the common blessing which can alone make a man a Christian, or confirm him in the faith."[264] Here again Fletcher seems to teach more than one baptism. Laurence Wood believes Fletcher's point is that it may take a number of crisis points before the habit of entire sanctification is established.[265] A better explanation would come from Fletcher's own words:

> A manifestation of the Spirit last year will no more support a soul this year, than air breathed yesterday will nourish the flame of life to-day. The sun which warmed us last week must shine again this week. Old light is dead light. A notion of old warmth is a very cold notion. We must have fresh food daily, and though we need not a new Christ, we need, perpetually, new displays of his eternal love and power.[266]

More recently Wood wrote a more accurate reflection of Fletcher:

> Fletcher believed the baptism with the Spirit was an ongoing dynamic event always being updated in one's daily life. It was never a static, absolute attainment, representing a final achievement. For Fletcher, today's reception of the Spirit's fullness became tomorrow's promise of greater infillings of the Spirit.[267]

Robert Fraser explained that Fletcher shifted his emphasis on the work

---

[263]Purkiser, *Biblical Foundations*, 109. Purkiser mistakenly placed Fletcher in another category, however.

[264]Fletcher, *Works*, 4:287.

[265]Wood, *Pentecostal Grace*, 204-206.

[266]Fletcher, *Works*, 4:289.

[267]Wood, *Meaning of Pentecost*, 366.

of the Spirit as an attempt at reconciliation with the Calvinists. The Calvinists had been offended by the disputed minutes of the Methodist Conference for August 7, 1770, where it was stated "We have leaned too much towards Calvinism." Two years earlier John Wesley had warned that Calvinism was "the direct antidote to Methodism, the doctrine of heart-holiness." Wesley had also warned that the "predestinarian poison" created a false sense of security.[268]

On the other hand Walter Shirley feared the doctrine of Christian perfection would "necessarily lead seekers into a miserable bondage and the professors of it into Enthusiasm and spiritual pride." Therefore, he determined "to oppose Perfection with my utmost might."[269] As a result Shirley convinced his cousin Selina, Countess of Huntington that all Arminians must be expelled from Trevecca College. Joseph Benson, the head master was then dismissed just after Christmas 1770.

The Countess had spent much time and money promoting the Calvinist wing of Methodism under George Whitefield. She had declared, "I will suffer no one in *my* society that even *thinks* of perfection."[270]

Yet she had encouraged more collaboration between Whitefield's followers and Wesley's followers. Thus, she had hired both Fletcher and Benson. As president of the college, Fletcher's concern for Christian unity caused him to seek biblical metaphors for Christian perfection which would not be so offensive. He may have asked Benson to also attempt this task. Apparently, Fletcher's "discovery," which equated Christian perfection and Spirit baptism, was first developed and published by Benson around 1770 in "The Baptism of the Holy Ghost."[271]

In March of the following year Fletcher resigned, believing his usefulness at Trevecca was at an end. During Fletcher's last visit as president, Shirley attacked a work by Benson on the "Baptism of the Holy Ghost." According to a letter from Fletcher to Benson, Shirley "abused it under the name of 'Perfection.'" Fletcher closed his letter to Benson, "I rejoice that your desires after a larger measure of the Holy Spirit increase. Part rather with your heart's blood than with them."[272]

---

[268]Wesley, *Works*, 8:336.

[269]Coppedge, *Wesley in Theological Debate*, 219.

[270]*Letter* from John Wesley to Joseph Benson, 26 December 1769.

[271]This work by Benson is no longer extant.

[272]The letter from Fletcher, 22 March 1771, is found in several sources [see Wesley, *Works*, 11:298-299; Benson, *Life of Fletcher*, 145-147; Tyerman, *Wesley's Designated Successor*, 198-199]. It is reprinted in its unabridged form by Fraser, *Strains in the Understandings of Christian Perfection*, Appendix G, pp. 485-489. This

In another document Fletcher wrote that he felt "bound in conscience to maintain the doctrine of the baptism of the Holy Ghost."[273] Thus, Fletcher continued to employ the expression and develop the doctrine concerning Spirit baptism. In fact, the promise of the Father, the gift of the Holy Ghost was his favorite subject.[274]

However, a recently discovered manuscript of John Wesley's apparently is his evaluation of Benson's work on "The Baptism of the Holy Ghost." In it Wesley declared, "I never yet baptized a real penitent who was not then baptized with the Holy Ghost." He noted that the "One Baptism includes the Outward Sign and the Inward Grace." He also wrote, "Every *Penitent* is then baptized with the Holy Ghost; i. e. receives righteousness and peace and joy in the Holy Ghost." Later he wrote, "I doubt if the word *Baptism* is ever used (unless twice or thrice metaphorically) for any but Water Baptism. And we can sufficiently prove our whole Doctrine, without laying any stress on those metaphorical Expressions."[275] According to Maddox, "It is clear from the manuscript that the treatise Wesley was critiquing was arguing that persons can be justified but not yet have 'received' the Spirit or experienced the 'new birth' by the Spirit. Moreover, the text apparently used a distinction between water baptism and a subsequent Spirit baptism to articulate a *personal recapitulation* model of Christian life. Wesley rejected this correlation. He insisted that the 'baptism' or initial 'receiving' of the Holy Spirit comes at justification as the initiation of Christian life."[276]

In his famous letter to Joseph Benson, Wesley gave his opinion on John Fletcher's terminology for entire sanctification:

> If they like to call this "receiving the Holy Ghost," they may: Only the phrase, in that sense, is not scriptural, and not quite proper; for they all "received the Holy Ghost" when they were justified. God then "sent forth the Spirit of His Son into their hearts, crying, Abba, Father." O Joseph, keep close to the Bible both as to sentiment and expression! Then there will never be any material difference between you and me.[277]

---

explanation of Fletcher's "pneumatocentric shift" is given by Fraser, 355-369.

[273]Tyerman, *Wesley's Designated Successor*, 203.

[274]Benson, *Life of Fletcher*, 186.

[275]Fraser, *Strains in the Understanding of Christian Perfection*, Appendix H, pp. 490-492; see also Maddox, "Wesley's Understanding" 109-110.

[276]Maddox, "Wesley's Understanding," 84-85.

[277]Wesley, *Letter*, 28 December 1770.

In a second letter to Benson on March 9, 1771, Wesley asked Benson to abstain from speaking of Fletcher's "late discovery" since "the Methodists in general could not bear this." John Telford explained

> Fletcher's discovery was his doctrine of "Receiving the Holy Ghost," which Wesley thought unscriptural and prejudicial to the spread of the truth. Wesley held that it was improper to separate the work of sanctification from justification, and that all who were justified had received the Holy Spirit.[278]

Fletcher's "Last Check to Antinomianism," written in 1775, seems to reflect Wesley's moderating influence. In referring to Luke 24:49 and Acts 2:17, 33, 38 Fletcher wrote, "This promise, *When received in its fullness*, is undoubtedly the greatest of all 'the exceeding great and precious promises . . . of pure love and unmixed holiness."

In his reference to John 14:15, 23 Fletcher cited from Wesley's *Notes* that Jesus "implies such a large manifestation of the Divine presence and love, that the former, in justification, is nothing in comparison of it." Yet Wesley's implication is that the disciples had not yet received either justification or entire sanctification.

Fletcher also stated, "And if one outpouring of the Spirit, one bright manifestation of the sanctifying truth, so empties us of self, as to fill us with the mind of Christ, and with pure love, we are undoubtedly Christians in the full sense of the word." What follows for the next two pages is an extended quote from Wesley which distinguishes between the initial baptism of the Spirit and Christian perfection.[279] William Greathouse believes that such qualifications would not have occurred in Fletcher's earlier writings, prior to Wesley's correction.[280]

However, Laurence Wood has labored to demonstrate that Wesley had misunderstood Fletcher and Benson. According to Wood, Wesley thought they meant that only the fully sanctified had received the witness of the Spirit. This theory is highly unlikely because the doctrine of Christian assurance was a

---

[278]Wesley, *Letters*, Telford, ed, 5:228. Although Smith disputed this explanation in "How John Fletcher Became the Theologian of Wesleyan Perfectionism, 71-72, his objections were rebutted by Dayton, *Theological Roots of Pentecostalism*, 59.

Ten years later Benson published *Two Sermons on Sanctification* (1781), which included no Spirit-baptism terminology. These two sermons were included in *Sermons on Various Occasions* (1802) and included in *Glory of the House of God*, 128-166.

[279]Fletcher, *Works*, 2:630-634.

[280]*Historical Development*, 241-244; also personal correspondence with the author, 26 May 2007.

primary emphasis of early Methodism and held to be the birthright of all believers. Workman commented, "Never before in the history of the Church since the writings of St. Paul had the doctrines of Assurance been so clearly enunciated."[281]

Wood also speculated that Wesley thought Fletcher and Benson had adopted the view of Zinzendorf. Yet Zinzendorf denied the doctrine of Christian perfection. It is not likely that Benson and Fletcher had adopted the theology of Zinzendorf with whom Wesley broke fellowship and began the Methodist societies. Yet Wood concluded that Wesley is satisfied with Fletcher and Benson once he understands they are merely asserting that only the fully sanctified have an abiding witness.[282] Wood concluded that after Wesley understood, he was in substantive agreement with Fletcher and Benson.[283] The logic of Wood's argument is:

1. John Fletcher was a great man intellectually and spiritually.
2. John Fletcher frequently used pneumatological language or made references to the Holy Spirit.
3. John Wesley put his seal of approval on Fletcher's writings.
4. Therefore, Wood concludes that Wesley connected the baptism with the Holy Spirit and Christian perfection.[284]

---

[281]Townsend, Workman, Eayrs, *New History of Methodism*, 1:21.

[282]Wood, *Meaning of Pentecost*, 122; 346. Wood covers the same ground in "Origin, Development, and Consistency,"45-51.

[283]Wood, *Meaning of Pentecost*, 37-51. Wood has argued that since Wesley approved and published Fletcher's writings, he must have approved of his terminology. However, Kenneth Collins concluded that Wesley did not link the baptism of the Holy Spirit and Christian perfection. Collins pointed out "that the Hill brothers charged Wesley with inconsistency due to some of the teachings expressed in his *Christian Library*. Wesley simply distinguished his thought from what he had reprinted. The same caveat applies" to those who attempt to confuse Wesley's thought with Fletcher's [Collins, *Faithful Witness*, 79; *Theology of John Wesley*, 139]. Wood admits that in principle Collins is right ["Origin, Development, and Consistency," 51]. Furthermore, we have also noticed that Charles Wesley also published some hymns which John did not necessarily approve. See p. 478.

[284]Wood says the clearest indication that Wesley approved of Fletcher's use of the baptism with the Holy Spirit as a designation for full sanctification is found in Wesley's edition of Fletcher's *Equal Check to Antinomianism and Phariseeism* ["Rediscovery of Pentecost,"24]. However, in the preface of this essay Fletcher declares that believers under inferior dispensations did not always have assurance. Fletcher argues that with the opening of the Christian dispensation at Pentecost, "Nobody therefore can truly believe, according to this dispensation, without being immediately conscious both of the forgiveness of sins, and of peace and joy in the Holy Ghost."

The problem is that Wood himself tends to equate Christian assurance with Christian perfection[285] and he projects that revision first upon Fletcher and Benson, then upon Wesley who supposedly corrected them at this very point. However, the subject of Wesley's discussion with Fletcher and Benson was not assurance of salvation, it was the baptism with the Holy Spirit.

According to Wood, Fletcher distinguished between justifying faith and being sealed by the Spirit in a letter to Miss Hatton. Wood defines this sealing as Christian perfection and said that Fletcher referenced the case of the Samaritans in Acts 8 as an example of those who received the seal of the Spirit after their justification.[286] This is not at all what Fletcher wrote and the attempt by Wood to equate Christian assurance with Christian perfection skewed his analysis of Wesley's concerns with Fletcher and Benson. Fletcher wrote to Miss Hatton on 1 November 1762,

> That there is a seal of pardon, and an earnest of our inheritance above, which you are as yet a stranger to, seems clear from the tenor of your letter. . . . I believe many people know when they receive faith, and all people when they receive the seal of their pardon. When they believe in Christ, they are justified in the sight of God. When they are sealed by the Spirit, they are fully assured of that justification in their own conscience. Some receive faith and the seal of their pardon in the same instant, as the jailor for example; but others receive faith first, as the dying thief, the woman of Canaan, David, the people of Samaria (Acts 8:12-16), and the faithful at Ephesus (Eph 1:13).
> Suppose then that God gave you faith, i.e. a hearty trust in the blood of Christ and a sincere closing with Him as your righteousness and your all, while you received the sacrament (which seems to me very probable, by the account you give me),

---

While this most important truth had been derided and denied, it had been gloriously revived by Wesley and his associates [Fletcher, *Works*, 1:429]. Note that Fletcher says nothing of Christian perfection, but of the witness of the Spirit in the new birth!

[285]See his latest attempt in "Origin, Development, and Consistency,"40. Peter Forsaith expressed reservations about Wood's use of primary sources in *The Meaning of Pentecost in Early Methodism*. Forsaith wrote that Wood's *Meaning of Pentecost* "sails again the wind as it seeks to read Fletcher — and, indeed Methodism — against the themes of the Wesleyan holiness movement. Wood's arguments have been challenged and the work is undermined by poor use of primary sources [*"Unexampled Labours"* 7].

[286]Wood, *Meaning of Pentecost*, 23.

> your way is exceeding plain before you. Hold fast your confidence, but do not rest in it. Trust in Christ; and remember He says, "I am the way," not for you to stop, but to run on in Him. Rejoice to hear that there is a full assurance of faith to be obtained by the seal of God's Spirit, and go on from faith to faith until you are possessed of it.[287]

Randy Maddox explained what actually was Wesley's concern with Fletcher and Benson.

> He insisted that the "baptism" or initial "receiving" of the Holy Spirit comes at justification as the initiation of Christian life. Turning the point around, he claimed that the baptism of the Spirit does not bestow Christian Perfection but only the Christian faith of a "babe." He willingly allowed that individuals may subsequently experience deeper immersions in the Spirit who indwells them at justification, but Wesley argued that these deeper immersions should not be confused with the "new birth." In particular, he rejected the "metaphorical" use of "baptism" to refer not to initiatory Christian baptism but to some subsequent immersion in the Spirit.[288]

In a letter to Charles Wesley, 24 November 1771, Fletcher stated that he was writing his third and last *Check.* "I shall introduce *my*, why not *your* doctrine of the Holy Ghost, & make it one with your brother's perfection. He holds the truth, but this will be an . . . improvement upon it, if I am not mistaken. In some of your *pentecostal hymns* you paint my light wonderfully. If *you do not recant* them we shall perfectly agree."

Patrick Streiff explained that this work appeared as *The Last Check to Antinomianism.* Fletcher quoted John Wesley more copiously than elsewhere in this book. "He was concerned to make clear the extent to which they agreed, since the stress Fletcher laid on being filled with the Holy Spirit could lead to differences, as in fact John Wesley had already pointed out in connection with the *Equal Check.* John Wesley has recognized and warned Fletcher that he occasionally overlooked the fact that even the so-called 'babes in Christ' had received the Holy Spirit, though not yet in such full measure as 'fathers in

---

[287]*Letters of Fletcher*, Edward Cook, ed, 26-27. Fletcher was giving this same counsel to Miss Hatton as Wesley preached in his sermon on the witness of the Spirit, that none who were seeking God were to rest without the witness of the Spirit.

[288]Maddox, "Wesley's Understanding," 84-85.

Christ.'"[289]

Wesley reviewed Fletcher's *Last Check to Antinomianism* and replied to Fletcher,

> It seems our views of Christian Perfection are a little different, though not opposite. It is certain that every babe in Christ has received the Holy Ghost, and the Spirit witnesses with his spirit that he is a child of God. But he has not obtained Christian perfection. Perhaps you have not considered St. John's threefold distinction of Christian believers: little children, young men, and fathers. All of these had received the Holy Ghost; but only the fathers were perfected in love.[290]

Fletcher evaluated their differences in a letter to Mary Bosanquet, whom he later married:

> You will find my view of this matter in Mr. Wesley's sermons on Christian Perfection and on Spiritual Christianity; with this difference, that I would distinguish more exactly between believers baptized with the Pentecostal power of the Holy Ghost, and the believer who, like the Apostles after our Lord's ascension, is not yet filled with that power.[291]

According to William Greathouse, Fletcher differed from Wesley in speaking of further effusions or baptisms of the Spirit subsequent to

---

[289]Streiff, *Reluctant Saint?* 183-184. The direct quote from Fletcher's letter to Charles Wesley was also contained in *Reluctant Saint?*

[290]Wesley, *Letter*, 22 March 1775.

[291]7 March 1778; cited by Tyerman, *Wesley's Designated Successor*, 433-434. Wood cited a letter from John Wesley to Fletcher, 18 August 1775, which stated "I do not perceive that you have granted too much, or that there is any difference between us." In the context of the letter Wesley made specific reference to papers he had received and proofread for Fletcher. He does not specify their content except to refer to "The Address to the Perfect" which is found in Fletcher's "Last Check to Antinomianism." However, Wood stretched the statement from Wesley that there was no difference between Wesley and Fletcher to a carte blank endorsement and absolute approval of everything Fletcher ever wrote [*Meaning of Pentecost*, 65-66]. Essentially, Wood has attempted to reinterpret Wesley through the writings of Fletcher, but Wood is deeply confused concerning what Fletcher actually taught.

regeneration.[292] However, he did not make a one-to-one equation between entire sanctification and the baptism with the Holy Spirit.[293] Instead he taught there were two or more baptisms with the Spirit.

In a sermon outline on Acts 1:5, Fletcher applied the promise to both the unconverted and to believers. To the unconverted he warned "rest in no baptism, but that of the Holy Ghost and fire." To the believer, he explained "you want a fresh baptism, till the Holy Ghost, which is grace, fill your soul."[294] In the fragments of a sermon on 2 Corinthians 13:5, Fletcher declared, "There is a day of pentecost for believers; a time when the Holy Ghost descends abundantly. Happy they who receive most of this perfect love, and of that establishing grace, which may preserve them from such falls and decays as they were before liable to."[295]

In his personal life Fletcher sought a fresh baptism of the Spirit many times.[296] Thus, when Laurence Wood asserts that in over thirty instances Fletcher linked "the baptism with the Spirit" with Christian perfection, without a word of censure from Wesley, this does not make the case for Wood's theology.[297]

According to David Cubie, "Fletcher teaches that the baptism with the Holy Spirit is repeated in a succession of events beginning with the new birth and concluding with glory."[298] Robert Tuttle came to the same conclusion, "In short, Fletcher sees Holy Spirit baptism repeated in a succession of experiences beginning with the new birth and concluding in glory."[299] Greathouse explained

---

[292]Greathouse, *Historical Development*, 244.

[293]Staples, "The Current Debate," 19. "Although Fletcher differed from Wesley in making an *association* between the baptism with the Holy Spirit and the experience of entire sanctification, this association was not an *equation*" [p. 29].

[294]Fletcher, *Works*, 4:196.

[295]Fletcher, *Works*, 4:270.

[296]Benson, *Life of John Fletcher*, 139; 174. For example see his letter to John Valton, July 1783, "O for a deeper baptism of the Spirit! I want that promise *more fully* accomplished, 'I and my Father will come, and will make our abode with you'" [Tyerman, *Wesley's Designated Successor*, 541-542].

[297]Wood, "Biblical Sources," 111. This article is a summary of the argument is Wood's 2002 book, *The Meaning of Pentecost in Early Methodism* and does not demonstrate the biblical basis for his thesis.

[298]Cubie, "Perfection in Wesley and Fletcher," 25. See also Cubie's appendix [pp. 29-30].

[299]Tuttle, *Sanctity without Starch*, 108.

that Fletcher believed in degrees of Spirit baptism.[300] This is why Fletcher wrote:

> Should you ask, how many baptisms, or effusions of the sanctifying Spirit are necessary to cleanse a believer from all sin, and to kindle his soul into perfect love; I reply, that the effect of a sanctifying truth depends upon the ardour of the faith with which that truth is embraced, and upon the power of the Spirit with which it is applied, I should betray a want of modesty, if I brought the operations of the Holy Ghost, and the energy of faith, under a rule which is not expressly laid down in the Scriptures. . . . if one powerful baptism of the Spirit "seal you unto the day of redemption, and cleanse you from all (moral) filthiness," so much the better. If two or more be necessary, the Lord can repeat them.[301]

Mary Fletcher, his wife, wrote in her journal for 1 December 1792,

> I was much encouraged in considering that it is the office of Jesus to "baptize with the Holy Ghost." How is it we so neglect to look for the fulfillment of that office of our Lord! Did he not say, "He that believeth on me, . . . out of his belly shall flow rivers of living water? But this he spake of the Spirit, which they that believe on him should receive." This gift of the Holy Ghost is therefore the very thing believers are to look for no matter what they call it — a clean heart, salvation from evil tempers, purity, or what they will — it makes no difference. There is a baptism of the Spirit for believers to receive and which I have had a taste of; but I want the fullness. Yes, I see it; I come near it; I feel a touch of it while writing. Yea, my faith wants a further life. Lord, it must be all thine own doing![302]

She wrote on 17 October 1801,

> You may say, "I have asked a clean heart, a stayed mind, a

---

[300]Greathouse, *Historical Development*, 244.

[301]Fletcher, *Works*, 2:632-633. According to Laurence Wood, R. S. Foster quoted this statement to make the point that entire sanctification is instantly attained through the baptism with the Holy Ghost [*Meaning of Pentecost*, p. 305]. That was not Foster's point [see *Christian Purity*, 187-188] nor was it Fletcher's point.

[302]Moore, *Life of Mary Fletcher*, 192.

> baptism of the Spirit. Well, they are mine; I shall enjoy them. They are given as an estate left to me; but I now want to enter into the possession. My Jesus is preparing my heart for his own abode. He will enter and with him all his fullness to fill up every aching void.[303]

These entrees, nearly nine years apart, illustrate the fact that the Fletchers continuously sought fresh baptisms of the Spirit. In his survey of Fletcher's emphasis, McGonigle recognized:

> John Fletcher does not have much to say concerning the baptism of the Spirit. He sees the promise of the Spirit as applying equally to sinners and believers. The unconverted are warned not to rest because they have been baptised with water, but they must seek the baptism of the Holy Ghost and fire. Believers need a fresh baptism till the Holy Ghost fills their souls. Fletcher plainly interprets the baptism of the Spirit as applying equally to the experience of the new birth and to the subsequent experience of being sanctified wholly.[304]

It was this emphasis on entire sanctification as receiving the Spirit to which Wesley objected. John Knight noted that

> Wesley did not distinguish between "receiving the Holy Spirit" and "being baptized with the Holy Spirit" as some in the holiness movement have done. Nor did he connect Christian perfection or entire sanctification with Pentecost.

Knight was wrong, however, in stating that Fletcher apparently did make this identification.[305] Fletcher connected Christian perfection with the events in Acts 4, writing

> Some time after, another glorious baptism, or capital outpouring of the Spirit, carried the disciples of Christ farther into the kingdom of grace which perfects believers in one. And therefore we find that the account which St. Luke gives us of them after this second, capital manifestation of the Holy Spirit, in a great

---

[303]Moore, *Life of Mary Fletcher*, 230-231.

[304]McGonigle, "Pneumatological Nomenclature," 68.

[305]Knight, "John Fletcher's Influence," 27.

degree answers to our Lord's prayer for their perfection.[306]

Timothy Smith thought that Fletcher's "persistent use of both the terms baptism and fullness of the Spirit to denote the experience of perfect love, is in fact clear from the direct correspondence between him and the two Wesleys. . . . So also is John Wesley's gentle insistence that such usage much not obscure the biblical teaching that the Christian's life in the Spirit begins with the new birth."[307] In another article Smith asserted that John Fletcher equated the experience of entire sanctification with the baptism of the Holy Ghost.[308] The truth is that Fletcher saw both regeneration and Christian perfection as accomplished through baptisms of the Holy Spirit.

In his introduction to Fletcher's unpublished manuscript on the new birth, Wood asserted that Fletcher made a distinction between the birth of water (justification) and the birth of the Spirit (full sanctification).[309] Fletcher's incomplete essay on the doctrine of the new birth is apparently based upon John 3:5. However, Fletcher's essay says something different than what Wood claims it says.

It may be the opinion of Dr. Wood that John 3:5 teaches two works of grace, but early Methodism taught that water baptism was the outward sign of Spirit baptism, which is regeneration. Fletcher said the Wesleys earnestly contended "for the birth or baptism of the Spirit and for the perfection of Christianity." Fletcher argues against baptismal regeneration by preaching that those who are born again are not only baptized with water, but with the Holy Spirit. In these statements Fletcher is clearing not associating the baptism of the Spirit with Christian perfection.

Fletcher then refers to John Wesley's sermon, "Salvation by Faith," in which Wesley compares the faith of the apostles before and after Pentecost. According to Wesley saving faith is faith in the death and resurrection of Christ. The apostles did not have this faith before Pentecost and Wesley did not view them as born again. Or, to use the words of Fletcher in his essay on the new birth, Wesley makes a distinction between "the faith of ante-Pentecostal, imperfect Christianity; and the faith of Pentecostal, perfect Christianity." Note that Fletcher is not defining Christian perfection, but saving faith. He continues by connecting

---

[306]Fletcher, *Works*, 2:631.

[307]Smith, "How John Fletcher Became the Theologian of Wesleyan Perfectionism," 72.

[308]Smith, "Doctrine of the Sanctifying Spirit," 106.

[309]Wood, "Rediscovery of Pentecost," 25; Wood, *Meaning of Pentecost*, 117-119.

“this important distinction” of “faith in Christ” with the full dispensation, baptism, or seal of the Spirit. Fletcher declares,

> in the language of the Scriptures the giving - the pouring out - the shedding forth - and the baptism of the Holy Ghost, are phrases of the same import. And to receive the Holy Ghost, - to be sealed with the Spirit of promise - to be baptized with the Holy Ghost - and to have the Holy Ghost falling upon one -and to be endued with power from on high, are expressions, which convey the same meaning.

The context continues to describe what it means to be born of the Spirit.[310] Fletcher, however, did modify Wesley’s approach to Christian perfection. Donald Dayton noted that while there was not one text from the book of Acts in Wesley’s thirty basic texts for Christian perfection, Fletcher quoted Acts more than any other book. Dayton concluded, “Thus we may detect between Wesley and Fletcher a significant shift in exegetical foundation, one that may even indicate a shift from a basically Pauline or Johannine orientation to a Lukan one.”[311]

However, this shift was misunderstood by the American holiness movement which felt it necessary to defend a crisis second work of grace. Fletcher did not believe in an absolutely fixed manner in which God is prescribed to work in the life of the believer. When asked whether Christian perfection is received instantaneously or gradually, Fletcher replied that “both ways are good.”[312]

It was not Fletcher’s emphasis on the work of the Holy Spirit which created the problems within the holiness movement (which will be discussed). It was Fletcher’s emphasis on a subsequent baptism of the Spirit coupled with a tendency to minimize initial sanctification, an insistence that this work of the Spirit must be instantaneous, and the concept that this resulted in a permanent state which all worked together to create a distinct theology. And while the holiness movement continued to appeal to Wesley and Fletcher, their writings were mixed with the teachings of men such as Finney who did not accept a basic Wesleyan framework of theology and redefined their terminology.

---

[310] Fletcher, “Essay on the Doctrine of the New Birth,” 44-45.

[311] Dayton, *Theological Roots of Pentecostalism*, 53.

[312] Fletcher, *Works*, 2:636; see also Wood, *Pentecostal Grace*, 203-204.

Adam Clarke (1762?-1832)

Clarke is most famous for his scholarly commentary on the entire Bible on which he worked for over thirty years. In his commentary Clarke defined the new birth as not only

> what is termed justification or pardon, but also sanctification or holiness. Sin must be pardoned, and the impurity of the heart washed away, before any soul can possibly enter into the kingdom of God. As this *new birth* implies the renewing of the whole soul in righteousness and true holiness, it is not a matter that may be dispensed with: heaven is a place of holiness, and nothing but what is like itself can ever enter into it.[313]

In his sermon "The Doctrine of Holiness," Clarke described David as a sinner who recognized that he was formed by God in a state of purity and holiness. David was also convinced that God could restore that state of righteousness and true holiness — which is the image and likeness of God. Clarke declared that man is not now what God made him. Man enters this world with a perverted nature and a distorted concept of spiritual things. But God can recreate us. The creator of heaven and earth can purify us. "The depth of our impurity is not argument so long as the eternal mercy of God through Christ Jesus comes in." God can renew a constant spirit in us. Our heart can be fixed and established. "Let us pray to God for this fixedness and certainly of character." God formed man in a state of happiness. It is impossible to be formed in the likeness of God and be unhappy, especially when we consider that God is with us and in us. Sin produces universal misery but the presence of God brings abiding joy. To take away from man his mental misery, the power of guilt must be broken and the impurity of sin must be purged away. Man must be created anew. We must abide in this state of purity if we are to persevere. To walk in the presence of God we must have the Spirit of God. We are uncertain, fickle, and vile, unless we are upheld by the Spirit. The divine Spirit will uphold us so that we will not sink into sin and that we may live up to the dignity to which we are called. We receive this image and demonstrate by a holy life that we have the Spirit of God.[314]

His comments in the book of Acts on the six outpourings of the Holy

---

[313]Clarke, *Commentary*, 5:530-531.

[314]Clarke, "The Doctrine of Holiness," Sermon #49, *Works*, 8:99-114. The text was Psalm 51:10-12. This sermon was reprinted in *Selected Sermons*, 83-94. See also Hunt, *Letters on Sanctification*, 83 and Letter 40, "Entire Sanctification Necessary to Happiness," 272-275.

Spirit make no reference to Christian perfection. When Paul is filled with the Holy Spirit in Acts 9:17, Clarke wrote that receiving the Spirit made him a Christian.[315] Again in Acts 19, Clarke concluded that the disciples at Ephesus were not in the Christian dispensation until they received the Holy Spirit.[316] Commenting on 1 John 4:18, Clarke explained perfect love as "another baptism of his Spirit" which purges out the old leaven and fills the soul with love which is the fulfilling of the law.[317]

Laurence Wood claimed that Adam Clarke linked Pentecost and Christian perfection in his comments on Acts 1:5.[318] However, if Clarke's comments are read in their entirely it becomes obvious that he interprets this verse as describing the work of the Holy Spirit "to illuminate, regenerate, refine, and purify the heart."[319] He makes no reference to Christian perfection.

"Clarke strongly emphasized the Holy Spirit in conversion."[320] Clarke believed that Paul was filled with the Holy Ghost in order "to make him a thorough *Christian convert*."[321] Concerning the falling of the Holy Spirit on the household of Cornelius, Clarke explained that "The promise of the Holy Spirit is given to the whole body of Christians — to all that believe on Christ as dying for their sins, and rising for their justification."[322] Clarke also believed that the Ephesians were not Christians prior to their contact with Paul.

> Genuine disciples of Christ are distinguished from false religionists, and from nominal Christians, by being made partakers of this Spirit, which enlightens their minds, and convinces of sin, righteousness, and judgment; quickens their souls, witnesses to their conscience that they are the children of God, and purifies their hearts. Those who have not received these blessings from the Holy Spirit, whatever their profession may be, know nothing better than John's baptism: good, excellent in its kind, but ineffectual to the salvation of those who

---

[315]Clarke, *Commentary*, 5:752.

[316]Clarke, *Commentary*, 5:841.

[317]Clarke, *Commentary*, 6:920.

[318]Wood, "Rediscovery of Pentecost,"16.

[319]Clarke, *Commentary*, 5:683.

[320]Tracy, *When Adam Clarke Preached*, 124.

[321]Clarke, *Commentary*, 5:752.

[322]Clarke, *Commentary*, 5:769.

live under the meridian of Christianity.[323]

When Wesley Tracy analyzed the sixty published sermons of Clarke, he found only three references to the baptism of the Spirit and Tracy concluded that Clarke did not tie entire sanctification to the baptism of the Spirit at Pentecost, in any direct way.[324] Tracy did notice that Clarke emphasized the crisis aspect of entire sanctification much more than did Wesley, urging seekers to get on with it.[325]

Clarke declared, "In no part of the Scriptures are we directed to seek holiness *gradatim*. We are to come to God as well for an instantaneous and complete purification from all sin, as for an instantaneous pardon."[326] Clarke wrote,

> Let us never rest till we are *adult Christians* — till we are saved from all sin, and are filled with the Spirit and power of Christ. . . . God is ever ready by the power of his Spirit, to *carry us forward* to every degree of light, life, and love, necessary to prepare us for an eternal weight of glory. There can be little difficulty in attaining the *end* of our faith, the salvation of souls from all sin, if God *carry us forward* to it; and this he will do if we submit to be saved in his own way, and on his own terms. Many make a violent outcry against the doctrine of *perfection*; i.e. against the heart being cleansed from all sin in this life, and filled with love to God and man, because *they* judge it to be impossible! It is too much to say of these that *they know neither the Scripture nor the power of God*?[327]

Yet in his letter to John Wesley from Norwich in 1784, Clarke wrote concerning his own state of grace,

> But to this day I am in doubt respecting the work in my own soul, not being able with propriety either to affirm that it is (fully) done, or to deny it as undone. I am in a strait betwixt two; a fear of denying, lest thereby I should forfeit what I have

---

[323]Clarke, *Commentary*, 5:841.

[324]Tracy, *When Adam Clarke Preached*,124.

[325]Tracy, *When Adam Clarke Preached*, 173.

[326]Clarke, *Christian Theology*, 207-208.

[327]Clarke, *Commentary*, 6:723.

> received, or grieve the blessed Spirit; and again, a fear of affirming that it is done, lest I should deceive myself. When you consider this, dear sir, you can easily perceive how much I stand in need of your advice and direction.[328]

Seven weeks before his death Clarke wrote in his journal, "I have redemption through His blood; and I am waiting for the fulness of the blessing of the Gospel of Jesus."[329] Clarke died having committed his soul into the hands of his God and trusting in the merits of his Savior,[330] but with no definite statement regarding the fulness of the blessing.

George Failing believed that Clarke threw Methodism off center by an overemphasis on the instantaneous phase of sanctification.[331] Yet Clarke did emphasize growth in grace and Grider overstates the case when he declares that the holiness movement followed Clarke instead of Wesley.[332]

Clarke said water baptism was typical of Spirit baptism. He then asked:

> Reader, hast thou never had any other baptism than that of water? If thou hast not had any other, take Jesus Christ's word for it, thou canst not in thy present state enter into the kingdom of God. I would not say to thee merely, "Read what it is to be born of the Spirit"; but "Pray, O pray to God incessantly till He give thee to feel what is implied in it!" Remember it is Jesus only who baptizes with the Holy Ghost. He who received not this baptism has neither right nor title to the kingdom of God; nor can he with any propriety be termed a Christian, because that which essentially distinguished the Christian dispensation from that of the Jews was, that its author *baptized* all his followers *with the Holy Ghost.*[333]

Clarke's advice to the seeker for entire sanctification at one point sounds

---

[328]Etheridge, *Life of Clarke*, 416. Wesley's only reply was, "I do not remember ever to have seen that letter from Norwich, else I should certainly have answered it" [12 Feb 1785].

[329]Etheridge, *Life of Clarke*, 439.

[330]Etheridge, *Life of Clarke*, 411.

[331]Failing, "Developments in Holiness Theology After Wesley," 14-17.

[332]Clarke, *Christian Theology*, 203-204; Grider, *Wesleyan-Holiness Theology*, 399.

[333]Clarke, *Commentary*, 5:531.

much like John Fletcher when he said, "Arise, then, and be baptized with a greater effusion of the Holy Ghost, and wash away thy sin, calling on the name of the Lord."[334] William Greathouse observed that Clarke took a holistic view of the baptism of the Holy Spirit, as Wesley and Fletcher did. For Clarke this baptism encompasses the total work of the Spirit within the heart.[335]

Richard Watson (1781-1833)

Watson is most famous for his *Theological Institutes,* first published in 1823, which was the first Methodist systematic theology. In 1877 Daniel Curry wrote, "To no other single agency is the continued doctrinal unity of Methodism indebted as to the extensive use of Watson's *Theological Institutes*. . . . This great work has been the standard of Methodist theology for a full half century."[336] Asbury Lowrey said of Watson's *Institutes:*

> Methodism has assigned to perfect holiness a distinct chapter in systematic theology. Watson, who wrote the first body of theology after Wesley's time, leads the way and indexes the topic as a benefit of the atonement under the head of "Entire Sanctification." No other conspicuous writer has such a division. No other consensus of faith has such a crowning credo.[337]

In his chapter on entire sanctification Watson wrote, "That a distinction exists between a regenerate state and a state of entire and perfect holiness will be generally allowed."[338] However, Watson and Clarke differed in their presentation of the doctrine. John L. Peters observed that while Clarke emphasized the instantaneous nature of entire sanctification, Watson emphasized the gradual aspect. Peters felt that Watson's emphasis led to a merging of sanctification with

---

[334]Clarke, *Christian Theology*, 206. While Wood insisted that Clarke borrowed his doctrine from Fletcher [*Meaning of Pentecost*, 272], Clarke himself declared, "No man ever taught me the doctrine I embraced; I received it singly by reading the Bible. From that alone I saw that justification by faith, the witness of the Spirit, and the sanctification of the heart were all attainable [Etheridge, *Life of Clarke*, 358].

[335]Greathouse, *Historical Development*, 247.

[336]"Introduction" in Raymond, *Systematic Theology*, 1:13.

[337]Lowrey, *Possibilities of Grace*, 28-29.

[338]Watson, *Theological Institutes*, 2:450.

the doctrine of regeneration.[339] However, in his *Institutes,* Watson did make a distinction, saying, "The regenerate state is, also, called in Scripture sanctification; though a distinction is made by the Apostle Paul between that and being 'sanctified wholly.'"[340] Watson noted,

> Some contending that all attainable degrees of it are acquired by the process of gradual mortification and the acquisition of holy habits; other allege it to be instantaneous, and the fruit of an act of faith in the Divine promises. That the regeneration which accompanies justification is a large approach to this state of perfected holiness; and that all dying to sin, and all growth in grace, advances us hearer to this point of *entire* sanctity, is so obvious, that on these points there can be no reasonable dispute. But they are not inconsistent with a more instantaneous work, when, the depth of our natural depravity being more painfully felt, we plead in faith the accomplishment of the promises of God. The great question to be settled is, whether the deliverance sighed after be held out to us in these promises as a present blessing? And, from what has been already said, there appears no ground to doubt this, since no small violence would be offered to the passages of Scripture already quoted, as well as to many others, by the opposite opinion. All the promises of God which are not expressly, or from their *order*, referred to future time, are objects of *present trust*; and their fulfilment *now* is made conditional *only* upon our faith. . . . Then to this faith shall the promises of entire sanctification be given, which supposes an instantaneous work immediately following our entire and unwavering faith.[341]

Dale Dunlap said of both Clarke and Watson that they were more

---

[339]Peters, *Christian Perfection*, 107-109. Greathouse noted that among Watson's published sermons not a single sermon on entire sanctification or Christian perfection was included [*Historical Development*, 254].

Barry Hamilton, however, thinks the distinction that Peters made between Clarke and Watson may be overstated. The holiness movement used Clarke more because it was a commentary which remained in print, while Watson's works became largely unknown to them
[Hamilton, *William Baxter Godbey*, 129].

[340]Watson, *Theological Institutes*, 2:269.

[341]Watson, *Theological Institutes*, 2:455.

scholastic and less dynamic than the theology of Wesley, but in general they were faithful to the essential emphases of John Wesley.[342] Greathouse evaluated three volumes of Watson's sermons and concluded that not one emphasized entire sanctification, although there were references to the gradual phase. He also concluded there is no reference in the *Institutes* to the baptism with the Holy Spirit.[343] However, in his *Conversations for the Young*, Watson wrote,

> The apostles ground all holiness upon that regeneration of the soul which is effected by the Holy Spirit; and make all its pure and benevolent and heavenly affections "the fruits of the Spirit." The entire sanctification of the soul from sin is held forth, both as necessary to qualify us for heaven and as the result of that "baptism" of the Spirit, which we receive in answer to prayer, and through faith in Christ. Hence the constant exhortation we see addressed to believers to cleanse themselves from all filthiness of the flesh and spirit, perfecting holiness in the fear of the Lord.[344]

Then Watson quoted 2 Corinthians 7:1. It is unusual to find an early Methodist attributing entire sanctification to the baptism of the Spirit. Perhaps in this instance Watson placed the word "baptism" in quotes because he was accommodating a younger audience and used it in the figurative sense of an outpouring or effusion and not in the technical sense of initiation into the body of Christ. The previous statement is sufficient to show that Watson believed regeneration was holiness begun and that this new birth is accomplished by the Holy Spirit. Perhaps, as well, Watson was also thinking of Wesley's caution that "all 'received the Holy Ghost' when they were justified."[345]

In Watson's sermon entitled "Power from on High," based on Luke 24:49, Watson declared, "If the Apostles needed the direct influence of the Holy Spirit to make them Christians, so do we."[346] In his sermon "The New Birth," Watson declared that regeneration was a change from darkness to light which implies the utter destruction of sin's power in the heart. We are born of the Spirit by the direct influence of the Spirit of God on the soul. All the earlier editions of true religion were dispensations of the Spirit to the extent it pleased God to pour

---

342Dunlap, "Methodist Theology," 218.

343Greathouse, *Historical Development*, 253-254.

344Watson, *Conversations for the Young*, 349-350.

345Wesley, *Letter* to Joseph Benson, 28 December, 1770.

346Watson, *Sketches of Sermons*, 2:89.

out his influence.

John, however, especially designated the dispensation of the Messiah as the dispensation of the Spirit. He shall baptize you with the fire of the Holy Ghost. "If you hope ever to enter the kingdom of God in heaven, bow now, before the throne of God, and ask for the Holy Spirit, the Spirit of regeneration."[347]

In his *Biblical and Theological Dictionary,* Watson does not define entire sanctification or Christian perfection. This according to Thomas Jackson was "purely accidental." Jackson encouraged all who would question Watson's orthodoxy to consult his *Institutes.* Jackson noted that while Watson affirmed both God's mercy and the Sonship of Christ, that both of these subjects were also left out of the *Dictionary*. Regarding entire sanctification, Jackson also noted that Watson, like Wesley, "did not himself profess to have attained it; but during the subsequent part of his life he exhibited its fruits in full maturity and beauty."[348]

Joseph Benson (1748-1821)

Benson was admitted into the Methodist Conference in 1771 and apparently came to accept Wesley's advice to keep close to the Bible both in sentiment and expression.[349] Yet there is a period of about ten years, from 1770-1780, in which he is still struggling to formulate his theology.[350] In 1781 he wrote "Thoughts on Perfection" in which he echoed the theology of Fletcher,

> Allowing, what (I think) neither Reason nor scripture forbids us to allow, that God *may*, and that he often *does*, *instanteously* so baptize a soul with the Holy Ghost and with fire, as to purify it from all dross, and refine it like gold, so that it is *renewed in love*, in *pure* and *perfect* love, as it never was before; yet ought not those who have experienced this, to be repeatedly told . . . That there is a further, and still further renewal to be experienced

---

[347]Watson, *Sketches of Sermons*, 3:411-418.

[348]Jackson, *Memoirs of Richard Watson*, 405; 424.

[349]See p. 493.

[350]Marsh Jones wrote that Benson's ideas were in a state of flux during the seventies and "it is not clear to me that he was sure what he meant" about the baptism of the Holy Spirit at that time ["Letter," 4]. In his dissertation Marsh Jones wrote that Benson seemed to use the terms "fill," "receive," and "baptize" interchangeably with reference to salvation and entire sanctification [Jones, *Pulpit, Periodical, and the Pen*, 77].

day by day.[351]

After his death in 1821 Benson's seven-volume *Sermons, and Plans of Sermons on Many of the Most Important Texts of Holy Scripture* was printed (1825-28), which contains 262 sermons covering Genesis to Revelation. The sermon on Matthew 3:11 makes no connection between the baptism of the Spirit and Christian perfection. In it Benson said the Holy Spirit is compared to fire because He enlightens the previously dark mind, He quickens the soul previously dead to God, He warms the heart, the affections of which were previously cold, He purifies the Spirit, naturally polluted and corrupt. He consumes our sins, lusts, vanities, He transforms us into his own nature. He is offered on terms of repentance and faith.[352]

Benson declared that to be born of the Spirit is not merely a relative but a real change, a change of nature, termed in 2 Corinthians 5:17; Galatians 6:15 *a new creation*, and described in Ephesians 4:22-23 as created to be like God in righteousness and true holiness.[353] This was followed up by his declaration,

> Knowest thou not that thou must be born of the *Spirit*, as well as of *water*; that the baptism of water is but "the outward and visible sign," and that this will never avail thee without "the inward and spiritual grace," even a "death unto sin, and a New Birth unto righteousness?[354]

Benson's collection of sermons contains no sermon from Acts 2. The theme of his sermon on Acts 19:2 is the absolute necessity of receiving the Holy Ghost in order to be saved. In it he declares "without the Holy Spirit, our faith cannot be a saving faith"and cites Romans 8:9. The thrust of the message is to seek spiritual life. We receive the Spirit as truth, life, grace which both converts and regenerates us, adoption, power, comforter, and holiness to carry on and complete the change begun in our regeneration. Those who have received the Spirit are exhorted to seek to be filled with the Spirit.[355]

Benson did declare that we are made members of the body of Christ by

---

351Benson, "Thoughts on Perfection," 553.

352Benson, "The Baptism of the Spirit," Sermon #57, *Sermons*, 2:182; 185.

353Benson, "No Admission to Heaven but by the New Birth," Sermon #102, *Sermons*, 4:19.

354Benson, "Nature and Causes of the New Birth," Sermon #103, *Sermons*, 4:45.

355Benson, "On Receiving the Holy Ghost," Sermon #121, *Sermons*, 4:212-220.

being “baptized”with and “made to drink into one Spirit.” Members of this one body are all inhabited by one Spirit.

> As a Spirit of truth, he enlightens them in the knowledge of themselves, of God, and of Christ, and of the way of salvation: as a Spirit of grace, he quickens them, begets in them repentance, faith, the new birth: as a Comforter, he assures them of their justification and adoption, and inspires them with hope and joy, as a Spirit of power, he strengthens them; as a Spirit of holiness, he renews them.

Here Benson makes the usual connection in Methodist theology between water and Spirit baptism when he says that the “one baptism” is baptism of water, “an emblem of regeneration; the same sign and the same thing signified.”[356]

Benson had two sermons on 1 Thessalonians 5:23. In them he preached that the Holy Spirit is termed the *Holy* Spirit and the Spirit of *holiness* not only because he is holy in himself, but because it is his office to sanctify and make us holy. In the Old Testament inanimate objects were said to be sanctified or separated from common use, dedicated to the worship and service of God. The whole body of priests were also sanctified in a ceremonial manner and consecrated to the service of God.

Our sanctification also implies a separation and dedication, not ceremonial and figurative, but a real separation from sin and dedication to God. Benson defined the human spirit as the faculties of the mind: understanding, will, conscience, and memory. The human soul refers to our passions and appetites, while the body means that which is material. Our spirit stands in great need of sanctification because it is naturally overspread with gross darkness and used as an instrument of iniquity. Our understanding is darkened, our will perverted, and our conscience is naturally blind, hardened, and insensible.

By sanctification the understanding is freed from its darkness and enlightened. By sanctification the will acquiesces to the will of God and is made obedient. By sanctification the conscience is acquitted from guilt, accepted by God and justified. The memory must also be sanctified so that the things of God make a deep and lasting impression upon us.

The passions or emotions are prone to love what ought to be hated and hate what ought to be loved; desire what ought to be abhorred and abhor what ought to be desired; hope for what should be feared and fear what should excite our hopes; rejoice in what ought to give sorrow and sorrow for that which should afford us joy. By sanctification our passions are properly restrained and regulated, made subject to the will of God. Our emotions are brought under the

---

[356]Benson, “Christians Exhorted to Unity,” Sermon #185, *Sermons*, 6:51-54.

influence of the love of God and we hate sin. Our appetites are not eradicated, any more than our passions, but they are restrained and regulated. The body is also sanctified so that sin does not reign in our mortal body so that we obey its evil desires. Our eyes are open to the Word of God and the discovery of his work. Our ears are open to receive instruction, our tongue proclaims the goodness of the Lord, our hands work in honest labor and reach out in acts of charity, and our feet convey us to the house of God.

Paul sets no bounds upon this sanctification, but instead uses the word ὁλοτελής (*holoteles*),[357] which means that every part should be sanctified perfectly or complete in all respects. Paul's prayer that we be perfectly sanctified means that we walk in light, that our will is wholly conformed to the will of God, that our conscience should continually feel the cleansing virtue of the blood of Jesus, and that we should continually rejoice in the testimony of a good conscience. Our passions and appetites are so regulated and inflamed with divine love that we do all to the glory of God.

We cannot produce this change in ourselves, but the God of peace himself sanctifies us. God begins this work by giving us his Spirit and he maintains it by causing his Spirit to continue with us. Our sanctification can be increased only by an increase of the Spirit's influences. Yet God is able to do for us more than we can ask or think. Shall he not with Christ freely give us all things? He invites us to come to him for this blessing (v 24). This sanctification is promised and God is faithful.

For those who have experienced this sanctification to any degree, has God sealed upon your heart the pardon of sin and wrought in your soul a hatred to sin? Has he given you power over it and are you groaning for its entire destruction? Have you submitted to the will of God? Is he the center of your desires, the foundation of your hopes and the source of your comforts? Do you long for him and delight in him? Are your appetites under restraint? Being made free from sin, are you a servant to righteousness? If not, you are not in a state of salvation and do not possess even that measure of sanctification.

But it is highly needful that you should possess this sanctification and to the degree stated in our text. God has appointed certain means with a view to our sanctification: faith, which comes from hearing the Word, prayer and watchfulness. If sanctification is so valuable and necessary, and if God is faithful to his Word and has indeed promised it; then let your prayers for it be fervent and persevering.[358]

---

[357]ὅλος (*holos*) - all or altogether, whole, entire, complete + τέλος (*telos*) - the end, goal, or completion.

[358]Benson, *Two Sermons on Sanctification*. Reprinted in *Glory of the House of God*, 128-166. Not in the seven-volume set, *Sermons, and Plans of Sermons.*

In a letter to John Pawson, Benson wrote on 27 April 1780:

I have been looking over Mr. Wesley's former Journals again, and as I proceeded I could scarcely avoid drawing the conclusion, that many of us have departed in doctrine and experience from the faith to which Mr. Wesley and others then bore their testimony. Have we not, leave room for a second blessing, set justification too low, by allowing that a person may be justified from all things, who has neither the witness nor fruits of the Spirit, neither peace, sensible peace with God, nor power over inward sin? Or if we affirm that all must have these at first, as evidences and fruits of justification; do we not allow many to think they are in a justified state, who are now, and have been for many years, as truly devoid of these, as if they had never received them? And if so, do we not mislead our hearers and cry, "Peace, peace, when there is no peace?"There is no peace to the earthly, sensual, and devilish; to the proud, the passionate, the covetous; to the carnally-minded, the lovers of the world, the unholy. And if we encourage such, directly or indirectly, to believe that they are justified, and of course children of God; do we not encourage them to believe that without holiness they may see the Lord? For certain it is, he that is a child of God hath everlasting life. If, therefore, I teach that a man may be justified, and yet carnal, unholy, and unrenewed, I teach that a man may be carnal, unholy, and unrenewed, and yet dwell with God. I doubt not that there is weak, as well as strong faith, and that a man is made a babe in Christ before he is a young man or father; but I ask, whether any are properly and savingly Christ's who have not crucified the flesh with its affections and lusts? Whether they are so in Christ, as to be free from condemnation, who walk after the flesh, not after the Spirit; who are not new creatures; the Spirit of life from Christ Jesus having not made them free from the law of sin and death? Hath not Jesus assured us, if he shall make us free, we shall be free indeed? Hath not St. Paul confirmed his Master's declaration, affirming, "Where the Spirit of the Lord is, there is liberty?" And hath not St. John borne the same testimony, in declaring, "He that is born of God overcometh the world, and does not commit sin?" And in the mouth of these three witnesses, is it not established, that it is a greater thing than many imagine to be truly justified, and made the children of God?"[359]

Early Methodism

Although there were variations in the doctrinal expression of the early Methodists, the similarities outweigh the differences. The emphasis of the early Methodists was both Biblical and balanced, but best stated by John Wesley, himself. Charles becomes skeptical, while Fletcher is too mystical.[360] Clarke overemphasized the crisis and perhaps Watson made too little of it. They did tend to have a holistic understanding of the Spirit's work, however, that was not fragmented by limiting his operation to a second blessing only.

According to early Methodism, the baptism of the Spirit was not a common privilege in the Old Testament. Since the Holy Spirit was given at Pentecost, believers have been added to the body of Christ through the baptism with the Spirit (1 Cor 12:13). The Methodist understanding of Spirit baptism should be clear by their consistent connection of it to water baptism.[361]

Not only does the Spirit bring assurance of adoption into the family of God, but He indwells the believer leading him into Christian perfection. This is not an absolute perfection, but a maturation of the fruit of the Spirit. There are fifteen clear testimonies to entire sanctification among the forty-one *Lives of Early Methodist Preachers*. However, not one refers to his experience in terms of the baptism of fullness of the Holy Ghost. "This is very convincing evidence that such terminology was not current among the early Wesleyans."[362] In 1745 George Whitefield changed the title of his sermon, "The Marks of the New Birth," to "Marks of Having Received the Baptism of the Holy Ghost."[363]

---

[359]MacDonald, *Memoirs of Joseph Benson*, 81.

[360]See Fletcher's work "On Evangelical Mysticism," in *Works*, 4:7-13. However, some mysticism, including dreams, were edited out of his works by second generation Methodists. In a letter dated 10 October 1775 Fletcher wrote that truth lies between driving Methodism and still mysticism [Forsaith, *Correspondence of Fletcher*, 289].

[361]Reasoner, "American Holiness Movement's Paradigm Shift Concerning Pentecost," 132-134.

[362]McGonigle, "Pneumatological Nomenclature," 68. McGonigle surveyed Jackson, *Lives of Early Methodist Preachers.* This set was edited by Telford as *Wesley's Veterans*. One exception was the testimony of John Oliver in 1779. He does equate Christian perfection with the baptism with the Holy Ghost [Sangster, *Path to Perfection*, 125].

[363]Smith, "John Wesley and the Second Blessing,"147. Smith labored to avoid the obvious implication that the two phrases were considered interchangeable. He

Flew summarized the testimonies in *Wesley's Veterans*,

> (I) The goal is uninterrupted communion with God. It is also described as Love, including both Love to God and love to man.
> (ii) The attainment is the gift of God, just as the entrance on the Christian life (conversion) is His work.
> (iii) The entrance on this larger experience is instantaneous, i.e. it is given in a moment, and can be dated.
> (iv) There is a process of struggle and quest leading to the decisive moment.
> (v) There is full consciousness of the need for progress in love and growth in the spiritual life after the Great Salvation has been received.
> (vi) The experience includes a deliverance from all conscious sin. The recipients believed that indwelling sin had been rooted out of them. They were conscious of a liberty beyond anything previously experienced.
> (vii) But all of them are most careful not to claim perfection, or sinlessness, or even enjoyment of that Great Salvation, at the time at which they write.[364]

Wesley said he never saw before or since anyone who had mastered biblical knowledge like Thomas Walsh.[365] In his sermon on Acts 2:4, "The Pouring Out of the Holy Ghost Upon the Apostles," Walsh said that the Lord had previously breathed upon the apostles in John 20:22, but now under the Gospel dispensation the rushing mighty wind far exceeds a gentle breathing. In the same

---

claimed Wesley avoided using Pentecostal terms in reference to entire sanctification during this time frame in order to avoid evangelical opposition. The fact is that he rarely ever used such language. In *Whitefield and Wesley on the New Birth*, Smith reprinted two sermons by Whitefield: "The Nature and the Necessity of our Regeneration or New Birth in Christ Jesus" and "The Indwelling of the Spirit, the Common Privilege of all Believers." Smith noted Whitefield's use of pentecostal language and tried to distinguish a different terminology for Wesley [pp. 64-65]. However, both men were Methodists, even if both were not Arminian. Wesley actually edited Whitefield's other sermon, "The Indwelling of the Spirit, the Common Privilege of all Believers" and did not delete Whitefield's association of the new birth with the baptism and infilling of the Holy Spirit. While Smith asserted that Wesley changed his doctrine a few months later, he offers no proof of that assertion [p. 92].

[364]Flew, *Idea of Perfection*, 323.

[365]Wesley, "On Charity," Sermon #91, 3.5.

way the grace and knowledge given to Christian believers far surpasses that which was given to the Israel of God before the Gospel.

Walsh explained that the Apostles were filled with the Holy Ghost, first of all, because they needed it for their own salvation. Without the Spirit of Christ they could be none of his. They were justified and in favour with God, while Christ was upon earth, yet they had not so strong and comfortable assurance of the love of God until afterwards. They also needed the Spirit of adoption to assure them that they were heirs of God, to fill them with love both to God and man, and to sanctify them throughout in soul, body, and spirit.

Yet Walsh does not necessarily claim all of this happened at Pentecost. In his conclusion he urges those who are partakers of the Holy Ghost not to stop short of the complete accomplishment of all the great and precious promises. But the emphasis throughout the sermon is that every true Christian is inspired of God; that is was absolutely necessary for sinners to receive the Holy Ghost, to make them the children of God and heirs of the kingdom of heaven. The Apostles were commanded to wait at Jerusalem until they were endued with power from on high, since Christ would not send anyone to preach in his name that knows him not nor have themselves been make partakers of his Spirit.[366]

The experience of early Methodists was not static; they sought fresh outpourings of the Spirit. Unfortunately sometimes these fresh anointings were called "baptisms." This term, however, would best be reserved to describe a person's entrance into the kingdom of God. John Fletcher probably opened the door to a less precise usage by his own broad use of the term. There are many infillings or anointing, but baptism connotes initiation. Bloesch argued that it is more in accord with the pattern of the New Testament to restrict the term *baptism* to the experience of being incorporated into the body of Christ and to speak of subsequent communications of the Spirit as fillings, anoints, outpourings and so on.[367]

Later holiness writers read into the devotional writings of early Methodism a static concept of the Spirit's work which was confined largely to a second crisis experience. It has been established, however, that early Methodism and the later holiness movement did not agree on the work of the Spirit and the point is that early Methodistic statements about the Holy Spirit must be understood in the context of that day and not in a later camp meeting context. What the holiness movement must prove, but cannot, is that Methodism spoke of a Spirit baptism exclusively in reference to a second crisis.

Charles Carter recognized Wesley's reticent to use "baptism with the Holy Spirit" language, but argued that more recent Holiness writers have

---

[366]*Sermons by Thomas Walsh*, 129-140.

[367]Bloesch, *Holy Spirit*, 299-300.

"improved upon the structure and expression" of Wesley. He argued that Wesley meant essentially the same thing as they believe and teach.[368] Leo Cox recognized the discrepancy between Wesley and his successors, but argued that "the idea is implicit in Wesley" that entire sanctification is the equivalent of the Pentecostal experience in Acts.[369] Dunning wrote, "In the light of the overwhelming evidence to the contrary, this can only be evaluated as a case of special pleading."[370]

Since it is the work of the Spirit to lift up Christ, the early Methodists were sound in putting the emphasis on Christ, his atonement, and being restored to his image. Although their preaching was fervent, there is no correlation between their emphasis and the later teaching of the pentecostal movement. Wesley cannot legitimately be called "charismatic." His handling of George Bell should give a clue as to how he would react to the modern charismatic movement. Wesley and early Methodism were not Pentecostal. Outler wrote that the pneumatology of the Wesleys had no exact equivalence in Western spirituality up to their time nor does it correspond to the "holiness associations" and Pentecostalists which so often invoked their authority.[371]

Maddox conceded some parallels and precedents in Wesley for later emphases of the Pentecostal and Charismatic movements, but said there are also significant differences. Wesley's distinctive concern was always more on the fruit of the Spirit than on the gifts of the Spirit, particularly more than on the gift of tongues."[372] In a letter to the Lord Bishop of Gloucester, John Wesley explicitly denied having the gift of tongues.[373] The leap from Wesleyan to Pentecostal could only come through the American holiness movement's distortion.[374] Yet

---

[368]Carter, *Person and Ministry*, 188-189.

[369]Cox, *Perfection*, 132.

[370]Dunning, "Wesleyan Perspective on Spirit Baptism," 203.

[371]Outler, "Preface" in *John and Charles Wesley*, xv-xvi.

[372]Maddox, *Responsible Grace,* 136.

[373]Wesley, *BE Works*, 11:469. According to charismatic author William R. Davies, "the only explicit reference to any of the Methodist preachers using the gift of tongues is to be found in the extracts from the diary of Thomas Walsh" [*Spirit Baptism*, 11]. The reference cited by Davies is found in Telford, *Wesley's Veterans*, 5:129-130.

[374]Bloesch recognized that the holiness movement laid the ground for Pentecostalism, "which encouraged seeking after charismatic endowment in addition to sanctifying grace" [*Holy Spirit*, 132; 182]. While Walvoord was not Wesleyan, he identified the problem in Wesleyan doctrine with those who did not follow accurately the theological guidelines of the originator. To understand that the baptism of the Spirit occurs when a person believes and is born again "would do much to prevent Pentecostal misuse of Wesleyan truth. . . . Had the teachings of John Wesley been followed closely

despite distortion and reduction, Wesley influenced every theological development which follows.

with caution, most of the proper grounds for criticism of Wesleyan theology would have been precluded" [Walvoord, "Augustinian-Dispensational," 56-57].

CHAPTER 7
A THEOLOGY of EXPERIENCE:
THE AMERICAN HOLINESS MOVEMENT

Early American Methodism

Francis Asbury brought Methodism to America in 1771. On December 24, 1784, the Methodist Episcopal Church was organized with sixty ministers present. From 1773-1790 the American population increased 75% and during the same period Methodism increased 5,500%. By 1850, the Methodists were the largest Protestant church in America and one-third of all church members were Methodist.[375]

The emphasis of the early American Methodists was that of Wesley. In describing their theology, Allan Coppedge explained:

> The terminology employed is predominately atonement language and its accompanying connection with the work of Christ, rather than pentecostal terminology with its relation to the Holy Spirit. Methodists tended to use the concepts and vocabulary of Paul and John more than those of Luke.[376]

Asbury preached frequently on Christian perfection. In his journal for 1803, he recorded, "I do not consider sanctification—Christian perfection, commonplace subjects, yet I make them the burden, and labour to make them the savour of every sermon."[377] Again, in 1814, he wrote, "I am divinely impressed with a charge to preach sanctification in every sermon."[378] Yet Darius Salter concluded that Asbury rarely focused any sermon exclusively on sanctification.[379] His emphasis was victory over sin and conformity to the will of God. He was

---

[375]Robb, "American Methodism at 200," 21.

[376]Coppedge, "Entire Sanctification in Early American Methodism," 45.

[377]Asbury, *Journal*, 2:383.

[378]Asbury, *Journal*, 2:751.

[379]Salter, *America's Bishop*, 150.

much more concerned about Christian character than emotionalism.[380] Concerning Christian perfection he wrote:

> One of the doctrines, as you know, which we particularly insist upon, is that of a present salvation; a salvation not only from the guilt and power, but also from the root of sin; a cleansing from all filthiness of flesh and spirit, that we may perfect holiness in the fear of God; a going on to perfection which we sometimes define by loving God with all our hearts.[381]

A survey of his journal and letters, however, yields no reference to this doctrine in pentecostal terminology. "Asbury did not make a technical connection between the work of the Holy Spirit and the experience of entire sanctification. Neither was there any reference to a permanent filling of the Holy Spirit. This reflects Asbury's conviction that present, ongoing experience was far more important than theological explanation." For Asbury, holiness was a never-ending pursuit.[382]

While there was no definite moment which Asbury identified as the time he was entirely sanctified, sometime in 1786, at age forty-one, there was a turning point. From that point on, he testified to a constancy of purity and to power over sin. Yet he continued to seek to be more holy.[383] This same emphasis could be said of those who followed immediately after Asbury.[384]

One exception often cited is that of Captain Thomas Webb. He was evidently somewhat of a novelty wearing his uniform in the pulpit and laying down his sword before preaching. It is reported that he took some text about the Holy Ghost from one of the epistles and went on to say,

> The words of the text were written by the apostles after the act of justification had passed on them. But you see, my friends, this was not enough for them. They must receive the Holy Ghost after this. So must you. You must be sanctified. But you are not. You are only Christians in part. You have not received the Holy Ghost. I know it. I can feel your spirits hanging about me like so

---

[380]Salter, *America's Bishop*, 216-217.

[381]Asbury, *Journal*, 1:211.

[382]Salter, *America's Bishop*, 342; 362.

[383]Salter, *America's Bishop*, 158; 152-153.

[384]Mitchell, *Wesley Century*, 478-487.

much dead flesh.[385]

However Webb was not preaching from Acts nor did he explicitly use the Spirit-baptism metaphor.[386] Joseph Pilmore described Webb, "His preaching, though incorrect and irregular, is attended with wonderful power."[387]

A more accurate picture of early Methodist doctrine can be gained from the first major American Methodist systematic theology. *A Complete System of Christian Theology* was published by Samuel Wakefield in 1869. It was basically a revision of Richard Watson's *Theological Institutes.* In it Wakefield stated that "the regeneration of a sinner is emphatically a work of the Holy Spirit."[388] For Wakefield, entire sanctification does not differ in essence from regeneration. He explained, "It introduces no new principle into the experience of the Christian, but is only the growth and perfection of that moral change which is effected in 'every one that is born of the Spirit.'"[389] Nowhere did Wakefield describe entire sanctification as receiving or being baptized with the Holy Spirit.

Ezekiel Cooper (1763-1847), an early American Methodist, preached from Acts 2:4 on the importance of receiving the Holy Ghost for salvation, lest his hearers should perish eternally. He did not use the text to press believers on to perfection, but to encourage unbelievers to become Christian. Fraser concluded that American Methodist preachers during the period of 1784-1801 began to read the writings of Fletcher, but did not appropriate Fletcher's terminology of Spirit-baptism and Spirit-reception.[390] Letters written by Methodists during the 1790s frequently mentioned holiness, but none used Spirit-baptism terminology.[391]

Devereaux Jarratt, Anglican clergyman in Virginia who identified with Wesley's teaching, wrote in 1792

---

[385]Hurst, *History of Methodism*, 3:1252.

[386]See the discussion of Fraser, *Strains in the Understanding of Christian Perfection*, 387-389. He pointed out that this description by Henry Moore, recorded by Hurst in *The History of Methodism*, was based on an event probably fifty years earlier in New York. Yet Moore was an Irish Methodist who never traveled to America. Other references to Webb do not mention this emphasis in his preaching [Norwood, *Sourcebook of American Methodism*, 23-30].

[387]Pilmore, *Journal*, 30.

[388]Wakefield, *Christian Theology*, 2:429.

[389]Wakefield, *Christian Theology*, 2:446.

[390]Fraser, *Strains in the Understandings of Christian Perfection*, 413.

[391]Fraser, *Strains in Understanding of Christian Perfection*, 415.

> By gospel holiness, which some term Christian perfection, I mean that maturity of grace and universal conformity to the holy will and image of God which every believer is enjoined to press after and which fathers in Christ do actually attain under the gospel dispensation. In other words, it is a ripe, settled, and confirmed habit of willing, thinking, speaking, and acting according to the evangelical law of Christ.[392]

Noah Levings (1796-1849) defined Christian perfection as a matured faith, the perfection of our love to God and all mankind, the perfection of our souls in humility and in meekness, and a complete resignation to all the dispensations of divine Providence. He preached that we must believe it is attainable and understand the nature of the blessing. It must be sought by simple faith through fervent, unceasing prayer and through the means of grace by those in possession of present justification.[393]

While the early Methodist circuit riders in America did preach on this deeper Christian life, in the rough frontier culture the new birth became the primary emphasis. Timothy Smith suggested, "The moral needs of rural and western America directed attention to the more elemental work of saving sinners." According to him, the doctrine of Christian perfection was not emphasized in early American preaching despite the efforts of Asbury.[394] Charles Edwin White observed that in Peter Cartwright's *Autobiography* he"often speaks of people getting saved, but rarely, if ever, speaks of them experiencing sanctification."[395]

The Articles of Religion, which Wesley prepared for the American church, did not include an article on Christian perfection.[396] There was also a period of twenty years from 1812-1832 in which Wesley's *Plain Account* was out of print. In the conference of 1812, the American Methodists voted to remove the *Doctrinal Tracts,* including Wesley's *A Plain Account of Christian Perfection,* from the *Discipline.* These tracts were to be bound in a separate volume, but according to Peters they did not get printed until 1832. He commented that "a

---

[392]Jarratt, *Life of Devereaux Jarratt*, 48-52; see also Asbury, *Journal*, 1:207-212.

[393]Clark, *Methodist Episcopal Pulpit*, 137-154.

[394]Smith, *Revivalism and Social Reform*, 115.

[395]White, *Beauty of Holiness*, 296.

[396]The article "On Sanctification" was added by the Uniting Conference of 1939 and was adopted from the Methodist Protestant Church, one of three bodies in the merger. The other two bodies were the Methodist Episcopal Church North and South. Neither the northern nor southern church had a statement on sanctification.

generation or two of Methodist ministers were rounding out their doctrinal views" without widespread circulation of literature on Christian perfection.[397] Yet Frank Baker pointed out that there were at least fifteen editions printed from 1812 to 1832.[398]

During this era the camp meeting replaced the class meeting and many seekers were lost in the crowd. A large crowd might create excitement, but could not provide accountability. Early Methodism had maintained spiritual growth through the discipleship of the class meeting. Howard Snyder believed the shift from small groups to large crowds was also a shift from ethical living to the emotional.[399] Fraser wrote,

> Frequently in British Methodism, the Eucharist was the focal point for critical moments of grace; seekers hoped in faith that God would justify or sanctify them while they took the sacrament at the altar. With the campmeeting and the development of the mourners' bench for penitents, the altar became less a place for celebration of the Lord's Supper and more a place of repentant prayer. The seeker was encouraged to "pray through" until every sin was confessed and God must immediately justify the repentant sinner or until remaining sin and unbelief was put on the altar as part of the "all" at which time God must sanctify the person who had become the gift on the altar, perfectly cleansing the heart. Such a shift in the understanding of the altar and the sacrament demonstrates the shift from theocentrism to anthropocentricism. God was no longer sovereign.[400]

During the nineteenth century in England the message was toned down. Abraham Scott preached before the Conference in the 1830s on Christian sanctification. He taught that purification was to be obtained by not resisting the Spirit, by prayer and by faith in the blood, by a diligent and devout use of divine ordinances. Regular church attendance, Bible reading and following Methodist ways formed the path of holiness. It is hard to discover exactly what William

---

[397]Peters, *Christian Perfection*, 98.

[398]Baker, *From Wesley to Asbury*, 176-180; see also Coppedge, "Entire Sanctification," 34-50.

[399]Snyder, "Church as Holy and Charismatic," 19.

[400]Fraser, *Strains in the Understanding of Christian Perfection*, 432-433.

Arthur's book *The Tongue of Fire* (1856) was recommending.[401] In 1882 George Osborn preached at Conference that the Holy Spirit is "competent to purify the heart continually by His indwelling, by His incessant operation." But Hugh Price Hughes, president of the Primitive Methodist Conference declared in the 1870s that the Methodist doctrine of entire sanctification was simply wrong because 1 Kings 8:46 declared, "For there is no man that sinneth not."[402] However, this statement is from the prayer of Solomon at the dedication of the Temple almost a thousand years before the new covenant.

In America during the nineteenth century the Methodist Church was torn over the slavery issue. Some Northern Methodists preached abolition, while some Southern Methodists justified slavery. The Methodist Episcopal Church split into northern and southern denominations. The church was caught on both sides of the slavery issue. In 1843, the Wesleyan Methodist Connection of America was formed in Utica, New York, because they desired the church to take a "more positive stand against slavery."[403] Then in 1845, the Methodist Episcopal Church, South was founded in Louisville, Kentucky, and there was controversy between the northern and southern churches until after the Civil War.[404] In 1860, B. T. Roberts founded the Free Methodist Church as a reaction to the modernism of the Methodist Episcopal Church and over theological trends away from entire sanctification.[405]

However, this period was not only marked by strife but prosperity. The upward mobility of urban Methodism saw the construction of Gothic cathedrals and with them, the need to attract a higher class who could carry the debt load.

---

[401]White concluded that the book "hints at the equation of entire sanctification with the Pentecost experience and states that if Christians would allow themselves to be baptized in the Holy Ghost, in the revival which would result, the whole world could be won for Christ" [*Beauty of Holiness*, 128]. However, Arthur's pentecostal language was not equated with entire sanctification but more generally with empowerment for service. Arthur anticipated a general revival which would result in a new Pentecost [Reasoner, *Hope of the Gospel*, 378-380]. According to Dayton it "implicitly conveyed for many the idea of Pentecostal sanctification" [*Theological Roots of Pentecostalism*, 74]. Grider felt that Arthur's book was not very definite or specific or even expressly on the subject of entire sanctification. Nor did it teach Spirit-baptism as entire sanctification [*Entire Sanctification*, 38; 71]. Bebbington described William Arthur as urging the reader to embrace full salvation, "but in blunted terms that make it hard to discover precisely what he is commending" [*Holiness*, 66].

[402]These examples are all drawn from Bebbington, *Holiness*, 66-68.

[403]Dieter, *Holiness Revival*, 21.

[404]Dayton, "American Methodist Churches," 655.

[405]Dieter, *Holiness Revival*, 45.

These people were often attracted to a higher liturgy, but not to soul-searching humility.

Methodism may have enjoyed more prosperity than was good for it. Particularly under the influence of Bishop Matthew Simpson, the church moved away from an earlier simplicity. The Methodists built their first Gothic cathedral in Pittsburgh, in 1855, with the encouragement of Simpson.[406] Other churches followed with elaborate architecture and the result was often heavy debt. The church was then placed in a position of courting the wealthy.[407] Along with the ornate buildings came more formalistic liturgy and an operatic style of church music. George Hughes said that the ministry became conformed to the spirit of the age and that holiness was referred to only in "glittering generalities."[408] Apparently Bishop Simpson never professed the experience of entire sanctification.[409]

These five factors, a twenty-year omission of Wesley's *Plain Account*, a shift in the emphasis of preaching away from Christian perfection, the shift from an ethical holiness to a more emotional emphasis, division over slavery, and upward mobility, all help explain why there was at least some decline in the emphasis on Christian perfection during the first half of the nineteenth century. Delbert Rose cited "reactions to the autocratic character of the Methodist episcopacy" as a factor in the decline.[410] According to A. M. Kiergan, the episcopal system of church government "was a prime factor in its spiritual decline."[411]

By the mid 1800s, for whatever reason, there was "a decline in the spiritual fervor and holiness emphasis of the Methodist Church," according to Delbert Rose.[412] Benjamin Lakin, an itinerant Methodist minister, wrote in his diary for March 15, 1814, "we have preached the gospel but have been deficient

---

[406]Clark, *Life of Matthew Simpson*, 192.

[407]Hughes, *Days of Power*, 13; 23-24.

[408]Hughes, *Days of Power*, 20.

[409]White, *Beauty of Holiness*, 43-44.

[410]Rose, *Vital Holiness*, 29.

[411]Kiergan, *Historical Sketches*, 3.

[412]Rose, *Vital Holiness*, 29. See also Clark who dates a general decline from the year 1840 ["History of the Doctrine of Christian Perfection," 238-240]. See also Gaddis, *Christian Perfection in America*, 304 who stated that perfectionism was on the decline in Methodism since the first quarter of the nineteenth century and definitely by the 40s and 50s.

in enforcing the doctrine of sanctification."[413]

Writing in 1850, Nathan Bangs conceded that a majority of Methodist preachers did not know the experience of Christian perfection. Many preached it more as a theory, than as something which they knew from their own experience. Bangs felt this had been the general state of the Church from its beginning and this lack in the ministry and the membership was always a defect painfully manifest.[414]

In 1824, the Bishops of the Methodist Episcopal Church warned:

> If Methodists give up the doctrine of entire sanctification, or suffer it to become a dead letter, we are a fallen people. It is this that lays the axe to the root of the Antinomian tree, in all its forms and degrees of growth — it is this that inflames zeal, diffuses life, rouses to action, prompts to perseverance, and urges the soul forward to every holy exercise, and every useful work. If Methodists lose sight of this doctrine, they will fall by their own weight. Their successes, in gaining numbers, will be the cause of their dissolution. Holiness is the main cord which binds us together. Relax this, and you loosen the whole system.[415]

From the pastoral address of the General Conference of 1832 is the lament that "among primitive Methodists the experience of this high attainment in religion may justly be said to have been common; now a profession of it is rarely to be met with among us."[416]

In 1841, Bishop L. L. Hamline wrote that in his opinion forty-nine fiftieths of the members of the Methodist Episcopal Church were not entirely sanctified and that part of the reason was that neither was most of the ministry.[417] According to Peters not one article on Christian perfection appeared in the *Methodist Quarterly Review* between 1836 and 1840.[418]

---

[413]Sweet, *Religion on the American Frontier*, 4:249.

[414]Bangs, *Present State, Prospects, and Responsibilities*, 59-60.

[415]Elliott, *Life of Robert Roberts*, 286.

[416]Wood, *Perfect Love*, 151.

[417]Wilcox, *Be Ye Holy*, 194.

[418]Peters, *Christian Perfection*, 101.

12. The American Holiness Movement and the Second Blessing

Unfortunately, those who felt called to reemphasize Wesley's doctrine also modified it. And by forming a movement to reemphasize one doctrine, they destroyed a balance of truth by making the *experience* of holiness the objective or end.

Outler wrote, "The ironic outcome of this process (especially in America) was that the keystone in the arch of Wesley's own theological "system" came to be a pebble in the shoes of standard-brand Methodists, even as a distorted version of Wesley's doctrine of sanctification (as "a second and separate work of grace *subsequent* to regeneration") was becoming a shibboleth of self-righteous Methodists who professed themselves holier than the rest."[419]

According to Kenneth Grider the holiness movement began "at about the year 1835."[420] This date is chosen because of the influence of Phoebe Palmer and Charles G. Finney on the doctrine of holiness. Palmer was entirely sanctified and began her ministry in 1835, and Finney began as professor of systematic theology at Oberlin College in Cleveland, Ohio in the same year. Finney redefined what Christian perfection was and Palmer redefined how it is attained.

According to Donald Metz, the shift in emphasis in the holiness movement was in the area of practical procedures: "*how* to arrive at experiential holiness and *what* was involved in the experience."

> Among the modifications made by the Holiness Movement were: (1) a strong emphasis on the "second blessing" as something to be experienced *now* (2) the introduction of a simplistic method of entering the experience; and (3) an emphasis on Pentecost and the baptism with the Holy Spirit.[421]

Melvin Dieter wrote that by the end of the nineteenth century both mainline Methodism and the holiness revival had "turned away from Wesley to something new."[422] Dale Dunlap wrote,

> In the beginning the message of the holiness people sounded and was enough like the orthodox Methodist understanding of Mr. Wesley's heritage of scriptural holiness that the movement was

---

[419]Outler, *Evangelism and Theology*, 118.

[420]Grider, *Entire Sanctification*, 62.

[421]Metz, *Some Crucial Issues*, 112-113.

[422]Dieter, "Development of Holiness Theology," 66.

seen and welcomed as a revival of authentic Methodist religion. And until about the time of the Civil War this was true. But then subtle shifts and changes began to emerge in the Holiness Movement that sooner of later had to lead to an "agonizing reappraisal." In general the Methodist theologians supported the emphasis on sanctification, for they were concerned for a renewal of traditional Wesleyan "holiness of heart and life conformable to the same," — the vital experience of personal and social holiness. But with the developing second blessing peculiarities and growing pentecostalism they began to shift to criticism.[423]

Phoebe Palmer

Charles Edwin Jones stated, "While the holiness movement always regarded John Wesley as its great authority, the movement owed many of its distinctive ideas and practices to Phoebe Palmer."[424] While Wesley's preaching produced "a generation of seekers after Christian perfection; Mrs. Palmer's, a century of holiness professors. . . . Wesley's followers developed a discipline for seeking perfect love; Mrs. Palmer's, a discipline for the sanctified life."[425] She was the mother of the holiness movement.

Palmer's father, Henry Worrall, was converted under Wesley and seven years later emigrated to the United States. Phoebe was a lifelong Methodist, but people from many denominations came to her home Bible study and prayer meetings. In time it became known as the Tuesday Meeting for the Promotion of Holiness, the birthplace of the holiness movement. Over the next thirty years the meeting influenced denominational leaders not only from the Methodist Church, but from other persuasions as well. By 1840, she was leaving New York City to speak in churches and camp meetings. Later she took her message to Canada and Great Britain. In 1864, she became the editor of *The Guide to Holiness,* a nationally circulated paper begun in 1839.[426]

In 1859, she wrote *The Promise of the Father,* in which she argued for a woman's right to minister in the Church. Charles White believed that Palmer came to emphasize the baptism of the Holy Spirit as a result of her research for

---

[423]Dunlap, "Tuesday Meetings," 102.

[424]Jones, *Perfectionist Persuasion*, 5. See the evaluation of DeNeff, *Whatever Became of Holiness?* 95.

[425]Jones, *Perfectionist Persuasion*, 4.

[426]Raser, "Phoebe Palmer: Ambassador of Holiness,"20-23.

this book.[427] Through her influence and her book, the holiness movement also accepted women preachers.

Palmer's basis of knowledge was experience. For Palmer Scripture must be experienced, while for Wesley experience must be assessed by Scripture.[428] Ironically, her experience taught her that Scripture is superior to experience. While she taught two works of grace as scriptural, some of her followers, such as Upham, claimed to experience three blessings. She argued that there was no scriptural foundation for three works of grace, but she inconsistently put great confidence in dreams. Near the end of her life she embraced the doctrine of Christ's imminent return because of a dream and the impression it made upon her.[429] She also felt that the Lord had made it clear to her that she would never fall from grace.[430]

As early as 1857, the Tuesday Meeting had picked up a pentecostal theme. An observer reported they were "similar to the upper room at Jerusalem, where the early disciples assembled with Mary, the mother of Jesus . . . till God gave them power from on high, the tongue of fire."[431] She utilized this pentecostal terminology, equating sanctification and the baptism of the Holy Spirit, in *The Promise of the Father*.

Those who came to her Tuesday Meeting were often more spiritually mature than those who attended her revival meetings. However, when she preached holiness to the unconverted, the backslider or the lukewarm they felt they were entirely sanctified when, in fact, they were converted or "healed of their backslidings."[432] This is why Wesley preached sanctification "scarce at all to those who are not pressing forward. To those who are, always, by way of promise; always drawing, rather than driving."[433]

In 1870, she reluctantly published Asa Mahan's *The Baptism of the Holy Ghost.* At first the Palmers suggested a Calvinistic publisher. Even though she was using Pentecost as the model of entire sanctification, she feared Mahan's

---

[427]White, *Beauty of Holiness*, 128.

[428]Bassett, "Theological Identity of the North American Holiness Movement," 86.

[429]White, "Holy Spirit Can and Cannot Do," 110-114.

[430]White, *Beauty of Holiness*, 24.

[431]Dieter, "Concept of the Church," 283.

[432]White, *Beauty of Holiness*, 180-184.

[433]Wesley, *BE Works*, 10:192; *Works*, 11:387.

presentation would be too controversial.[434] Mahan also realized that he was presenting an old doctrine in a new way. Donald Dayton concluded

> But the context of this development is more Reformed than Methodist—not only in the illustrations used and the broader Biblical base developed, but also in the extent to which the themes of "cleansing from sin" are largely relegated to a single discourse. Indeed, the "consequences" of the baptism are described primarily in terms of "permanence and power."[435]

Phoebe Palmer's most important contribution, however, was her "altar theology." In 1843, she published her first book, *The Way of Holiness,* in which she described how she had found a shorter way to the blessing of entire sanctification. It went through at least fifty editions. The book begins with these words:

> "I have thought," said one of the children of Zion to the other, as in love they journeyed onward in the way cast up for the ransomed of the Lord to walk in; "I have thought," said he, "whether there is not a shorter way of getting into this way of holiness than some of our * * * brethren apprehend?" "Yes," said the sister addressed, who was a member of the denomination alluded to; "Yes, brother, THERE IS A SHORTER WAY! O! I am sure this long waiting and struggling with the powers of darkness is not necessary. There is a shorter way." And then, with a solemn feeling of responsibility, and with a realizing conviction of the truth uttered, she added, "But, brother, there is but one way."[436]

This represented a conversation she had with Dr. Ball, a Presbyterian

---

[434]Dayton, "Asa Mahan," 63.

[435]Dayton, *Theological Roots of Pentecostalism*, 89.

[436]Palmer, *Way of Holiness*, 15. Greathouse gives the date as 1848 and calls the book *The Way to Holiness* in *Historical Development*, 299. I assume that the brethren to whom Dr. Ball referenced were Methodist and that Palmer deleted that specific reference because she claimed continuity with Methodism.

elder.[437] Palmer could not point to a definite conversion experience.[438] And she struggled for years in her search for entire sanctification. She could not find the experience and witness she sought, so her solution was to develop a shorter way which emphasized that one could claim the blessing without any feeling.[439] Instead of a possibly long period of self-denial and other disciplines, the shorter way involved an act of consecration in which the seeker devoted his whole life to God. Palmer taught the act of consecration brought entire sanctification. It was a shorter way because it was accomplished as a decision.[440]

Phoebe saw a woman's absorption in her husband and children as a form of idolatry. She repeatedly relinquished her family in prayer, fearing that she loved them too much. Of her six children, only three survived to adulthood. She felt that God took a son at nine month, another son at seven weeks, and a daughter in tragic crib fire. It was the death of this daughter which became the springboard for Phoebe's entrance into public ministry.

One of Phoebe's eight struggles in consecration was to relinquish her husband. She had already interpreted the death of her two infant sons as judgments of God because of her idolatrous love for them. Heath conceded, "It is not clear from Palmer's autobiographic statements just how much of her suffering was due to psychological distress and how much was from 'powers and principalities.'" Palmer did describe episodes of darkness as mental conflicts. The spiritual depression, emotional anguish, "dark night of the soul," and intense mental conflicts surrounding the death of her children led to a detachment from the world and union with God.[441]

While Phoebe felt she must put all this on the altar in order to be sanctified, and while she taught this as "the shorter way," her mis-perception of God's purposes led to a lifetime of mysticism. Palmer adopted a view of marriage and family that amounted to a practical monasticism.[442]

437Hughes, *Fragrant Memories*, 182; White gave the name as "Bull" [*Beauty of Holiness*, 28].

438Raser, *Phoebe Palmer*, 266. See the comments of Truesdale that this struggle is an underlying thesis in Raser's book ["Reification of the Experience of Entire Sanctification," 115]. However, according to White, Palmer did receive assurance of her salvation *after* she had concluded that she must be justified in spite of the lack of emotion [*The Beauty of Holiness*, 12].

439Staples, "John Wesley's Doctrine of the Holy Spirit," 104-105.

440Powell, "Theological Significance of the Holiness Movement," 127.

441Heath, *Naked Faith*, 6-8; 21; 56-7.

442It must also be conceded that John Wesley had an unscriptural view of marriage. This is documented by Headley in "Marriage and Ministry," 83-96, as well

Her shorter way was entire consecration, faith in the written Word, and confession.[443] Palmer frequently emphasized a naked trust in the naked word of God. This was regarded as the exercise of faith. While Palmer rejected mysticism, emphasizing the written Word of God, Elaine Heath argues that Palmer must be understood as a mystic. The three steps of her altar theology are actually the threefold contemplative process of negation, purgation, and illumination.[444]

Palmer incorporated five types of extra-biblical mysticism. First, the sense of union with God which she felt on "the day of days," the day she was sanctified. Second, was a dream in which she had died and was being judged. Third, a distinctness of perception of the persons of the Trinity. Four, regular communion with her mother through dreams for years after her mother's death. Fifth, a vision of heaven and seeing the mansion prepared for her. [445]

Heath identified Palmer's visions and dreams, spiritual combat, and mystical union as kataphatic mystical experiences. Health also found at least three such apophatic aspects in Palmer's autobiographic records: the struggle to accept internal darkness and nothingness in order to enter the way of holiness or oneness with God, the ongoing experience of passive surrender, and dark nights of the soul as a purgative initiation into deeper levels of union with God.[446]

Yet the word *consecration* is not often used in the New Testament and perhaps never in close connection with the direct instruction regarding the higher spiritual life.[447] We are not sanctified wholly through consecration alone, but through faith in the provision of Christ.

J. C. Ryle wrote, "I doubt, indeed, whether we have any warrant for saying that a man can possibly be converted without being consecrated to God.

---

as his book, *Family Crucible*. However, Wesley wrote in 1749, "St. Paul slowly and gradually awakened me out of my mystic dream; and convinced me, 'The bed is undefiled and no necessary hindrance to the highest perfection.' Though still I did not quite shake off the weight, till our last conference in London" [Heitzenrater, *Elusive Mr. Wesley*, 1:182]. Heitzenrater was citing from a document written by Wesley and first published by Léger, *Wesley's Last Love*.

[443]Greathouse, *Historical Development*, 299.

[444]Heath, *Naked Faith*, 25. These levels are described in various terms under the section on mysticism, pp. 328-359.

[445]White, "Holy Spirit Can and Cannot Do," 114-115. See also Heath, *Naked Faith*, 36; 50-59. Oden also included a vision of Palmer's which had not been previously published [*Phoebe Palmer*, 322-325].

[446]Heath, *Naked Faith*, 49; 69.

[447]Lowrey, *Possibilities of Grace,* 152.

More consecrate he doubtless can be, and will be as his grace increases; but if was not consecrated to God in the very day that he was converted and born again, I do not know what conversion means."[448]

Huntington wrote that consecration, up to the measure of light, was a condition of justification. Entire consecration, kept up to increasing light, is a condition of retaining a justified state. Resistance to the known will of God in anything is sin — not "inbred sin," but our own voluntary sin — just like all other sin. To make an act of entire consecration a special condition of obtaining the "removal of inbred sin," rather than a universal condition of being saved at all, implies that partial consecration may exist in connection with a justified state. This lowers Christian experience to a dangerous standard and inevitably encouraged professed Christians to believe that they are accepted of God while they do not claim to have really and wholly surrendered themselves to his will.[449] Shelhamer also held that consecration was part of conversion.[450]

More recently, Chris Bounds wrote that Wesley assumed entire consecration on the part of Christians at or before the experience of conversion. "It would be difficult for Wesley to conceive of individuals being born again apart from full consecration." While entire consecration is essential to the realization of entire sanctification, it is not the equivalent of it. "A truly Wesleyan view will affirm that it is possible for a Christian to be fully surrendered to the Lord and not entirely sanctified."[451] Bounds continued,

> Wesley assumed entire consecration on the part of Christians at or before the experience of conversion. Wesley did not believe a person could be born-again apart from entire consecration. Entire consecration was essential in becoming a Christian. Palmer, on the other hand, saw entire consecration as an act of a believer subsequent to conversion and an essential element in appropriating entire sanctification. Along with the exercise of faith, entire consecration was the means by which Christians entered into the life of holiness. For Wesley and Palmer consecration was a means to holiness, but not the equivalent of it.
>
> In the American holiness tradition, a transition took place, particularly at the end of the nineteenth and beginning of the

---

[448]Ryle, *Holiness*, xv.

[449]Huntington, *Sin and Holiness*, 112-113.

[450]Shelhamer, *Popular and Radical Holiness*, 92.

[451]Online: Bounds, "Spiritual Transformation," 10-11.

> early twentieth century, making entire consecration synonymous with entire sanctification. The rationale: if people relinquished control of their lives and surrendered everything to the Holy Spirit, then of course the Holy Spirit would take complete control and exercise dominion in their lives. The Spirit always receives and takes control of what people freely give to Him. At the moment Christians fully surrender to Christ, the Holy Spirit performs the work of entire sanctification. Therefore, when people entirely consecrate their lives to Christ, they are said to be entirely sanctified, whether they have had a deeper cleansing work of the Holy Spirit or not. Over time as entire consecration rose to the fore as an equivalent to entire sanctification and the power and hold of sin was not broken, remaining patterns of sin and obvious sin were classified as "struggles," "infirmities," and "weaknesses." They were overlooked or explained away. An emphasis upon freedom from sin and perfection in love receded to the background.
>
> At this point, it may be helpful to clarify that while entire consecration is essential to the realization of entire sanctification, it is not the equivalent of it. A truly Wesleyan definition of holiness has affirmed that it is possible for a Christian to be fully surrendered to the Lord and not be entirely sanctified. To entire consecration faith must be added in the appropriation of entire sanctification.[452]

Not only was the believer sanctified through his own consecration, but the believer also produced his own assurance. Everett Stackpole described the syllogism on which Palmer's assurance was based:

> The major premise is this: God has promised salvation on certain conditions.
>
> The minor premise is: I have complied with those conditions.
>
> The conclusion logically follows: Therefore I am saved.[453]

As Grider described it, the seeker is instructed: "(1) put your all on the altar; (2) Christ is the altar; (3) the altar, Christ, sanctifies the gift. Therefore, if the seeker has put all on the altar, he or she is sanctified."[454] Charles Edwin Jones

---

[452]Online: Bounds, "Legitimate and Illegitimate."

[453]Stackpole, *Evidence of Salvation*, 27.

[454]Grider, *Entire Sanctification*, 116.

explained, "Once the scriptural requirements were met, the seeker had the right by faith to claim perfect love. . . . Having surrendered pleasures, ambitions and thoughts to the divine will, the Christian seeker had every right to claim the blessing."[455]

The result was a substitution of presumption for faith and the adoption of a theological syllogism: I am sanctified because I say I am. There is no divine assurance, but the certainty is based on a kind of autosuggestion. According to George Failing, she reduced entire sanctification to a three-step proposition, just as much of today's evangelism has done to justification.[456] Greathouse remarked that "syllogistic holiness is not scriptural holiness."[457] Ironically, a methodology for pursuing Christian perfection was never discussed until the nineteenth century.[458]

A. J. Smith warned, "'Only believe' is for those who have truly repented until there is nothing more to repent of. 'Only believe' is for those who have made full consecration and have entirely abandoned themselves to God and yielded themselves wholly up to Him. There is nothing in the Bible that directs a sinner or a believer to go to the altar and pray a bit, and then to get up and say that he is saved or sanctified. Oh, how many souls are deceived at the altar nowadays!"[459]

This "altar theology" was based upon a misunderstanding of Adam Clarke. Clarke had written on Hebrews 13:10, "The altar is here put for the sacrifice on the altar; the Christian altar is the Christian sacrifice, which is Christ Jesus, with all the benefits of his passion and death."[460] White explained, "Evidently Mrs. Palmer missed Clarke's subtle distinction between the altar and the sacrifice offered on the altar. She concluded that Jesus Christ is the altar upon which Christians make their sacrifices of themselves." However, Clarke actually

---

[455]Jones, *Perfectionist Persuasion*, 5.

[456]Failing, "Developments in Holiness Theology After Wesley," 20.

[457]Greathouse, *Historical Development*, 301.

[458]Gunter, "Aldersgate, the Holiness Movement," 131.

[459]Smith, *Jesus Lifting Chinese*, 80.

[460]Clarke, *Commentary*, 6:787. See also Clarke's comment on Exodus 29:37, "To this our Lord refers Matt 23:19 where he says the altar sanctifies the gift; and this may be understood as implying that whatever was laid on the altar become the *Lord's property*, and must be wholly devoted to sacred uses, for in no other sense could such things be *sanctified* by *touching the altar*"[*Commentary*, 1:455]. See Staples, "John Wesley's Doctrine of the Holy Spirit," pp. 104-105. However, Diane Leclerc repeatedly connects Adam Clarke's teaching with Phoebe Palmer, as though they are both saying the same thing [*Discovering Christian Holiness*, 60; 114; 203].

taught the altar signifies the sacrifice on the altar and that the sacrifice offered for believers is Jesus Christ himself.[461]

Palmer also relied on an out-of-context reference from Matthew 23:19 and a deduction she made from Romans 12:1. In *Faith and its Effects* Palmer gave this instruction:

> Imagine a Jew in ancient time, fully aware of the requirements of the law demanding the choice of his flock; for a moment he hesitates while covetousness, murmurs in his heart, as he gazes with increasing interest on the valuable sacrifice, until aroused by the consideration of what indulgence in the unhallowed propensity will head to, he, with decisive step, hastens at once with his offering to the hallowed altar. The sacrifice is presented; and the very moment it touches that "altar most holy" it is sanctified. The sanctification of the gift did not depend on any inherent good in the offerer, but upon the sanctify of the altar upon which it was laid. The altar sanctifieth the gift.[462]

But this is ceremonial sanctification which does not produce moral holiness.[463] Daniel Steele explained,

> When a thing is laid on God's altar it is not purified, but only consecrated. When the phrase "I laid myself on the altar," is used by a seeker of entire sanctification he has a wrong formula, for impurity has no place on the holy altar of God. Its place is in the cleansing stream issuing from the pierced side of the Son of God. In the Wesleyan sense no person in the scriptures was ever sanctified by being laid on the altar of God, or by touching it. The altar theory of sanctification is not found in the writings of either Wesley or in volumes of his great defender, John

---

[461]White, *Beauty of Holiness*, 289.

[462]Palmer, *Faith and Its Effects*, 63. Raser felt Palmer had been influenced to develop this statement from Hester Ann Rogers, "I feel I am very unworthy, yet offering up myself and my services on that *altar which sanctifieth the gift*, my God accepts a worthless worm, thorough his beloved Son" [*Experience*, 188; Raser, *Phoebe Palmer*, 247]. She also insisted on an instantaneous sanctification which resulted in the believer knowing the precise day and moment in which it occurred.

[463]See Taylor, *Theological Formulation*, 181-182. Staples concluded the only holiness such a model can convey is merely an imputed holiness, not an imparted holiness ["John Wesley's Doctrine of the Holy Spirit," 108].

Fletcher, nor in any of the standard Methodist theologians, Watson, Raymond, Pope and Miley. In fact it originated in America about the year 1840, in the writings of Mrs. Phoebe Palmer, who regard it as a great discovery. It was her *short way* to entire sanctification. Christ is the altar; the altar sanctifieth the gift; lay yourself on the altar and you are sanctified. The error is in confounding the two meaning of sanctify, or in substituting purification, the work of the Holy Spirit, for consecration, man's work.

Steele continued,

The more thoughtful friends of the precious doctrine of full salvation adhered to Wesley's statement that "no one ought to believe that the work is done till there is added the testimony of the Spirit witnessing his entire sanctification as clearly as his justification." [464] That souls have experienced entire sanctification while asserting "the altar sanctifieth," we do no deny. They had real faith in Christ despite the erroneous formula. But many have made the same assertion and have found themselves in great perplexity. The altar theory has become a snare to them. Their faith was *mere presumption*, an unwarranted inference that God does his part because they have done their part, as they suppose.

Steele concluded,

Many a person has, under erroneous instruction, thought that he laid himself on the altar and has been induced to say, "The altar sanctifies the gift," and has kept repeating this assertion for months and years, without realizing any inward change. Some continue thus till death, but many more in despair pass into a state of indifference and unbelief respecting the question of purity of heart in this life. Bishop William Taylor styles the altar theory "the devil's switch just outside the depot of full salvation, by which he switches off seeking souls, and causes them to wander round and round, and to fail of entering in." The so-called holiness evangelist is strongly tempted to adopt this

[464]Wesley's actual statement was, "none therefore ought to believe that the work is done, till there is added the testimony of the Spirit, witnesses his entire sanctification, as clearly as his justification" [*Works*, 11:402].

theory, because it enables him in his brief term of labor in any church to *count up* as sanctified as many as he can persuade to say, "I am on the altar, and the altar sanctifies the gift."[465]

Crane wrote,

> Altars are for sacrifice. Is this a sacrificial act? Does the one who ministers at this altar prepare, like Abraham, to slay his child? Does he leave his home and retire to a monastery? Does he *sell all* that he hath, *and give to the poor*? No, none of these things. What, then, is the practical shape of this act of consecration? It is simply a pious resolution and solemn vow that he will henceforth, by divine help, be a faithful servant of God, and, to the utmost of his powers and opportunities, do the divine will in his business, in his family, in the Church, in public and private, every-where, and at all times. Such an act is a solemn thing; nor do we wish to under-estimate its value. In fact, we do not see how any one can hope for the pardon of his sins till he is ready to make just such a surrender, nor how any one can be living a really Christian life who is not continually renewing this high purpose.[466]

Palmer's instruction is based upon the logical deduction that, if the seeker has put all on the altar, he or she is sanctified. The seeker has a duty to believe this even if there is not further evidence of sanctification.

If the seeker will, he may exercise faith. If he may exercise faith then he may exercise faith when he wills. Therefore, faith is an obligation at the very moment of consecration. To hesitate is to question the integrity of God. Such doubting constitutes sin and causes the seeker to lose the blessing of justification. Here Palmer quoted John 3:18.

Thus, Palmer can describe faith as "omnipotent."[467] In fact she taught, "The act, on your part, must necessarily induce the promised result on the part of God."[468]

Palmer argued that the entire voice of the Scriptures was the voice of the Holy Spirit. Palmer quoted Wesley's description of the witness of the Spirit and

---

[465]Quoted in Baldwin, *Lessons for Seekers of Holiness*, 114-115.

[466]Crane, "Christian Perfection and the Higher Life," 697.

[467]Palmer, *Faith and Its Effects*, 29; 132; 98.

[468]Palmer, *Faith and Its Effects*, 101-104.

then substituted the Word for the Spirit, arguing that if we receive the Word of God we have received the communication of the Spirit.[469] Stackpole wrote, "The general principles of salvation may be found in the written Word, but my salvation or yours is nowhere revealed in the Bible. The Word gives no testimony whatever with reference to that event. If I ever learn that for a certainly, it must be by special revelation to me."[470]

Around 1762 Thomas Maxfield had taught "Crede quod habes et habes" — "believe that you have [perfection] and you have."[471] Wesley wrote to Maxfield that he disliked "your affirming people will be justified or sanctified just now: (9) the affirming they are when they are not: (10) the bidding them say, "I believe."[472]

While Maxfield considered this formula the equivalent of Mark 11:24, Fletcher wrote that "the humble reason of the believer, and the irrational presumption of the enthusiast, draw this doctrine to the right hand or to the left. But to split the hair — here lies the difficulty."[473]

However, John Wesley taught that the Holy Spirit brought assurance of entire sanctification and that this assurance was verified indirectly by the fruit of the Spirit and a holy life. According to Wesley, the most common error of fanatics is to imagine themselves as Christians without any fruit or evidence.[474]

With regard to the meaning of Mark 11:24 Richard Watson explained,

> An ill use has sometimes been made of this passage, as though it meant, that, when praying, whatever we believe, that is, persuade ourselves that we receive, we do receive, — an absurdity and a self-contradiction. Here, however, to *believe*, does not signify to persuade ourselves into an opinion; but to trust, or to have faith in God. This trust must necessarily be regulated by God's own PROMISE and WARRANT, and it is exercised IN ORDER that we may receive. The sense therefore

---

[469]Palmer, *Faith and Its Effects*, 150-151. Bebbington told of a South African, George Rose, who read Palmer's *Way of Holiness* in 1859 and noted that it did not agree with Wesley's *Plain Account of Christian Perfection*, omitting the witness of the Spirit [*Dominance of Evangelicalism*, 203].

[470]Stackpole, *Evidence of Salvation*, 27.

[471]*Letter* from John Fletcher to Charles Wesley, 22 Aug 1762. See also Gunter, *Limits of "Love Divine,"* 223.

[472]Wesley, *Letter*, 2 November 1762.

[473]*Letter* from John Fletcher to Charles Wesley, 20 Sept 1762; *Works*, 4:317.

[474]Wesley, "The Nature of Enthusiasm," Sermon #37.

is, *believe*, trust, *that ye* shall *receive them*, and *ye shall* obtain *them*; that is, all things which God both expressly promises, and which are, as St. John states, "according to his will."[475]

Charles Wesley also penned these words which reflect Methodist theology:

How can a sinner know
His sin on earth forgiven?
How can my gracious Savior show
My name inscribed in heaven?

What we have felt and seen
With confidence we tell;
And publish to the sons of men
The signs infallible.

His Spirit to us he gave,
And dwells in us we know;
the witness in ourselves we have,
And all its fruits we show.[476]

Francis Asbury taught that "assurance is suspended on an evangelical act of faith, by which we apply the merits of Jesus Christ for the removal of our guilt; and that we then receive the testimony of the Spirit."[477]

Phoebe Palmer's theology, however, replaced the Spirit's witness with a written statement found in Scripture, sometimes even taken out of context. While the Bible does give instruction to the seeker, it cannot tell the seeker when God has met the need. According to Scripture that assurance is part of the Holy Spirit's ministry. Palmer's emphasis is humanistic and it also undermines the ethical emphasis of the indirect assurance.[478]

The views of Melville Horne, who left Methodism, represented a rising

---

[475]Watson, *Exposition*, 380.

[476]Charles Wesley, *Collection of Hymns*, #93; Young, *Methodist Hymnal* (1964), 114.

[477]Asbury, *Journal*, 1:81-82.

[478]Staples, "Wesleyan Perspectives on the Doctrine of the Holy Spirit,"223-229; see also Staples, "John Wesley's Doctrine of the Holy Spirit," 108; Collins, *Wesley on Salvation*, 127.

evangelical emphasis that taught a mere acceptance of Christ.[479] Yet Christian maturity will not occur simply by declaring that we have it. The concept of "appropriating faith" amounts to "name it and claim it." Within the holiness movement seekers were taught to use the paradigm saying, I must be filled with the Spirit, I may be filled with the Spirit, I would be filled with the Spirit, I shall be filled with the Spirit. "Such language means INSTANTANEOUS SANCTIFICATION by faith, for you NOW."[480] Therefore, it was taught that we are sanctified as an act of our will.

From the time of Phoebe Palmer it was asserted that a person was saved by saying that they were. It attained by a deliberate act of the will. She taught that it was our right to say, "I *must* and I *will* have it *now*."[481] No confirmatory feeling was necessary. Yet early Methodism preached that true religion was heartfelt. Assurance must be felt to be truly known. While Palmer urged a leap of faith, that for Wesley would amount to claiming something one did not really know.[482] Wesley required evidence, but Palmer taught that only "bare faith" was necessary.[483] Palmer, as Horne, replaced the witness of the Spirit with the witness of the Word.

David Bebbington explained, "For Wesley the empiricist, evidence was needed in experience; for Phoebe Palmer, in keeping with Romantic currents of thought, bare faith was all that was required. A new era had dawned in holiness teaching."[484] Thus, John Kent concluded that Phoebe Palmer's claim that John Wesley would have approved of her language was not well founded.[485]

The conclusion of Charles Edwin White is that Phoebe Palmer modified Wesley's doctrine in six different ways and that each of these changes was incorporated by the Pentecostal movement.

1. She linked entire sanctification with the baptism of the Holy Spirit.

479Reasoner, "Assurance or Presumption? 103-119.

480Hills, *Holiness and Power*, 279.

481Palmer, *Way of Holiness*, 234.

482Raser, *Phoebe Palmer*, 263-276.

483The Hebrew word אמת (*emet*), often translated "truth," also means a "sure sign" in Joshua 2:12. It describes the character of Yahweh, which we are to imitate in faithfulness. The root verb אמן (*mn*), denotes faith or belief. The adverb *amen* is used as a statement of self commitment, "let it be so." The point is that faith is associated with evidence, commitment, and character, not presumption.

484Bebbington, *Dominance of Evangelicalism*, 203.

485Kent, "Wesleyan Methodist to 1849," 2:237-238.

2. While Fletcher and Clarke did not connect entire sanctification with power, she "made it a central element of her teaching."
3. She stressed an instantaneous sanctification to the exclusion of the gradual.
4. She taught that entire sanctification is not really the goal of the Christian life, but rather its beginning. Thus, the new convert should quickly move on to it.
5. Her altar theology reduced the attainment of sanctification to three-steps. Pentecostalism uses the same three-steps to instruct seekers for the baptism of the Holy Spirit.
6. Finally, she held that no evidence other than the biblical text was needed to be assured of entire sanctification. While this is a major difference between Palmer and many modern Pentecostals, there are some who tell seekers that God has baptized them even if they do not feel any different.[486] Her "name-it-and-claim-it" theology is commonly used among Pentecostals seeking healing and prosperity. It is also used by most evangelicals regarding the assurance of salvation.

Despite the fact that none of this is Wesleyan, it is Timothy Smith's opinion that by 1867, "her views had won out."[487]

The Irish evangelist James Caughey who was influenced by Palmer, remodeled the Wesleyan tradition just as Finney had remodeled the Calvinist tradition. Both sought to maximize conversions. In his attempt to encourage as many people as possible to enter the experience of sanctification, Caughey taught that there was no need for long seeking, but that entire sanctification could be attained by a deliberate act of the will. No confirmatory feeling was necessary.[488]

Yet Hiram Mattison reminded Methodists that Bell and Maxfield were able to convince people to believe they were sanctified when they were not, by dismissing Wesley's doctrine of the witness of the Spirit and teaching that people received it whether they felt it or not on the strength of their faith. When Wesley opposed them, they claimed Wesley himself was not entirely sanctified and therefore they could not learn from him. Mattison warned that Palmer's emphasis

---

[486]White, "Phoebe Palmer," 198-208; White, *Beauty of Holiness*, 125-143. See also Lowery, "Fork in the Wesleyan Road," 187-222.

[487]Smith, *Revivalism and Social Reform,* 125. In 1894 Daniel Steele acknowledged "the fear of Palmerism" within American Methodism [*Half-Hours with St. Paul*, 287]. Dieter records some of the reaction to Palmer in *Holiness Revival*, 28-32; 42-45; 113-115.

[488]Bebbington, *Holiness*, 65; Bebbington, *Dominance of Evangelicalism*, 201. Caughey was influenced by Palmer [Raser, *Phoebe Palmer*, 3; 138]. See the reference to Caughey in Hughes, *Fragrant Memories*, 188. William Booth was converted under Caughey [Dieter, *Holiness Revival*, 53]; see also Rightmire, "Samuel Brengle," 105-106.

was the same.[489]

Mattison also linked Palmer to the New Divinity advocates of perfection at Oberlin College, such as Finney and Mahan. He warned that simply to emphasize consecration is to ignore the work of the Spirit. Sanctification is purification by the Holy Spirit, while consecration was based on human effort. Hence Palmer's emphasis was Pelagian and not Methodist.[490]

The following year Bishop Nathan Bangs, editor of the *Methodist Quarterly Review*, visited a Tuesday meeting of Mrs. Palmer to refute the teaching that Christians may believe they have the experience before they have the witness of the Holy Spirit. According to Bangs the "altar phraseology" was "unsound, unscriptural, anti-Wesleyan and no doubt in many cases had caused deception."[491]

W. P. Harrison also expressed concern that Palmer bordered on Pelagianism, emphasizing human agency over divine action. Thus she gave "great and real cause for anxiety upon the part of those who watch over the welfare of the Church."[492]

According to William Greathouse, "Mrs. Palmer herself recognized her view of faith as a departure from the commonly held Methodist views."[493] But in *Called Unto Holiness*, Smith said the leaders of the holiness revival constantly appealed to the memory of Wesley, Fletcher, and Asbury. "So successful were they in identifying sanctification with Methodist orthodoxy that opponents were hard pressed to find ground upon which to stand without laying themselves open to the charge of heresy.'"[494]

Therefore, the rising holiness movement modified the Wesleyan emphasis drastically, while at the same time affirming that they were Wesleyan and appealing to the honored names in Methodism for credibility. This amounts to

---

[489]Mattison, "Deceived Professors of Sanctification," (2 Aug 1855) 121; "Deceived Professors of Sanctification," (20 Sept 1855) 151. Mattison followed up his first two articles with two articles rebutting Palmer's teaching. Both were entitled "Believe that Ye Have It and Ye Have It," (29 Nov) 189 and (20 Dec 1855) 201. Much later, Palmer's teachings were also denounced by Ridout, *Beauty of Holiness*, in a chapter, "How to Attain Christian Purity."

[490]Mattison, "Dr. Perry, "3. J. H. Perry had written in defense of Phoebe Palmer. See White, *Beauty of Holiness*, 52-58; 143-144.

[491]See p. 589.

[492]Harrison, "Editors Table,"396-397. Harrison had published an annotated edition of Wesley's sermons [*Wesleyan Standards*].

[493]Greathouse, *Historical Development*, 300.

[494]Smith, *Called Unto Holiness*, 21.

historical revisionism.

Charles Edwin Jones said she passed over Wesley's emphasis of Christian perfection as a process and emphasized a sudden crisis accompanied by "emotional exuberance."[495] Since holiness was seen as a present duty, those who died without a conscious experience of entire sanctification would not be saved. This provided the basis for the "holiness or hell" teaching.[496] In contrast, John Wesley wrote to Elizabeth Hardy,

> "The doctrine of perfection," you say, "has perplexed you much, since some of our Preachers have placed it in so dreadful a light; one of them affirming, A believer, till perfect, is under the curse of God, and in a state of damnation: Another, If you die before you have attained it, you will surely perish."
>
> By "perfection," I mean "perfect love," or the loving God with all our heart, so as to rejoice evermore, to pray without ceasing, and in everything to give thanks. I am convinced every believer may attain this; yet I do not say, he is in a state of damnation, or under the curse of God, till he does attain. No, he is in a state of grace, and in favor with God, as long as he believes. Neither would I say, "If you die without it, you will perish;" but rather, Till you are saved from unholy tempers, you are not ripe for glory.[497]

Palmer was responsible for preachers extending altar calls exclusively for entire sanctification.[498] For her holiness was a "state" which was attained.[499] She

---

[495]Jones, *Perfectionist Persuasion*, 4; however see also p. 6.

[496]Greathouse, *Historical Development*, 301. See also Dieter, *Holiness Revival*, 28.

[497]Wesley, *Letter*, 5 April 1782; see also *Works*, 11:388. Benjamin Pettit asserted that Wesley could not state "holiness or hell" any more clearly than he did in his *Journal*, 21 March 1744, "I strongly enforced upon the m the apostles' Words, 'How shall we escape, if we neglect so great salvation?' If we do not 'go on to perfection', how shall we escape lukewarmness, antinomianism, hell-fire." It seems to me that Wesley is warning that unless we go forward, we will lose ground. He gives three increments, the last being hell. But there several stages between the failure to go forward and the ultimate apostasy [Pettit, *Great Privilege of All Believers*, 507].

[498]Raser, "Phoebe Palmer," 22. Invitational hymns such as "Is Your All On the Altar?" by Elisha A. Hoffman (1873), reflect Palmer's altar theology [White, *Beauty of Holiness*, 158].

[499]Peters, *Christian Perfection*, 112.

was also very insistent that a definite public testimony be given in order to retain the state.[500] While these teachings were not part of early Methodism, many of them became "distinguishing marks of what came later to be called the 'holiness movement.'"[501] Dieter concluded:

> The result was that the American holiness revival came to emphasize crisis stages of salvation at the expense of an emphasis on growth in grace. Dramatic and even revolutionary experience frequently became the hallmark of Christian life and witness. This distinctive eventually became a vital element of pentecostalism.[502]

Thomas Oden concluded that Palmer was the missing link between Methodism and Pentecostalism.[503] The emphasis that Palmer placed upon claiming and verbally affirming sanctification as a means of receiving it, was transferred by E. W. Kenyon to health and wealth.[504] However, historic Methodism understood true faith as the gift of God. It will not do to appropriate what we do not have.

Alice Hertel has documented that Palmer had contact with and influenced Boardman, Mahan, Upham and Robert Pearsall Smith. Her theology not only formed the American holiness movement, but was very influential upon Keswick theology.[505]

Charles Finney and Oberlin College

Charles Finney's greatest impact upon evangelicalism was his understanding of the baptism in the Holy Spirit. John L. Gresham, Jr. documented Finney's large impact on the Wesleyan-holiness movement, the Keswick movement, Pentecostalism, and dispensationalism.[506]

During the first half of the nineteenth century, Methodist theologians did

---

500Dieter, *Holiness Revival*, 30-32.

501Peters, *Christian Perfection*, 113.

502Dieter, "Wesleyan-Holiness Aspects of Pentecostal Origins," 62.

503Oden, *Phoebe Palmer*, 16-19.

504Simmons, *E. W. Kenyon*, 158-159; 171-172.

505Hertel, "Missing Links."

506Gresham, *Finney's Doctrine of the Baptism of the Holy Spirit*, iii; 64-85.

not use pentecostal language to speak of entire sanctification.[507] According to Timothy Smith, "the man chiefly responsible for the adoption by American Wesleyans of the terms "filling" or "baptism of the Spirit" to describe the experience of sanctification was Charles G. Finney."[508] Yet Finney did not explicitly connect Pentecost with entire sanctification. A. M. Hills said, "Finney failed to connect the obtaining of sanctification with the baptism of the Holy Ghost," although "sometimes he almost got the truth."[509]

The Oberlin faculty, of which Finney was president, was adamant that they had not received their doctrine from Wesley. Mahan had been raised in traditional Calvinistic theology and spent much of his early years seeking assurance that God had elected him to salvation.[510] According to Mahan it was "new light" Calvinism, yet he acknowledged "the terms by which we designated it were those by which it had been presented since the times of Wesley and Fletcher, namely Christian Perfection, Entire Sanctification, and Full Salvation."[511]

George Marsden described Finney's teaching as a synthesis of the Methodist holiness tradition with the Puritan and Reformed concept of the Christian life.[512] However, Allen Guelzo has written that Finney was involved in an intramural argument within Calvinism, between New England followers of Jonathan Edwards and the Princeton old school. The holiness movement misread Finney as being Wesleyan, when in fact he constructed a perfectionist theology which was drawn more from Jonathan Edwards.[513]

---

[507]Berg, "Theological Context," 50; see also White, *Beauty of Holiness*, 284-285.

[508]Smith, "The Cross Demands," 23. Smith conceded that Wesley, Fletcher, and the early Methodists almost never spoke of believers being "baptized" or "filled" with the Spirit. Instead Wesley almost exclusively used "Calvary language" to "declare the promise and describe the experience of sanctification" [p. 22]. See also "Preface" in Smith, *Charles G. Finney on Christian Holiness*, n. p.

[509]Hills, *Life of Finney*, 226.

[510]Garrison, *Forty Witnesses*, 226-228.

[511]Mahan, *Autobiography*, 367.

[512]Marsden, *Fundamentalism and American Culture*, 73-74.

[513]Guelzo, "Heir or a Rebel? 61-94; "Oberlin Perfectionism,"159-174. See also an earlier article by Guelzo making the same claim that Finney was not preaching Arminianism, but a New England brand of Calvinism associated with Edwards ["Making of a Revivalist," 28-30].

Even J. A. Wood recognized that Finney had mixed the holiness doctrine with "some new-school Calvinistic sentiments." However, Wood was wrong is his evaluation

"Old School" Calvinism opposed Finney because he confused an outward act with the new birth, because of his superficial view of conversion, because he taught that obedience to the direction of the evangelist was necessary to become a Christian and compliance with these commands was considered assurance, because this lowered the standard for membership within the church, and because revival was regarded as normal and continuous, not extraordinary and occasional.[514] While the "old school" erred in viewing regeneration as an irresistible act of God in which the elect were passive, Finney erred at the opposite extreme by teaching "that sinners can regenerate themselves, and repent and believe just when they please."[515] Thus, regeneration is the moral change which results when we choose to change. This teaching makes the new birth merely a change of purpose.

In 1837 Wilbur Fisk objected to a new Calvinistic theology which he described as self-conversion by an act of the will. While the Holy Spirit is involved in moral persuasion, the sinner resolves to give himself up to God and this is defined as regeneration. Fisk objected that this teaching was inconsistent with the doctrine of depravity, that it reduces sin to nothing more than a voluntary exercise, that it reduces regeneration to an act of the will which results in no transformation of character, and that it makes entire sanctification take place at the time of true regeneration.

Fisk did affirm the conditional agency of man in salvation. While the new birth hinges on believing on the name of Christ, the terms regeneration, born, and birth imply the efficient agency which God himself accomplishes. Fisk objected that this position teaches that man has power to lay down his life and then after he is "dead in trespasses and sins," he has power to take his life again. "Truly this is giving man a power that approaches very near to one of the divine attributes. To Christ alone does it belong 'to quicken whom he will.'"[516]

The basis of Finney's theology is free moral agency. No one has to sin. Finney objected that to talk of a sinful nature is to ascribe sinfulness to the Creator, who is the author of nature. Even selfishness is our choice. Finney taught that everything required by God's moral law is possible. What we cannot do through the power of our choice to do is outside the realm of moral law and moral obligation. Partial obedience to moral law is impossible. Either we love

---

that in the great essentials Finney harmonized with the Wesleyan view [*Perfect Love*, 274]. See also Warfield, *Perfectionism*, 2:18-19. Leclerc calls Oberlin theology "a new kind of Calvinism" [*Discovering Christian Holiness*, 117].

[514]Murray, *Pentecost - Today?* 49-53.

[515]This was the critique of Hodge, *Systematic Theology*, 2:277.

[516]Fisk, *Calvinistic Controversy*, 226-235. Another Methodist, Francis Hodgson was also critical of Finney in *Examination of the System of New Divinity*.

God with all our heart and our neighbor as ourselves, or we do not. Sin is a unit. Thus, we cannot be partly holy and partly sinful at the same time.[517]

Finney probably did more harm as a theologian than he did good as an evangelist. Finney was used as an evangelist, probably due to the intercessory work of Father Daniel Nash. Nash traveled with Finney for seven years. Recently, *Reader's Digest*, listed Rochester, New York, as one of the most desirable cities in the United States in which to live because of the 1830-1931 revival that took place under Evangelist Charles Finney.[518] After Nash died in 1831, however, Finney left the field of evangelism within three to four months.

After a decade of revival preaching in the 1820s, Finney became increasingly concerned with the quality of conversion which occurred through his "new measures." He wrote, "I was often instrumental in bringing Christians under great conviction, and into a state of temporary repentance and faith but, falling short of urging them up to a point, where they would become so acquainted with Christ as to abide in him, they would of course soon relapse again into their former state."

Writing in 1838 Joseph Ives Foot said, "During ten years, hundred, and perhaps thousands, were annually reported to be converted on all hands; but not it is admitted that his real converts are comparatively few. It is declared, even by himself that 'the great body of them are a disgrace to religion'; as a consequence of these defections, practical evils, great, terrible, and innumerable, are in various quarters rushing in on the Church."

James Boyle wrote to Finney in 1834, "Let us look over the fields where you and others and myself have labored as revival ministers, and what is now their moral state? What was their state within three months after we left them? I have visited and revisited many of these fields, and groaned in spirit to see the sad, frigid, carnal, contentious state into which the churches had fallen — and fallen very soon after our first departure from among them."

Asa Mahan wrote that the people were left like a dead coal which could not be reignited. The pastors were shorn of all their spiritual power. With the exception of Finney and Nash, the evangelists all lost their unction after a few years and became equally disqualified for the office of evangelist or pastor.[519]

---

[517]This paragraph was drawn from Jepson, *Don't Blame It All on Adam*, 19-32; 53-56; 61; 87; 109-111; 122.

[518]Tompkins, "Our Kindest City," 53-56. This ranking was based on the high rate of volunteerism.

[519]Warfield, *Studies in Perfectionism*, 2:23-27. The bane of shallow evangelism would reach a new low with the methods and manipulation of Billy Sunday between 1908-1920. His music director for seventeen years, Homer Rodeheaver, finally quit the crusades after pointing out the dishonesty of Sunday's practices. "When he

Thus, Finney became motivated to emphasize sanctification along with conversion during his remaining years. Nearly all his writings on sanctification were written after 1830. Finney believed that entire sanctification occurred at conversion when the Christian became fully obedient and entirely consecrated to God.[520] It is primarily the entire consecration of the human will. Finney defined sanctification as entire consecration to God, "nothing more nor less than entire obedience, for the time being, to the moral law."[521]

Yet Turner said that *consecration* is what man dedicates to God and *sanctification* describes the spiritual renewal of the soul by God.[522] The baptism, or baptisms, in the Spirit is the prerequisite to that union with Christ which keeps the soul in a state of sanctification.[523]

The Christian then experienced "perfect sanctification" as a process following conversion. Christians have the moral ability to freely choose the life of holy love and sinless perfection, yet they should use all the means of grace to prevent them from sinning. The struggle against temptation for singlemindedness to please God increased the process of sanctification. Sanctification occurs through the constant appropriation of faith through Christ.[524]

After going to Oberlin College to serve as professor of systematic theology under President Asa Mahan, Finney became the next president and was associated with the school until his death.[525] The school was a hotbed for the

---

makes his proposition for everyone to come it loses its effect because people cannot see any definite, specific thing for which they should come."
It is estimated that perhaps no more than 5% of those who "hit the sawdust trail" were actually born again [Dorsett, *Billy Sunda*y 136; 108. See also McIntyre, *Graham Formula*, 44-53].

520Oberlin theology taught the unity or simplicity of moral action. At no time can there be mixed character. Thus a moral agent is always as sinful or holy as with their knowledge they can be. According to J. H. Fairchild, "One of the most obvious consequences of the doctrine is, that conversion is entire consecration (sanctification)" [Hills, *Fundamental Christian Theology*, 2:252]. See the rebuttal of Daniel Steele in *Love Enthroned*, 31-32; see also Peck, *Christian Perfection*, 193 in which he says that this sweeps away the doctrine of Christian perfection with a stroke. Taylor said that Finney's emphasis was on the will and his teaching at Oberlin led to "an unhappy lot of legalists" [*Holiness*, 56-57].

521Finney, *Systematic Theology*, 431.

522Turner, "Doctrine of Sanctification," 87.

523Gresham, *Finney's Doctrine,* 37; 54.

524Hollon, "Love as Holiness."

525McIntire, "Charles Grandison Finney," 415-416.

abolitionist movement, radical feminism, and vegetarianism. Finney was a follower of Sylvester Graham, who taught that bad eating habits were as sinful as drinking alcohol. Oberlin adopted Graham's notions, forbidding coffee, tea, tobacco, gravy, most sweets, pepper, oil, vinegar and mustard. Graham also advocated a meatless diet of vegetables, fruits, and grains.[526] Graham and John Harvey Kellogg, advocated a Seventh-Day Adventist meatless died which would reduce "bestial sexual impulses. Thus, one's children would grow up with less original sin.[527]

B. B. Warfield described the atmosphere at Oberlin where "fads were exaggerated into fanaticism, foibles into gospels."[528] At one point Mahan was almost forced to resign from Oberlin because the faculty and trustees objected to his self conceit and his tendency to attribute unworthy motives to his brethren. Then he resigned in 1850. Oberlin did become more moderate after he left, but five years after leaving he demanded back pay from the college. He had to be brought face-to-face with Finney to clear up rumors he had spread about Finney.[529]

Oberlin is most famous, however, for its doctrine of perfection. Writing about Finney and Mahan, Peters observed:

> [They] were outspoken advocates of Christian Perfection in a period when it was neglected in many sectors of American Methodism. They came, therefore, to be considered as champions of the doctrine among Methodist groups similarly interested in its promotion. Their Reformed interpretation tended to become the standard view even in these quarters.[530]

---

[526]Madden and Hamilton, *Freedom and Grace*, 57-59; Miller, "Did You Know?" 4. Graham is best known for inventing the Graham cracker in 1829.

[527]Jordan, *Pig Out?* 50.

[528]Warfield, *Studies in Perfectionism*, 2:6-7; see also Dayton, *Discovering An Evangelical Heritage*, 15-98.

[529]Hardman, *Charles Grandison Finney*, 405-406. In a letter to Mahan, Lewis Tappan wrote that he was so self-conceited, so sensitive about his reputation, so idolatrous of his influence that he had hone immense injustice to Finney and himself [Miller, "Gallery,"18]. Finney wrote, "But circumstances had occurred here that seemed to render it necessary for the stability of our college that I should return" [Rosell and Dupuis, *Memoirs of Finney*, 516]. Hills, however, said that Mahan was opposed because of his doctrine of holiness [*Life of Finney*, 228-229; 234-235]. Madden and Hamilton devote an entire chapter to why Mahan left Oberlin [*Freedom and Grace*, 99-126; 136-139].

[530]Peters, *Christian Perfection*, 116; 189.

Fredrick Bruner said Finney was "the major historical bridge between primitive Wesleyanism and modern Pentecostalism."[531] Finney had no formal theological training, but his views were generally those of New School Calvinism. He does not consistently fit any theological pattern, however.[532] Timothy Smith is certainly wrong in asserting that Finney's views on sanctification were "precisely the same doctrine as taught by Fletcher."[533] Finney himself said:

> I had known considerable of the view of sanctification entertained by our Methodist brethren. But as their view of sanctification seemed to me to relate almost altogether to states of the sensibility, I could not receive their teaching.[534]

Finney not only misunderstood Wesley's emphasis on perfect love, but his teaching on sanctification differed from Wesley's in at least three important areas. First, Finney did not accept total depravity. The only bondage a man was under was a voluntary bondage to his own selfishness and love of the world. Finney said:

> To talk of a sinful nature, or sinful constitution, in the sense of physical sinfulness, is to ascribe sinfulness to the Creator, who is the author of nature. It is to overlook the essential nature of sin, and to make sin a physical virus, instead of a voluntary and responsible choice.[535]

A. M. Hills wrote, "President Finney had a marvelous experience, but a faulty philosophy on this subject. He held a peculiar theory of sin and depravity. *All sin was in the wrong use of the will.*"[536] Hills complained that many Methodist theologians had borrowed the doctrine of original sin as usually held by Calvinists. Hills denied that Adam's sin was imputed to us. However, he concluded that we were born with "propensities to sin." *Propensity* means a bend, a natural inclination or tendency. Later Hills affirms that man is totally depraved.

---

[531]Bruner, *Theology of the Holy Spirit*, 40.

[532]Shelly, "Charles Finney," 376.

[533]Smith, *Revivalism and Social Reform*, 260.

[534]Rosell and Dupuis, *Memoirs of Finney*, 391; see also Finney, *Lectures to Professing Christians*, 358-359; Gresham, *Finney's Doctrine*, 68; 88.

[535]Finney, *Systematic Theology*, 172.

[536]Hills, *Fundamental Christian Theology*, 2:252.

He seems to have confused original sin and original guilt. Although influenced by Finney, Hills said Finney "held a peculiar theory of sin and depravity."[537] Concerning Finney's theology, J. W. Jepson stated:

> Finney did not think much of this doctrine of original sin. In fact, he was quite opposed to it. For one thing, he did not believe that the Bible really teaches that we are born with a sinful nature or a natural disposition toward sin per se.[538]

In 1854 John McClintock, editor of the *Methodist Quarterly Review*, call this a "flippant denial" of man's depravity.[539] Thus, Finney's doctrine falls under the condemnation of 1 John 1:8. However, A. M. Hills, who was trained by Finney, declared concerning Finney's teaching that "with regard to total depravity, he accepts it as a Biblical doctrine, that all the acts of men since the fall, and previous to regeneration, are sinful."[540] But this description given by Hills does not define total depravity. Hill, himself, defined total depravity as the whole man being *injured* in every department and faculty of his being.[541]

On the other hand, Wesley did teach original sin very clearly. Original sin refers to a state of sin in us inherited from that original act of sin by Adam. Wesley preached that all who denied original sin are but heathens still. He claimed this as "the first grand distinguishing point between heathenism and

---

[537]Hills, *Fundamental Christian Theology*, 1:392-438; 2:252.

[538]Jepson, *Don't Blame It All On Adam*, p. 109; see also Hills, *Holiness and Power*, 33.

[539]McClintock, "The Conflict of the Ages," 176; 189-190.

[540]Hills, *Life of Charles G. Finney*, 210. Yet Hills acknowledged that Finney taught no moral depravity of human nature [*Holiness and Power*, 30-31; 40-43].

[541]Hills, *Fundamental Christian Theology*, 1:409. Hills, the first theologian of the Church of the Nazarene, both affirmed and denied the doctrine of original sin. He denied "moral inability" [1:368] and declared that man possesses the natural ability to obey all the requirements of God [1:369-375]. He declared Finney's rejection of gracious ability or prevenient grace to be unanswerable [1:373]. While he declared that "the tap-root of all sound theology is the sin question," yet he rejected the doctrine of original sin [1:379; 393-406]. With Finney he rejected the "theological fiction of imputation,"[1:395], but said that infants have inherited a depraved nature [2:133]. Men are not born with an sinful nature, but they are born with a sinful propensity [1:406]. Hills continued in the following chapter to affirm total depravity [1:409; 2:129]. He rejected "federal headship" [1:325], but wrote of a "law of natural descent" [2:141; 128]. See also Metz, *Some Crucial Issues*, 149.

Christianity."[542] He also wrote *The Doctrine of Original Sin,* running 272 pages in length, in which he defended the doctrine against the liberal views of his day.

Finney is not in agreement with Wesley at this point, but with Pelagius. W. B. Pope objected to Finney's Pelagianism and his denial of original sin.[543] Kenneth Grider wrote that Finney "sometimes tended to be Pelagian and humanistic, as for example when he wrote, 'The human will is free, therefore men have the power or the ability to do all their duty." However, Grider later wrote, "Finney does teach Pentecostal entire sanctification quite clearly in these 'Letters.' We could wish, however, that he were more specific on the matter of cleansing from original sin."[544] However, if Finney was clear on original sin, he would not be Pelagian! Yet Grider finds support for his teaching which equated entire sanctification with the baptism with the Holy Spirit from one who rejected a fundamental Bible doctrine.

In 1841 S. B. Canfield warned that the Oberlin doctrine of perfection was "Pelagian Perfectionism," not Arminian.[545] Luther Lee, theologian of the

---

[542]Wesley, "Original Sin," Sermon #44, 3.1. Mudge objected to the term "original sin," claiming the only original sin was the sin of Adam. But he went on to contend for "depravity," which he defined as the results entailed upon human nature by the original sin of our first parents, stating that "men come into the world to-day with a bias or tendency to sin or to that self-gratification which is sure to eventuate in sin" [Mudge, *Growth in Holiness*, 59-63, 65]. Steele found no fault with Mudge for substituting "depravity" for "original sin," provided he meant all that original sin means without the implications of voluntariness and guilt [Steele, *Defense of Christian Perfection*, 29]. Yet Mudge seemed to think that this bias or depravity itself was not sin. However, mankind may freely adopt it through their own choices resulting in a settled state or condition of sin [Mudge, *Growth in Holiness*, 73]. This view leans toward Pelagianism, emphasizing the human condition as the privation of good. Granbery felt that Mudge did not reject the doctrine of original sin as stated in the seventh Article of Religion, even though he rejected the term. But Granbery, writing in 1896, expressed concern that a tendency to Pelagianism had developed and was on the increase [Granbery, "Dr. Mudge," 206].

[543]Pope, *Compendium*, 3:73-74. See also Pope, *Higher Catechism*, 273, where he objected to the teaching of the Oberlin school, of which Finney was president, that there is no moral law incumbent on man but that which is accommodated to human weakness. This statement is amplified by Berkhof in which he explained that both Roman Catholic and Oberlin theologians teach that the demands of the law are adjusted to man's present ability [Berkhof, *Systematic Theology*, 538]. George Duffield described this as perfection on a sliding scale [Warfield, *Studies in Perfectionism*, 2:70].

[544]Grider, *Entire Sanctification*, 20; 67. Ironically, Timothy L. Smith declared that Finney was "never a Pelagian" ["Doctrine of the Sanctifying Spirit," 104].

[545]Canfield, *Exposition of Oberlin Perfectionism*, 83.

Wesleyan Methodist Church, wrote in 1856 that the power of sin is broken at the moment of regeneration. Yet there is still a warfare within and the state of things is explained as the remains of original sin, indwelling sin, or the depravity that remains after regeneration. "Rev. Charles G. Finney, denies that it is moral depravity, and hence he denies that there is any sin or moral depravity remaining in the soul after regeneration." After reviewing Finney's comments, in which he declared that sanctification designates "a phenomenon of the will or a voluntary state of mind,"[546] Lee declared,

> The conclusion appears undeniable, that every man is entirely sanctified the moment he wills right, and as Mr. Finney contends for the freedom of the will, that man has natural power to will right, all can sanctify themselves by an act of will in a moment. . . . The fact cannot be overlooked that Mr. Finney's view of sanctification differs very materially from that commonly held by all other schools of theology. It differs by being grounded upon a denial that moral depravity extends to the states of the intelligence and sensibility of the soul, depravity being confined wholly to the state of the will.[547]

Because Finney denied original sin, he also denied the need for prevenient grace. According to Finney, prevenient grace, the doctrine of gracious ability "is an absurdity."[548] Roger Olson concluded that Finney "vulgarized Arminian theology by denying human moral inability and the need for prevenient grace.[549] Finney taught that enough power remains in the will to initiate the beginnings of salvation and reason, illuminated by the Holy Spirit, turns the heart toward God.

According to Leland Scott, Nathan Bangs was the first Methodist to use

---

[546]Finney, *Systematic Theology*, 340-341. Finney also said, "Moral depravity is a depravity of choice. . . . Moral depravity, as I used the term, does not consist in, nor imply a sinful nature, in the sense that the substance of the human soul is sinful in itself. It is not an involuntary sinfulness. . . . Moral depravity is sinfulness, not of nature but of voluntary state. It is a sinfully committed state of the will to self-indulgence. . . . Moral depravity is sin itself, and not the cause of sin. It is not something prior to sin, that sustains to it the relation of a cause, but it is the essence and the whole of sin" [pp. 165-172].

[547]Lee, *Elements of Divinity*, 212-213. First edition published in 1856.

[548]Finney, *Systematic Theology*, 278.

[549]Olson, *Arminian Theology*, 27-28; 30.

the words "gracious ability."[550] Yet Bangs was only perpetuating the teaching of Wesley, who believed all cooperation with grace is of grace.[551]

It should be obvious that sanctification for Finney could not be a cleansing from the root of sin since he did not believe in a sinful nature. The problem with Finney's theology is that it emphasizes human will instead of divine grace. This humanistic emphasis ignores man's depravity by teaching that we perfect ourselves by choosing what is right. Finney's theology underestimates sin and the holiness doctrine overestimates eradication. Perkins concluded that Finney's theology emphasized obedience while the Methodist theology of perfection emphasized love.[552]

Quite naturally the shift in emphasis is from heart purity to power. This is reflected in the title of a holiness class by A. M. Hills, *Holiness and Power*.[553] Hills was the first theologian of the Church of the Nazarene to write a systematic theology and he was educated at Oberlin College under Finney.[554]

Secondly, Wesley taught that regeneration was accomplished by receiving the Holy Spirit. However, in his teaching, Finney saw regeneration as a moral change.[555] He called conversion "a change of mind," and compared it to a vote for the Lord.[556] In the words of one sermon title, Finney called on sinners to "change their own hearts."[557] According to Gresham, the change of regeneration is effected when the sinner turns from his selfishness to God.[558] Finney taught regeneration is an instantaneous change from entire sinfulness to entire holiness.[559] Richard Lovelace wrote, "He taught justification by sanctification and not by faith, and

---

550Scott, "Methodist Theology in America," 48-52.

551Pope, *Compendium*, 2:78-80.

552Perkins, *Evangelical Perfection*, 228.

553Hills failed to integrate the two concepts. "Holiness" emphasizes the Methodist concept of cleansing, while "power" emphasizes the Keswick concept of victory over sin.

554Grider, *Entire Sanctification*, 80.

555Jepson, *Don't Blame It All On Adam*, 122.

556White, *Beauty of Holiness*, 179.

557Finney, *Sermons*. Sermon #1, "Sinners Bound to Change Their Own Hearts;" Sermon #2 "How to Change Your Heart."

558Gresham, *Finney's Doctrine*, 34.

559Finney, *Systematic Theology*, 227.

sanctification by will power more than by grace."[560] In his systematic theology he devoted one chapter to justification, overlooking the real significance of regeneration, and spent six chapters on sanctification.

In *Power from on High,* Finney explained that the disciples were Christians before the Day of Pentecost and had "a measure of the Spirit," but in order for them to be successful they needed to pray for the promised baptism of the Spirit which would endue them with power.[561] He wrote in the *Oberlin Evangelist,* "The baptism of the Holy Ghost is . . . universally promised . . . to Christians," and "this blessing is to be sought and received after conversion."[562] The believer needs this baptism for sanctification and for service. Gresham explained why Finney felt a subsequent work was necessary:

> The regenerate person is fully sanctified—for the moment. However, after regeneration, Christians find themselves falling back into sin and needing to do again their "first works" and return to Christ. In that sense, they are not yet entirely sanctified. . . . Entire sanctification refers to a state of "entire and continued obedience to the law of God."[563]

While Wesley never taught regeneration is full sanctification, he did teach that those regenerated by the Holy Spirit do have victory over outward and willful sin. Wesleyans would call Finney's regeneration "reformation." No wonder Finney taught you have to get sanctified to keep saved; it was all a human effort until the Spirit came in "sanctification." Warfield accused Finney of teaching a system of morals which could operate just as well without God's grace. "God might be eliminated from it entirely without essentially changing its character. All virtue, all holiness, is made to consist in an ethical determination of will."[564] Obviously, such a decision for Christ would not result in a transforming grace which breaks the bondage of sin. Thus, in Finney's theology we need a second experience in order to maintain the first.

Third, Finney taught every person is at any given instant perfectly sinful or perfectly holy. Wesley did not teach absolute perfection and he allowed for "sin

---

[560]Lovelace, *Dynamics of Spiritual Life*, 194.

[561]Finney, *Power from on High*, 5-20.

[562]Grider, *Entire Sanctification*, 66.

[563]Gresham, *Finney's Doctrine*, 34.

[564]Warfield, *Studies in Perfectionism*, 2:193.

in believers."[565] It seems that Finney came to his understanding of the baptism of the Holy Spirit through the influence of the other three theological faculty members at Oberlin: Asa Mahan, John Morgan, and Henry Cowles. Morgan was the first to argue that the baptism of the Holy Ghost is the common privilege of all believers.[566]

Of the three, Mahan was by far the most influential. He stated that the one theme of his was "the two great doctrines" of Christian Perfection and the Baptism of the Holy Ghost.[567] However, Mahan's book *Scripture Doctrine of Christian Perfection* (1839) did not deal with the baptism of the Spirit. Finney's first explicit teaching on the baptism of the Spirit began in 1839-1840.[568]

Finney described his own conversion in 1821 as "a mighty baptism of the Holy Ghost."[569] Later in *Power from on High,* Finney seems to separate this experience from regeneration even though it occurred the same evening as his conversion.[570] A. M. Hills, writing from a holiness perspective, said:

> I question if there is a parallel to this in all the literature of the saints—a man receiving such a Baptism with the Spirit so soon after conversion, without asking for it or expecting it, and when he was too utterly ignorant of the whole subject to even think about it.[571]

The early Methodists would have tied Finney's baptism with the Spirit to the rest of his conversion process. A. M. Hills, however, equated Spirit baptism and entire sanctification. While Finney believed the state of sanctification is entered through the baptism of the Spirit, he saw the Christian life as a series of baptisms in the Spirit.[572] Finney himself professed sanctification in 1843, twenty-two years after his conversion.[573] As Hills tells the life of Finney, though, he is

---

[565]Hardman, *Charles Grandison Finney*, 332-333.

[566]Dayton, "Asa Mahan," 62.

[567]Warfield, *Studies in Perfectionism*, 2:66.

[568]Gresham, *Finney's Doctrine*, 17.

[569]Rosell and Dupuis, *Memoirs of Finney*, 23; see also Grider, *Entire Sanctification*, 66.

[570]Finney, *Power from on High*, 9.

[571]Hills, *Life of Charles G. Finney*, 21.

[572]Gresham, *Finney's Doctrine*, v; 9-11; 19.

[573]Rosell and Dupuis, *Memoirs of Finney*, 456-459.

forced to explain Finney's subsequent baptisms as necessary because he had let the blessing leak away and needed to be sanctified again.[574] Thus, multiple interpretations are offered to explain Finney's experience!

Although Finney's teaching was heretical, he influenced the holiness movement to accept the position that the baptism of the Holy Spirit was subsequent to regeneration. The holiness movement took Wesley's rationale for Christian perfection, fused it with Finney's teaching that the baptism of the Spirit was an experience subsequent to regeneration, concluding that the baptism of the Spirit was Christian perfection. Obviously, such as emphasis will lead to an emphasis on Pentecostal *power* and the gifts of the Spirit instead of upon Christlikeness and the fruit of the Spirit. By the turn of the century, a majority of the holiness movement had become Pentecostal. The emphasis had shifted from purity to power.

Like Finney, Asa Mahan did not acknowledge the doctrine of original sin.[575] He seems as well, to have overlooked the significance of regeneration. According to Mahan there is no real inner change produced by the Holy Spirit in conversion. The converted individual has a new attitude toward God and God has forgiven him, but he cannot maintain this relationship without taking the second step, which is the baptism of the Holy Ghost.[576] Mahan felt the Holy Spirit was "with" believers, but was not "in" them until they received this baptism.[577] B. B. Warfield said concerning his proof text, Acts 19:2:

> It is an inconvenience to Mahan that he has to depend for the scriptural ground of his doctrine of the baptism of the Spirit on passages which teach that the Spirit is given to all believers. . . . It would be a curious speculation to inquire into the effect it would have had on his constructions, had Mahan learned that what Paul really said was, "Did you receive the Holy Spirit when you believed?"[578]

Mahan had first written *The Scriptural Doctrine of Christian Perfection* in 1839. According to Donald Dayton, it was the major expression of holiness

---

574Hills, *Life of Charles G. Finney*, 155.

575Warfield, *Studies in Perfectionism*, 2:126. Yet as he grew older Mahan moved closer to Wesleyan theology and away from Finney's Pelagianism [Dayton, "Asa Mahan," 60-61].

576Warfield, *Studies in Perfectionism*, 2:109-110.

577Greathouse, *Historical Development*, 307.

578Warfield, *Studies in Perfectionism*, 2:122-123.

theology before the Civil War.[579] Mahan taught that none are actually saved who are not perfect in the sense of being in full compliance with known duty. "The first holy act of the converted sinner is as perfect as any act of any intelligent being in existence." Yet this infant Christian must be taught there are two types of perfection and he must press on to a condition of being confirmed, settled and strengthened in the way of holiness and peace.

According to Mahan God seems to promise perfection on the express condition of perfection.[580] Perfection in holiness is "a full and perfect discharge of our entire duty, of all existing obligations in respect to God and all other beings. It is perfect obedience to the moral law."[581] Not believing in original sin, Mahan did not emphasize a cleansing from the inner nature of sin

In 1870, Mahan wrote *The Baptism of the Holy Ghost,* which Phoebe Palmer published. Grider called this second book a "milestone" and said it had a

---

[579]Dayton, "Asa Mahan," 60-61. George O. Peck wrote, "Though it is not to be maintained that he expresses himself Methodistically upon all the points of this great doctrine, we are satisfied that the thing which we mean by Christian Perfection is truly set forth in that work ["Christian Perfection," 308]. Dieter mistakenly cited this passage as approval of Finney's views [*Holiness Revival*, 58].

Peck devoted an entire chapter to the differences between the Wesleyan and Oberlin theories on perfection in *Christian Perfection*, 174-193. In his original edition of 1842 Peck concluded that regardless of the differences, "there may be a perfect agreement as to the doctrine of Christian perfection" [p. 192]. However, in the revised edition of 1848 Peck added a lengthy footnote stating that he had seem material from Finney which he had not previously seen. He then labels the views of Finney as not only "novel and eccentric, but several of them exceedingly objectionable" [p. 186]. There he revised his original conclusion of "perfect agreement" to say that he had charitably concluded this agreement with all the light he had at the time he originally wrote. "But I am not compelled to fear the case is otherwise." He then reluctantly concluded that Wesleyans can have no sympathy with Finney's views on Christian perfection [pp. 192-193]. In his autobiography Peck wrote, "At first glace it look as if they had embraced the Wesleyan theory of Christian perfection, but a close examination of the language they employed convinced me that they had a theory of their own, and on several vital points were in error"[Peck, *Life and Times of George Peck*, 237].

However, Rader concluded that other than disagreement on cleansing of human depravity, "in regard to the attainability of the experience of entire sanctification, the prerequisites of attainment, the condition of attainment, and the results of entering into this experience, both Wesleyans and Finney are in substantial, if not absolute agreement" [Rader, "Doctrine of Sanctification," 103].

[580]Hamilton, "Nineteenth Century Philosophy and Holiness Theology," 59-60.

[581]Mahan, *Christian Perfection*, 1.

major impact both in Europe and America.[582] It represented a major hermeneutical shift from a Christocentric doctrine to an emphasis on the Holy Spirit and Pentecost.[583] As would be expected, Mahan's second book emphasized power, not purity.[584] According to Donald Dayton, Mahan later seemed to conclude that entire sanctification was for purity and it prepared the heart for the baptism of the Spirit which came later and produced power.[585]

According to Timothy Smith, the influence of Finney's pentecostal teaching was "direct and immediate." George O. Peck, editor of the *Methodist Quarterly Review*, does refer to the work of the Holy Spirit in sanctification as "the baptism of the Holy Ghost."[586] In so doing, Smith said George Peck became "the first Methodist since John Fletcher to equate the experience of entire sanctification with the baptism of the Holy Ghost."[587] This means, however, that the early Methodists did not emphasize baptismal language to describe entire sanctification and when it reappeared in the American holiness movement it was

---

[582]Grider, *Entire Sanctification*, 72.

[583]Marsden, *Fundamentalism and American Culture*, 75.

[584]Grider, *Entire Sanctification*, 21; see also Dayton, *Theological Roots of Pentecostalism*, 77.

[585]Dayton, *Theological Roots of Pentecostalism*, 96. See the evaluation by Madden and Hamilton, *Freedom and Grace*, 184-191.

[586]Peck, "Christian Perfection," 151. Yet Peck did not emphasize this connection in *Scripture Doctrine of Christian Perfection*, mentioning only once on p. 412.

[587]Smith, "Doctrine of the Sanctifying Spirit," 106; 113. This disregards the atypical Captain Thomas Webb and White's more specific statement that "no Methodist *theologian* between John Fletcher and George Peck identified sanctification with the baptism of the Spirit" [White, *Beauty of Holiness*, 284-285].

The article cited by Smith contains numerous quotations from early Methodists, but no reference to Finney or Mahan [Peck, "Christian Perfection," 123-154]. It is the April 1841 issue in which Peck actually reviews Mahan's *Christian Perfection*. Peck noted that while Mahan did not express himself Methodistically upon all the points of this great doctrine, we are satisfied that the *thing* which we mean by *Christian perfection* is truly set forth in that work. Mahan's primarily failure was the failure not to sufficiently distinguish between legal and evangelical perfection [Peck, "Christian Perfection" 308]. Note, however, that Peck is not reviewing Mahan's *The Baptism of the Holy Ghost* which would not be published for another twenty-nine years.

In "The Blessing of Abraham," Smith said that in the *MQR* for January 1841 George Peck pronounced Mahan's volume "virtually Wesleyan" [*Christian History*, 26]. Again it must be pointed out that it is the April issue and that Peck later retracted his endorsement [see ftnt #2276].

imported from outside mainstream Methodism and brought that baggage with it.

Certainly by this time there were shifts taking place in Methodist theology, but not everyone was changing. The prince of Methodist theologians, W. B. Pope, lamented this new emphasis, saying:

> There has been a tendency among some teachers of religion in modern times so to speak of Christian perfection as to seem to make it the entrance into a new order of life, one namely of higher consecration under the influence of the Holy Ghost. That this higher life is the secret of entire consecration there can be no doubt. But there is no warrant in Scripture for making it a new dispensation of the Spirit, or a Pentecostal visitation superadded to the state of conversion. *Have ye received the Holy Ghost when ye believed?* means *Did ye receive the Holy Ghost when ye believed?* In other words entire consecration is the stronger energy of a spirit already in the regenerate, not a Spirit to be sent down from on high. This kingdom of God is already within, if we would let it come in its perfection. Neither SINCE in this passage, nor the AFTER in *after that ye believed*, has anything corresponding in the original Greek. The teaching tends to diminish the view of regeneration, which is itself a life *hid with Christ in God.*[588]

John McClintock and James Strong, both Methodists, wrote in their *Cyclopedia of Biblical, Theological, and Ecclesiastical Literature:*

> Under the Christian dispensation it appears to be the office of the Holy Ghost to enter into and dwell within every believer (Rom. viii, 9, 11; 1 John iii, 24). . . . We have said that these two great blessings [the witness of the Spirit and the baptism of the Spirit] properly attend the conversion of the soul. . . . This baptism is neither the same with entire sanctification, nor is the latter the invariable result of the former. Some may have, unwittingly, but not therefore harmlessly, confounded the two under the vague name of "the second blessing."[589]

Daniel Steele was the first major Methodist theologian to embrace the

---

[588]Pope, *Compendium*, 3:64.

[589]McClintock and Strong, *Cyclopedia*, 9:947; 950-951.

Pentecostal position developed by Mahan and Finney.[590] In 1874 he encouraged his brethren "to cease to discuss the subtleties and endless questions arising from entire sanctification or Christian Perfection, and all cry mightily to God for the baptism of the Holy Spirit."[591] Steele linked the baptism of the Holy Spirit with entire sanctification in his first book, *Love Enthroned,* published in 1875. Writing in 1896, Steele considered the methodology of S. A. Keen a hopeful sign. Keen had held "Pentecostal Meetings" in about seventy conferences of the Methodist Episcopal Church, including the General conference of 1892.

Daniel Steele reported, "The distinctive Wesleyan doctrine of entire sanctification was not made conspicuous, but was merged in the broad doctrine of the fullness of the Holy Spirit as the supply of the believers' utmost needs." According to Steele, Keen felt this approach, emphasizing the fullness of the Spirit would "clear away the difficulties that exist in some minds respecting Christian perfection as taught in our standards."[592] At the time Steele thought he was right, although recognizing this was not the traditional Methodist approach but by 1912, when he published *Steele's Answers,* he seemed to be having second thoughts when he wrote, "The phrases 'baptism of the Spirit, and fulness of the Spirit,' do not specifically designate entire sanctification, or perfect love."[593]

The Holiness Camp Meeting

After the Civil War, The National Camp-Meeting for the Promotion of Christian Holiness was organized in 1867. This organization still exists as the Christian Holiness Partnership.[594] Since Methodism was the largest denomination at that time and a majority of those who attended these camp meetings were Methodists, the leadership of the Methodist Church exerted a restraining influence in this movement.

However, the movement was interdenominational and gradually picked

---

[590]Greathouse, *Historical Development*, 312.

[591]Steele, "Baptism in the Spirit," 37-38.

[592]Steele, *Defense of Christian Perfection*, 135-136; 7.

[593]*Steele's Answers*, 156-157. Donald Dayton also noted this later ambivalence about identifying entire sanctification with the baptism of the Spirit [*Theological Roots in Pentecostalism*, 84].

[594]Although critics sometimes claim more souls were conceived than born again at camp meetings, I am not critical of everything about the camp meeting movement. From 1989-2005 I served on the board of Mt Olivet Camp Meeting in Hinton, WV. I was camp president 2001-2005. This camp was originated by John L. Harris in 1916. See his biography, *Tears and Triumphs*.

up more support from non-Methodists. Those within Methodism who were advocates of the holiness message felt a greater loyalty to the holiness movement than to the Methodist Church. Over time, frustration was expressed with the mother church.

Methodism believed in holiness. Wesley said the purpose of Methodism was to spread scriptural holiness across these lands. Yet the holiness message had been modified and reduced into a speciality. Huntington wrote,

> Wherever this theory of Christian holiness is taught, it generally becomes a specialty. Special meetings for the "promotion of holiness" are thought to be necessary, the implication being that other religious meetings are not for that purpose. Associations are formed, other than Church organizations, for the special work of promoting sanctification as understood by those who accept this view. Certain religious papers are devoted specifically to this subject, and are known as "holiness papers." Some ministers come to regard themselves as specially called to the work of "preaching holiness," and conducting "holiness meetings." This specialism has been fruitful in the development of the class idea in Churches.[595]

The Methodist Church was also alarmed that holiness evangelists were accountable to no one. Not everyone in this movement was holy.[596] On the other hand, Methodism was accused of wanting to control the movement. In reality both sides needed each other, but each side was repelled by the extremes each saw in the other.[597]

Kevin Lowery concluded, "It can be said that the Methodist neglect of Christian perfection is what sparked the Holiness Movement, but it can also be argued that the excesses of the Holiness Movement fueled the Methodist aversion

---

[595]Huntington, *Sin and Holiness*, 254-255.

[596]Bryant, *"A Survey of the Field"* said the number of those connected with the holiness movement whose lives were not up to the common standards of Christian morals was larger that he would like to name [p. 3]. Bryant referred specifically to those who divorced and married again for other than Bible causes and those who went out as evangelists when their domestic relations make it their duty to stay at home and attend to the raising of their young families [p. 25; see also pp. 5, 7-8]. Bryant was rebutting John P. Brooks, editor of the *Banner of Holiness*. See Oblinger, "John P. Brooks"; Oblinger, "Religious Mimesis."

[597]Peters, *Christian Perfection*, 192.

to the doctrine."[598] In time the more radical holiness movement broke with Methodism and began to form separate organizations. I want to contrast the radical holiness message, preached at the turn of this century, with historic Methodist doctrine.

The teaching of Palmer and Finney, as well as a growing number of less influential ministers, focused new attention on the doctrine of sanctification. After the Civil War there was a mood of national optimism and these holiness leaders felt their time had come. They believed "the sanctification of the church meant the salvation of the world."[599] It was J. A. Wood who first suggested a camp meeting for the promotion of holiness. The National Camp-Meeting for the Promotion of Christian Holiness issued a call to all "irrespective of denominational ties" to meet in Vineland, New Jersey, on June 17, 1867, "to realize together a Pentecostal baptism of the Holy Ghost."[600] As many as 25,000 attended and they came from nearly every state in the Union.[601] By 1872 there were regional associations modeled after the national association. By 1887 the national association had sixty-seven national camp meetings. By 1891 they listed 304 holiness evangelists. By 1892 there were forty-one holiness periodicals.[602]

Through the influence of Finney and Mahan, the doctrine of holiness was linked to Pentecost and holiness expositors routinely identified entire sanctification with the baptism with the Holy Spirit. They also thought of Pentecost, not only as a first century event, but as a promised eschatological event. They believed that before the return of Jesus, the Holy Spirit would be poured out again. This would be the eschatological event which would prepare the world for the return of Jesus. The leaders of the holiness movement believed that their movement was that eschatological event. The ecumenical character of the movement seemed to confirm this belief, since it seemed the holiness movement was uniting Christian and overcoming denominational barriers.[603]

The movement constantly appealed to Wesley, Fletcher, and Asbury to give credibility to their message. Timothy Smith declared, "So successful were they in identifying sanctification with Methodist orthodoxy that opponents were hard pressed to find ground upon which to stand without laying themselves open

---

[598]Lowery, *Salvaging Wesley's Agenda*, 33.

[599]Rose, *Vital Holiness*, 59. Rose was describing the convictions of John Inskip, a founder of the holiness camp meetings.

[600]Hughes, *Days of Power*, 55.

[601]Jones, *Perfectionist Persuasion*, 21.

[602]Peters, *Christian Perfection*, 138-139.

[603]Powell, "Theological Significance of the Holiness Movement," 129.

to the charge of heresy."[604] However, John Peters recognized the change by his chapter title, "The Doctrine Modified, 1865-1900."[605] According to Grider, by this time pentecostal terminology was almost synonymous for entire sanctification.[606] Yet at a 1867 meeting of Methodist preachers on the subject of sanctification, which met in part to respond to Inskip and other holiness evangelists, S. D. Brown objected to the assertion that the baptism of the Holy Ghost on the day of Pentecost was entire sanctification.[607] It was also claimed that holiness preachers ignored partial sanctification, speaking only of simple pardon. They entirely ignored regeneration and all gradual sanctification.[608]

However by 1880 J. A. Wood wrote, "That the disciples were all sanctified at the day of Pentecost, is taught by nearly all the authorities and standards of Methodism."[609] Grider observed, "There seemed to be at this time a groundswell toward viewing entire sanctification as being wrought by the baptism with the Holy Spirit."[610] In 1910 A. M. Hills could write:

> We are now prepared to give a formal definition of sanctification or Scriptural holiness, which would probably be accepted by the three hundred teachers and preachers in the National Holiness Association of America. . . : Entire Sanctification is a second definite work of grace wrought by the Baptism with the Holy Spirit in the heart of the believer subsequent to regeneration, received instantaneously by faith, by which the heart is cleansed from all corruption and filled with the perfect love of God.[611]

---

[604]Smith, *Called Unto Holiness*, 21.

[605]Peters, *Christian Perfection*, 133.

[606]Grider, *Entire Sanctification*, 76.

[607]Janes, *Perfect love*, 70.

[608]Janes, *Perfect love,* 27-37.

[609]Janes, *Perfect love*, 291.

[610]Grider, *Entire Sanctification*, 74.

[611]Hills, *Scriptural Holiness and Keswick Teaching Compared*, 29. Here Hills is citing from the doctrinal statement adopted at the General Holiness Assembly of 1885. According to Hills the "scriptural" teaching is eradication, while the Keswick position is "counteraction." Yet both are figures of speech used to describe how God deals with sin in the human heart. To the question of whether sin was suspended or destroyed, Wesley replied "call it what you please. They are all love today" [*Works*, 11:442-443]. In a letter to Mrs. Maitland, Wesley wrote, "And whether sin is suspended or extinguished, I will not dispute. It is enough that they feel nothing but

Yet George Failing recognized this definition was not Wesleyan and asked, "Can any comparable definition be found in Wesley's works?"[612] The first doctrinal statement of the National Holiness Association contained no pentecostal language, but connected sanctification with the cleansing blood of Christ's atonement, using 1 John 1:7. The formulation by the General Holiness Assembly of 1885 associated justification with the work of Christ on Calvary and sanctification with the work of the Holy Ghost at Pentecost.

The writings of J. A. Wood illustrate the solidification of the theology of the holiness movement. Wood originally published *Perfect Love* in 1861, six years prior to the organization of the National Association for the Promotion of Holiness. By 1880 *Perfect Love* had gone through 28 editions. In it Wood quoted from some eighty theologians and it contains a breadth not found in his later writings. However, in *Perfect Love* Wood used the phrase "merely regenerate" some ten times,[613] betraying a depreciation of the new birth contrary to Methodism. There is nothing mere about the regenerating work of the Holy Spirit. Huntington wrote,

> As the result of their forgiveness and renewal in righteousness, they have "redemption through his blood, even [not merely] the forgiveness of sins." They are "born of the Spirit." They are "new creatures" — a "new creation." They are "in Christ." They are "reconciled to God." They have "no condemnation." They "have the Spirit of Christ." They are "in the Spirit." They are "children of God." They are "made free from sin. They are "saved." They are "sanctified." They have "passed from death unto life." Christ is in them. "The love of God is shed abroad in their hearts by the Holy Ghost, which is given unto them." "Whether they live or die, they are the Lord's." They are "holy."

---

love" [12 May 1763].

[612]Failing, "Developments in Holiness Theology After Wesley," 23.

[613]Janes, *Perfect love*, 11, 43, 55, 59 (twice), 60 (twice), 61, 64, 120. This fact is noted by Quanstrom, *Century of Holiness Theology*, p. 45. See also Peck, *Central Idea of Christianity*, p. 11. Mudge objected to this depreciation of the work of grace wrought in the soul at the time of conversion by the holiness movement [*Growth in Holiness*, 23-24; 110; 172]. Huntington also reacted to Wood saying, "There is an undertone in this phraseology which conveys the impression that religious experience which falls short of this particular idea of holiness, does not amount to much" [*Sin and Holiness*, 105-106]. Ironically, Steele seemed to defend the use of the phrase "merely justified" [*Defense of Christian Perfection*, 88]. Yet Kenneth Collins warned that referring to regeneration as "mere" constituted a "grave danger" [*Wesley on Salvation*, 125].

> They are "delivered from the power of darkness, and translated into the kingdom of God's dear Son." They are "made meet to be partakers of the inheritance of the saints in light."[614]

Nor did Wesley view regeneration as "mere." He declared , "No man is able to work it in himself. It is a work of omnipotence. It requires no less power thus to quicken a dead soul, than to raise a body that lies in the grave. It is a new creation; and none can create a soul anew, but he who at first created the heavens and the earth."[615] Wesley warned that the grand device of Satan, was to destroy the first work of God in the soul, or at least to hinder its increase, by our expectation of that greater work.[616]

Wood also taught that faith must be "naked" to be pure. In other words we are to claim entire sanctification without any divine assurance.[617]

Hiram Mattison observed that J. A. Wood ignored Fletcher's formal definition of the nature of perfect love. Fletcher had declared

> We give the name of "Christian perfection" to that maturity of grace and holiness which established adult believers attain to under the Christian dispensation: and thus we distinguish that maturity of grace, both from the ripeness of *grace*, which belongs to the dispensation of *the Jews below us*; and from the ripeness of *glory*, which belongs to *departed saints above us*. Hence it appears, that by "Christian perfection" we mean nothing but the cluster and maturity of the graces which compose the

---

[614]Huntington, *Sin and Holiness*, 114-115.

[615]Wesley, *An Earnest Appeal to Men of Reason and Religion*, ¶ 9, *Works*, 8:5.

[616]Wesley, "Satan's Devices," Sermon #42, ¶ 5.

[617]Wood, *Perfect Love*, 104-105; 117; 121. The term "naked faith" is synonymous with "bare faith," see p. 540 of this book. Although Wood cites Fletcher as though Fletcher was advocating "naked faith," Fletcher only used this term once [*Works*, 2:661] and the context was not faith for entire sanctification. Notice that on p. 121 Wood actually contradicts Wesley's teaching that we should not believe we are sanctified wholly *before* we have the witness of the Spirit. Wesley declared that faith was indeed naked "if it be stripped both of love and peace and joy in the Holy Ghost!" ["The Wilderness State," Sermon # 46, 2.2.2]. As Collins noted, in Wesley's later years he did urge several people to anticipate perfect love by the basis of "naked faith." However, Wesley meant that believers were to wait for Christian perfection on the basis of faith, without works added. J. A. Wood and Phoebe Palmer, however, taught that Christian perfection should be claimed on the basis of "naked faith" or "bare faith" without any assurance [Collins, *Real Christian*, 154-155].

> Christian character in the Church militant. In other words, Christian perfection is a spiritual constellation made up of these gracious stars, perfect repentance, perfect faith, perfect humility, perfect meekness, perfect self denial, perfect resignation, perfect hope, perfect charity for our *visible* enemies, as well as for our *earthly* relations; and, above all, perfect love for our *invisible* God, through the explicit knowledge of our Mediator Jesus Christ.[618]

Yet Mattison complained that when Wood asked, "What constitutes Christian perfection?" that he proceeded to give answers professedly from Wesley, Fletcher, and others, after which he proceeds to define what *he* understood by Christian perfection. Mattison charged that Wood has not only ignored or suppressed Fletcher's definition but instead cited a passage certainly never written as a definition and which Mattison could not find in Fletcher's *Works* at all.

Furthermore, Wood could not tell him where it could be found. The quote which neither of them could find, is found in Fletcher's *Works*, volume 2, page 567. But Wood had taken a hypothetical statement by Fletcher and edited it into a definitive statement. Wood did not include it in the second edition of *Perfect Love* (1880). Nor did Wood include the more definitive statement Mattison suggested, probably because it did not lend itself to his artificial distinction between purity and maturity. Mattison claimed that Wood had substituted an inferior definition for Fletcher's formal definition because Fletcher's definition is too high for Wood.[619]

Fifteen years later, Wood wrote *Purity and Maturity* in 1876, which he claimed was a defense of Wesleyan doctrine. But it tended to redefine the terms. According to Wood, a babe in Christ is pure when cleansed, but still immature.[620] Yet according to 1 Corinthians 2:6-3:3, Ephesians 4:13-14, and Hebrews 5:11-6:3 the spiritual babe (νήπιος - *napios*) is not entire sanctified. These three references contrast the babe with the mature (τέλειο - *teleio*) and the implication is that if the believer is mature he would no longer be a babe.

Purity and Maturity reflects Wood's own theology and does not rely on extensive citations, as did *Perfect Love*. According to Barry Hamilton, the paradigm of purity and maturity was a popular rhetorical device among holiness

---

618Fletcher, *Works*, 2:492-493.

619Janes, *Perfect love*, 23-24; 26-27.

620Wood, *Purity and Maturity*, 190.

preachers. W. B. Godbey probably borrowed the concept from Wood.[621]

In *Purity and Maturity* Wood asserted that "it is necessary that we keep in mind the idea that GROWTH, PURITY, and MATURITY are distinct."[622] He contended that *purity* is a state arrived at by an instantaneous second experience. It cannot be obtained by growth in grace.[623] After the crisis experience we then grow into maturity.[624] However, Wood had little to say about maturity in *Purity and Maturity*.[625] In contrast, John Hunt defined entire sanctification as purity *and* maturity.[626]

While Methodism taught that entire sanctification was the culmination of a process of growth, the holiness movement taught entire sanctification was the basis for spiritual growth. They represented the time between conversion and sanctification as a temporary, and hopefully short, period marked by frustration and spiritual defeat. Entire sanctification represented the solution to this frustration and defeat. Thus, the holiness movement was a "single-issue movement."[627]

It was not until his 1880 revision of *Perfect Love*, which was about one-

---

[621]Hamilton, *William Baxter Godbey*, 127. Godbey relied on Wood's book *Perfect Love*, in his book *Sanctification*, 9 and Godbey recommended Wood's book, *Wesley on Perfection* in his book, *Christian Perfection*, 128. *Wesley on Perfection* was a cut and paste job, in which Wesley was brought into conformity with the theology of the holiness movement.

[622]Wood, *Purity and Maturity*, 157.

[623]R. S. Foster expressed dissent from those who deride the doctrine of progress in holiness [*Christian Purity*, 188; see also pp. 183; 185]. However, Dunning felt that it was hard to determine whether Foster held that entire sanctification was gradual or instantaneous [*Grace, Faith, and Holiness*, p. 453]. Stephen Merrill also declared "there is no growth in grace without an increase in holiness" [*Doctrinal Aspects of Christian Experience*, 263; see also pp.219; 221].

[624]The irony is that in *Perfect Love* Wood had originally written, "The approach to entire sanctification may be gradual" [p. 19].

[625]This fact was noted by Abbott, "Christian Maturity," 304. What Wood had to say on maturity is found on pp. 55-59 of *Perfect Love*, an earlier work. Wynkoop noted that relatively little literature on the Christian maturation process has been produced by the Wesleyan-Arminian writers [*Foundations*, 107]. It would have been more accurate to say the American holiness movement.

[626]Hunt, *Letters on Sanctification*, 7.

[627]Powell, "Theological Significance of the Holiness Movement," 131-132. As a representative of this viewpoint, Powell cited Wood, *Perfect Love* (1880 edition), 30-33; 170-182.

third larger than the first edition, that Wood "viewed entire sanctification as being wrought by the Spirit baptism."[628] Grider also noted that in the second edition Wood is even more vigorous in his opposition to gradual sanctification.[629] In it Wood declared,

> The idea that deliverance from indwelling sin, and a state of entire sanctification may be secured by the ordinary process of growth, we regard as a serious mistake and productive of much evil. The reader will find this question treated with special attention in *Purity and Maturity*, pp. 128-185.

In 1885 Wood compiled *Christian Perfection as Taught by John Wesley*, but he tended to use only quotes from Wesley with which he agreed. Randall Stephens observed holiness adherents were not interested in the full range of Wesley's works, "especially his writings that seemed to make sanctification anything less than an instantaneous experience. Also, they frequently read Wesley through later holiness redactors who had significantly modified his theology."[630] For example, chapter 8 is entitled, "Sanctification Instantaneous, by Faith, and Not by Growth in Grace." Leo Cox observed that Wesley did not make the same distinction that Wood made concerning purity and maturity, noting that "where Wood emphasized the instantaneous character of cleaning as in a moment, Wesley was more insistent on a gradual cleansing from the beginning of sanctification at regeneration to its completions in entire sanctification."[631] For Wesley *purity* began at regeneration while *maturity* referred to Christian perfection. J. M. Boland wrote in 1888, "Of all the books I have read *Perfect Love* and *Purity and Maturity* by Rev. J. A. Wood excel in this work of confusion."[632]

---

[628]Grider, *Entire Sanctification*, 22.

[629]Grider, *Entire Sanctification*, 100.

[630]Stephens, *The Fire Spreads*, 322.

[631]Cox, *Perfection*, 93; 121; see also Quanstrom's evaluation, *Century of Holiness Theology*, 50. In reaction to the theology that growth and sanctification are radically different ideas, Granbery wrote that partial and entire sanctification are one in kind, different in degree. "All growth in grace, unless perfection has already been gained, is a dying to sin, is the destruction of impurity. . . . If a believer is being more and more cleansed from defilement, waxing whiter day by day, do not tell us that to wash him from the last and least stain, so that he shall be every whit pure, is an operation of an altogether different nature" [Granbery, *Entire Sanctification*, 38].

[632]Boland, *Problem of Methodism*, 199-201. Boland contended that the regenerate are entirely sanctified and hence they are morally pure. He also advocated Christian perfection as Christian maturity [pp. 28; 196]. While my concern with Wood

In *Perfect Love* Wood said that regeneration is a partial purity,[633] but he used the term "purity" exclusively to describe entire sanctification in *Purity and Maturity*. Wesley affirmed that every man, as soon as he believes is "a new creature, sanctified, pure in heart."[634] Ironically, Wood quoted Wesley's statement that "sanctification begins in the moment a man is justified" in *Perfect Love*.[635] Yet in *Purity and Maturity* Wood defined *purity* as the second work of grace and *maturity* was what followed that work.

By 1905 Wood could claim his distinction between purity and maturity "relieves the subject of entire sanctification of difficulties which have perplexed many good men. . . . It also harmonizes some conflicting items in Mr. Wesley's works on Christian Perfection."[636] However, as Wood shifted his emphasis toward an instantaneous experience he declared, contrary to Wesley, that "there are 'babes,' 'young men' and 'men of full age" in a state of entire sanctification."[637] In this reference to 1 John 2:12-14, Wesley saw only the fathers as perfect men. Thus, according to him, growth would occur prior to perfection.[638] According to Wood, on the other hand, perfection was instantaneous and growth would occur *after* perfection. While Wood allowed for growth only after entire sanctification, Wesley said inward sanctification begins in the moment a man is justified. "From that time a believer gradually dies to sin, and grows in grace."[639]

In *Mistakes Respecting Christian Holiness* Wood declared that "spiritual life, moral purity and Christian maturity are three prominent facts, distinct in Christian experience. . . . No one grows into a state of purity, that is by faith, is instantaneous, and is wrought by the Holy Spirit, and the cleansing blood of

---

is similar to the concerns of Boland, the difference is that I would hold with Wesley that sin remains, but does not reign in the regenerate. Boland, on the other hand, rejected what he called "the residue theory of regeneration."

633Wood, *Purity and Maturity*, 39.

634Wesley, *Works*, 8:291.

635Wood, *Perfect Love*, 22.

636Wood, *Mistakes*, 73.

637Wood, *Mistakes*, 72.

638Wesley, "On Sin in Believers," Sermon #13, 3.2; "Christian Perfection," Sermon #40, 1.9; "On Patience," Sermon #83, §10; "On Working Out Our Own Salvation," Sermon #85, 1.2-3; "On the Discoveries of Faith," Sermon #117, § 15-17.

639Wesley, *Works*, 11:387.

Christ."[640] James Mudge responded, calling the idea preposterous that

> if growth be conceded to have anything to do with removing or diminishing depravity, some dishonor is cast upon the spirit of truth, the blood of Christ, and the office of faith. But surely no one of any evangelical school of thought for a moment supposes or claims that growth in grace is secured in any other way than by faith — joined, of course, with works — and through the perpetually operating efficacy of the atonement and through the ever present Holy Spirit.[641]

In *Soul Food*, G. D. Watson taught a deeper death of self after the soul has been sanctified. "This deeper crucifixion to self is the unfolding and application of all the principles of self-renunciation which the soul agreed to in its full consecration." Since sanctification is instantaneous, this progress sanctification which Watson describes must take place *after* sanctification. He conceded, "The very largest degrees of self-renunciation, crucifixion, and abandonment to God, take place after the work of heart-purity." Watson wrote,

---

[640]Wood, *Mistakes*, 71-72. Leslie Wilcox echoed the emphasis of Wood, "Entire sanctification is purity, never maturity or development. This is the key of the Wesleyan idea of sanctification" [*Profiles*, 2:264].

[641]Mudge, *Growth in Holiness*, 228. Laurence Wood claimed that Mudge "misunderstood Wood to say that there was no growth toward perfection" and cited Wood's earlier statement that the approach to entire sanctification may be gradual [*Meaning of Pentecost*, 319].

Mudge did describe the holiness teaching, as represented by J. A. Wood, G. D. Watson, and William McDonald, that "no matter how much we grow in grace, we are brought by it no whit the nearer to entire sanctification and become in no degree or particular purer in heart." Mudge called this one of the most singular notions connected with this subject [*Growth in Holiness*, 226].

And the fact is that J. A. Wood did became more rigid in its insistence upon a crisis experience. I have traced this shift in my article "American Holiness Movement's Paradigm Shift Concerning Pentecost," 137-138, and in my dissertation "Spirit and Sanctification: Changes within American Wesleyanism," 41-45, which was mentored by Laurence Wood.

Laurence Wood concluded that "Wood and Mudge simply passed by each other like two ships in the night" [*Meaning of Pentecost*, 321-322]. In a sense both men were attempting to defend the Wesleyan message and both men may have overstated their case. Coming down on the side of J. A. Wood, Laurence Wood wrote that J. A. Wood's *Perfect Love* "represented the end of an era, and it was largely unsuccessful in stopping the erosion of the Wesleyan heritage largely because it did not engage in a constructive contemporary restatement of Wesleyan theology" [p. 322].

"There, are innumerable degrees of interior crucifixion on these various lines. Perhaps not one sanctified person in ten thousand ever reaches that degree of experimental death to self that Paul and Madame Guyon, and similar saints reached."

While Watson is locked into a rigid two-works-of-grace paradigm, he seems to realize from experience that Christian perfection it not all attained in a moment of time. Thus he borrows from the mysticism which Wesley rejected

> In contra-distinction from heart-cleansing this finer crucifixion to self is gradual; it extends through months or years. The interior spirit is mortified over and over on the same 'points, till it reaches a state of Divine indifference to them.
> A great host of believers have attained heart-purity, and yet for a long time have gone through all sorts of "dying daily " to self, before they found that fixed union with the Holy Ghost which is the deep longing of the child of God.
> Again, In contra-distinction from heart-cleansing, which is by faith, this deeper death to self is by suffering. . . . When the soul undergoes this phase of death to self, it enters into a great wideness of Scriptural comprehension and love — a state of almost uninterrupted prayer, of boundless charity for all people, of unutterable tenderness and broadness of sympathy, of deep, quiet thoughtfulness, of extreme simplicity of life and manners, and of deep visions into God and the coming ages.
> In this state of utter death to self, suffering, sorrow, pains, and mortification of all kinds are looked upon with a calm, sweet indifference. Such a soul looks back over its heart-breaking toils, its scalding tears, its mysterious tribulations with gentle subduedness and without regret, for it now sees God in every step of the way.
> Into such a soul the Holy Spirit pours the ocean-currents of His own life; its great work henceforth is to watch the monitions and movements of the Spirit within it, and yield prompt, loving, unquestioning co-operation with Him.
> Such a soul has, at least, in deed in the truth, reached the place where there is "none of self, and all of Christ.[642]

Quoting Wood and Steele, Huntington also objected to their teaching that "no amount of growth in grace serves in any degree to remove or destroy 'inbred

---

[642]Watson, *Soul Food*, 11-14. See Billheimer, *Don't Waste Your Sorrows*, 76-78.

sin.'" He asserted,

> It follows, then, that there can never be more than two degrees in sanctification — the lowest, which is regeneration; and the highest, which is entire sanctification. Between these least and greatest measures of sanctification, then, there is no removal, or destruction, or decrease of what is termed "inbred sin," in any believer, in any degree; but every Christian either has no "inbred sin" whatever, or he has all he had at the moment of his regeneration. Is it, then, destroyed at all? . . . If, however, entire sanctification is an instantaneous work of the Holy Spirit, by which "inbred sin" is destroyed or removed from the soul, the statement that this work was begun in regeneration, but left incomplete, seems utterly without explanation."[643]

While Huntington went too far in denying inbred sin, which he called the theory of passive sin, with the passage of time J. A. Wood developed a more rigid doctrinal position which justified the existence of the holiness movement. Wood came to emphasize a perfected state, not perfecting grace. As the holiness movement rose to national prominence, with Wood as a leader and spokesman, this position was perpetuated throughout the twentieth century as "Wesleyan."

George Hughes, the secretary for the national association, recorded that from the first call for a holiness camp meeting some looked on with suspicion, fearing the movement would cause division.[644] The holiness movement was interdenominational from its beginning and its converts did not always feel at home in the Methodist church. It was inevitable that the loyalty of holiness professors would be with the smaller group, the holiness "band" or regional association, and not with the Methodist Episcopal Church.[645]

The holiness movement further alienated itself from Methodism by preaching such non-Methodist doctrines as premillennialism and faith healing. In 1901 the General Holiness Assembly, meeting in Chicago, largely due to concerns over fanaticism, adopted a doctrinal statement that only contained six items and one of the six was a statement favoring divine healing.[646] Martin Wells Knapp

---

[643]Huntington, *Sin and Holiness*, 128-129; 131.

[644]Hughes, *Days of Power*, 50.

[645]Rose, *Vital Holiness*, p. 70; see also Smith, *Called Unto Holiness*, 35; 127; Oblinger, "Separatist Tendencies."

[646]Kostlevy, "Nor Silver, Nor Gold," 96-126.

explained, "One Holiness Movement had been superseded by another."[647] Thornton explained that Methodist holiness had given way to Pentecostal holiness.[648] By the mid-1890s the more radical leaders of the holiness movement were all premillennial. This set the stage for the four-fold emphasis of early pentecostalism: Christ as Savior, Baptized with the Holy Ghost, healer, and coming king.[649]

Between 1896 and 1902, W. B. Godbey wrote his *Commentary on the New Testament* in seven volumes starting first with Revelation and working back to the gospels. In the "Introduction" Beverly Carradine explained that while Adam Clarke and Richard Watson were both sanctified men, their writings did not emphasize the doctrine of sanctification enough. Godbey's *Commentary* was written to make up for the deficiency.[650] We also learn from his autobiography that the commentary was dictated to a secretary while Godbey continued his ministry as a traveling evangelist.[651] The commentary is filled with personal anecdotes and dogmatic assertions, usually shedding little light upon the text.

In his doctoral dissertation on the life and theology of W. B. Godbey, Barry Hamilton described Godbey's commentary as an apologetic for holiness premillennialism. He concluded that "Godbey's theology could be called 'Wesleyan,' but it lacked Wesley's emphasis on prevenient grace over the whole course of the Christian life."[652]

Godbey commented on Acts 1:8:

> "You shall receive dynamite of the Holy Ghost having come on you"; I. e., if you will receive the Holy Ghost as a personal, indwelling Sanctifier and abiding Comforter, He will supply you with all the dynamite you need to blow all sin out of you and to qualify you to blow up the Devil's kingdom wherever you go, and enjoy an everlasting victory in your heart and life.[653]

---

[647]Knapp, "God Answering by Fire," 1, 6.

[648]Thornton, "Revivalist Movement," 180.

[649]Dayton, *Theological Roots of Pentecostalism*, 115-171. The phrase "fourfold gospel" was coined by A. B. Simpson in 1890 [Nienkirchen, *A. B. Simpson*, 2]. The phrase was used by Seth Rees in his dedicatory sermon for God's Bible School in 1900 [Knapp, *Back to the Bible*, 45-52].

[650]Godbey, *Commentary*, 1:4.

[651]Godbey, *Autobiography*, 369.

[652]Hamilton, *William Baxter Godbey*, 101; 181.

[653]Godbey, *Commentary*, 5:12-13.

On 1 Corinthians 14:25 he admonishes the holiness movement to maintain the "old-style knock-down power."[654] He believed that the filling of the Holy Spirit was "sanctification" and on Acts 2:4 he asserted that "Spirit-filled people alone constitute the Bridehood of Christ."[655] Apparently it took a second blessing to be part of the church. This kind of thinking does not exalt regeneration very high nor does it take very seriously Acts 2:47.

Randall Stephens wrote that "Perfectionist leaders like Godbey never acknowledged that they were, in many ways, responsible for the 'tongues movement.' But Godbey, Martin Wells Knapp, and G. D. Watson focused much attention on the fourfold gospel — Jesus as savior, sanctifier, healer, and coming king — and contributed significantly to the rise of pentecostalism."[656]

Stanley Horton claimed pretribulational premillennialism became a bigger barrier between the older holiness groups and the newer pentecostal groups than was either group's teaching on the baptism in the Holy Spirit.[657] Donald Dayton believed that doctrines of entire sanctification and postmillennialism go together. One is a personal progressive transformation and the other is a progressive social transformation. On the other hand, the baptism in the Holy Ghost and the rapture of the church go together because they both emphasize instantaneous events.[658] Yet he also observed that the shift to Pentecostal formulation of holiness teaching predated the adoption of premillennialism by a decade or so.[659]

The southern Methodists feared the holiness camp meeting was a tool of the north to proselytize.[660] Thomas L. Boswell, a theologian within Southern Methodism, taught that sanctification is developed by a gradual growth under the gracious influence of the Spirit. He denied that the influence of the Spirit,

---

[654]Godbey, *Commentary*, 4:234.

[655]Godbey, *Commentary*, 6:25; 5:34.

[656]Stephens, *The Fire Spreads*, 224.

[657]Horton, "Pentecostal Perspective," 233.

[658]Dayton, *Theological Roots of Pentecostalism*, 165.

[659]Dayton, "Doctrine of the Baptism of the Holy Spirit," 124.

[660]Turley, "A Wheel Within a Wheel," 295-320; see also Stephens, *The Fire Spreads*, 15-135; 140; Dieter, *Holiness Revival*, 103-104. Peters concluded that during the fourteen years leading up to the Civil War, the quarterly review of the Methodist Episcopal Church, South never once mentioned the subject of entire sanctification [*Christian Perfection*, 131-132]. According to Merrill Gaddis, the Methodist Episcopal Church, South had declined in their emphasis on perfection and had ceased to be a "holiness sect" [*Christian Perfection in America*, 426; 455].

however powerful, eliminated a tendency to sin.[661] Particularly in the southern church, holiness pastors were assigned to "hard scrabble" circuits to lessen their influence. If they were successful anyway, the next pastor to be sent would attempt to tear down the doctrine. In 1894, Atticus Haygood, a holiness fighter, was elected bishop in the southern church and he began a "war of extermination."[662] However, during this same time period two southern bishops, Eugene Russell Hendrix and J. C. Granbery, wrote articles which favored the gradual approach to sanctification, but which allowed for the instantaneous approach. This was printed in pamphlet form and circulated widely.[663]

I disagree with Peters' assessment of Granbery, along with his evaluation of Whedon.[664] Peters cited Granbery as declaring that God does not complete purification "a little before death," as Wesley held, but "at the instant of death."[665] However, in the context of his review of *Growth in Holiness* by Mudge, Granbery took exception to a position taken by Mudge. Mudge argued against the holiness position that only the sanctified will see the Lord. Mudge then declared that all God's children will be admitted into heaven regardless of their stage of maturity. Here Granbery declared his belief that God will perfect the immature believer. Since God requires no time to do his work, believers who die suddenly will be made fit for heaven. However, Granbery should not be categorized as holding that we are sanctified by the article of death or that complete deliverance from sin is never accomplished in this life.

In *Entire Sanctification* Granbery argued against Zinzendorism,

---

[661]Boswell, "Salvation and Its Individual Relations," 224.

[662]Synan, *Holiness-Pentecostal Tradition*, 37-38.

[663]Hendrix, *Perfecting of the Saints* and Granbery *Entire Sanctification*. The article by Hendrix had previously been published in the *Quarterly Review of the M. E. Church, South* and the editor John J. Tigert believed that this effort would do much to put an end to controversy. "If the spirit of crush-outism has anywhere found expression, let it not be so as mentioned among brethren" ["Editorial Departments," 120]. In a review, Tigert also wrote that this booklet, containing both articles, was "wise and timely, modest and moderate, the views in this pamphlet are also scriptural and Wesleyan. The work has contributed materially to the peace of the Church and ought to prove the end of controversy" ["Brief Reviews," 456]. While Tigert himself did not profess entire sanctification, he believed in it and closed the columns of the journal to all material which contradicted traditional Methodist theology [Smith, *Called Unto Holiness*, 43].

[664]Peters, *Christian Perfection*, 176; see p. 420 of this book for Peters' assessment of Whedon.

[665]Peters, *Christian Perfection*, 169; see also Tillett, *Personal Salvation*, 482. This statement is found in Granbery, "Dr. Mudge," 204.

Calvinism, and the holiness teaching. Against the teaching of Zinzendorf he declared that the Methodist doctrine is that the carnal mind lingers in believers, but is not dominant. Rather it is hated, resisted, and overcome. Yet it causes great grief and trouble, but undergoes gradual weaning and extinction.[666] He argued that Calvinism puts an arbitrary limitation on the provisions of grace. Any restriction on the full work of purification seems unwarranted by the Scriptures.

Granbery argued that the holiness movement denied all progressive cleansing after the new birth. However, he stated that the Methodist position, while holding that entire sanctification may be obtained progressively does not deny its attainment by this process. "If we progress toward the goal, why may we not reach it?"[667] "Let us so look and seek for this fullness of blessing as not to despise our present state as the sons of God in the enjoyment of his favor and fellowship, and not to neglect daily growth in piety, but so as to quicken our progress and to abound in the work of the Lord"[668]

In the article by Hendrix, which was also published together with the article by Granbery, Hendrix declared, "It is possible to be made perfect in love in this life, and the final act is an instantaneous one, usually occurring somewhat late in life, after the 'saint' has been 'perfecting holiness in the fear of the Lord,' and putting on 'as the elect of God, holy and beloved, bowels of mercies, kindness, humbleness of mind, meekness, long-suffering.'"[669]

Reaction to the holiness movement encouraged Methodism to go to the opposite extreme. The Methodist seminaries were moving toward Darwinism and their German trained professors were introducing higher criticism.[670] A. M. Kiergan, a Missouri holiness preacher in the Methodist Church, discussed the doctrine of holiness with his presiding elder around 1878. The elder admitted Kiergan was Wesleyan in his views, but replied that "the church does not now believe Wesley's theory."[671]

Between 1880 and 1905 some 100,000 holiness believers left the Methodist Church.[672] Peters stated that by 1900 most holiness advocates had

---

[666]Granbery, *Entire Sanctification*, 34.

[667]Granbery, *Entire Sanctification*, 38.

[668]Granbery, *Entire Sanctification*, 44.

[669]Hendrix, *Perfecting of the Saints*, 21. Hendrix quoted from 2 Cor 7:1 and Col 3:12.

[670]Peters, *Christian Perfection*, 143-144.

[671]Kiergan, *Historical Sketches*, 9; 18.

[672]Wacker, "Holiness Movement," 333.

either withdrawn or had been encouraged to leave the Methodist Church.[673] As many as fifty denominations came into being as a result of conditions within the Methodist Church and in response to local situations.[674] Merrill Gaddis gave four reasons for the rise of the holiness movement:

- The institutionalization of Methodism
- The holiness sects felt unwelcome
- The holiness emphasis on absolute morality
- Modernism within Methodism[675]

Gaddis said the most severe shock of all was the Methodist adaptation of the historical critical method, which he called the scientific approach to the Bible. Writing in 1929, Gaddis said the impact of evolutionary presuppositions had not ceased to resound in holiness circles.[676]

The holiness movement originally had interdenominational influence. They expected their message of Christian holiness would bring in the millennium.[677] However, instead of reforming all of Christendom, ultimately they created a whole series of new denominations.

Originally, those who were part of the holiness movement were required to be members in good standing of some denomination. But as these denominations began to react both to the growing popularity and the excesses of the holiness movement, their loyalty was primarily to the reform movement and not the denomination.

By the turn of the twentieth century it was clear that they were being excluded from the mainline denominations. In order to justify their own existence and the new churches which were being organized, they had to define their distinctives and in the process became more radical. What happened was that the experience of holiness became their justification and their end instead of the means to the end. They developed a theological rigidity which had not characterized early Methodism. Dieter wrote that

---

[673]Peters, *Christian Perfection*, 150.

[674]Smith, *Called Unto Holiness*, 27.

[675]Gaddis, *Christian Perfection in America*, 449-458.

[676]Gaddis, *Christian Perfection in America*, 407; 454-455; 530-531.

[677]Edmund S. Janes, writing the Introduction to Foster, *Christian Purity*, declared, "A holy Church would soon make a holy world" [p. 13]. Although Dale Yocum held a dispensational eschatology, he declared, "The quality of abundant life in the sanctified individual is a quality which, if made universal, would usher in the Millennium" [*Conformed to Christ*, 84].

the confrontations were often bitter as two increasingly divergent paradigms for understanding Christian perfection vied for the loyalties of Methodism. Wesley was used against himself as both sides of the conflict drew heavily upon one polarity or the other of this crisis-growth dialectic of holiness. Holiness advocates in the church commonly took up crisis; their opponents emphasized process. Purity was put over against maturity; the "now" against the "not yet."[678]

On the other side, Elmer Clark wrote,

> Vital holiness was passing out of Methodist faith and practice. Finally all graces of the doctrine were carefully eliminated from the songs of the church in the hymnal published in 1935. . . . Nothing was allowed to remain that might remind Methodists that their church had ever endorsed a second work of grace.[679]

Seventeen Warnings

While it is often true that the victor writes the history, when we go back into this time period I have found at least seventeen voices which were raised in opposition to this new theology of holiness:

1. In 1849 John Hunt wrote that the equation of Spirit-baptism with entire sanctification placed the subject of entire sanctification too low.[680]

2. In response to controversy over the teaching of Phoebe Palmer, the pastoral address of the General Conference of the Methodist Episcopal Church in 1852 warned

> We advise you in writing of holiness, to follow the well sustained views, and even the phraseology employed in the writings of Wesley and Fletcher, which are not superceded by the more recent writers on the subject. Avoid both new theories, new

---

[678]Dieter, "Development of Holiness Theology," 65.

[679]Clark, *What Happened at Aldersgate?* 58. Clark gave the example from Charles Wesley's hymn "Love Divine" in which "let us find that second rest" was altered to "let us find the promised rest."

[680]Hunt, *Letters on Sanctification*, 183. See additional relevant comments on 20; 45; 209; 258.

> expressions, and new measures on the subject, and adhere closely to the ancient landmarks.[681]

3. In 1856 Jesse T. Peck warned that "holiness must not be taken out of its proper connections." He stated that the doctrine of holiness supersedes no doctrine of the gospel. It is dependent upon the atonement, conviction, repentance, justification by faith, regeneration, adoption, sanctification commenced, and growth in grace. Peck warned of schism,

> Any organization of the friends of holiness as a distinct work is highly dangerous. It must lead to invidious distinctions which are by no means intended by the friends of the measure. It must place distance, more or less, between the members of such associations and their brethren and lead to jealousies, heart-burnings and divisions. It must cut off from the sympathies of the masses those whose special graces are intended by our heavenly Father to be like leaven in the measures of meal, to permeate the entire church.[682]

4. In 1857, Bishop Nathan Bangs, editor of the *Methodist Quarterly Review*, visited a Tuesday meeting of Mrs. Palmer to refute the teaching that Christians may believe they have the experience before they have the witness of the Holy Spirit. According to Bangs the "altar phraseology" was "unsound, unscriptural, anti-Wesleyan and no doubt in many cases had caused deception." Bangs felt so strongly that Palmer was in error that he insisted if his diary was ever published, the report of this incident must be included verbatim.[683]

---

[681] *Journals of the General Conference*, 160.

[682] Peck, *Central Idea of Christianity*, 180-186; see Hughes, *Beloved Physician*, 246-248. See also Peck's statement at #7.

[683] Stevens, *Life and Times of Nathan Bangs*, 396-402. This was reprinted in Stackpole, *Evidence of Salvation*, 79-86. In 1851 Bangs also warned against consecrating oneself to God in order to become happy and attain excellence, then claiming the blessing without feeling any consciousness of an impure heart [Bangs, *Necessity, Nature, and Fruits*, 58-59]. He also warned against believing oneself to be sanctified without any evidence of the fact [pp. 175-176]. But then he quoted Palmer's declaration of a shorter way to substantiate his claim that God is able to save from all sin now; this very moment [p. 178]. Apparently between 1851 and 1857 Bangs became more definite in his rejection of Palmer's teaching.

Incredibly Melvin Dieter wrote, "Most Methodists, however, followed Nathan Bangs and other prominent Methodists in sanctioning Palmer's teachings as essentially Wesleyan" [*19th-Century Holiness Movement*, 133.

5. In 1860 the bishops of the Methodist Episcopal Church warned that a few persons have introduced variation into the standard statements of Christian perfection.

> These individuals claim to be strictly Wesleyan in their views of the doctrine, and probably are so substantially. . . . But, in our judgment, in denouncing those in the ministry and laity who do not sympathize with them and adopt their measures, and in some instances, by employing and encouraging erratic and irresponsible persons to conduct religious services, they have erred, and unhappily agitated some of our societies, and in a few instances caused secessions. It is our opinion that there was no occasion for these specialties.[684]

6. In 1869 Bishop R. S. Foster wrote in *Christian Purity* concerning Phoebe Palmer's teachings,

> It has been indiscreetly said, "We are to believe the work is done, and it will be done." Persons seeking the blessing have been told that they must believe they are sanctified, and they will be sanctified. What a misfortune that so great, so dangerous an error should be taught, in connection with so important a subject! What a manifest absurdity! Making our sanctification to depend upon the belief of an untruth; namely, a belief that it is now wrought, in order that it may be wrought! This is a great delusion. It is not the doctrine of the Bible. It is not, and never was, the doctrine of any branch of the Church. Some sincere and honest Christians have fallen into this delusion without perceiving its absurdity; and it has gained considerable currency.[685]

---

[684]Peters, *Christian Perfection*, 131.

[685]Foster, *Christian Purity*, 209-210. Foster analyzes the theology of Palmer in pp. 204-217. See also the analysis of Langford, *Practical Divinity*, 95-96. See also the discussion on pp. 529-539 of this book.

Jesse T. Peck, another Methodist bishop, was also apprehensive that Palmer's teachings would result in schism. He addresses her teaching, without naming her, in *Central Idea of Christianity*, 136-137; 148-149; 226. Contrast this teaching with A. M. Hills who taught that there must be a definite act of appropriating faith *before* the witness of the Spirit could be expected [*Holiness and Power*, 281-296]. In this section Hills cited F. B. Meyer, Asa Mahan, and Samuel A. Keene for support of his position.

He also expressed concern regarding the extravagant and inconsistent professions of holiness. Professors have separated themselves from their brethren and "appear to be forming into a separate body. They are acquiring a nomenclature of their own — having a charmed circle within whose inclosure only certain persons are expected to be found — becoming known to and specially sympathetic with each other."[686]

7. In 1877 Jesse Peck addressed the Southern Illinois Conference, elaborating on the questions asked of ministerial candidates seeking full connection with the conference. He told them that perfect love is a perfection of Christian character and that this perfection in love demands perpetual growth in grace. However, those who doubted whether entire sanctification or perfect love was a definite blessing which ought to be sought and those who did not expect to be made perfect in love in this life ought not to be Methodist preachers. He then declared the doctrine of holiness to be the central idea of Methodist religion.[687] He reminded them that they were to pastor the whole flock, not just a dozen persons devoted to holiness. Perhaps ninety-nine in a hundred of them cannot readily understand the matter. Then he warned "it is possible for a man to be so filled with zeal for holiness as to give it a technical position that will do some harm." He counseled his audience to preach the whole gospel which includes "'repentance before God and faith toward our Lord Jesus Christ,' a justification by faith, and regeneration, and the beginnings of sanctification at the time of regeneration, and then going on to perfection."

Peck declared that he had found men everywhere who were out of harmony with Methodism. They call themselves evangelists, but they prove to be erratic men who assume the title but enter a pastoral charge without acknowledging or consulting with the pastor. They harshly accuse brethren, preach in a way we cannot approve and in this way do much harm. Peck did not counsel that they should be fought, but that the true doctrine of Wesleyan holiness should be preached and lived. In fact, a person who is filled with perfect love will not need to testify to it because the people will know it. "If your soul if filled with love, my brother, it makes little difference when it happened; only let a man be sure of it, and let him go on; don't call him back and insist upon knowing the time." Peck then exhorted his audience not only to groan after perfection but to

---

[686]Foster, *Christian Purity*, 273-277.

[687]Later in the address Peck referred specifically to his 1856 book, *Central Idea of Christianity*. He admonished prospective Methodist pastors to led indecisive members to the highest standards of Christian excellence, "not by the 'Central Idea of Christianity,' but by the Bible" [p. 94].

obtain the blessing.[688]

While this address defended the Methodist doctrine of Christian perfection, it was obvious that the Methodist Church was upset by those who misrepresented it. The following year D. D. Whedon, editor of the *Methodist Quarterly Review*, reviewed Bishop Peck's address declaring:

> The holiness association, the holiness periodical, the holiness prayer-meeting, the holiness preacher, are all modern novelties. They are not Wesleyan. We believe that a living Wesley would never admit them into the Methodist system. They seem to distort the healthy symmetry of our religion. Wisely was it asked by one of our bishops, "Are not all our meetings holiness meetings?" Is not the purpose of our whole system to "spread Scripture holiness?"[689]

8. In 1879 the Illinois Annual Conference passed resolutions urging its ministers to preach *all* the doctrines, including perfect love — plainly, clearly, and in the spirit of Christ." The same resolution, directed at free lance holiness evangelists, encouraged Methodists to allow no services and invite no evangelists without the

---

[688] Jesse Peck, "Bishop Peck's Address," 92-98.

[689] Whedon, "Quarterly Book-Table," 177-179. This was a review of Jesse Peck's "Address to the Ministerial Candidates of the Southern Illinois Conference." Melvin Dieter confused this article with Crane's article in the October issue [*Holiness Revival*, 128].

Whedon charged the holiness movement with a theology of "hyper-Wesleyanism" [p. 176]. In the previous review Whedon responded to a complaint from George D. Watson to J. O. A. Clark's article on holiness [see p. 412 of this book]. Whedon replied that Clark's article was "less perniciously divergent from Wesley than Inskip, McDonald, or this Dr. Watson" ["Quarterly Book-Table," 172-177]. All three were early holiness leaders and Whedon is making a distinction between Richard Watson and George Watson.

William McDonald responded to Whedon by calling him the "chief umpire in Methodism" to which every Methodist preacher must gracefully bow and silently submit ["Methodist Quarterly Review," 64].

According to Timothy L. Smith, Peck had urged the Methodist General Conference of 1872 to revise the doctrinal statement on sanctification so as to commit the church wholly to the "second blessing" view [*Called Unto Holiness*, 19]. Yet this Address in 1878 by Peck did not favor the separation of holiness churches from Methodism. And Peck had previously declared in 1856 that "any organization of the friends of holiness, as a distinct work, is undesirable and highly dangerous" [see #3 above].

consent and supervision of the pastor.[690]

9. The Missouri Annual Conference of 1880 reported problems including, "self-constituted specialists, who, in some instances, are members of our own Church and yet pay little or no regard to our rules of discipline.[691]

10. William Burt Pope, considered the prince of Methodist theologians, wrote in 1880 against the modern tendency to teach a new dispensation of the Spirit or a Pentecostal visitation superadded to the state of conversion. He warned that those who teach Acts 19:2 as an experience after regeneration diminish the value of regeneration.[692]

11. T. J. Bryant, a Methodist editor, expressed reservations about the holiness movement. He explained, "Holiness has always been the watchword of Methodism," but there was a "growing opposition in the Methodist Episcopal Church to the so-called holiness movement in the West." He expressed concern that

> the number of those at one time and another connected with it, whose lives were not up to the common standards of Christian morals, is larger than we like to name. And then, some without moral offense have been sadly lacking in the spirit of Christ. Their righteousness has been that of the Pharisees; the most charitable have not been able to detect even a trace of perfect love in their lives. They are captious, arrogant, ready in finding fault, wanting in Christian courtesy, over-anxious apparently to assert and show their disregard for proper authority.[693]

12. Daniel Curry, editor of the *Methodist Review*, complained, "They not only use their own methods, but they have a peculiar dialect, and words and phrases as used by them have come to have special and somewhat technical significations. 'Sanctification,' and 'holiness,' and many like terms, that in Holy Scripture and in general religious discourse are used to designate the ordinary fruits of the Spirit in believers, are narrowed down so as to indicate only a specific and ultimate work

---

[690]Peters, *Christian Perfection*, 145-146.

[691]Peters, *Christian Perfection*, 146.

[692]Pope, *Compendium*, 3:44; 64.

[693]Bryant, *Survey of the Field*, 2-4. See also Bryant, *Plain Things to Holiness People* and *Protest and Criticism*.

of grace."[694]

13. In 1894 the bishops' address to the General Conference of the Methodist Episcopal Church, South reaffirmed the doctrine of entire sanctification, but issued a warning:

> The privilege of believers to attain unto the state of entire sanctification, or perfect love, and to abide therein is a well-known teaching of Methodism. Witnesses to this experience have never been wanting in our Church, though few in comparison with the whole membership. Among them have been men and women of beautiful consistence and seraphic ardor, jewels of the Church. Let the doctrine still be proclaimed and the experience still be testified. But there has sprung up among us a party with "holiness"as a watchword; they have holiness associations, holiness meetings, holiness preachers, holiness evangelists, and holiness property. Religious experience is represented as if it consists of only two steps, the first step out of condemnation into peace, and the next step into Christian perfection. The effect is to disparage the new birth, and all stages of spiritual growth from the blade to the full corn in the ear, if there be not professed perfect holiness. Such Scriptural terms as "saints," "sanctified," "pure in heart," "holy," "dead to sin," "filled with the Spirit," and "made meet to be partakers of the inheritance of the saints in light," are restricted to the few who have reached the height of perfect purity and love and improperly denied to the body of believers; and not only to those who are new or weak in the faith, but also the mature Christians who by walking with God in blessed fellowship and by patient continuance in well-doing, ever increasing in the knowledge of God, and being fruitful in every good work, adorn the doctrines of God our Saviour in all things, and are pillars in the Church. We do not question the sincerity and zeal of these brethren; we desire the Church to profit by their earnest preaching and godly example; but we do deplore their teaching and methods in so far

[694]Curry, "Book Notices," 152. Curry was reviewing Asbury Lowrey's *Possibilities of Grace*. Yet Lowrey expressed concern about holiness propagated through irregular agencies and desired for the Methodist Church to return to their proclamation of holiness [*Possibilities of Grace*, 453].

Curry's doctrine of holiness was included in Janes, *Perfect love*, 39-60. Foster included an extended excerpt in *Christian Purity*, 94-103.

> as they claim a monopoly of the experience, practice, and advocacy of holiness, and separate themselves from the body of ministers and disciples.[695]

They objected that many holiness evangelists were accountable to no one. Since fanaticism can grow from a misapplication of truth, it was felt that the ministry should preach "the whole counsel of God" and not specialize on one subject.[696] Therefore, the bishops rejected the separate office of evangelist as an attempt to squelch itinerant holiness evangelists.

In 1896 the northern Methodist conference issued a similar statement. The bishops wrote, "We have insisted on the glorious privilege and duty of all men becoming saints, of immediately being made perfect in love, and of gradually ripening into Christian maturity in all faculties. This doctrine was never more definitely stated, clearly perceived, nor consistently lived by greater numbers than now." But they cautioned that "it is not vital that we hold the work done instantaneously" and concluded that "it is not essential that a man make a specific profession of the experience."[697]

14. Everett Stackpole, a Methodist missionary to Italy, returned home and in 1894 wrote about "a current error." He wrote, "To 'receive the Holy Ghost,' to be 'filled with the Holy Ghost,' to be 'baptized with the Spirit,' according to New Testament phraseology mean substantially the same thing". . . . To make the baptism of the Spirit synonymous with perfect purity of heart or to say that one baptized with the Spirit is thereby and always entirely sanctified is a proposition we have long distrusted."[698]

15. In 1895, James Mudge, the secretary of the New England Conference of the Methodist Episcopal Church, wrote *Growth in Holiness Toward Perfection*.[699] He

---

[695]*Journal General Conference, M. E. Church, South, 1894*, 25-26; "Bishops on Christian Perfection," 283.

[696]Peters, *Christian Perfection*, 145-146.

[697]*Journal of the General Conference of the Methodist Episcopal Church, 1896*, Appendix III, 497-498.

[698]Stackpole, *Evidence of Salvation*, 46; 67. See also my comments in the foreword to the centennial edition, viii.

[699]Editor William V. Kelley, who had known Mudge for thirty years, said Mudge *was* this book before he ever wrote it. In his review Kelley also concluded that Mudge had made a notable contribution toward the necessary reconstruction of the doctrine for which Whedon had called [Book Notices,"663-665].

devoted an entire chapter to the "Baptism with the Holy Ghost" noting that the phrase "is of frequent occurrence in the devotional writings and religious meetings of our time," but that it is used only seldom in Scripture.[700] After giving an accurate survey of the Biblical data, he concluded:

> Our conclusion is that all true Christians, when they are born of the Spirit, are filled with the Spirit up to their capacity at that time, are baptized with the Spirit, and receive the gift of the Holy Ghost, even the spirit of adoption, or the spirit of holiness, whereby they cry to God, "Father!" and are made holy. Then, as they go on, having it for their chief business to perfect this holiness which has been planted in them, to grow out of infancy into manhood, to become of full age, mature, perfect, they will

---

In the November issue Asbury Lowrey responded by claiming that the very title itself implied never ending growth and was a departure from Methodism. According to Lowrey, Wesley taught that "Christian perfection or perfect love is a grace put within the reach of every man and receivable any moment by faith." Yet this quote cannot be found in Wesley's *Works*. Lowrey objected that Mudge repudiated the doctrine and formula of original sin, that he rejected the Methodist definition of sin, that he substituted empowering for cleansing, that his definition of holiness was Zinsendorfian and not Wesleyan, and that Mudge invalidates the testimonies of our best saints and the exegesis of our best scholars ["Dr. Mudge," 954-959]. The first three concerns of Lowrey carry some validity (see ftnt # 98; 107; 171; 517; 596; 1870). However, the big concern of Lowrey with Mudge is that Mudge did not restrict holiness to a second work. Lowrey himself did not accurately represent Wesley's views and Lowrey's final objection is over the top.

Lewis R. Dunn also reacted to the *MQR* favorable review of Mudge in *Manual of Holiness*. Dunn objected to Mudge's definition of sin which rejects depravity, original sin, and birth sin. Mudge accepted Whedon's term "racial impairment," but Dunn said that does not go far enough. Dunn said the focal point of the whole contention is the definition of regeneration. He accused Mudge of calling it holiness. This can only be true in a limited or preliminary sense. Dunn associated this teaching by Mudge that God's people are holy and perfect in regeneration with Zinzendorf. Dunn objected to Mudge's view on the baptism of the Holy Ghost, arguing that the disciples were justified and regenerated before the day of Pentecost [pp. 92-93]. Dunn had previously contributed an article, "Entire Sanctification" to the *MQR* for 1867, pp. 555-572, arguing that in most cases the work of sanctification is gradual, but there comes a point when it is complete and entire.

See also Granbery, "Dr. Mudge on Growth in Holiness,"198-210, where Granbery said the book by Dr. Mudge was helpful, but a little more deference to Mr. Wesley and the other leaders of thought in Methodism would have improved this treatise.

[700]Mudge, *Growth in Holiness*, 235.

have, from time to time, other special quickenings, or baptisms, of blessings, from the Holy Spirit.[701]

---

[701]Mudge, *Growth in Holiness*, 261. Laurence Wood insinuated that this amounted to revisionism of Wesley which was influenced by theological liberalism and resulted in a view similar to Calvinism [*Meaning of Pentecost*, 314-316]. However, it is Wood himself who has attempted to impose his revision upon Wesley. Wood accused Mudge of being influenced by Borden Parker Bowne and his liberalism [p. 316]. However, Mudge only mentioned Bowne once [p. 189]. Therefore, it is difficult to determine how accurate this analysis is. Wood concedes Mudge is not a liberal [p. 317], but continues to try to dismiss him as a liberal [pp. 325, 328; 330-331]. In fact, Bowne was a liberal, but Mudge appeals to him only on the question of whether there could be a witness of the Spirit to a perfection that was never absolute.

Mudge did view theology as a progressive science and felt Wesley could be improved [pp. 7, 9]. Steele was willing to make some concessions, but stated his sympathy was with Richard Watson who said "anything essentially new in Christian theology is essentially false" [*Defense of Christian Perfection*, 17]. To the degree that Mudge was influenced by the liberalism of his day, I reject his opinions. However, he realized that the holiness movement of his day was not reflecting the emphasis of Wesley and at this point his protest was valuable.

Yet Mudge held a restricted definition of sin [p. 38; see Steele, *Defense of Christian Perfection*, 42] which misled him regarding depravity and the possibility of cleansing from that depravity [p. 62, 68, 221; *Perfect Life*, 296]. He suggested empower was a better term [p. 107; see Steele, *Defense of Christian Perfection*, 46], which sounds similar to the Keswick position. Ironically, Tillett had a positive evaluation of the Keswick movement in *Personal Salvation,* 419-421. In his review of Mudge, Granbery said that "power" was a good scriptural word, that we are impotent and need to be empowered. But we are also defined and need to be purified. Thus, we should not give up on cleansing and the washing in the blood of the Lamb ["Dr. Mudge on Growth in Holiness," 207-208].

Mudge denied that 1 John 1:7 referred to anything beyond regeneration [p. 107] and conflated love with perfect love [p. 89; see Steele, *Defense of Christian Perfection*, 86-87]. Granbery called these comments unfortunate and said there was no need to make "love" and "perfect love" synonyms ["Dr. Mudge on Growth in Holiness, 207-208]. Mudge also had an inadequate definition of holiness [p. 83; see Steele, *Defense of Christian Perfection*, 20].

Wood concluded his extended analysis of Mudge, saying that "Wesleyans have Mudge to thank for raising a number of issues which had not been adequately addressed. These include: the need to clarify the use of holiness terms and metaphors; the practical implications of living a sinless life defined evangelically; the psychological implications of emphasizing the instantaneous moment of increased holiness; the importance of growth and maturity, and the meaning of Pentecost." Finally Wood ended with the evaluation that Mudge "was a transitional figure who was caught between reactionary forces on the one hand and revisionists on the other hand"[p. 331]. I assume this means Mudge was struggling with both the reactionary holiness movement and liberal trends within Methodism.

The following year, Daniel Steele wrote *A Defense of Christian Perfection,* which was a rebuttal to Mudge, whom he accused of "great error."[702] However, Steele admitted "that the phrase, 'baptism of the Spirit' was not used by Wesley to describe Christian perfection. He wrote that Wesleyan theologians do not ground the doctrine of Christian perfection, as initiated by entire sanctification on texts which emphasize the fullness of the Spirit, such as Acts 19:2. Steele also conceded that the phrase "'baptism or fullness of the Spirit,' may mean something less than entire sanctification."[703] In 1911 Mudge wrote *The Perfect Life in Experience and Doctrine* which was dedicated to Daniel Steele among others. Mudge states that all full-fledged believers received, were baptized with the Holy Ghost, and indwelt by the Spirit.[704]

16. During this same time frame John McClintock and James Strong, both Methodist professors at Drew, wrote in their *Cyclopedia* that the baptism of the Spirit properly belongs with conversion. "This baptism is neither the same with entire sanctification, nor is the latter the invariable result of the former. Some may have, unwittingly, but not therefore harmlessly, confounded the two under the vague name of 'the second blessing.'"[705]

17. In 1916 Joseph H. Smith warned the most serious defect of the holiness movement was its lack of discipline. "We have doctrine; we have experience; we have much liberty for both ministry and laity, at least in our own fellowship; *but we have no discipline. . . .* We have no court of trial; no authorized committee of investigation; no power to stop us from witnessing, or even evangelizing, when our lives have become a stench and reproach. Thus there is in some quarters a growing cause for challenging our standards upon such matters as social purity and divorce, as well as libel, defamation of character, business integrity in the care of trusts, payments of subscriptions to churches, schools, papers, etc. . . . We find lapses into unholy living by some of our people and preachers with no adequate power to restrain or to rebuke them, or to offset the pernicious influence of their example." Smith concluded, "The grace of entire sanctification has not suspended the need of discipline. . . . Perfect love is not free love. . . . Liberty is not license!"[706]

---

[702]Steele, *Defense of Christian Perfection*, 5.

[703]Steele, *Defense of Christian Perfection*, 108-111.

[704]*Perfect Life*, 269. As Wood demonstrated, Mudge made a number of concessions in this book [*Meaning of Pentecost*, 327-330].

[705]McClintock and Strong, *Cyclopedia*, 9:951.

[706]Smith, *Things Behind*, 33-36.

The Doctrine Debated

In 1896 L. L. Pickett and M. A. Smith, both of the Methodist Episcopal Church, South debated entire sanctification as a second blessing for four days in Terrell, Texas. Pickett represented second-blessing holiness at its worst and Smith represented the views of J. M. Boland that Wesley changed his mind and later rejected the "residue theory" of inbred sin. Both men appealed to Wesley, but both men misrepresented his teachings. Both men tended to promise more than they delivered.

Smith denied there was a distinction between sanctification and entire sanctification. Pickett gave his personal testimony and Smith objected that his experience was of no benefit to anyone else. Smith claimed that Pickett's interpretation of Hebrews 12:14 amounted to, "Without the second blessing no man can see God." Smith continued to object that the holiness movement represented the regenerate heart as in a state of defilement, a state of pollution, a dirty state, a filthy state, a state of idolatry. He quoted popular holiness writers who described the regenerate heart as hard or stony, impure, bound, blind, and in a state of unbelief. He objected to the teaching that the regenerated man was not part of the bride of Christ and that the regenerate heart was depicted as diseased, dark, and in a state of wretched bondage to a body of death. He objected to language of Pickett which referred to"the spirit of evil that lurks within the bosom of the spiritual babe." Smith rejected the holiness or hell argument.

Pickett argued for the second blessing based on such distinctions as the Spirit with us and in us (John 14:17), that the Christian had a cold, stony, hard heart until he received a new heart in entire sanctification. Pickett argued from Romans 7 that the man there described is regenerated, but needed entire sanctification. He argued that the distinction between the way and the highway in Isaiah 35:8 illustrated the distinction between regeneration and sanctification. Pickett also appealed to the different between being made "white as snow" (Isa 1:18) and "whiter than snow" (Psalm 51:7) as illustrating two works of grace.

Pickett contended there was a difference between receiving the Spirit at regeneration and the baptism of the Holy Ghost. Smith observed that Clarke understood the baptism of the Spirit to be equivalent to the new birth.

Smith objected to the concept that salvation is to be divided, cut up into fragments, and parceled out. Pickett continually tried to pin the label of "Zinzendorf" on him. It was Smith's position that the regenerated man was cleansed and sanctified, but that he grew in grace toward perfection. He emphasized that the heart was purified at conversion. Yet he noted that after the Apostles had received the second blessing at Pentecost, according to Carradine, that there was contention between those who had been filled with the Spirit (Acts 11:2).

Smith argued that Cornelius was unregenerate and Pickett held that he was regenerate. Pickett argued for the second blessing from 1 Thessalonians 4:3 and Smith pointed out that according to Pickett these people in a regenerate state were a group of fornicators, since they were not sanctified. Pickett countered that the fornication here spoken of was spiritual adultery or worldliness. "It requires entire sanctification to save us from the love of the world."

Thus, this debate, filled with redundancies and sarcasm, runs 352 pages. It generated much heat, but little light. However, it illustrates the polarization taking place within Methodism toward the end of the nineteenth century.[707]

In an address at a conference in Cincinnati under the auspices of the National Camp Meeting Association, John P. Brooks first advocated coming out of sectarian denominations in 1877.[708] He later wrote that "holiness cannot successfully be propagated under sectarian conditions."[709] Yet as late as 1916 Joseph H. Smith advocated the holiness movement be interdenominational. He argued for permeation, not extraction. "Whether we be Baptists or Methodists, Nazarenes or Friends, etc., we thrust not what is peculiar to our sect upon the holiness movement, though we continue to prefer and enjoy them in our own churches."[710] Timothy L. Smith was right,

> Evangelical denominations are not subject to a spiritual second law of thermodynamics. The order, force, and beauty of Christian institutions do not inevitably waste away, requiring, at some dark time of crisis down the road, new and freshly anointed ones to arise and replace them. The promise of the continual, sanctifying presence of the Holy Spirit in the Body of Christ is as trustworthy now as it was at Pentecost.[711]

While both the holiness movement and the pentecostal movement was sectarian, the charismatic movement has had a greater influence on the entire Church because it has largely remained interdenominational.

---

[707]Pickett, *Pickett-Smith Debate*. See Truesdale, "Reification of the Experience of Entire Sanctification," 108-109.

[708]Brooks, "What are the Chief Hindrances," 85-102. See Dieter's evaluation of this address, *Holiness Revival of the Nineteenth Century*, 184-188.

[709]Brooks, *Divine Church*, 271. Timothy L. Smith called this book the textbook of "come-outism" [*Called Unto Holiness*, 29]. Yet Wesley would not tolerate "come-outism." See ftnt # 1279.

[710]Smith, *Things Behind*, 50; 53-54.

[711]Smith, *Nazarenes and the Wesleyan Mission*, 3.

D. S. Warner also sounded remarkably like Alexander Campbell in his call for the unity of all Christians. But if Campbell had sought to unite God's people by recovering the doctrines and practices of the primitive Church, these holiness advocates sought to restore the primitive church by restoring the holy lifestyle of early Christians.[712] Wesley was greatly influenced by William Cove's *Primitive Christianity*, which he abridged in 1753. Cove emphasized the morality of the early Church.

Melvin Dieter wrote concerning Warner's doctrine of the Church, "The dominant theme, however, was the strong primitivism which was present in all holiness concepts of the church. The original Pentecost experience and the church which lived close to that period were looked upon as the models of the pure church."[713] Describing the holiness movement at the turn of the twentieth century, Dieter wrote, "The church of Pentecost became the model for many in the holiness movement. It was a Christian primitivism, not seeking to return to the doctrinal formulas or ecclesiastical structures of the early church, but, rather, to experience again the power and purity of which they believed the first Christians had experienced because of Pentecost."[714] Is apostolic measured by organization, lifestyle, or experience?

Wynkoop wrote, "Holiness theology grafted into non-Wesleyan roots produced interpretations of sanctification that clashed with historic Christian faith — and with it, Wesley."[715]The new doctrine was promoted under Wesley's name, but it rested upon a different hermeneutical foundation. Formerly, salvation history was divided into covenants with the atonement of Christ as the pivotal point between the old and new covenant. It was easier for the holiness movement to adopt dispensationalism because their view of salvation history emphasized a third shift with their emphasis on Pentecost.[716] They emphasized the emotional over the ethical, gifts instead of fruit, and power instead of purity. Without realizing it, the holiness movement set itself up for the rise of pentecostalism. In fact, Richard Hughes contrasted the holiness movement with the Pentecostals by calling one "ethical primitivism" and the other "experiential primitivism."[717]

The American holiness movement claimed to restore primitive Wesleyan, but actually modified Wesley in three major areas:

---

[712]Hughes, "Christian Primitivism as Perfectionism," 240-243.

[713]Dieter, *Holiness Revival*, 213.

[714]Dieter, *Holiness Revival*, 251.

[715]Wynkoop, "Theological Roots," 78.

[716]Staples, "Current Debate," 12.

[717]Hughes, "Christian Primitivism as Perfection," 239-250.

1. A Distinct Holiness Exegesis

Wesley's defense of Christian perfection is based upon Scriptural promises, commands, prayers, and examples. His presentation is marked by reasonableness and carefulness. If anything, he tended to understate his position. Wesley was writing for the general church. Edmund Gibson, the bishop of London once asked Wesley what he meant by perfection. After he explained himself, the bishop replied, "Mr. Wesley, if this be all you mean, publish it to all the world."[718]

By the turn of the century, holiness exponents were writing for the holiness movement. They tended to depreciate the new birth, emphasizing what it did *not* accomplish. Their description of the new birth would often better correspond to what Wesley variously described as "the almost Christian," "the legal state," or "the faith of a servant. What Wesley described as "the new birth," "the evangelical state," or "the faith of a son" would often correspond to the holiness movement's description of entire sanctification.[719] Collins warned that the danger of "Pentecostal" sanctification "is that it runs the risk of underestimating the value of regeneration, of depreciating the glorious state of the children of God who are free from both the guilt and power of sin and who have the Holy Spirit very much in their lives."[720]

Thus, the holiness movement could not preach Christian perfection based upon the historic Methodist teachings. Mark Quanstrom explained that the Church of the Nazarene felt the need to produce their own theologies because the older Methodist theologies did not stress the instantaneous nature of sanctification, they did not state strongly enough that sanctification accomplished nothing less than the eradication of the sinful nature, they did not use Pentecost as the paradigm of entire sanctification, and they did not describe the results of entire sanctification in the extravagant terms of many in the holiness movement.[721]

Over the next thirteen pages, I will discuss eight characteristics of holiness exegesis. In order to promote their doctrine of a second blessing the holiness movement resorted to a restricted definition of "sanctification" in which

---

[718]Wesley, *Plain Account of Christian Perfection*, ¶ 12, *Works*, 11:374.

[719]Kenneth Prior made a similar observation, that on the basis of Scriptural teaching some examples of "second blessing" could be more accurately described as conversion [*Way of Holiness*, 103]. J. C. Ryle made the same observation in *Holiness*, xv.

[720]Collins, *Faithful Witness*, 81; see also Collins, *Wesley on Salvation*, 114-115; 125. Keith Drury referred to his efforts to get people sanctified who actually needed to get saved ["Response 1," 116; 25].

[721]Quanstrom, *Century of Holiness Theology*, 58-59.

holiness is restricted to the second blessing. Wesley said the term *sanctification* refers to those who are justified unless it is qualified by another word such as "wholly" or "entirely." Yet with the holiness movement initial, progressive, and final sanctification tend to be ignored. Lindström objected that "sanctification has been limited to the instantaneous experience of 'the second blessing.' The fact that it also comprises a gradual development of the Christian life has not been realized."[722] Howard Snyder wrote that the holiness movement narrowed John Wesley's concept of Christian perfection, emphasizing the second crisis and de-emphasizing sanctification as a process of growth that begins with conversion.[723] Of the conservative holiness ministers I surveyed, 48% said *sanctification* as used in the Bible usually meant the second work of grace.[724]

This restricted definition creates interpretative problems with 1Thessalonians 4:3. "Paul is not calling them to an entire sanctification while they are in fornication."[725] Nor does Hebrews 12:14 teach "holiness or hell." In passages such as 1 Corinthians 1:30; 2 Thessalonians 2:13; Hebrews 12:14 *hagiasmos* refers to the total process of sanctification.

The Scriptures do not use the term "second blessing." Gamertsfelder objected that the term "second blessing" is not biblical.[726] The phrase "second benefit" in 2 Corinthians 1:15 simply refers to a second visit from Paul to Corinth. Wesley advised, " Avoid all magnificent, pompous words: indeed, you need give it no general name; neither perfection, sanctification, the second blessing, nor the

---

[722]Lindström, *Wesley and Sanctification*, 123. Dunning said that Wesley would have been appalled that many of his nineteenth and twentieth century successors denied that there was a gradual work of sanctification [*Grace, Faith, and Holiness*, 485].

[723]Snyder, *Divided Flame*, 71.

[724]"Spirit and Sanctification: Changes Within American Wesleyanism," 98. In 1993 I surveyed the Inter-Church Holiness Convention asking a 5% random sampling of ministers within the movement to list their three favorite texts for a second blessing. The three most popular texts were Heb 12:14, 1 Thess 4:3, and John 17:17, none of which will bear the weight placed upon them as second-blessing proof texts. Evidently they were popular because they contain the word "holiness" or "sanctification." Four texts from Acts were also on the IHC list (1:8; 2:4; 15:8-9; 19:2). The implication from their use of these texts is that believers do not yet have the Holy Spirit [p. 100]. Mudge also rejected the use of the Heb 12:14 and 1 Thes 4:3 as description of Christian perfection [*Growth in Holiness*, 168-169].

[725]Shaw, *Spirit in Redemption*, 139; Gibson, *Sincerity of God*, 28.

[726]Gamertsfelder, *Systematic Theology*, 529-544.

having attained."[727]

There is something ambiguous about the phrase "second blessing." Since it is not a scriptural phrase, we cannot become contentious over it. Some have reasoned, if a second, why not a third or fourth? This tends to fragment the grace of God and create a caste system within the Church. Those who use the term "second blessing" properly mean by it that sin is two-fold in its nature, both an outward expression and an inner disposition. Thus, salvation is also twofold. The new birth enables a person to live holy in his outward expressions, but while the old nature of sin no longer reigns, it still remains.

In a letter to Joseph Benson, Wesley wrote of a "second change, whereby they shall be saved from all sin, and perfected in love."[728] In "The Repentance of Believers," Wesley spoke of the Lord speaking "to our hearts again, to speak the second time, Be clean."[729] In a letter to Jane Hilton, Wesley referred to a "second deliverance."[730] Thus, there is a "secondness" about the perfecting grace of God which deals with those inner attitudes.

Yet holiness exegesis tended to arbitrarily divide such passages as Acts 2:38; Acts 26:18; Ephesians 5:25-26; Titus 3:5 into two works of grace.[731] For example, Beverly Carradine taught "peace with God" (Rom 5:1) was justification and "the peace of God" (Rom 4:7) was sanctification.[732] Leon Hynson also referred to the holiness interpretation of Acts 19:2 as imposing experience on Scripture:

> The apostolic question to the disciples of Ephesus, "Have ye received the Holy Ghost since ye believed" (Acts 19:2), was

---

[727]Wesley, *Works*, 11:434-435. Wesley violated his own advice a total of five time, and always in correspondence. *Letter* to Jane Hilton [Barton], 8 Oct 1774; *letter* to Sarah Crosby, 14 Feb 1761; *letter* to Thomas Olivers, 24 March 1757; *letter* to Jane Salkeld, 9 Aug 1772; *letter* to Samuel Bardsley, 3 April 1772.

[728]Wesley, *Letter*, 28 December 1770.

[729]Wesley, Sermon #14, 1.20.

[730]Wesley, *Letter* 1 March 1769.

[731]For examples, see Wood, *Pentecostal Grace*, 33; Hills, *Holiness and Power*, 143-145; Doty, *Lessons in Holiness*, 27; Keen, *Salvation Papers*, chapter 2; McLaughlin, *Acts*, 32. Staples described the attempt to divide Acts 2:38 as "misguided" and "strained" [*Outward Sign*, 150]. Wood even divides Titus 2:14 into two stages of Christian life [*Pentecostal Grace*, 62].

[732]Carradine, *Better Way*, 30. Wood distinguished between "being in Christ" and "Christ dwelling within" as the distinction between justification and sanctification [*Pentecostal Grace*, 75].

> interpreted as the description of a two-stage reception of God's grace. It would be a personal, identifiable experience: "Your Pentecost," "My Pentecost." In the experience of regeneration, the Spirit is "with you" and in Pentecostal experience "in you." This Pentecostal dimension was to take the holiness tradition beyond Wesley's position on Pentecost, as seen in his *Notes on the New Testament.*[733]

In holiness exegesis, sanctification was contrasted to regeneration, instead of viewed as a continuation. The first and second blessing were contrasted and the first work depreciated in order to demonstrate the necessity of the second. The first work was reduced to justification — something done *for* us, while sanctification was something done *in* us. Those in the holiness movement who recognized that the Holy Spirit comes in regeneration, tend to teach that he came as a guest, not as a resident. Others taught that in regeneration he was resident, but not president.

Samuel Logan Brengle, for example, viewed the work of the Spirit prior to entire sanctification as preparatory. "The concept of a new nature's being wrought in the believing heart by regeneration is curiously absent from Brengle's theology. He does say that 'in some measure' the indwelling of the Holy Spirit begins at conversion" but "justification, with its corollary, regeneration, is viewed as an intermediate state in the work of salvation."[734]

Jonathan Raymond observed that while Brengle emphasized the second blessing as a crisis experience, Frederick Coutts, the eighth Salvation Army general, put an equal stress on the process of becoming more and more like Christ over time. This was an attempt to bring balance to Brengle's view.[735]

While William Booth could write in *The War Cry*, "All of us got such a baptism we had not had for a long time," John Larsson, General of the Salvation Army 2002-2006, explained

> Forty years later William Booth would have found it difficult to express himself in the same terms without being misunderstood, for by then the phrase "baptism in the Spirit" would have become associated with a highly distinctive, rigid and controversial doctrinal structure. But when William Booth wrote his letter, the term was in the main used to convey the idea of an infilling or enduement of spiritual power which could be repeated

[733]Hynson, "Wesleyan Quadrilateral," 20.

[734]Rightmire, "Samuel Brengle," 116.

[735]Raymond, "Social Holiness," 170.

> many times in the life of a believer. It was the kind of experience one could pray for and expect every Sunday morning in the prayer meeting. "Spirit of the living God, fall afresh on me!" It was *a* baptism with the Spirit, rather than *the* Baptism with the Holy Spirit—with definite article and capital B. "All of us got such a baptism we had not had for a long time!"[736]

Wesley warned that many persons have spoken of the work of sanctification as if it were quite different from justification.

> But this is a great and dangerous mistake, and has a natural tendency to make us undervalue that glorious work of God which was wrought in us when we were justified; whereas in that moment when we are justified freely by his grace, when we are accepted through the Beloved, we are born again, born from above, born of the Spirit. And there is as great a change wrought in our souls when we are born of the Spirit as was wrought in our bodies when we were born of a woman. There is in that hour a general change from inward sinfulness to inward holiness."[737]

Wesley continued to explain that entire sanctification

> does not imply any new *kind* of holiness: let no man imagine this. From the moment we are justified till we give up our spirits to God, love is the fulfilling of the law. . . . Love is the sum of Christian sanctification: it is the one *kind* of holiness which is found, only in various *degrees*, in the believers who are distinguished by St. John into "little children, young men, and fathers." The difference between one and the other properly lies in the degree of love.[738]

Pope explained, "Never do we read of a *higher life* that is other than the intensification of the lower; never of a *second blessing* that is more than the unrestrained outpouring of the same Spirit who gave the first."[739] Instead we

---

[736]Larsson, *Spiritual Breakthrough*, 59-60.

[737]Wesley, "On Patience," Sermon #83, ¶ 9.

[738]Wesley, "On Patience," Sermon # 83, ¶ 10.

[739]Pope, *Compendium*, 3:44.

should understand that "Entire Sanctification is the perfection of the regenerate state."[740]

Holiness exegesis tended to resort to Old Testament typology. The "promised land" motif is a popular type of the victorious life. Yet typology cannot prove doctrine; it only illustrates it. Richard S. Taylor taught that passages which illustrate a doctrine are not properly proof texts in support of that doctrine.[741] The fact that Fletcher does uses such figurative language to illustrate a point does not justify the use of typology to establish doctrine.[742]

Holiness authors such as Godbey, Carradine, Knapp, and G. D. Watson could find holiness everywhere and thus begged the question.[743] The complaint concerning George McLaughlin was that he could preach the second blessing from two humps on a camel. It has been reported that Bud Robinson once retorted, "If we can see second-blessing holiness where it ain't, then you ought to be able to see holiness where it IS."[744]

In 1907 Leonidas McDougle offered his own variation of holiness typology.

> Israel crossing the Red Sea is made to typify conversion, the wanderings in the Wilderness the varied experiences of regeneration, and entrance into Canaan entire sanctification. My version differs widely. The Wilderness experience does not typify regeneration; too carnal, vacillating and unreal. The conquest of Canaan began in Canaan, not in the Wilderness. Sanctification begins in regeneration, not in wandering, doubt and condemnation. Israel did not have peace for seven years after entering Canaan.[745]

Essentially, *Pentecostal Grace* by Laurence Wood is a attempt to link Pentecost to Christian perfection through typology. Wood applied Israel's corporate deliverance from bondage to individual salvation under the new

---

[740]Flew, *Idea of Perfection*, 320.

[741]Taylor, *Preaching Holiness Today*, 94-95. See p. 214 of this book.

[742]Fletcher, *Works*, 2:546.

[743]For example Knapp, *Out of Egypt into Canaan*.

[744]Online: Metcalfe, "Life Begins With Thanksgiving," McLaughlin acknowledged the objection that he "sees Holiness every where in the Scriptures because he is determined to see it there" [*Acts*, 5].

[745]McDougle, *Salvation*, 16. Yet the two crossings are used by Dale Yocum as types of two-fold salvation [*Holy Way*, 91-92].

covenant. Chapter 2, "The Promised Land Motif as a Prefiguration of the Promise of the Father," and Chapter 3, "Pentecostal Language as Canaan Land Language" advances the same approach of Knapp while utilizing neo-orthodox theologians to give a weak argument more academic clout. Yet Wood conceded early in his book that "this theological parallel is not systematically developed as such in the New Testament."[746]

Wood also attempted to prove his thesis from the two stages of the Christian life: Easter and Pentecost. Yet Easter and Pentecost do not correspond to the Exodus and the Conquest of Canaan as Wood asserted.[747] Nor does the Exodus prefigure the Resurrection of Christ.[748] In fact the word ἔξοδος (*exodus*) occurs three times in the New Testament. It refers to the historic exodus of Israel from Egypt in Hebrews 11:22; in Luke 9:31 and 2 Peter 1:15 it refers to physical death.

Pentecost is the appropriation of the resurrection life, not a second stage of conquest. Furthermore, 1 Corinthians 12:13, which speaks of Spirit baptism, should be linked to 1 Corinthians 10:1-4 which connects this "baptism" with Israel's exodus through the Red Sea. Thus, a better argument could be made from typology that Spirit baptism should be connected with the initial salvation of Egyptian deliverance rather than with the Christian perfection of Canaan. Furthermore, the generation which crossed over the Red Sea became apostate. Therefore, unless the doctrine of unconditional election is presupposed, the "baptism" of Israel in the Jordan River was not a second work, but the initiation of a new generation.[749]

In holiness exegesis, the "old man" is put off through sanctification. But the three passages which use this phrase, Romans 6:6; Ephesians 4:22; Colossians 3:9 are describing the former way of life. "If anyone is in Christ, he

---

[746]Wood, *Pentecostal Grace*, 26.

[747]Wood, *Pentecostal Grace*, 20.

[748]Wood, *Pentecostal Grace*, 50.

[749]The third analogy Wood used concerning birth and circumcision might be a legitimate figure of two stages of growth, but does not advance his thesis linking the second stage to Pentecost. Nor does it fit how spiritual circumcision is used in the New Testament. See ftnt # 49.

In his final analogy Wood borrowed from the Roman Catholic theology of infant baptism and confirmation. Yet Wesley considered the Roman Catholic doctrine of confirmation "an abuse" [Wesley, *Works*, 10:117; 135-136; 150-151]. According to Ole Borgen, Wesley showed no interest in the rite of confirmation, but instead connected confirmation with the inner assurance of the Holy Spirit [Borgen, *John Wesley on the Sacraments*, 170; 276].

is a new creation: the old has gone, the new has come" (2 Cor 5:17).[750] Robert Lyon concluded,

> Paul states categorically that a Christian — every Christian — is one who has died to sin and his old man has been crucified for the destruction of the body of sin. This is the common experience of the believer and not only of the few who have gone on to perfection. . . . It is worth noting how often these passages have been employed within the holiness movement as a basis for the exhortation to Christian perfection when in reality they are descriptive of what has happened in the lives of all believers.[751]

Holiness literature such as *The Old Man* by E. G. Marsh describes the new Christian as a very unstable individual who really should not be trusted. Marsh wrote, "It is a sad fact according to experience that many regenerated saints do not always suppress the old man. They, at times, give way to his stirrings and must repent and ask God's forgiveness. Thus man lives an up and down life for a time."[752]

In *The Man in Black*, F. M. Lehman told of a young couple who are saved, but not sanctified. Before their evening of relaxation was over, however, she had thrown a shell which broke his favorite lamp, and he had used an ax to make kindling wood of her piano.[753]

In *Gospel Dynamite* a saved man who was not "sanctified" killed another man.[754] John T. Hatfield testified that before he was sanctified he "could no more keep the 'old man' down than he could keep down a sick stomach." He later explained to the cow, "I have been mean to you; I have kicked, cuffed, and beat you with milk-stools and buckets; I have pulled hair out of your back, but now I want you to understand I am sanctified; I've got the blessing and the kick is taken out of me."[755]

Jack Jones cautioned that the new birth can be expounded in such a way

---

[750]Grider, "The Meaning of 'Old Man,'" 15-16, 46; Dunning, *Grace, Faith, and Holiness*, 474; see also Reasoner, *Romans*, 231-236.

[751]Lyon, "Baptism and Spirit-Baptism," 22; 26.

[752]Marsh, *Old Man*, 57-63. For examples, see Jones, *Perfectionist Persuasion*, 83-88. One wonders what the practical differences are between an up and down life and the back and forth "seesaw" life depicted by Walvoord [see p. 667].

[753]Lehman, *Man in Black*.

[754]Hudson, *Gospel Dynamite*, 174-176.

[755]Hatfield, *Thirty-three Years a Live Wire*, 36; 39.

that awakened sinners conclude they are born again. Then they seek entire sanctification and are disappointed. Wesley's description of the grace conveyed in the new birth exceeds the grace of entire sanctification as proclaimed by many of its current exponents.[756] In fact, when the testimony of Kenneth Collins was published, in which he told of his discovery that faith in Christ had provided not only forgiveness of sins, but power over sin, the editor of the article inserted two sidebars on the doctrine of entire sanctification. Yet Collins was not writing about his entire sanctification, but about his new birth.[757]

Holiness exegesis tended to misinterpretation of the transitional nature of the book of Acts. According to Laurence Wood, "The primary issue for the Wesleyan tradition is whether the doctrine of Christian perfection is to be equated with Pentecostal language."[758] Yet the result, according to Kenneth Collins, is that Wood "has for the most part emptied out what it means to be justified and born of God, and all for the sake of his pentecostal paradigm." According to Collins, "the net result of Wood's hermeneutical move is to diminish the first work of grace in his celebration of the second. But if regeneration is not properly understood, neither is entire sanctification." Collins concluded that Wood's pentecostal paradigm is a failed one.[759]

W. T. Purkiser claimed that all examples of the baptism with the Spirit and entire sanctification are found in the book of Acts.[760] Yet Ken Lesta objected that Purkiser was using an historical book about a transition period to reach a supposedly permanent activity of the Holy Spirit. "The isolated and unique events of Acts 2,8,10, and 19 are claimed as universal and permanent." Ultimately Lesta concluded that the Wesleyan position was faulty, although true Wesleyan theologians never based their doctrine on this foundation.[761]

Those who receive the Spirit in Acts are Jews entering into the new covenant, not Christians receiving a second blessing. Staples explained that while the disciples were saved previous to Pentecost, they were saved under the terms of the old covenant. Thus Wesley viewed the disciples as becoming Christians at

---

[756]Jones, "First and Second Blessing Holiness," 1-2.

[757]Collins, "Free!" 6-8; see Reasoner, "Spirit and Sanctification: Changes Within American Wesleyanism," 48.

[758]Wood, *Pentecostal Grace*, 13. Yet according to Mitchell this debate is "merely academic, of small profit, and rather boring" ["Response to Smith," 10].

[759]Collins, "The State of Wesley Studies in North America," 28-36.

[760]Purkiser, *Conflicting Concepts of Holiness*, 29.

[761]Lesta, "Nature of Sanctification," 156.

Pentecost, when by faith they entered the new covenant and received the Spirit.[762] A survey of the *Ancient Christian Commentary on Acts* produces no passage where the early Church fathers made a direct association between Christian perfection and the six outpourings of the Spirit. They consistently wrote of baptism (both of water and the Spirit) as the scriptural entrance into the Church and Christ's Kingdom with the perfecting of believers following later.

Donald Dayton concluded that Wesley's articulation of Christian perfection contained "few real crossovers to the Pentecostal accounts and vocabulary."[763] In the Sangster list of Wesley's primary texts, the book of Acts, along with any reference to Pentecost, is conspicuous by its absence.[764] However, my survey of the conservative holiness movement revealed their reliance upon four proof texts for entire sanctification from Acts.[765] Yet Acts is primarily a historical narrative, not a doctrinal treatise. While all Scripture is profitable for doctrine, care must be taken not to make prescriptive that which is merely descriptive.

In holiness exegesis the baptism of the Spirit was equated with entire sanctification. H. C. Morrison, the founder of Asbury Theological Seminary, wrote a booklet in 1900 entitled *Baptism with the Holy Ghost.* It is typical of the pentecostal emphasis of the holiness movement. Morrison asserted that "the baptism with the Holy Ghost is bestowed subsequent to regeneration."[766] He argued that the disciples' names were written in heaven before Pentecost and since no sinner's name is written there, the disciples must have been regenerated men. Therefore, the blessing of Pentecost was a second work of grace.

While Morrison felt he was defending Wesleyan teaching, he failed to grasp Wesley's understanding of the privileges of the new covenant. Wesley taught the Holy Spirit was promised to all believers in this dispensation and the result is regeneration. Morrison, on the other hand, declared, "The baptism with the Holy Ghost is for believers only, and is never bestowed upon the unregenerated."[767] According to Morrison, we are first regenerated; then at another point in time we are baptized with the Holy Spirit.

762Staples, *Outward Sign*, 153-154.

763Dayton, "Doctrine of the Baptism of the Holy Spirit," 121.

764Sangster, *Path to Perfection*, 37-52. Donald Dayton noted this fact, yet observed that Fletcher cited the book of Acts more than any other book in his writings [*Theological Roots of Pentecostalism*, 52-53].

765Reasoner, "Spirit and Sanctification: Changes Within American Wesleyanism," 100. This was also reported in Reasoner, "American Holiness Movement's Paradigm Shift," 141. The four texts were Acts 1:8; 2:4; 15:8-9; 19:2.

766Morrison, *Baptism with the Holy Ghost*, 14.

767Morrison, *Baptism with the Holy Ghost*, 19.

In 1911 W. B. Godbey participated in a debate on water baptism and the baptism with the Holy Ghost. He argues at one point that the water ordinance is only a sign or symbol of the real baptism — the baptism with the Holy Ghost. However, at another point in the debate Godbey argued for two works of grace — the birth of the Spirit and the baptism with the Holy Ghost. He said Spirit baptism and sanctification meant the same thing. The context of the statement indicates he was referring to entire sanctification, when "the old man got burned up."[768]

Greg Hudson noted the change of emphasis in the followers of Wesley, concerning the essence of sanctification, from an emphasis on "perfect love" to an emphasis on the "baptism of the Spirit."[769] American Methodism did not use pentecostal language to describe entire sanctification until it was introduced primarily from those outside Methodism. Donald Dayton dates the rise of the doctrine to a period from 1855-1870.[770] This new emphasis came at a time when Christian perfection was not receiving the attention it deserved within Methodism. While the holiness movement was an attempt to bring Methodism back to Wesley's doctrine, the final outcome left neither the holiness movement nor the Methodist Church with Wesley's emphasis. Quanstrom wrote that Pentecost was regarded as the biblical paradigm for the doctrine of entire sanctification in early Nazarene theology. "Interpreting Pentecost as the moment of entire sanctification was fundamental to the Holiness Movement's argument concerning the nature of the doctrine."[771]

The question is not whether anyone prior to the holiness movement every used pneumatical or pentecostal language to describe Christian perfection. Before the conclusion is reached that there was a historical precedent for the holiness emphasis on Pentecost as entire sanctification we must ask these questions:

- If a writer connected Pentecost and perfection, did he also connect Pentecost and the new birth?
- Did the writer teach that Christians did not have the Spirit prior to their perfection?
- Did the author connect the baptism of the Holy Spirit with Christian perfection?

768McWherter, *Godbey-Maupin Debate*, 7-9; 15-16.

769Hudson, "Wesleyan Minister's Guide," 81. See also Faupel's discussion of the paradigm shift which equated Christian perfection with the baptism of the Holy Spirit, in his preface to *Six Tracts by W. B. Godbey*, ix-x.

770Dayton, *Theological Roots of Pentecostalism*, 186.

771Quanstrom, *Century of Holiness Theology*, 23; 35.

- Did the author teach that Christian perfection is an instantaneous experience?

Kenneth Grider concluded that before the 1970s, "perhaps not a single book was authored by a holiness scholar in the previous 100 years or so, that had not taken the position that Pentecost was the time of the entire sanctification of the 120 disciples."[772]

Elmer Long was tried in 1947 for teaching that all believers had the Holy Spirit.[773] Around 1948 A. J. Smith collaborated with Elmer Long, James E. Church, and Wallace Memmer on a twelve-page tract which consisted primarily of quotations from early Methodist writers demonstrating Pentecost made believers Christians.[774] This tract stirred extreme reactions. Even some of the employees at the print shop lost their jobs as a repercussion over the tract.[775]

The tract created enough of a stir that A. L. Vess also published a booklet entitled *Were the Disciples Born Again Before Pentecost?*[776] Vess made ten inferences and then moved to seventeen direct reasons why the disciples were born again before Pentecost. His logic fails to grasp the real meaning of regeneration and he makes no attempt to demonstrate that anyone received the Holy Spirit before Pentecost. However, Smith did not face the repercussions until he returned from his expedition in search of Noah's ark.[777]

Under pressure, then president Jim Green dismissed Smith over doctrinal

---

[772]Grider, *Entire Sanctification*, 89-90. However, Grider overlooked Smith's *Bible Holiness* (1953). McGonigle's 1973 article, "Pneumatical Nomenclature" is often regarded as the "opening shot." See McCumber's editorial in 1979 that scholars are not debating the reality of the experience but the appropriate terminology for understanding and describing the experience ["Lively Debate," 18].

[773]Reasoner, "Paradigm Shift Concerning Pentecost,"140.

[774]The tract was titled *The Holy Spirit and the Born Again Man*. It is included as Appendix C in Smith, *Bible Holiness*, 165-176.

[775]See my "Introduction to the Second Edition" of A. J. Smith, *Bible Holiness*, 9-10; also pp. 128-129. I interviewed William D. Gale on 2 December 2009. He not only heard Dr. Smith preach at the Bible school he was attending in Tabor, Iowa, but along with Kathryn Dunn wrote a biography of Winnie Crouch [*Miss Winnie Crouch*]. According to Gale, Miss Crouch was influenced by Dr. Smith and held to his view concerning the work of the Spirit in the new birth.

[776]Vess, *Were the Disciples Born Again?*

[777]This was the first such expedition after World War II and its significance is acknowledged by LaHaye and Morris, *Ark on Ararat*. Chapter 5 is entitled "A. J. Smith: 1949." See also Cummings, *Noah's Ark*, 87-90.

issues from the People's Bible College where he was dean (now Laurel University in Highpoint, NC). Jim Green later apologized publicly to Smith at Camp Free near Valdese, North Carolina.

In 1950 Dr. Smith was elected president of Southern Wesleyan Bible College in Intercession City, Florida.[778] In 1951 he was brought before the board and charges were preferred again him. A. L. Vess, the former president of the college, stirred up the opposition to Smith.[779] Six charges were brought against Smith:

> 1. The disciples were born again at Pentecost instead of entirely sanctified.
> 2. The disciples were not born again before Pentecost. (In the New Testament evangelical sense).
> 3. There is a difference between being saved (under the law of the Old Testament dispensation) and born again (by the power of the Holy Ghost in the New Testament dispensation).
> 4. The statement that Mr. Wesley makes little distinction between the two works of grace (so far as the outward life of the believer is concerned).
> 5. One is baptized with the Holy Ghost when born again.
> 6. The Old Testament saints (generally) did not have a born again experience.[780]

Smith affirmed these six propositions, but he added the bracketed material in 1953 for clarification. Smith was first interrogated by two examiners. There were twelve members of the panel beside school board members. The notes indicate that Smith was vindicated. However, the final decision rested with the board.

In his 1953 work, *Bible Holiness and the Modern, Popular, Spurious*, Smith said that in 1951 he promised before a panel meeting "to refrain from making any further statements about the matter of the Disciples and their spiritual state before and after Pentecost." However, after studying the scriptures and the

---

[778]Smith had founded Intercession City Biblical College and Academy in 1939 and served as president from 1939-1946. This institution had been purchased by the Wesleyan Church and renamed Southern Wesleyan Bible College. They asked Smith to return and build up the school in 1950.

[779]Letter by L. A. Carpenter, 31 December 1951.

[780]"Minutes of the Board-Panel Meeting."

writings of Wesley, Clarke, and Fletcher, he retracted that promise.[781]

Smith explained that at that time, while before the panel meeting, he was not sure of his position. The panel had objected primarily to the conclusion of the tract, that the disciples were not born again in the New Testament evangelical sense until Pentecost. Prior to the conclusion, the tract had been a collection of statements by early Methodists. Under examination Smith confessed that Wallace Memmer had written the last two pages, the conclusion, and that it could be misunderstood to mean that the disciples would have gone to hell had they died before Pentecost.

It seems that between 1948-1951 Smith had signed his name to the tract, left for his expedition, returned home to be dismissed as dean of a college, moved to Florida to assume the presidency of a college, and was subsequently called upon to defend something he had not written. He resigned the presidency in May 1952.

In his resignation letter he expressed amazement over the inconsistencies taught at the college, such as the born again man has a devil in him and the regenerated man has no Holy Spirit in him. Smith said he had often been lonesome for fellowship, but found few like-minded people. His own church ostracized him. Smith wrote that he had seen four powerful revivals, but in each case the Spirit was grieved away and never returned because those who grieved the Spirit did not repent. Smith warned that they would not have a real Holy Ghost revival in Intercession City if those who are pointing at other people's sin and wrongs fail to humble themselves and confess their own.

About the same time O. C. Seevers wrote,

> I was here through the storm last winter and watched the crucifixion of Dr. A. J. Smith by his foes; if he did not behave himself more like Jesus than any man I have ever known in such a time of crisis, and under such terrific opposition and hate, then I must have been dreaming. Never once did I see him act or talk in a resentful way or manifest a spirit of retaliation.[782]

Smith returned to Greensboro, North Carolina in 1952 and was diagnosed with cancer. While he assisted two other men in the administration of the college which had previously dismissed him, this perhaps was the first time Smith actually had to research the accusations made against him. In 1953, his magnus opus, *Bible Holiness*, defends all charges. Then, in the 1951 minutes of the panel

---

[781]*Bible Holiness and the Modern, Popular, Spurious*, 18-19. Second edition, *Bible Holiness*, 110.

[782]Letter by O. C. Seevers.

meeting, he also inserted strong assertions in brackets. Six years after *Bible Holiness* had been published Smith wrote to John R. Church that no one had offered any refutation of his research. Until his death in 1960, Smith continued to dialog with the leading holiness theologians of his day.[783]

Wesley Tracy noted that it was common for those in holiness schools from the 1940s into the 1960s to complete their education without being expected to read a single page of Wesley.[784] Ever since Zondervan reprinted the works of John Wesley in 1958 students within the holiness movement have been discovering the holiness movement is not purely Wesleyan.[785]

Samuel Powell wrote that until the 1970s there was a consensus that entire sanctification was identified with the baptism with the Holy Spirit. There is a greater diversity of thought today within the holiness movement because of an increase in historical knowledge. The "back to Wesley" movement which began in the 1960s revealed that Wesley's understanding of holiness differed in significant respects from that of the holiness movement. This variance between Wesley and the holiness movement put denominational leaders in an awkward position. While entire sanctification had been identified with Pentecost, toward the end of the 1970s the exegetical propriety of this understanding was debated and found to have little warrant. The revelation that the most popular exposition of the movement's central doctrine had shaky biblical foundations was shocking to that generation.[786]

Although passages such as 1 Corinthians 12:13 and Galatians 3:27 clearly associate Spirit baptism with the new birth, it has been claimed that there are two baptisms; that the Holy Spirit baptizes believers into the body of Christ

---

[783]Such as John R. Church who opposed his teaching. However, Claude A. Ries at Houghton College wrote, "Yes, I'm fully convinced that the Scriptures teach that one received the Holy spirit when he become born again. The Holy Spirit in the born again believer is the only power that enables him to stop the sin business as a practice in his life" [19 November 1956]. In the minutes of the 1951 meeting, Smith also referred to a personal letter from H. Orton Wiley who wrote, "The Holy Spirit comes in regeneration as a life-giving Spirit."

[784]Wesley Tracy, "Foreword" in Dunning, *Layman's Guide to Sanctification*, 10-11.

[785]Rob Staples wrote that he first became aware of the shift in the early 1960s. "It became abundantly clear, as I read everything Wesley had published on the subject that Wesley did *not* understand the outpouring of the Holy Spirit upon the disciples on the day of Pentecost, as recorded in Acts 2:4, to be the equivalent of the experience of entire sanctification which he believed in and preached so fervently" ["Current Debate," 2].

[786]Powell, "Theological Significance of the Holiness Movement," 134-135; 137.

and that subsequent to the new birth, Christ baptizes believers with the Holy Spirit.[787] Upon examination of every passage in Scripture which refers to Spirit baptism, we will discover that this artificial distinction between Christ's baptism and the Spirit's baptism does not exist. Christ is always the baptizer. He baptizes *with* the Spirit *into* the body of Christ or *into* the realm of the Spirit and the Church (the body of Christ).[788]

By making the baptism with the Holy Spirit an experience subsequent to entrance into the kingdom of God, the modern holiness movement has obscured the significance of water baptism. Water baptism and Spirit baptism are two halves of one act or the one baptism. That one act or baptism is entrance into the

---

[787]Riggs taught, "This experience is as distinct from conversion as the Holy Spirit is distinct from Christ. His coming to the believer at the Baptism is the coming of the Third Person of the Trinity, in addition to the coming of Christ, which takes place at conversion"[*The Spirit Himself*, 79-80]. For other variations, see Bloesch, *Holy Spirit*, 190.

[788]Pentecostal scholar Howard Ervin advocates two aspects in 1 Cor 12:13. While he concedes that the baptism in the Spirit takes place at conversion, he believes that to be given to drink of the Spirit represents a progression and subsequent experience [*Spirit-Baptism*, 31-36]. The result of this interpretation is that Spirit baptism is associated with conversion, a position Ervin does not hold, or that "one baptism" is separated into two and that conversion is associated only with water baptism. Furthermore, the parallelism of the verse is destroyed. It is much better to understand the second phrase as an expansion and explanation of the first, which commentators often call "epexegetical."

Ervin holds that the parallelism between the two phrases "we were baptized" and "we were made to drink" are not synonymous, but that the second metaphor supplements the first. He concedes that the phrase "into one body" weighs in favor of Christian initiation, but then argues that initiative and incorporative significance cannot be imposed on both phrases. Yet he fails to demonstrate that they are describing two *different* experiences [*Conversion-Initiation*, 100-102]. Both verbs ("were baptized" and "were given to drink") are aorist tense verbs that point to a single act which occurred in the past.

Writing for the Pentecostal/Charismatic viewpoint, Oss concluded, "There is no evidence in the context that Paul has two experiences in mind. Furthermore, his use of a closely related metaphor in 1 Corinthians 10:1-4 cannot be take this way" ["Pentecostal/Charismatic View," 58]. Referring to an earlier work by Ervin [*These are not Drunken*, 44-47] where he argued that the phrase "into one body" means something quite different from that of the Gospels and Acts, Dunn concluded, "For Paul, to become a Christian and to become a member of the Body of Christ are synonymous. Thus, unless recourse is had to semantic sleight-of-hand with ἐν or εἰς, there is no alternative to the conclusion that the baptism in the Spirit is what made the Corinthians members of the Body of Christ, that is, Christians" [*Baptism in the Holy Spirit*, 128-129].

kingdom of God. Baptism consists of an inward effusion of the Holy Spirit, outwardly typified by the application of water as its emblem. Water baptism, properly understood, is an outward sign of this inward grace. This is one event, not two; it is an act of initiation which occurs at the time of regeneration.[789]

In 1979 when Rob Staples wrote "The Current Debate on the Baptism with the Holy Spirit," he concluded with a plea that the Church of the Nazarene could live with both the Wesleyan tradition and the holiness tradition of Spirit baptism. He now believes that such a strategy is unworkable. Honest biblical exegesis cannot sustain both positions. "I do not believe the doctrine of sanctification is well served by basing such an individual religious experience on a text in the Book of Acts where the focus is on the creation of Christ's Church by the Holy Spirit." Staples also polled fourteen New Testament professors, all with doctorates in their field. He asked, "Was the outpouring (baptism) of the Holy Spirit on the Day of Pentecost the equivalent of entire sanctification as our holiness tradition has understood it? (In other worlds, do you see that corporate event as a proof-text for the "secondness" of entire sanctification as an individual experience?) Not a single professor answered "yes."[790] Ken Schenck also reported

> An informal polling at the Salvation Conference of The Wesleyan Church two years ago yielded the striking result that not a single Bible scholar at Wesley Biblical, Nazarene Theological, Asbury Seminary, Indiana Wesleyan, Houghton, Southern Wesleyan, Bartlesville, or Bethany was found who understood the Spirit-fillings of Acts to be experiences of a second work of grace. In this conclusion Wesleyan Bible scholars have apparently come to agree with the virtually unanimous sense of biblical scholarship in general that receiving/being baptized with the Holy Spirit in Acts is an entry experience rather than a secondary experience subsequent to conversion.[791]

Holiness exegesis often used Romans 7 to demonstrate the need for entire sanctification. Yet, James Arminius demonstrated that the Church fathers, until Augustine in the fifth century generally interpreted Romans 7 as pre-

[789]Wood divides water baptism from baptism with the Holy Spirit, putting the baptism of water with regeneration and the baptism with the Spirit with full sanctification [*Pentecostal Grace*, 56].

[790]Online: Staples,"Things Shakeable," 3-4.

[791]Online: Schenck,"Church and the Holy Spirit," 2.

Christian experience. Methodism uniformly held that Romans 7 was not the description of one who was born again.[792] According to Romans 6 sin is no longer our master; we have been set free from sin. According to Episcopus, a follower of Arminius, one of the basis principles of Arminius was that "it is possible for a regenerate man to live without sin."[793] Yet the holiness movement adopted a Calvinistic interpretation in order to make their case for the need for entire sanctification. Their characterization of the new birth as a defeated life does not do justice to the enabling, liberating, transforming, as well as, perfecting grace of God.

H. C. Morrison wrote that Romans 7 depicted a regenerated person who needed the baptism with the Holy Ghost, which he thought was entire sanctification.

> The Christian reader will at once recognize the undoubted truthfulness of these Scriptures for they are corroborated by the every-day experience of believing souls, who, struggling against the "old man," have often been made to cry out, "O wretched man that I am, who shall deliver me from the body of this death."[794]

Isaiah Villars, a Methodist preacher, wrote of a conversation he had with a holiness preacher who had used Romans 7 to characterize the justified person. Villars objected that Romans 7 describes one in radical need of justification. "The Scriptures paint no truly justified heart as a cage of unclean birds, or as a whitened sepulchre full of all manner of uncleanness." Then Villars asked him, "Do you not believe that four-fifths of the [sic] these persons professing this 'second blessing' so happily, are simply *reclaimed* and are filled with the joy of their *first love*, and yet take it for the so-called 'second blessing?' He finally answered: 'Yes, but you dare not tell them so.'" Villars concluded that they mistook conviction for conversion. The truly converted or reclaimed backslider thus had obtained the second blessing. The faithful pastor who opposed the shibboleth of the perfectionist was accused of being opposed to holiness.[795]

---

[792]Reasoner, *Romans*, 285-295.

[793]Steele, *Defense of Christian Perfection*, 13.

[794]Morrison, *Baptism with the Holy Ghost*, 24. Grider labeled this interpretation as eccentric [*Wesleyan-Holiness Theology*, 363], but the entire pamphlet by Morrison is reprinted as a "great holiness classic" in *Holiness Teaching Today*, Harper, ed, 24-47.

[795]Villars, *Theory of the Second Blessing*, 15-17. Yet, as was often the case, Villars also held a wrong view of Christian perfection. See p. 416.

Holiness preaching created the dilemma of holiness or hell. This error is based upon a misinterpretation of Hebrews 12:14 and the belief that justification is partial and the believer remains in an unholy state. According to Quanstrom it was reflected in the writings of Asbury Lowrey, A. M. Hills, and much of the early Nazarene teaching.[796] W. B. Godbey wrote *Holiness or Hell?* in 1893.[797]

Merrill Gaddis observed that a transition from a "holy people" to "holiness people" made entire sanctification a necessary condition for salvation.[798] In an attempt to correct this problem within the holiness movement, Daniel Steele wrote,

> An ill use is sometimes made of Heb. 12:14, by quoting it as a threatening against the regenerate who do not realize the completion of the work of inward cleaning. There are no threatenings in the Word of God against the persevering sons of God. . . . Hence it is neither scriptural nor wise to Mt. Sinai for your pulpit when you preach entire sanctification.[799]

In contrast to the holiness or hell emphasis, Wesley wrote,

> I am convinced every believer may attain this; yet I do not say he is in a state of damnation or under the curse of God till he does attain. No, he is in a state of grace and in favour with God as long as he believes. Neither would I say, "If you die without it, you will perish; but rather, Till you are saved from unholy tempers, you are not ripe for glory."[800]

2. A Distinct Holiness Theology[801]

In the third volume of *Great Holiness Classics*, Richard S. Taylor edits

---

[796]Quanstrom, *Century of Holiness Theology*, 44-45.

[797]Godbey, *Holiness or Hell?* See also the comments by W. C. Wilson on Godbey's doctrine of "holiness or hell" [*Well Glory!*, 58-60].

[798]Gaddis, *Christian Perfection in America*, 454.

[799]Steele, *Half-Hours with St. Paul*, 108-109.

[800]Wesley, Letter to Elizabeth Hardy, 5 April 1758.

[801]Diane Leclerc describes ten myths about sanctification which parallel this section [*Discovering Christian Holiness*, 178-182].

a collection of the writings of the eighteen leading Wesleyan thinkers. Yet he found it necessary on sixteen occasions to correct them or impose the later holiness paradigm upon what they were saying. Ironically, as the anthology moves into the more modern era, fewer corrections are necessary. Some of his "improvements" are noted throughout this book. This illustrates the point that the holiness movement deviated from Wesleyanism while at the same time claiming to defend it.[802] Here are five examples of the more narrow perspective of the holiness movement:

In holiness theology, the holy life is restricted to the second blessing. Disregarding such passages as Romans 6 and 1 John 3:9, the doctrine of initial sanctification, and statements by Wesley that "a Christian was so far perfect as not to commit sin,"[803] holiness is confined to the second blessing. E. O. Chalfant was more correct in his reference to "first and second blessing holiness."[804]

The 1896 debate between Pickett and Smith highlighted the difference in emphasis between Methodism and the holiness movement. Smith objected that the holiness movement was built upon the idea that the regenerate soul is unclean, impure and unprepared for heaven. He cited eighteen instances from the writings of Pickett, Carradine, and Godbey which displayed a clear departure from Methodism.[805]

In Methodist theology, purity begins with "the washing of regeneration" (Titus 3:5) and *maturity* is growth in Christian perfection.[806] In holiness theology, *purity* is a state which is attained by a crisis second blessing and *maturity* is the result of growth after Christian perfection. Yet Hebrews 6:1, "let us go on unto perfection" (KJV) is translated "let us go to maturity" (NIV).

However, if I arrive at Christian perfection in a crisis moment, and that perfection is conceived of as a state of perfection, there will be little emphasis upon the maturity to follow. How can perfection be improved? Nor is there much emphasis in holiness theology upon growth *before* perfection, since it is taught that the sin nature prevents purity and maturity.

Mildred Wynkoop observed three problems in holiness theology. There is a tendency to make too sharp a distinction between justification and sanctification by considering them as totally unrelated. Here too much confidence is put in the 'crisis experience to solve all human problems. The means (the

---

[802]Taylor, *Leading Wesleyan Thinkers.*

[803]Wesley, "Christian Perfection," Sermon #40, ¶ 20.

[804]Jack Jones, "First and Second Blessing Holiness,"1. Chalfant was a Nazarene district superintendent. See *Forty Years on the Firing Line.*

[805]See pp. 599-600 of this book.

[806]Marston, *From Chaos to Character.*

crisis) becomes the end (perfection). And the consequence is an almost complete neglect to relate real-life problems to the experience of grace.[807]

Stephen Gibson wrote that the conservative holiness movement still relies most on the second crisis. "We have tended to expect it to solve every spiritual problem. The statement has been made, 'If everyone in the church was sanctified, the church wouldn't have any problems.'"[808]

While Christian perfection was the goal of early Methodism; it is the beginning point of the Christian life in holiness teaching. Thus, according to holiness theology, the person who does not meet God's requirement for holiness is not ready for heaven and is subject to backsliding. Therefore, it is holiness or hell.

In an apology for the conservative holiness movement, Stephen Gibson conceded (1) that they have not always made it clear in what sense all believers are holy/sanctified even before a second crisis, though the Bible says they are. (2) Some have implied that a believer does not have the Holy Spirit until entire sanctification. (3) They tend to depreciate the justified state in order to promote entire sanctification. (4) They have used such terms as *holiness*, *sanctified*, and *carnal* to refer to concepts much more specifically than does the Bible.

> One well-known evangelist would read his text, "Without holiness no man shall see the Lord," the say, "Either this verse means what is says, or it doesn't." He would go on to preach that a Christian will not make it to heaven if he has not been entirely sanctified. To him, the term *holiness* could not refer to anything but a second work of grace.[809]

In holiness theology, holiness is perceived as a crisis experience, not an ethical lifestyle. In holiness theology, progressive sanctification is ignored in favor of a crisis experience. Miley defined "the second-blessing view" as built on the incompleteness of regeneration, but that the regenerate attain the fullness of sanctification instantly. Yet he warned that "any insistence upon such a mode as the only possible mode of sanctification must be without definite warrant of Scripture."[810] However, the early holiness movement gave so much attention to

---

[807]Wynkoop, *Theology of Love*, 47; 332; 341. "No holiness preacher or teacher can justifiably reject the Calvinist's distinction between common and saving grace who himself makes a distinction between 'saving grace' and 'sanctifying grace.' Certainly the Bible makes no such distinctions" [Wynkoop, *Foundation*, 97].

[808]Gibson, *Held by Conviction*, 78.

[809]Gibson, *Held by Conviction*, 71-73.

[810]Miley, *Systematic Theology*, 2:369-370.

the instantaneous nature of entire sanctification "that the gradual nature of the grace had been all but abandoned."[811]

Harald Lindström wrote that the concept of salvation has been concentrated too often on the new birth and complete sanctification as "two isolated phenomena unconnected organically with the doctrine of salvation as a whole."[812] Charles Edward White wrote that in Wesley's doctrine of Christian perfection there is a tension between sanctification as a gradual process and sanctification as an instantaneous blessing. "Phoebe Palmer uncoupled this tension between gradual and instantaneous sanctification in Wesley's thought, placing all her emphasis on the instantaneous."[813] Merrill Gaddis observed that the holiness movement emphasized crisis and lightly passed over the connecting states of life so that the result is a series of steps with little or no continuity.[814]

Steven Cooley identified four types of holiness experience advocated within holiness literature: affective piety, sacramental piety, mysticism, non-experiential piety of reason and faith.

By "affective piety" is meant the revelation of truth and the knowledge of God through emotions or religious feelings. "Sacramental piety" emphasized the real presence of the sacred through ritual, fellowship, symbols, and physical surroundings. Cooley demonstrated the sacramental nature of the holiness campmeeting.[815]

"Mysticism" involves meditation, visualization, or contemplation of a sacred scene from the Bible. The most popular were the experience of Jacob at Peniel, fire falling from heaven, and Pentecost. Then the believer was to particularize or concentrate on a few elements of the scene, involving a direct engagement with the physical senses. This concluded in a cathartic burst of feeling and action.[816]

The fourth type of experience, according to Cooley, is the rational, matter-of-fact, non-experiential kind of experience. It is based on a formula in which the congregation is exhorted first to consecrate themselves, then step out on

---

[811]Quanstrom, *Century of Holiness Theology*, 135.

[812]Lindström, *Wesley and Sanctification*, 105.

[813]White, *Beauty of Holiness*, 129-130.

[814]Gaddis, *Christian Perfection in America*, 539. Pentecostalism would simply add another step on the ladder.

[815]Cooley, *Possibilities of Grace*, 107-139.

[816]A modern example of this mysticism would be the Emmaus Walk program. Cooley documented the erotic language sometimes found within the piety of holiness mysticism [69-73]. Cooley also demonstrated that a metaphor can lose its influence on a culture. Yet the Word of God is always relevant.

God's promise. Then there was an emotional ratification of this act.[817]

It might be argued that these various emphases on experience correspond to various personality temperaments.[818] Cooley demonstrated historically how both liberalism and fundamentalism were a threat to the emphasis on experience.[819] A later generation would attempt to legitimize experience through a philosophy of existentialism.

While I have argued that our relationship with God includes emotions and feelings, my concern here is with auto-suggestion, that we assume we are in a real relationship with God because of an emotional experience which is not validated by an ethical lifestyle.

Phoebe Palmer insisted that the seeker testify definitely to entire sanctification in order to retain it.[820] No doubt seekers were often pressured into claiming something they did not understand. Yet the mere profession of this blessing does not produce Christian perfection. Contrary to Wesley, Palmer taught no evidence was necessary other than the witness of the Word that God would do the work if we met the conditions.[821] This profession of holiness tended to produce bigotry, not sensitivity to the Spirit. A standardized profession of holiness has not necessarily produced the practice of holiness.

The all important issue is to testify to the experience, when the emphasis should be upon living the life. This emphasis upon seeking an experience, coupled with the teaching that the baptism with the Holy Spirit was an experience following regeneration, led to pentecostalism a generation later. Holiness is claimed presumptively and must be testified to definitely.

Is there a direct witness to entire sanctification?[822] Those who view

---

[817]Cooley, *Possibilities of Grace*, 5; 64-82.

[818]See the discussion of sanctification and temperaments on pp. 813-815.

[819]Cooley, *Possibilities of Grace*, 204-233.

[820]Cooley demonstrated that Phoebe Palmer was a genuine mystic, although she never testified publically to her experiences [*Possibilities of Grace*, 75-78]. Ironically, her teaching advocated the fourth type of experience, a rational non-experiential piety [pp. 78-81].

[821]Howard, "Wesley Versus Phoebe Palmer," 34-36.

[822]John Hunt felt that a direct testimony to entire sanctification was not necessary, but the person who is entirely sanctified must know it [*Letters on Sanctification*, 45; 79]. Among those who answer "no," see Mudge, *Growth in Holiness*, 183; *Perfect Life*, 271; Banks, *Manual of Christian Doctrine*, 255-256; Huntington, *Sin and Holiness*, 233; Pope, *Higher Catechism*, 262; Flew, *Idea of Perfection*, 328-330; 336-338; Williams, *John Wesley's Theology Today*, 187. Wesley may have gone too far in teaching that "none therefore ought to believe that the work

entire sanctification as a permanent condition or state tend to argue for a direct witness to that state. Those who understand entire sanctification to be a goal which we progressively move toward would naturally deny that there could be divine assurance to something not yet realized. Bounds explained,

> Sometimes in the Wesleyan tradition there have been attempts to declare Christians entirely sanctified too hastily, either as a result of a deficient view of entire sanctification or an attempt to solidify or strengthen faith in entire sanctification. For example, if a Wesleyan sees entire sanctification as simply entire consecration, then the Wesleyan may ask if a Christian is fully surrendered to Christ and assume entire sanctification if there is a testimony to such personal consecration. However, a person may be fully surrendered and not have faith to appropriate entire sanctification. Or if a person has gone to the altar to be entirely sanctified, the person may be instructed to testify to this work of grace as a way to strengthen faith. However, in subsequent days the Christian may realize that entire sanctification has not happened.

---

is done, till there is added the testimony of the Spirit, witnesses his entire sanctification, as clearly as his justification [*Works*, 11:402]. Sangster called this emphasis the "least defensible part of Wesley's doctrine" [*Path to Perfection*, 160]. Staples pointed out that the New Testament dies not speak unequivocally of a witness of the spirit to entire sanctification. The New Testament usually, if not always, associated the witness of the Spirit with our adoption into the family of God or to our new birth, not to the degree of our holiness. "The Spirit witnesses not to a state of sanctify but to the reality of a relationship. The Scriptures which Wesley used to support his position deal primarily with assurance that we are children of God and only by implication can they be applied to entire sanctification ["Wesley's Doctrine of the Holy Spirit,"103]. According to Maddox there is little biblical warrant for a distinct witness of the spirit to entire sanctification [*Responsible Grace,* 189].

Turner admitted the biblical grounds are not as sure, *Vision Which Transforms*, 260. While this point is conceded by Miley, he still argued that such a witness was possible [*Systematic Theology*, 2:380-382]. Jesse Peck conceded that no special Scripture in so many words affirms this witness, yet argued for a consciousness of purity communicated by the Holy Spirit [*Central Idea of Christianity*, 147-152]. Miner Raymond argued for a direct witness to entire sanctification [*Systematic Theology*, 2:396-397]. Steele argued against Mudge and for a direct witness in *Defense of Christian Perfection*, 65. Brengle also emphasized the necessity o the witness of the Spirit to claim entire sanctification. Merrill, *Doctrinal Aspects of Christian Experience*, 198, argued that the witness was to adoption, not specifically to regeneration or sanctification. See also Foster, *Christian Purity*, 206-207; 225; 229; Lowrey, *Possibilities of Grace*, 405-408.

Bounds concluded, "It is possible for Christians to be entirely sanctified and not have the internal witness of the Spirit."[823] But if we allow that our perfection is moment-by-moment can we not allow that at those moments when we are being perfected we are conscious of the fact? Stackpole has a valid point.

> With increasing knowledge of the truth and prayerful meditation upon it, assurance becomes clearer and the fruit of the Spirit more abundant. . . . If this spiritual law be rightly stated, then when one grasps the promise of purity of heart through the blood of Jesus, there would naturally be expected the witness of the Spirit thereto with special clearness and this is the general testimony of saints in all ages. . . . The Spirit bears witness to truth and a powerful manifestation of His presence and indwelling may accompany other truth as well. . . . It is an intensification of the abiding witness of the Spirit.[824]

According to George Peck the satisfactory evidence of the state of entire sanctification was the witness of the Spirit, a consciousness of victory over inward sin such as rebellion or unholy elements, a deep and constant love flowing toward God and all mankind, perfect submission to the will of God, unwavering confidence in God, and uninterrupted communion with God. Furthermore, the person will be able to mark the successive steps through which he passed. Peck declared that a person would be conscious of the time when they became aware of their struggle with inward corruption, when they resolved to seek deliverance, when it began to appear near and when they first claimed it as their own.[825]

Assurance should be the common privilege of a child of God. However, those who emphasis process sanctification have made it a rare thing, because they like to limit what the Holy Spirit can do now. Those who move toward a closer walk with God should have a greater assurance from him. Wesley taught this was the full assurance of faith. He declared, "If any deny the witness of sanctification and occasion disputing in the select society, let him or her meet therein no more."[826] He wrote that the witness of sanctification as well as of justification is

---

[823]Online: Bounds, "Spiritual Transformation," 12-13.

[824]Stackpole, *Evidence of Salvation*, 111.

[825]Peck, *Christian Perfection*, 439-449. Perhaps on the last point Peck is describing his own experience. His experience is recorded in *Holiness Miscellany* [Inskip, ed, 79-89] and it does follow the paradigm he gave. I am not convinced that it will be the same in every case, however.

[826]Wesley, *Letter* to John Mason, 15 November 1768.

the privilege of God's children. "And you may have the one always clear as well as the other if you walk humbly and closely with God."[827]

Perhaps the real issue is not where there is assurance of entire sanctification or not but whether that witness is to a permanent state or to a present condition. If there is not a specific witness to entire sanctification, at least there should be a clearer witness to a deeper relationship.

In holiness theology the state of holiness is claimed presumptively and must be testified to definitely. Yet, Wesley counseled that it was not necessary to testify to having attained a specific blessing — "neither perfection, sanctification, the second blessing, nor the having attained. Rather speak of the particulars which God has wrought for you. You may say, "At such a time, I felt a change which I am not able to express; and since that time, I have not felt pride, or self-will, or anger, or unbelief; nor any thing but a fulness of love to God and to all mankind."[828] According to Hester Ann Rogers, Fletcher said he lost the blessing four or five times by not testifying to it.[829] This report made a great impression upon Phoebe Palmer who insisted that the seeker testify definitely to entire sanctification in order to retain it. No doubt seekers were often pressured into claiming something they did not understand.

But the mere profession of this blessing does not produce Christian perfection. Yet Palmer taught no evidence was necessary other than the witness of the Word that God would do the work if we met the conditions. This profession of holiness tended to produce bigotry, not sensitivity to the Spirit. A standardized profession of holiness has not necessarily produced the practice of holiness.

H. A. Ironside sought and claimed entire sanctification. He noticed that after his experience he tended to exalt himself more and Christ less. He found that the "sanctified" were very little different from their brethren who were "only justified." He observed among holiness denominations a continual pattern of breaking off and forming new groups. He concluded that there was more immorality among holiness groups than an outsider would suspect. He expressed sorrow over many who sought an experience that was unattainable. Although he became labeled a "holiness fighter" and Henry Brockett attempted to rebut him in *Scriptural Freedom from Sin*,[830] Ironside offered the holiness movement some

[827]Wesley, *Letter* to Peggy Dale, 18 June 1767.

[828]*Works*, 11:434-435. See the advice given by Haney, *Inheritance Restored*, 146-147.

[829]See p. 483 of this book.

[830]Brockett, *Scriptural Freedom from Sin*. Brocket pointed out that Ironside taught that the sin nature dwells in the mortal body. This is the old Gnostic error [pp. 43-44].

sound advice when he wrote, "Let a full Christ be preached, a finished work be proclaimed, the truth of the indwelling Spirit be scripturally taught, and all these excrescences disappear."[831]

The doctrine of eradication was taught by holiness theology. Claude Thompson declared that the eradication question has caused more difficulty than all other questions in the discussion of sanctification.[832] Yet, the Bible does not use the term "eradicate," nor did Wesley ever use it in his explanation of entire sanctification.[833] Yet, according to Romans 6:6, the consequence of entire sanctification or perfect love is that the sin nature is destroyed (καταργέω - *katargeo*). This verb has been variously translated: to render inactive, to render powerless, to abolish, to destroy, to annihilate, to nullify, or to release. Without question, it is a strong word. James Dunn said it was one of the most difficult of Paul's words to pin down to a precise meaning, yet he argues for the much stronger sense because Paul is dealing with God's ultimate purpose through Christ.[834] This verb carries the meaning of "nullify" in Romans 3:3, 31; 4:14 It is used in 7:2, 6 to describe release from the law.

While Romans 6:6 does teach that the "body of sin" is destroyed, "destruction" can be explained in such a way that is not biblical. Here the Greek philosophy of stoicism with its concept of perfection as impassible (that our human emotions are unaffected), can be substituted for the biblical idea that perfection is to love God with your whole being.

"The Stoics taught that the perfect person submits — but neither sullenly nor triumphantly, neither sadly nor gladly. The perfect person submits precisely because he or she realizes that the human being is simply one expression of nature coordinating with the rest of nature. To be perfect is to be completely natural, to be completely rational."[835] Wesley wrote, "I now see a Stoic and a Christian are

---

[831]Ironside, *Holiness, the False and the True*, 39.

[832]Thompson, "Witness of American Methodism," 810.

[833]Dayton conceded "there was no clear precedent in early Wesleyan theology" for use of the term to describe cleansing or purification [*Contemporary Wesleyan Theology*, 1:530]. White also conceded that Wesley did not use the term, but argued that he believed in the concept [*Eradication*, 38].

[834]Dunn, *Romans 1-8*, 319. Godet concluded that "the translation *destroyed* probably renders the thought best" [*Commentary on Romans*, 245]. Herman Cremer described Paul's use of this term, "With him it always denotes a complete, not a temporary or partial ceasing. Elsewhere it signifies a putting out of activity, out of power or effect; but with St. Paul it equals to *annihilate*, to put an end to, to bring to naught" [*Biblico-Theological Lexicon*, 261].

[835]Bassett, *Holiness Teaching*, 44-45.

different characters."[836]

"In no religion is the perfection of the saint as something won and realized during life so emphatically conceded and insisted upon as it is in early Buddhism." Yet Buddha taught that desire is the root of suffering. Desire causes attachment, which leads to suffering and which causes others to suffer. This produces negative karma. The goal is to become enlightened, as Buddha. In the enlightened state one eliminates desire and stops causing suffering. The perfect or ideal state was spoken of by the negative term "nirvana," which meant extinction or the elimination of all sinful qualities and painful conditions.[837] But is desire always a bad thing? Murphree wrote,

> Being human we find it impossible not to want. Even when we are wanting not to want, we are still wanting. Sanctification is not a cessation of desire. The idea is not to stop wanting, but to redirect one's wants, to replace inferior desires with worthy ones.[838]

Sam Powell explained that sin does not lie in the object of desire but in the fact that we desire created things instead of God.[839]

Yet isn't the desire for enlightenment within Buddhism still desire? If so, how can one ever attain enlightenment? Pope objected to the final perfection of Buddhism, claiming that nirvana was an abyss of absolute extinction.[840] If perfection is the finite absorbed by the infinite, how would one know if he had arrived at this state of perfection having lost all self consciousness?

Therefore, carnal traits such as pride, anger, jealousy and desire are not removed but redirected.[841] A holy person is fully human and no human emotion is destroyed. For example, ζέω (*zeo*) is used both in a positive sense (*zealous* - Rom 12:11) and a negative sense (*jealous* - Rom 13:13). God does not remove

---

[836]Wesley, *Letter* to Miss J. C. March, 30 November, 1774; see also 27 December, 1774 in which Wesley wrote, "I desire no apathy in religion; a Christian is very far from a Stoic."

[837]Rhys Davids, "Perfection (Buddist)," 9:727; see also Jones, *Christ of the Mount*, 42.

[838]Murphree, *Love Motive*, 18.

[839]Powell, *Discovering our Christian Faith*, 140.

[840]Pope, *Compendium*, 3:231.

[841]Lowery described perfection as the reordering and reformulating of one's value system and maxims. "This entails real moral change while emphasizing both human responsibility and divine assistance" [*Salvaging Wesley's Agenda*, 294].

our passion; instead he redirects it.

God himself is jealous (Exod 20:5). He is angry with the wicked (Psalm 7:11). Jesus Christ experienced such human emotions as anger (Matt 21:12; John 2:14-15; 11:33) and sorrow (John 11:35). Seamands explained that there are no sinful emotions, only sinful uses of emotions. We should not pray that anger be eradicated, but that it be redirected to that which makes God angry.[842]

If holiness is full conformity to the image of Christ and Christ was angry, we should not pray for anger to be removed but redirected. The sinful nature is a twisting or perversion of that which is natural and normal, not a physical substance. Meekness (πραΰτης - *praotes*) is the balance between excessive anger and passivity. It is power under control. A man who is meek is the man who is always angry at the right time and never angry at the wrong time.[843] Wesley declared that "anger at sin, accompanied with love and compassion to the sinner, is so far from being itself a sin, that it is rather a duty."[844]

While there is a promised cleansing from the sinful nature, the questions is how do we realize that deeper cleansing? Miley observed that while the Scriptures are "full of the idea of entire sanctification, they are quite empty of any such [second-blessing] teaching respecting the mode of its attainment."[845] While the atonement of Christ provides complete and radical victory over sin, when the metaphoric expression, "the body of sin," is interpreted substantively and coupled with the strongest sense of this verb, it can lead to the use of eradication language.

We make a mistake when we fail to recognize that *katargeo* is a figure of speech. Then the sin nature is conceived as being a physical or material substance that is destroyed or annihilated through a crisis experience. While *katargeo* can mean utter destruction, how can a figure of speech be utterly destroyed? Paul is using phenomenal language to describe spiritual victory. Zink declared that the terms uncleanness, defilement, and filthiness do not suggest something material to be removed. Nor do the terms washed, cleansed, purified suggest something material has been removed. "These Bible terms have no material meaning."[846]

If sin is considered to be a substance, when it is removed the result is a spiritual state of sinlessness. This substantive concept is referred to as "ontological," meaning that sin and sanctification are granted the status of being or objective reality. But sin should be considered to be a brokenness relationally and sanctification should be considered as teleological, meaning a gradual moral

---

[842]Seamands, *Putting Away Childish Things*, 45-50.

[843]Barclay, *New Testament Words*, 241.

[844]Wesley, Letter to a Member of the Society, 31 May, 1771.

[845]Miley, *Systematic Theology*, 2:370.

[846]Zink, *Review of Dr. Huntington*, 11-12.

transformation.[847]

While scripture uses phenomenal language, it is a mistake to interpret this language concretely. Al Truesdale calls this tendency "reification." Reification is the fallacy of treating an abstraction as substantive.[848] The problem is, that in our attempt to explain entire sanctification, preachers have used phenomenal language to explain a spiritual process. In other words, we have tried to make a spiritual process more easily understood by comparing it to physical processes. For example, our old life of sin is compared to a tree, which is cut down when we get saved. But the old life attempts to come back by growing new shoots. So, when we get sanctified the stump is pulled out. Or, the sinful nature is likened to a rotten tooth which must be extracted. Or it is Leviathan, a crocodile which must be killed. I have seen a holiness evangelist wrestle that crocodile all over the platform. It made for very entertaining preaching, but these attempts to explain a spiritual process in physical terms are very misleading.

Eradicate means to pull up by the roots. The danger in using this term is that it conveys the concept that sin is a physical substance that can be removed once and for all, like a tooth is extracted or the roots of a tree dug out. This would result in a permanent state of sinlessness, yet Wesley taught that there was no state of grace from which we could not fall. We must always watch and pray, while trusting the present tense cleansing of the blood as we walk in light (1 John 1:7). Therefore, Sangster wrote that the controversy could not, and cannot, be settled by quoting καταργηθῇ.[849] While the word "eradication" is not found in scripture, the Bible contains metaphoric expressions which are incorrectly interpreted literally as proof of the doctrine of eradication. John L. Peters set the stage for the holiness movement's distinctive doctrine of eradication.

> In later holiness history two terms came to be the shibboleths of opposing factions. These were "eradication" and "suppression." The first symbolized the position of the out-and-out perfectionist; the second often characterized his not-so-certain brother. In Wesley's day the issue was between "destroyed" and "suspended." Wesley, though favoring the first as to terminology, was hardly partisan enough in his teaching to give aid and comfort exclusively to either camp. It is true that Wesley, again following Pauline analogy, uses such terms as

---

[847]Lowrey, *Salvaging Wesley's Agenda,* 282.

[848]Truesdale, "Reification of the Experience of Entire Sanctification," 95-119.

[849]Sangster, *Path to Perfection*, 115. The Greek word Sangster cited is the third person singular aorist passive subjunctive form of *katargeo*, the form used in Rom 6:6.

"eradicate" and "destroy." "I used the word 'destroyed,'" he said, "because St. Paul does; 'suspended' I cannot find in my Bible."[850] But in his immediate context he states, "Indeed, the unclean spirit, though driven out, may return and enter again; nevertheless he was driven out." What Wesley means by "destroyed," then, is "driven out." For Wesley taught, it should be remembered, that whatever it was that happened in entire sanctification (or any other phase of the Christian life) was sustained on a moment-by-moment basis. Consequently, the terms "eradication" and "destruction" may be used, if at all, only in the most qualified fashion. They are not congruous with a teaching which calls for such a sense of momentary reliance nor which allows the possibility of backsliding and restoration. A term far more appropriate to Wesley's thought is the term "expulsion." "Entire sanctification," he said, ". . . is neither more nor less than pure love — love expelling sin and governing both the heart and life."[851] And this is what he preached: It is love excluding sin; love filling the heart, taking up the whole capacity of the soul. . . . For as long as love takes up the whole heart, what room is there for sin therein?[852] Here in Wesley is the explicit teaching of the "expulsive power of a new affection." But again Wesley does not contend for a term: "Call this the destruction or suspension of sin, it is a glorious work."

"The expulsive power of a new affection" was the description of Thomas Chalmers (1780-1847). The phrase describes a dynamic present-tense relationship, not a permanent, static state. Until we reach Eternity there must be continual maintenance. According to 1 John 4:18, perfect love drives out (present tense) or displaces fear.[853] Thus, entire sanctification is a condition in which the love of God expels or displaces sin and this condition must be maintained moment by moment as we walk in the light. Colin Williams called this "a perfection of

---

[850]Wesley, Letter to Joseph Benson, 5 October, 1770. In this same letter Wesley said that in the sanctified person holy tempers presently reign to the point of driving out opposing tempers, although they may return.

[851]Wesley, Letter to Walter Churchey, 21 February, 1771.

[852]Wesley, "The Scripture Way of Salvation, Sermon #43, I.9; III.14.

[853]After evaluating eradication language, Murphree opted for the term "replacement" [*Love Motive*, 44-46]. Leclerc says that love excludes sin [*Discovering Christian Holiness*, 151].

unbroken conscious dependence upon Christ."[854]

Wesley taught that in the soul of a person entirely sanctified love reigns to the point of driving out sinful affections. He spoke of "love filling the heart, expelling pride, anger, desire, self-will."[855] Wesley believed that we could be so full of the love of God that there was no room for sin, but it is only as we are filled with divine love that sin is displaced. Wesley used the phrase "love excluding sin."[856] He described this love as sitting "upon the throne which is erected in the inmost soul; namely, love of God and man, which fills the whole heart, and reigns without a rival."[857]

Stephen Merrill taught that sanctification began with regeneration, but it was not then completed. It is something that never becomes a past experience. "So by faith the cleansing process goes on, washing away the defilements that otherwise would gather upon the soul, and purging the corruptions that survive the beginning of the new life."[858] Thomas Cook wrote, "We teach, therefore not a *state of purity*, but a *maintained condition of purity*, a moment-by-moment salvation consequent upon a moment-by-moment obedience and trust."[859] Peters described entire sanctification as an expulsion which was sustained on a moment-by-moment basis.[860] Olin Curtis wrote that Wesley held "that the civil war in the perfect Christian is rendered impossible by love, supreme love toward God and man. Whether the natural disposition is extirpated or only overwhelmed, it does not appear in a consciousness full to the brim of pure love."[861]

Over time, however, this emphasis on divine love was replaced by an emphasis on human will and our ability to make moral choices, which were restored in regeneration. Perfect holiness was viewed as an ideal to be pursued

---

[854]Williams, *John Wesley's Theology Today*, 179.

[855]Wesley, *Works*, 11:418.

[856]Wesley, "Scripture Way of Salvation," Sermon #43, 1.9; see also *Journal*, 29 October 1762. Perkins said the doctrine of Christian perfection rests on the hypothesis that the divine love is continually striving to overcome the sinfulness of human nature [*Evangelical Perfection*, 13].

[857]"On Zeal," Sermon #92, 2.5.

[858]Merrill, *Doctrinal Aspects of Christian Experience*, 190. Merrill also wrote, "Sanctification is neither identical with regeneration nor Christian perfection, while it accompanies both and has specific relation to each" [p. 192].

[859]Cook, *New Testament Holiness*, 43.

[860]Peters, *Christian Perfection*, 56-59.

[861]Curtis, *Christian Faith*, 383.

through habitual rational control over our lower nature.[862]

Finally there was a growing emphasis from the holiness movement that the baptism of the Holy Spirit eradicated the sinful nature producing a spontaneous rational control.[863] In 1897 Seth C. Rees wrote, "Holiness is a state; entire sanctification is an experience; the Holy Ghost is a person. We come into the state of holiness through the experience of entire sanctification, wrought by the omnipotent energies of the Holy Ghost."[864]

In *Entire Sanctification: The Distinctive Doctrine of Wesleyanism*, J. Kenneth Grider linked the popularity of eradication language to leaders in the American holiness movement, such as J. A. Wood in *Perfect Love* (1861), H. C. Morrison in *Baptism with the Holy Ghost* (1900), S. S. White, *Eradication* (1954). While Grider said that the holiness movement does not use the term much any more, he argued for the validity of the term.[865] Grider felt it was appropriate to use physical analogies, like getting the stump pulled out, to illustrate spiritual truths. However, Ralph Earle conceded that he regarded terms like "eradication" as misleading.[866] Recently Leclerc, representing the same Nazarene tradition,

---

[862]For example, see the reference to Merritt Caldwell on p. 408 of this book. This amounts to a shift from free grace to free will. Leclerc said that at times Wesleyans have embraced a practical Pelagianism [*Discovering Christian Holiness*, 168]. However, this is the result of Finney's influence and certainly a reflection of Wesley's teaching.

[863]This shift was traced by Maddox, "Reconnecting the Means to the End," 41-50.

[864]Rees, *Ideal Pentecostal Church*, 13. McDonald declared, "In regeneration sin does not *reign*; in sanctification it does not *exist* [cited by A. M. Hills, *Holiness and Power*, 77].

Yet Wesley wrote that he disliked talking of a *state* of sanctification. In an open letter, Wesley commented on a statement in the minutes, "Does not talking of a justified or a sanctified state tend to mislead men? almost naturally leading them to trust in what was done in one moment? Whereas we are every hour and every moment pleasing or displeasing to God according to our works, according to the whole of our inward tempers and our outward behaviour." His comment was, "Every hour God is more or less pleased with us according to the whole of our inward and outward behaviour" [*Letter*, 10 July 1771]. However, Sangster said Wesley appears inconsistent in speaking of sanctification sometimes as a state and sometimes as a moment-by-moment life [*Path to Perfection*, 144].

[865]Grider, *Entire Sanctification*, 138. Although eradication language is not utilized much, according to Grider, on p. 28 he himself uses the same analogy of getting the stump pulled out.

[866]Earle, Letter to Robert Shank, 9 Jan 1960.

declared that the word has lost its power and relevance in the present context.[867]

In his *Systematic Theology*, John Miley raised the question, "Is the inner work of entire sanctification in the mode of repression or in that of eradication?" Miley cites some of the Methodist writers of his day and argues against eradication because the theory of eradication allows "no possible lapse from that state."[868] Miley rejected the implications of eradication, but concluded "sanctification is entire when the spiritual life attains complete dominance."[869]

Daniel D. Whedon wrote concerning the "abuse of figurative terms" that sanctification is

> less the taking away any thing than the bestowment of a repressive power over our inward tendencies. We do not say that the idea of taking away is excluded; but that the idea of bestowing is the predominant and literal, while the idea of *taking away* is the subordinate, inferential, and often metaphorical. When, for instance, a governor bestows pardon on a criminal, you can say, less properly, he takes away his guilt. And so of the sanctified man, as the Spirit enables him to live thus purely, you can say that "sin is all cast out," "evil tempers are abolished," "lusts are wholly removed," "the roots of sin are plucked out," "our inbred corruption is ejected." These metaphors, like all metaphors, are literally untruth, but they have legitimate place and use of rousing and inspiriting our feelings and actions. Only let them keep their place, and not be used in the process of exact analysis of actual realities.[870]

Bishop Foster first wrote *Christian Purity* in 1869,

> It is not the office of grace to eradicate human passions. There is nothing in them, when existing in a normal state, of the nature of sin. They were at first implanted in the holy pair. They will remain in humanity while the earthly life remains. Holiness requires their proper subjugation and use. They are in their nature physical, and wholly void of moral character except as

---

[867]Leclerc, *Discovering Christian Holiness*, 203.

[868]Miley, *Systematic Theology,* 2:363-366. Richard S. Taylor felt it necessary to correct Miley at this point [*Leading Wesleyan Thinkers*, 222].

[869]Miley, *Systematic Theology*, 2:365.

[870]Whedon, *Statements*, 345-348.

they become instruments of righteousness or unrighteousness.[871]

Foster seemed to teach a repression of sin when he wrote,

> It may be well to explain here, more particularly, both with respect to the natural dispositions and propensities. These are not supposed to be destroyed when a soul is entirely freed from sin, but only brought under right government and restored to a proper character — not allowed to be instruments of sin. Evil dispositions and propensities are but perverted forms of good ones; and hence, holiness or sanctification consists not in the eradication of them, but in the restoration of them to their legitimate character and use. Nothing is further from the truth than the idea that any work of grace destroys any power either of the soul or body, or imparts any new faculty. Grace enters the soul to restore dead affections, make them alive, make them grow, and to exscind and pluck up false growths; to make the soul right, not to destroy any part of it or create any new parts. The passions of the body are not, any more than the faculties of the soul, removed. They are but regulated; they remain, and have their appropriate use as much in the entirely sanctified as in the unfallen Adam; but they are servants of righteousness now, and not of sin.[872]

Huntington argued that inbred sin was not a physical entity. He described depravity as a perversion, not a creation. He argued that sanctification was not a work of removal or destruction, but a permanent subjugation.[873] J. Agar Beet wrote in *Holiness As Understood by Writers of the Bible*:

> This complete and abiding victory over all sin in thought, word, or deed marks, I venture to believe, a stage of the Christian life higher than justification and sufficiently definite to be an object of thought and faith. The discovery that by faith Jesus saves us now by his power from all sin has been an era in the spiritual life of thousands. It may be suitably called full salvation, or, as we

---

[871]Foster, *Christian Purity*, 68-69.

[872]Foster, *Christian Purity*, 74.

[873]Huntington, *Sin and Holiness*, 77; 122; 104; 137. However, I do not accept the distinction made by him and Boland between inbred sin and depravity. Mudge also rejected eradication [*Growth in Holiness*, 212, 214, 224].

> look at its positive side, entire sanctification. But, although day by day as we trample them under foot the inward forces of evil become weaker and by their increasing weakness reveal our spiritual growth, yet I do not find anywhere in the Bible reason to believe that they may now by our faith or at any future time in our lives be entirely annihilated.[874]

John Brash, a Wesleyan minister who joined with three other such ministers in 1872 to form *The King's Highway* in order to promote full salvation, found the literature coming from America "very mechanical" and preferred to emphasize that holiness was "living union with a living Saviour." He felt eradication language was unscriptural and "the figure is one that has no application to the case, and no correspondence to anything the Spirit does in the human heart."[875] S. J. Gamertsfelder wrote

> The carnality that must be removed in entire sanctification is not material substance. It cannot be weighed nor measured, nor handled with hands nor moved with a derrick. It is some form of moral or ethical activity; it is evil tendencies and desires. The only way to eradicate these evil tendencies and desires is to fill the soul with good tendencies and desires. When these new affections completely fill the soul and engage all its powers, there will be no room for any evil affection to arise in the mind.[876]

Edward Sugden, who edited a critical edition of Wesley's *Works*, in his introduction to Wesley's sermon "Christian Perfection," Sermon #40, accused Wesley of creating confusion by teaching that the carnal mind is something which can be removed "like an aching tooth or a cancerous growth."[877] W. E. Sangster, in *The Path to Perfection*, has a chapter "Can Sin be Eradicated?" He thinks

---

[874]Beet, *Holiness As Understood*, 69; see also Beet, *Shorter Manual of Theology*, 124. However, Charles W. Rishell wrote that in all of Methodist literature, this statement by Beet is the only exception to Methodism's usual optimism of grace. Rishell expressed surprised that Beet had not been challenged on this statement ["Doctrine of Sanctification Psychologically Developed," 518].

[875]Page, *John Brash*, 38; 33.

[876]Gamertsfelder, *Systematic Theology*, 516.

[877]Sugden, *Works of John Wesley*, 2:148-150.

Sugden was right in his assessment of Wesley, but argued against eradication.[878] Wynkoop also accused Wesley of holding a substantival concept of sin.[879]

However, Laurence Wood demonstrated that the term "carnal" was a metaphor and that Paul did not think of sin as a physical substance. He concluded it was not Wesley, but Sugden himself who came closest to a materialistic concept of sin.[880] Cox was aware that both Sangster and Flew were critical of Wesley's definition of sin, but Cox concluded "a careful study of Wesley reveals that for him sin was no 'thing.'" But Wesley thought of sin in scriptural terms and if the scripture speaks of sin metaphorically, then Wesley is guilty of conveying that same metaphor in his writings. However, Wesley did not attach sin to the human body as Calvinism has tended to do. "Sin had no existence in material essence any more than love did."[881]

More recently, H. Ray Dunning, in *Grace, Faith, and Holiness: A Wesleyan Systematic Theology*, referenced the Sugden criticism and argued that sin in believers is not substantival in nature, but a condition contrary to the mind of Christ.[882] Nazarene theologians such as Mildred Bangs Wynkoop and Ray Dunning have a more relational understanding of sin and holiness,[883] while Kenneth Grider[884] and Richard S. Taylor contend for the American holiness emphasis. In *Exploring Christian Holiness* Taylor argued for the necessity of

---

[878]Sangster, *Path to Perfection*, 113-117. See also Turner, *More Excellent Way*, 247.

[879]Wynkoop, *Theology of Love*, 153.

[880]Wood, *Pentecostal Grace*, 146. Yet in *Meaning of Pentecost* Wood cited one example in which an early Methodist, James Creighton, gave his testimony to holiness speaking of Christian perfection as the means "to eradicate sin" [p. 335; Creighton, "Account of the Experiences," 402].

[881]Cox, *Perfection*, 125-126.

[882]Dunning, *Grace, Faith, and Holiness*, 481-485. Miley wrote that "Depravity is a moral state of the soul, not a substance within it" [*Systematic Theology*, 2:358]. Foster wrote that a substantive view of sin grossly corrupts our understanding [*Christian Purity*, 119].

[883]Greathouse declared, "If the quintessence of sin is a perverted relationship to God, the quintessence of holiness is a grace-restored right relationship" [*Historical Development*, 207].

[884]See Grider's attempt to defend eradication language and reconcile it with the relational view in *Entire Sanctification*, 27-29. Yet on p. 138 he conceded that eradication language was misunderstood and is not used much any more.

eradication.[885] He argued that a substance may be either material or nonmaterial.[886] This seems like a case of "special pleading" to me.

In his essay "Why the Holiness Movement Died," Taylor lays the blame with Mildred Wynkoop because she advocates a relational view of sin instead of Taylor's more substantive or materialistic view. Taylor felt that his concept of eradication is essential to the holiness message. Thus carnality is perceived as something, often compared to a tree stump, which was removed by the second blessing.[887] Although Taylor tries to distance himself, and the holiness movement, from a substantive view of sin, he previously argued that it was reasonable to believe that the sin nature was passed down through the genetic code.[888] While this has been debated across the last twenty years, according to Samuel Powell, an "uneasy truce" now exists.[889]

Wynkoop rejected eradication as a magical elimination of a thing and a mutilation of personality.[890] At a more popular level David Seamands wrote that the perfect love, described in 1 Corinthians 13, will not be found "until there is *katargeo*." Seamands admitted that it was hard to distinguish between original sin and damaged emotions. A parishioner told him, "David, all this time I've heard it was the 'old man,' and now you're saying it is a 'little child' within me causing the problem." Seamands wrote that "putting away childish things" is both the ultimate crisis and a never-ending process. God can reprogram those old ways and lead us to Christian maturity, but we must break its power and render it inoperative by taking responsibility and seeking the healing power of the Holy Spirit.[891] Wesley advised seekers to "rejoice, if sin is suspended till it is totally

---

[885]Taylor, *Theological Formulation*, 104.

[886]Taylor, *Theological Formulation*, 3:100.

[887]Taylor, "Why the Holiness Movement Died," 50-55.

[888]Taylor, *Theological Formulation*, 3:96-98.

[889]Powell, *Holiness in the 21st Century,* 11. Powell had previously written that "holiness has become a problematic topic in Wesleyan circles" ["Introduction," 13].

[890]Wynkoop, *Theology of Love*, 73; 164. She also rejected the doctrine of eradication as based on a Calvinistic view of human nature. She described "Calvinistic Wesleyanism" as holding to a sort of dual human nature. This always creates the dilemma of how to distinguish between human nature and carnal nature. Eradication is the removal of the carnal nature [*Foundations*, 77-78]. Geisler pointed out that the stanch Calvinist, B. B. Warfield, himself embraced a form of eradicationism [*Systematic Theology*, 3:585-586].

[891]Seamands, *Putting Away Childish Things*, 10, 13, 17, 49, 127. In his *Systematic Theology*, 3:580 Norman Geisler quotes me as arguing that Wesley did not believe in eradication since Wesley emphasized the need for believers to continue the

destroyed."[892] The danger is not that we preach a complete cleansing; the danger is that we infer such a cleansing produces automatic sinlessness. We must always watch and pray.

In holiness theology, the second blessing results in a permanent state of sanctification. The teaching that the sinful nature is eradicated leads to the conclusion that entire sanctification is a permanent state. Wesley taught that whatever it was that happened in entire sanctification (or any other phase of the Christian life) was sustained on a moment-by-moment basis. Oden declared, "If the complete eradication of all possibility of sin were God's way of dealing with our fallen nature, then there would be little point in talking further of the continuing work of the Spirit."[893]

Does eradication result in a sinless state? Does this eradication include the subconscious mind? If the sin nature were eradicated in parents, how could it be passed on to their children? If it comes through Adam and not immediately through the parents, would the sanctified parents still be in need of the cleansing blood moment by moment? If sin is eradicated and then the person backslides, does the sin nature return? Some in the holiness movement have taught that the entirely sanctified person who back slid would need forgiveness, but not cleansing since eradication would result in a permanent state. Thus, they teach "once sanctified, always sanctified."

This dogmatic paradigm was demonstrated in the case of A. L. Brewer. In 1878 at the annual conference of the Southern Methodist Church of North Missouri, A. L. Brewer was to be ordained. The bishop asked him, "Are you going on to perfection? Do you expect to be made perfect in this life? Are you groaning after it?" Brewer interrupted the bishop saying, "Bishop, if you please, I cannot answer this and the other two questions in the affirmative." The bishop asked why not and Brewer answered, "Because I have that experience now." This was reported as "a grand victory for holiness."[894] More properly it distinguishes the contrast between the emphasis of the holiness movement and the emphasis of historic Wesleyan teaching.

1. Anyone who professes not to be pursuing holiness because they have obtained it, is disobedient to the admonition of Hebrews 12:14.

---

process of breaking sin's power in their lives. Then Geisler quotes David Seamands and the emphasis of Seamands that sanctification is both the ultimate crisis and a never-ending process [*Systematic Theology*, 3:580].

[892]Wesley, *Works*, 11:405.

[893]Oden, *Life in the Spirit*, 234.

[894]Keirgan, *Historical Sketches*, pp. 12-13; see also Jones, "Anti-Ordinance," 7-23. Jones traced the career of Brewer to its conclusion where Brewer admitted to being a fanatic who felt that Jesus was just another great moral teacher like Buddha.

2. Everyone who is truly regenerate has received the Holy Spirit and is therefore made holy. John Wesley taught that while sin remained, it did not reign in the believer.

3. It is the work of the indwelling Spirit to make us more like Christ; more holy.

4. Those who are the most like Christ have the deepest realization that they need to be made more like Christ. Those in whom the Holy Spirit is working the strongest have the greatest hunger for more holiness. One of the surest signs a person is holy is that he is seeking more holiness. Those who have truly been filled are those who have the greatest spiritual appetite.

5. How can we pursue what we have already obtained? Whatever degree of holiness we have obtained is derived from God. Just as the moon has no light of its own, but reflects the light of the sun, so I have no holiness of my own. Only God is absolutely holy. He is the source of all holiness. I am made holy only so long as I am in communion with him. I am not "saved and sanctified" as though that was a permanent state; it is as I walk in the light that his blood cleanses me. In 1 John 1:7, the Greek present tense for *cleanse* means that his blood *keeps on cleansing* us from all sin. I am not perfect; but his perfecting grace is at work within me.

Some earlier holiness writers did not think there would be any need to pray "Forgive us our debts" if sin had been eradicated. Later writers felt there were at least infirmities which were appropriate for the sanctified to confess.[895]

A misunderstanding of this concept of deliverance from sin has also left

---

[895]See Watson's answer, *Theological Institutes*, 2:456, which was repeated by Wakefield, *Christian Theology*, 454; Richard Treffry, *Treatise on Christian Perfection*, 65-67. Yet Charles Hodge answered Watson by arguing that the use of the Lord's Prayer by all Christians is an acknowledgment that no Christian in this life is perfect [*Systematic Theology*, 3:249-250]. See the rebuttal by Lowrey, *Possibilities of Grace*, 246-251 and Quanstrom's discussion, *Century of Holiness Theology*, 106-107. Vincent Perronet, Vicar of Shoreham, responded to the question of how a Christian could pray the collects of the church asking for forgiveness if he enjoyed "sinless or Christian perfection." In 1746, even before he attended his first Methodist conference in 1747 but two years after he began a long conversation with Wesley, he wrote that however holy or perfect, the believer must still grow in grace, striving to love God fully as well as loving even his worst enemies. At the least, any believer must confess every day and even every hour, "for where is that Saint upon Earth, who can say, he has spent the preceding Day, or even Hour, with all that Care, and Watchfulness, and Diligence; and with all that Patience, and Self-denial, and Christian Love, and universal Charity; and that he has improved himself as much in Faith, and Grace, and the Knowledge of Christ; and in the Fear, and Knowledge, and Love of God, as it was possible for him to do" [Perronet, *Some Reflections*]. Bloesch observed that the public prayer of confession of sin is generally absent in the worship services of holiness churches [*Holy Spirit*, 142].

holiness theologians to struggle over whether a backslider loses one work or two and whether a reclaimed backslider has to come back to God in two stages.[896]

John Wesley was once asked in open conference if any one could fall from a sanctified state without at the same time losing justification. Wesley's only reply was to read his brother's hymn

O may the least omission pain
My well-instructed soul,
And drive me to the blood again
Which makes the wounded whole.[897]

Christian perfection is a moment-by-moment experience. The fact that I am victorious over sin at one moment is no guarantee that I will conquer it in the next moment, although the tendency may become more and more habitual. Sugden then introduced this statement by Wesley, saying it was one of the wisest things he ever said:

> Does not talking of a justified or a sanctified *state* tend to mislead men? Almost naturally leading them to trust in what was done in one moment? Whereas, we are every hour and every moment pleasing or displeasing to God, according to our works; according to the whole of our inward tempers, and our outward behavior.

---

[896]See Smith, *Backslider and His Recovery*. S. I. Emery taught that carnality, once eradicated cannot return. One may need forgiveness for backsliding, but never need to be sanctified again. John Knight explained that original sin is not a material entity which cannot return once its roots are destroyed. Understood relationally, the sin nature that was cleansed in a moment must continue to be cleansed moment by moment [*Holiness Pilgrimage*, 84].

J. A. Wood taught that persons could lose the grace of entire sanctification without necessarily losing their justification [*Perfect Love*, 291-292]. But Huntington asked, "If souls forfeit and lose this state of salvation from the existence of 'inbred sin,' this loss must result from the fact of sin. And does a sanctified soul fall into a justified state by committing sin? Is this not depreciating justification? And if a soul, in whom all the effects of ancestral sin have been destroyed, does fall into sin, is it not sin against superior light? Is not the guilt of sin graded by the light which is sinned against? In case a soul 'merely justified' should thus sin against his light, would he retain his justified state?" [*Sin and Holiness*, 108-109]. Shelhamer argued that one could not lose holiness and retain justification [*Bible Holiness*, 115-118]. Leo Cox argued that one could be lost without necessarily losing the other [*Perfection*, 178-179].

[897]Tillett and Nutter, *Hymns and Hymn Writers of the Church*, 173.

Sugden concluded that "geometry loses none of its value because there never was . . . a perfectly straight line or an absolutely true circle." Christian perfection is an ideal "to which the believer approximates ever more closely, though it may be impossible to say that he has absolutely attained it."[898] Donald Bloesch wrote, "We should never speak of a sinless perfection attainable in this life (as do some in the wider Wesleyan movement), but we can hold up the possibility of perfect love, love that comes from God and takes us into itself, though this is something momentary, something that has to be received again and again."[899]

3. A Distinct Holiness Subculture

Writing in 1929 Merrill Gaddis concluded that the holiness movement suffered from misinformation, provincialism, and hyper-individualism. He explained that "primary group" control is quite essential to the peaceful continuity of a "Spirit-guided" order of things in a local congregation. The result of such control, however, is smaller congregations. Thus, in 1929, the average membership of a holiness congregation was about one-third that of the Methodist Church.[900]

Yet the holiness movement taught that only they would go up in the rapture. It is not unusual for cults and religious fringe groups who feel disenfranchised to teach a partial rapture. There is some sense of superiority in teaching that only the special, the elect, or the super-spiritual will be so favored by God. Actually, this doctrine of election has only substituted sanctification for predestination.

G. D. Watson taught that "the Bride of Christ does not comprise all of those who are saved, but a select company out from that body who have been conformed to Christ in His life and sufferings and ministry in a special degree." Just as Eve was taken from Adam's body, so the Bride is taken from the Church. "Those who make up the Bride must not only be saved but sanctified in the most

---

[898]Sugden, *Works of John Wesley*, 2:149-150. The quote from Wesley was from "Minutes of Several Conversations between Wesley and Others," (1770) *Works*, 8:338.

Wynkoop said that when Wesley related perfection to the human situation, the "absolute" of sanctification was no longer "perfect." "Whenever perfection is understood in an absolute sense — a point beyond which there can be no further development — it can be called perfectionism. New Testament writers knew nothing of this kind of thinking" [*Theology of Love*, 270; 274].

[899]Bloesch, *Jesus Christ: Savior and Lord*, 183.

[900]Gaddis, *Christian Perfection in America*, 533-534; 540.

thorough degree."[901]

W. B. Godbey also made this distinction between the church and the bride. Just as the church was called out of the world, so the bride was the elect from within the church which had received the second work of grace. Godbey wrote an entire chapter entitled "the pentecostal experience indispensable to a place in the bridehood."[902] By this time Godbey had equated pentecost with entire sanctification. Godbey taught that only the bride, or the "sanctified," would be raptured.[903] Therefore, when Christ returned with his saints to set up the millennial kingdom, only the "sanctified" would reign with him. While Wesley had preached that holiness was the wedding garment which prepares us for the marriage of the Lamb, the holiness of which he referred included justification by faith.[904]

The holiness movement became a different class of people, with a different emphasis and a different world view. In many instances they had no choice but to leave Methodism and with the more conservative element gone, Methodism quickly turned liberal. As the new movement assimilated more and more people from outside Methodism, they moved further from the emphasis of Wesley. They became more rigid in their insistence on a second crisis experience and for them holiness became a static state. The experience could be received instantaneously and was to be confessed emphatically. Progressive growth after the crisis was not emphasized and the experience became an end in itself.

The later holiness movement did demand a second crisis experience whether or not the professor demonstrated godly character. There was a move away from the fruit of the Spirit toward the gifts of the Spirit. Power was stressed over purity. James Dunn observed that toward the close of the nineteenth century, especially in America, there was a shift from sanctification and holiness to an emphasis on power and spiritual gifts.[905] Douglas Frank writes about the rise of Christian heroes who have God's power through the baptism of the Holy Spirit. He finds this theme is characteristic of the American church at the turn of the nineteenth century. He concluded that all too often the hero's message was manipulative and superficial and that his confidence was in the flesh.[906]

Wesley Tracy observed that the early Wesleyans were quick to seek

---

[901]Watson, *Bridehood Saints*, 4-7.

[902]Godbey, *Church-Bride-Kingdom*, 88-97.

[903]Godbey, *Commentary*, 1:232-233; 254.

[904]Wesley, "On the Wedding Garment," Sermon # 127, § 18-19.

[905]Dunn, *Baptism in the Holy Spirit*, 2.

[906]Frank, *Less Than Conquerors*, 232-270.

sanctifying grace but slow to profess it. Today there is a real danger that people are pressured into a profession of sanctifying grace prematurely. The result is spiritual confusion.[907] The positive confession teaching counsels people to "just say it." However, we are not made holy merely because we profess it, claim it, or confess it to be so. Early Methodism was quick to seek and slow to profess Christian perfection. Later holiness people were quick to profess, but often short on living it. Methodism taught holy living through the discipline of a method, utilizing the means of grace. The holiness movement taught an emotional experience through an act of the will.

There is little seeking after holiness today within any theological camp. Among the holiness denominations people are not often pursuing holiness because they profess to be holy and they see no need to pursue what they have already obtained once and for all. Yet A. W. Tozer wrote, "to have found God and still to pursue him is the soul's paradox of love."[908]

The popular teaching of the holiness movement requires two trips to the altar instead of one. A Christian is "up and down" or "carnal" until he becomes "Spirit-filled." The second work of grace is promised as a cure-all to rectify the deficiencies of the new birth. It is obtained by the name it and claim it method,[909] and the seeker who professes it at some point faces the realization that he is still haunted by the same old sins. The modern holiness movement is as powerless as the rest of the nominal church and is not exempt from the antinomianism that plagues every other denomination. In practical experience there may be little difference between the godly Calvinist who "sins every day" and the careless holiness professor who excuses his sins as "mistakes."

When Wesley said Methodism was raised up to "spread scriptural holiness" he certainly had far more in mind than one specific doctrine. Yet the primary purpose for the existence of the American holiness movement was the preservation and proclamation of one doctrine. This is too narrow a purpose. The contemporary holiness movement cannot go back to eighteenth century Methodism or to the nineteenth century camp meeting. It cannot make tradition or experience the ultimate authority. The only way to avoid drowning in a sea of subjectivity is to accept the Word of God as the sole authority for faith and practice and preach it expositionally. In formulating a Biblical theology for today, the early Methodists with their careful exegesis of Scripture and their balanced understanding of theology, have much to contribute.

In contrast to Palmer's "shorter way," which the holiness movement adopted, Bounds identified two other positions in the larger Wesleyan-Arminian

---

[907]Tracy, "Entire Sanctification and Uncertain Trumpets," 6-7.

[908]Tozer, *Pursuit of God*, 15.

[909]DeNeff, *Whatever Became of Holiness?* 90.

tradition. He described "the middle way" as entire sanctification by seeking until you receive. Sanctifying grace is seen as a gift of grace, more grace than is made available at conversion. "The longer way"sees entire sanctification as a long process of growth. Some will realize entire sanctification in the present life, but most will not experience it until just before death or at the point of glorification.[910] While the "shorter way" separates perfect love and maturity, "the longer way" requires maturity in order to have perfect love. We need the balance of "the middle way," a perfect love which leads to a progressive perfection.

---

[910]Online: Bounds, "Spiritual Transformation," 2-5.

CHAPTER 8
A THEOLOGY of EXPERIENCE: THE HOLINESS-PENTECOSTAL MOVEMENT

We are tracing in history seventeen theological positions on holiness. Early in the twentieth century, there were three new evangelical movements teaching about the Holy Spirit. Dispensationalism had a Keswick emphasis on the "higher life," the holiness movement had its modified Wesleyan emphasis, and pentecostalism stressed tongues as the evidence of the Holy Spirit. All three movements overlapped to some extent and men like R. A. Torrey were highly regarded in all three traditions.[911] While chapter 7 dealt with the holiness movement, this chapter will look at the Keswick view and dispensationalism, then trace the rise and growth of pentecostalism. Then we will attempt to look at some contemporary developments.

13. The Keswick View of Consecration

Keswick is the name of a resort town in England where annual conventions have been held since 1875. The Keswick formulation is based on Oberlin theology.[912] The Keswick convention teaches that believers live defeated lives until they discover victorious, Spirit-filled living. Until Christians receive a baptism or filling of the Spirit, they believe that they are not delivered from the power of sin.

Keswick theology teaches that the believer must consecrate his life completely and the Holy Spirit will counteract the sin nature which frees the believer from the power of sin in his life and empower him for service. Thus, the baptism with the Spirit is a deeper experience which empowers, sanctifies, and transforms. By the power of the Spirit the flesh is kept under as we walk in the Spirit. H. C. G. Moule, probably Keswick's best theologian, summed up the message as "crisis with a view to a process."[913]

---

[911]Noll, *Eerdmans' Handbook to Christianity in America*, 335.

[912]Faupel, *Everlasting Gospel*, 86.

[913]Quoted in Cook, *New Testament Holiness*, 43. Cook, representing a Wesleyan perspective was in agreement, as is Nazarene theologian Ray Dunning in

Watchman Nee taught that the normal Christian life begins with knowing that we were crucified with Christ. That crucifixion occurred at the cross, but that knowledge must be revealed personally. Then we reckon based upon fact. "Our reckoning must be based on knowledge of divinely revealed fact, for otherwise faith has no foundation on which to rest. When we know, then we reckon spontaneously." Nee taught the third step is presenting and the fourth step is walking in the Spirit. It is only after this presenting that we are indwelt by the Spirit and have deliverance from sin.[914]

The Keswick emphasis is a more optimistic version of the Reformers, who taught that the sin nature will always be with us. Yet Keswick theologians were influenced by Wesley's two-step view of sanctification. "Keswick made the idea of entire sanctification palatable to those in the Calvinist tradition."[915] They teach the Holy Spirit counteracts the sin nature and helps us suppress it. Wesleyans agree that this is our condition in regeneration (Gal 5:17-24), but believe God's grace can take us beyond this.

The Keswick movement originated from the ministry of Robert Pearsall Smith[916] and his wife Hannah, who wrote *The Christian's Secret of a Happy Life*

Reflecting the Divine Image, 43. Richard Taylor wrote a presumably unpublished paper for an area National Holiness Association seminar in the early 1960s in which he concluded that the Keswick and Wesleyan views are very similar [Grider, *Entire Sanctification*, 20].

[914]Nee, *Normal Christian Life*, 42-43. According to Roberts, Nee's books *The Latent Power of the Soul* and *The Spiritual Man* teach "gnostic psychoanalysis." The key to Christian maturity is based on extensive Bible studies, the spiritual knowledge of the mature, and a series of spiritual enlightenments [*Understanding Watchman Nee*, 150]. Nee was not yet twenty-five when he wrote *The Spiritual Man* and later in life he affirmed several times his desire that the set of books not be reprinted [Kinnear, *Against the Tide*, 77;183].

[915]Bebbington, *Dominance of Evangelicalism*, 208.

[916]See Warfield, *Studies in Perfectionism*, 2:494-558. Smith disappeared from public ministry after the first Keswick Convention in 1875 under the cloud of moral failure. His reputation was not enhanced by the account of his son Logan Pearsall Smith in *Unforgotten Years*, 54.

Nearly ninety years later J. C. Pollock was commissioned to write a history of the Keswick convention and discovered a letter of confession written by Smith. It turns out that Smith had carelessly put his arm around a young woman in distress while they were in his hotel room. She embellished the account and Smith was called to give an account. In a state of exhaustion from the recent meetings, he told all expecting sympathy, forgiveness and encouragement. Instead the council, reacting to a scandal that very week in the news and the reputation of immorality among the American holiness movement, "treated Smith as a surgeon would a cancer" [Pollock, *Keswick*

(1875), and William E. Boardman. Broadman's *The Higher Christian Life* (1858) has been considered the most influential book within holiness literature.[917] Broadman sought to present the holiness doctrine in non-Methodist terms. He was heavily indebted to Finney and Mahan. He taught that Christ is not only the door to salvation, but he is the way of salvation. Many Christians enter the door through trust in Christ's atoning work, only to seek to walk the way in their own power. Thus a second crisis is necessary to experience "full trust" through which we enter "full salvation."

As a Presbyterian, A. B. Simpson read Broadman's *The Higher Christian Life* and this marked the beginning of his identification with the deeper life movement. Simpson taught the baptism of the Holy Spirit was a necessary experience in the life of the believer subsequent to and distinct from conversion-regeneration. This crisis met the deeper need of sanctification and held the secret to holiness and happiness. Spirit baptism introduced Christians into a life of repeated baptisms which take them even deeper into the fullness of God. This doctrine became a nonnegotiable tenet of the Christian and Missionary Alliance, which Simpson founded in 1887.[918]

This is the *Christian's Secret of a Happy Life* and only a few had learned this secret. The secret is passivity; to cease from our works and trust in the life of Christ within us. H. C. G. Moule described the believer's part as "a blessed and wakeful Quietism."[919]

This is often called the exchanged life or a substituted life. Not only did Christ die for us on the cross, but he lives within us and gives us the victory. Personal effort only frustrates the grace of God. Therefore we are encouraged to give up or let go.[920]

Story, 36; Bebbington, *Holiness*, 77; Dieter, *Holiness Revival*, 154-157]. However, Henry had access to some 6,000 letters and twelve volumes of journals of Hannah. She portrayed Robert as straying throughout much of their marriage [*Secret Life of Hannah Whitall Smith*, 61; 78-88].

A rumor concerning Beverly Carradine also persisted for almost ninety years, but was recently dispelled by Long, *Beverly Carradine*, 191-196.

[917]Boardman, *Higher Christian Life*. On Boardman, see Warfield, *Studies in Perfectionism*, 2:466-494.

[918]Nienkirchen, *A. B. Simpson*, 59-64.

[919]Moule, *Veni Creator*, 197.

[920]William Broadman wrote, "There's nothing to get hold of, it is letting go all hold of everything but Jesus" [*Work for Jesus*, 34]. Charles Trumbull counseled, "We must not try not to sin" because such efforts "can and do effectually prevent such victory." "Therefore, stop trying. Let him do it all" [Palmer, *Person and Ministry of the Holy Spirit*, 89-90]. The phrase "let go and let God" apparently was first used by

James McConkey taught that all believers have been baptized with the Holy Ghost and this indwelling of the Spirit is irrevocable. However, this should not be confused with yielding to Christ. The consciousness that we are indwelt is based upon an obedient walk with God. This consciousness of his presence can be constant if we learn the secret of abiding in Christ. Thus, the threefold secret of the Holy Spirit is union with Christ, yielding to Christ, and abiding in Christ. However, the second and third steps may be compromised without forfeiting our union with Christ.[921]

Ruth Paxon spoke at the 1936 Keswick Convention on John 15:5. From this verse she taught positional sanctification based on our oneness in Christ, progressive sanctification based on our likeness to Christ, and personal sanctification based on the fullness of Christ. She taught that the Christian must make a choice between the continued sovereignty of sin or that of the new master, Christ. When we let the Holy Spirit, who indwells all believers, have absolute control he counteracts all the works of the flesh. The flesh remains with the believer through life, but the Spirit can keep the flesh from having dominion and power over us when we make Jesus our Lord.[922]

Born into a Methodist family, J. Hudson Taylor (1832-1905) learned to abide, not struggle. He found the secret of resting in the joy of a complete salvation from all sin. He felt that practical holiness was to be gradually attained by a diligent use of the means of grace. Then he saw the truth of our oneness with Jesus. According to 2 Timothy 2:13, even if we are faithless, he will remain faithful. Faith is strengthened by resting in his faithfulness, not striving for faith. Taylor's son wrote, "Surrender to Christ he had long know, but this was more; this was a new yieldedness, a glad, unreserved handing over of self and everything to Him."[923]

More recently, Francis Schaeffer adopted the Keswick emphasis on

---

Trumbull. On Trumbell, see Warfield, *Studies in Perfectionism*, 2:563-611. See Packer's critique of this passivity or quietism in *Keep in Step with the Spirit*, 146-147; 155-157. John Frame wrote that we should not wait passively for God to sanctify us. He said "let go and let God" is not biblical because God is sovereign and does not need to wait for us to let go before he can work. And we should not let go because God commands us to fight in the spiritual battle, working out our own salvation (Phil 2:12-13) [Frame, *Salvation Belongs to the Lord*, 215].

[921]McConkey, *Three-Fold Secret of the Holy Spirit*.

[922]Paxon, *Called Unto Holiness*, 17; 52-60. However, Wynkoop warns that we should not conceive of sanctification as being possessed by the Holy Spirit in such a way that he controls us and suppresses our evil nature [*Theology of Love*, 215-216; see also *Foundations*, 73-77].

[923]Taylor, *Hudson Taylor's Spiritual Secret*, 155-166.

holiness. The parents of Edith, his wife, had served under Taylor's China Inland Mission. Neither Francis nor Edith believed Christians could be perfected, but they did believe in the constant pursuit of sanctification and "substantial healing."[924] He taught that we break the tenth commandment before we break any of the rest. He taught a resignation to the will of God which resulted in loving God enough to be contented and loving men enough not to envy. Thus, we love God with our whole heart and our neighbor as ourselves. This resignation comes as we take up our cross and die daily. As I die, I am resurrected to live in the power of the Spirit.[925]

While Schaeffer opposed existential philosophy, he conceded that at the point of sanctification as a moment-by-moment life of faith the existentialist is right.[926] Schaeffer felt that Wesley's terminology was wrong and that his theology was mistaken, but that he certainly had the right aspiration. "He knew a direct working of God in his life on the basis of the finished work of Jesus Christ."[927]

However, the Keswick message is not a complete theology; it is a special emphasis. It does not address the ethical and social dimensions of Christianity, but tends to focus on inner piety.[928] Mysticism was also a major influence on the Keswick message. J. Gregory Mantle, a popular Keswick author, declared in *The Way of the Cross* (1896) that "utter abandonment to God is, then, the only way of blessing. . . . there must be a total loss of self."[929] Mantle also quoted Upham, "What is it to be inwardly crucified? It is to have no desire, no purpose, no aim but such as comes by Divine inspiration." Within this quote, Upham cites the mystic John Tauler.[930] Mantle also devoted six pages to Tauler.[931] This is an example of the theological crossover which sometimes occurs among different approaches to holiness.

Everett Cattell concluded that the major issue between Wesleyan holiness and Keswick holiness has been a fuzzy and ambiguous definition on both sides of

---

[924]This reference to substantial healing is the basis of four chapters at the conclusion of Schaeffer's book, *True Spirituality* in *Works*, 3:315-372.

[925]Schaeffer, *Works*, 3:199-253.

[926]Schaeffer, *Works*, 3:272; 280. See also 2:360-364.

[927]Schaeffer, *Works*, 3:295; 288.

[928]McQuilkin, "Keswick Perspective," 186.

[929]Mantle, Reprinted as *Beyond Humiliation*, 46-47.

[930]Mantle, *Beyond Humiliation*, 62.

[931]Mantle, *Beyond Humiliation*, 142-148.

the sinful nature and eradication.[932] According to Ralph Thompson, "Wesleyanism teaches that the soul itself is delivered from all sin. Keswick, on the other hand, teaches that the sanctified themselves are not made holy, but only that they are made completely victorious over the sin nature, which still remains in their hearts. They distinguish between a state of holiness and a condition of holiness."[933]

While this more Calvinistic holiness movement has debated with the more Wesleyan holiness movement over terminology, my greatest concern is not terminology but the inference that those who are born again are still defeated and under the power of sin. William Boardman and Robert Pearsall Smith "maintained that the majority of contemporary Christians never experienced salvation as it had been intended because they expected, after justification, to continue to sin. God had provided for 'victory' over sin in each individual experience; it could be achieved by allowing Christ to reign in the heart 'moment-by-moment.'"[934] When this discovery is made and the believer learns the secret of holiness through consecration and faith, he moves "out of Romans 7 into Romans 8."[935] And yet this victory, the normal Christian life of Romans 8, is not the "higher life." It is regeneration.

Higher life teachers often use justification passages in order to teach sanctification. I have exactly the same concerns with the emphasis of the American holiness movement. Theodore Monod represented Keswick theology in declaring, "We ought not to sin, and we need to not sin, but as a matter of fact we do sin."[936] Wesley, on the other hand, wrote, "We know no gospel without

---

[932]Cattell, "Keswick and Wesleyan," 274-275. Cattell wrote that eradication was a figure of speech and that Christian holiness is a relationship which must be maintained moment by moment. Yet in 1895 Reader Harris of the Pentecostal League of Prayer, representing what he thought was the Wesleyan tradition, offered a reward of a hundred pounds to anyone who could prove from Scripture that sin must remain in the believer. Since he held to eradication, no one within the Keswick movement could respond to his satisfaction [Bebbington, *Holiness*, 87].

[933]Thompson, "Appraisal of the Keswick and Wesleyan," 14. Yet Thompson noted Thomas Cook's statement that purity is not a state, but a maintained condition [p. 18]. And Cook is Wesleyan. Greathouse also declared, "Entire sanctification is not so much a state as a condition preserved moment by moment as we walk in the light" [*From the Apostles to Wesley*, 27].

[934]Blumhofer, "Purity and Preparation," 264.

[935]See Packer, *Keep in Step with the Spirit,* 161.

[936]Pollock, *Keswick Story*, 65.

salvation from sin."[937] Chris Bounds concluded that "entire sanctification as freedom from willful sin falls short of a truly Wesleyan Holiness view, because it does not take seriously the possibility that Christians can be set free from the 'bent toward sinning' or the sin nature."[938] A. W. Tozer explained, "To save us completely Christ must reverse the bent of our nature; He must plant a new principle within us."[939] We can be bent toward love.

According to the Baptist preacher J. Sidlow Baxter, Romans 6:6 is the battle ground for holiness theories. Yet it does not refer to inward sanctification at all, but to the judicial act of Christ in destroying our legal bondage. The whole human connection with Adam was done away in this judicial reckoning. But this must be realized experimentally, which is the message of Romans 7-8. According to Baxter the bondage of sin, described in Romans 7 is counteracted and overcome by the indwelling Holy Spirit.[940] Therefore, Baxter contends for a second blessing after regeneration — entire sanctification. This does not imply an eradication of sin, but the outpouring of the Holy Spirit.

This deeper work is not different from regeneration, but is a maximum development of it. However, Baxter is critical of the doctrine of two natures and holds that those who are born again have one nature which is restored and renewed by grace. Those who emphasize the two natures concept fear that if this concept is not held, that the believer always has two natures, the door is opened to the error of eradication. Those who emphasize the changed nature believe that the expectation of a transformed character is limited if the believer expects always to have two natures.

The two natures view emphasizes the struggle with sin, while the changed nature emphasizes the victory over sin. Baxter does not believe the pursuit of holiness is one part of the human nature subduing or counteracting another part. Yet the new nature received in regeneration is not the human nature, but the indwelling Holy Spirit. The Wesleyan understanding is that while the old nature remains, the new nature reigns.

Baxter rejected the "dismal dogma" of Calvinism which teaches that sanctification cannot be perfected in this life. Baxter also rejected the Wesleyan view, which he identifies with eradication, and the Keswick view which emphasizes an inward union of the believer with the crucifixion of Christ. Instead he advocates a complete possession by the Holy Spirit. This is an instantaneous

---

[937]Wesley, Letter to Mary Bishop, 18 October 1778.

[938]Online: Bounds, "Legitimate and Illegitimate."

[939]Tozer, *Knowledge of the Holy*, 38.

[940]Baxter, *New Call to Holiness*, 73-104. Lesta categorized Baxter as a Keswick author ["Nature of Sanctification in the New Testament," 150].

surrender which initiates the process of a deeper work. "From the moment the Holy Ghost fully possesses us, He begins to correct, purify, refine, inbreathe and renovate all the qualities, tempers, urges, propensities, and functions of the mind, the sensations, and the will. This is how holiness begins and continues to be inwrought."[941]

14. Dispensationalism and the Spirit-Filled Life

John Darby adapted the three dispensations of Joachim of Fiore to premillennialism, not the dispensational theology of John Fletcher.[942] This resulted in the teaching of an "any moment" rapture of the church. According to W. E. Blackstone, this doctrine of the imminent return of Christ was an incentive to purity, abiding in Christ, and separation.[943] In order to evangelize the world rapidly and efficiently, these dispensationalists concluded they needed an enduement with power for service. This experience was not considered to be a work of grace and it did not sanctify, but it was an empowerment for evangelism. However, they also recognized this enduement also contributed to the overcoming life. They rejected instantaneous sanctification, but emphasized walking in the Spirit and the overcoming life, along with a crisis experience of baptism with the Holy Spirit as enduement with power for service.[944]

According to John Darby, perfect holiness is one and the same with justification. It is not personal, but positional in Christ. Thus, he distinguished between our standing in Christ and our state. Regeneration has no effect on the old man and holiness is imputed.[945] Writing of the same antinomian doctrine of an earlier period, Fletcher said, "People, it seems, may now be 'in Christ,' without being 'new creatures,' and 'new creatures' without casting 'old things' away. They may be God's children without God's image; and 'born of the Spirit'

---

[941]Baxter, *New Call to Holiness*, 116. See also Baxter, *His Deeper Work in Us* and *Our High Calling*; Bloesch, *Holy Spirit*, 140.

[942]See Reasoner, *Hope of the Gospel*, 85; 202-203; 225-226; 256; Reasoner, *Revelation*, 45-46.

[943]Blackstone, *Jesus is Coming*.

[944]Blumhofer, "Purity and Preparation,"269-270. Later dispensationalists equated the baptism with the Spirit with regeneration, for example Walvoord, "Augustinian -Dispensational Perspective," 211-213.

[945]Steele, *Substitute for Holiness*, 10; 33; 69-74. At the Keswick convention Evan Hopkins also clashed with John Brash over the distinction between state and standing. To Methodists such as Brash, such a distinction was unacceptable [Bebbington, *Holiness*, 86].

without 'the fruits of the Spirit.'"[946] Steele warned, "Let none ever presume to rest in any supposed *standing* in Christ while his actual *state* of character is not radiant with all the excellencies of Christ. Let no one who is in a state of wilful sin, imagine that he has a standing in Christ pure and clear before the throne of God, for his standing in heaven is the same as his state on earth."[947]

C. I. Scofield asserted that Romans 7 personified the struggles of the two natures within the believer.

> Romans 7 is a record of the conflict of the regenerate man with his old self, and is, therefore, intensely personal. "I would," "I do not," "I would not," "I do," is the sad confession of defeat which finds an echo in so many Christian hearts. In the eighth chapter the conflict still goes on, but how blessedly impersonal! There is no agony, for *Paul* is out of it; the conflict is now between "flesh" — Saul of Tarsus — and the Holy Spirit. *Paul* is at peace and victorious.[948]

Lewis Sperry Chafer, a disciple of Scofield, developed this two-natures theory. He taught that regeneration was the addition of a new nature rather than the re-creation of the old. He said the new nature was possessed in conjunction with the old nature so long as we are in this body. "The presence of two opposing natures in one individual results in conflict."[949] Chafer taught that positional sanctification occurred at the moment of conversion, but that experimental sanctification is progressive and never completed in the course of this life.[950]

Chafer claimed that a believer could be a new creation and yet remain a carnal Christian without any change in character. He stated that the carnal Christian is also characterized by a walk that is on the same plane as that of the natural man.[951] He asserted that a carnal Christian may not exhibit any spiritual

---

[946]Fletcher, *Works*, 1:108.

[947]Steele, *Substitute for Holiness*, 41.

[948]Scofield, *New Scofield Reference Bible*, 1219; *Rightly Dividing the Word of Truth*, 58.

[949]Chafer, *He That Is Spiritual*, 142.

[950]Chafer, *Systematic Theology*, 6:284-285. Greathouse said that sanctification is more than positional, it is relational. "At the moment this new relationship is established through faith in Christ, the justified believer receives the Holy Spirit and experiences the beginnings of ethical sanctification" [*From the Apostles to Wesley*, 14].

[951]Chafer, *He That Is Spiritual*, 12.

fruit. Chafer wrote elsewhere that the fruit of the Spirit is the experience of every believer *who comes into right adjustment with the Spirit.*[952] However, the fruit of the Spirit is characteristic of all believers. John Wesley taught that this was the indirect witness that one was actually born again.[953]

Charles Swindoll wrote in admiration of Chafer, and later became president of Dallas Theological Seminary, of which Chafer was the first president. Swindoll taught that a Christian could deliberately choose to disobey his Lord and remain in that state of carnality, grieving the Spirit of God living with him. The promptings of the Spirit may be ignored and the wickedness intensified until the "believer" is sucked into a kind of black hole, winding up in misery and filth. According to Swindoll some Christians could die in that condition, but he warned that such a lifestyle was an abuse of grace. While Swindoll's larger point was that "we don't have to sin on a constant, day-after-day basis," he conceded that "the Christian can be temporarily addicted to sin."[954]

Yet Romans 6 asserts that justification and initial sanctification are bound together and we cannot have the one without having the other. Randall Gleason wrote that Chafer over emphasized the discontinuity between justification and sanctification and underestimated the transforming power of regeneration. "To imagine that a person can be justified without any change for the better in his condition demonstrates a deficient view of both justification and sanctification."[955]

John MacArthur said Chafer's concept of two classes of believers is an example of dispensationalism methodology carried too far.

> There is a tendency, however, for dispensationalists to get carried away with compartmentalizing truth to the point that they can make unbiblical distinctions. An almost obsessive desire to categorize everything neatly has led various dispensationalist interpreters to draw hard lines not only between the church and Israel, but also between salvation and discipleship, the church and the kingdom, Christ's preaching and the apostolic message, faith and repentance, and the age of law and the age of grace.[956]

MacArthur wrote that when Chafer's book, *He That Is Spiritual*, was first

---

[952]Chafer, *Grace*, 338. Italics added.

[953]Wesley, "The Witness of Our Own Spirit," Sermon #12. See also Sugden, *Works of John Wesley*, 1:220-221.

[954]Swindoll, *Grace Awakening*, 57-58; 137-139.

[955]Gleason, "Warfield and Chafer," 241-256.

[956]MacArthur, *Gospel According to Jesus*, 25.

published in 1918 it was extremely controversial. "Prior to this century, no serious theologian would have entertained the notion that it is possible to be saved yet see nothing of the outworking of regeneration in one's life-style or behavior." MacArthur went on to say that Chafer's concept of two classes of Christians, carnal and spiritual, "was a foreign concept to most Christians in Dr. Chafer's generation, but it has become a central premise for a large segment of the church today." It "became the basis for a whole new way of looking at the gospel."[957]

Chafer asserted that grace is rendered ineffectual if we preach that a sinner must surrender to God. He labeled it an error of the first magnitude to require the unregenerate to surrender to the Lordship of Christ. He also said it creates confusion to demand that the unsaved must dedicate themselves to God's will in their daily lives as an added condition.

Chafer taught that all Gospel preaching should avoid the life to be lived beyond regeneration. When believers are taught that they may voluntarily dedicate their lives to God, the preacher must remind the unsaved repeatedly that issues of Christian character, conduct, and service have no application to them. Nor should sinners be exhorted to confess sin, make restitution, or seek God. All that was necessary was to believe. Chaffer admonished preachers to preach the Lordship of Christ exclusively to Christians and the Saviorhood of Christ to the unsaved.[958]

Thus, Dwight Pentecost wrote that "there is a vast difference between being a Christian and being a disciple. Not all men who are saved are disciples . . . ."[959] This is known as "free grace theology." They claim the difference between a Christian and a disciple is the difference between salvation and sanctification — which is optional. Biblically, this distinction cannot be substantiated. Yet Lawrence O. Richards holds that the church should not use the discipleship process in training believers, as Jesus did with his disciples while on earth, because the church is a community of equality between brothers and sisters.[960] But the imperative in Matthew 28:19 is "make disciples."

---

[957]MacArthur, *Gospel According to Jesus*, 23-25.

[958]Chafer, *Systematic Theology*, 3:372-389. Laurence Wood claimed that it was one thing to be a member of the kingdom of God and yet another thing for the kingdom of God to be established within each believer. Presumably the believer would come under the reign of Christ "through the sanctification of the Spirit." Wood then claimed that Wesley taught this "twofold differentiation" [*Pentecostal Grace*, 39-40]. In neither of the passages from Wesley which Wood cited is the immediate subject Christian perfection, however. He cited from "The Way to the Kingdom," Sermon #7, 1.12 and "Christian Perfection," Sermon #35, 2.13 where Wesley simply taught that the kingdom was established on earth when the Spirit was given at Pentecost.

[959]Pentecost *Design for Discipleship*, 14.

[960]Richards, *Practical Theology of Spirituality*, 228-229.

Richard Foster wrote that some hold to a practical theology that will not allow for spiritual growth. "Having been saved by grace, these people have been paralyzed by it. To attempt any progress in the spiritual life smacks of 'works righteousness' to them. Their liturgies tell them they sin in word, thought, and deed daily, so they conclude that this is their fate until they die."[961]

Chafer declared that the child of God is free. "He has been delivered from every aspect of the law — as a rule of life, as an obligation to make himself acceptable to God, and as a dependence on the impotent flesh." Chafer declared that "the Christian's liberty to do precisely as he chooses is as limitless and perfect as any other aspect of grace." According to this lawless teaching, neither the carnal Christian nor the Spirit-filled Christian are subject to the law. But while the carnal Christian knows liberty, the surrendered Christian discovers victory if he chooses voluntarily to yield.[962] Chafer said that a Christian is a Christian because he is rightly related to Christ, but "he that is spiritual" is spiritual because he is rightly related to the Spirit, in addition to his relation to Christ in salvation.[963] While Chafer acknowledged that all Christians are baptized with the Spirit, he said not all are Spirit-filled. Chafer gave seven manifestations of the Spirit which he said are experienced only by the higher class of Christians, the Spirit-filled believer.[964]

Among those who call themselves Reformed Arminians, there is also a tendency to separate growth from salvation. The Christian's obedience to the commands of Scripture is unrelated to salvation. Imparted righteousness is seen as a matter of progressive sanctification, not of salvation.[965] This is based on the teaching that the active obedience of Christ is imputed to the believer. While a believer ought to obey the commands of Christ, there is no real consequence if he does not.

In the second century Irenaeus wrote in *Against Heresies* against the three stages of fleshly, soulish, and spiritual persons, calling this teaching a gnostic heresy. While we may talk of our flesh, our soul, or our spirit, a human being

---

[961]Foster, "Spiritual Formation Agenda,"29.

[962]Chafer, *Grace*, 344-5; see also Chafer, *Major Bible Themes*, 182. Walvoord writes, "Christ stated that no one can serve two masters. The issue facing Christians after their conversion is whether they will submit completely to the will of God" ["Augustinian-Dispensational Perspective," 217]. Implied in this statement is that regenerate believers who have not submitted are serving two masters. According to this position the filling of the Spirit comes when this condition is met.

[963]Chafer, *He That Is Spiritual*, 15.

[964]Chafer, *He That Is Spiritual*, 45.

[965]Ashby, "Reformed Arminian View," 183.

consists of all three together. They do not designate types of persons. Irenaeus probably would have also rejected the modern distinction between carnal Christians and Spirit-filled Christians. In his sermon on "The More Excellent Way," Wesley described two orders of Christians, those who take the higher road and those who take the lower road.[966] However, Outler overstated the case when he called this sermon an implied admission that Wesley had changed his mind on the order of salvation and had moved away from his earlier standard of true faith and salvation.[967]

Kenneth Collins regards this assessment as a serious mistake that lowers both the standards and promises of what it means to be a child of God.[968] The "almost Christian," as described in "The Almost Christian," cannot be equated with "the generality of Christians," as described in "The More Excellent Way."

The description Chafer gives of the "Spirit-Filled Life" is the biblical description of regeneration. It is also significant that dispensationalism teaches that the baptism of the Spirit is a "non-experiential work of the Spirit." Thus, the believer can be regenerated, indwelt, sealed and baptized by the Spirit without necessarily being conscious of the Spirit.[969] Walvoord wrote that the baptism of the Holy Spirit is not an experiential, but a positional truth.[970] Even John MacArthur said the baptism with the Spirit is a fact, not a feeling.[971]

Thus, the only assurance of salvation is the rational acceptance to certain propositional truths. For David Needham, sanctification comes as we grasp the concept of our position in Christ. He believes we are hindered by not knowing

---

[966]Wesley, Sermon #89, §6-8.

[967]Wesley, *BE Works*, 3:262.

[968]Collins, "Motif of Real Christianity," 49-62. Collins observed that Wesley referred to the faith of a servant in two ways. In the broad sense, the faith of a servant lacks assurance because he is under the spirit of bondage. He is under the power and dominion of sin. Thus he is not justified nor born of God. Wesley also taught the faith of a servant, in the narrow sense, as descriptive of those who lacked assurance due to ignorance of the gospel promises or some bodily disorder. Although these *are* justified and born of God, they are "exempt" or exceptional cases ["Real Christianity as Integrating Theme," 15-45; see also Collins, *Theology of John Wesley*, 134-136]. One exceptional case was Wesley's own brief bout with depression, recorded in his *Journal*, 4 January, 1739.

[969]Ryrie, *Holy Spirit*, 77.

[970]Walvoord, *Holy Spirit*, 146.

[971]MacArthur, *Charismatic Chaos*, 189-191.

who we really are in Christ.[972] Yet George Whitefield warned, "If I had a mind to hinder the progress of the Gospel, and to establish the kingdom of darkness, I would go about telling people they might have the Spirit of God, and yet not feel it."[973]

Walvoord explained that Scripture reveals positional perfection to be the possession of every Christian. "It is, therefore, absolute perfection, which Christ wrought for us on the cross. There is no reference here to the quality of the Christian life. The issue of sinlessness is not in view. All saints (Sanctified ones) are partakers of the perfection accomplished by the death of Christ." Thus, this positional perfection or sanctification was the work of Christ for every believer and "is the possession of the believer from the moment of saving faith."[974]

Modern dispensationalists have sometimes carried their doctrine of the carnal Christian to such absurdities as claiming that you can't tell a carnal believer from a lost man because they both act the same way. This explains how Christians can steal, lie, commit adultery or suicide and still go to heaven. It has even been taught that a carnal Christian can fall away from the faith, cease to believe, and still be eternally secure.[975] The result of such teaching is a shallow profession of faith and not much emphasis on imparted holiness.

Henry Holloman in his *The Forgotten Blessing: Rediscovering the Transforming Power of Sanctification* argued for victory over sin. He wrote that Christians can conquer sin by grace. "Grace then does not give us freedom to sin. Grace is our great liberator from sin and not our license to sin." Yet he considers

---

[972]Needham, *Birthright*. See Walvoord's complaint that Needham so emphasizes the concept of a Christian as a new creation that he almost eliminates the concept of sin in the believer ["Augustinian-Dispensational Perspective," 207].

[973]Quoted by Steele, *Antinomianism Revived*, 48.

[974]Walvoord, *Doctrine of the Holy Spirit*, 208-210.

[975]"It is not lying, cheating, stealing, raping, murdering, or being unfaithful that sends people to hell.... Neither do we become unsaved by acting unsaved... . Even if a believer for all practical purposes becomes an unbeliever, his salvation is not in jeopardy" [Stanley, *Eternal Security*, 70-71; 94]. Statements from Charles Stanley, Tony Evans, Chuck Swindoll, and others are compiled by Corner, *Believer's Conditional Security*, Chapter 9, "The Carnal Christian," 153-164. See also MacArthur, *Gospel According to Jesus*, where he documents the teaching of some that believers out of fellowship may be "unbelieving believers," even agnostics or atheists, yet even those who deny God are still eternally secure [p. 98]. Ray Dunning objected to the imbalance articulated by Swindoll, who declared that Abraham would never again have to worry about where he stood before God. "He was, once and for all, declared righteous" [Swindoll, *Grace Awakening*, 24; Dunning, *Reflecting the Divine Image*, 13].

Romans 7:14-25 to describe "the struggle of a true believer."[976] Throughout the book he urges believers to live holy and yet affirms that regeneration is permanent and cannot be reversed.

In *Five Views on Sanctification* John Walvoord represents what is called the "Augustinian-Dispensational" view. Walvoord advocated the two-nature view of Chafer and McQuilkin, who represented the Keswick position, claimed the position of Walvoord was nearly the same as the Keswick position.[977] This label of "Augustinian" is actually a misnomer since there is little theological relationship between Chafer's view of sanctification and his dispensational distinctives. Walvoord claimed that both men held to a two-nature view of the believer. Then Walvoord conceded that Augustine typically did not refer to two natures.

Calvinism, which follows Augustine, tends to reject the two-natures theory.[978] However, they tend also to affirm Luther's concept of a believer being simultaneously just and sinful. My impression of Calvinistic writing is that the believer is typically described as having one nature, a new nature, but that he habitually falls short. This still amounts to a dualism, even though it is expressed as one nature which can choose to sin.[979] Augustine, and most Calvinists, teach that the believer will never get beyond the Romans 7 struggle.

Sproul explained, "All Christians are 'carnal' insofar as we continue to struggle with the old nature of flesh. But no true Christian is carnal in the sense that the flesh totally dominates his life. If the carnal aspect were in total dominion, we would know that we are still unregenerate."[980] Thus, the evidence of regeneration is partial victory over sin.

The Wesleyan view is that while two natures exist within the regenerate, only one nature can control. The old nature remains, but the new nature reigns. While Calvinism teaches that we only have one spiritual nature, sin still reigns in our bodies. Thus, a dualism still exists.

---

[976]Holloman, *Forgotten Blessing*, 114-115; 229. In the Spring of 1984, I took the first third of systematic theology under Dr. Holloman at Talbot Theological Seminary.

[977]Walvoord, "Augustinian-Dispensational Perspective," 194; 237.

[978]See Warfield, *Studies in Perfectionism*, 2:585-586. Warfield saw salvation as a unitary event. Justification and sanctification were so joined that to experience one necessarily involved experiencing the other [pp. 326; 356]. See also Warfield's review of Chafer's book *He That Is Spiritual* in *Princeton Theological Review* (April 1919) 322-327. Also see Hoekema, "Reformed Perspective," 231.

[979]See my discussion at p. 364.

[980]Sproul, *Pleasing God*, 159.

Richard Treffry argued that it was absurd to hold that the seat of sin is in the body, because then the body may be sinful and the soul sinless at the same time.[981] Yet positional theology has apparently adopted this dualism. The dispensational view teaches that the believer slips back and forth between the two natures. Hoekema called this description by Walvoord "a spiritual seesaw."

> . . . he fails to do full justice to the fact that a decisive break with sin was brought about by Christ for believers - so that sin, though still present in the believer, no longer has dominion - and to the amazing truth that the believer is now indeed, a new creature, old things having passed away. . . . He gives the impression that the Christian is something like a spiritual seesaw with two contradictory types of inner tendencies. With both tugging at one's heart, a believer can go either way.[982]

James R. Graham expressed a Wesleyan understanding

> Some say that there are three classes of men: the natural man, the carnal man, and the spiritual man. The natural man, is, of course, the unsaved child of the world. The carnal man is a saved man who, however, still walked in the flesh. The spiritual man is the higher quality of saved man, who walks in the Spirit and in the course of obedience. Much of this is directly contrary to the teaching of the eighth chapter of Romans ... the teaching, then of the three classes: natural man, carnal man, and spiritual man is deeply pernicious and is deluding many who are continuing in sin into thinking they are saved. . . . It is the worst kind of

---

[981]Treffry, *Treatise on Christian Perfection*, 93.

[982]Hoekema, "Reformed Perspective," 231. Representing a Calvinistic interpretation, Hoekema declared that the Bible never speaks of a third class of people called "carnal Christians." The New Testament distinguishes between those who have been born again and those who have not ["Reformed Perspective," 189].

See also Shank, *Life in the Son*. Shank asserts that the believer is a single spiritual entity and whatever he does, he does as a whole man [pp. 212-216]. Murray wrote in *Principles of Conduct*, "The believer is both old man and new man; when he does well he is acting in terms of the new man which he is; when he sins he is acting in terms of the old man which he also still is. This interpretation does not find support in Paul's teaching. . . . The old man is the unregenerate man; the new man is the regenerate man created in Christ Jesus unto good works. It is no more feasible to call the believer a new man and an old man, than it is to call him a regenerate man and an unregenerate. . . . Our old man has been crucified" [pp. 211-218].

antinomianism and is part of the base alloy of fundamentalist instruction that is abroad today. . . .The Scripture knows of two places — heaven and hell; two beings - God and Satan; two ways — the narrow way that leadeth to life and the broad that leadest to destruction; two principles of walk — the Spirit principle and the flesh principle.[983]

15. Pentecostalism and the Power of the Spirit

Throughout Church history there have been movements which emphasized emotionalism and supernatural manifestations of the Spirit. This was the emphasis of the Montanists in the second century, of Edward Irving in the early nineteenth century, of Pentecostalism which began in 1906, and the Charismatic movement which began in 1960.

Around A. D. 160 Montanus, a priest of Cybele, was converted to Christianity. He was soon joined by Maximilla and Priscilla, two women who deserted their husbands with the approval of Montanus, to proclaim the true faith. All three claimed their prophecies were God's final word to men. They were "spiritual," while the rest of the Church was "carnal." Montanus declared himself to be an incarnation of the Holy Spirit, the revealer of "things to come." However, Ted Campbell rejected this claim as a distortion of his words.[984]

The followers of Montanus preached the imminent coming of the kingdom of God, when Christ and the New Jerusalem would descent to Phrygia (in present day Turkey). All believers were called to point them there to await the return of Christ. Tertullian championed this cause late in his life, believing its purpose was to restore the church to its purity. However, by this time the original three had died and the movement had moderated. Montanism advocated a strict asceticism, a perfectionistic lifestyle motivated by an apocalyptic expectation of the end of the age and by new prophetic revelations. They also courted martyrdom. It was considered a sign of spirituality to want to die for Christ. Montanism emphasized the miraculous gifts of the apostolic age, the priesthood of all Christians, and premillennialism, along with their ascetic discipline.

According to Pope, Montanus taught that the Holy Spirit, as the Paraclete, was not given to the Apostles, but was reserved for a fuller, deeper

---

[983]Graham, "Are There Carnal Christians?" Reprinted as Appendix B in Smith, *Bible Holiness*, 158-164. See also Smith, *Bible Holiness*, Chapter 10, "Were There Carnal Christians in the Corinthian Church?" 73-79.

[984]Campbell, "Charismata in the Christian Communities," 13. Campbell claims that Montanus spoke in the first person singular as a prophet spoke the words of God. But we must still determine whether Montanus was a true or false prophet.

baptism of the Spirit than Pentecost under Montanus.[985] Tertullian claimed, "The Paraclete has revealed greater things through Montanus than Christ revealed through the Gospel."[986]

The Church condemned Montanus as heretical.[987] Anderson explained that Wesley's adversaries accused Methodism of closely resembling Montanism. Wesley conceded the point in order to refute their argument — that both groups were heretical. In so doing Wesley was functioning as a debater, not a

---

[985]Pope, *Compendium*, 3:63.

[986]Migne, *Patrologia Latina*, 2:91.

[987]Yet Charles Williams upheld the Montanists in his *Descent of the Dove*, 34. While John Wesley rejected fanaticism, he inconsistently approved of Montanus in sermon #61, "The Mystery of Iniquity," ¶ 24; "The Wisdom of God's Counsels," sermon #68, ¶ 9; and "The Real Character of Montanus" in *Works*, 11:485.

In his *Journal*, 15 August 1750 Wesley logged that he had read an odd book, but that it convinced him that the Montanists were real, scriptural Christians. The book was by John Lacy, *General Delusion of Christians*. Lacy was a participant in the French Prophets movement. His book was also reprinted by Edward Irving in 1832. Thus, Montanism, the French Prophets, Irving, and the charismatic movement all share a common view of prophecy.

Lacy noted that Irenaeus had charged that Montanus had prophesied by an evil spirit. Lacy is concerned that this resulted in the church council's condemnation of all charismatic phenomenon. However, Lacy argues for charismatic prophecy and therefore is defending the Montanists. He cites fourteen charges against Montanism and then attempts to demonstrate that the church passed sentence against Montanus without conclusive proof. This exercise amount to the setting up of a straw man and then pulling him down. While Lacy is not successful in exonerating Montanism, he would have had Wesley's sympathy when he argued that everything must be evaluated by Scripture.

Lacy concluded that there were false prophets within the Montanist movement, but not all were false. There was demonic influence, but there was also the work of the Spirit. Yes, the devil worked openly in some cases, but he was not at work in all cases. Yet history has condemned the Montanist movement without considering all the evidence and submitting it to the authority of Scripture. The result was more ecclesiastical regulations and the lost of charismatic phenomenon within the church.

While Wesley was concerned that the same circumstances were at work against Methodism, he made a poor choice in identifying the Montanists as real, scriptural Christians. It is significant that Lacy declared that the maxims of the French prophets in London were the same as those of Montanus [p. 233]. While Wesley could not personally interview the Montanists of an earlier era, he did interview and ultimately reject the French prophets [see p. 474 of this book]. Had he been present during the time of Montanus there is every reason to believe he would have rejected Montanism as well.

historian.[988] According to Perkins, Montanism was restated in modern times in Quakerism.[989]

Edward Irving was a Presbyterian minister serving in London from 1822-1834. Irving was talented and well educated but perhaps never regenerated. Irving first began to move away from the absolute authority of Scripture, then to a heretical view of Christ, and then to a speculative view of prophecy — expecting the Lord's return in 1835 or 1836. He also became persuaded that the gifts of the Spirit, especially prophecy, tongues, and healing, should occur in the church as a latter day rain. He taught Spirit baptism as subsequent to regeneration and sanctification, with tongues as the "standing sign." Spoiled by his own success, Irving was eventually dismissed from his congregation, deposed from the ministry, and died at the age of forty-two.[990]

After surveying church history, Stanley Burgess concluded that "while the concept of Spirit baptism was very common throughout the Christian centuries, the modern Pentecostal identification of glossolalia as the 'initial evidence' of such baptism is completely novel until the nineteenth-century Irvingites." Burgess conceded that in almost two millennia of Christian life and practice, tongues was not associated with the advent of life in the Spirit.[991]

Glenn Hinson wrote that glossolalia was uncommon in church history until recent times.[992] The earliest reference is from Montanus, which was not so much tongues as prophecy. Iraneaus mentioned tongues three times: one passage citing Acts 2 without comment, one referring to the ability to speak foreign languages,[993] A third reference refers to an abuse of spiritual gifts.[994]

Tertullian makes one reference to tongues.[995] Origen makes two statements, one supposing Paul had the gift of speaking the languages of all people and the other disassociating Christianity from the unintelligible words spoken by Montanists. Chrysostom and Augustine were both unfamiliar with tongues speaking and were cessationists, believing the practice had only occurred

---

988Anderson, *Clement of Alexandria*, 296-298.

989Perkins, *Evangelical Perfection*, 135.

990Dallimore, *Forerunner of the Charismatic Movement.*

991In two chapters Burgess covered "The Ancient and Eastern Churches" and "The Medieval and Modern Western Churches" in *Initial Evidence*, 3-38.

992Stagg, Hinson, Oates, *Glossolalia*, 45-62.

993Iraneaus, *Against Heresies*, 5.6.1, *ANF*, 1:531.

994Iraneaus, *Against Heresies*, 1.13.3, *ANF*, 1:334.

995Tertullian, *Against Marcion*, 5.8, *ANF*, 3:446-7.

in very early times and had ceased.

This accounts for all the references to tongues through the fourth century. There are only scanty references from fifth century through middle ages. Glossolalia cropped up among the Cévenols in France beginning in 1688,[996] then among the Irvingites.

Yet, "the single most important aspect of Pentecostal pneumatology is the doctrine of Spirit baptism."[997] Pentecostal scholar, Vinson Synan, stated the overriding thesis of his work was to demonstrate that "the historical and doctrinal lineage of American pentecostalism is to be found in the Wesleyan tradition."[998] On the other hand, Charles Carter, in a book endorsed by the Christian Holiness Association, tied pentecostalism to the early Mormons and Shakers in America. Carter declared:

> Any attempt to trace "pentecostal tongues speaking" to Methodistic origins through the Topeka, Kansas and Azusa Street Mission outbreak of this phenomenon lacks convincing evidence, even where the mere historical facts are subjected to careful scrutiny. . . . Any attempt to establish this position, whether for the greater respectability of Pentecostalism or otherwise, comes near, if it is not actually, to a falsification of history.[999]

Both men may have overstated their case. Fredrick Bruner, who is neither pentecostal nor holiness, is more accurate in concluding that "eighteenth-century Methodism is the mother of the nineteenth-century American holiness movement which, in turn, bore twentieth-century Pentecostalism."[1000]

The emphasis of early Methodism would have never produced pentecostalism, but the shift of emphasis in the holiness movement was a transition which did lead to pentecostalism. A survey of the holiness literature around the turn of this century indicates the nearly universal emphasis on pentecostal terminology by the holiness movement. Fraser concluded that Merritt, in a sermon from 1821, was the first American Methodist to appropriate

---

[996]see John Wesley's *Letter* to Dr. Conyers Middleton, 4 January 1749, 5.3.

[997]Kärkkäinen, *Pneumatology*, 95.

[998]Synan, *The Holiness-Pentecostal Tradition*, xi.

[999]Carter, *Person and Ministry*, 183-184.

[1000]Bruner, *Theology of the Holy Spirit*, 37.

Fletcher's Spirit-baptism language.[1001]

The Guide to Christian Perfection was begun in 1839 by Timothy Merritt. This was the first periodical dedicated solely to promote Christian perfection. According to Dieter, Merritt's publication with its call for a special emphasis on Christian perfection marked a new emphasis which eventually led to the creation of "holiness churches. . . . The application of the revivalist's methods to the promotion of this particular doctrine and the adoption by revivalism of the experiential goals and possibilities of 'a higher Christian life,' marks a change both in revivalism and the advocacy of Christian perfection."[1002]

The name had been changed to *The Guide to Holiness and Revival Miscellany* before the Palmers purchased the periodical in 1865.[1003] By 1897 the title was *The Guide to Holiness and Pentecostal Life.* After reviewing the contents of *The Guide to Holiness* at the turn of the century, Donald Dayton noted:

> Sermons were published in a column called the "Pentecostal Pulpit," women's meetings were reported as "Pentecostal Womanhood," prayers were held in the "Pentecostal closet," music was provided by "Pentecostal choirs," and the Scriptures were distributed by "Pentecostal Bible Houses."[1004]

Other holiness periodicals included *The Pacific Pentecost, The Pentecost Century, The Pentecostal Era, The Pentecostal Herald,* and *The Pentecostal Evangel.*[1005] Classic holiness books from this period include: *Pentecostal Papers* (1895) by S. A. Keen; *The Ideal Pentecostal Church* (1897) by Seth C. Rees; *Holiness and Power* (1897) by A. M. Hills, and *Lightning Bolts from Pentecostal Skies* (1898) by Martin Wells Knapp. According to Leon Hynson, the

---

[1001]Fraser, *Strains in the Understanding of Christian Perfection*, 425-427. This language was used in Merritt, *Address to Christians and Ministers on Christian Perfection*. However, his book *Christian's Manual* does not use such language.

[1002]Dieter, *Holiness Revival*, 2-3; 17.

[1003]The Palmers also bought another periodical at the same time, *Beauty of Holiness and Sabbath Miscellany*. The two magazines were merged to avoid any rivalry [Hughes, *Fragrant Memories*, 61; 161-180]. Hughes said the name was changed from "The Guide to Christian Perfection" to "The Guide to Holiness" under D. S. King, who followed Merritt as editor. Hughes speculated that the term "holiness" would arouse less prejudice than "perfection" [p. 173].

[1004]Dayton, "Doctrine of the Baptism of the Holy Spirit,"119.

[1005]Rose, *Vital Holiness*, 274.

"geographical center" of this teaching was God's Bible School.[1006] Thus, Pentecost was normative and "Back to the Bible" was interpreted to mean "Back to Pentecost." According to Thornton, Martin Wells Knapp sought nothing less than the replication of Pentecost.[1007]

Across the nation holiness groups were organized in reaction to the "formalism" of the Methodist Church.[1008] Through a series of mergers the Pentecostal Church of the Nazarene was organized in Pilot Point, Texas in 1908 and became the largest holiness denomination. The word "Pentecostal" was not dropped from their name until 1919.[1009]

Leon Hynson noted that holiness was more likely to be interpreted in terms of "categories of the Spirit and Pentecost, than of the Son and Calvary or the resurrection."[1010] Holiness preaching often used typology and allegory to teach holiness from any passage in the Bible. At times in holiness preaching, experience took priority over exegesis. Robert Coleman wrote, "I am afraid that in Wesleyan circles, to our shame, far too much emphasis has been given to the recitation of personal testimonies to the neglect of solid biblical exegesis. This is one reason, I am convinced, holiness teaching so often is compromised."[1011]

"As the nineteenth century progressed, holiness teaching and preaching focused less on Christ and the atonement and spoke more in terms of the Holy Spirit."[1012] Leon Hynson was told by an old holiness preacher, "Anyone can preach about Jesus. We need preaching about the Holy Ghost."[1013] The attitude still prevails among many holiness people that a good service is one in which the Holy Spirit takes over and there is no preaching at all. This attitude, in essence, is what the charismatic meant who had written on the flyleaf of his Bible, "I don't care what the Bible says, I've had an experience."[1014] Jimmy Swaggart concluded

---

[1006]Hynson, "They Confessed Themselves Pilgrims," 227.

[1007]Thornton, "God's Trustee," 148-157.

[1008]Yet Joseph H. Smith, writing as late as 1916 observed, "Dead and degenerate, formal and fashionable as the churches are, *I have found none of them yet from which the Holy Spirit has entirely withdrawn His membership*" [*Things Behind and Things Before*, 49].

[1009]Smith, *Called Unto Holiness*, 9; 320.

[1010]Hynson, "Wesleyan Quadrilateral," 22.

[1011]Coleman, *Nothing to Do but to Save Souls*, 89.

[1012]Parsons, *Living the Holy Life Today*, 23.

[1013]Hynson, "Wesleyan Quadrilateral," 25.

[1014]MacArthur, *Charismatics: A Doctrinal Perspective*, 59.

a plea for Pentecostalism with this statement: "Those who are opposed to the baptism in the Holy Spirit (with the evidence of speaking in tongues) have an argument. Those who have received it have an experience."[1015]

As early as 1881 there is a record of a holiness woman speaking in an unknown tongue. The ministers present did oppose the phenomenon, but the camp was divided in their opinion of whether it was a wonderful manifestation of divine power or of the devil. While this was a new problem for the leaders of the holiness camp meeting in Missouri, Kiergan reported that "similar things had occurred in Illinois."[1016] In 1896 a group of southern holiness people who later helped form the Church of God (Cleveland) claimed to have spoken in tongues in a revival held in Cherokee County, North Carolina. Yet they did not make the connection between Holy Ghost baptism and the gift of tongues.[1017]

In 1878 Alma White was converted under the ministry of W. B. Godbey. In Denver, Mrs. Alma White organized the Pentecostal Union in 1901 which became the Pillar of Fire Church in 1917. In 1918 she was consecrated a bishop by W. B. Godbey. The Pillar of Fire emphasized "unfettered emotion in worship" and the evidence of sanctification was the "holy dance."[1018] In Zarephath, New Jersey the Pillar of Fire developed a commune that was self-sufficient. Alma also taught that sexual relations within marriage were legitimate only when the couple knew that God wanted them to have a child.[1019]

While she considered tongues speaking "the climax of demon worship," her husband, Kent, spoke in tongues. Neither believed that they should divorce, so he moved to England where he joined the first British pentecostal denomination, the Apostolic Church.[1020] He returned home in his final year and his wife claimed that on his deathbed he recanted.

Much of the holiness movement in Texas taught sinless perfection, freedom from death, marital purity, a third work of grace called "the fire," abstinence from pork and coffee, and no doctors or drugs. According to C. B. Jernigan, they divided the plan of salvation into seven steps: repentance,

---

[1015]Swaggart, *Is Speaking in Tongues Scriptural?* 44.

[1016]Kiergan, *Historical Sketches*, 31.

[1017]Hunter, "Spirit Baptism," 8-9.

[1018]Smith, *Called Unto Holiness*, 231; Synan, *Holiness-Pentecostal Tradition*, 95. In 1906 the Pillar of Fire lost a congregation in Los Angeles to tongues advocates [Synan, *Holiness-Pentecostal Movement*, 143; Ward, "Anti-Pentecostal Argument,"103].

[1019]Stanley, *Feminist*, 11; 79; 65; 69; 97.

[1020]See his book, White, *Word of God Coming Again*. See her book, *My Heart and My Husband*.

justification regeneration, entire sanctification, the baptism with the Holy Ghost, the gift of healing, and faith. Those who obtained the seventh step, faith, could never see death. They reasoned that God had not only removed sin, he also removed the penalty of sin. "Those who were thus sanctified and cleansed were thereafter freed from the penalty of sin and would never die." Since they believed they would not die, but live to see Jesus come in his millennial glory which would be only a short time off, they started a meeting in Corsicana, Texas which was to run until Jesus descended from heaven with a shout. They also taught that if a man's wife did not believe as he did, particularly on the doctrine of holiness, it was sufficient ground for a scriptural divorce.

Related to the Corsicana Enthusiasts were the Belton Sanctificationists, a group of women in the region of Belton, Texas who decided they should not have physical relations with their husbands. These Belton women, led by Martha McWhirter, later became known as the "Sanctified Sisters" and officially as the Woman's Commonwealth.[1021]

Jernigan was not specific when this occurred, but earlier in his book he recorded the first convert to holiness teaching was in 1872. He then specified the next phase of fanaticism came in 1884. All denominations were call Babylon. The come-outers did not need to read the Bible because they had the one who had inspired it in their hearts. They no longer needed to pray, since they had the very spirit of prayer all the time. They did not take the Lord's Supper because they were in constant feasting on the living bread. They did not keep Sunday, because they were not sun worshipers. The leader of this group eventually left his wife for a woman in Kansas that God sent him to marry.

Jernigan said "the fire" teaching reached Texas and Louisiana in 1897. B. H. Irwin came to teach them this new doctrine. G. D. Watson even came through Texas teaching "the fire." Some of the fire teachers also taught that demons were God's servants sent into sanctified people to chastise them.

About this same time the doctrine of marital purity sprang up.[1022] The teaching that husband and wife should not have sexual relations brought about

---

[1021]Hamilton, *William Baxter Godbey*, 89.

[1022]Ironically, there have been both Catholic and Protestant versions of this teaching. In Roman Catholicism perfection was attained through poverty, chastity, and obedience. "Chastity" was interpreted to be celibacy. Thus, virginity meant purity. The Protestant version taught purity was maintained *after* marriage through "male continence" and "marital purity," which meant that sexual intercourse was only allowable for the purpose of procreation. See also ftnt #1054 of this volume. According to Robeck, William Seymour had to oppose this teaching at Azusa Street [*Azusa Street Mission and Revival*, 164; 309-310].

their separation in some cases.[1023] Delbert Rose felt the fanaticism of the movement in Texas was because of "the unschooled leadership," but it was not representative of the whole movement either then or now.[1024] While it certainly cannot be traced back to Methodism, the fanaticism of the early holiness movement cannot be isolated to Texas alone. According to the record left by Kiergan, many of these same teachings had surfaced in northern Missouri during the same time frame.[1025]

According to Gary Maxey, scattered autonomous holiness groups taught against sex within the marriage union except for procreation. They preached against Coca-Cola, chewing gum, neckties, and life insurance. They emphasized such controversial issues as divine healing, premillenialism, and a third blessing or "the fire" which was often accompanied by the "holy dance" and "hallelujah earthquakes."[1026]

In Nebraska B. H. Irwin, a member of Iowa's Holiness Association, concluded that there was a third blessing called "the baptism with the Holy Ghost and fire." His conclusion was based on a misreading of John Fletcher.[1027] Fletcher had suggested that there were many baptisms or outpourings of the Spirit in the Christian life. Holiness teachers often read their own presuppositions into early Methodist literature. For them there was no continual filling of the Holy Spirit, therefore every outpouring of the Spirit had to mean either the blessing of sanctification had been lost and was regained or it was a new work of grace. In the milieu of the holiness movement, Irwin concluded by 1900 that there were six works of grace, adding the baptisms of dynamite, lyddite, and oxidite.[1028] He was influenced by Godbey's translation of the Greek word for "power" as "dynamite." According to W. C. Wilson, Godbey was to blame for the introduction of this new doctrine. He said Godbey's translation encouraged people to believe that the incoming of the Holy Spirit is always a spectacular, explosive experience, creating

---

[1023]Jernigan, *Pioneer Days*, 193-202. Jernigan argued that there had never been a great spiritual awakening which was not followed by a scourge of fanatical teaching.

[1024]Rose, *Vital Holiness*, 73. Yet Jernigan said all the leadership of the holiness movement in the early days in Texas "seemed to be well educated men" [*Pioneer Days*, 193].

[1025]Kiergan, *Historical Sketches*, 55.

[1026]Maxey, "Wesleyan-Holiness Roots," 1:10. Writing in 1881 Doty rejected a third blessing [*Lessons in Holiness*, 104]. However, Doty called upon holiness people to give up tea and coffee [pp. 82; 182-185]. See also Stephens, *Fire Spreads*, 123.

[1027]See Fletcher, *Works*, 2:632-633, quoted on p. 497 of this book.

[1028]Synan, *Holiness-Pentecostal Tradition*, 57.

a big noise and a big smoke.[1029]

> Taking advantage of the discovery or invention in his own lifetime of dynamite, which is derived from the Greek word translated "power" in the text where Jesus promised that with the coming of the Holy Spirit the disciples should receive power, he translated the expression, "You shall receive Dynamite." This has many times encouraged people to believe that the incoming of the Holy Spirit is always a spectacular, explosive experience, creating, as it were, a big noise and a big smoke. One group in Texas actually added several experiences to the baptism of the Holy Spirit. That was to be a separate baptism of fire, then of dynamite, then of lyddite, then of TNT, and so on.

Those receiving "the fire" would often shout, scream, speak in other tongues, fall into trances, or get the jerks.[1030] These baptisms of fire, subsequent to entire sanctification were intended for empowerment, special gifting, deeper mystical experiences in heavenly places, and deeper cleansings which delivered from coffee and pork. It also produced new phenomenon including "wheel-in-a-wheel" and leaping.[1031]

In 1895 Irwin organized Fire-Baptized Holiness Associations in Iowa, Kansas, Oklahoma, and Texas. In 1897 he went south and added associations in Florida, Georgia, South Carolina, North Carolina, and Virginia. The same year associations were begun in Ontario and Manitoba, Canada.[1032] In 1899 it was discovered that Irwin was living in "open and gross sin" and later he left the movement in disgrace. He was arrested in Kansas City for drunkenness and bad conduct late in 1899. Pictures of his luggage with the insignia "blood and fire" and "holiness unto the Lord" were displayed on the front pages of the Kansas City newspapers.[1033] The report that Irwin had walked the streets of Omaha drunk and smoking a cigar was circulated widely through H. C. Morrison's *Pentecostal Herald*.[1034]

In 1906 Irwin came in contact with the Azusa Street meetings. He

---

[1029]Wilson, "Well Glory!"59-60.

[1030]Synan, *Holiness-Pentecostal Tradition*, 52.

[1031]Davidson, *Upon This Rock*, 290; Conn, *Like a Mighty Army*, 39-43.

[1032]Synan, *The Holiness-Pentecostal Tradition*, 54.

[1033]Pheobus, "Fire Baptized Holiness Church," 55.

[1034]Jones, "Irwin, B. H," 583.

abandoned his doctrine of baptisms of fire, dynamite, lyddite, and oxidite, proclaiming that the "tongues" baptism was the one he had been seeking all along. By 1907 a restored Irwin was preaching this new doctrine on the West coast.[1035]

In 1911 most of the Fire-Baptized movement merged with the Pentecostal Holiness Church.[1036] Among the remaining minority doctrine was flexible and people who held to two-works, as well as those who held to three-works coexisted in the same organization. Floyd Martin preached a third work until asked, "What does this fire do for a feller?" Unable to give an answer, Martin concluded he could no longer advocate seeking the "fire." He visited each church where he had preached a third work and apologized for teaching false doctrine.

A compromise was reached in 1934. Those seeking credentials were asked, "Do you understand that God pours out his spirit upon His believing children again and again? Will you earnestly desire such out-pourings?" Finally the preaching of a third work was banned in 1948 and in 1995 their name was changed to the Bible Holiness Church (Independence, Kansas).[1037]

During this same time period Ralph C. Horner (1854-1921), a maverick holiness evangelist in Canada, founded two small denominations. He taught that the disciples were saved *and* entirely sanctified before Pentecost. He taught Pentecost as a third blessing. He recognized that Wesley did not connect sanctification with Pentecost.

> Wesley taught holiness by the commands, prayers, and promises in the Word, given to God's people. He selected commands from the Old and New Testaments, but did not use any that were given by the Lord Jesus to the apostles regarding the Pentecost. They were told to tarry in the city of Jerusalem until they would be endued with power from on high. Wesley did not quote this command given by the Lord Jesus to the disciples. The question is why did he not? Simply because he knew that they had received holiness, and this command was for the special anointing for service, which they received on the day of Pentecost.

Horner then observed that Wesley also collected biblical prayers for entire sanctification, "but did not intimate that any of these prayers were answered on the day of Pentecost." Horner felt John 17:17 could have been used if Wesley had connected Pentecost and entire sanctification. Promises such as Acts 1:5 and

---

[1035]Synan, *Holiness-Pentecostal Tradition*, 127-128.

[1036]Synan, *Holiness-Pentecostal Tradition*, 59.

[1037]Black, *Holiness Heritage*, 243-248.

Acts 1:8 could have also been cited by Wesley to prove that their fulfilment on the day of Pentecost was the instantaneous blessing of entire sanctification. Horner was correct in his observation that Wesley did not make the connection. He also defended Wesleyan theology in his book refuting J. M. Boland,[1038] but he was incorrect in his conclusion that the baptism of power at Pentecost was a third blessing.[1039] Horner arrived at his doctrine of a third blessing as a result of refuting Boland. With that emphasis on "soul-winning power," physical manifestations such as "prostration, ecstasy, immediate laughter" were common in Horner's ministry and alienated him from the Methodist people with whom he began his ministry.[1040] His emphasis on a third blessing allowed for prophecy and speaking in tongues, dividing the Holiness Movement Church, which he formed in 1895.

While the entire holiness movement did not adopt all these extreme notions, those who did not adopt them often had to fight hard to keep these notions from taking root. In doing so, they laid themselves open to the charge of hindering the work of the Holy Spirit. Howard Snyder asserted:

> Holiness theology in the late nineteenth century logically leads either to Pentecostalism or to some disillusionment with the second crisis experience. By its very nature, a spiritual peak experience cannot be permanently satisfying. . . . But without normative structures for nurturing the life of holiness, and with the increasing stress on subjective crises typified by the growing use of Pentecostal crisis language, many Holiness people no doubt felt an inner lack in their lives, a sense that there must be something deeper, something more, in Christian experience. So then, after the turn of the century the question logically became, could this "something more" be the new phenomenon of speaking in tongues? Many concluded that it was. Other groups staunchly resisted this new Pentecostalism, and on that issue the Holiness Movement divided.[1041]

[1038] Horner, *Notes on Boland.*

[1039] Horner, *Pentecost*, 137-139; 66-68. Horner was also influenced by the writings of Simon P. Jacobs, Methodist president of the Southwestern Holiness Association. Jacobs realized that the doctrine of pentecostal sanctification was a late development [Dayton, *Theological Roots of Pentecostalism*, 98-99]. See Jacobs, *Real Christian.*

[1040] Dayton, *Theological Roots of Pentecostalism*, 98-100.

[1041] Snyder and Runyon, *Divided Flame*, 72-73; see also Snyder, "Church as Holy and Charismatic," 21.

While there was a new emphasis on the Holy Spirit and experience, there was often a lack of emphasis on the Holy Spirit and the Word of God. It was the influence of Phoebe Palmer that opened the door to women preachers although at first she hesitated to preach.[1042] Oberlin College became the first coeducational college in the world and Antoinette Brown, a graduate of Oberlin College was the first woman to be fully ordained. Her ordination sermon was preached on September 15, 1853 by Luther Lee of the Wesleyan Methodist Church.[1043] Eventually Ms. Brown became a Unitarian.

Twenty-five percent of the clergy of the early holiness movement were women.[1044] When the Church of the Nazarene was founded, 20% of the ministers were women.[1045]

When John Wesley used women in the Methodist societies it must be remembered that Methodism was a parachurch organization. Wesley felt it was possible to do things within Methodism that could not be done within an ecclesiastical organization.[1046] Methodist societies were divided into classes and Wesley did allow both men and women to be class leaders. He made it clear, though, that the class leader was to be under the pastor.[1047] To allow a woman to exhort a class for four or five minutes was not the same to Wesley as preaching. Women were not allowed to take a text. Wesley allowed for men to be lay preachers and still prohibited them from administering the Lord's Supper because they were not ordained. Wesley did not allow women to preach or administer the sacraments and to ordain them was unthinkable.[1048] To claim Wesley opened this door to women is to misunderstand the Methodist structure.

In *A Letter to a Person lately joined with the people called Quakers* Wesley stated the differences between Quakerism and Christianity. He took exception to Robert Barclay's statement that it was no longer unlawful for a woman to preach. He answered the argument that in the last days daughters would prophecy by making a distinction between preaching and prophesying. The

---

[1042]White, *Beauty of Holiness*, 188-189.

[1043]Dayton, *Discovering an Evangelical Heritage*, 41; 83. While Lee was happy to preach the sermon, he refused to perform the act of ordination and refused to provide a certificate of ordination [Kaufman, *"Logical" Luther Lee*, 163-166; 228.

[1044]Dayton, *Discovering an Evangelical Heritage*, 97-98. Maddox, "Christian Feminist Critique," 109.

[1045]Schwartz, "Your Daughters Will Prophesy," 32.

[1046]Clouse, *Women in Ministry*, 14.

[1047]Wesley, *Works*, 13:16.

[1048]Wesley, *BE Works*, 9:573.

letter runs eleven pages and nearly a full page is devoted to rebutting the error among the Quakers that women may preach.[1049]

Wesley wrote to Sarah Crosby, "The Methodists do not allow of women Preachers. . . ."[1050] Eight years later he cautioned her, "keep as far from what is called preaching as you can."[1051]

In his notes on 1 Corinthians 14:34 he may have given too much latitude when he commented that women are to be silent "unless they are under an extra-ordinary impulse of the Spirit." But Wesley understood that preaching and prophesying were not the same and may have had that in mind when he wrote the comment. He continued, "*For* in other cases *it is not permitted them to speak* — By way of teaching in public assemblies; *but to be in subjection* — To the man, whose proper office it is to lead and instruct the congregation."[1052]

After Wesley's death, Methodism became a church and there was "clear embarrassment about the existence of women preachers which led to the denial of ordination for women in the main Methodist church until the mid-twentieth century."[1053] Maggie Van Cott was the first woman licensed to preach in the Methodist Church. She was given a local preacher's license in 1869. In 1870 over seventy women received local preacher's licenses. However, in May 1880, the judiciary committee of General Conference ruled that church law did not permit the ordaining or licensing of women and rescinded all local preacher's licenses from 1869 on. Full clergy rights were not granted to women in the Methodist Episcopal Church until 1956.

An emphasis on experience above Scriptural authority also produced extremes regarding sexual purity. A book from the holiness movement in South Africa warned,

> There is a teaching extant among so-called holiness people, termed "sexual purity" which is unnatural, unscriptural and harmful. It is on the line of living together in the married relation, but practicing celibacy. Some good people have been pushed into this heresy by Satan and have fallen into secret sins more revolting in God's sight than that condemned in Hebrews

---

1049 Wesley, *Works*, 10:180.

1050 Wesley, *Letter*, 14 February 1761.

1051 Wesley, *Letter*, 18 March 1769.

1052 Wesley, *Notes*, 440.

1053 Maddox, "Christian Feminist Critique,"109.

13:4.[1054]

The early holiness groups also opposed a problem they called "free love." Apparently souls were not only born again at some camp meetings, but souls were also conceived in the emotional environment. More recently a professor at Oral Roberts University told his class that sometimes during sexual intercourse he spoke in tongues.[1055] Apparently "freedom in the Spirit" can easily lead to a loss of other inhibitions.

A. M. Kiergan recorded that they had to deal with the "free love" problem in Missouri and that it had been influential in Illinois some years earlier. Apparently a holiness preacher had set up a "free love" establishment there.[1056] W. T. Hogue, a Free Methodist bishop, warned against the minister who had a "spiritual affinity" for those of the opposite sex. He warned that this almost always led to free love.[1057]

During this era holiness was sometimes pursued in communal settings. Mother Ann Lee, influenced by radical Quaker teaching, believed that perfection was attainable through the elimination of greed, pride, and sex. In the early nineteenth century the Shakers urged new revival converts to "go on unto perfection," as they understood it. According to Shaker theology God is bisexual, as was Adam until Eve was taken from his side. Redemption is deliverance from physical lust and the realization of spiritual love.[1058]

The most famous advocate of free love was John Humphrey Noyes. He established two communities, Putney, Vermont (1840-48) and Oneida, New York (1848-81), where his ideas of perfection, communism, complex marriage, male continence, and population control were practiced.[1059]

[1054]Shephard, *Bible Lessons*, 146; see also "the continent life" described in Shelhamer, *Auntie Coon*, 147-150. The Hephzibah Faith Missionary Association, a holiness group headquartered in Tabor, Iowa practiced "social and marital purity" [Jones, "Anti-Ordinance,"18].

[1055]Sholes, *Prime-Time Religio*, 80.

[1056]Kiergan, *Historical Sketches*, 31; see also Harris, *Tears and Triumphs*, 335-339.

[1057]Hogue, "Fallen Ministers" 46. McDougle in *Salvation* had to disassociate holiness from "free love"[p. 40]. However, see the explanation by Hamilton that anyone who challenged an abusive marriage would be labeled a "free lover" in order to discredit them by appealing to force or intimidation ["Corsicana Enthusiasts,"184].

[1058]See Gaddis, *Christian Perfection in America*, 223-224.

[1059]Pitzer, "John Humphry Noyes," 718. See also Warfield, *Perfectionism*, 2:219-333. Presumably this is the group Asa Mahan referenced in *Christian Perfection*,

Timothy Smith called Noyes the most radical "perfectionist" of them all, explaining that he tied together revivalism and socialism, selective breeding along with biblical communism, theocratic democracy, divine healing, and male continence in order to usher in the Kingdom of God.[1060] Noyes believed that the second advent had already occurred in A. D. 70. Christ had returned spiritually making perfection available to all who accepted the inner presence and reign of Christ. Noyes believed the marriage relationship, with its emphasis on special love, was a hindrance to perfection. Since the kingdom of heaven has come and according to Matthew 22:30 those who are resurrected do not marry, Noyes taught that no man has exclusive right to any one woman or vice versa. Instead all live as "angels."

Within the holiness movement there were other attempts to live communally. D. S. Warner led a band of people who lived communally and their publishing house had these arrangements for the first thirty-two years of operation.[1061] An associate of Warner's taught that sexual relations within marriage were carnal and not compatible with "holy living." Warner's wife accepted this teaching and later divorced him.[1062] Christ's Sanctified Holy Church traveled communally for their first twenty-five years.

Martin Wells Knapp first advocated a radical view of property ownership in *Lightning Bolts from Pentecostal Skies* (1898). In 1899 God was formally listed as the proprietor of the *Revivalist*. In 1900 when Knapp opened a Bible school, it was named God's Bible School, with Knapp as the sole trustee. Knapp believed the accumulation of property for personal gain was sinful and Knapp did not pay workers a salary.

This conviction influenced the Metropolitan Church Association, known as the Burning Bush Movement. They preached a consecration which included the teaching that ownership of private property was contrary to apostolic teaching and threatened one's eternal destiny. Based on Acts 2:44-45, they insisted that those who wanted to be disciples of Christ must forsake all, surrendering their assets to the church. Beginning in 1906 they operated a communal home in Waukesha, Wisconsin until 1956.[1063]

65-68; 170). Originally this book was published in 1839.

[1060]Smith, *Revivalism and Social Reform*, 162. See also Warfield, *Perfectionism*, 2:219-333; Miller, "Gallery," 14. "Male continence" refers to sexual discipline. "Complex marriage" means all members were married to each other.

[1061]Smith, *Quest for Holiness and Unity*, 67.

[1062]Smith, *Quest for Holiness and Unity*, 65.

[1063]Kostlevy, "Nor Silver, Nor Gold." Kostlevy claimed that between 1870 and 1917 as many as a dozen evangelical communal societies flourished in the U. S. For

In 1892 Joseph B. Lynch left the Methodist Church in Chincoteague, Virginia over the issue of sanctification. He led a band who traveled and held revivals. They called themselves Christ's Sanctified Holy Church, based on Ephesians 5:25-27 and Hebrews 12:23. Their main emphasis was on sanctification.

> Salvation is accomplished by two separate works of the grace of God through faith in Jesus Christ, the Son of God. The first work of grace is repentance before God, or asking for forgiveness of the sins that we have committed. The second work is the baptism of the Holy ghost, or Sanctification, which is the indwelling of the Holy Spirit, eradicating the nature of sin.[1064]

Although small in number, their importance can be easily overlooked.[1065] Like many small holiness groups, they would be suspicious of higher education and book learning. "They believed that there was no school or college that could reveal the secrets of the Bible as well as the great teacher from Heaven could teach and inspire an individual."[1066] Consequently they left very little written history, but their "grass roots" theology impacted a class of people who would never read the more scholarly and balanced literature.[1067]

For twenty-five years their itinerant groups, sometimes on houseboats, traveled going as far west as California and preaching in over a hundred cities. Passages such as Matthew 19:29; Mark 10:29-30; Luke 14:26; 18:29 were interpreted as a test of sanctification. The truly sanctified were expected to leave

---

another example, see the House of Prayer movement in Brown and Brevard, *History of the Churches of Christ in Christian Union*, "Rise and Expulsion of 'All Things Common,'" 125-139. The House of Prayer movement originated with Edward Wayne Runyan who was influenced by the Metropolitan Church Association. In 1918 the Churches of Christ in Christian Union expelled 14 ministers, including one of its founders, for advocating Runyan's teaching.

1064Collins and Hagan, *Christ's Sanctified Holy Church*, v.

1065Collins and Hagan, *Christ's Sanctified Holy Church*, stated the church was composed of over a thousand people in 17 cities in nine states [p. 1]. Yet they claimed to have influenced tens of thousands through their itinerant ministry.

1066Collins and Hagan, *Christ's Sanctified Holy Church*, 5.

1067An exception would be Cornelius P. Haggard, president for thirty-six years of what is now Azusa Pacific University. The parents of Cornelius, Neal and Lillie Haggard, were influenced by "the sanctified people" and Lillie preached with them [Haggard, *Intrepid Builder*, 7].

all behind and travel with the band.

The men were carpenters and they carried their tools with them. They all moved in a big house using it both for a church and living quarters. They were self supporting and stayed and preached until the Lord led them to move on. They had a motto, "No creed but Christ; no law but love; no guide but the Bible."[1068] They had no song leader, but when it was time to start someone was led of the Spirit to begin a song. They did not believe in musical instruments. They had no pastor, but during the course of the service the Bible would be handed to the one whom the leader felt should bring the message. After the message someone was asked to back the preacher. He sanctioned the character of the speaker and the message. Others testified that they knew by experience the message was true and seekers were invited forward. They emphasized feeling the Spirit which was a tingling sensation. When the Spirit was moving they felt they must jump or they would quench the Spirit. For them this jumping blessing was the witness of the Spirit. In their early days they were also called "Holy Jumpers."[1069]

They felt that all sinners were living in adultery. They also felt they must separate from an "Egyptian wife" or a companion whom they married before they were sanctified. Since they were to be led of the Spirit and since the Spirit could not have led them to a proper mate before conversion, they felt the Lord could lead them to a new partner within the group. Thus, they left their spouse when they were sanctified.[1070] This led to the doctrine of the righteous generation, that holy parents produced holy children who had no sinful nature. Sanctified parents would bear sinless children and this would bring in the millennium.[1071]

[1068]Collins and Hagan, *Christ's Sanctified Holy Church*, 4; 16.

[1069]The Burning Bush movement (Metropolitan Church Association), which began in 1894, was also known as jumpers since they regarded jumping as the evidence of the baptism of the Holy Spirit.

[1070]Waite, *Goodly Heritage*, 34 explained that Ben Milam's first wife "never came out with the sanctified," so he remarried.

[1071]According to a phone interview with Harry Collins, this has not been taught nor practiced since the 1930s [3 Dec 1995]. However, the original teaching is referenced by West, *Holiness Groups*, 8-9]. West reported that their teaching on marriage aroused such public indignation that they were taken to court, declared to be a common nuisance and ordered to leave the state. Thus, by living on houseboats they could avoid state restrictions on their marriage doctrine. In 1894 Lynch and two other "sanctified ones" were sentenced from 4-8 months of jail for lasciviousness in a high profile case tried in Accomack County, Virginia. The newspaper account described their believe that "all marriages were unholy in divine sight except those of the sanctified" ["'Sanctified Ones' Go to Jail," *New York Times*, 6 Nov 1984]. A *New York Times* special report described the bigamy, gross immorality and vice practiced by some, implying that the promise of a "holy wife" enticed some men to leave their wives and

The atonement of Christ was for sanctification. Sanctification is through Christ's shed blood. The church does not observe the sacraments, but allows women to preach. They do not believe in Christ's literal second coming and do not emphasize tongues, but do stress divine healing. They put little emphasis on the law of God since they believe a sanctified person will naturally do what is good. Marriage vows are not considered important in the wedding ceremony.

The church registered their name with the U.S. Patent Office in 1982 stating in the legal document that the origin of their church dates back to John and Charles Wesley. However, their statement of doctrine makes no reference whatsoever to regeneration and claims no one is saved without the second work of grace. In 1887 Joseph Lynch became convinced "that he could not be truly saved without Holiness, even though he was living in a Justified state."[1072] Since Romans 7 is interpreted as the life of one converted and Romans 8 the sanctified life, they taught must get sanctified to avoid going right back to sinning again.[1073]

They claim water baptism is superceded by the baptism of the Holy Ghost. "The second coming of Christ occurs at the time we are sanctified" and this also is the resurrection. "There will never be a general resurrection of people from the grave in this life. The resurrection is spiritual."[1074]

In 1930 a split occurred in Birmingham, Alabama, at least in part, over the doctrine of marriage and in 1936 the Sanctified Church of Christ was formed in Columbus, Georgia to affirm holy matrimony. Christ's Elect Sanctified Holy Church, under the leadership of Cashier Grey, practiced open marriage teaching that they were all sheep of one fold. Although such groups represent an extreme fringe, the issues were the same with little groups across the nation.

In the mountains of West Virginia everything has been taught. I interviewed a lay leader who verified that at least as far back as the 1940 and up to the 1990s there were charismatic leaders who taught that a believer should not be unequally yoked to an unbeliever. Sometimes a believer claimed that God led

---

families and join the band ["Lynch's Sanctified Band," *New York Times*, 24 Sept 1899]. See also Bell, "Sanctified Band Controversy," 25-30, which chronicles the arrival of the sanctified "ark"in North Carolina after fleeing Virginia. It was reported that they preached, "Sanctification does not regard the marriage relationship." In a public debate Sarah Collins denied that a man is saved when he is converted and affirmed that a sanctified man is sinless. They taught that no matter what they do so long as they are "sanctified," it is no sin. They told women that after sanctification they can be any man's spiritual wife.

[1072]Collins and Hagan, *Christ's Sanctified Holy Church*, 2.

[1073]Waite, *Goodly Heritage*, 29; 91.

[1074]*Christ's Sanctified Holy Church*, no pagination; *Association of Churches Under the Name Christ's Sanctified Holy Church*, 1-20.

them to a spouse other than the one to which they were presently married. While this was not generally accepted within the Church of God Reformation Movement, some churches broke away because of this issue. It still crops up occasionally in rural areas, although it has generally died out. My friend knew of two instances within the last six to eight years. He said the Helms movement taught this strongly, even picking couples out of the church to be married to each other although they were already married to someone else. Often these groups felt that no church government was necessary. Autonomous local churches had little control. Credentialing committees faced this issue and were about the only means of controlling it.[1075] Merle Strege explained the feeling of early Church of God (Anderson, Indiana) people that if the Holy Spirit is to guide us into all truth, why even vote on an issue? They felt that the sectarian Babylonian churches (every other church other than theirs), were ruled by men and not by God.[1076]

The early days of the Church of God (Holiness) were also filled with debate over how much government was necessary. They felt that to be amenable to a local congregation was joining and God was the One who should add to the church. To be subject to the discipline of a local congregation meant to be in subjection to human authority and thus the church was no longer God's, but man's.[1077]

In addition to these tendencies there was a move away from observing the sacraments. Although Jesus commanded that we keep his Supper, many holiness groups felt it was too formal and unspiritual. John Wesley had emphasized both evangelicalism and the means of grace. He did not divorce preaching from the sacraments. He demanded both and exhorted those who heard him preach to "attend the offices of the Church."[1078]

But within the holiness movement water baptism was not nearly so important as Spirit baptism.[1079] When John Brooks wrote *The Divine Church* in 1891, he devoted sixty-four pages or almost a fourth of the book defending the sacraments. While Brooks used both terms, *sacrament* and *ordinance*, his

---

[1075]Don Page, 6 Feb 2009. See also Helm and Cullum, *Voice in the Wilderness*, 125, where Helm claimed the Holy Spirit revealed to him that 87% of all marriages in the United States are out of divine order. Yet having made those vows, whether or not it *was* God's will, it is now God's will that they remain marriage.

[1076]Strege, "God's Ways Are Not Our Ways," 4.

[1077]Cowen, *History of the Church of God (Holiness)*, 41-42.

[1078]Wesley, *Works*, 8:62; Borgen, *John Wesley on the Sacraments*, 282.

[1079]Bloesch observed that in some holiness churches only spiritual baptism has merit and the rite of water baptism has been discontinued [*Holy Spirit*, 142; 366].

emphasis was on ordinances.[1080] In the Church of God Reformation Movement, the term *sacrament* is rejected. They observe believer's baptism by immersion, communion, and footwashing as ordinances. These are seen as symbolic and acts of obedience, but not means of grace.

Today several holiness denominations do not believe in observing the sacraments. While some prefer the term *ordinances*, much of the the holiness movement puts very little emphasis on them. A. M. Kiergan said the controversy over water baptism and the Lord's Supper were really only a symptom of a deeper problem, a spirit of anarchy which was sweeping the country.[1081]

While the movement in general had adopted pentecostal terminology, there were those on the fringes who not only had received their baptism, but were claiming the Spirit had revealed new truth to them. A. M. Kiergan described a spirit of anarchy which led some in northern Missouri around 1885 to recognize no human responsibility or authority in church government. They rejected the sacraments and taught

> the resurrection was regeneration; the second coming of Christ was the indwelling Spirit; the millennium was an ineffable third experience, glorification. With them the resurrection was past, Christ had come the second time and they were glorified.[1082]

One woman said she was resurrected, glorified, and walking the golden streets of the New Jerusalem. When a brother questioned her, she replied, "Oh, you need the third experience." A minister claimed, "The bullet was never moulded [sic] that could penetrate his body, it was a spiritual body. That he would be the same young and healthy man he was then a thousand years hence." One man boasted that "he could write a better Bible than the one we have." Another preacher taught the blood of Christ was not efficacious and someone else discarded the atonement putting Christianity on a par with Judaism or pagan religions.[1083]

[1080]Brooks, *Divine Church*, 137-201.

[1081]Kiergan, *Historical Sketches*, 55.

[1082]Kiergan, *Historical Sketches*, 55.

[1083]Kiergan, *Historical Sketches*, 55; see also Jones, "Anti-Ordinance" 12-13. Wesley dealt with some of this same fanaticism, see his *Journal*, 5 February 1762. Notice this doctrine of immortality was taught by the Cathari [p. 424 of this book; see also pp. 475; 661]. This teaching also surfaced within Pentecostalism in 1948. The Manifest Sons of God had already received their redeemed bodies and would not die [Riss, "Latter Rain Movement," 133-135]. They taught sinless perfection not only as a possibility, but a biblical promise. This perfection culminates in physical immortality

Pentecostal Theology and Azusa Street

Most of the doctrines and expectations of the pentecostal movement were shaped in the holiness movement.[1084] According to Vinson Synan, all the teachings and practices of pentecostalism, including their style of worship, their music, and their basic theology were adopted "whole cloth from the Holiness milieu," except the teaching that tongues was the evidence of the baptism of the Holy Spirit.[1085] Donald Dayton declared, "I find it difficult, if not impossible, to conceive of the rise of modern Pentecostalism without the background of the Wesleyan doctrine of 'Christian Perfection' transmuted into the doctrine of 'Pentecostal sanctification.'"[1086] Howard Snyder concluded, "Whereas early Methodism grew up around the recovery of the doctrine of the new birth, the Holiness Movement sprang from a recovery of Wesley's doctrine of entire sanctification as a deeper experience beyond conversion. In this sense, at least, the Holiness Movement has more affinities with modern Charismatic Christianity than does early Methodism. . . . From this perspective, late-nineteenth-century Holiness theology logically leads either to Pentecostalism or to a denial of the validity of a second crisis experience."[1087]

Writing for the Southern *Methodist Quarterly Review* in 1925, J. M. Steadman observed that the tongues movement was not distinctive of Methodism. Steadman said that some Methodists had identified with it, "but those who claim this gift usually pass into some other Church." He recalled that some years ago some members of the Methodist Episcopal Church, South went to the Wesleyan Methodist Church because of extreme views on the question of sanctification or holiness. "In these sections where this occurred, the unknown tongue movement followed. These excesses brought the doctrine of holiness into disrepute."[1088]

---

prior to the general resurrection. This elite group of overcomers would have the power to defy the laws of gravity, to walk upside down, as well as attain present immortality [Reeves, *Other Side of the River*, 124; 171-175].

[1084]Marsden, *Fundamentalism and American Culture*, 72.

[1085]Dayton, "Pentecostalism,"836. In a review of *Christian Spirituality: Five Views on Sanctification* John Hughes noted that each view could point to a major theologian to articulate their view, "but the Pentecostals have no guiding theologians" ["Five Paths to Holiness," 35]. Bruner noted that Finney's theology is the only one stocked by the average pentecostal book room [*Theology of the Holy Spirit*, 40].

[1086]Dayton, "Baptism of the Spirit," 122.

[1087]Snyder, "Church as Holy and Charismatic," 19; 21.

[1088]Steadman, "Gift of Tongues," 713. Steadman was reviewing two books which both had the title *The Gift of Tongues*. One was by D. A. Hayes and the other by

However, as early as 1907 *The Wesleyan Methodist* addressed the Apostolic Faith Movement publishing twenty-one articles that year. While S. A. Manwell and P. B. Campbell rejected tongues as the only biblical evidence of the baptism of the Holy Ghost, they did equate the baptism of the Holy Ghost with entire sanctification.[1089]

Larry Martin collected fifty-eight articles which appeared in holiness periodicals in 1906-1907 which were critical of the new movement at Azusa Street. Of these articles, twenty-one were from the *Burning Bush*, the periodical of the Metropolitan Church Association and nine were from the Pillar of Fire periodical. Yet both of these holiness groups were radical in their worship and they were both very hostile to each other. Alma White had begun as an evangelist of the MCA, but withdrew over a property dispute. To the uninitiated, both groups seemed to worship interchangeably as "jumpers." Alma White's husband embraced pentecostalism and A.G. Garr of the MCA was the first white to speak in tongues at Azusa Street.[1090]

In 1908 Charles P. Pumphrey addressed the "gift of tongues" in the mainline *Methodist Review*. He concluded that the baptism of the Holy Spirit is a baptism of common sense resulting in a quickening of mental and moral

---

Alexander Mackie.

[1089]Campbell, "Gift of Tongues," I-III, 8; 9; 9; "Present Tongues Movement, I-VI," 3; 2; 2; 2; 2; 2; Manwell, "Speaking with Tongues," I-II, 8-9; 8-9. See also Jennings, "Be Wise as Serpents, Harmless as Doves," 1; "Fundamental Principle," 8; "But It Improves Religious Experience," 8; "What Would Convince You?" 8; "Some Things in the Tongues Movement," 8; Besse, "Speak With Tongues," 2-3; Cox, "Speaking With Other Tongues," 2; Waddell, "Revival and Tongues," 11; Hill, "Paul on Tongues," 11; James, "Doctrine Of Tongues," 2-3.

[1090]Other holiness denominations reacting to the Azusa Street phenomenon which Martin included were the Free Methodists with four articles, Church of God (Anderson) with four articles, the Church of God (Independent Holiness People) with three, the Church of the Nazarene with two, and the Christian & Missionary Alliance, and God's Bible School with one each. In the previous paragraph I already referred to the Wesleyan Methodist Church which published twenty-one articles in 1907. Martin referenced three of these articles. At least one article in Martin's collection was not from a holiness church.

A. M. Kiergan, who was referenced on p. 577 of this book, became part of the Church of God movement which split in 1897 into the Church of God (Holiness) and the Church of God (IHP).

In general the groups reacting to Azusa Street were the groups closest to pentecostalism in their own practices. See Kostlevy, "Nor Silver, Nor Gold" concerning the controversy between the MCA and the Pillar of Fire. Larry Martin's book is *Skeptics and Scoffers*.

precepts.[1091]

The United Methodist Church issued its evaluation of the movement in 1976, concluding that when "United Methodist charismatics adopt a classical Pentecostal line, they are no longer United Methodists — at least in the Wesleyan sense. . . . Pentecostals have a predictable interpretation of the Wesleyan revival. Although Pentecostalism has its roots deeply imbedded within that tradition, it has little in common with Wesley's theology."[1092] Synan was aware of this report, but he observed that United Methodism welcomed tongues speakers, including Oral Roberts in 1969.[1093] Roberts separated from the Methodists in 1988.

Elmer Clark concluded in *The Small Sects in America* that most of the pentecostal churches "were the direct or indirect creations of A. J. Tomlinson."[1094] Tomlinson is considered the founder of the Church of God (Cleveland) in 1907 and the Church of God of Prophecy in 1923. However, Clark was relying on information given him by Tomlinson.[1095] It is generally agreed that the American pentecostal movement began with Charles F. Parham in 1901. Tomlinson did not receive his "baptism" until 1907.[1096]

Parham began his ministry as a supply pastor in the Methodist Episcopal Church. Later he came in contact with B. H. Irwin and was influenced by his teaching of a third work of grace. In 1898 he operated Bethel Healing Home in Topeka, Kansas and in 1900 Parham began Bethel Bible School. Parham adopted his own Bethel Bible School from Frank W. Sandford's Holy Ghost and Us facility near Durham, Maine.

By December of that year Parham concluded that tongues was the evidence of the baptism of the Holy Ghost. In many holiness groups tongues

---

[1091]Pumphrey, "Gift of Tongues," 764.

[1092]Tuttle, *Guidelines*, 6; 8. The Guidelines themselves were approved by action of the 1976 General Conference. The second half of the document was derived from a paper by Robert G. Tuttle and is not to be considered official. Instead it is "commended to the church for study as background to the 'Guidelines.'" The citation I have given is from that second part.

[1093]Synan, *In the Latter Days*, 124.

[1094]Clark, *Small Sects in America*, 101.

[1095]Synan, *Holiness-Pentecostal Tradition*, 80.

[1096]Tomlinson, *Last Great Conflict*, 210; Tomlinson, *Diary of A. J. Tomlinson*, 1:51-53 gives the date of 12 January 1908.

According to Thornton, Tomlinson attended God's Bible School ["Revivalist Movement" 174]. He apparently attended prior to 1899 [Hunter, "Ambrose Jessup Tomlinson," 846-847]. This reference does not appear in the second edition, *New International Dictionary of Pentecostal and Charismatic Movements* (2002).

would have been accepted as *an* evidence of the Spirit, but Parham was apparently the first to demand that there must be *the* evidence of tongues.[1097] Parham designated himself as the Projector of the Apostolic Faith Movement. Thus, his emphasis was on experiential primitivism through the restoration of the experience of the apostles. Without grasping the shift in emphasis his wife later wrote, "He preached sanctification as a second definite work of grace, as taught by John Wesley and the early Methodists."[1098]

During the nineteenth century restorationism or a return to primitive Christianity, however it was perceived, was promoted by groups as diverse as the Christian Church, as envisioned by Alexander Campbell, the Jehovah's Witnesses, the Seventh-Day Adventists, and the Apostolic Faith movement.[1099]

Yet Parham believed that sanctification not only purified the soul from sin, but it cleansed the body from disease. Infirmity signified sin's physical remnant. "Just as Wesley proposed sanctification as the means for removing the remnant of sin in the soul, Parham prescribed sanctification to remove sin's vestiges in the body."[1100]

Parham's Apostolic Faith Movement was based upon the beliefs that:

1. Tongues was the absolutely indispensable evidence of the baptism with the Holy Spirit.

2. The gift of tongues was given for the purpose of world evangelism and would thus hasten the premillennial return of Christ. Tongues were initially believed to be actual foreign languages which would enable this last generation to evangelize (but not necessarily convert)[1101] the whole world.

[1097]Parham, *Sermons: Voice Crying*, 38.

[1098]Parham, *Life of Parham*, 21.

[1099]Robeck also lists the Mormons as a restorationist group which originated in this same era [*Azusa Street Mission and Revival*, 121]. While Mormonism saw itself as a restoration of the Church of Jesus Christ, Joseph Smith's new revelation places the church in a category of movements which attempt to improve on apostolic Christianity, such as Islam and liberalism. Both extremes, whether restorationist or evolutionary, are examples of institutional perfectionism. See the discussion on p. 422.

[1100]Callahan, "Fleshly Manifestations," 2; 42; 182. Ironically, Parham was ill his entire life. Parham originally had wanted to be a physician, but felt it was impossible to be both a Christian and a physician [Callahan, "Fleshly Manifestations," 17]. His quest for physical perfection is also clouded by the allegations of his homosexuality.

[1101]Faupel, *Everlasting Gospel*, 21. The postmillennial emphasis was on the conversion of the world until, as Wesley put it, we would see a Christian world

This position raises the question of why anyone would need to speak in tongues if he had no intention of traveling to a foreign mission field. Parham's answer, which really did not answer the question, was that speaking in tongues was the remedy for all of the years that people preached in their own languages in order to propagate their own creed or gain financial benefit. On the other hand, when the preacher spoke as a medium of the Holy Spirit, the message of God, when interpreted, came undiluted.[1102]

Essentially Parham claimed the purpose of tongues was to cross linguistic barriers. But when there were no linguistic barriers, Parham defended the practice of tongues on the basis that the message, when spoken in another tongue and then interpreted, was pure and undistorted. This would only be true if the original message in another language was inerrantly interpreted. But the original purpose for the gift of languages was to avoid the need for translation.

However, in pentecostal eschatology, tongues were not only a sign to the individual that he had been baptized with the Holy Spirit, but they were also a sign that the last days were here. This was the "latter-day rain."

3. Those who received the baptism with the Spirit were sealed for the rapture and constituted the five wise virgins who comprised the bride of Christ and who alone would be taken in the rapture. This teaching was "borrowed" from the radical holiness teachings of W. B. Godbey and George Watson.[1103] The first full-length book to come from the Azusa Street revival was George Taylor's book on the bride, which claimed only pentecostals would make up the bride.[1104] Pentecostals claimed that only believers who had experienced the baptism of the Holy Spirit would be taken up in the rapture.[1105]

Parham's own eschatology was even more complex. He distinguished between the apostate Christianity and the Church. These apostate "saints" would be sanctified through martyrdom. Secondly, he distinguished between the Church and the Bride. Only Pentecostals would comprise the Bride of Christ. They were the 144,000 who had come out of the institutional church.[1106] The Bride would escape once again to the wilderness, while the rest of the Church endures the

---

["Scriptural Christianity," Sermon #4, 3.1].

[1102]Parham, *Sermons: Voice Crying*, 31.

[1103]Godbey, *Church-Bride-Kingdom*, 88-97; Watson, *Bridehood Saints*, 4-7. See also Bloesch, *Holy Spirit*, 202.

[1104]Taylor, *Spirit and the Bride*.

[1105]Wacker, *Heaven Below*, 253.

[1106]Parham, *Sermons: Voice Crying*, 86.

Tribulation. While in the wilderness, the Bride becomes pregnant with the Man-child. The Man-child is the most elite and very few in number. Parham never explained how one becomes part of the Man-child, but they alone will experience the rapture.[1107]

Charles Parham, along with the students, sought the baptism of the Holy Spirit with the evidence of tongues. The first recipient of glossolalia, Agnes Ozman, was unable to speak in English for three days. She even claimed to be able to write Chinese. However, later she rejected the idea that persons who did not speak in tongues were not "baptized in the Holy Spirit."[1108]

It was claimed that the students spoke in twenty-one known languages, Chinese being the first. According to Robeck, "Chinese" was among the favorite languages identified by those at Azusa Street. However, they never specified whether it was Mandarin or Cantonese or any other Chinese dialect — it was always just "Chinese."[1109]

Parham claimed that reporters brought with them professors of languages, foreigners, government interpreters and they all claimed the students of the college were speaking in the languages of the world.[1110] Yet the reporters were actually skeptical. A Chinese man claimed, "Me no understand. Takee to Jap."[1111]

It was also claimed that if missionaries would receive this baptism, they could go anywhere and preach the gospel.[1112] "Charles Parham originally believed that the gift of tongues would allow Spirit baptized missionaries to preach in foreign countries without learning the native language. Scholars call this xenoglossa. . . . Although there were a few remarkable instances where this also took place on the mission field, for the most part, the gift of tongues was of little xenoglossaic value."[1113] Most of their early missionaries failed to communicate,

---

[1107]Parham, *Sermons: Voice Crying*, 90.

[1108]Ozman, "When the Latter Rain First Fell," 2. In this article she stated "tongues was not the only evidence of the Spirit's Baptism."

[1109]Robeck, *Azusa Street Mission and Revival*, 237.

[1110]Parham, *Life of Parham*, 54-55.

[1111]"Queer Faith," 2.

[1112]Synan, *Holiness-Pentecostal Tradition*, 92.

[1113]Martin, *Life of Seymour*, 235-236. Horton wrote of three couples who believed they could preach the gospel in foreign lands without having to learn the language, but they were disappointed ["Pentecostal Perspective,"52]. Packer wrote that the unanimous opinion of professional linguistic scholars is that glossolalia has no language-character at all ["Charismatic Renewal,"16-17]. See also the discussion by Ridgway, "Psychology," 2:916-920; Faupel, "Glossolalia as Foreign Language," 95-109.

however, and had to learn their new language "in the more conventional manner."[1114]

In 1914 Charles Shumway made a thorough search for Parham's "professors of languages," but failed to find anyone willing to corroborate his claims. Shumway interviewed Parham at length and tried in vain to identify the government interpreters. A Methodist pastor in Topeka, John T. McFarland, stated that he had been unable to find any outside source to verify Parham's claim.[1115] Two of Parham's students left and both expressed doubt that the tongues were authentic languages.[1116]

Finally in 1925 Charles Parham conceded, "To my knowledge not a single missionary in the foreign field speaks in the tongue of the natives as a gift from God."[1117] Later pentecostals claimed the tongues could be those "of men or of

---

Faupel concluded that "the present practice of glossolalia is not known language. Charismatics and Pentecostals are gradually coming to accept this view" [p. 109].

[1114]Synan, "Introduction,"178.

[1115]Shumway, "Study of 'The Gift of Tongues,'" 168; 42; 45; 170. Ironically, Shumway predicted that the tongues revival would soon vanish into obscurity [p. 192]. Shumway also did a doctoral thesis, "Critical History of Glossolalia."

[1116]Goff, *Fields White Unto Harvest*, 79-81.

[1117]Parham, "Critical Analysis," 2. See also the evaluation by Godbey, *Spiritualism*, 22-24. Burdick knows of no recorded sample of "tongues" which linguists have ever been able to identify as a human language [*Tongues*, 60]. Eugene A. Nida, internationally known linguist of the American Bible Society, with a team of linguists from twenty-five countries examined recordings of tongues speaking. They concluded that their recordings bore "no resemblance to any actual language which has ever been treated by linguists" [Edman, "Divine or Devilish"14]. Goodman discovered this phenomenon in a variety of religious settings, but concluded that it is not a language in terms of grammar and syntax. Instead it is a form of ecstatic vocalization marked by certain acoustic patterns [*Speaking in Tongues*. She explains glossolalia as an altered state of consciousness. See also Maloney and Lovekin, *Glossolalia*.

Samarin concluded that glossolalia does not match with a semantic system of language and that it is a "learned behavior" [*Tongues of Men and Angels*, 104-109; 199; 231; 235]. He defined glossolalia as "a meaningless but phonologically structured human utterance believed by the speaker to be a real language but bearing no systematic resemblance to any natural language, living or dead" [p. 2]. See the summary of this book by Geisler in *Systematic Theology*, 4:666-670; see also Samarin, "Glossolalia as a Vocal Phenomenon,"128-142. Samarin believes glossolalia is a learned behavior and does not follow the patterns of normal human language. "A *glossa* is never a natural language" [p. 131].

angels." What they spoke was not xenolalia, but ecstatic utterances.[1118]

When a Baptist preacher denied that it was possible to speak in a foreign language without learning it, Parham said he had a Ph.D., a D.D., and a LL.D. at the rear of his name and a Rev. in front of it. Parham challenged the man to come to his school for just one week.

> I would have gotten him so humble before God, and so willing to let God use him, that he would have come out of the post-graduate course with A.S.S. on the end of his name. Could I have gotten him to become as humble as was Balaam's mule, God would have talked through him in tongues.[1119]

After spreading his message through Kansas and Missouri, Parham moved to Houston, Texas in 1905. By the end of 1905 there may have been as many as twenty-five thousand pentecostal believers in Texas.[1120] It was here that W. J. Seymour, a Negro evangelist who had previously attended God's Bible School,[1121] was taught by Parham. No blacks were allowed in the Topeka school and they were not allowed to mix with the whites in Texas, but Mrs. Parham reported Seymour "was so humble and deeply interested Mr. Parham could not refuse him."[1122] Thus, Seymour was allowed to sit in an adjoining room where he heard through an open door.

Seymour stopped by to visit the Pillar of Fire Bible School in Denver on his way to Los Angeles. They believed he was "devil possessed."[1123] Seymour took the teaching to an old abandoned African Methodist Church building at 312 Azusa Street in Los Angeles.

Alfred G. Garr was an evangelist with the Metropolitan Church

---

[1118]On the failure of xenolalia, see Anderson, *Vision of the Disinherited*, 16-19; 90-92.

[1119]Parham, *Sermons: Everlasting Gospel*, 67.

[1120]Quebedeaux, *New Charismatics*, 29.

[1121]Although this fact has been disputed by Lewis in "William J. Seymour," 175-176, it is confirmed by Thornton, "God's Trustee." See also Nelson, "For Such a time as This," 35; Sanders, *William Joseph Seymour*, 52-54; Synan, *Holiness-Pentecostal Tradition*, 93. According to Stephens, there is an oral tradition that Seymour attended God's Bible School [*Fire Spreads*, 192]. Cecil Robeck concluded that while no known list of students at GBS from that period exists, "it seems likely that William Seymour was among them" [*Azusa Street Mission and Revival*, 31-35].

[1122]Parham, *Life of Parham*, 63; 137.

[1123]White, *Demons and Tongues*, 67.

Association, better known as the Burning Bush Movement. Garr closed the Burning Bush Mission and took its members to Azusa Street. In doing so Garr moved from a holiness church which accepted tongues as *an* evidence of the baptism to a pentecostal church which considered tongues as *the* evidence.[1124]

On June 14, 1906 Garr became the first white man to speak in tongues at the Azusa Street Mission. Alfred had announced that he had received the Hindustani language of India, while Lillian announced that she could speak Chinese. Convinced that they had spoken in Indian and Chinese dialects, Garr and his wife headed for India as the first missionaries to be sent from Azusa Street. However, when Garr could not be understood in Calcutta, he turned his attention to other missionaries, attempting to promote the merits of speaking in tongues to them.[1125]

After arriving in China in 1908, Alfred wrote, "I supposed He would let us talk to the natives of India in their own language, but He did not, and as far as I can see, will not use that means by which to convert the heathen . . . . So far I have not seen anyone who is able to preach to the natives in their own tongue with the languages given with the Holy Ghost. Here in Hong Kong, we preach the word to the Chinese through an interpreter."[1126]

S. C. Todd was in Macao, China under the Bible Missionary Society. He investigated the work of A. G. and Lillian Garr, T. J. McIntosh, as well as other Apostolic Faith missionaries in China, India, and Japan who had come "expecting to be able to preach to the natives of those countries in their own tongues." By their own admission, he found that in no single instance have they been able to do so.[1127] In an open letter Todd concluded that a "dual movement" was at work, "one from heaven, the other from hell." He described the Pentecostal message as

---

[1124]Kostlevy, "Nor Silver, Nor Gold, 237-244.

[1125]Robeck, *Azusa Street Mission and Revival*, 239; 252.

[1126]Garr, "Letter from Garr," 21-22. This British periodical printed a letter from Garr, written from China. While Garr spoke in tongues, it was not the language of Hong Kong. Eventually the translator and other converts spoke in tongues, but it was not English [Robeck, *Azusa Street Mission and Revival*, 256-257].

[1127]Todd, "Some Sad Failures," 1-2. Hills wrote that the Garrs had studied under him and showed great promise until their delusion. Toward the end of his book, he cites an unnamed missionary friend and is probably quoting from the open letter of Todd [Hills, *Tongues Movement*].

The Christian and Missionary Alliance listed Samuel C. Todd as a district superintendent in Laurens, SC from 1898-1900. He helped N. J. Holmes establish the Altamont Bible Institute. Todd left for China in 1904, but maintained contact with J. O. McClurkan's Pentecostal Mission in Nashville. Todd was later listed as both Baptist and Presbyterian.

- No Pentecost, if no tongues
- Do not question, hold in abeyance your reasoning powers
- Accept every manifestation as from God
- Follow every tongue, impression, voice and interpretation
- Look for, expect, and do not be satisfied without manifestations
- Noise is essential to earnestness
- The experience now proclaimed is different from that referred to in 1 Corinthians 14, hence all are free to exercise tongues as often as they like, for any length of time, no interpreter being necessary, and they all may speak at once if they desire
- One's whole personality must be absolutely abandoned to impressions, impulses and "the power."

The result was false prophecies, contrary tongues in the same individuals, demonic possession, anathemas pronounced on those who questioned, urged caution, or withstood the work. Salvation by grace was buried under the doctrine that without the "sign" of tongues one will be lost.

"One marked feature of the work has been the absence of conviction on the unsaved; the heathen have been unmoved; and carnal Christians have not been attracted to a better life by the movement. . . . *There has been no soul set on fire for other souls*, who with flaming tongue has gone out to warn the multitude; there has been no upheld Cross and no exalted Blood proclaimed; the theme has been the marvelous; the spectacular demonstrations of the Spirit." Todd clarified that while the cross and the Blood had been mentioned, the emphasis was on the spectacular.

Yet Todd observed, "At no time has there been any *known* tongue spoken, all has been an *unknown* utterance." Todd concluded that the Apostolic Faith missionaries had been influenced by "a real spirit of evil, personal demons, sweeping down upon God's children, marked as an angel of light — but who comes from the pit." The result was that the Church in South China was divided.[1128]

George Ridout wrote in the 1920s that this fanaticism, which first attracted attention in Los Angeles, was reaping some sad results.

> The craze has led some to abstain from food until death resulted. Some have gone insane. Others have killed friends or enemies. Many have made spiritual shipwrecks. One young man, an industrious mechanic, imagined that he had the Chinese tongue,

---

[1128]Todd, "Open Letter." This open letter was apparently written later in 1908 than the January 23 article in *The Baptist Argus*. It may be an abstract of a prior circular letter which Shumway titled "'Tongues' and Missions" in his 1914 thesis.

> and was called to mission work in China. He sold all, and with his wife, went there, only to be undeceived. The Chinese did not understand his mutterings and would not have him. After great hardships they reached our shores again, and he is a hopeless inmate of an asylum.[1129]

From 1906-1909 people came from all over the world to Azusa Street and took the doctrine home with them.[1130] For them it was a restoration of the "apostolic faith" or a "latter rain" of the Spirit. Since the Holy Spirit was primarily associated with "power," the evidence of the Spirit was the miraculous.[1131] It should also be realized that within this time frame some pentecostal phenomenon occurred in Africa independent of the Azusa Street influence.[1132]

In September 1909 a group of over fifty pietist-holiness leaders in Germany issued the Berlin Declaration, in which they declared the Apostolic Faith movement was "not from on high, but from below."[1133]

> The undersigned brothers raise their voices in warning against the so-called Pentecostal Movement.
>
> 1. After serious joint examination of the comprehensive and reliable material before the Lord, we have come to the following conclusion:
> a) The movement is inseparably connected with the movement of Los Angeles, Christiana, Hamburg, Kassel, Grossalmerode. The attempts to deny this connection fail because of the actual facts.
> b) The so-called Pentecostal movement is not from above but from below; it has many phenomena in common with Spiritism.

[1129]Ridout, *Deadly Fallacy of Fanaticism*, 13.

[1130]In 1909 Henke noted an increase in phenomena such as speaking in tongues, tongues of fire, rushing of a mighty wind, interpretation of tongues, jerking, writhing, and falling to the ground in the past two years ["Gift of Tongues"].

[1131]Williams wrote, "The central purpose for the gift of the Holy Spirit is *power*"[*Gift of the Holy Spirit Today*, 43].

[1132]Kalu, "Historical Perspectives," 7. For example, the Liberian prophet William Wadé Harris (born around 1860-1865, died 1929), who was raised by his uncle who was a Methodist pastor. See Jenkins, *Next Christendom*, 48-49. See also Shaw, *Global Awakening*, 55-65.

[1133]Robeck, *Azusa Street Mission and Revival*, 245-246.

Demons are at work in it that, led by Satan's cunning, mix lies and truth in order to deceive the children of God. In many cases, those who have been said to have "received gifts from the Spirit" later prove to have been possessed.
c) Regarding this conviction, that this movement is from below, we cannot be misled by the personal faithfulness and devotion of individual leading brothers and sisters nor by the healings, tongues, prophecies, etc. by which the movement is accompanied. Such signs have often been connected with similar movements, e.g. Irvingianism, even, indeed, with Christian Science and Spiritism.
d) The spirit in this movement produces spiritual and bodily effects of power. Nevertheless, this is a false spirit. It has been exposed as such. The ugly phenomena like falling down, facial twitches, trembling, crying out, revolting loud laughter, etc. also appear in meetings at this time. We leave it open as to how much of this is demonic, how much hysterical or psychological; such phenomena are not brought about by God.
e) The spirit of this movement introduces itself via the Word of God, but the Word is pushed into the background by so-called "prophecies." Cf. 2 Chronicles 18,18-22. In general, these prophecies contain a great danger: not only do they turn out to have clear contradictions within themselves, but they now and then bring brothers and their entire work into slavish dependence on these "messages." The latter resemble the messages of spiritual mediums in the way they are sent. The senders are mostly women. At certain points of the movement this has led, contrary to the clear prophecies of Scripture, to women, even young girls, being at the center in leadership positions.

2. It is impossible for us to acknowledge such a movement as sent by God. It is, of course, not excluded that the proclamation of the Word of God in the meetings will produce fruit by the same internal power. Inexperienced brothers and sisters let themselves be deceived by such blessings of the Word of God. But this does not change at all the fact that this movement as a whole has the character of a lie. Cf. 2 Cor. 11,3.4.14.

3. The church of God in Germany has reason to reflect deeply on the fact that this movement could start. We are all guilty because of our lacks and omissions, particularly with respect to

intercession. The lack of biblical knowledge and grounding, of holy seriousness and vigilance, a superficial view of sin and grace, of conversion and rebirth, an arbitrary exegesis of the Bible, the desire for new, exciting phenomena, the inclination to exaggerate, but above all also arrogance — all this paved the way for this movement.

4. But in particular, the non-biblical teaching of so-called "pure heart" has become disastrous for many circles and beneficial for the so-called Pentecostal movement. This concerns the fallacy that "internal sin" is eradicated in a pardoned and sanctified Christian. We hold to the truth that the Lord can and will preserve his own from all stumbling and falling (1 Thess 5,23; Jude 24,25; Hebr 13,21) and that they have power to reign over sin through the Holy Spirit. But no one receives, while yet on earth, a pure heart - with all God-given and lasting preservation - that goes beyond Paul's humble confession: "I am conscious of nothing against myself, yet I am not by this acquitted." Even the most advanced Christian has to bow before God who alone judges the true state of the heart, cf. 1 Cor. 4:4. "If we say that we have no sin, we are deceiving ourselves and the truth is not in us" (1 Jn 1:8).

The believer in Christ does receive a spotless, purified heart, it is true, but the fallacy that the heart can reach a state of sinlessness has already brought many children of God under the curse of insincerity with respect to sin, has deceived them about sins that are still present in their thoughts, in their omissions or in their falling short of the high commandments of God in their lives. One cannot be admonished enough to keep an eye open for those sins, an eye that is not blinded by a humanly produced sanctification or by an imagined teaching that the sinful nature is removed.

Inadequate attention to one's own sin bars the way to new blessings and brings one under the influence of the devil. Unhappy experiences at present show that where one claims to have reached a state of sinlessness, the believer can come to such a point that he is no longer capable of admitting an error, let alone confessing it. A further unhappy consequence of a false doctrine of sanctification is its associated disparagement of the biblical divinely ordained married life, by presenting marital intercourse between man and woman as incompatible with true sanctification. Cf. Gen. 1,28 and Eph. 5,31.

5. Pastor Paul appears in public as the leader in the so-called "Pentecostal Movement." At the same time he is the chief representative of the unbiblical teachings rejected above. We love him as a brother and wish to serve him and the flock of his followers in truth. It pains us to have to take a position against him. There has been no lack of discussions with him and admonitions in narrower and wider brotherly circles. Since everything was in vain, we must now for his sake and for that of God's affairs state herewith: We, the undersigned brothers, can no longer recognize him as a leader and teacher in the church of Jesus. We command him in love, faith and hope to the grace of the Lord that restores all things.

6. We believe that there was only one Pentecost, Acts 2. We believe in the Holy Spirit, who will remain in the church of Jesus Christ for eternity; cf. Jn 14:16. We are aware that the church of God has always received and needed renewed visitations of grace by the Holy Spirit. The admonition of the apostle applies to everyone: "Be filled with the Spirit" (Eph 5:18). The way to that is and remains complete fellowship with the crucified, resurrected and exalted Lord. In him the fullness of the Spirit dwells in person, from whom we take grace upon grace. We do not expect a new Pentecost; we wait for the Lord's return.
Hereby we request all our brothers and sisters, for the sake of the Lord and his affairs, which Satan wants to ruin: Keep away from this movement! But whoever among you is caught by the power of this spirit, he should renounce it and ask God for forgiveness and liberation. Do not despair in the battles through which many, perhaps, will go. Satan will not surrender his dominion easily. But be assured: The Lord will support us throughout! He has freed many and wants to give them the true equipment of the Spirit.
Our sure confidence in this difficult time is this: God's people will emerge blessed from these battles! You too may say that to yourselves, beloved brothers and sisters, who stand shaken by the facts before which our words place you. The Lord will give light to the simple and the humble and strengthen and preserve them. We entrust ourselves to Jesus, the Chief Shepherd. If everyone makes room for the Lord and his Word, as is due to

> him, then he will carry out the work of his Spirit that he began so graciously in Germany, to his glorious, divinely ordained end. We entrust ourselves to him who said: "Ask Me about the things to come concerning My sons, And you shall commit to Me the work of My hands" Isa 45:11
>
> Berlin, September 15, 1909[1134]

Two weeks later the Second Pentecostal Conference at Mühlheim-Rhor in Germany published the Mülheim Declaration as a response. Mülheim was the center of the pentecostal work in West Germany.[1135] There were 2800 in attendance at the conference.[1136]

The declaration was brief and conciliatory in tone. It admitted mistakes were made, but declared the movement was from above. The document stated that in all revivals there are manifestations from God, from humanity, and in some cases demonic. It defended the teaching of a clean heart and declared that Pastor Jonathan Paul did not teach a sinless state.[1137] In an interview Pastor Paul stated

> Then there are those also who have received the Baptism, but have not spoken in Tongues. I know personally those who have undoubtedly received the Baptism. Their lives and power and love show this, and I could not say that they were not baptized with the Holy Ghost. I myself received the Baptism twenty years ago, and had all the evidences which I have to-day, though I did not speak in Tongues. But when I came in contact with the dear people in Norway I recognised that it was the very same Spirit in them that had been in me all these years. Later I spoke also in Tongues, but I had the Baptism twenty years before.[1138]

1134Online: "Berlin Declaration."

1135Dennis, "Letter to *Confidence*,"190-192.

1136Dennis, "Mulheim Conference," 208-211.

1137Kok, "Mulheim Declaration," 228-230. English translation by Arie Kok. The declaration was dated 29 Sept 1909. There were no signatories.

1138Boddy, "Germany,"233. Boddy was an Anglican vicar who was converted to pentecostalism under Thomas Ball Barratt of Norway. Barratt was the leading Methodist pastor in Norway. In 1906 he came to the United States to raise money for a city mission and came in contact with the Azusa Street influence.

Boddy challenged the Keswick conference to consider this "new Pentecost," but this suggestion was rejected by the Keswick leaders. In 1908 he began the

Vinson Synan listed the five major teachings of Azusa Street as justification by faith, sanctification as a definite work of grace, the baptism of the Holy Spirit as evidenced by speaking in other tongues, divine healing provided in the atonement, and the premillennial rapture.[1139] For them this constituted the "full gospel." This, however, was the same position as the holiness movement, except for the gift of tongues. The editor of the *Pentecostal Advocate,* a holiness journal, reprinted a letter which described the "tongues people."

> They preached the full gospel, emphasizing the ministry of holiness and also the universality of the gospel invitation. They taught with great conviction the immediate return of our Lord, and the necessity of being filled with the Holy Spirit as a preparation for the rapture. They taught divine healing; in fact, the full gospel as we understand it, with this addition, the gift of tongues.[1140]

However, the early pentecostals taught the disciples were sanctified in John 20:22 as a second definite work of grace. This sanctification made them a clean vessel for the Holy Spirit to fill. The baptism of the Holy Spirit at Pentecost represented the third blessing.[1141] Although the idea of a third work of grace was not new to the holiness movement,[1142] the rise of the pentecostal movement helped the holiness people to insist on two and only two definite works of grace.

It was Frank Bartleman who spread the news of the Los Angeles "revival" by writing accounts for the holiness press. As late as 1914 his articles were still appearing in holiness periodicals, including *God's Revivalist.*[1143] Bartleman was

---

publication of the pentecostal magazine *Confidence.*

Jonathan Paul was a leader in the German holiness movement who was also converted to pentecostalism through a visit to Barratt in Oslo, Norway in 1907.

[1139]Synan, "Introduction," xx.

[1140]Huckabee, "Gift of Tongues, Again," 8.

[1141]Horton, "Pentecostal Perspective,"106-107.

[1142]In 1906, Leonidas I. McDougle, a Methodist who was heavily influenced by the holiness movement, self-published a booklet which places the baptism with the Holy Ghost *after* entire sanctification. According to McDougle this is a threefold blessing. Thus the sinner surrenders in order to be regenerate and the Christian consecrates in order to be entirely sanctified. Only then is the gift of the Holy Ghost bestowed for service in response to faith. Yet tongues and other extraordinary manifestations passed with the apostolic age [*Salvation*, 29-32].

[1143]Dieter, "Wesleyan-Holiness Aspects," 74-75; 79.

saved in 1893 in the Baptist Temple of Philadelphia. He turned down a chance to go to college and began preaching. Four years later he joined with the Salvation Army and became a captain. He was soon disillusioned and left to be ordained in another holiness group. During this period he experienced emotional instability ranging from suicidal depression to falling unconscious at camp meetings under "electric shocks" of blessing. After marriage, he pastored a Wesleyan Methodist congregation and shortly thereafter moved to Denver to work with the Pillar of Fire Church. In 1902 he was arrested in Boulder for painting scripture on the canyon walls near the city. In 1904 he was in charge of Peniel Mission in Sacramento, California. At times his wife had to scrounge through garbage cans to feed their two children after he left Peniel. Then he moved to Los Angeles and worked with several missions before joining with a Baptist pastor who started the New Testament Church.

When Seymour came to Los Angeles in 1906 preaching that tongues was the "initial evidence" of the baptism of the Holy Spirit, Bartleman was in the group that moved to the historic 312 Azusa Street mission with the evangelist. Although Bartleman focused international attention on the new movement through his glowing reports, Phineas Bresee, who was founding the Church of the Nazarene in Los Angeles at the same time, said the meetings "attracted some attention, especially among that class of people who are always seeking for some new thing." Because it bordered on fanaticism and heresy, Bresee preferred not to mention the matter.

> But some parties who had the confidence of editors in the East sufficiently to secure the publication of what they have written, have given such marvelous statements of things as occurring in connection with this thing, that for the sake of those at a distance, and the many who are writing us about it, we deem it wise to say a simple word. Locally it is of small account, being insignificant both in numbers and influence. Instead of being the greatest movement of the times, as represented — in Los Angeles, at least — it is of small moment. It has had, and has now, upon the religious life of the city, about as much influence as a pebble thrown into the sea; but what little influence it has had seems to have been mostly harmful, instead of beneficent. It seems not only to have had at least some of the elements of fanaticism, but to be trying to inculcate such erroneous or heretical doctrines as mark it as not of the Spirit of truth. The two principal things which are emphasized, and wherein they claim to differ from others, is, that Christians are sanctified before they receive the baptism with the Holy Ghost, this

> baptism being a gift of power upon the sanctified life, and that the essential and necessary evidence of the baptism is the gift of speaking with new tongues. As far as has come under our own observation, or that we have seen experted by competent examination, the speaking with tongues has been a no-thing — a jargon, a senseless mumble, without meaning to those who do the mumbling, or to those who hear. Where in a few instances the speaker or some other one has attempted to interpret, it has usually been a poor mess.[1144]

In 1911 Bartleman had joined with William Durham who denied sanctification as a second blessing. In 1914 when the "Jesus Name" movement came to Los Angeles, Bartleman identified with it and was rebaptized. When he died in 1935 he was not a member of any church.[1145]

Donald Gee told of the president of a holiness association who was asked to go to Los Angeles and convince Seymour that the baptism of the Holy Ghost was sanctification. After hearing Seymour the man said he wanted the baptism accompanied by tongues.[1146]

However, things did not go as well when Parham came to preach for Seymour in October of 1906. On August 27, 1906 Seymour wrote asking Parham to come to Los Angeles because "Satan is working." Mrs. Parham said that Seymour continued to write "urgent letters appealing for help as spiritualistic manifestations, hypnotic forces and fleshly contortion as known in the colored Camp Meetings in the south had broken loose in the meeting."[1147] Parham first visited in Zion City, Illinois where John Alexander Dowie, a faith healer had been discredited. Parham said if Dowie would place himself under his care he would soon be restored to his former self.[1148]

1144 Bresee, "Gift of Tongues," 6.

1145 Synon, "Introduction,"ix-xxv.

1146 Gee, *Pentecostal Movement*, 12.

1147 Parham, *Life of Parham*, 155-156. William Faupel argued that Seymour had invited Parham to bridge the racial divide in the city of Los Angeles and to restore unity between black and white pentecostals there [*Everlasting Gospel*, 207-208].

1148 Parham, *Life of Parham*, 160. In 1876 Dowie married his cousin. By the time of Parham's visit, Dowie had been accused of polygamy and misappropriation of funds. Having suffered a stroke in 1905, Zion City was placed by a federal judge under control of a receivership in July 1906.

Dowie held a Keswick theology, but his vision was to merge the major Keswick and holiness groups as an end-time movement which would establish the kingdom of

When Parham arrived at Azusa Street in October 1906, he was shocked at the emotional excesses and declared it seemed the hypnotists and spiritualists had taken over. He found things even worse than he anticipated. Parham spoke for the rest of his life of the Azusa Street meeting as a case of "spiritual power prostituted." Mrs. Parham said that Seymour sat helpless.[1149] However, when Parham tried to take over, Seymour was "possessed with a spirit of leadership" and sought to prove that Azusa Street Mission was where the baptism of the Holy Spirit first fell. Parham pleaded with Seymour to repent for deceiving the people, to reject the spirit of leadership, and to repent for exalting self or God would humble him.[1150] Seymour did not repent or at least did not submit to Parham. Parham was soon invited to leave and he went to the corner of Broadway and Temple to conduct services. Seymour and Parham were never reconciled.[1151] Parham warned,

> I have witnessed great dangers in the work here in Los Angeles, and in pointing them out I shall not refer to individuals, but to the work itself as a whole, that we all may see the error of our way and get back to God. . . .
> Let me speak plainly with regard to the work as I have found it here. I found hypnotic influences, familiar-spirit influences, spiritualistic influences, mesmeric influences, and all kinds of spells, spasms, falling in trances, etc. All of these things are foreign to and unknown in this movement outside of Los

---

God on earth. In 1890 he also visited the Mormons in Salt Lake City and even negotiated with them about becoming one of their apostles. Dowie planned to return to Salt Lake City and declare that God had shown him the reinstitution of plural marriage was part of God's end-time program of preparing for Christ's return and ushering in the millennium. He planned to invite all Mormon converts to join him as he initiated the practice in Mexico. Instead, he had a stroke [Faupel, "Missionary Strategy," 201; 207; "Theological Influences," 226-253].

Catherine Booth-Clibborn, daughter of William and Catherine Booth, came in contact with Dowie while her husband was a follower of his. She objected to his luxurious lifestyle, advocating self-sacrifice and self-denial [Strahan, *Maréchale*, 272-286].

1149Parham, *Life of Parham*, 163-164. Parham declared that Azusa Street was animalism [Shumway, "Study of the Gift of Tongues," 178].

1150Parham, *Life of Parham*, 163-164.

1151Synan, *Holiness-Pentecostal Tradition*, 102-103. Synan speculated that Seymour may have resisted submission to Parham because it was frequently charged that Parham was a practicing homosexual.

Angeles, except in the places visited by the workers sent out from this city.

A word about the baptism of the Holy Ghost. The speaking in tongues is never brought about by any of the above influences. In all our work the laying on of hands is practiced only occasionally, and then for the space of only a minute or two. No such thing is known among our workers as the suggestion of certain words and sounds, the working of the chin, or the massage of the throat.

Nonsense! The Holy Ghost needs no help! When the recipient of the Holy Ghost comes into proper relations with God the speaking in tongues comes as naturally as any other gift from Him. There is always the real and the false, and anything outside of the operation of the Holy Ghost is counterfeit.

There are many in Los Angeles who sing, pray and talk wonderfully in other tongues, as the Spirit gives utterance, and there is jabbering here that is not tongues at all. I know that people sometimes fall under the power of God, and that there are times that God thus deals with his creatures that resist Him; but these cases are exceptional and not general. The falling under the power in Los Angeles has, to a large degree, been produced through a hypnotic, mesmeric, magnetic current.

The Holy Ghost does nothing that is unnatural or unseemingly [sic], and any strained exertion of body, mind, or voice is not the work of the Holy Spirit, both of some familiar spirit, or other influence brought to bear upon the subject. . . .

Having guarded this Pentecostal blessing from it's earliest infancy, I feel that it is still my duty to stand against anything and everything that will in any way prove a hindrance to others, or to the advancement of the work. . . . The Holy Ghost never leads us beyond the point of self-control or the control of others, while familiar spirits or fanaticism lead us both beyond self-control and the power to help others.[1152]

[1152]Parham, *Life of Parham*, 167-170. This letter was originally written from Los Angeles on 1 December 1906 and was then published in the January issue of *The Apostolic Faith*. *The Apostolic Faith* was issued from Topeka, Kansas in 1899-1900; from Melrose, Kansas and Houston in 1905-1906. It was issued from Los Angeles in 1906-1908 by Seymour, from Portland beginning in July 1908 when Florence Crawford took Seymour's mailing list there; and from Baxter Springs, Kansas from 1910 by Parham. Note that the first issue with the Portland address was Vol 2, Number 15. See their "100-Year Commemorative Edition," *Higher Way* (July-Sept 2006).

Nettie Harwood, a Pillar of Fire missionary, visited Azusa Street and reported that "kissing between the sexes" was a common occurrence.[1153] W. B. Godbey visited in 1909 and was asked to preach. When asked if he had spoken in tongues, he replied that he thanked God that he could say with Paul that he spoke in tongues more than all of them (1 Cor 14:18). He then proceeded to quote in Latin, "Johannes Baptistes tinxit, Petros tinxet et Christus misit suos Apostolos, ut gentes tingerent."[1154] The pentecostals claimed Godbey as one of them and wanted to put him "at the front of the movement." Disillusioned, Godbey said he had a language, but they had a demonic counterfeit. He concluded it was the product of "spiritism," calling them "Satan's preachers, jugglers, necromancers, enchanters, magicians, and all sorts of mendicants."[1155] Godbey also detected a good deal of "hell-hatched free lovism" in these circles, reporting that gamblers, atheists, whores and thieves also spoke in tongues.[1156] The conservative holiness crowd often claimed that the congregation at Azusa Street was made up of backslidden holiness people. In his later years apparently Seymour reverted back to his holiness heritage and taught that love was the evidence of a Holy Spirit baptism.[1157]

When Crawford took the *Apostolic Faith* to Portland, she left her husband in Highland Park, California and they never reunited. Her justification for breaking with Seymour was that she had heard rumors he had compromised his teaching on sanctification; that he no longer taught the Wesleyan position that entire sanctification was a second work of grace [Robeck, *Azusa Street Mission and Revival*, 300].

[1153]White, *Demons and Tongues*, 73.

[1154]The English translation of Godbey's utterance is, "John the Baptist baptized, Peter baptized and Christ sent his apostles to baptize the Gentiles."

[1155]Godbey, *Tongues Movement, Satanic*, 5; see also White, *Demons and Tongues*, 121. Godbey also dealt with the tongues "heresy" in *Current Heresies*, 20 and *Try the Spirits*, 8-12.

Charles Parham wrote an article which claimed that Godbey's perspective would have been different had he visited a service of the original Apostolic Faith Movement "as upheld and practiced at the National Camp Meeting at Baxter Springs, Kansas." In contrast to "wildfire and fanaticism," Parham claimed that a visitor to his own meetings would be "convinced that Pentecost has returned in dignity, in power and in 'decency and order'" ["Godby" 7].

[1156]Godbey, *Tongues Movement, Satanic*, 27-28. Even Parham frequently alluded to sexual impropriety around the altar, accusing the participants at Azusa Street of "freeloveism" [Callahan, "Fleshly Manifestations,"162]. According to Robeck, Seymour fought this free loveism [*Azusa Street Mission and Revival*, 164; 309-310].

[1157]Lewis, "William J. Seymour,'"182. See also Robeck, *Azusa Street Mission and Revival*, 177-178. In the sermons of Seymour, which Larry Martin compiled from

Cecil M. Robeck, Jr. elaborated on this shift in Seymour's thinking which began about the middle of 1907. Seymour had experienced harshness from Parham, as well as racial prejudice in general. Seymour rejected Parham's doctrine of annihilation and therefore eventually concluded Parham could also be mistaken on tongues as the evidence of baptism in the Holy Spirit. Within six months of Parham's arrest, Seymour declared that divine love was the real evidence that a person had received the baptism with the Holy Ghost. Ultimately Seymour's position on Parham's initial evidence "had hardened into a clear rejection." By 1915 Seymour wrote, "Some people to-day cannot believe that they have the Holy Ghost without some outward signs." Seymour declared, "that is Heathenism."[1158]

In his *Doctrines and Discipline of the Asuza Street Apostolic Faith Mission*, Seymour the founder and general overseer declared, "Wherever the doctrine of the Baptism in the Holy Spirit will only be known as the evidence of speaking in tongues, that work will be an open door for witches and spiritualists, and free loveism." Later in the same work, Article V was amended to read, "The speaking in tongues being one of the 'signs following' the baptised believers and other evidence of the Bible casting out devils, healing the sick and with the fruits of spirit accompanying the signs."[1159]

The report was often made and repeatedly denied by Parham that he was a practicing homosexual.[1160] Parham was arrested in San Antonio, Texas on July 19, 1907 on charges of sodomy. He was released on bail four days later and no formal indictment was ever filed. Goff wrote that there is neither enough hard evidence to condemn him nor enough doubt to sufficiently clear him.[1161] However, Leslie Callahan evaluated the evidence and concluded "the specific charge had some basis in fact."

While Parham never answered the specific charges against him in print, he claimed that the charged were trumped up by Wilbur Voliva. Voliva and Parham both attempted to gain control of the aging John Dowie's empire, Zion City, Illinois. Parham had been a threat to Volvia when he showed up in Zion City in September 1906. Yet Callahan argued that Parham was no longer a threat after he left Zion City for Azusa Street. "It strains credulity to think [Voliva] able to orchestrate Parham's arrest from hundreds of miles away, complete with an

---

1907-1908, there was a greater emphasis on tongues [Martin, *Azusa Street Sermons*].

1158Robeck, "William J. Seymour,'" 80-89; Seymour, *Doctrines*, 8.

1159Seymour, *Doctrines*, 6; 82.

1160White, *Demons and Tongues*, 121.

1161Goff, *Fields White Unto Harvest*, 141.

eyewitness, affidavits, and the participation of the constable."[1162]

On the other hand, Howard Goss, a friend of Parham's wrote, "One of our leading ministers fell into an awful sin, which turned out to be only a temporary affair. He repented, confessed, was forgiven, and afterward led an exemplary life so far as I ever heard."[1163] This was the basis for R. A. Torrey's conclusion that the movement was founded by a "Sodomite."[1164]

Parham did believe in the annihilation of the wicked[1165] and accepted the British Israel theory.[1166] There was a heavy emphasis on speculative prophecy in his preaching. Parham did not believe the church should be organized, but later became involved in support of the Ku Klux Klan.[1167]

[1162]Callahan, "Fleshly Manifestations,"141-142; 153-159.

[1163]Goss, *Winds of God*, 134. According to Callahan it is clear that Goss was referring to Parham ["Fleshly Manifestations," 158].

[1164]Jones, *Guide to Pentecostal Movement*, 1:350; 354; Mezies, *Anointed to Serve*, 73.

[1165]Callahan, "Fleshly Manifestations," 210-214.

[1166]Parham, *Sermons: Voice Crying in the Wilderness*, 20; 105-108; *Everlasting Gospel*, 92-95; 111-117. See also Hollenweger, *Pentecostals*, 22; Cargill, *How God Communicates with Man*, 38.

[1167]Parham, *Sermons: Everlasting Gospel*, 91-110; 115-118. See also Synan, *Holiness-Pentecostal Tradition*, 182; Goff, *Fields White Unto Harvest*, 128-132; Grady, "Pentecostals Renounce Racism," 58.

Throughout Parham's life he advocated white supremacy based on his theology of Anglo-Saxon superiority as the ten lost tribes of Israel (also called British Israelism). He supported racial segregation on the basis of two creations: those created on the sixth day were created in God's image; the Adamic race was formed on the eighth day. The punishment of the Noahic flood was because the sixth day creation had intermarried with the eighth day creation [see Callahan, "Fleshly Manifestations," chapter 3, "Azusa's Shame: Racial Boundaries and Apostolic Faith," 101-140].

Frank Bartleman is often quoted as saying that at Azusa Street, "the color line has been washed away in the Blood" [Bartleman, *How Pentecost Came to Los Angeles: As It Was in the Beginning* (Los Angles: the Author, 3rd ed, 1925), 54; *Azusa Street*, xviii]. However, the truth is that Parham was a racist and many of the early pentecostal denominations were segregated. See Jones, "'Color Line,'" 252-265. The early Pentecostal interracial unity lasted about ten years until the movement split along racial lines [Alexander, *Black Fire*]. Yet the 1994 "Miracle in Memphis" was a major breakthrough in race relations among pentecostal denominations [Synan, *Holiness-Pentecostal Tradition*, 186].

It should also be noted that Alma White, bishop of the Pillar of Fire, one of the most vocal critics of pentecostalism, was also a regular speaker at Ku Klux Klan rallies [Stanley, *Feminist*, 85-90].

While the conservative segment of the holiness movement rejected tongues, the pentecostal revival made its greatest inroads where the holiness movement was already prospering.[1168] Among the pilgrims to Azusa Street was G. B. Cashwell from North Carolina. Through his influence the Pentecostal Holiness Church, organized in 1898 as a holiness church, became pentecostal in 1908.[1169] C. H. Mason brought tongues to the Church of God in Christ, originally a holiness group founded in 1897. This split the church and those not accepting the doctrine of tongues formed the Church of Christ (Holiness).[1170] The Church of God (Cleveland, Tennessee) was another holiness church dating back to 1886. Initially it was influenced by the teachings of the Fire-Baptized leader, B. H. Irwin and his doctrine of the third blessing.[1171] Its leadership did not embrace pentecostalism until ten years later.[1172] As an indication of the Methodist influence, even if not the Methodist doctrine, all three of these groups retained the episcopal form of government even after becoming pentecostal.[1173]

According to David Michel, such early Pentecostal groups were in general agreement with Wesley's emphasis that sanctification was subsequent to the new birth and that it entailed the eradication of the sinful nature. It does not follow, however, that all early Pentecostals had a clear grasp of the Wesleyan understanding of sanctification. For them, sanctification was reduced as a means to an end. It was preparatory to the third blessing, the baptism of the Holy Spirit. Michel found that Wesley's emphasis on perfect love was virtually missing in the first fifty years of Church of God theological history.[1174]

According to Synan, the only major holiness group in the South that did not embrace tongues was the Pentecostal Mission, which eventually merged with the Church of the Nazarene, the Wesleyan Methodist Church, and the Methodist

---

[1168]Pierard, "American Holiness Movement,"518.

[1169]Synan, *Holiness-Pentecostal Tradition*, 112-123. Ultimately, Cashwell returned to the Southern Methodist Church [Synan, *Holiness-Pentecostal Tradition*, 128].

[1170]Synan, *In the Latter Days*, 53; Thuston, "C. H. Mason," 227-236.

[1171]Woods, "Our American Holiness Heritage,"13; see also Phillips, "Baptist Rejection of Holiness Revives the Church of God, 9.

[1172]Conn, *Like a Mighty Army*, xxii; 25. The Church of God revival in Cherokee City, NC in 1896 was an isolated phenomenon and did not spread Pentecostalism in the same rapid manner as Azusa Street [Grady, "Memories of Azusa," 8].

[1173]Quebedeaux, *New Charismatics*, 41.

[1174]Michel, "Revisiting the Methodist Legacy," 196-205.

Episcopal Church, South.[1175] In 1901 H. F. Reynolds, general superintendent of the Church of the Nazarene, reported that the "so-called Tongues Movement" had taken every Nazarene church in Florida except one. The Wesleyan Methodists were also affected, especially in the South.[1176] Jones said that the pentecostal movement swept "almost the entire independent Holiness movement of the southeastern United States into the pentecostal camp."[1177]

The pentecostal movement grew because of those who crossed over from the holiness movement and because of their zeal. Within fourteen years there were twenty-five separate pentecostal denominations and these groups were the fastest growing churches during the first half of this century.[1178] By 1983 the Church of Christ (Holiness), which had remained within the holiness movement, had nine thousand members and 151 congregations. The Church of God in Christ, which was pentecostal, began with a bare majority after the split. Over the same period of time they had grown to over three million members and seven thousand congregations.[1179]

By 1920 the pentecostal movement had experienced two controversies that left the lines clearly drawn. One issue was the doctrine of the Trinity. About a fifth of all pentecostals in the United States practice baptism in Jesus' name only.[1180] To add to the confusion there are trinitarian groups which baptize in Jesus' name only and non-trinitarian groups which use the formula given in Matthew 28:19.

In 1913 at a camp meeting at Arroyo Seco, California, a Canadian evangelist, Robert McAclister preached that the Apostles understood that they were commanded to baptize in the name of Jesus. Frank Ewart and Glenn Cook began to preach this and re-baptize in Jesus' name only. G. T. Haywood also advanced the doctrine of Oneness Pentecostalism.[1181]

The other controversy within pentecostalism was over sanctification as

---

[1175]Synan, *Holiness-Pentecostal Tradition*, 126;

[1176]Dieter, "Wesleyan-Holiness Aspects," 75.

[1177]Jones, *Guide to the Study of the Pentecostal Movement*, 1:252.

[1178]Snyder, *Divided Flame*, 42.

[1179]Synan, *In the Latter Days*, 53.

[1180]Synan, *Holiness-Pentecostal Movement*, 162-163 counted "about one-fourth." In his update, twenty-six years later, Synan reported "about a fifth" [*Holiness-Pentecostal Tradition*, 165]. However, Kenneth Gill wrote that Oneness Pentecostals worldwide "make up only a fraction of one percent of the world's Pentecostals" ["Dividing Over Oneness," 22].

[1181]Alexander, "G. T.Haywood," 275-283.

a second work of grace. Up until 1910 all those associated with the pentecostal movement accepted holiness presuppositions and added the baptism of the Spirit as a third work. At that time W. H. Durham began to preach his doctrine of "the finished work." Durham, a holiness pastor from Chicago, had visited Azusa Street in 1907.[1182] After receiving his pentecostal experience he vowed never again to preach the traditional holiness doctrine of sanctification as a second work. As large numbers of people with no holiness background became pentecostal, they were attracted to Durham's doctrine that sanctification was a process and that there were only two works of grace: conversion and the baptism of the Holy Spirit.

However, when Durham came to preach his doctrine at Azusa Street, in 1911, the opposition was so great that he was locked out.[1183] Charles Parham prayed that God would take Durham's life if the doctrine of a second work was true and Durham did die six months later.[1184] Durham was so influential, though, that most of the pentecostal groups formed after 1911 adopted his view. Of these groups, the Assemblies of God is the largest with over 32 million members in 1995.[1185]

According to Kärkkäinen, there are two versions of *ordo salutis* (order of salvation) among Pentecostals.[1186] According to Synan, this issue of sanctification divides the pentecostal world about evenly on both sides.[1187] There are currently at least thirty-five pentecostal denominations in the United States with a Wesleyan-Arminian tradition.[1188]

However, even the Assemblies of God, a non-holiness group had in their statement of faith a section entitled "Entire Sanctification," until 1961 when the word "entire" was dropped.[1189] Dayton explained the move away from the original holiness emphasis, saying:

[1182]See Kerwin, *Rejected Blessing*.

[1183]Bartleman, *Azusa Street*, 151.

[1184]Synan, *Holiness-Pentecostal Tradition*, 151.

[1185]Synan, *Holiness-Pentecostal Tradition*, 133.

[1186]Kärkkäinen, *Pneumatology*, 96.

[1187]Synan, *Holiness-Pentecostal Tradition*, 165. According to "Global Statistics" from Barrett and Johnson, there are 240 Pentecostal denominations which teach three crisis experiences and 390 which teach two crisis experiences [pp. 293-294].

[1188]Jones, *Guide to the Study of the Pentecostal Movement*, 1:251-345.

[1189]Horton, "Pentecostal Perspective," *Sanctification*, 112; "Pentecostal Perspective," *Spirit Baptism*, 238.

> A study of the Biblical doctrine of "perfection" does not naturally lead to the account of Pentecost and vice versa. This constitutional instability of the synthesis may help to explain why the concern for sanctification tended to drop out of the Pentecostal movement.[1190]

The "Apostolic Faith" movement of Charles Parham failed to restore apostolic Christianity because Parham did not have an adequate grasp of apostolic doctrine (Acts 2:42) nor did his life exemplify Christian perfection. A grasp of the history of the Christian Church will help us discern the work of God, an adequate theology will help Church leaders keep the work of God on track, but we must also seek Christian holiness and maintain a vital relationship with Jesus Christ. A genuine movement of God will be characterized by the seeking after more of God's love. For as Wesley cautioned

> If you are seeking anything but more love you are looking wide of the mark, you are getting out of the royal way. When others ask, "Have you received this or that blessing?" if they mean anything but more love, they are leading you out of the way and putting you on a false scent.[1191]

We are not to seek a particular gift; the Holy Spirit divides them as he wills. After giving a listing of spiritual gifts (χάρισμα - *charisma*) in 1 Corinthians 12, at v 11 Paul teaches that the Holy Spirit gives them to each man, just as he determines. If there are as many as twenty-one gifts of the Spirit, why insist that only one is the initial evidence of the Holy Spirit?

Tongues advocates do not agree among themselves as to what tongues evidences. Among Roman Catholic charismatics it is renewal, not salvation. Among The Way and United Pentecostals it is the evidence of salvation. Among Assemblies of God and non-holiness pentecostals, it is the second work. Among Pentecostal Holiness members it is the third blessing.

"Any tracing of tongues phenomenon through church history faces the hazzard of the common lack of clear-cut distinctions between tongues and prophecy and between the use of foreign languages and ecstatic utterances."[1192]

[1190]Dayton, "Asa Mahan," 65. In his evaluation of the Pentecostal approach to Christian spirituality, Hinson noted that Splitter's essay said little about sanctification. While Splitter had described Pentecostal spirituality, no special attention had been given to sanctification ["Contemplative View,"168].

[1191]Wesley, *Works*, 11:430

[1192]Farrell, "Outburst of Tongues," 5.

Furthermore, tongues is not a distinctly Christian phenomenon. Plato mentions it among pagan religions. It was common in the worship of Venus. It was common among Mother Ann Lee and the Shakers and among Mormons.[1193] When their temple was dedicated in Salt Lake City, hundreds of elders all spoke in tongues. Tongues is common among Hindus. In the occult world, spiritualists list tongues as a manifestation of their church.[1194] Walter Hollenweger observed that speaking in tongues is not even supernatural. In Africa or Mexico speaking in tongues and healings are not considered extraordinary. They can even be found in some indigenous pagan religions. Third-world Pentecostals focus on corporate worship, singing together, and Christian education, not tongues.[1195]

According to 1 Corinthians 12:30, "not all speak with tongues." However, Stanley Horton argued that Paul "is not talking about tongues as the initial evidence of the baptism in the Holy Spirit. The Corinthian believers all had that experience. Paul, in this context, is talking about the gifts of the Spirit and makes clear that not everyone will be used by the Spirit for every spiritual gift in the local assembly." In other words, Horton says not everyone will continue to speak in tongues.[1196] Here Horton presumes what he has not proven, that the Bible requires tongues as the initial outward evidence of Spirit baptism. He then reads into the text his own theological distinction. Two pages later he concedes that "no Scripture passage says specifically that tongues is the normative evidence."[1197]

While Jack Hayford subscribes to Pentecostal doctrine that tongues is a "sign gift," he "does not think the point can be conclusively proven one way or the other from Scripture."[1198] Donald Gee concluded

---

[1193]Smith, *History of the Church of Jesus Christ of Latter-Day Saints*, Period 1,1:295-297; 322-323; 4:485; 541.

[1194]See Behm, γλῶσσα, 1:722-724 for this phenomenon in non-Christian religions. "Glossolalia is not to be thought confined to Christian groups and offshoots. This emphasizes the fact that the practice is not self-authenticating" [Farrell, "Outburst of Tongues," 5]. Koch, *Strife of Tongues*, 32 refers to tongues associated with pagan religions.

[1195]Hollenweger, "Pentecostalism's Global Language," 42.

[1196]Horton, "Pentecostal Perspective,"*Spirit Baptism*, 76. This is also the interpretation of Gee in *Speaking in Tongues*, 7-8.

[1197]Horton,"Pentecostal Perspective," *Spirit Baptism*, 78.

[1198]Stafford, "Pentecostal Gold Standard," 28. Ironically, Hayford wrote *The Beauty of Spiritual Language*, a 204-page book which advocates speaking with tongues.

> Now the doctrine that speaking with other tongues is the initial evidence of the Baptism of the Holy Spirit rests upon the accumulated evidence of the recorded cases in the book of Acts where this experience is received. Any doctrine on this point must necessarily be confined within these limits for its basis, for the New Testament contains no plain, categorical statement anywhere as to what must be regarded as THE sign.[1199]

Pentecostal theologian Russell Spittler conceded that "the Bible gives no direct answer to this question."[1200] Six times in Acts the Holy Spirit was given; three times the phenomenon of tongues was present and three times it was absent.[1201] Surveying the four major outpourings of the Spirit in Acts, Danny McCain concluded that the baptism of the Holy Spirit in Acts follows no

---

[1199]Gee, *Speaking in Tongues*, 3. This statement was omitted in later editions. See Bibliography. However, Gee argued that since results in character and ministry will take some time to manifest themselves, they cannot be the initial evidence of Spirit baptism. Nor can the evidence be an inner personal consciousness of the recipient alone because that would be inconclusive as evidence to any others who were present. Here Gee, relied on logic to argue for a physical manifestation and then later in this tract conceded with sorrow and shame that those who have spoken with tongues may not live consistent lives. In contract, Methodist taught an inner witness of the Spirit which would be confirmed by an outward ethical standard of holy living.

[1200]Spittler, "Pentecostal Tradition, Part IV," 4.

[1201]Gee acknowledged that there is no indication whatever concerning the outward manifestation of Spirit baptism at Samaria. But he concluded that "we are as much justified in believing it was 'tongues' as in believing it was anything else." He also acknowledged that there is no separate record of Saul receiving the fullness of the Spirit, but he said it is implied as part of the commission given to Ananias in Acts 9:17. Again Gee concluded there is every reason to believe that Paul spoke in tongues because of his testimony in 1 Cor 14:18 [*Speaking in Tongues*, 5].

While William Durham acknowledged the Scriptures are silent concerning the phenomenon in Acts 8:17, yet he wrote "There is not a doubt in our mind, however, that they spoke in tongues" [*Articles by Durham*, 24]. However, an argument from silence convinces no one except those who have already formed their conclusion. Larry Hurtado admitted, "The question of what constitutes 'the initial evidence' of a person having received the 'baptism in the Spirit' is not raised in the New Testament." However, he argued that this does not render invalid the doctrine that tongues are the initial physical sign of Spirit baptism, even if we cannot show anywhere that this was the intent of the biblical writer. Experience can fill in the needed evidence where the scripture is silent [Hurtado, "Normal, but Not a Norm," 191].

consistent pattern.[1202]

According to 1 Corinthians 14:22 tongues is a sign to the unbeliever, not a sign to the believer that he or she has the Holy Spirit.[1203] In other words, their purpose is evangelistic, not confirmatory. Therefore, tongues are to be interpreted so that everyone will know what has been said (14:31). And tongues are to be used one at a time, at the most three (14:29).

I object to the atmosphere of confusion which frequently prevails in pentecostal/charismatic worship services in which these scriptural commandments are disregarded. We cannot say "amen" to what we cannot understand (1 Cor 14:16).[1204] The Holy Spirit is not the author of such confusion. Oral Roberts teaches that "on rare occasion the Holy Spirit manifests tongues and interpretations in a way seemingly not in accordance with rules laid down in Scripture."[1205] The same Spirit that inspired the scriptures would not contradict his own word.

The genuine gift of tongues is real languages. In Acts 2:8-11, 15 regions or dialects are mentioned. Everyone heard in their own language. In both Acts and 1 Corinthians the word "unknown" is italicized and not in the original text. Glossolalia means known languages.

Some concluded that they were speaking the language of angels, not men (see 1 Cor 13:1). However, this is a third class condition, meaning "even if I could."[1206] Here Paul uses an exaggeration or hyperbole to make a point. Nowhere else in scripture is an angelic language mentioned and this verse does not establish such a fact.

Tongues can be easily counterfeited. Today people are coached. They are to abandon control and just say anything. But according to 1 Corinthians 14:32 "the spirit of the prophets are subject to the control of the

---

[1202]McCain, "Baptism of the Holy Spirit," 1-5. See also McCain, *Lord, Lift Me Up!*, 85-86.

[1203]A booklet by the Full Gospel Businessmen's Fellowship asserted that speaking in tongues is a sign of the believer, as well as to the unbeliever. However, the only proof that tongues is a sign to the believer is the citation of John 7:38-39. It is assumed that the overflowing life described by John is evidenced by tongues, although the scriptural passage never says so [Jensen, *Methodists and the Baptism of the Holy Spirit*, 5].

[1204]Thus, Thomas Walsh objected to the error of the Church of Rome in allowing her ministers to speak to the people in an unknown tongue [*Sermons*, 136].

[1205]Roberts, *Baptism with the Holy Spirit*, 96.

[1206]The conditional particle ἐάν (*ean*) occurs five times in 1 Cor 13:1-3. While the KJV translates it "though," it would be better translated "if." In each case Paul uses it to state a hyperbole and in no case is he stating an actual reality.

prophets." The indwelling of the Spirit gives us greater self-control. It is a dangerous practice to open yourself to anything and become passive. God does not bypass our minds, but enlightens our mind. A physical phenomenon therefore does not evidence a spiritual reality. An emotional experiences does not override an ethical disobedience.

Tongues-speaking does not necessarily produce holy living. Stanley Horton, Assemblies of God scholar admitted, "the baptism in the Holy Spirit is not of itself a sanctifying experience."[1207] Another pentecostal leader, Jack Stiles, wrote that a great host of people, who have spoken in tongues, are not manifesting holiness, but are conducting themselves in ways in which any Christian knows is

---

[1207]Horton, "Pentecostal Perspective," *Sanctification*, 132. McQuilkin expressed surprise at such a statement ["Keswick Perspective, "144]. One can only wonder, then, why he includes six pages on the subject in a book devoted to the explanation of sanctification. However, Lloyd-Jones also declared that there is no direct connection between the baptism with the Holy Spirit and sanctification [*Joy Unspeakable*, 136].

Lloyd-Jones made a distinction between the baptism *by* the Spirit, which all Christians received at regeneration, and the baptism *with* the Spirit. He taught this second baptism of the Holy Spirit was not sanctification, but power for service which could be often repeated—like an anointing. He taught that a believer might not be conscious that he had received the Spirit in regeneration. He equated the assurance taught here with the baptism *with* the Spirit and with the sealing of the Spirit and taught that this produced assurance, not sanctification. He would not have wanted this doctrine to be identified with a second work of grace, yet it was something distinct from regeneration [*Life in the Spirit*, 41; see also *Christian Conduct*, 190, 222, 232]. Lloyd-Jones also stated there is no direct association between the sealing of the Spirit, the baptism of the Spirit, the witness of the Spirit, and sanctification [*Sons of God*, 381]. Although Lloyd-Jones devoted over 200 pages to establish his unusual view, his argument is based primarily upon the experiences he cited [*Sons of God*, 194-399]. It seems Lloyd-Jones was trying to reconcile cold, academic Calvinism with the great revival outpouringsof the Spirit. Therefore, he made the conscious reception of the Spirit somethingother than the new birth. However, if the human heart is deceitful and unreliable, how can anyone know they are justified unless by a conscious revelation? While Lloyd-Jones taught a person can be a Christian and yet know little or nothing about this Spirit of adoption [*Sons of God*, 246], the Spirit of adoption is received at the time of adoption. Without the Spirit of adoption, we have no basis for claiming to be adopted. It seems that Lloyd-Jones is trying to articulate the Puritan distinction between faith and assurance. This position taken by Lloyd-Jones is critiqued by Schreiner, *Romans*, 427; Stott, *Romans*, 235-236. Stott contended that all believers have received the Spirit of adoptionand cry "Abba, Father" as the Spirit himself witnesses to them that they are God's children.See also Murray, *David Martyn Lloyd-Jones*, 2:483-491. Murray said that Lloyd-Jones was reacting to the prevalent view among evangelicals that there was no larger giving of the Spirit after conversion. Murray, however, concluded that his interpretation was mistaken and caused confusion.

displeasing to God.[1208] Donald Gee observed that it seemed possible to exercise a spiritual gift and "yet be out of touch with the Lord."[1209] Jimmy Swaggart taught that one does not seek tongues. "One asks for the Holy Spirit, and the tongues will automatically follow."[1210] However, Swaggart also conceded, "We do not believe, nor do we teach, that speaking in other tongues will automatically produce a better Christian."[1211]

While the *Full Life Study Bible* teaches that the baptism in the Holy Spirit results in "enhanced sensitivity to sin," "a greater seeking after righteousness which conforms to Christ," and "a deeper awareness of the judgment of God against all unrighteousness," William and Robert Menzies think this is an invalid association of Spirit baptism with holiness of life and Christian maturity. They argue that it confuses the fruit of the Spirit and Paul's admonition to be filled with the Spirit with Luke's description of Pentecost. According to them, Luke does not describe the Spirit as the direct source of ethical transformation. "Spirit-baptism in the Lukan sense, cannot be linked with holiness or Christian maturity."[1212]

Across the twentieth century the pentecostal movement has been characterized by flamboyant evangelists such as Aimee Semple McPherson who made their own rules and were accountable to no one. McPherson was the role model for Kathryn Kuhlman. In 1938 she married Burroughs A. Waltrip who had left his previous wife because he had fallen in love with Kathryn. They divorced in 1947. She operated independently and was never ordained.[1213] In *Occult ABC* Kurt Koch evaluated the ministry of Kuhlman after a thorough investigation which included a personal interview. He raised serious doubts concerning whether she was operating under the power of the Holy Spirit or as a medium.[1214]

William Branham claimed to be the new Elijah, the forerunner of Christ's return and the head of the seventh Church age. He taught annihilation, denying

---

[1208]Stiles, *Gift of the Holy Spirit*, 80-82. See his letter in *Christianity Today*, 17 in which he wrote, "There is a growing minority among Full Gospel people who do not believe that tongues is the 'only" or 'necessary' evidence of the initial receiving of the Holy Spirit. We do accept that it is *an* evidence."

[1209]Gee, *Concerning Spiritual Gifts*, 67.

[1210]It was once explained to me that when you buy a pair of shoes, the shoe strings come along with the shoes. I could not help but realize that at that time that I did not own a single pair of shoes *with* shoestrings.

[1211]Swaggart, *Is Speaking in Tongues Scriptural?* 37; 3.

[1212]Menzies, *Spirit and Power*, 205. Stamps, *Full Life Study Bible*, 244.

[1213]Liardon, *God's Generals*, 284-288.

[1214]Koch, *Occult ABC*, 110-121.

the eternal punishment of hell (as did Parham), adopted the Jesus Only teaching, and was expected by his followers to raise from the dead.[1215] The coroner's report on the death of A. A. Allen in 1970 reported a very high and concentrated level of alcohol in the blood stream. The cause of death included "acute alcoholism."[1216] Oral Roberts, Robert Tilton, Jim and Tammy Bakker, Jimmy Swaggart, Earnest Ansley, Benny Hinn, Paul Crouch, and Todd Bentley represent an egocentric pentecostalism at its worst.[1217]

The pentecostal movement seemed to struggle with an inferiority complex and at the same time with a feeling of superiority. Touting the growth of their movement seemed to pragmatically justify their doctrine. Not only did they refuse accountability, it seemed they did not even believe scriptural commands applied to them as long as they had the Holy Ghost. The emphasis was on power, not purity; upon emotional experience not ethical holiness; the gifts instead of the fruit of the Spirit. Thus, they separated the Holy Spirit from Christian perfection and holy living. It is no longer acceptable to point out this departure from holiness, since they have experienced such phenomenal growth in the twentieth century. Yet their success has, in some ways, hurt the entire church of God. Truth must ultimately win out. The truth must be spoken in love, but it must be spoken.

I used to feel that the rhetorical question in James 3:11 amounted to a wholesale condemnation of the pentecostal movement. Bitter water and fresh water cannot come from the same source. The historical roots of pentecostalism

---

[1215]Liardon, *God's Generals*, 334-343.

[1216]Liardon, *God's Generals*, 408. Tragically, *Charisma* reported that Liardon himself confessed to a homosexual relationship with his youth pastor and then returned to his pulpit three months later [Butcher, "Roberts Liardon," 36; Lawson, "Most Students," 16-18; Lawson, "Liardon Preaches," 26-27].

[1217]Hanegraaff, *Christianity and Crisis*, 29-39; 331-361. Fisher and Goedelman, *Confusing World of Benny Hinn*. In "Best-selling Author Admits Mistakes, Vows Changes," Hinn retracted his statement that there were nine members of the Godhead and repudiated his claim to receive some of his controversial doctrines directly from God [Frame, 44-46]. However, "Same Old Benny Hinn, Critics Say" indicates that he has not changed [Frame, 52-54]. Hinn later renounced the "word-of-faith" movement [Feraiuolo, "Christian Leaders Admonish Hinn," 38-39]. See Frame, "Account of Hinn's Healings Challenged," 84. See also Fisher and Goedelman, "Welcome, Holy Spirit," 49-50. In *Anointing*, Hinn teaches that Christian live at four levels: saved, baptized in the Spirit, the presence, and the anointing. Unless Christians progress on to higher levels, God cannot bless or use them. Hinn taught that we must abandon self, die to self, and empty ourselves to get the anointing, which is the highest level and which liberates from sin. However, the Scriptures teach that the saved are liberated from sin and that all who are God's children have an anointing (1 John 2:20; 27).

were sufficiently corrupt to condemn the entire movement. However, I have met too many good pentecostal pastors who were helping their congregations find a spiritual balance and had genuine saints in their congregation. In some instances people were attracted to pentecostalism because they were sick of the dead formality of the mainline denominations. And in many instances, those who identify themselves as pentecostal or charismatic have not even spoken in tongues. They simply believe in the gifts of the Spirit. And Pentecostalism must be given credit for breaking the mindset of Western rationalism and making a supernatural worldview legitimate.

A survey by Gallup Poll indicated that 19% of all adult Americans (29 million) consider themselves to be Pentecostal or charismatic, yet only 17% of these people (5 million or 4% of the general population) have spoken in tongues.[1218] More recently, the Pew forum on Religion and Public Life found that 49% of all Pentecostals and 32% of all Charismatics never speak in tongues.[1219]

Unlike pentecostals, charismatics do not believe the gifts of tongues is a sign of a higher level of Christian experience nor are they promised as part of normal Christian experience, yet they believe God may give these gifts today. The movement is perceived as a lay-ministry movement or a prayer cell movement and in some locations it may be the best available option. Whether or not these lay ministries and small group movements are aware of their heritage, the fact is that no one did it better than John Wesley.

Stanley Horton objected to Wesley's balance of law and love. Instead he explained that Pentecostals are led by the Spirit to do the good things God intended when he gave the law.[1220] Yet we demonstrate our love for God by keeping his commandments (John 14:15). True faith produces love and obedience. Horton's rejection of ethical holiness in lieu of an emotional experience, differentiates between the Wesleyan and Pentecostal emphases. Jesus warned that it is possible to be lawless and to have never know God, yet to be able to prophesy, drive out demons and perform many miracles. Therefore, the fruit of the Spirit (Gal 5:22-23) should be sought instead of the gifts of the Spirit.

[1218]Kantzer, "Charismatics Among Us,"25. Olsen cited an October 2006 survey by Pew Forum on Religion and Public Life which revealed that at least 40% of Pentecostals in six of the ten countries surveyed said they had never prayed or spoken in tongues. Only half of U. S. Pentecostals had spoken in tongues [Olsen, "What Really Unites Pentecostals?"18]. According to statistics in the *New International Dictionary of Pentecostal and Charismatic Movements* only 5%-35% of all Pentecostals had spoken in tongues, either initially or on an ongoing basis [Barrett and Johnson, "Global Statistics," 291].

[1219]McMullen, "Holding Their Tongues," 16.

[1220]Horton, "Pentecostal Perspective,"*Sanctification*, 51, 96.

Bloesch concluded, "It is not extraordinary gifts of the Spirit but the fruits of the Spirit that constitute the evidence of whether our conversion is genuine."[1221]

The Charismatic Movement

Just as the early holiness leaders thought their doctrine of holiness would unite all Christians, so the early pentecostal leaders thought their emphasis would bring unity. While both movements resulted in more denominations, the charismatic movement has crossed every denominational line and at this point in time it has not yet institutionalized. The pentecostal/charismatic movement worldwide is estimated at half a billion members.[1222] In the United States only one third of those who identify themselves as Pentecostal belong to one of the 300 traditional Pentecostal denominations.[1223]

The modern charismatic movement differs from classic pentecostalism primarily in the fact that it exists outside classical pentecostal denominations.[1224] The old- line Pentecostals feel that charismatics who stay in non-Pentecostal denominations are attempting to put new wine in old wineskins.[1225] For almost all neo-Pentecostals, as well as classic pentecostals, "Spirit baptism is linked directly to the glossolalia phenomenon," according to Quebedeaux.[1226] Much of the difference between pentecostals and charismatics is cultural. The old line Pentecostal groups have become institutionalized and represent old "wineskins" to the charismatics. On the other hand, for members of mainline denominations, which originally rejected pentecostalism, to speak in tongues is putting new wine into old wineskins according to pentecostals. Many Pentecostals have spoken in tongues only once. Unlike charismatics they do not exercise tongues as a private prayer language. Neo-pentecostals or third wave pentecostals refuse to make tongues the one evidence of the Spirit's infilling [1227] Among charismatics there

---

[1221]Bloesch, *Holy Spirit*, 300.

[1222]Barrett, Kurian, and Johnson, *World Christian Encyclopedia*, 1:19-21. The worldwide count for Jesus Only pentecostals is 2.4 million; 5.6 million for holiness pentecostals; 49 million for Baptist/Keswick pentecostals, 1.5 million for Apostolic pentecostals, and 3,000 for classic pentecostals [1:16].

[1223]Wacker, "America's Pentecostals,"16.

[1224]Williams, "Charismatic Movement," 205.

[1225]Swaggart, "Pentecostals and Charismatics," 4-9.

[1226]Quebedeaux, *New Charismatics*, 130.

[1227]Farah, "Differences Within the Family," 25. Packer identified twenty-three characteristics of charismatics, including the claim that none of the elements of New

are differing viewpoints concerning whether the baptism in the Holy Spirit is subsequent to conversion and whether it is a sign of the baptism in the Spirit.

The charismatic movement began in 1960 when Dennis Bennett, rector of St. Mark's Episcopal Church in Van Nuys, California, spoke in tongues and introduced the experience to his congregation.[1228] Charismatics may be Protestant or Catholic, Reformed or Wesleyan, Trinitarian or even Unitarian-Universalist.[1229] The charismatic experience of speaking in tongues unites people through a common experience who could not agree theologically. In spite of the diversity within the movement, it is united by a common experience: the baptism of the Holy Spirit with accompanying gifts.[1230]

Bennett taught that every Christian is indwelt by the Holy Spirit, "but he or she still needs to speak in tongues. . . . It is not an optional 'gift' among many." "You start speaking in tongues the same way you start speaking any language, by beginning to make sounds." He taught two ways that tongues were used, as a prayer language and the gift of tongues. The prayer language does not need interpretation, but the less common practice of public speaking in tongues does require interpretation. "With the prayer language you can speak in tongues any time you decide to do so, but you do not just decide you'd like to bring a gift of tongues." Yet he cautioned, "Speaking in the Spirit doesn't show how holy you are and you don't do it to prove you have the Holy Spirit living in you."[1231]

Jack Stiles taught there need be no tarrying or preparation to receive the Spirit other than being a believer in Christ. One should have no fear of getting in the flesh, for speaking begins as a fleshly act and then the Holy Spirit takes over supernaturally during that speech.[1232]

According to Multmann, the church was born at Pentecost and

Testament ministry and experience have ceased. Charismatics make an empirical claim that a post-conversion Spirit-baptism can be enjoyed. Tongues are understood as deliberately uttering language-like sounds primarily in private devotions. None of the twenty-three emphases address the subject of sanctification. Packer quoted Richard Lovelace who observed, "Gifts of the Spirit are more prominent than the call to sanctification" ["Piety on Fire," 18-21].

1228Williams, "Charismatic Movement," 205.

1229Quebedeaux, *New Charismatics*, 127.

1230Quebedeaux, *New Charismatics*, 5.

1231Bennett, *How to Pray*, 75; 54; 18; 27; 56. Bennett actually taught connected childish babbling with glossolalia and claimed "it is not unusual to find a person who has been speaking in tongues ever since childhood but who did not know the significance of what he or she was doing ["The Gifts of the Holy Spirit," 26].

1232Stiles, *Gift of the Holy Spirit*, 43-44.

glossolalia was the sign of its birth.[1233] Clark Pinnock emphasized that the baptism in the Spirit, for charismatics, does not refer to a doctrine to be believed, but it is an encounter which must be experienced.[1234]

Theology is not extremely important to either group, yet the older Pentecostal movement struggled over a two-step or three-step paradigm. Such issues are relatively unimportant to charismatics. For Catholic charismatics tongues is a renewal. It is part of initial salvation for unitarian pentecostals.[1235] It is a second work of grace for evangelical pentecostals and it is a third crisis experience for holiness pentecostals. Larry Hart explained, "Strictly speaking, Spirit baptism is a metaphor, not a doctrine. Further, it is a metaphor whose usage is clearly not univocal within the New Testament." Hart argued that in the New Testament Spirit baptism refers to the eschatological redemptive work of Jesus, Christian initiation, the Christian life, and empowerment for Christian mission and ministry. He concluded, "There is no one 'Charismatic position' on spirit baptism."[1236] Many charismatics have come to believe that being filled with the Spirit is an experience which begins with justification and continues one's whole lifetime. For them Spirit-baptism is not one but many gifts, not two but

---

[1233]Multmann, "The Spirit Gives Life: Spirituality and Vitality," 26.

[1234]Pinnock, *Evangelical Theology*, 1-9. See also "Theological Evaluation and Critique,"128-141, in which Pinnock argued that the gift of tongues must be evaluated Scripturally and not on the basis of experience. It can be harmful for a Christian to seek a gift which the Scriptures do not explicitly promise. Yet nowhere are we commanded either to be baptized with the Spirit or to seek the gift of tongues. "The reason why Paul did not ask the Corinthian Christians to be baptized with the Spirit is simple: they had already been baptized with him (1 Cor 12:13)." We must formulate our doctrine from the epistles, not the historical account of Acts. "Paul knows nothing at all about a second work of grace subsequent to conversion which is called a 'baptism.'"

However, see Pinnock's defense ofPentecostalism in "Truce Proposal," 6-9 and "Reflections of a Well-Wisher," 6-10. Pinnock later declared, "It is not a *doctrine* of the Spirit that we need, but a *movement* of the Spirit, pervading and filling us, setting our convictions on fire" ["Opening the Church," 16]. See also Pinnock's testimony to healing and being filled with the Spirit in 1967 through the charismatic renewal ["Revolutionary Promise, "19]. In *Flame of Love*, Pinnock described salvation in relational terms as the embrace of God. The goal of salvation is glorification and union with God, the Spirit. Pinnock employs sexual imagery to describe our union with God. This oneness is the ancient concept of *theosis*. Pinnock does not require everyone to speak in tongues, but *glossolalia* is one of the evidences of the Spirit.

[1235]Hall, "Oneness Pentecostal,"184.

[1236]Hart, "Charismatic Perspective," 108-109.

many experiences.[1237]

John L. Peters, author of *Christian Perfection and American Methodism* (1956), had been raised and educated in the Church of the Nazarene. He testified that as president of World Neighbors he had become completely exhausted. He found himself in a charismatic prayer group which emphasized the baptism with the Holy Spirit. He began to realize this is what the church in general needed. Later he went forward in a service and tarried until he spoke in tongues. He reported a new and deeper intimacy in the quality of his relationship to his Lord, a new and deeper bond with those who know and love him. He also found a more rewarding method by which to pray and praise; a new key to personal worship and edification, a new joy, a new fellowship, a new dimension. While this testimony is one of fourteen experiences shared by Methodists, there is no attempt to correlate their experience with Methodist theology.[1238]

Neo-orthodoxy is existential in its emphasis on subjective experience. Faith becomes a mystical "leap in the dark" and "tongues" can become an attempt to find meaning in the irrational. Modern theologians such as Paul Tillich taught existentialism, which says that human experience is not describable in scientific or rational terms. Tillich taught "God above God."[1239] By this phrase Tillich meant that God was undefined, but experienced through an irrational leap of faith. Tongues then becomes a non-rational experience or a "leap in the dark." Without necessarily understanding the philosophical terminology, it is common for pentecostal preachers to exhort their congregation to quit trying to understand with their minds and "just let go." But how can the will surrender to what the intellect cannot grasp? Paul asked, How can we say "amen" to what we do not understand? (1 Cor 14:16).

The charismatic movement did not produce a systematic theology for over thirty years.[1240] Experience becomes all important, yet without the absolute truth of Scripture experience can mean anything. Yet their emphasis on the Holy Spirit forced all the denominations influenced by charismatics to develop or redefine the role of the Holy Spirit. While the early Church held councils to state the ecumenical doctrines concerning the Father and the Son, no such council has ever been held to deal with the doctrines of the Spirit. While not every answer can be

---

[1237] Tuttle, "Guidelines," 7.

[1238] Jensen, *Methodists and the Baptism of the Holy Spirit*, 30-32.

[1239] Tillich, *Courage to Be*, 186-190. Oral Roberts was especially impressed with existentialists. While he did not forsake his beliefs, he simply found new language to express them [Robinson, *Oral*, 95].

[1240] Farah, "America's Pentecostals," 24-25. J. Rodman Williams completed his *Renewal Theology*, a systematic theology from a charismatic perspective, in 1992. The three volumes were reprinted in one volume by Zondervan in 1996.

accepted as adequate, the charismatics can at least be thanked for forcing the question.

Ironically, the holiness movement has tended to abandon their tradition in order to share in the growth of this newer movement. While the Church of the Nazarene had taken an official stand against tongues as the evidence of Spirit baptism, they have had their problems. In 1955 they merged with Calvary Holiness Church of Great Britain. This church had broken with its former denomination in 1934 partially over the issue of spiritual gifts.[1241] They merged with the Church of the Nazarene understanding that they would be granted "freedom of conscience."[1242] Maynard James was president of Calvary Holiness Church at the time of the merger and he stated in a 1976 interview that his church:

> would never have joined the Church of the Nazarene" without the assurance that its followers could follow their own conscience in the matter of tongues. "We have happy fellowship with godly pentecostal (charismatic) people. There is no issue here. As far as we in Britain are concerned there is no need to bring it up.[1243]

The Church of God (Anderson, Indiana), started around 1880 as a holiness church, has also experienced problems over the tongues issue. In1973 the executive secretary reported to the General Assembly that "in some states there is a lot of controversy about speaking in tongues and the charismatic movement. A few of our congregations have encountered serious schisms over the issue." His solution was to permit, but not encourage, glossolalia.[1244]

As a result of the charismatic convention held in Kansas City in 1977, a charismatic caucus developed among churches of the Wesleyan tradition. There was a Wesleyan Charismatic Conference held in Cincinnati in 1979.[1245] Warren Black, vice-president of the Wesleyan Charismatic Fellowship, said his group includes several hundred pastors and laymen. He sees a mellowing among younger Nazarene and Wesleyan leaders, although many are not yet willing to publically identify with his movement. Black understands the baptism of the Spirit as a third work. While entire sanctification purifies, this baptism empowers and affects different levels of the soul and spirit, bringing more deliverance. Black, who once

---

[1241]Purkiser, *Called Unto Holiness*, 2:261.

[1242]Purkiser, *Called Unto Holiness*, 2:263-265

[1243]Allison, "Issue Sharply Divides Church of Nazarene,"1.

[1244]Smith, *Quest for Holiness and Unity*, 425.

[1245]Snyder, *Divided Flame*, 85.

was a Nazarene, had a hunger for greater power and sought this baptism.[1246]

The Wesleyan Holiness Charismatic Fellowship, also known as Fellowship of Charismatic Nazarenes, states in their newsletter that they are "a network of believers of Wesleyan Holiness background who have come into a new dimension of their Christian walk in the scriptural baptism in the Holy Spirit, accompanied by the scriptural manifestations of the Spirit described in 1 Corinthians 12, including the ability to speak and worship God in tongues as the Spirit gives the utterance."[1247] In 1967 the National Holiness Association (now the Christian Holiness Partnership) admitted into their membership Bethany Fellowship, a group that practices speaking in tongues.[1248]

Free Methodist author and pastor Howard Snyder claims that John Wesley's theology is charismatic and Methodism was a charismatic movement. He does not think Wesley would have "necessarily opposed the modern phenomenon of glossolalia." He says the pentecostals and charismatics are here to stay and that the holiness bodies are "softening their opposition" and taking a second look.[1249] Snyder's conclusion is that "tongues-speaking is legitimate whenever it is prompted by the Holy Spirit, regardless of one's theology!"[1250]

Lowell O. Ferrel proposed a much more valid Wesleyan position toward the charismatic movement by arguing from Wesley's reaction against subjectivity, lack of discipline, and misguided priorities that Wesley would reject the modern charismatic movement.[1251]

The Third Wave

Peter Wagner coined the term "third wave" in 1983 to refer to a third wave of pentecostalism with Azusa Street representing the first wave and the charismatic movement representing the second wave. Wagner did not consider himself to be pentecostal or charismatic, but had been teaching a class on signs

---

[1246] Black, interview, 20 April 1989.

[1247] *Wesleyan Holiness Charismatic Fellowship Newsletter* (1990): 1. Jones give the date as 1985, but the newsletter advertizes "Indianapolis 1990" [*Wesleyan Holiness Movement*, 1:508; 782].

[1248] Synan, *Holiness-Pentecostal Tradition*, 217.

[1249] Snyder, "Church as Holy and Charismatic," 16; 22.

[1250] Snyder, *Divided Flame*, 21.

[1251] Ferrel, "John Wesley and the Enthusiasts," 180-187. See also Maddox, *Responsible Grace*, 134-136; Jennings, *Supernatural Occurrences*.

and wonders at Fuller Theological Seminary.[1252] Those within the third wave are evangelicals who exercise the gifts of the Spirit without accepting the previous labels. They see the work of the Holy Spirit in divine healing, new prophecies, and casting out of demons. However, they deny any "second blessing," instead teaching that believers are baptized with the Spirit at the time of their conversion.

John Wimber declared that conversion and Holy Spirit baptism are simultaneous experiences. "How can we experience Spirit baptism? It comes at conversion."[1253] They do not always insist on glossolalia.[1254]

The Vineyard movement, led by John Wimber, emphasized healing and deliverance, connecting this with power evangelism.[1255] "For Wimber, the heart of the Christian faith resides in an experience of the power and love of God, not in a creed."[1256] Wimber emphasized a paradigm shift away from biblical doctrine toward experience.[1257] Wimber emphasized that God is bigger than His Word. "All that is in the Bible is true, but not all truth is in the Bible. We integrate all truth, both biblical and other, into our experience of living."[1258]

For Wimber the power of God lies in activity — signs, wonders, healings, miracles, church growth. Thus, the third wave emphasizes evangelism through signs and wonders. The Vineyard movement taught multiple fillings of the Holy Spirit and did not understand tongues to be the "initial evidence." The emphasis was on empowerment by the Holy Spirit. This empowerment was demonstrated through the charismatic gifts of prophecy and healing more than speaking in tongues.[1259]

[1252]Wagner, "Signs, Wonders and Church Growth,"42-49. See also Chandler, "Fuller Seminary,"48-49; Patterson, "Cause for Concern,"20 both of which reported the course had been cancelled due to problems.

[1253]Wimber, *Power Points*, 136, see also Storms, "Third Wave," 176-185. Yet Storms defines being "filled with the Holy Spirit" as a continuous, ongoing experience. "To be filled with the Spirit is to come under progressively more intense and intimate influence of the Spirit" [p. 179]. Storms also argues for "postconversion encounters or experiences with the Holy Spirit that are related to but not identical with infilling" [p. 181].

[1254]Pawson, "Mixed Blessing," 84.

[1255]Stafford, "Testing the Wine," 17-22.

[1256]Percy, *Words, Wonders and Power*, 83.

[1257]Wagner, *Acts of the Holy Spirit*, 123.

[1258]Online: Goodwin, "Testing the Fruit of the Vineyard."

[1259]Poloma, "Reconfiguration of Pentecostalism," 102-103. According to Oropeza another of the Kansas City "prophets" achieved no more than a 65% success

Although the phenomenon of "holy laughter" had occurred as early as 1986 under Wimber's ministry, between 1994-1996 this became known as the "Toronto Blessing" at the Toronto Airport Vineyard congregation.[1260] A Church of England Board of Mission report defined the "Toronto Experience" as particular phenomena in congregations when members of the congregation exhibit not only common manifestations of charismatic worship, including praying in tongues, ecstatic ululation etc, but also shaking, falling down ("being slain in the Spirit"), an imperative need to laugh or to cry, or to make unusual noises, especially sounds analogous to animal noises such as "roaring" or "barking."[1261] Dixon explained that "some began to seek a sign rather than an inner work of grace."[1262]

Pastor John Arnott had been influenced by Benny Hinn and Rodney Howard-Browne. Browne became known as "God's bartender" because people under his ministry experienced "Spirit drunkenness." They also made animal sounds and often spent "carpet time," meaning that they fell to the ground when prayed for and often lay for an hour or more.[1263] Observers wrote that early in the service two or three people would be brought forward to share their testimonies. These testimonies would tend to create the expectation for others to imitate later in the service.[1264]

Kevin Springer explained, "You don't understand the Vineyard if you don't understand the worship music. That is probably the greatest contributor to the growth and advancement of the Vineyard movement."[1265] While the hymns of Charles Wesley communicate theology, Wimber believes that people's feelings are

---

rate in the fulfillment of his prophecies [*Time to Laugh*, 56].

1260Woodward, "Giggles Are for God," 54.

1261Richards, *Toronto Experience*, 1; Beverley, "Toronto's Mixed Blessing," 22-27; see also Hanegraaff, *Counterfeit Revival*; Hanegraaff, "Rodney Howard-Browne," 8-18; 45-46. On Howard-Browne's background, see Duin, "Evening with Howard-Browne," 5-6; 43-45.

1262Dixon, "Altered Christian Consciousness," 92.

1263Poloma, *Main Street Mystics*, 43; 70-74. Much of this phenomena has been explained psychologically as an altered state of consciousness [Dixon, "Altered Christian Consciousness," 91-98]. Poloma explained this altered state of consciousness as triggered by the music [pp. 37-49].

1264Philip Foster reprinted two pages of Vineyard Christian Fellowship tips for leaders regarding who should be selected and how the worship time should be managed ["Suggestibility, hysteria and hypnosis," 70-71].

1265Poloma, *Main Street Mystics*, 56. John Wimber was a converted rock musician [Wimber, *Power Evangelism*, 14].

to be changed first through worship. "The ideology, helped by the music, establishes and fixes a relationship between God and the believers that is intimate, at times passive, passionate and sensual, and occasionally, almost sexual. The combination of 'soft contemporary rock' and 'romantic/intimate' tunes clearly help 'carry' the textual ideology of the songs."[1266] Percy wrote that while Wesley's hymns were essentially didactic, to help unread people learn theology, Wimber's choruses are existential — to help people experience God in new ways.[1267] Instead of an emphasis on expositional preaching, it is typical to have an hour of praise choruses led by a praise team. Reeves described this music as monotonous frequency and endless repetition.[1268] However, at one point Wimber gave his staff Andrew Murray's *The Holiest of All* and told them they needed more new choruses about the blood and holiness.[1269]

David Hilborn concluded that this "Toronto Blessing" cannot be considered to be revival or an awakening. Nick Gumbel stated, "I don't talk about it now. It divides people. It splits churches. It is very controversial."[1270] On December 5, 1995 Wimber expelled the Toronto Airport Vineyard church because it did not reflect the Vineyard priorities.[1271]

Paul Cain, one of the "Kansas City Prophets," had warned Wimber and the Vineyard in 1988 that he must give greater priority to holiness within the movement.[1272] Concerning the controversial phenomenon, however, Cain explained that "God offends the mind to reveal the heart. The issue is one of control. God wants to know who among his people will be willing to play the fool

---

[1266]Percy, *Words, Wonders and Power*, 79.

[1267]Percy, *Words, Wonders and Power*, 64.

[1268]Reeves, *Other Side of the River*, 132-133; 158-162.

[1269]Ravenhill, interview, 13 July 2006.

[1270]Hilborn, "Introduction," 24-25.

[1271]Stafford and Beverley, "God's Wonder Worker," 47. Wimber disagreed with their use of scripture to justify the phenomena and did not want the Toronto "model" to permeate the Vineyard movement. While Arnott felt they should not "touch the ark," Wimber felt they should exercise more pastoral oversight. They were repeatedly warned not to promote, encourage, or theologize the animal behavior and the accompanying sounds [Ford, "Toronto's Church Ousted from Vineyard,"12].

[1272]In 1989 Leonard and David Ravenhill gave the Vineyard movement what was to be Leonard's last seminar and the subject was holiness. Ultimately, however, Wimber's message was on the fatherhood of God and the emphasis on holiness was downplayed in favor of the message of acceptance. Wimber and the Kansas City movement split over this issue. It is one thing to come to Jesus "just as you are," it is another matter to remain in that same state [Ravenhill, interview, 13 July 2006].

for his glory."[1273]

Howard-Browne also claimed, "You can't understand what God is doing in these meetings with an analytical mind. The only way you're going to understand what God is doing is with your heart."[1274] Brownsville leader John Kilpatrick said, "God will choose to offend our minds in order to reveal what is in our hearts." "The Lord is saying, 'I'm bypassing your mind and going straight to your heart,'" according to Lindell Cooley.[1275] Yet Wesley wrote, "It is a fundamental principle with us, that to renounce reason is to renounce religion; that religion and reason go hand in hand; and that all irrational religion is false

---

[1273]David Hilborn, "Chronicle of the Blessing," 140; 156. According to Poloma the Arminian emphasis on holiness was a source of tension between Wimber and the Kansas City prophets [*Main Street Mystics*, 151]. Paul Cain provided the acronym of IHOP for the four essentials of the Kansas City Fellowship: Intercessory prayer, Holiness through which men and women became "lovers of God," Offerings (extravagant giving to the poor), Prophetic ministry [Poloma, *Main Street Mystics*, 149]. In the few references I find to holiness within this movement, this reference to "lovers of God" is about all the definition I have found. In asking questions I have been told that holiness was presented as faithfulness to God based on love.

During the first anniversary of the "Toronto Blessing," the question was asked why this "revival" did not place a strong emphasis on the holiness of God and the depravity of man. Randy Clark replied that God decided to throw a party for his people because they "already feel so icky about themselves" [Hanegraaff, "Visionary Hoaxes and Revisionary History," 45].

In 1993 Wayne Grudem wrote a defense of the Vineyard, but conceded that they needed to teach a more thorough doctrine of sanctification [*Power and Truth*, 62].

Paul Cain traveled in the 1950s with William Branham, whom he considered to be the greatest prophet of the twentieth century. Wimber also considered Cain to be a prophet, like the apostle Paul. It was claimed that God had cleansed Cain from all erotic thoughts [Percy, *Words, Wonders and Power*, 56; 112]. However, in 2004 Cain was exposed as an alcoholic and practicing homosexual. His letter of confession was posted online, but later removed [Online: Cain, "Letter of Confession"]. See also Hayword, "News," 26. Another third wave leader, Bob Jones, was removed from ministry in 1991 for sexual misconduct.

Mike Bickle launched the International House of Prayer (IHOP) as a direct fulfillment of a prophecy he received in 1983 from Bob Jones. While Bickle emphasizes self-denial holiness and Sermon-on-the-Mount living, he also sees IHOP as an elite forerunner movement within the church which will prepare the way for the Great Tribulation and the return of Jesus [Jackson, "Forerunner Eschatology," 20-29].

[1274]Duin, "Praise the Lord," 26.

[1275]Hanegraaff, "December 1997 Meetings," 4.

religion."[1276]

John Stott expressed three concerns with the Toronto Blessing. First, it is a self-consciously anti-intellectual movement. While advocates cautioned, "Don't analyze, don't ask questions. Simply receive," this is both foolish and dangerous. The Holy Spirit is the Spirit of truth.

Second, Stott was grieved by the animal noises. "The whole Bible tells us that we are different from the animal creation; it rebukes us when we behave like animals and calls us to be distinct. Nebuchadnezzar's animal behavior was under the judgment, not the blessing, of God."

Stott was also troubled over all the falling. "On the few occasions in the Bible when people have fallen over, they have all fallen forwards on their faces, and they have all done so *after* they have been granted a vision of the majesty, holiness, and glory of God. In the Toronto experience, however, people fall backwards without any previous vision of God."[1277]

Since Toronto there was a "revival" at the Brownsville Assembly of God in Pensacola, Florida, which began on Father's Day, June 18, 1995 and ran four years. While there was some Toronto-style phenomenon, the emphasis was more on holiness, repentance, and the preaching of the cross. Yet the Brownsville leadership had received "an impartation" by John Arnott in Toronto and members of the Toronto staff had been to Pensacola.[1278] Kevin Reeves claimed the Brownsville phenomenon is merely a Toronto clone.[1279]

In 1996 there was the Smithton Missouri Revival, which moved to

---

[1276]Letter to Dr. Rutherforth, 28 March 1768, 3.4. According to Poloma, pentecostals and charismatics qualify as "mystics." She gave five characteristics of mysticism and gave examples of all five from the Toronto "revival" [*Main Street Mystics*, 24-33]. According to Wesley, Polema said, we find no authority from Scripture to reject reason since Jesus and Paul were strong reasoners and books like Hebrews are based upon a close chain of reasoning. Therefore, we must reject the "mystic divines" who decry the use of reason in religion [see "An Earnest Appeal to Men of Reason and Religion," §30, Wesley, *BE Works*, 11:55-56].

[1277]McCloughry, "Basic Stott," 32.

[1278] Rabey, "Pensacola Outpouring,"54-57. See also Hanegraaff, "Separating Fact from Fabrication,"10-20; 42. Ultimately, on December 6, 1997 it was revealed that the Brownsville church had not paid taxes on organizations set up by individual leaders and that the pastor's salary had been concealed. Pastor Kilpatrick admitted being unwise and said "we are very, very sorry" [Hilborn, "Chronicle of the Blessing," 314]. The editor of *Charisma* wrote an evaluation of the Brownsville revival, concluding with a prayer that the Lord would do it again and a prayer that the next time he does, "I pray we will transport the ark the way God intended — and keep our hands off it" [Grady, "Don't Drop the Ark," 6].

[1279]Reeves, *Other Side of the River*, 13.

Kansas City in 2001. Recently it has been reported that this church has experienced new revival.[1280] David Pawson expressed hope that there would be a *fourth wave*, in which the Word and the Spirit would be integrated as they were in the New Testament. He wrote,

> Now I fear that Word and Spirit are drifting apart again, with some seeking the spirit but less interested in Scripture; others are returning to the bible but shying away from direct encounters with the Spirit. At least part of the blame for this sad situation must be laid at the door of the events associated with Toronto.[1281]

In an attempt to justify their phenomenon, third wave advocates like to cite from Wesley's *Journal,* "About three in the morning, as we were continuing instant in prayer, the power of God came mightily upon us insomuch that many cried out for exceeding joy and many fell to the ground."[1282] However Wesley did not encourage or attempt to elicit this behavior. Those who would attempt to justify such phenomena by linking them with early Methodism should consider these incidents: Wesley recorded that several of his friends went with him to a house where they met a woman who was connected with a movement of French Prophets.[1283] She went into convulsive motions and spoke a prophetic message. Wesley wrote that "two or three of our company were much affected and believed she spoke by the Spirit of God. But this was in no wise clear to me. The motion might be either hysterical or artificial. And the same words any person of a good understanding and well versed in the Scriptures might have spoken. But I let the matter alone, knowing this, that 'if it be not of God, it will come to nought.'"[1284]

However, Wesley did not have to wait long to observe the fruit of this movement. Five months later he called on one who "did run well," until he was hindered by "some of those called French Prophets." Wesley concluded that these prophets were not sent by God and "earnestly exhorted all that followed after holiness to avoid as fire all who do not speak according 'to the law and the testimony.'" That same day Mr. Wesley came to the Methodist society with the text from 1 John 4:1, "Beloved, believe not every spirit, but try the spirits whether they be of God." He told them not to judge the Spirit on the basis of appearances,

---

1280 Ghiringhelli, "Kansas City Church Enters Revival Season," 18-19.

1281 Pawson, "Mixed Blessing," 87.

1282 Wesley, *Journal*, 1 January 1739.

1283 See Schwartz, *French Prophets.*

1284 Wesley, *Journal*, January 28, 1739.

common report, or by their own inward feelings. "No, nor by any dreams, visions, or revelations supposed to be made to their souls, anymore than by their tears or any involuntary effects wrought upon their bodies." Wesley declared the only certain test was "the law and the testimony," a reference to Isaiah 8:20, which is a description of God's Word.[1285]

On May 9, 1740 Mr. Wesley wrote, "I was a little surprised at some who were buffeted of Satan in an unusual manner, by such a spirit of laughter as they could in no wise resist, though it was pain and grief unto them." In fact, John Wesley remembered an earlier incident when he and Charles could not stop laughing. But he did not attribute this phenomenon to the Holy Spirit. In his *Journal* for May 21, 1740 Wesley recorded,

> In the evening such a spirit of laughter was among us that many were much offended. . . . One so violently and variously torn of the evil one did I never see before. Sometimes she laughed till almost strangled; then broke out into cursing and blaspheming; then stamped and struggled with incredible strength, so that four or five could scarce hold her . . . At last she faintly called on Christ to help her. And the violence of her pangs ceased.

Most within the Methodist society believed "those under this strange temptation could not help it." Two women, however, felt it could be controlled until they themselves were seized with this same spirit and laughed for two days. Again, Wesley did not promote this phenomenon as revival, but recorded that prayer was made for them and that they were "delivered in a moment."

Wesley received a report of some congregations in Wales.

> It is common in the congregations attended by Mr. William Williams and one or two other clergymen, after the preaching is over, for anyone that has a mind to give out a verse of an hymn. This they sing over and over with all their might, perhaps above thirty, yea, forty times. Meanwhile the bodies of two or three, sometimes ten or twelve, are violently agitated, and they leap up and down, in all manner of postures, frequently for hours together.

[1285]Wesley, *Journal*, June 22, 1739; see also "The Witness of the Spirit, II," Sermon #11, 4.2; *The Principles Of A Methodist Father Explained*, 4:2; *A Letter To The Rev. Dr. Conyers Middleton*, 5:3; Letter to Mr. T.H., 12 Dec1760. Charles Wesley went so far as to say that one he spent the night with was demon possessed [*Journal of Charles Wesley*, 11 Dec 1738].

Wesley commented, "I think there needs no great penetration to understand this. They are honest, upright men, who really felt the love of God in their hearts. But they have little experience, either of the ways of God or the devices of Satan. So he serves himself of their simplicity, in order to wear them out and to bring a discredit on the work of God."[1286] Finally, Wesley recorded his dislike of fanaticism he had witnessed.

> Satan strives to push many of them to extravagance. This appears in several instances. (1) Frequently three of four, yea, ten or twelve, pray aloud all together. (2) Some of them, perhaps many, scream all together as loud as they possibly can. (3) some of them use improper, yea, indecent expressions in prayer. (4) Several drop down as dead and are as stiff as a corpse, but in awhile they start up and cry, Glory! Glory! perhaps twenty times together. Just so did the French Prophets, and very lately the Jumpers in Wales, bring the real work into contempt. Yet whenever we reprove them, it should be in the most mild and gentle manner possible.[1287]

Apologists for the extraordinary phenomenon within the "third wave" have sometimes appealed to the precedent of the "jerks" or religious exercises associated with the Cane Ridge Camp Meeting in 1801. Peter Cartwright described these manifestations and concluded that the jerks were either a judgment sent from God to bring sinners to repentance or to show professors that God could work sovereignly. Cartwright was sure that there was a great deal of "copy-cat" manifestations, but for others it was perfectly involuntary. However, unlike the more modern variation in which manifestations are sought and encouraged, in those days prayer was advocated as a remedy for the jerks. Concerning the "running, jumping, barking exercise," Cartwright reported, "The Methodist preachers generally preached against this extravagant wildness."[1288]

In 1859 G. W. Henry wrote *Shouting, Genuine and Spurious.*[1289] In reviewing the book, Whedon said, "We love a piety blending holy emotion with intellect. We thank God for the religion which has in all ages made men weep and

---

[1286]Wesley, *Journal*, 27 August 1763.

[1287]Wesley, *Journal*, 3 April 1786.

[1288]Cartwright, *Autobiography*, 45-46. It has been claimed that the expression "barking up a tree" originated from the Cane Ridge Camp Meeting.

[1289]Henry, *Shouting, Genuine and Spurious*. The author was known as "Blind Henry."

shout, and has even resulted, through human infirmity in jerks and catalepsies [falling out], but we desire no effort to promote the weeping, shouting, jerking, and catalepsy as a distinct institution." But Whedon went on to argue that no premium should be put on noise or manifestations. Whedon concluded that the author advocated fanaticism.[1290]

We can expect these movements and similar ones to either burn out as they veer away from orthodox Christianity or to be used by God as they move toward orthodox Christianity. Every legitimate move of the Holy Spirit will result in an emphasis on holy living.

Colin Urquhart, who was involved in the charismatic renewal movement in the United Kingdom during the 1960s-1970s, wrote *Holy Fire* in 1984. In this book he wrote, "In recent years people have been seeking the Lord for experiences of the Holy Spirit: His power, love, gifts, healings, joy, etc. But how many have truly been seeking Him for the holiness that God wants the Spirit to bring into their lives?"[1291] He declared that the Gospel will impact modern society when the church exemplifies holiness.

16. Legalism: Sanctification by Works

In the book of Galatians Paul refutes the notion that faith in Jesus Christ is not sufficient for salvation and that some observance of the law is necessary. "Having begun by the Spirit, are you now being perfected by the flesh?" (Gal 3:3).

The weakness of the Law was its powerlessness to produce the love which motivates a person to strive to please God. According to Romans 8:3 the sinful nature overrides any desire to please God in the life of the unregenerate. The law reveals God's holy nature and man's sinful nature. The law demonstrates man's need for salvation (Gal 3:19). Yet the law cannot save. The law drives man to Jesus Christ who alone can save (Gal 3:24). But the law defines how a believer is to walk *after* he is saved (Gal 5:14).[1292]

In 1 John three tests of truth are repeated. The doctrinal test is what we *believe* about Jesus Christ. The social test is whether we *love* the people of God. The moral test is whether we *obey* God's commandments. These are three marks of the new birth, propositional, relational, and behavioral, and amount to an

---

[1290]Whedon, "Quarterly Book-Table," 666-667. Also in Whedon, *Statements*, 286.

[1291]Urquhart, *Holy Fire*, 179. Urquhart described holiness as a walk, not a state [p. 27].

[1292]Wesley, "The Original, Nature, Properties, and Use of the Law," "The Law Established Through Faith, Discourse I & II," Sermons #34-36.

indirect witness which corresponds to the direct witness of the Spirit promised in 3:24; 4:13; 5:10. It is no accident that the three words, "Believe, Love, Obey" are on John Wesley's personal seal.[1293]

Kevin Lowery explained that if the concept of sin is expanded to entail a breach or neglect of duty, then perfection must necessarily be broadened to include the fulfillment of duty. We have a duty to love, to believe, and to keep the moral law — as well as duties to ourselves.[1294]

However, we must distinguish between the law and legalism. Legalism is the attempt to earn salvation through works. The Hebrew word for law is תורה (*torah*) which means instruction or guidance. It refers to a way of life. John Barton explained that "'Torah' is a system by which to live the whole of life in the presence of God. . . . ethics is not so much a system of obligations as a way of communion with God, which is the cause of joy."[1295] Thus the Torah defines holiness not as rigid adherence to regulations but as life lived in obedient love. This definition of godly character, through the giving of the law, implies that God wants us to take on his holy character.

The entire book of Galatians is a warning against legalism. Legalism is the attempt to earn salvation and assurance through works. But salvation is a relationship. Whenever religion loses the supernatural emphasis, it will always revert into legalism and works. The legalist will attempt to justify himself or herself through strict rules. Whenever they fall into difficulty they will try harder, but they do not have the Spirit, they do not have victory over sin, nor do they have any assurance. This is also the situation found in Romans 7.

Ray Dunning wrote that the majority of the apostolic fathers held a moralistic or legalistic understanding of Christian life, stressing the new religion as a new law. The doctrine of justification by faith is noticeably absent from their writing. "Their stress on the holy life would be sound if it were placed within the context of justification."[1296]

Legalism is inherent within Pelagianism and liberal Arminianism because they deny original sin. According to them man is born morally neutral and is condemned only for his own sin. For Pelagius, human perfectability is the result of man's freedom and moral nature. Pelagius maintained that the will is naturally

---

[1293]"On the Motto of a Seal," 439-442.

[1294]Lowrey, *Salvaging Wesley's Ethics*, 296-299.

[1295]Barton, "Approaches to Ethics in the Old Testament," 120.

[1296]Dunning, *Grace, Faith, and Holiness,* 49; see also Greathouse, *From the Apostles to Wesley*, 33. Dunning wrote that when justification is made central, the tendency is toward antinomianism. When sanctification is central, the tendency is toward legalism. Wesley sought to maintain a proper balance, adopting Gal 5:6 as his motto: "faith working by love" [*Grace, Faith, and Holiness*, 48-49].

free to do good and is not at all impaired by the fall, that there are not special influences of the Spirit in regeneration, but all the help that is necessary in that work is instruction. Through such education a man can perfectly keep the law.[1297]

Yet legalism cannot be restricted to any denomination or doctrine. Both legalism and/or antinomianism may crop up within any movement or theological position. However, as legalism relates to the doctrine of Christian perfection three examples will be given.

Ellen G. White had a Methodist heritage, but her family also embraced the teachings of William Miller and ultimately were expelled from the Methodist Church. She taught that salvation by obedience to the law is impossible, but salvation *without* obedience is also just as impossible. She declared that we are justified only by faith in the merits of Christ, but such faith will never excuse transgression. Implicit in her teaching that men cannot be saved without obedience was her notion that the Sabbath must be observed in order to be saved.[1298] "The Sabbath is a sign of memorial of sanctification." It is her understanding of the Sabbath as the seventh day that distinguishes her understanding of the law from Methodism. Yet there is a fine line between demanding obedience to the law as a *condition* for salvation and as a *result* of salvation.

White's most challenging and perplexing statement is that the sealed believers will have "to stand in the sight of a holy God without a mediator. Their robes must be spotless, their characters must be purified from sin by the blood of sprinkling."[1299] She taught that "when the decree shall go forth enforcing the counterfeit sabbath, and the loud cry of the third angel shall warn men against the worship of the beast and his image, the line will be clearly drawn between the

---

[1297]Peck, *Christian Perfection*, 90; Pope, *Compendium*, 3:70; see also Arminius, *Works*, 1:684-688 where Arminius labeled such a view as "heretical."

The Hebrew term מוסר (*mussar*), is from the book of Proverbs 1:2 meaning instruction, discipline, or conduct. The term can be used to refer to Jewish moral or pious literature in general. The Jewish spiritual path of Mussar teaches that each of us is born with an inner soul that is irrevocably pure, but the outer layers constantly engage in the age-old struggle between good and evil. By determining our soul curriculum, or "issues that repeatedly challenge [us]," we can strengthen our souls and therefore every aspect of our lives. Specifically, he addresses 18 soul traits: humility, patience, gratitude, compassion, order, equanimity, honor, simplicity, enthusiasm, silence, generosity, truth, moderation, loving-kindness, responsibility, trust, faith and *yirah* (a combination of fear and awe, without a true English counterpart) [Morinis, *Everyday Holiness*].

[1298]Whidden, *Ellen White on Salvation*, 25; see also Whidden, "Adventist Soteriology,"173-186.

[1299]Whidden, *Ellen White on Salvation*, 134.

false and the true. Then those who still continue in transgression will receive the mark of the beast."[1300]

While most conservative holiness denominations claim the Bible is their sole authority for faith and practice, there tend to be other unwritten rules. Elmer Parsons explained, "The techniques for obtaining entire sanctification sometimes received more attention than holiness itself. Probably more serious was the temptation to legalism: trusting rules-keeping for merit. . . . Though discipline is implied in discipleship, mere outward adherence to rules proves a poor substitute for heart purity and overflowing love."[1301] David Kendall observed that most of the American Holiness movement rightly rejected legalism as a condition for salvation, but embraced the very same legalism as the path to perfection. Yet this was the very error Paul sought to expose in Galatians 3:3.[1302]

Ray Dunning compared the terms *teleological* and *deontological*. The first term, from the Greek word *telos*, means that Christian perfection should be viewed as a lifelong pursuit of maturity. The second word is based on the word "ought." In other words, is Christian perfection an aspiration or an obligation? Dunning concluded that many in the American holiness movement turned this teleological emphasis into a deontological one. The result was a "perfected perfection," rather than a "perfectible perfection."[1303] Thus, I am "sanctified" because I keep certain rules. It is even possible to keep church rules, while breaking God's law (Matt 15:3). While Christian perfection does include the fulfillment of our duties, this implies keeping God's law and not extra-biblical rules. And even the keeping of divine principles would not alone be the basis of our assurance.

Charles Edwin Jones felt that the emphasis on standards and personal disciplines in the holiness movement was an attempt to facilitate an inward struggle which would identify the carnal nature, so that the crisis event of entire sanctification could remove it.[1304] Only a focus on intentionality keeps Wesley's perfectionism from becoming a harsh legalism.[1305]

[1300]White, *Questions on Doctrine*, 83; *Bible Readings for the Home Circle*, 420; 422. See the evaluation of Martin, *Kingdom of the Cults*, 492-496.

[1301]Parsons, *Living the Holy Life Today*, 22-23.

[1302]Kendall, "Jesus and a Gospel of Holiness," 61. See also Reasoner, "How to Be a Pharisee," 1-3; Beckham, "The Conservative and Truth," Online: John Johnson, "Divine Intervention or Historical Accident?"

[1303]Dunning, *Reflecting the Divine Image*, 34-36; see also Dunning, "Ethics in a Wesleyan Context," 8-9.

[1304]Jones, *Perfectionist Persuasion*, 83-88.

[1305]Bence, "John Wesley's Teleological Hermeneutic," 65.

If the experience of holiness is received through an act of the will, it is consistent for that holiness to be maintained through legalism instead of grace. The conservative holiness movement was organized into the Inter-Denominational (later Inter-Church) Holiness Convention in 1951. Although it has been labeled the Glenn Griffith movement,[1306] it was actually organized by H. Robb French and H. E. Schmul.[1307] The movement centered around a reaction to centralized government, television, wedding rings[1308] and jewelry, and music.[1309]

[1306]Melton, *Encyclopedia of American Religions*, 35-39; 323-349. The first rupture within the Church of the Nazarene occurred in 1955 when Griffith formed the Bible Missionary Church. However, the IHC had been organized since 1951.

[1307]Thornton, "Inter-Church Holiness Convention," 138-140. I served as chairman of the Southern California IHC from 1985-1988 and appreciated the breadth of H. E. Schmul's knowledge and ministry. However, few in the movement had his understanding, wisdom, or grace. He wanted me to relocate to Colorado or Kansas City and assist with the IHC work [personal letter, 17 March 1988].

Schmul was aware of my masters research and when it was printed as *The Hole in the Holiness Movement*, he ran an ad for it in the Nov/Dec 1991 issue of the *Convention Herald*. Although Fundamental Wesleyan Publishers had paid for the same ad to appear in the next issue, under fire, Schmul asked permission to discontinue running the add and when I consented, he wrote that I was a kind and gracious fellow. "It makes life a little easier to work with the likes of Vic Reasoner" [personal letter, 8 January 1992]. However, in the Jan/Feb 1993 issue of the *Convention Herald* a review was published, Edsel Trouten, "Holes in The Hole of the Holiness Movement," 4-5. By this time Leonard Sankey was the editor and Trouten called me on January 11, 1993, ahead of the magazine release to apologize. He had not released his review draft for publication and it was printed without his permission. In the March/April 1993 *Convention Herald* a small-print explanation by Trouton appeared on p. 5, but the editor never assumed responsibility for his mistake. The board of publication for the *Arminian Magazine* asked me to publish a rebuttal to what was published. "Plugging the Holes," 2-4 was printed in the Fall 1993 issue.

Schmul, who served as general secretary of the Inter-Church Holiness Convention, also sought permission in April 1992 from the IHC board to give me access to the IHC mailing list in order to survey their constituency in connection with my doctoral dissertation. My request was denied. In his letter, dated 13 Jan 1993, Schmul informed me that Sankey was the editor of the *Convention Herald*. Schmul died in 1998.

[1308]The Puritans were the first movement in the history of Christianity to ever protest the wedding ring and they did so in the 1550s on the basis that it furthered the Roman Catholic teaching that marriage was a sacrament [Packer, *Quest for Godliness*, 53]. Wesley was influenced by the Puritans at this point, but early Methodism did not make an issue of the wedding ring. Clarke was not opposed to the wedding ring [*Christian Theology*, 265-266; see also Wesley's *Advice to the People Called Methodists with Regard to Dress* [*Works*, 11:466-477; "On Dress," Sermon #88].

Purkiser characterized this movement as a struggle over standards.[1310] According to Oden "a *standard* is literally a flag, a banner, an ensign distinctive of a community. It is metaphorically that which is set up visibly and established by authority as a rule for the measure of value of something."[1311] Based on this definition, the Scriptures must be our standard. Our philosophy, priorities, attitudes, conversation, entertainment, and appearance should be in conformity to God's Word. This may necessitate a separation from the world. However, extrabiblical standards, primarily of dress, came to be mandatary in order to be accepted by the radical holiness subculture. In some cases, they replaced the witness of the Spirit as the basis for assurance.

Grider explained, "People were to be Holiness 'in life and look' — the 'look' having to do with dress. Donald W. Dayton's research shows that simplicity of dress was encouraged to free more money for evangelism and for helping the destitute."[1312] In time, however, the means became the end. Interest in world evangelism waned, but dress preferences became legislated. Thornton observed that while Wesley's emphasis concerning plain dress was on stewardship, the later holiness movement made it the proof of entire sanctification.[1313] In the best sense "standards" were an attempt to uphold and ethical holiness through separation from the world. At their worse, they were reductionistic, legalistic, and subjective.

Today the Inter-Church Holiness Convention annual convention would draw about five thousand[1314] and continues to emphasize "sweet radical

---

Telford wrote that Wesley disliked all display of jewelry. However, when a Methodist itinerant preacher took hold of a girl's hand, drawing Wesley's attention to a number of rings that she wore, Wesley simply replied, "The hand is very beautiful" [*Life of Wesley*, 338].

[1309]Gary Maxey, unpublished lecture notes. Maxey's reference to music was the struggle within the Free Methodist Church over the use of instrumentation. See also Schmul and Fruin, *Profile of the I. H. Convention*, 3-5.

[1310]Purkiser, *Called Unto Holiness*, 256-258; 266-274.

[1311]Oden, *Doctrinal Standards in the Wesleyan Tradition*, 15.

[1312]Grider, *Wesley-Holiness Theology*, 393.

[1313]Thornton, *Radical Righteousness*, 30.

[1314]Taylor, "Why the Holiness Movement Died," 39. See my description of the IHC in my dissertation, "Spirit and Sanctification: Changes Within American Wesleyanism," 13-16; 86; 91-95; 104-116.

holiness."[1315] While the sweetness of this emphasis has not always been apparent, they have attempted to maintain a balance between love and holiness, mercy and judgment, charity and austerity.

In an apology for the conservative holiness movement, Stephen Gibson refers to God's presence among them which is sometimes evidenced by shouting.[1316] The early Methodists shouted for joy, but did not regard such phenomenon as a divine sanction of their superiority.[1317] Deductive reasoning, such as that demonstrated by Gibson, concludes that the sect must be right because they have God's presence among them. Yet Wesley emphasized ethical holiness, not any emotional phenomenon, as the indirect evidence of the Holy Spirit.

Writing from a fundamentalist perspective, Fred Moritz emphasized two kinds of separation: personal and ecclesiastical. There is to be a personal separation from the practice of sin and it is not legalism to live in obedience to biblical commands to separate from sin.[1318] There is an outward and inward separation from the world which begins with salvation (2 Cor 6:14-18).

Moritz also cited such passages as Matthew 18:15-17; 1 Corinthians 5:1-11; Galatians 5:19-21, 1 Thessalonians 3:6-15, and Titus 3:9-11 as teaching ecclesiastical separation.[1319] These passages teach the necessity of a separation from false brethren, from false doctrine and apostasy. According to Bob Jones, Jr. the issue is not "second-degree separation," but the two kinds of separation: personal and ecclesiastical.[1320]

It was proper for Protestants to separate themselves from the errors of

---

[1315]Thornton, "Sweet Radical Holiness," 248-249. For a scholarly defense of the conservative holiness movement, see Thornton, "Embourgeoisement and the Formation of the Conservative Holiness Movement," 172-197; Thornton, *Radical Righteousness*.

[1316]Gibson, *Held by Conviction*, 47-48.

[1317]Ruth, *Little Heaven Below*, 74-78; 229-233.

[1318]Moritz, *Be Ye Holy*, 37.

[1319]Moritz, *Be Ye Holy*, 74-81.

[1320]Jones, "What is 'second-degree separation'"? 4. Yet Sidwell defined first degree separation as refusing to cooperate with false teachers in religious actions. Second degree separation was refusing to fellowship with someone who does not practice first-degree separation [*Dividing Line*, 5]. Sidwell connected separation with sanctification [pp. 2-3; 16-21] and described fundamentalist teaching on holiness as more Keswick than Methodist [p. 77].

Rome and it is still sometimes necessary to separate from error,[1321] yet the danger is that ecclesiastical purity is substituted for personal purity of life. While Jesus himself found it necessary to cleanse the temple, those who have been the most outspoken in their denunciation of that which is false have not always exemplified the spirit of Christ. It is easier to fall into a pattern of ecclesiastical separation than to make every effort to maintain the unity of the faith in the bond of peace (Eph 4:3). The body of Christ has been unnecessarily torn by divisions over personal preference and notions.

In 1970 the Southern Methodist Church, in reaction to this type of influence, ruled that faith and not affiliation is the scriptural basis for Christian fellowship. Southern Methodist ministers were free to fellowship with believing ministers who are in apostate or liberal organizations.[1322]

While the believer should be separate from sin, all too often believers have separated from each other over nonessentials. An emphasis on separation from the world can be Manichaean, based on the belief that the physical world is evil and that we should retreat from it. This can lead to monasticism or legalism. While we are not to love the world system (1 John 2:15), we must realize that the earth is the Lord's and everything in it (Psalm 24:1).

17. A Psychological/Philosophical Theology of Sanctification

Relational Sanctification

When the Pentecostal Church of the Nazarene was formed through a series of mergers culminating in 1908, they believed at the time that the entire holiness movement would come under their organization. They were optimistic that they would see national revival which would bring in the millennium. Their distinctive doctrine was the American holiness movement's understanding of entire sanctification. Entire sanctification was taught as an instantaneous second work of grace, through the baptism of the Holy Spirit, which eradicated the sin nature, which was received through "appropriating faith," and resulting in a society free from sin.

H. Orton Wiley taught sanctification as instantaneous because of the use

[1321]For defenses of this principle see Sidwell, *Dividing Line*; Cohen, *Biblical Separation Defended*; Murray, *Evangelicalism Divided.*

[1322]Comfort, "Statement,"6. Wesley also taught that the Methodists should attend the Church of England services regardless of the spiritual state of the priest. "The validity of the ordinance doth not depend on the goodness of him that administers, but on the faithfulness of him that ordained it" ["Sermon on the Mount, XII," Sermon #32, 3.8; see also "On Attending the Church Service," Sermon #104, § 27-33; *Works*, 8:280-281; 322].

of the aorist tense. He therefore taught the progressive nature of salvation was the progression of instantaneous acts of God in the life of the believer.[1323] Wiley also backed off of the extravagant claims made by some earlier holiness writers, who were more interested in proclaiming the wonderful possibilities of this experience which resulted in almost a glorified state. With Wiley this began to change as he distinguished between purity and maturity, sin and infirmities, and the possibility of temptation.[1324]

By 1940-1950 the Nazarene Church had tempered their expectations, producing many books during this era which distinguished between being blameless and faultless, and between willful transgressions and mistakes. Quanstrom wrote that there were two agendas at work within the Nazarenes by this time: traditionalism and realism. William Deal wrote *Problems of the Spirit-filled Life*. An earlier generation felt that to be Spirit-filled would end most problems. Deal distinguished between thoughts of evil and evil thoughts, carnality and humanity-humanity. Deal and Richard S. Taylor in *Life in the Spirit* wrote about nervous or sensitive temperaments, saying entire sanctification would not change this. Nor did it do away with all irritability.

Ironically Wesley's *A Plain Account of Christian Perfection* was not part of the Nazarene ministerial training until 1952.[1325] Then in 1958 Zondervan reprinted *The Works of John Wesley*, providing his writings for the first time in nearly a century. The problem, however was that Wesley's writings "were not entirely consistent with the holiness writings that the Church of the Nazarene had recommended."[1326] Wesley did not emphasize instantaneous sanctification, instead using "sanctification" to describe the whole salvation process.

Leo Cox, founder of the Wesleyan Theological Society, was also pivotal with his book on *John Wesley's Concept of Perfection* (1964). In 1985 there was even a move in the General Assembly to replace the phrases "baptism with the Holy Spirit" and "eradication"in the Nazarene Articles of Faith. While the move was defeated at that time, it reflected a shift in understanding. The word "eradicated" was dropped by the Nazarene General Assembly from their Articles of Faith in 1997.[1327]

[1323]Wiley, *Christian Theology*, 2:479-483; Quanstrom, *Century of Holiness Theology*, 81-82. E. Stanley Jones wrote of a series of crises, compared to passing through the locks in the Panama Canal. Yet his description seems to infer a series of two crises, then a permanent state of higher living [*Christ of Every Road*, 217].

[1324]Quanstrom, *Century of Holiness Theology*, 85-89.

[1325]Quanstrom, "Doctrine of Entire Sanctification,"185.

[1326]Quanstrom, *A Century of Holiness Theology*, 129.

[1327]Quanstrom, *Century of Holiness Theology*, 220.

In 1976 the Articles of Faith on entire sanctification was modified for the first time in fifty years, adding two qualifying paragraphs. Both paragraphs referred to growth in grace. Quanstrom explained, "So much attention had been given to proclaiming the instantaneous nature of entire sanctification that the gradual nature of the grace had been all but abandoned."[1328]

Quanstrom concluded, "Entire sanctification eradicated sin in its entirety, but sin in its entirety was understood quite particularly. . . . There had been such redefinition of what should be considered sin over against what could be considered infirmity, the second work of grace was in danger of becoming an experience without any significant consequence."[1329]

In 1973 Mildred Bangs Wynkoop wrote *A Theology of Love*. She questioned the terminology of a "second work of grace."[1330] She taught sin was not a substance to be eradicated, but a wrong relationship with God. Wynkoop taught the decisive moment of salvation was justification and that believers received the Holy Spirit at that time. She did not connect the baptism of the Spirit with entire sanctification. As Wynkoop focused more on "love" she moved more toward relational theology. While existentialism emphasizes experience, this more modern form emphasizes relationship and Wynkoop saw that emphasis as positive.[1331]

[1328]Quanstrom, *Century of Holiness Theology*, 135.

[1329]Quanstrom, *Century of Holiness Theology*, 115; 135-136. See the negative review of Quanstrom by Cunningham, "Book Review," 230-234. Cunningham complained that the book did not welcome theological development and asked rhetorically if Wiley had uttered the final word.

[1330]Wynkoop, *Theology of Love*, 334.

[1331]Leclerc, "Mildred Bangs Wynkoop," 328-329. However, Mark Olson argues that Wynkoop was not Wesleyan in her relational view of the image of God as all that is essential to human beings and therefore not lost in the Fall. This affects her doctrine of sin as perverted love and holiness as love locked into Christ, the true center. Faith, then, is an essential element of personality, the rational link between the divine and the human.

Olson concludes that Wynkoop's system is more aligned with Charles Finney than with John Wesley. Olson describes Wynkoop's approach as moralist, if not Pelagian. However, Olson concedes that Wynkoop and Finney disagreed over the doctrine of prevenient grace. While Wynkoop attempted to express Wesleyan theology in more psychological language, and while her existential philosophy may have resulted in language which Wesley would not have used, I think Olson has overstated his case in "Strange Bedfellows,"196-217.

It may be significant that Olson's publisher, Truth in Heart, Fenwick, Michigan, is committed to reprinting Finney and Mahan, as well as advancing their moral government theology. The publisher states that he does not agree with everything

This interpretation of Spirit baptism became the position of Rob Staples who was almost refused tenure at the Seminary because of this. In 1984 the board of General Superintendents ruled that Staples' teaching was compatible with Nazarene doctrine.[1332] In 1979, Ray Dunning was asked by the board of General Superintendents to write a new theology to replace Wiley. Dunning did not identify the baptism of the Spirit with entire sanctification either. Dunning placed more emphasis on the radical nature of the first work than on the second.[1333]

Yet Donald Metz declared that theological confusion existed in the Church of the Nazarene because the baptism with the Holy Spirit was taught occurring at the time of regeneration, while others within the church taught that it was a second crisis. Throughout his book Metz expressed concern that the Church of the Nazarene was not teaching classic Wesleyan doctrine with regard to essential doctrines such as the inspiration of the Bible, the nature of original sin, the Trinity, and even Christology. However, when he came to the baptism with the Holy Spirit, he argued that the church need not become fixed on the "Wesley mound." He declared, "The idea of a second crisis called entire sanctification does not depend entirely upon the authenticity of the Wesleyan origin of the idea."[1334]

Quanstrom concluded, "At the end of the 20th century, there was no substantial agreement in the denomination over what it meant to be 'entirely sanctified.' The Church of the Nazarene no longer had a precisely articulated definition of their distinctive doctrine, the doctrine that at one time had been their sole reason for being."[1335]

Essentially all five major components of holiness teaching which the Church of the Nazarene originally emphasized are now questioned by some Nazarene theologians. This has resulted in competing doctrines of holiness. In 2002 a "Global Theology Conference" was held to try to reach a consensus, but there was no consensus reached. More recently Rob Staples declared, "I suspect it would be more accurate to say there were upwards of 10 to 15 views of holiness in play in the denomination at the end of the 20th century than only the two that

---

Wesley taught or did, but makes no disclaimer about Finney or Mahan [Online: "Truth in Heart"].

[1332]Quanstrom, *Century of Holiness Theology*, 150-157.

[1333]Quanstrom, *Century of Holiness Theology*, 162.

[1334]Metz, *Some Crucial Issues*, 170-174. Metz warned that identifying the baptism with the Holy Spirit with regeneration generally introduced the idea of progressive holiness. He did not elaborate on how this would necessarily follow.

[1335]See also Greenberg, "Identity 'Crisis,"17.

Quanstrom enumerates."[1336] But at least the Church of the Nazarene has tolerated discussion.

According to Donald Metz, the Church of the Nazarene came under the influence of naturalistic evolution, humanistic psychology, and liberal theology and philosophy. In 1993 he expressed concern that Ray Dunning's theology in *Grace, Faith and Holiness* had the liberal, humanistic thought of Paul Tillich as its reference point. He also charged Dunning with having a relational view of sin.[1337]

William Greathouse wrote a letter to Metz in which he defended Dunning. Greathouse asserted that Paul used relational language in Romans 1:18 and then referenced his own commentary. Greathouse defined depravity as the depravation of the Holy Spirit which resulted in idolatry, a perverted relationship to God, and moral perversity in human relationships. Greathouse also quoted Wesley's statement that when man fell into sin he fell off from God and turned into himself. Wiley amplified this statement, describing sin as self-separation from God.[1338]

The kingdom of God is not a matter of eating and drinking, but it is relational. It is righteousness, peace, and joy in the Holy Spirit (Rom 14:17). The indwelling of the Holy Spirit does not describe a physical location, but a personal relationship.[1339]

Dunning built on Wynkoop's concepts of relational holiness. The philosophical foundation for Dunning's theology is found in John Macmurray's book *Persons in Relation*.[1340] This philosophy emphasizes that God is a relational God. He is not static, passive, and indifferent.

Relational theology may offer help in explaining sanctification, but when the result is that God is so identified with the world that he is no longer transcendent from his creation, it has created far greater problems. In relational

[1336]Online: Staples, "Things Shakeable," 8

[1337]Metz, *Some Crucial Issues*, 118; 137-138; 147; 151-156.

[1338]Greathouse, *Letter*, 31 January 1994. See Greathouse, *Romans*, 8:50-59; Wesley, *Works*, 9:456; Wiley, *Christian Theology*, 2:84. Dunning also wrote Metz, claiming that Richard S. Taylor had serious questions about relational theology until he understood it. Then he ceased objecting [Dunning, *Letter*, 2 February 1994]. See also Dunning's reference to a conversation with Taylor in *Grace, Faith, and Holiness*, 16-17. However, Taylor did continue to express concerns. Dunning is existential [*Grace, Faith, and Holiness*, 30; 248], in the tradition of Kierkegaard and Paul Tillich, and relational [pp. 14-16], but not a process theologian. See Dunning, "Holiness: Experience or Relationship," 44-45.

[1339]Hanegraaff, "Indwelling of the Holy Spirit," 54.

[1340]Macmurray, *Persons in Relation*. Macmurray held to a personalist philosophy.

thought, the future is not fixed or certain. Even the mind of God is partly open. Part of his essence is to provide freedom. This loving act means that God cannot override the freedom he has given away.

To be created in the image of God is understood in relational terms only, as some aspect of human personality which makes us resemble God. A degree of goodness is possible for those who do not know God because of the creative presence of God in the world. It is sometimes denied that Adam's sin caused the rest of us to have a sinful nature. Yet it would seem consistent with a relational emphasis to emphasize that we do have a sinful nature because we are related to Adam, the head of our race.

In 2004 Samuel Powell at Point Loma Nazarene University wrote *Holiness in the Twenty-first Century*. He explained holiness in relational language, but not in terms of process thought. According to Powell, holiness begins with God. People and things are regarded as holy because of their relationship to God. While Wynkoop and Staples based their relational theology of the philosophy of Buber, Powell recommends a more biblical view of relationship based on God's calling and our consecration which leads to an obedience based on love. Just as God has chosen Israel to be a holy people without any regard for their righteousness, so God has called us into his Church to be a holy people by existing in relation to him. To be holy is to be part of the body of Christ. It is holy in the same way Israel was holy. Holiness is not only about our relationship to God as individuals, but about our relationship to the Church, and the relationship of the Church to God.

This understanding of holiness is primarily corporate. The sanctification of each believer presupposes the sanctification of the church as the body of Christ. Each believer shares in the church's holiness. Every believer is a saint by virtue of his or her participation in the church, although each believer's status as holy must be matched by faithful obedience and righteous conduct. The Christian life is a call to actualize in practice the holiness that is ours because we are members of the holy and elect people of God.

We participate in God's holiness through responding in consecration to God's *call*. This call is not individualistic, as Calvinists suppose, but the called are the Church. Holiness is also *consecration*, faithful *obedience*, and perfected *love*. Powell says that consecration may or may not be marked by a momentous decision. It could come at conversion. These three qualities: consecration, obedience, and love are ongoing, but shape the holy life. Powell writes that although believers have crucified the flesh (Gal 5:24), the flesh has an amazing power to resurrect itself after we have crucified it. We are never so free from the flesh as to be exempt from temptation or falling away. Powell's understanding of lingering sin rules out any eradication. But we are also enabled by the Spirit to live without sin and overcome the flesh, living in consecration, obedience, and love. Yet this life of entire sanctification is not necessarily entered through an instantaneous experience. Holiness is not a permanent state, but requires a continual decision to abide in Christ and walk in the Spirit. In principle it is possible to walk in and be guided by the Spirit perfectly and continuously in such a way that our consecration is unchanged, or obedience and our love undiminished. Yet this requires a continual decision, every moment, between the flesh and the Spirit. The Church is the means God uses to call us, elicit our consecration, lead us into faith, and kindle our love. The means of grace is vital to our becoming holy.

Entire sanctification is the affirmation that the Christian life is a journey from the world of sin into the Kingdom of God. However, this definition does not really distinguish it from the entire salvation process. Within this life of consecration we can identify moments of particular significance: the moment of initial awakening, acts of repentance, the first acts of faith in Christ as Savior, and the critical moment of presenting ourselves to God as living sacrifices. Sanctification, or holiness, is our coming to participate in the Trinitarian life of God. To live in the Spirit is to be drawn into the Trinitarian life of God.

How, then, do we participate in the holiness of God? "To be holy is to be part of the body of Christ."[1341] Thus, the Church is a means of our holiness. Stanley Hauerwas explained that holiness was not an individual achievement, but the work of the Holy Spirit building up the body of Christ. "Holiness is the result of our being made part of a body that makes it impossible for us to be anything other than disciples."[1342] William Kostlevy observed that virtually all the authors in *Embodied Holiness* "argue that the real presence of embodied holiness is in the regeneration of baptism and the celebration of the Eucharist."[1343]

While God is the means of holiness, Wesley said "there is no holiness but social holiness." Powell argues for a social holiness through the means of grace, interaction with its members, and submission to its authority. The Church is the means God uses to call us, elicit our consecration, lead us into faith, and kindle love.

While this statement is not wrong, it denies everything taught by the holiness movement and destroyed the argument for a "holiness" church comprised of holy individuals.[1344] Oord and Lodahl argue that the temple of the Holy Spirit

---

[1341]Powell, *Holiness in the Twenty-first Century*, 41. *Holiness Today* excerpted three articles based on Powell's book in 2004-2005.

[1342]Hauerwas, "Sanctified Body," 20; 28

[1343]Kostlevy, "Book Review,"271.

[1344]As early as 1971 Richard S. Taylor warned against this dynamic and relationship concept of holiness which reduced "what has been traditionally thought of as a definite work of grace to a mere work of man, and thus fall into the Pelagian trap.

in 1 Corinthians 3:16-17 is not the body of an individual believer, but the church itself.[1345] Frederick Platt observed that the defects frequently associated with most theories of Christian perfection have been an exaggerated individualism and a preference for the unsocial habit of life. The tenor of New Testament teaching is that the perfection of the individual Christian is not something apart from his relation to the Christian community, but is realized in it and through it. He pointed out that the use of *katartizo*, a medical term used to denote Christian perfection, means the setting of each man in his right moral relation to the body of Christ.[1346]

Steve DeNeff said a person could get saved without benefit of the Church, but he could not stay saved without the Church. He said a person could not become entirely sanctified outside of the Church.[1347] Steve Harper made a similar statement, "No one can develop a mature spirituality alone. To be a Christian is to be called into community. It is to become a functioning part of the body of Christ."[1348]

The Church is one, holy, catholic, and apostolic. But we cannot separate the holiness of the Church based on its Head and the holiness of the body. We cannot emphasize corporate holiness at the expense of personal holiness. The whole cannot be more holy than the sum of its parts.

Building on the theology of Mildred Wynkoop, some recent Nazarene theologians have developed a theology of relational holiness. Under the umbrella

---

This does not do justice to the full biblical concepts of either sinfulness or holiness, which sees both as what a man is, not just what he does." Taylor proceeded to articulate a paradigm which saw the sin principle as a unit and emphasized its removal through a direct work of divine grace [Taylor, "Some Recent Trends,"10-12]. I do not necessarily agree with Taylor's concerns, but state them to demonstrate the different emphasis between what he says God instantaneously does *for* us and what relational holiness theology says God progressively does in relationship *with* us. See also his 1983 warning in *Contemporary Wesleyan Theology*, 1:68.

In defending the relational holiness model, Leclerc refuted the charge that it is simply positional holiness [*Discovering Christian Holiness*, 189]. She also defends Wynkoop at this point [Leclerc, "Mildred Bangs Wynkoop," 329].

1345 Oord and Lodahl, *Relational Holiness*, 116-118.

1346 Platt, "Perfection," 9:736. Platt cited Eph 4:12; Heb 13:21; Gal 6:1, 1 Peter 5:10, 2 Cor 13:9 as examples.

1347 DeNeff, Asbury College chapel, 14 Sept 2005. According to 1 John the love of God in the believer will lead him to fellowship with other believers. Yet throughout church history there was been a distrust of organization from the early monks who fled to the desert to the Quakers.

1348 Harper, *Devotional Life*, 54.

of relational theology some theologians may also be open or process or feminist or liberation, but not necessarily. Relational theologians point out that God interacts with creation. He makes covenants with Israel and all creation. In Jesus Christ we have the fullest revelation of God's relational nature. The church is relational. While all this cannot be disputed, they may go too far when they claim that God's primary attribute is love.[1349]

In advocating relational holiness, Thomas Oord and Michael Lodahl believe that a contemporary statement of holiness must be built upon something besides a word-study of biblical terms. Holiness should not be presented as rules and regulations because that emphasis leads to legalism. If purity is considered the core notion of holiness, that also leads back to rules and regulations. Certain problems also arise when separation is promoted as the core notion of holiness. Holiness as God's transcendence does not account for *why* we should value holiness *for us*. Separation can foster an exclusive attitude of superiority and encourage people to be different simply for the sake of being different. Holiness in terms of total commitment is vague. Even terrorists operate on the basis on utter devotion to their deity. The main problem with equating holiness with perfection has to do with the various meanings of perfection. And the main problem with considering Christ-likeness the core notion of holiness is the lack of clarification. Does that mean wearing sandals or speaking Aramaic?

Thus, in *Relational Holiness*, Oord and Lodahl propose that holiness and sanctification be expressed within the framework of relationship with both God and others. The postmodern world view is relational. "To 'be' is to be in relation." Personhood is largely determined and shaped in terms of relationships.[1350] Once a relationship has been established, relational theology helps explain the perfection of that relationship. Therefore, love is proposed as the core notion of holiness. It provides the foundation and framework for faith. Yet this concept is, itself, vague. While Oord and Lodahl say "the core meaning of holiness is love" and "love is the core of holiness,"[1351] Kenneth Collins objected that we must qualify "love" with the word "holy."[1352] Steve DeNeff warned that if we say God is love, but do not tie it to his holiness, then his love lacks discretion.[1353]

[1349]See the discussion on pp. 17-19.

[1350]Oord and Lodahl, *Relational Holiness*, 31-32. Oord and Lodahl are cousins and both are Nazarene theologians. See also <crivoice.org/relational.html>

[1351]Oord and Lodahl, *Relational Holiness*, 72.

[1352]Collins, *Theology of John Wesley*, 7-9. See also the Collins review, "Book Notes," 94-95 and the concerns raised by Staples, "Book Review," 248-249].

[1353]DeNeff, *Whatever Became of Holiness?* 23.

In his more recent *Discovering our Christian Faith*, Powell wrote that holiness is to be in relationship with God. It is participation in the divine life or union with God. It is freedom from sin which results from living in the Spirit. But while sin is dead, it can live again. Love is the definition and measure of holiness for us. Entire sanctification is the perfection of that love. We attain this perfect love through God's grace, through using the means of grace, through spiritual disciplines, and through consecration. The path to this perfect love is characterized for some as a momentous event of faith and consecration. For others it is characterized by a development that culminates in the perfection of love.[1354]

Process Sanctification

Prior to the 1970s there was not much diversity of opinion regarding the doctrine of holiness in the Church of the Nazarene. Today a far greater diversity exists than did a generation ago. An useasy truce now exists regarding particular terminology.[1355] According to Quanstrom, by the end of the twentieth century there was no substantial agreement in the Church of the Nazarene over what is meant to be entirely sanctified.[1356]

The older view in the holiness movement was that sanctification was crisis with a view to a process. Sanctification is a crisis *and* a process. Wesley taught, "All experience, as well as Scripture, show this salvation to be both instantaneous and gradual."[1357] Kenneth Waters wrote that holiness is a present process and a present possession, as well as a future goal.[1358] Kevin Lowery suggested that perfection is a process that has specific thresholds, degrees of attainment, or culminations points, but these should not be regarded as a termination point.[1359]

But now that crisis has been eradicated, the process is endless. Somehow the balance has been lost as the scale has tipped too far to the other side in order to compensate for excesses of the past. Process philosophy holds an attraction to some contemporary holiness theologians because it offers a way to reconcile and explain process and crisis. But the explanation raises more questions than it answers.

[1354]Powell, *Discovering our Christian Faith*, 245-254.

[1355]Powell, *Holiness in the 21st Century*, 8-11.

[1356]Quanstrom, *Century of Holiness Theology*, 174.

[1357]Wesley, "On Working Out Our Own Salvation," Sermon #85, 2.1.

[1358]Waters, "Holiness in New Testament Perspective,"44-45.

[1359]Lowery, *Salvaging Wesley's Agenda*, 300.

In 1995 Roger Olson asked, "Has God been held hostage by philosophy?"[1360] This section will deal with the attempt to give theology credibility by establishing Christian holiness on a philosophical basis. Yet theology is not validated by philosophy. Rather philosophy should be evaluated on the basis of biblical revelation. Alan Padgett warned against wedding any particular philosophy to Christian theology in such as way that the philosophy is allowed to set the agenda for theology.[1361] Furthermore, the philosophical basis is always in flux. By definition process theology must evolve into something else.[1362] In this section we will look at the shift from personalism to existentialism to process philosophy.

Each of these philosophies compromise the nature of God. Personalism teaches that God is finite, denying his omnipotence. In his critique of openness theology, Douglas Kelly concluded the advocates of this position feel that God cannot be infinite and personal at the same time. To deal with us personally God must be finite or at least refrain from employing infinitude.[1363] Grider denies God is omnipresent and immutable.[1364] Process theology denies God's omniscience, especially with regard to foreknowledge. And yet Psalm 139 affirms the omniscience, omnipresence, and omnipotence of God! While our ultimate concern is its contribution to the doctrine of sanctification, there is a connection between how we view God and how we understand holiness.

Personalism is the transitional link between Wesleyan theology and process theology.[1365] Not all contributions of personalism, existentialism, or

---

[1360]Olson, "God Held by Philosophy,"30-34.

[1361]Padgett, "Putting Reason in Its Place," 263-278.

[1362]John Cobb concluded, "Process theology, under that unattractive name, will not continue indefinitely. From its own point of view it should change and develop, and in due course what it becomes will be known by other names" [Online: Cobb, "Process Theology"].

Clark Pinnock's replied to criticism by explaining that he was still in process ["Pilgrim on the Way," 43]. The introduction to *Embodied Holiness* claimed not to have offered the final word on the subject of holiness [Powell, "Introduction," 13]. This is both a valid expression of humility and a reflection of process thought. Staples declared that there is no final theology, even for Wesleyans. We have only a Final Word ["Present Frontiers of Wesleyan Theology," 6].

[1363]Kelly, "Afraid of Infinitude,"32.

[1364]Grider, *Wesleyan-Holiness Theology*, 118-121. Yet see Oden's defense of immutibility [*Living God*, 113].

[1365]Oord, "Boston Personalism,"379-392; Oord, "Boston Personalism's Affinities," 114-129; Oord, "Types of Wesleyan Philosophy," 159-160.

process philosophy should be rejected, but the trend is to formulate theology based on something other than on Scripture. Personalism tends toward humanism, relationalism is psychological, and process theology is philosophical.

Personalism

Personalism holds that reality is personal and the ultimate reality is personality. This proposition is based philosophically on the centrality of human freedom. The world is God's thought externalized. Personalism, existentialism, and process philosophy are all forms of idealism. Idealists believe that all physical reality is purely mental. Only minds and the contents of minds exist. This is applied neoplatonism, following the philosophy of Plato who taught that perfection and happiness could be achieved through philosophical contemplation.

Based on Descartes, the human person is the starting point. The Cartesian world is no larger than man's ego. Personalism holds that reality is made up of persons and their experiences. Thus, it is mystical. The primacy of consciousness is emphasized. If a person is not conscious, it is questioned whether or not he exists. Since human consciousness is the starting point of modern philosophy, they reason from the known to the unknown and determine that God must be like us.

Personality was first introduced by Frederich Schleiermacher in 1799. Bordon Parker Bowne (1847-1910) taught at Boston University School of Theology, the oldest United Methodist seminary in America, where he developed the philosophy of personalism.[1366] However, Bowne felt that a new interpretation of basic reality was needed. He concluded that personality was the key to reality and that God was the ultimate "person." Bowne taught that it is impossible for the entire universe to exist apart from a person to experience it. Thus man is the starting point and personality is the ultimate reality. Thus, God is a personal being because we are created in his image.

Martin Buber, a Jewish personalist, proposed that the human form of relationship is "I-Thou" as opposed to "I-it."[1367] Buber believed that all relationships should be based on treating people as people, not as objects Yet

---

[1366]McConnell, *Borden Parker Bowne*, 13-14. While McConnell described this personalism as based on the theme of Christian perfection, I would submit that personalism is based more on free will than on Christian perfection. Bowne was charged with heresy in 1904. George A. Cooke charged Bowne with denying the Trinity, miracles, and substitutionary atonement, as well as being at variance with Methodist doctrine at numerous other points [Langford, *Practical Divinity*, 23].

[1367]Buber, *I and Thou*; Buber, *Between Man and Man*.

Buber was apparently so pantheistic[1368] that he insisted a tree and a cat could have an "I-thou" relationship.[1369]

This "I-Thou" concept was picked up by Emil Brunner, in reaction to Karl Barth who described God as "the Wholly Other." In his 1938 commentary, Brunner wrote, "Thus there is no human existence without a relation to God. The pagan religions testify of this, too. They would not exist if God did not at first and inescapably declare himself to everyone since the dawn of humanity in his works, in nature and history. The denial of such a 'general revelation' preceding the historical revelation of grace in Jesus Christ can appeal neither to Paul nor to the Bible at large. It contradicts the facts of responsibility. If man did not know God, how could he be responsible? But he is responsible, for he knows about God on the strength of the divine self-revelation. The apostle does not speak of a past, now buried, possibility but of something actually present; for it is true of everyone that he is inexcusable in his godlessness."[1370]

Thus, Brunner emphasized the "I-Thou Encounter" between the individual and God.[1371] This is relational and not merely theoretical. For Brunner the problem in theology was that the subject and object were both made third person and impersonal. Thus God communicates truth about himself rather than communicating himself. Wynkoop declared, "There is no place in Wesley's thought for any God-man relationship which in its arbitrariness and 'itness' (Martin Buber) violates the moral/personal reality of mankind. It is impossible for salvation to take place — or to come into the sphere of salvation — without this beginning and ongoing self-contribution to the event."[1372] However, truth is also objective and propositional, as Dunning seems to concede.[1373] The marks of the new birth in 1 John are propositional, relational, *and* behavioral.

Thus, Gerald Heard asserted that natural theology is the first pier in the bridge of faith. Without natural theology, we cannot produce saints.[1374] Apparently Heard concluded that sainthood develops from mysticism and not from intellectualism. Sangster evaluated and ultimately rejected this conclusion as a

---

[1368]or panentheistic - see ftnt # 3013.

[1369]Hall, *Imaging God*, 55.

[1370]Brunner, *Romans*, 17.

[1371]Brunner, *Truth as Encounter*, 24; *Christian Doctrine of God*, 139.

[1372]Wynkoop, *Theology of Love,* 90-91; 71; 169-174.

[1373]Dunning, *Grace, Faith, and Holiness*, 128-129.

[1374]Heard, *Is God Evident?*

false dichotomy.[1375] Understanding does not necessarily destroy faith. However, both Barth and Brunner operated from a neo-orthodox foundation which denied that Scripture is the infallible revelation of God. Saving faith is based upon this Word. However, because their doctrine of inspiration undermines faith, Barth is pessimistic regarding any progress toward the recovery of holiness in man. Brunner, while more optimistic, based his optimism on natural revelation and not the special revelation of Scripture. Yet properly understood, the intent of special revelation and natural revelation is to reveal God.[1376]

We can have a personal relationship with God without sacrificing objective reality. We need not sacrifice God's transcendence in order to maintain his immanence. Samuel Powell wrote that Wynkoop and Staples made prominent use of Buber. While they emphasized the relational character of holiness, they failed to see this relationship to God in terms of calling, consecration, purity, and obedience. Instead they emphasized only love.[1377] For Powell, God is trinitarian and participating in God involves calling, consecration, obedience, *and* love.[1378]

However, the humanistic approach of personalism amounts to "I think, therefore God is." This, of course, is an adaptation of Rene Descartes famous statement, *cogito ergo sum* (I think, therefore I am). This Enlightenment philosophy began with the autonomous human mind as its presupposition and went on to prove the existence of God. As a personalist philosopher John Macmurray wrote, "We should substitute the *I do* for the *I think* as our starting point and centre of reference, and do our thinking from the standpoint of action."[1379] In contrast, I would advocate Anselm's position, *credo ut intelligam* (I believe that I may understand).

Robert Chiles wrote, "For the personalist, even more than the existence of God, the reality of the self, or soul or 'I,' is *the* fundamental presupposition."[1380] Thus a relational approach to theology developed as personalists attempted to describe a personal relationship with God.[1381] God and

---

[1375]Sangster, *Pure in Heart*, 211-214.

[1376]Reasoner, *Romans*, 52-57.

[1377]Powell, *Holiness in the 21st Century*, 9-10, 12, 21.

[1378]Powell, *Holiness in the 21st Century*, 17-19.

[1379]Macmurray, *Self as Agent*, 84.

[1380]Chiles, *Theological Transitions*, 110.

[1381]Wynkoop's theology of relationalism is based on personalism, see *Theology of Love*, 81; 87-91; 164-172. "Wesleyan theology stresses the *personal*. God has made man a *person*. The image of God has to do with whatever a person is . . . . We simply regard man in this study as the Bible does — a person to whom God speaks and one

man share the characteristic of personhood. But Sam Powell argued that God is utterly different from all other beings. God is infinite, while humans are finite. This preoccupation with God as a person undercuts the doctrine of God as Trinity.[1382]

Bowne was the most important person in the Methodist transition toward liberalism. Personalism was perpetuated at Boston University by Albert C. Knudson, Olin A. Curtis, Edgar S. Brightman, Harris F. Rall, Geogria Harkness, and L. Harold DeWolf — all Methodist theologians. Since almost every student who attended the Boston University School of Theology in the twentieth century was taught philosophy of religion and theology by a personalist, it is not surprising that most Methodist ministers and bishops were of the personalist persuasion.[1383]

Methodism historically has emphasized a personal relationship with God, not simply a legal righteousness imputed by God. Yet this presupposition of personalism leads to distortion because it starts with man and is based on a rejection of human depravity. Traditional Wesleyan theology insisted that freedom was lost in the fall and that its partial restoration was based upon prevenient grace, but Knudson appealed to neither Scripture nor tradition in arguing for a freedom, essentially unimpaired by sin.[1384]

The long-standing attraction of Methodism to personalism was based on four emphases. Boston Personalism's core conception was that God is personal, interactive, and relational. Second, it emphasized the freedom of persons,[1385] opposing mechanistic, behavioristic, or theistic theories that denied persons a measure of self-determination. For personalism, humanity is defined by intentionality. Personalism starts with man, not God and emphasizes human freedom in reaction to Calvinism. Hence the emphasis is upon free will, not free

---

who can answer back in a genuine conversation" [p. 166]. There is a close connection between Wiley and Wynkoop.

[1382]Powell, "Trinitarian Alternative," 144; 158; 167. Since process thought continues on the basis of personalism, Powell argued that it must also be regarded as misguided. Peterson asserts that in process thought God cannot be considered either as a definite being or personal. Thus process theology reduces personhood to a series of events ["Orthodox Christianity,"50-51]. The God of process theology is dipolar, both as abstract essence and concrete actuality, but not trinitariam.

[1383]Langford, *Practical Divinity*, 119-124; Langford, *Wesleyan Theology*, 149-151.

[1384]Chiles, *Theological Transition*, 182-183.

[1385]"personalism. . .holds to the libertarian as against the deterministic view of men" [Knudson, *Philosophy of Personalism*, 74].

grace. Depravity is not total. The image of God is not lost. Salvation is not a surrender, but a deliberate choice.

The personalist claim that God created persons with the capacity to act freely corresponds well with the central Wesleyan doctrine that prevenient grace enables humans to act in free response to God. John Cobb emphasized this theme of responsibility.

> In my opinion, the greatest theological contribution of Wesley was his way of affirming human responsibility for our ultimate destiny and daily life while strongly maintaining the primacy of faith. This provided a third way between Calvinism and deism. Calvinists thought that they must exclude any human contribution to salvation to avoid allowing Christians to believe that they were saved by their virtue. Deists thought that God gave us free will and that everything else is up to us. Wesley found both views deeply alien to the Bible. . . . Wesley changed this picture by locating the working of God within the human being. He kept the view that human nature is entirely sinful, but he regarded human nature in this sense as an abstraction from real human beings. An actual human being, even a baby is already the union of God's grace and human nature. Thus an actual human being makes choices that result from the particular way in which grace and nature are united in that person. This choice is constantly affecting the way in which grace can function in the next moment. It clearly affects the question of whether justification will occur and how far one will go on to perfection in love. In this way Wesley gives a large role to actual human decisions. But these decisions are never made independently of grace. To the extent that they are oriented to the reception of more grace, they are already informed by the grace that has worked there before. No one can boast of any achievement as if that were not dependent on the working of grace. One can only thank God for the great gifts bestowed on one and pray for continued strength to make the decisions for which one is responsible.[1386]

While I think this emphasis on responsibility is biblical, I do not think it necessarily leads to process theology. Powell demonstrated that because of the

---

[1386]Online: Cobb, "Wesley the Process Theologian." See also Cobb, *Grace and Responsibility*; Cobb, "Human Responsibility and the Primacy of Grace." Randy Maddox also emphasized *Responsible Grace* and "Seeking a Response—able God."

Wesleyan interest in freedom and responsibility, later Wesleyans turned to personalism Powell explained, "In the debate with the Calvinists in which freedom was the disputed concept, the personality of God was invoked to guarantee human freedom. The concept of the Trinity, not able to perform such a feat, fell by the wayside."[1387]

Third, Boston Personalism offered Wesleyans a structure to support the Christian demand for personal morality and social responsibility. "Personality implies freedom and moral responsibility," argued Knudson.[1388]

Finally, Wesleyans were attracted to Boston Personalism by its emphasis on love. The process understanding of sanctification is based on the image of God as love, sanctification is the restoration or perfection of this image

According to Daniel Berg, personalism provided a philosophical basis for perfection, by its focus on the will as the center of the Christian and the core of Christian perfection. Berg said that personalism applied the word "perfection" to humanity rather freely.[1389] Yet, according to Grider, while personalism corrected the tendency of idealism toward pantheism, it depreciated the physical world. It emphasized human freedom, but denied original sin.[1390]

Yet personalism subordinated the ultimate authority of the Scriptures to reason. Curtis Jones argued that personalism neither begins nor really ends with Christianity. It begins with some speculations about he self and ends with an hypothesis about God.[1391] Brightman's notion of a finite God, for whom evil is something of a "given" within the divine self, is not biblical.[1392] Even Knudson admits that "the traditional doctrines of the Trinity, Incarnation, and Atonement do not easily fit into the framework of our current personal idealism." He maintained, however, that "this may point to the need of the reformulation of these doctrines rather than to any want of harmony between personalistic philosophy and the essentials of the Christian faith."[1393]

H. Orton Wiley defined personalism as "the philosophy that gives priority to the personality, regarded as constituting the chief reality and highest value."

[1387]Powell, "Trinitarian Alternative," 147. This emphasis on personalism was promoted early by Whedon in *Freedom of the Will* and Miley who defined God as "an eternal personal Being" [*Systematic Theology*, 1:60].

[1388]Knudson, *Philosophy of Personalism*, 83.

[1389]Berg,"Theological Context of American Wesleyanism," 52-53.

[1390]Grider, *Wesleyan-Holiness Theology*, 40.

[1391]Jones, "Personalism as Christian Philosophy," 213; 196.

[1392]See Bloesch, *God the Almighty*, 244.

[1393]Knudson, *Philosophy of Personalism*, 80.

In turn, Wiley influenced Wynkoop, Dunning, Staples, and Lodahl.[1394]

Richard S. Taylor, who earned his doctorate from Boston University in 1953, also articulated personalism by declaring, "Man, for all his finiteness, is the most godlike being on earth, and perhaps in the universe." He quoted Oswald Chambers who declared, "God created man to counteract the devil." Then Taylor continued by declaring the first respect in which man was made like God was the possession of personhood. This personhood implies self-awareness, the power to act, and the ability to communicate with other people.[1395]

Yet the opening paragraph of this chapter, "Holiness in Man," in *Exploring Christian Holiness*, attempted to avoid some of its more radical implications. In a footnote, Taylor labeled process sanctification "the new face of Pelagianism."[1396] Later in the book he tries to mediate between the traditional holiness theology and relational theology.[1397] In other writings he lashed out against relationalism,[1398] but relationalism is part of the personalism which Taylor embraced. Thus, Taylor is a conservative personalist, while other Nazarene theologians have carried this philosophy to more radical conclusions.

John Cobb conceded that after the decline of Boston Personalism, United

---

[1394]Price, "Influence of Personalism," 142-160; Online: Price, *We Teach Holiness*, 51-68. Price concluded that Wiley was "saturated in personalistic thought." See Wiley's chapter, "God as Perfect Personality" [*Christian Theology*, 1:290-319]. While it is not denied that God is a person, yet the description of divine personality is largely inferred from the personalism which defines human personality. Thus God is the ultimate personality and this is deduced from his creation. Based on human reason many personalists have denied that God is infinite or omnipotent.

[1395]Taylor, *Theological Formulation*, 29-32. See Harper, "Personalism,"397; Grider, *Wesleyan-Holiness Theology*, 39-40.

[1396]Taylor, *Theological Formulation*, 78. Taylor had written that he was "afraid of the inroads of Whitehead's process philosophy via process theology (Cobb)." Process theology "translated into Wesleyan terms becomes a holiness theology which accents process at the expense of crisis, of relation at the expense of nature, which discounts any true doctrine of original sin as an inherited proclivity, and which leaves little place for supernatural works of grace which make a radical instantaneous change in the inner self, both conscious and subconscious" [*Letter* from Richard S. Taylor to Ray Pollard, 23 Sept, 1981].

[1397]Taylor, *Theological Formulation*, 99-101.

[1398]In "Why the Holiness Movement Died," Taylor blamed Mildred Wynkoop as a major contributor to the staggering of the holiness ranks [p. 50]. Yet it seems a bit presumptuous for Taylor to single out Nazarene theologian Mildred Wynkoop (1905-1997) as the scape goat of a movement that was off track before she was ever born.

Methodism lost its way theologically.[1399] Yet he explained that the departure was generally because personalism advocated metaphysical positions which were out of step with the scientific community. The general movement toward openness and process thought is driven partially by the promise of a dialog with the scientific community.

Existentialism

Before modern Wesleyan theologians looked at process theology, personalism's emphasis on self-consciousness and experience led to existentialism. Mildred Wynkoop was more open to existentialism.[1400] Existentialism does not fit as well with relationalism. Nor does existentialism lead to process, but they are all idealist philosophies. Existential philosophy deals with our act of existing. We have being or existence, but no essence. According to existentialism, we must define ourselves.

The existential theology of Kierkegaard, as well at the later existential interests of Martin Buber, Paul Tillich, and Rudolf Bultmann have aspects that are useful in theology, according to Nazarene theologian Kenneth Grider.[1401]

Wynkoop advocated three major conceptual adjustments. The first concerned an understanding of the nature of persons. She advocated a return to the Hebrew definition of personhood as a unity, as opposed to the Greek dualism which regarded the human body as evil. She advocated a relational view of sin, as opposed to a substantial concept of sin. And she promoted a moral interpretation of salvation, as opposed to a magical understanding. Salvation was not something which happened to man, but a right relationship with God and man, based on love.[1402]

Process Philosophy

Personalist and process philosophers have generally appreciated each other's views since the early decades of the twentieth century. In fact, Brightman called both Whitehead and Hartshorne "personalists," and he praised Whitehead,

---

[1399]Cobb, *Grace and Responsibility*, 8. In fact, most process theologians are United Methodists according to Suchocki ["Coming Home," 36]. See also Langford, *Practical Divinity*, 229-235; Stafford, "Frontiers in Contemporary Theology,"1:23-25.

[1400]Wynkoop, "Existential Interpretation"; Wynkoop, "Existential Interpretation of the Doctrine of Holiness," "Sanctification is Existential," 1-5; "Love is Existential," 16-20; "Practical Norm," 29-31; "Life Spiritualized," 12-13.

[1401]Grider, *Wesleyan-Holiness Theology*, 41-42.

[1402]Quanstrom, *Century of Holiness Theology*, 143-144.

saying that "the greatest Anglo-American philosopher of recent times, A. N. Whitehead, came from a realistic tradition, but his doctrines. . .all point to panpsychistic personalism."[1403] Brightman's published work and personal correspondence reveal that, through his reading of Whitehead and his exchanges with Hartshorne, he slowly drifted away from hard-core personal idealism toward doctrines more characteristic of process thought. Hartshorne considered Brightman to be a process theist and was influenced somewhat by Brightman.[1404]

Writing in 1972, Wynkoop felt that process theology made "a much need correction to the dualisms of a former day. . . . Its insights are inescapable in a biblical theology. The dynamic emphasis in relation to God, man, love, grace, nature, and salvation and interpersonal relations is crucial to the Christian faith." She categorized Wesley's thought as perceiving man "in process." Yet she expressed reservation about its metaphysical foundations.[1405]

In an attempt to make the doctrine of holiness palatable for the post-modern mind, process sanctification theologians emphasize relationships and community. As early as 1977 Rob Staples called process theology "the hottest thing in town today." Although Staples expressed severe questions about process theology, he felt it might offer some models which would help Wesleyans clarify their doctrines of man, sin, and sanctification. Staples thought perhaps Whitehead's philosophy might show "how sanctification is not merely a crisis, not merely a process, not merely *both* a crisis *and* a process held in some loose and undefined conjuncture, and not merely a *series* of crises unrelated to one another as in the Oberlin theology and as in a strictly existentialist interpretation."[1406]

[1403]Brightman, "Personalism,"344. *Panpsychism* literally means that all is soul. It is the doctrine that mind is a fundamental feature of the world which exists throughout the universe. The universe or nature is filled with mind and purpose. Murphree explained that Eastern pantheism leads directly to panpsychism, "Because everything and every person is of the same spiritual substance, every object is a part of God and every person is a spark in the divine flame" [*Divine Paradoxes*, 90]. Much earlier, in the seventh century, Baruch Spinoza held that since all things are produced by the consummate perfection of God, reality and perfection are one and the same thing. If we fail to perceive perfection everywhere, the problem is due to the inadequacy of our understanding [*Ethics*, Proposition XX].

[1404]Auxier, "God, Process, and Persons,"175-199.

[1405]Wynkoop, *Theology of Love,* 11; 81.

[1406]Staples, "Present Frontiers," 9-10. Whitehead taught the relationship of one occasion of experience to its predecessors. What he termed "prehension" was defined as the way one momentary experience incorporates earlier such moments. Basically, the experience of any one moment is a crisis experience, but what happens at any one

Whitehead taught that the world is made up of actual entities, which are brief events. The objects of our everyday life are "societies" of these brief events. Relationships between actual entities form the nexus or web of reality. Every actual entity "prehends" or is related either positively or negatively to all previous actual entities. Thus, the actual entity connects all of reality in its brief moment. What we experience as the material world is basically a constant flux of subjective, experience-based events which link together to form our experience. This process thought emphasizes relationality just as much as it does process.

Process thought is a reaction against the position that there is objective, static, changeless reality. The only reality is the fact that everything is in process or becoming. Everything is contingent and everything is interdependent. The result is an inclusive theology in which Methodist theologian John B. Cobb, Jr. can speak of a "Christianized Buddhism and a Buddhized Christianity."[1407] The universe is characterized by process and change carried out by the agents of free will. Self-determination characterizes everything in the universe. Process theology stresses experience, internal relations, contingency (every event could have been otherwise), and co-creativity (finite beings work with God to make the world what it is here and now).

Cobb, who studied under Hartshorne, is one of the most prominent spokesmen for process theology.[1408] At the time they wrote in 2001, Bryan Stone and Thomas Oord claimed *Grace and Responsibility* by Cobb was the most important published interpretation of Wesley's theology in light of process thought.[1409] Yet *Grace and Responsibility* declared that "it is not Wesley's actual

---

moment is influenced by the past. Thus any crisis is interpreted in terms of an overarching process. This interconnectedness between experiences is based upon the idea of panentheism. *Panentheism* claims that God is not all, but in all and all is God, by means of prehension. According to process theology, we influence God's nature, decisions, and actions since we are "in" God [Cobb and Griffin, *Process Theology*, 41-62]. Thus the world is in God and whenever the world changes, God changes with it.

Leclerc wrote, "It is not necessary to embrace this understanding in order to affirm God's more empathetic qualities. It is more than possible to hold to God's independence and God's passionate relationality at the same time" [*Discovering Christian Holiness*, 141].

[1407]Cobb, *Christ in a Pluralistic Society*, 209. See also Cobb, "Can a Christian Be a Buddhist Too?"1-20.

[1408]Nietzsche had said "without Hegel there could be no Darwin." Rushdoony asserted without Hegel, "there could be no Hartshorne either" [*To Be as God*, 189]. Rushdoony regarded Charles Hartshorne to be a more able proponent of process theology than either Alfred Whitehead or Pierre Teilhard de Chardin [p. 186].

[1409]Stone and Oord, "Introduction," 12. See Cobb's *Grace and Responsibility* in which he interacts with the theology of John Wesley.

view that all who have been born again are free from voluntarily transgressing the commandment of love."[1410] Cobb also doubted whether Wesley's doctrine of perfection could be transposed unchanged into our own time.[1411] Without advocating a return back to Wesley, Cobb stated that Wesley's emphasis on growth in grace made a lot of sense, especially his conviction that we should not set any limits to where this process can bring us.[1412] Cobb was initially resistant to a "back to Wesley" movement, until he realized that Wesley could be the starting point for a discussion on how to move forward.[1413] Thus, Thomas Langford could write that while the Methodist tradition cannot be understood apart from John Wesley, it also cannot be understood except as it has moved beyond Wesley.[1414] It is significant that this statement is quoted with approval by process theologian Schubert Ogden.[1415]

Cobb used Wesley's words, that sin cleaves not only to our words but to our actions as well, to suggest that regenerate believers remain under the power or dominion of sin. This may be the view of process theology, but it does not accurately reflect Wesley's teaching.[1416]

Process theologians hold that the Greek philosophical system provides only static categories which do not provide for real relationships and for real change to occur. Jon Tal Murphree has argued, however, that this "guilt by association" argument against classical theology does not necessarily prove classical theology to be wrong. Process theology offers a God who is immanent but not transcendent, finite rather than infinite, a part of the system rather than above the system. God is interdependent with the world and relies on the world to actualize his potential and thus realize fulfillment. He is not able to prevent evil and is constantly updating himself to be relevant to a changing culture.[1417]

1410Cobb, *Grace and Responsibility*, 104.

1411Cobb, *Grace and Responsibility*, 112.

1412Cobb, *Grace and Responsibility*, 10.

1413Cobb, *Grace and Responsibility*, 8-9.

1414Langford, *Practical Divinity*, 260.

1415Ogden, "Process Theology," 33. Ogden also denied that Christ was the sole mediator through whom God speaks his Word ["Bultmann's Project," 165].

1416Wesley's words are from his sermon, "The Repentance of Believers," Sermon #14, 1.11. See the reaction to Cobb and explanation of Wesley by Collins, *Theology of John Wesley*, 220-221. Collins said this interpretation, as stated by Cobb, is becoming increasingly popular in American Methodism.

1417Murphree, *Divine Paradoxes*, 8-11. See Process Theology website, http://www.ctr4process.org

Actually this description fits modern theologians, not God.

While process thought can be traced back to the ancient philosopher Heraclitus, in the more modern era Georg W. F. Hegel (1770-1831) introduced his theory of dialectics which provided an evolutionary theory of history. He explained the endless process on the basis of thesis, antithesis, and synthesis.[1418] For Alfred North Whitehead events are the primary realities, not objects or substances. Reality is not static essence, but process. God is not being but is becoming. He is a combination of actuality and potentiality. He is temporal and limited. Yet Whitehead himself admitted that he had never fully worked out his doctrine of God and the question has been raised by Dorothy Emmet as to whether God's reality is really integral to Whitehead's view of the world.[1419]

Whitehead proposed that each moment in time should be viewed as connected with all other moments of time. Reality is perceived as moments of experience which join together, grasping previous actual occasions incorporating them into the universe, thus forming a synthesis. Thus, a crisis moment is itself part of a larger process and each moment shapes other occasions. Yet this process understanding of time presupposes a kind of panentheism.[1420]

Bradford McCall has suggested that Wesley anticipated the concept of panentheism in his sermon on the omnipresence of God. But Wesley's declaration that there is no point of space where God is not,
avoids the extreme of McCall's panentheism. McCall declared, "Panentheism seeks to stress that the infinite God is as ontologically close to finite things as can possibly be thought without dissolving altogether the distinction between Creator and created." Thus, he is advocating a position as close to pantheism as we can possible get without actually blurring the distinction between Creator and created.[1421] Wesley, on the other hand, would have maintained a balance between the immanence and transcendence of God.

Clark Pinnock has argued for open theism as a via media between classical and process theology. Yet open theism amounts to a "halfway house of conservative process theism," to quote Royce Gruenler.[1422] Writing from an

---

[1418]Murphree, *Divine Paradoxes*, 101-102; Oden, *Living* God, 266.

[1419]Henry, *God, Revelation and Authority*, 6:60.

[1420]*Panentheism* is a belief system which posits that God personally exists, interpenetrates every part of nature and timelessly extends beyond it. *Panentheism* differs from *pantheism*, which holds that God is not a distinct being but is synonymous with the universe.

[1421]McCall, "Emergence Theory and Theology," 196-207.

[1422]Pinnock, "Between Classical and Process Theism,"321; 325. See Bloesch, *God the Almighty*, 254-260; Picirilli, *Grace, Faith, Free Will*, 41.

Openness perspective, Pinnock argued for the longevity and not the timelessness of God himself: "Timelessness limits God. If he were timeless, God would be unable to work salvation in history, would be cut off from the world, have no real relationship with people and would be completely static."[1423] Yet Murphree argued that God can be active in time without being confined to time.[1424] The problem is that this model is built upon evolutionary presuppositions in which God himself is portrayed as being in process. Process theology prefers to describe God as "everlasting," but part of history. They see the word "eternal" as Neoplatonistic, meaning that God exists outside time. But Deuteronomy 33:27 uses both words to describe God; he is both transcendent or outside time and immanent, acting within history.

Process theology over-reacts to a rigid view of God found within some Calvinistic theologians in which God is immutable and incapable of relationships. It is claimed that the traditional view of God originated in Greek philosophy, not Scripture. Yet in their attempt to correct our understanding of God, process theology proposes a God who is relational, but finite. This God can only exist by being in the process of change. The result is a God who needs the world as much as the world needs him. Thus, his sovereignty is diminished and our freedom is magnified.[1425] We resemble God and he needs us.

Process thought seems to lean toward Pelagianism in its denial of original sin and emphasis on human ability. Yet without a proper view of sin there cannot be a proper understanding of sanctification. Process sanctification seems to infer that we can evolve beyond sin and the result is that we are moving toward universalism. Marjorie Suchocki declared that process thought affirms and requires pluralism.[1426] She advocates both process theology and feminist theology, which she describes as a form of liberation theology, as a contemporary extension of Wesley's doctrine of Christian perfection.[1427] Mary Elizabeth Mullino Moore argued that a process understanding of Wesley's emphasis on love should lead to gay, lesbian, bisexual, and transgendered persons being fully accepted and

---

[1423]Rice, Sanders, and Pinnock, *Openness of God*, 121. By 2007 this book was in its twelfth printing. See also Online: Oord, "Emergence of Open Theology."

[1424]Rice, Sanders, and Pinnock, *Openness of God*, 28.

[1425]Lodahl believes that God shares his power with us. This results in the free will of man. Therefore, when God creates, he "let's thing be." Thus, God's creation is out of love, not out of nothing. Lodahl defines the sovereignty of God as the fellow sufferer who understands. Therefore, God is not responsible for evil; he is doing the best that he can do [*Story of God*, 59-61; 219-224].

[1426]Suchocki,"Coming Home," 63.

[1427]Suchocki, "Coming Home," 62; 64.

included within human community.[1428] Thus, "holiness" is reduced to an all-inclusive love which condones sexual deviancy.

About all that remains of the doctrine of Christian perfection is the assertion that while the church remains susceptible to sin, there are moments when we fully walk in the Spirit. Thus, "being" was replaced with "becoming" and in a process universe God is no exception. God's words to Moses, "I am that I am" (Exod 3:14) are interpreted as a refusal to be named in a way that can be conceptually circumscribed. God is conceived as a verb, not a noun. Yet to be coherent there must be a subject as well as a verb. Certainly God is active, but doing flows from being. Yet it is asserted that God needs us in order to become actualized.[1429] This amounts to a deification of process. According to existential philosophy, we are not finished either, but are always on the way to expressing more fully who we are.[1430]

Process philosophy did not enter Christian theology until the last half of the twentieth century. Applying this concept theologically, Whitehead taught the interdependence of God and the world. God is not aloof from, nor unaffected by, the world. God works in the world primarily through persuasion, not coercion. God should be thought of in terms of suffering with the world, not in terms of omnipotence.[1431]

The result is a God who is only different from us in quantity, not quality. They end up with an immanent God who is actually caught up in the evolutionary process. He does not superintend the world; he is a part of the world.[1432] Both God and creation are involved in an ongoing process. Yet "nothing can be added to that which is full."[1433] Process thought is opposed to materialism. It sees the whole universe as alive and growing. Hartshorne believed that God is not absolutely perfect, but is ever growing toward such perfection. The process emphasis has created a new interest in the Eastern concept of perfecting grace, deification, and Eastern mystical philosophy.

Teilhard de Chardin also viewed the universe as a christologically guided movement toward perfection which he explained in terms of a rationalistic

---

[1428]Moore, "Compassion and Hope," 330.

[1429]Gruenler, "Reflections,"353. Gruenler once championed process theology, but later forsook it and returned to evangelical orthodoxy.

[1430]Gruenler, "Reflections,"340; Stafford, "Frontiers in Contemporary Theology,"1:21-22.

[1431]Grenz and Olson, *Twentieth Century Theology*, 135-138.

[1432]Bloesch rejected this finite God of process philosophy (Whitehead) and philosophical personalism (Brightman) [*Theology of Word and Spirit*, 126].

[1433]Oden quoted Gregory Nazianzen, *Word of Life*, 72.

evolutionary mysticism.[1434] Chardin's process thought comes close to pantheism in which the world process is practically equated with deity. "When God is depicted as Creative Process or as the Life Force, a pantheistic world view is again evident. God is not longer a person but now a process."[1435] According to Grider, Chardin was a devout Catholic who applied the view of biological evolution to a whole spectrum of understandings, including God. Yet Grider himself declared that immutability was not an attribute of God.[1436]

Veli-Matti Kärkkäinen summarized the emphases of a process theology of the Holy Spirit:

- Process pneumatology takes the immanence of God seriously; God in Spirit is present in all creation and all people. However, this may open the door to universalism.
- The Holy Spirit is passible, meaning he is able to experience emotions, and sensitive — even vulnerable.
- If the Spirit of God is love, this presupposes relationality, the ability to suffer, and change.
- The Holy Spirit, as the consequent nature of God, signifies God's intimate responsiveness to creation.
- Life in the Spirit is not flight from the world, but the fullest possible actualization of our capacities for creaturely existence.
- The relationship between the Spirit of God and the human spirit is mutual. While all persons have the power to shape their own destinies, the fulfillment of this creative potential is grounded in the presence of God's Spirit.
- The Holy Spirit is not a miraculous supernatural energy which overwhelms and fills up persons so as to depersonalize them. Rather the Spirit denotes the fullest expression of the potential for creaturely existence.[1437]

Bryan P. Stone and Thomas Jay Oord discussed the similarity between Wesleyan theology and process theology, saying both "understand the perfecting of God's creation in general, and human growth in grace, in particular, primarily

---

[1434]Chardin, *Phenomenon of Man*.

[1435]Bloesch, *God the Almighty*, 190; See Laurence Wood, "An Appendix on the Concept of Substance" in *Pentecostal Grace*, 161-175, where Wood argued that to embrace a relational theology does not dispense with the concept of substance.

[1436]Grider, *Wesleyan-Holiness Theology*, 41; 118-119.

[1437]Kärkkäinen, *Pneumatology*, 153-154.

in relational and processive terms."[1438] Process thought has been influenced in particular by evolutionary theory. Thus, the goal of sanctification is to participate in what God is becoming. "For process thought, however, all reality is social and, therefore, conditioned by and, in some sense, dependent on others. This applies even to God, who is not merely social and conditioned by others but is eminently so."[1439]

Although a literal, prehistorical Fall has been abandoned in favor of evolutionary theory, process theology redefines original sin as our being embedded in sinful structures. Original sin is no longer the sins of our ancestral parents. Borden Parker Bowne, an earlier Methodist theologian, taught that sin was "a relic of the animal not yet outgrown."[1440] He also declared, "Sin itself, as we find it among men, is largely the willfulness of freedom which has not learned self-control."[1441] Since we are influenced by the decisions of other people, one can never be free from combined negative influences. But the "means of grace" are positive influences which cooperate with the divine lure. The victory over sin is a communal victory.[1442] Thus, salvation is not deliverance from the penalty and power of sin, but integration — the realization of significance, health, wholeness and the process of exchanging egocentricity for concern for others.[1443]

While progressive sanctification may result in all of the above, initial sanctification is deliverance from sin. Without adapting a process philosophy framework, which teaches that God is also in process, sanctification is progressive in nature. Furthermore, the new birth also involves both process and crisis. But process theology tends to describe salvation in evolutionary terms.

Kenneth Collins has argued against the liberal view of the Christian life as a process of incremental changes without any crucial events. Collins argued

---

[1438]Stone and Oord, "Introduction," 9.

[1439]Stone, "Process and Sanctification,"78.

[1440]Bowne, *Studies in Christianity*, 145. Delbert Rose rejected the teaching that Adam cannot be regarded as a real person, but symbolizes mankind. Therefore, the fall is not a sudden event in the past, but a continuing process in each person's life. Original righteousness is not something from which the first Adam fell, but the destiny for which we were all intended and toward which we should be moving ["Wesleyan Understanding of Sin,"10]. Yet this teaching was advocated by Williams, *John Wesley's Theology Today*, 55-56. Romans 5:12-21 treats Adam and Jesus as representative of the human race. One cannot be mythical and, on the other hand, historical.

[1441]Bowne, *Christian Life*, 41.

[1442]Stone, "Process and Sanctification,"82-83.

[1443]Demarest, "Process Reduction of Jesus and the Trinity," 72.

for the crisis of salvation as a logical necessity based on sovereign grace, but he concedes that while conversion is a crisis, it may not be dramatic nor memorable. He allows for process, but argues that process must have actualization and not be opened ended where we are always seeking but never arriving. "The continuity of the process of growth in grace must be matched by the discontinuity, the concluding work of actualization."[1444] Thus, Collins opposes an evolutionary or process model of salvation. He argues for a qualitative, not incremental, change. However, he also distances himself from the instantaneous emphasis of the holiness movement in which the seeker is admonished to claim the work is done in an instant. Thus, he argues for a divine work, not a human work. The process has a *telos* or goal, but it is not all process nor crisis.[1445]

Yet Young wrote, "A process theology of sanctification begins with the notion that all actual entities receive God's loving acceptance, lure, and empowerment. . . .Sanctification is not a test to be passed, a state to be entered, or an achievement to be gauged. It is a creative project of love in which, as co-creators with God, we are led increasingly to reflect the image of God discovered in Christ and offered to us by the power of the Holy Spirit as a gift, as demand, as lure."[1446] "This process of sanctification continues on an inward and outward basis as the person regenerated in Christ moves toward perfection. One is never completely exempt from committing sin in this life but is always living in a state of renewal in Christ."[1447]

Young has abandoned all deliverance from sin in his statement, "One is never completely exempt from committing sin in this life but is always living in a state of renewal in Christ."[1448]

[1444]Collins, *John Wesley: Theological Journey*, 195.

[1445]Collins, "Other Thoughts," 10-25; see also Collins, *Faithful Witness*, 149-161. Collins expresses concern over the "gradualism" of Maddox which places an undue stress on process in explaining entire sanctification ["Recent Trends," 68. See also Collins, *John Wesley: Theological Journey*, 83]. In 1909 Burns objected to the new emphasis on entire sanctification which denied it to be an instantaneous work. Sheldon's *System of Christian Doctrine* (1903) was challenged by Burns as teaching "that the *Christian life is an evolution*." Thus evolutionary theory caused Sheldon to teach sanctification as a process that extends into the next life [Burns, *Crisis in Methodism*, 35-36; 58]. Yet it does not necessarily follow that all who teach progressive sanctification are working from evolutionary presuppositions. Collins maintains the proper balance between process and crisis.

[1446]Stone, "Process and Sanctification," 76; 94.

[1447]Young, "Spirituality and Social Transformation," 347-348.

[1448]Young, "Spirituality and Social Transformation," 347-348. See also Maddox, *Responsible Grace*, 190 and the objection from Collins to the emphasis from

Sanctification is a life of dancing with God in which God is responsive to our moves. Randy Maddox described the relationship between God and man as "a *dance* in which God always takes the first step but we must participate responsively, lest the dance stumble or end."[1449] "Sanctification depends upon the movement of God and it never ends. It is the image of God throughout all time."[1450] This mystical description, however, presupposes that human beings are not capable of sustained, uninterrupted intimacy or union with God. Collins also objects that this image omits about half of Wesley's emphasis, that of free grace which is the activity of God *alone.*[1451]

John Culp felt that the theology of John Cobb provided a model for relating the crisis and progressive aspects of the experience of entire sanctification. Cobb held that events are the basic nature of reality, thus the second crisis is the moment of decision which is carried out and developed by succeeding events. Culp explained,

> Without the crisis experience in which the person decides to realize fully the possibilities which God provides, there is no ongoing experience of the greater possibilities. Likewise, without the continuing development of the influence of the crisis, the crisis event would have no meaning. The process is initiated in the event, and the event is continued through the process of the following events. Neither exists apart from the other, and there can be no debate about the greater importance of one or the other.[1452]

Cobb represented Wesley's theology of perfect love as taking one of two

---

Maddox that believers must struggle under the plage of sin for much of their lives ["Recent Trends in Wesley Studies," 75]. Collins said that this paradigm of responsible grace emphasizes process by focusing on the possibility of attainment in a lengthy process rather that what graces can now be actualized ["State of Wesley Studies in North America," 20].

[1449]Maddox, *Responsible Grace*, 151. See also Oord and Lodahl, *Relational Holiness*, 136-140.

[1450]Coleman, "The World At Its Best," 141; 143.

[1451]Collins, "State of Wesley Studies in North America,"16. The free grace of God is revealed in creation, prevenient grace, and in regeneration and entire sanctification.

[1452]Culp, "Dialog with the Process Theology," 39-40.

forms — either a gradual growth in grace or a second instantaneous blessing. Cobb felt this second emphasis led to so many negative consequences that much of the Wesleyan movement abandoned the entire doctrine of perfection. Cobb felt if Wesley had limited himself to the first form, the problems his doctrine of perfection raised would have been less severe.[1453]

However, Michael Peterson held that there is more to the experience of sanctification than what process thought can explain. He observed that process philosophy was generally weak in its understanding of supernatural intervention and implied that the issues of crisis and process in sanctification can be better explained in terms of the work of God, not in terms of process theory.[1454]

The next generation of Nazarene theologians tended to define the core of holiness as love. We abide and participate in the life of God. Not only do they emphasize that holiness is an individual relationship with God, which is characterized by love, but that holiness is social and includes our relationship with the Church.[1455] Oord and Lodahl said that "no one, including God, is wholly independent or isolated from others. God is not entirely independent, because God is love, and love is expressed in relationships."[1456]

Michael Lodahl has developed this relational view into a process view of sanctification in which he described God as limited except in good intentions. The difference between God and man is a matter of quantity, not quality. God has more of what we have a little of. He is the risk taker who does not know the future.[1457] Yet he needs creation for his self actualization and thus creation is a big experiment driven by his love. In fact God did not create out of nothing (*ex nihilo*), for this is considered too coercive. Thus, Lodahl teaches that God creates out of love.

Lodahl defined sin as lovelessness, a lack or privation of authentic, loving relationship with God. Being filled with the Spirit does not describe God controlling us like robots, but it means that we are workers together with God.[1458]

[1453]Cobb, *Grace and Responsibility*, 109-110. In his lecture at Point Loma Nazarene University in Feb 2000, "Wesley the Process Theologian," Cobb argued for a third way between the determinism of Calvinism and the freedom of deism. While Wesley was not a process theologian, Cobb felt he was open to process thought on the basis of his emphasis on human responsibility.

[1454]Peterson, "Orthodox Christianity," 55.

[1455]Oord and Lodahl, *Relational Holiness* is a popular level introduction to this approach. See also Powell and Lodahl, *Embodied Holiness*.

[1456]Oord and Lodahl, *Relational Holiness*, 34-35.

[1457]Lodahl, *Story of God*, 88-89.

[1458]Lodahl, *Story of God*, 88-89.

So long as a person continues in a response of entire consecration he or she is sanctified. While the self is never destroyed, when we live in a relationship in which the love of God fills the heart, expelling sin, we are perfect in the sense we are being what we are created to be.[1459] "We are holy when we love wholly."[1460]

In his address "Revisioning Article X: Fifteen Changes in the Church of the Nazarene's Article on Entire Sanctification," Thomas Oord conceded some of the changes he advocated were cosmetic, but that other were substantial. While some of his suggestions would be an improvement, the overarching theology driving this reform is process theology. Oord suggested that the word "entire" be dropped. He advocated dropping the language that implies sanctification is a singular, completed work. He explained that two definite experiences may be descriptive for some, but should not be prescriptive for all. He held that sanctification is a component of and not an addition to salvation. He described sanctification as a relationship between God and creation. He affirmed a necessary role for both church and individual in the initiation and ongoing experience of sanctification. He described sanctification as God's empowering to love and avoid sin, not removal of a body of sin. Here his language goes beyond a rejection of the concept of eradication and seems to deny freedom from original sin. He advocated deleting mention of the baptism of the Spirit. He denied sanctification can be ultimately lost and said it should primarily be understood as love.[1461]

Ultimately, the process theory of sanctification is not inadequate because it deals with the progressive nature of sanctification. The older view was that sanctification was crisis with a view to a process. But now all crisis has been eradicated and the process is endless. Somehow the balance has been lost as the scale is tipped too far to the other side in order to compensate for excesses of the

---

[1459]Lodahl, *Story of God*, 196-197.

[1460]Oord and Lodahl, *Relational Holiness*, 131.

[1461]Online: Oord, "Revisioning Article X." His proposed statement on sin is also a concern. He stated that the Nazarene article on sin should address the efficacy of sanctification in response to sin. His proposal was "Sanctification cancels guilt, breaks sinful habits and propensities, and frees the Christian from living a life oriented toward sin." If this is defining *initial* sanctification, it would be a good statement. But it is ambiguous and if it is describing *entire* sanctification, it has lowed the biblical standard.

See also Oord's online "Eleven Suggestions for a Reformulated Article X," which is less controversial. Several of Oord's suggestions were approved at the 2009 general assembly [Online: Oord, "Changing Sanctification"].

Donald Metz fears that revisioning causes Nazarenes to reject their heritage. If they reject their heritage, they may lose their identity. If they lose their identity, they do not have any reason to exist as a church ["Theology in Crisis,"5].

past. Why do both extremes have to be Pelagian?

The problem is that this model is built upon evolutionary presuppositions in which God himself is portrayed as being in process. His sovereignty is diminished and our freedom is magnified. We resemble God and he needs us. It seems to lean toward Pelagianism in its denial of original sin and emphasis on human ability. Without a proper view of sin there cannot be a proper understanding of sanctification. Process sanctification seems to infer that we can evolve beyond sin and are in some process toward universalism. Yet sin is inevitably personal and our holiness is understood to be a corporate holiness. Yet how can there be a corporate holiness when corporate sin is denied. Romans 5:19 declares that through the disobedience of the one man, Adam, many were made sinners.[1462]

While the church remains susceptible to sin there are moments when we fully walk in the Spirit. This is about all that remains of the doctrine of Christian perfection. Thus, to accept the concept of progressive sanctification does not mean it is based upon process philosophy. Our perfection may be in process, but the perfection of God is absolute. According to a process theology application to the doctrine of Christian perfection, Matthew 5:48 would need to be amended to read, "Become perfect, therefore, as your heaven Father is becoming perfect." Is such a God in any position to make us what he has not yet become? How can he confirm us to his image, when he himself is a moving target?

Into the Future

William Bradford reported the farewell speech Pastor John Robinson made to the Pilgrims in 1620 before they left on the Mayflower,

> We are now ere long to part asunder, and the Lord knoweth whether ever he should live to see our faces again: but whether the Lord had appointed it or not, he charged us before God and his blessed Angels, to follow him no further then he followed Christ. And if God should reveal anything to us by any other instrument of his, to be as ready to receive it, as ever we were to receive any truth by his Ministry: For he was very confident the Lord had more truth and light yet to breake forth out of his holy Word. He took occasion also miserably to bewaile the state and condition of the Reformed churches, who were come to a period in Religion, and would goe no further then the instruments of their Reformation: As for example, the *Lutherans* they could not be drawne to goe beyond what *Luther* saw, for whatever part of

---

[1462]Reasoner, *Romans*, 195-198.

God's will he had further imparted and revealed to Calvin, they will rather die then embrace it. And so also, saith he, you see the Calvinists, they stick where he left them: A misery much to bee lamented; For though they were precious shining lights in their times, yet God had not revealed his whole will to them: And were they now living, saith hee, they would bee as ready and willing to embrace further light, as that they had received. Here also he put us in mind of our Church-Covenant (at least that part of it) whereby wee promise and covenant with God and one with another, to receive whatsoever light or truth shall be made known to us from his written Word: but withall exhorted us to take heed what we received for truth, and well to examine and compare, and weigh it with other Scriptures of truth, before we received it; For, saith he, *It is not possible the Christian world should come so lately out of such thick Antichristian darknesse, and that full perfection of knowledge should breake forth at once.*[1463]

We do not yet know what new movements will arise in the future, but they will come as the Spirit works within the Church. As we seek to evaluate men and movements, we need a grasp of what God has done throughout Church history.

The ministry of the Holy Spirit is to glorify Christ (John 16:14). Those truly led by the Spirit will put the emphasis on Christ and his atonement. The message of early Methodism was Christocentric. However, the holiness movement moved away from the Wesleyan balance and placed the emphasis on the Holy Spirit. In their desire to be led by the Spirit, they departed from the Word of God and emphasized experience.

Leo Cox conceded, "It seems probable that the teaching would have fared better if it had been favorably retained in the Methodist church. That there have been extremes in the holiness groups is readily admitted."[1464]

The American holiness movement explained Christian perfection in terms of power and taught it was the baptism with the Holy Spirit. Kenneth Grider taught Spirit baptism as one of the "non-negotiables" of holiness theology. Within one generation there were those within the holiness movement who concluded that speaking in tongues was the initial evidence of the baptism with the Holy Spirit. The holiness movement became a transition to pentecostalism and today there is a growing tolerance of glossolalia among holiness churches.

There had been glossolalia in the holiness movement before Charles Parham, but he was the first to insist there must be tongues if the experience is

[1463]Winslow, *Hypocrisie Unmasked.*

[1464]Cox, *Perfection*, 202-203.

really the baptism of the Holy Spirit. While the holiness movement did not accept tongues as the evidence of the Holy Spirit, it did teach an experience after regeneration called the baptism of the Holy Spirit. Often the physical manifestations allowed in the holiness tradition varied only in degree from their pentecostal counterpart. The emphasis of both movements was on "power," although Jesus taught that the ability to drive out demons and perform miracles does not necessarily prove you have ever been saved (Matt 7:21-23).

The Methodists emphasized purity of intention, not power to do the spectacular. The Wesleys emphasized the fruit of the Spirit, not the gifts of the Spirit. For them receiving the Spirit did not result in an emotional manifestation, but in an ethical transformation. Laurence Wood raised the question, "Can Pentecostals be Wesleyan? Then he gave a very misleading answer, "They can if Wesley was!"[1465]

And I object to the use of process philosophy to explain sanctification because theology should be based upon revelation, not philosophy. The holy life we must live is not emotionally based nor based on philosophy. It is based on biblical ethics. It is unnecessary to use process philosophy to explain the biblical process of sanctification. The Bible itself teaches sanctification is a process, but it does not base this doctrine on a philosophy which appeals to Pelagianism, pantheism, a mutable God who is not transcendent, or evolution as its foundation. The explanation of the process of sanctification, through the lens of process philosophy, ends up with an endless process and never a realization of the end. Thus to accept the concept of progressive sanctification does not mean it is based upon process philosophy. The concept of progressive sanctification is not in error because of its emphasis on the process of sanctification. The error is to project this process on the nature of the God who is sanctifying us.

The biggest problem with process thought is that God himself is in process. Our perfection may be in process, but the perfection of God is absolute. According to a process theology application to the doctrine of Christian perfection, Matthew 5:48 would need to be amended to read, "Become perfect, therefore, as your heaven Father is becoming perfect."

[1465]Wood, "Can Pentecostals Be Wesleyans?" 130; Wood, "Appreciative Reply," 163-172. For problems with Wood's methodology, see Dayton, "Response to Wood," 355-361, Dayton, "Rejoinder," 367-375, and "Final Round with Larry Wood,"265-270. Dayton contends that Wesley's thought is fundamentally christological and that one or two texts where Wesley seems to speak of pentecostal sanctification are hardly characteristic of Wesley. It is possible to attribute the work of entire sanctification to the Holy Spirit, who came at Pentecost, without holding that Pentecost was entire sanctification.

Ironically, Laurence Wood offered a very thorough critique of the areas in which pentecostalism erodes the distinctives of the Wesleyan tradition in "Third Wave of the Spirit," 110-140.

Is such a God in any position to make us what he himself has not yet become? And would such a God even know whether or not we will ever be made perfect in love? If God is the source of our holiness and he is in process, how can we know what holiness is? Thus, the goal of Christian perfection becomes a moving target. And the process is never complete. "There is no end. The end is not the end because God is luring us, over and over again, to perfect love."[1466] Surely, the Holy Spirit can lead us into something less ambiguous than this. We must look again to the Word of God.

John Wesley did not create a new doctrine of holiness. He drew from the Roman Catholic mystics, the Eastern Orthodox tradition, the Calvinistic Reformers and synthesized the best into the Methodist doctrine of Christian perfection. It is not necessary to argue for a theological label and reject every other approach which does not neatly fit our adopted label. Often one emphasis arises as a counterbalance to an extreme which has arisen within another tradition.

While Wesley appreciated the place of tradition, reason, and experience, his ultimate authority was the Word of God. Jesus prayed, "Sanctify them by the truth; your word is truth" (John 17:17). Adherence to the Word of God will keep us from danger and extremism. Obedience to the Word will keep us from sin and will drive us to seek holiness.

We may pray earnestly that God will bless our activities, but God cannot bless what is out of conformity to his Word. If God did bless and revive the institutional Church in many cases he would be perpetuating error. Rather than ask God to bless our program, we must get back to his plan and then we can expect his blessing. We must have a reformation before we will ever see a revival.

A. W. Tozer warned, "To beg for a flood of blessing to come upon a backslidden and disobedient Church is to waste time and effort. . . Unless we intend to reform we may as well not pray."[1467] David Wells declared,

> We need reformation, rather than revival. The habits of this modern world, now so ubiquitous in the evangelical world, need to be put to death, not given new life. They need to be rooted out, not simply papered over with fresh religious enthusiasm.[1468]

We must reaffirm not only the inerrancy, but the sufficiency of God's Word. We dare not add to nor take from the Scriptures. It is our sole authority for faith and practice. When John Wesley first was taught the doctrine of justification by faith, he went to his Greek New Testament "resolving to abide by 'the law and

---

[1466]Coleman, "World at its Best," 152.

[1467]Tozer, *Keys to the Deeper Life*, 17-18.

[1468]Wells, *No Place for Truth*, 301.

the testimony.'"[1469] A later generation of holiness leaders did not have the grasp of Bible doctrine and elevated their experience to a source of truth. This always leads to confusion. While experience may illustrate or confirm truth, it does not determine truth. They wrote books to prove entire sanctification as a second work of grace by giving the testimonies of famous Christians who had such a second crisis experience.[1470]

Kenneth Prior observed that a particular experience may be valid for the person who had it, but it is not necessarily meant as the norm for all Christians. "Still less should other Christians be urged to seek such crises for themselves. Surely the ground for what we believe about the Christian life is the Bible, not another person's experience. The only kind of experience we have any right to press on others is what Scripture clearly teaches."[1471]

If entire sanctification is true, it is true because it is taught in 1 Thessalonians 5:23, for example, not because of anyone's experience. Roman Catholics have claimed healing through the Virgin Mary, Mormons have spoken in unknown tongues, women have fainted under the influence of Father Divine, and Hindus have had powerful experiences of Krishna. Why stop with two experiences, when some have experienced three or six works of grace? Wynkoop called this "religious mathematics."[1472]

When a group of people unite on the basis of a common experience, they eventually develop their own tradition and tradition becomes a source of truth for them. Many small holiness denominations demand conformity of their members in areas of dress and lifestyle that cannot be substantiated by Scripture. Just like Jesus said of the Pharisees, they substitute their tradition for God's law (Matt15:1-9). In too many instances the holiness movement today is both legalistic and antinomian. It is no accident that at the same time the holiness movement was developing their emotional emphasis they were also adopting a new view of the atonement which taught that God was not bound to keep his own law. Greg Bahnsen observed:

> In this present day there is a grave heresy which has permeated large areas of the Christian Church; it claims that the Christian life of victory is produced solely by an inward guidance of the Holy Spirit. In matters of Christian ethics, whether it be in reference to how to love one's neighbor or to deciding if any

---

1469Wesley, *Journal*, 23 March 1738.

1470For example, Edman, *They Found the Secret*; Turner, *Witnesses of the Way*.

1471Prior, *Way of Holiness*, 102.

1472Wynkoop, *Theology of Love*, 199; 347.

> particular activity is wrong, many Christians claim that for moral authority they depend only upon the guidance of the Spirit. Whichever way the Spirit moves them is the way which they trust to be right.[1473]

R. C. Sproul stated, "God's kingdom will never come where His name is not hallowed. . . . It is foolish to look for the kingdom anywhere God is not revered."[1474] The early holiness movement believed that "a holy church would soon make a holy world."[1475] But all too quickly holiness was defined in terms of an emotional experience and it became the label, but not necessarily the lifestyle of a new movement. There has been a shift from ethical holiness to emotional holiness. The wife of a holiness evangelist writes:

> In traveling the length and breadth of this land within the parameters of evangelical and holiness churches, I am repeatedly appalled and grieved to find every type of sexual sin and perversion surfacing again and again among our clergy and lay leaders, but creating very little ripple to mar our pious complacency.[1476]

It is often amazing what "sanctified" people can charge to nerves and poor health.[1477] Just as evangelicalism short-changed the new birth through decisional regeneration, the holiness movement short-changed the doctrine of the new birth in order to exalt the second blessing. This blessing is described in terms of a duplication of pentecostal power instead of an emphasis on being conformed to the character of Christ. We need a new emphasis on holy living. The holy life is not characterized by peculiarity, but by practicality. It is not a spectacular emotional experience, but consistent Christian living which is sensitive to the needs of others. When it falls short, it does not cling to an empty profession, but seeks a fresh infilling of God's love.

[1473]Bahnsen, *Theonomy in Christian Ethics*, 168-169; see also White, *Beauty of Holiness*, 111-116.

[1474]Sproul, *Holiness of God*, 25.

[1475]Bishop Edmund Janes in Foster, *Christian Purity*, 13.

[1476]Lawrence, "I Protest!" 12.

[1477]Reasoner, "Indulgences,"4-5.

III. PRACTICAL THEOLOGY

CHAPTER 9
LIVING THE HOLY LIFE TODAY

In 1879 the Congregationalist pastor R. W. Dale preached at the Wesleyan conference at Birmingham, declaring, "If Methodism had carried out its doctrine of entire sanctification in public as well as in private life, it would have effected the most profound and beneficent ethical revolution modern history has known."[1478] At the bicentennial of Wesley's birth in 1903, R. W. Dale was quoted:

> There was one doctrine of John Wesley's — the doctrine of perfect sanctification — which ought to have led to a great and original ethical development; but the doctrine has not grown, it seems to remain where John Wesley left it. There has been a want of genius or the courage to attempt the solution of the immense practical questions which the doctrine suggests. The questions have not been raised, much less solved. To have raised them effectively, indeed, would have been to originate an ethical revolution which would have had a far deeper effect on the thought and life — first in England and then of the rest of Christendom — than was produced by the Reformation of the sixteenth century.[1479]

As we have seen from our survey of legalism, Keswick theology, dispensationalism, pentecostalism, charismaticism, the third wave, relational sanctification, and process sanctification across the twentieth century, the doctrine of entire sanctification was often confused and misguided. By the twentieth century, both the Calvinist and Wesleyan tradition of holiness went into eclipse,

---

[1478]Cited by Steele, *Gospel of the Comforter*, 297.

[1479]*Wesley Bicentennial*, 72-73. George Jackson made the citation from Dale, *Evangelical Revival*, 89. Woodrow Wilson, then president of Princeton University, also gave an address.

although there was a revival of neo-Calvinism in the second half.[1480]

In his evaluation of American evangelicalism at the end of the twentieth century, Dallas Willard concluded that the biblical teaching on personal salvation, with an emphasis on repentance and real transformation into the image of Christ, has been reduced to a simple divine pronouncement of forgiveness and the bestowal of a "ticket to heaven." A preoccupation with imputed righteousness, to the neglect of the Holy Spirit's actual impartation of holiness, has rendered much of evangelicalism powerless to bring about true Christian discipleship.[1481] Harold O. J. Brown wrote

> Evangelical theology knows that there must *be* sanctification; yet, with its awareness of the radical fallenness of man, it hesitates to say that anything so corrupted can be set apart for the purposes of God. If there is a weakness in the emerging evangelical consensus, it is doubtless at this point.[1482]

J. I. Packer wrote that historically holiness has been a leading mark of evangelical people. Yet, "As holiness is a neglected priority throughout the modern church generally, so it is specifically a fading glory in today's evangelical world."[1483] Rodney Clapp added, "Holiness is not a popular subject in contemporary theology."[1484]

John Stott also observed that there is an absence of the quest for holiness in expressions of evangelical faith. He noted that "holiness" carries a rather sanctimonious feel to it and therefore people do not like to be described as holy. "But the holiness of the new Testament is Christlikeness. I wish that the whole evangelical movement could consciously set before us the desire to grow in Christlikeness such as it is described in Galatians 5:22-23."[1485]

[1480]Bebbington, *Holiness*, 93; Hansen, "Young, Restless, Reformed," 32-38; Biema, "New Calvinism," 50.

[1481]Willard, *Divine Conspiracy*, 1-60. Francis Chan in *Crazy Love* deals with the lukewarmness of the church and calls it to become counter-culture. *Crazy Love* is an impassioned plea to take the call to discipleship seriously. His *Forgotten God* is a call to the Spirit-filled life. According to Chan the "forgotten God" is the Holy Spirit. Chan is not a theologian but is on target in regard to easy believism. Chan, who is a pastor, cites such writers as A. M. Hills and A. W. Tozer as his inspiration.

[1482]Brown, "Conservative Option," 466-467.

[1483]Packer, *Keeping in Step with the Spirit*, 99.

[1484]Clapp, "Tacit Holiness," 62.

[1485]Stafford, "Evangelism Plus," 99.

Elsewhere Stott sketched Christlikeness by stating that Jesus Christ is the one who emptied himself and humbled himself. He is the one who served other people in their need. He is the one who loved his enemies. He is the one who trusted and obeyed God.[1486]

Yet among the 76% of all Americans who say they are Christians, there is an appalling ignorance of what is meant by that profession. In 1990 a Gallup Poll indicated that 74% of Americans had made a personal commitment to Jesus Christ. Of that group, 95% considered it a "born again experience."[1487] Yet George Gallup, Jr. observed that most Americans who profess Christianity do not know the basic teachings of the faith and are open for anything that comes along. Gallup also observed, "You really don't find much difference between the churched and the unchurched in terms of cheating, tax evasion, and pilferage."[1488]

George Barna surveyed 152 separate items comparing the world and the church and concluded there is virtually no difference between the two. The divorce rate is the same and there was only one percent difference on gambling.[1489] Over 100 million Americans think they are going to heaven because they have repeated a salvation prayer.[1490] Yet it is claimed that 90% of those who have prayed such a prayer show no fruit of salvation.[1491] Even 70% of the homosexual population in the United States identify themselves as Christians and 27% of them say they are "born again."[1492]

Polls currently place the number of Americans who profess to be born again at 45%.[1493] George Barna felt 36% of these were "notional Christians" who think they are Christians but do not meet the definition because they do not see Jesus as the reason they will go to heaven.[1494] The common perception and the standard preaching on this subject are shallow indeed. Nothing is more desperately needed in the evangelical churches of America than to experience what they have long professed.

[1486]Stott, *Understanding Christ.*

[1487]Dobson, *Newsletter*, 3.

[1488]Jones, "Tracking America's Soul," 22-25.

[1489]Cited in *Family News From James Dobson*, 9.

[1490]McIntyre, *Graham Formula*, 107.

[1491]Comfort and Cameron, *School Of Biblical Evangelism*, 133.

[1492]Hertz, "God and Gays,"86.

[1493]Online: Barna, "State of the Church 2006."

[1494]The term is defined in *State of the Church 2002*, 98. The 2006 online report for 2006 gave the figure as 36%.

George Gallup, Jr. did another survey in which he identified less than 10% of the population as "a breed apart." He described them as more tolerant of people, more involved in charitable activities, more involved in practical Christianity and absolutely committed to prayer. He says they are "far, far happier than the rest of the population."[1495] If everyone is a Christian and a third of the population is born again, then we must adopt another term to distinguish genuine Christians; Gallup calls them saints. Perhaps they are the real Christians. In 2002 Barna determined that most likely true Christians comprise 5-8% of our population.[1496]

A nationwide survey conducted by The Barna Group in 2006 indicates that most adults remain confused, if not daunted, by the concept. Overall, three out of every four adults (73%) believe that it is possible for someone to become holy, regardless of their past. Only half of the adult population (50%), however, says that they know someone they consider to be holy. And that's more than twice as many as those who consider themselves to be holy (21%).

The views of born again Christians are not much different from the national averages. Among born again adults, three-quarters (76%) say it is possible for a person to become holy, regardless of their past. Slightly more than half of the born again group (55%) say they know someone whom they would describe as holy. And roughly three out of ten born agains (29%) say they are holy, which is marginally more than the national norm. The adults most likely to say they know someone they consider to be holy are those who describe holiness primarily as possessing a positive attitude toward God and life. Adults who think of holiness as a spiritual condition are among the least likely to identify anyone they know as holy.

When pressed to describe what it means to be holy, adults gave a wide range of answers. The most common reply was "I don't know," offered by one out of every five adults (21%). Other responses fell into categories such as "being Christ-like" (19%), making faith your top priority in life (18%), living a pure or sinless lifestyle (12%), and having a good attitude about people and life (10%). Other response categories included focusing completely on God (9%), being guided by the Holy Spirit (9%), being born again (8%), reflecting the character of God (7%), exhibiting a moral lifestyle (5%), and accepting and practicing biblical truth (5%). Once again, the responses of born again and non-born again adults were virtually identical.

Holiness is a matter embraced by the Christian Church, but it is not one that many Americans adopt as a focal point of their faith development. This is partially because barely one-third of Americans (35%) contend that "God expects

---

[1495]Gallup and Jones, "Uncovering America's Hidden Saints," 26.

[1496]Barna, *State of the Church 2002*, 95-97.

you to become holy." A larger share of the born again public believes God has called them to holiness (46%) but that portion remains a minority of the born again population.

The types of people most likely to say that God expects them to become holy are evangelicals, revolutionaries, people with a biblical world view, and ethnic born again adults. In each of these segments, a majority stated that they firmly believe God expects them to be holy. The survey results also indicated that young adults (39 or younger) are less likely than middle-aged and older adults to believe that God expects holiness of his people.

The new survey findings, when combined with existing knowledge about the state of faith in America, caused the survey's director, George Barna, to suggest that churches need to take this body of information seriously. "Realize that the results portray a body of Christians who attend church and read the Bible, but do not understand the concept or significance of holiness, do not personally desire to be holy, and therefore do little, if anything to pursue it. However, the data identify a remnant that understands holiness, wants to live a holy life, and is engaged in its pursuit. The challenge to the nation's Christian ministries is to foster a genuine hunger for holiness among the masses who claim they love God but who are ignorant about biblical teachings regarding holiness."

Pointing to data from several of his recent surveys on spiritual maturity in the U.S., Barna noted, "To initiate the education of people regarding holiness, we must arrest their attention and teach its importance. To align their hearts with the notion of being holy, we must move them away from a 'cheap grace' theology and replace people's self-absorption with focus on God and his ways. To help them pursue holiness, we must help them comprehend and accept biblical theology regarding God, Satan, the purposes of life on earth, the nature of spiritual transformation and maturity, and the necessity of bearing spiritual fruit."[1497]

Even though entire sanctification is possible, most who profess to be entire sanctified aren't, according to Steve DeNeff.[1498] E. Stanley Jones wrote, "Entire sanctification would be the life of Christ entirely dominant in the soul. I have no quarrel with this. My only quarrel is that the sanctification, as usually presented, has not been sufficiently entire. If it is to be entire, it should begin at the individual man and go as far as his relationships – social, economic, racial, and international – extend."[1499]

If we need to recover an emphasis on holiness, which approach to holiness

---

[1497]Online: Barna, "Concept of Holiness Baffles Most Americans."

[1498]DeNeff, *Whatever Became of Holiness?*, 78.

[1499]Jones, *Christ of Every Road*, 186.

is the right one? There are elements of truth within every emphasis.[1500] R. S. Foster acknowledged points of disagreement, primarily concerning the time and manner of entire sanctification, but observed that all agree there is such a thing. He concluded the points of disagreement are not as important as the points of agreement.[1501] There is a broad agreement in *Five Views on Sanctification*[1502] and *Christian Spirituality: Five Views of Sanctification.* Oden called the breadth of consensus on sanctification among evangelicals and Catholics "surprising."[1503]

Across two thousand years of theology certain propositions perennially crop up. Holiness begins at the new birth and yet those who are initially sanctified are exhorted to purify themselves from all pollution of the flesh and spirit (2 Cor 7:1). The indwelling Spirit will give us power and spiritual gifts, as well as purity. While all believers have the Spirit, we can have more of the Spirit. We are to be conformed to the image of Christ. We must be separate from the world. The sacraments are a means of grace. Whatever holiness we experience will be the result of faith, not works. If regeneration and entire sanctification are the gifts of God's free grace, then they can be received by faith now. Yet they will result in good works and spiritual fruit.

Biblical holiness is not limited to a personal experience; it has social implications. Nor is it for a few elect, but it is God's will for all believers. The biblical call to a holy life cannot be relegated to a future life or dismissed as an exclusive attribute of deity.

Flew surveyed the idea of perfection in church history and then issued this challenge:

> We reach, then, this broad conclusion, that the seeking of an ideal that is realizable in this world is essential to Christianity. It is essential to the corporate life of the Church that this principle should be enshrined at the heart of its doctrines, its hymns, its confessions of faith, it institutions. It is essential for the individual Christian that the goal set before him should be not merely conversion, not merely a life of service, but perfection. Of if the term is disliked, let it be Wesley's phrase — "perfect love", or "sanctity", or "holiness". If we have no hunger and

[1500]J. Edwin Orr wrote that there are three schools of thought concerning sanctification: positional sanctification is credited at regeneration, critical sanctification which believers enter, and progressive sanctification in which believers automatically grow. Orr concluded the Scripture teaches all three [*Full Surrender*, 73-82].

[1501]Foster, *Christian Purity*, 59.

[1502]See "Foreword,"Dieter, *Five Views on Sanctification*, 7.

[1503]Oden, *Life in the Spirit*, 216.

thirst after that righteousness which is Christ, we are not Christians . . . at all. Christianity is not Christianity unless it is aiming at Perfection.

Flew continued his argument stating, "The ultimate consideration is not whether human beings have ever attained, but whether it is God's will that they should." He concluded, "Since holiness is given in response to faith, and since faith is no mere single response but a continuous succession of responses to the divine Giver, it follows that the ideal life is a 'moment-by-moment' holiness."[1504] As we open ourselves more deeply to God's grace, love becomes more and more the dominant motive of our lives. The more this disposition is acted upon the freer we become. Augustine advised,

> Love, and do what thou wilt: whether thou hold thy peace, through love hold thy peace; whether thou cry out, through love cry out; whether thou correct, through love correct; whether thou spare, through love do thou spare: let the root of love be within, of this root can nothing spring but what is good.[1505]

Finally, Flew concluded that the truest evangelism is to preach the full ideal for which power is offered in this present life. A vast evangelistic advance can only be sustained if the Christian ideal for this life is steadily set forth in all its beauty and its fullness as being possible to attain by the grace of God. And if this principle is valid, to ignore it brings poverty and stagnation to the Church.[1506]

Perkins concluded that whatever meaning we give to perfection, we must make it applicable to the present as well as to the future. "We can never concede that the hindrance is purely that of flesh and blood. Our aim must be to give an ethical content to Faith and Hope, and to make it plain that the full assurance of Faith and of Hope tends to fill the whole nature with the Divine Love. . . . The problem set before us is to define the state of perfection in such a way as to leave open the vista of such a consummation in eternity, while at the same time using terms which are applicable to the possibilities of this present life."[1507]

The seventeen emphases which I have attempted to catalog in historical sequence overlap and inter-pollinate to the point it is difficult to categorize them

---

[1504]Flew, *Idea of Perfection*, 398; 402; 405. See also Sangster's chapter, "Is It Possible to Live a 'Moment-by-Moment Life?" in *Path to Perfection*, 109-112.

[1505]"Homilies on First John, Homily 7, ¶ 8, *NPNF*, First Series, 7:504.

[1506]Flew, *Ideal of Perfection*, xiii.

[1507]Perkins, *Evangelical Perfection*, 14; 17.

separately. The holy life can only be lived by faith in the provisions of Christ. Yet it involves grace and discipline. There must be absolute surrender, commitment, and dependence on God. Yet while it is submissive, it is not passive. We are made holy and are perfected in that holiness through the process of suffering and denial. Through such experiences, as well as the illumination of God's Word, we receive knowledge of ourselves. But while it produces a full assurance of understanding, it is not philosophical gnosticism. The mature Christian keeps the law of God, but is not legalistic. We must die to sin, mortify the flesh, and separate ourselves from the world. Sin is mortified as the Spirit crucifies the flesh daily. The holy life is to be lived within the institutions of marriage and the Church, institutions which God ordained. We will not be made holy outside the ministry of the Church, yet we must cultivate personal discipline. We must submit to the rule of God's law and yet always be motivated by divine love. The holy life can never be lived without sanctifying grace and the power of the Holy Spirit. It is a relationship, not a static state. It is both a separation from sin and a positive influence in the world.

Yet these individual emphases, when taken to the extreme, can easily lead either to a works orientation, ritualism, faith as a cloak which covers unrighteousness, no impetus to seek more of God, or the perception that sanctification is an act of the will, emotionalism, or fanaticism. While Romans 8:14-16 promises that the indwelling Spirit will assure and guide, this sometimes leads to the charge of mysticism. Holiness has often been reduced to something which is named and claimed. Holiness is often propagated under sectarianism and in isolation from believers who are seeking the same thing from a different framework. Yet the contemplative may forget the needs of the world. The moralist may focus on sin and neglect compassion. The charismatic may seek the gifts instead of the Giver. The social activist may forget to pray. The Bible preacher may emphasis the centrality of the Scripture, but preach without the anointing of the Spirit. The ascetic may reduce Christianity to a discipline and reject the joy of life in Christ. The relational Christian may rely on the community of faith and lose his own individual identity. The Christian leader may focus on spiritual activities and yet forget he is still one of the flock.

In 1768 John Wesley wrote Charles confessing to be at "wit's end" with regard to the doctrine of Christian perfection because some of his lay preachers had distorted it. He asked, "Shall we go on in asserting perfection against all the world? Or shall we quietly let it drop?"[1508] Maddox concluded that

> Wesley was convinced that the Christian life did not have to remain a life of continual struggle. He believed that both Scripture and Christian tradition attested that God's loving grace

[1508]Wesley, *Letter*, 14 May 1768; 14 June 1768.

can transform our lives to the point where our own love for God and others becomes a 'natural' response. Christians can aspire to take on the disposition of Christ, and live out that disposition within the constraints of our human infirmities. To deny this possibility would be to deny the sufficiency of God's empowering grace — to make the power of sin greater than that of grace.[1509]

In another context Maddox wrote,

> Perhaps the best way to capture Wesley's affectional view of entire sanctification, then, is to say that he was convinced that the Christian life did not have to remain a life of perpetual struggle. He believed that our sin-distorted human lives can be responsibly transformed through God's loving grace to the point where we are truly freed to love God and other consistently. Christians can aspire to take on the disposition of Christ, and to live out that disposition within the constraints of our human infirmities. To deny this possibility would be to deny the sufficiency of God's empowering grace — to make the power of sin greater than that of grace.[1510]

According to Romans 5:20 grace is more powerful than sin. If the sinful nature of humanity is extensive, darkening our intellect, alienating our emotions, and perverting our will, then the sanctifying grace of God must not be reduced to anything less than a wholistic realignment of our total personality.

We are faced with the same question today that Wesley asked. We are now in a time of reevaluation. How do we best articulate this biblical doctrine? The contemporary holiness movement is at a crossroad. At one time Methodist chapels were being built at the rate of nearly two every day.[1511] Methodism was once the dominant religion in America. American Methodism, under C. C. McCabe, the secretary of the Methodist Extension Society, built more than one Methodist church for every day in the year and proposed to make it two a day.

Today all the holiness groups combined amount to .7% of the American

---

[1509]Maddox, *Responsible Grace*, 188.

[1510]Maddox, "Reconnecting the Means to the End," 44; Maddox, "Holiness of Heart and Life," 154.

[1511]Tyerman, *Life and Times of Wesley*, 1:3-13.

population[1512] and they continue to divide. Will they try to recapture the momentum of another era by embracing the charismatic emphasis? Or will they rediscover the balance of early Methodism?

Just as the holiness movement claimed it was promoting Wesley's doctrine while it was moving away from it, so the modern charismatic movement has attempted to rewrite Wesley. Wesley was not a charismatic and his theology will not logically lead to pentecostalism. His class meetings were not "tarry meetings" or charismatic prayer meetings. Their purpose was to provide accountability and to encourage practical holiness.

While the holiness people claim to be Wesleyan, all too often they have a spirit of antinomianism and anarchy. They are often suspicious of education and theology. They have sometimes discounted doctrine and the sacraments. They have sometimes rejected church organization and authority. They have tended toward emotional demonstrations in worship, extra-biblical standards of dress, faith healing and speculative prophecy. The move toward emotional experience is often a move away from ethical holiness. John Wesley counseled:

> Try all things by the written word, and let all bow down before it. You are in danger of [fanaticism] every hour, if you depart ever so little from Scripture; yea, or from the plain, literal meaning of any text, taken in connection with the context.[1513]

Today each major Wesleyan denomination is facing this same question, "Shall we go on in asserting perfection against all the world? Or shall we quietly let it drop?" The old Free Methodist Article of Religion on Entire Sanctification read:

> Entire sanctification is that work of the Holy Spirit, subsequent to regeneration, by which fully consecrated believers, upon exercise of faith in the atoning blood of Christ, are cleansed in that moment from all inward sin and empowered for service. The resulting relationship is attested by the witness of the Holy Spirit and is maintained by faith and obedience. Entire sanctification enables believers to love God with all their hearts, souls, strength, and minds, and their neighbors as themselves,

---

[1512]In 1995 the U. S. population was 262 million. According to Barrett, Kurian, and Johnson, *World Christian Encyclopedia* the holiness movement in the U. S. was 1.9 million [2:662]. Worldwide the holiness movement was 7.2 million.

[1513]Wesley, *Works*, 11:429. Wesley's word was *enthusiasm*.

and it prepares them for greater growth in grace.[1514]

In July 2007, delegates to the general conference of the Free Methodist Church of North America voted in favor of a proposed amendment to the Article of Religion on Entire Sanctification. At the World Conference in 2003 the amendment was referred to the Council of Bishops for review with power to act and put into referendum. Such constitutional changes or referendums are rare, and require a 2/3 vote to approve by each of the denomination's twelve general conferences as well as full approval by the World Conference. This was approved in March 2010 and became the new ¶ 119 in the Articles of Religion of the Free Methodist Church.

Notice the emphasis on work of the Holy Spirit, yet the absence of Spirit-baptism language. The new article, as revised by the Council of Bishops in September 2005, reads:

> Sanctification is that saving work of God beginning with new life in Christ whereby the Holy Spirit renews His people after the likeness of God, changing them through crisis and process, from one degree of glory to another, and conforming them to the image of Christ. As believers surrender to God in faith and die to self through full consecration, the Holy Spirit fills them with love and purifies them from sin. This sanctifying relationship with God remedies the divided mind, redirects the heart to God, and empowers believers to please and serve God in their daily lives. Thus, God sets His people free to love Him with all their heart, soul, mind, and strength, and to love their neighbor as themselves.

"While affirming the Wesleyan doctrine of entire sanctification, the revised article reframes our understanding of holiness within the entire work of salvation," according to Bishop David Kendall, a participant in the amendment process. "I am convinced that we are now on firmer biblical ground from which to engage our culture more effectively," Kendall said. "What's notable is that we have broadened our articulation of holiness beyond simply a focus on a second crisis experience, a second form of commitment," he added. "We still affirm that, but we are acknowledging that the Holy Spirit is at work to grow us up in Christ and make us like Christ from the very beginning … The commitments we make throughout our life, including the climactic one that settles the bent of our life, are

---

[1514]Cited by Taylor, *Finished Foundation*, 14. This book is an exposition of the ten "foundation stones" comprising Article 13 in the Articles of Religion of the Free Methodist Church.

all set within a lifelong process of conformity to Jesus."[1515]

Yet a follow-up article in the denominational magazine conceded that the Free Methodist Church had largely abandoned its early holiness emphasis, adopting instead a "live and let live" attitude.[1516]

Ken Schenck also reported on changes within The Wesleyan Church.[1517] I have documented shifts within the Church of the Nazarene.[1518] An ecumenical gathering of holiness leaders produced The Holiness Manifesto which declares

> God is holy and calls us to be a holy people.
>
> God, who is holy, has abundant and steadfast love for us. God's holy love is revealed to us in the life and teachings, death and resurrection of Jesus Christ, our Savior and Lord. God continues to work, giving life, hope and salvation through the indwelling of the Holy Spirit, drawing us into God's own holy, loving life. God transforms us, delivering us from sin, idolatry, bondage, and self-centeredness to love and serve God, others, and to be stewards of creation. Thus, we are renewed in the image of God as revealed in Jesus Christ.
>
> Apart from God, no one is holy. Holy people are set apart for God's purpose in the world. Empowered by the Holy Spirit, holy people live and love like Jesus Christ. Holiness is both gift and response, renewing and transforming, personal and communal, ethical and missional. The holy people of God follow Jesus Christ in engaging all the cultures of the world and drawing all peoples to God.
>
> Holy people are not legalistic or judgmental. They do not pursue an exclusive, private state of being better than others. Holiness is not flawlessness, but the fulfillment of God's intention for us. The pursuit of holiness can never be exhausted.
>
> God wants us to be, think, speak, and act in the world in a

---

[1515]Florian, "Lead On," 22. I was given a preliminary draft in October 2003 and asked for an evaluation. I felt it was an improvement over the original statement, which reflected too much of the American holiness movement's paradigm of sanctification as a state, without seeing the progressive nature of the work of sanctification. Yet the new statement, while correctly emphasizing the progressive nature of sanctification, does not make an adequate distinction between initial and entire sanctification.

[1516]Munshaw, "Keepers of the Flame," 8-11.

[1517]See p. 621.

[1518]See p. 760.

Christ-like manner. We invite all to embrace God's call to: be filled with all the fullness of God in Jesus Christ — Holy Spirit-endowed co-workers for the reign of God; live lives that are devout, pure, and reconciled, thereby being Jesus Christ's agents of transformation in the world; live as a faithful covenant people, building accountable community, growing up into Jesus Christ, embodying the spirit of God's law in holy love; exercise for the common good an effective array of ministries and callings, according to the diversity of the gifts of the Spirit, practice compassionate ministries, solidarity with the poor, advocacy for equality, justice, reconciliation, and peace; and care for the earth, God's gift in truth to us, working in faith, hope, and confidence for the healing and care of all creation. By the grace of God, let us covenant together to be a holy people.[1519]

Chris Bounds said of this attempt,

Recently, a group of Wesleyan holiness denominational leaders and scholars issued a Holiness Manifesto, contending for the necessity of a reminted statement and emphasis on sanctification in the twenty-first century. While they offered a helpful critique of contemporary evangelicalism and addressed the imperative of a socially driven, mission oriented expression of holiness, they were not able to offer any specifics as to what entire sanctification or holiness is, beyond the statement that "Holiness is Christ likeness."The Manifesto is indicative of the contemporary Wesleyan-Holiness tradition's inability to articulate clearly, succinctly, and persuasively her understanding of holiness.[1520]

[1519]Kevin Mannoia, a bishop in the Free Methodist Church is chairman of the Wesleyan Holiness Study Project, Azusa, CA, February 2006. See also Mannoia, "Wesleyan Holiness Study Project,"265-268; Thorsen, "Holiness Manifesto," 209-224. According to Diane Leclerc, the document's creators were comfortable with a statement that never mentioned secondness. Also, the first half of the document was apparently created entirely and solely by the document's editor Kevin Mannoia, without any input from the committee. but it was affirmed by the group. Diane didn't actually do a paper, but was interviewed by George Lyons at the Revisioning Holiness Conference held at Northwest Nazarene University, February 8-10, 2007, about her work in the Holiness Manifesto project. This information was confirmed by Thomas Jay Oord at Northwest Nazarene University in personal email correspondence [13 December 2007].

[1520]Online: Bounds, "What is Entire Sanctification?"

While the purpose of the book by the same title, which was published two years later, is to promote holiness, there is no attempt made to prop up the old holiness movement or to create a new movement.[1521] The book contains a dozen essays which argue that the concept of holiness is relevant in the twenty-first century. There is concern expressed that "this next generation could in fact be the generation that abandons belief in sanctification" unless it can be adapted to a postmodern culture.[1522] Yet for this new generation, "doctrinal purity is second to the relational nature of faith in Christian community."[1523]

Christian perfection or ethical holiness is not a new doctrine. It was not discovered within the last one hundred years. Neither does the holiness movement have any monopoly upon it. Within every tradition is an attempt to struggle with what this involves. Stephen Seamands declared that while the call to holiness has not changed, the way we present holiness must change. We must go back to the Bible and a fresh encounter with Jesus Christ.[1524] A survey of biblical prayers, promises, commands, and examples define the purpose of God's sanctifying grace:

- A heart cleansed from all unrighteousness (1 John 1:9). This ethical purity is implied in terms such as blameless and righteousness.
- Maturity of character (1 John 2:13-14). We are no longer children or young men, but spiritual fathers.
- It is the fruit of the Spirit perfected (Gal 5:22-23). It is an increase in love and all the fruit of the Spirit. "Every branch in me that bears fruit, he purges it that it may bring forth more fruit" (John 15:2). The fruit of the Spirit can increase in quality and quantity.
- Perfect love; an increase in love and all the fruit of the Spirit. It is a holy love; love expelling sin and governing both the heart and life. The term "perfect love" is used in 1 John 2:5; 4:12, 17, 18 (twice). 1 Corinthians 13 is the portrait of one who has the love of God perfected.
- A greater delight in God's law and a greater consistency in keeping it; a greater consistency in doing all to the glory of God.
- A greater sense of God's favor; a full assurance of faith.
- A greater consistency in performing our social, civil, and religious duties.
- A greater sensitivity toward spiritual realities and a greater compassion for his neighbor (Matt 22:37-39). More sensitivity toward our neighbor

---

[1521]Thorsen, "Integrated Streams of Holiness," 75.

[1522]Mannoia and Thorsen, *Holiness Manifesto*, 111; 129; 149; 200. See also Thorsen, "Holiness in Postmodern Culture,"123-135.

[1523]Mannoia, "Introduction," 4.

[1524]Seamands, *Holiness of Heart and Life*, 16.

and a purer ethic in our relationships; a maturity of character.[1525]

- Perfection of motive (Matt 22:37). It is a single eye (Matt 6:22). It is a united will. One thing I do (Phil 3:13). According to Søren Kierkegaard, "Purity of heart is to will one thing."[1526] It is a passion for righteousness and a compassion for men.[1527]
- A realignment of attitudes, healing of damaged emotions, in which we are made whole (2 Cor 13:9; Eph 3:16; Heb 13:20-21).
- An establishing grace which causes us to be rooted, grounded, and stable (1 Peter 5:10).
- The enlargement of our capacity to receive a greater measure of the Spirit (Eph 3:19; 5:18)
- A maturity in knowledge, spiritual insight, discernment (Eph 1:17; Phil 1:4-6; 3:10).
- A greater consciousness of God. It is a greater sense of God's presence, his acceptance and favor; a full assurance of faith and hope (Col 2:2; Heb 10:22). It is a life of confidence based upon a full assurance of understanding, faith, and hope, as well as a perfect love.
- A greater conviction of the substance of God's will and submission to his will.
- A greater comprehension of the Lordship of Christ
- A deeper surrender based upon a deeper revelation of ourselves (compare Rom 6:13-19; 12:1).
- A more perfect obedience based upon a greater knowledge of God and of the substance of the will of God.
- The possibility of unbroken praise to God, unbroken communion with God, unbroken awareness of God (1 Thess 5:16-18).
- The completion of sanctification, a restoration fo the full image of God (Rom 8:29; 2 Cor 7:1).
- It produces a holy optimism (1 Cor 13:7), a holy joy which is thankful in all circumstances (1 Thess 5:16). We can maintain a positive attitude while persevering.
- It produces a more consistent prayer life (1 Thess 5:17).
- It results in the ability to live in peace with one another (Heb 12:14).

[1525]Hunt, *Letters on Sanctification*, 7.

[1526]Dunning explained that this purity was intentional and that Kierkegaard distinguished purity from maturity ["Toward a New Paradigm," 161-162].

[1527]Jones, *Christ of the Mount*, 74.

- It produces a greater respect for and submission to spiritual authority and for the preaching of God's Word (1 Thess 5:19-20).
- A greater realization of our privilege, identity, and power (Eph 1:18-19).
- Death to selfishness - not self; death to carnal traits, not to personality
- A greater sense of God favor and assurance that we are pleasing God
- The characteristics described in 1 Corinthians 13:4-7 displacing all sin
- A heart cleansed from all unrighteousness (1 John 1:9).
- The mind of Christ; Christlikeness - especially humility and meekness.
- It is spiritual health.

Diane Leclerc wrote that entire sanctification is restoration to what God originally intended us to be. It is a completion that prepares us to live in communion with God forever. It is a foretaste of the kingdom of God. It puts us in a right relationship with God, others, self, and the world.[1528]

Anxiety disorders are the most common mental illnesses in America, surpassing depression and alcoholism. Edmund Bourne concluded that anxiety arises from a state of disconnection. And yet Christian assurance should produce a connection to God in which the peace of God rules our heart.[1529] John MacMillan declared, "Discouragement and depression are of the devil. Good cheer and victory are the right of those in Christ."[1530] James Mudge described the perfect life.

> It is the full assurance of faith and of hope. There is in it a deeper satisfaction, a larger bliss, a more abiding peace, a fuller contentment, a sweeter rest than can be found on the lower levels. It imparts courage in the face of danger, tranquility in commotion, independence of the world, indifference toward earthly possessions and positions, cheerfulness in view of the future triumph over every foe. Those in this path find duty turned into delight; they have an enthusiastic attachment to the Master, which He cordially reciprocates; they sing at their tasks because He is so close to them as they toil; they are not dependent on circumstances and worldly amusements for their pleasure. Their obedience is not a matter of calculation of

---

[1528]Leclerc, *Discovering Christian Holiness*, 186-187.

[1529]Anderson and Miller, *Freedom From Fear*, 13; 21; 25; 49.

[1530]King, *Believer with Authority*, 44.

> hesitation. They have settled it once for all that every command is to be promptly heeded. They find nothing too small to be of importance in the glad service of their King, nothing too hard to be welcomed for the sake of Him who appoints it. Constant and intimate is their fellowship with God and their glad recognition of His glorious presence. They live in sunshine, they are cheery, they take their religion with relish. They find an ever increasing conformity to the divine will, and ever increasing fondness for prayer, and they draw water with joy out of all the wells of salvation.[1531]

C. C. Cary preached about a perfect love which delivered from a slavish fear of God. We are not slaves nor do we dread God. We are delivered from a fear of want through a perfect faith in the Divine Providence. We are delivered from a fear of man. We are not afraid of what men may say nor think so long as God is pleased with us. We are delivered from a morbid fear of death. Not that we want to die, but perfect love makes us ready to live or die. We are delivered from the fear of evil and the vain imagination of impending calamity. We can be quiet, "without fear of harm" (Prov 1:33).[1532] Adam Clarke wrote similarly that the fear of *want*, the fear of *death*, and the fear or terror of *judgment* were all inconsistent with perfect love.[1533]

Perkins defined the marks of perfection as freedom, joy, expansion, and lordship. "There is a joyful sense of deliverance from the bondage of sin, and even from the burden of the world, in so far as that burden oppresses the soul. . . . Wherever the good tidings of great joy are proclaimed, they increase the beatitude of humanity. This is especially the mark of the higher state, in which the soul's freedom from sin and the world, and its bondage toward God, are more clearly recognized."

Perkins referred to Paul's words, "As sorrowful, yet always rejoicing" (2 Cor 6:10). While we must not overlook the sadness which accompanies all progress, this sadness often prevails where there is a specific denial of the possibility of attainment in this present life. Examples may be seen in the lives of

---

[1531]Mudge, *Perfect Life*, 149-150.

[1532]Cary, *Twentieth Century Holiness Sermons*, 81-83.

[1533]Clarke, *Commentary*, 6:921.

John Bunyan and David Brainerd.[1534] Even Augustine was convinced that such experiences of heavenly bliss, if they come at all, are momentary flashes in this present life. "The result may be seen in the gloom which rested on his theology, and which has so gravely and so detrimentally affected the Church."

The idea of expansion is that of continual, even eternal progress. "Spiritual Perfection in its very nature cannot be static." By "lordship" Perkins means "authority." We may say of the disciples what we say of the Master, "that their rule takes its authority from the love which fills their soul."[1535]

Every true Christian hungers for these dynamics. Some theologies offer little encouragement. Yet the Calvinist Robert Murray M'Cheyne prayed, "Lord, make me as holy as a pardoned sinner can be made."[1536] The Wesleyan emphasis is the most optimistic, teaching that these hungers are God-given. I am intrigued by the titles of Asbury Lowry, an old Methodist writer, who wrote *Positive Theology* (1853) and *Possibilities of Grace* (1884). It is unfortunate that, at times, the doctrine of holiness ever became associated with fanaticism and legalism.

God can save completely or to the uttermost (Heb 7:25). This phrase means salvation is to the farthest extent, to the greatest degree, to the most distant point. Full salvation is not only freedom from the guilt, the bondage, and the power of sin, but cleansing from the pollution and nature of sin and ultimately deliverance from the very presence of sin.

But how much of this complete salvation may be experienced in this life? Thomas Oden replied that the doctrine of sanctification is not primarily a teaching about the human capacity as such, but about the sufficiency of God the Spirit to transform all human capacities.[1537] "Now to him who is able to do immeasurably more than all we ask or imagine, according to his power that is at work with us" (Eph 3:20). William Burt Pope argued that the perfecting work of the Spirit ceases when Christ returns. It dishonors the Spirit to teach that he cannot

---

[1534]Wesley admired Brainerd and suggested reading Brainerd's biography as a means of reviving the work of God where it is in decay [*Works*, 8:328]. Yet in his diary Brainerd conceded that he never expected to make any considerable attainments in holiness in this life. In this instance, however, his experience was superior to his theology.

[1535]Perkins, *Evangelical Perfection*, 258-262.

[1536]Bonar, *Memoirs of McCheyne*, p. 209.

[1537]Oden, *Life in the Spirit*, 230.

administer the benefits of a perfect atonement in this life.[1538]

We can love God with all our heart, and soul, and mind, and strength and love our neighbor as ourselves. This occurs as we trust Christ moment-by-moment and are moment-by-moment cleansed by his blood and filled with his Spirit. Yet there will be moments when we realize an attitude, a word, or a deed was not Christlike. These may be revelations of deeper needs and become crisis points when we repent as believers and surrender anew to his Lordship.

This sanctifying work of the Spirit occurs in all true believers, whether or not they embrace Wesleyan theology. While it is not necessary to adhere to a particular theological system to experience this sanctifying grace, it is the duty of the Church to counsel, teach, and provide spiritual guidance for believers. Packer noted that we must maintain a balance between knowing, feeling, and doing. There must be a balance in our concern for truth, for experience, and for action.[1539] The Wesleyan synthesis is the most adequate frame work in which to diagnose spiritual needs, discern spiritual unbalance, and direct spiritual formation.

Larry Crabb has been advocating an expression of relational holiness as opposed to a spiritual formation model with involves experiencing God subjectively. He says self-centeredness is the cause of our problems. We need to focus on what God's mission is in us and not on our problems.[1540]

We are all out of balance because of the Fall. Christian perfection brings balance to life. Philippians 4:4-13 is a wonderful passage dealing with Christian maturity. Pope warned of two opposite errors about holiness. One is to regard it as attainable outside of Christ. The unregenerate waste vast amounts of energy in pursuit of these virtues only to have it thwarted by their sinfulness. The other error, after regeneration, is to neglect the obligations of morality and carelessly presume on a vicarious salvation from sin. Pope emphasized that the words "think on these things" (v 8) carry a strong injunctive to the regenerate.[1541]

Notice especially v 5, let your "moderation" be known. The *New International Version* translates this word "gentleness," but the real meaning of ἐπιεικής (*epieikes*) is reasonableness, tolerance, consideration, a magnanimous spirit. It has something to do with balance.

This issue of balance means that somehow the Holy Spirit works to bring

---

[1538]Pope, *Compendium*, 3:53-54.

[1539]Packer, *Rediscovering Holiness*, 167-170.

[1540]Crabb, "Spiritual Formation or Relational Holiness."

[1541]Pope, *Sermons,* "The Meditation and Practice of Holiness," 216.

us to a wholistic synchrony. To realize all that God intended us to be is to be fully human. When this concept is described in terms of moral development it can be expressed in evolutionary terms. Wynkoop warned us not to substitute developmental theories for the "two-ness" of Wesleyan theology or let attractive new trends lead us out of the narrow way.[1542] Samuel Powell noted the connection between holiness and moral development in Wesley's use of certain words, such as "temper" and "affection."[1543] Yet Powell questioned whether character can be equated with what the Bible emphasizes as holiness. Thus, Powell concludes that holiness must be distinguished from moral development.[1544]

However, in his research on moral development, Donald Joy began with the presupposition that morality originates outside of humanity, but that human morality is bestowed as the "image of God." The first level is a prudence in which self-interest dominates. The second level is a sense of "oughtness" or a conventional sense of right and wrong. The third level involves an internal control. "The authority that once lay outside has been written on the motives or 'the heart.'" These three levels correspond to Wesley's categories of the natural man, the legal man, and the evangelical man.[1545]

Other moral development philosophers, such as Erik Erikson recognized the goal is adulthood which is creative and productive, which contributes to the development of oncoming generations. Each state of development has a particular crisis. If that crisis is not faced, growth is impeded. Erikson recognized that this personal development can give into a tragic stagnation in which the individual devotes their energy to remedy or reclaim what was lost or never gained in their own earlier lives.[1546] Lawrence Kohlberg described stage seven of moral development as the highest level of maturity religiously, morally, humanistically, and mystically. The highest level for James Fowler was stage six or

---

[1542]Wynkoop, "Wesleyan Theology and Christian Development," 36-41.

[1543]See Wesley's *Notes*, 528, where he distinguished between transient affections and a fixed temper. This is discussed by Maddox, *Responsible Grace*, 69; 288.

[1544]Powell, "Contribution to Wesleyan Understanding,"167-168.

[1545]Joy, "Toward Christian Holiness," 207-231.

[1546]Fowler, *Becoming Adult*, 28-29. Using Erikson's paradigm, Newport argued that glossalalia should be understood as an immature or childish stage of religion and that agape love is a higher level ["Contemporary Glossalalia Movement,"115-117].

Universalizing Faith, including a commitment to the Kingdom of God, the unity of all persons, and the fulfillment of human rights and justice.[1547]

While writers in this field may come from any religious background and disagree on the best paradigm, the significance of their work is that they all seem to agree on the ideal of perfection — even if they are unable to explain how this development occurs except through a humanistic model. James Fowler describes the goal as a decentration from self and a resting of our hearts in which we are no longer driven by fear. In fact he even cites 1 John 4:18.[1548]

Joy also wrote about a hierarchically integrative trajectory in the beatitudes.[1549] But Joy also wrote about an arrested development. While this moral failure is typically explained as underdevelopment, a person may discontinue or arrest progress at any point.[1550] Thus it seems that the field of psychology is attempting to describe the process of perfection through the imperfect lens of natural revelation. Their attempt to research stages of growth is an empirical attempt to quantify what some of the earlier mystics attempted to describe in more spiritual language.

Rob Staples concluded that the biblical picture of a Christian, such as Ephesians 4:13, will not differ greatly from the picture of a mature person presented by responsible psychologists. "The only difference is that the Bible knows such personhood to be possible only by the grace of God."[1551] Richard S. Taylor described Christian maturity as coping grace which is manifested in a more relaxed manner, a happier disposition, a humbler spirit, greater interest in others, and a new capacity to empathize.[1552]

The highest level of the Methodist society was the select society. Wesley explained, "They had no need of being encumbered with many rules, having the best rule of all in their hearts. No peculiar directions were therefore given to

---

[1547]Hanford, "Relationship Between Fowler and Kohlberg," 306-310.

[1548]Fowler, *Becoming Adult,* 68-70.

[1549]Joy, "Wesleyan Theology and Developmental Structuralism," 83. See also Wesley, "Sermon on the Mount, I," 1.1; Urquhart, *Holy Fire*, pp. 124-147.

[1550]Joy, "Kohlberg Revisited," 51-55.

[1551]Staples, "Sanctification and Selfhood," 12. See also Murphree, *Love Motive*,10-13 for a brief reference to the psychology of Freud, From, Erikson, Rogers, Sullivan. Murphree holds that God works through structures that He Himself has built into human personality.

[1552]*Theological Formulation*, 225.

them," except a commitment to confidentiality, submission, and voluntary contribution. "Everyone here has an equal liberty of speaking, there being none greater or less than another. I could say freely to these, when they were met together, 'Ye may all prophesy one by one' (taking that word in its lower sense), 'that all may learn and all may be comforted.'"[1553] This is how Christian maturity looks.

While a popular, motivational writer like Wayne Dyer writes about the power of intention which enables us to connect to the field of energy,[1554] only the Holy Spirit can purify our motives so that we can realize all that God has intended us to be.

The New Testament uses the word ψυχή (*psuche*) over a hundred times. It is often translated "soul"or "life." Sometimes it has reference to the mind. The modern field of psychology is the study of the mind and behavior. Jesus is our "wonderful counselor" (Isa 9:6). However, the Great Physician often works through human physicians and the Great Counselor can also work through human counselors. A counselor is a temporary assistant to the Holy Spirit. The goal of biblical counseling is holy living. We have all received distorted views of God from those who have imperfectly reflected God. Thus, we need spiritual healing.

While humanistic psychology is based upon human reason as the source of truth, they may have truth which is consistent with Scripture but goes beyond it in specifics. Thus, we do not reject all psychology, but we reject psychological assumptions which are contrary to God's Word. Larry Crabb rejects a need-centered, anthropocentric understanding of human nature.

> We are already secure and significant in Christ. Our sins have been forgiven and we've been called and equipped to advance His kingdom. We have what we need to do what we should do. No one can rightly plead poor self-esteem or a damaging background or difficult circumstances as an excuse for ungodly living.[1555]

Crabb believes that soul care can best be provided within spiritual community. Yet church, as most Americans define it, no longer holds any hope

---

[1553]Wesley, "Plain Account of the People Called Methodists,"8.4; *BE Works*, 9:270. See also Watson, *Early Methodist Class Meeting*, 120.

[1554]Dyer, *Power of Intention*.

[1555]Crabb, *Safest Place on Earth*, 7.

for Crabb in his deep desire to experience more of God. Crabb describes the soul as having two rooms. The lower room is our lower nature. The upper room is the new self which Christ gives us. The four provisions of the new covenant are: a new purity, a new identity, a new inclination, and a new power. If these passions are aroused in us, as we meet with each other, we are part of a spiritual community. This spiritual community is the safest place on earth and the place of greatest danger. Most often we are disappointed, but we must journey on because lives are changed when we reach the sacred place of vulnerability.

Drawing from Madame Guyon and Teresa of Avila, Crabb invites us to enter the upper room and meet Christ. People long for relationship. It exists in the upper room. As a professional psychotherapist he has spent most of his professional life trying to understand why the furniture has been so poorly arranged in people's lower rooms. He describes the furnishings of the lower room as a passion for self, a passion to control, a passion to define, a passion to perform. The furnishings of the upper room are what Teresa called the seventh mansion: a passion to worship, a passion to trust, a passion to grow, and a passion to obey.

Thus, brokenness is the pathway to a deeper relationship with God. Through church we connect in ways that create a passion for God which is deeper than all other passions. The power of spiritual friendship is the best care for hurting souls.[1556]

David Seamands taught that the influence of the Spirit in the unconscious mind brings repressed memories to our consciousness so that we can confess our need and find grace. People who do not face their painful memories become hung up at a certain state of development. Victory comes through a progressive work of the Spirit culminating in a crisis "healing of memories." But Seamands warned that "the healing of memories does not automatically computerize us into perfect performance and guarantee different behavior." It must be followed up with "a great deal of hard work." Patterns must be changed "by the sanctifying power of the Spirit working through our daily disciplines."[1557]

Francis Schaeffer advocated a Keswick understanding of sanctification. In his book, *True Spirituality*, he taught a present freedom from the bonds of sin. While he believed that justification is once for all, and while he contended that

---

[1556]Crabb, *Safest Place on Earth*, 9, 16, 61-69, 87-94, 105-115.

[1557]Seamands, *Healing of Memories*, 31. In spite of the tremendous insights of David Seamands, he confessed to moral failure, shortly before his death in 2006, "with an adult female occurring over a number of years"[Patrick, "Moral Failure," A1, A5].

“substantial” did not mean “perfect,” he taught the believer could experience a substantial healing which goes beyond justification. Since sin has separated man from himself, this healing is a healing of conscience and a healing in our thought life. It is also a healing from psychological problems. He wrote of a healing for the total person; the integration of our personality. This included a deliverance from fear of the impersonal, of nonbeing, and of death. It also included a deliverance from feelings of superiority and inferiority. There is also a substantial healing in interpersonal relationships which comes when we no longer place ourselves at the center of the universe. This healing can even be extended to the Church, so that as a corporate body it demonstrates holiness and love.[1558]

More recently, Theophostics has taught emotional renewal through the reinterpretation of painful memories. Healing the past redeems the present. Emotional pain comes from past wounds, not present circumstances. Yet they are triggered by something in the present. The disturbing emotion comes from the lie embedded in the memory, not the memory itself. Freedom from the pain brought by the original lie comes when we receive truth from God. There is a higher level of victory than simply abstaining from sin. We will walk in victory when we know the truth experientially. This truth will result in God’s perfect peace.

In his evaluation of this teaching, Elliot Miller expressed concern that founder Ed Smith believed in imparted righteousness, not simply imputed righteousness, at regeneration. Miller insisted that Romans 7 describes Christian life and expressed concern that Smith held an inadequate view of sanctification. Miller argued that the persisting problem of sin in the lives of Christians is based the sin nature, not merely lie-based memories. Yet Smith distinguished between emotional pain and sin.[1559] But he felt that mind renewal can promote sanctification and victory over sin. While Miller expressed a more pessimistic view, Smith holds that Romans 6 teaches more than a positional sanctification. Smith calls it denial to proclaim the one is dead to sin when one is actually all too alive to it. We must reach the end of ourselves, as Paul did in Romans 7.[1560]

If holiness is anything, Diane Leclerc wrote that it is absolute dependence

---

[1558]Schaeffer, *Works*, 3:287-371.

[1559]Smith, *Theophostic Prayer*, 54. *Theophostic* comes from *theos* (God) and *phos* (light).

[1560]Miller, “Theophostic Prayer Ministry,” 12-21. In this article Miller concluded there was nothing unbiblical about the core theory and practice of TPM. See Miller, “Teachings in Transition,” 30-39. In this article Miller’s criticisms concerning victory over sin and sanctification surface.

on God. This weakness is strength because his strength is made perfect in our weakness (2 Cor 12:9-10). Thus, power and weakness are not in contradiction. Weakness elicits our dependence on God and on each other. We are holy through the broken body of Christ. The heart of God is present to the broken and weak.[1561]

Harald Lindström described entire sanctification as a perfecting of the personality.[1562] Around 400 BC Hippocrates wrote about four basic temperaments — sanguine, choleric, melancholy, and phlegmatic — elaborating on observations from the Greek philosopher, Empedocles. While Hippocrates thought these temperaments were governed by body fluids,[1563] his basic observation was an expansion of the basic introvert/extravert categories. Claudius Galen (AD 130-200) first established the classification of temperaments.

Tim LaHaye seems to teach a fifth temperament, the Spirit-controlled temperament, which is connected with the fruit of the Spirit.[1564] It is better to understand that sanctification does not change our temperament, but deals with the deficiencies and extremes of each personality type. Each personality type needs divine help with different manifestations of spiritual fruit. Different temperaments tend to gravitate toward different emphases on perfection. The sanguine understands perfection as the enthusiastic model. The phlegmatic may see perfection in terms of mysticism. The choleric tends toward a humanistic emphasis on perfection through asserting the will, while the melancholy seeks perfection through the ascetic approach. Yet the work of the Spirit in Christian perfection develops us in areas where we are not naturally inclined.

[1561]Leclerc, *Discovering Christian Holiness*, 250. See also her "Holiness and Power" 55-69.

[1562]Lindström, *Wesley and Sanctification*, 158.

[1563]Martin and Deidre Bobgan argue that it is a form of occult practice to utilize these personality types. They attempt to tie the basic personality types to astrology. However, the ancient observations concerning human nature may be correct even if their explanations for why such difference exist may be inaccurate or based upon their own pagan presuppositions. The Bobgans warn that we should not use our personality type as an excuse for sinful behavior and that concern is valid. They also have a section entitled "Self-Improvement or Sanctification?" [pp. 17-18]. They argue that an emphasis on temperaments leads to attempts to change oneself instead of relying on the work of the Spirit. But this discussion creates a false dilemma. While we may applaud any self improvement, even in the unsaved, it does not result in salvation. Yet sanctification in the believer is not a passive experience. The believer must cooperate with the sanctifying work of the Spirit [Bobgan, *Four Temperaments*].

[1564]LaHaye, *Spirit-Controlled Temperament*, 8; 45-46.

The sanguine needs to be made more sensitive to others and less self-centered. He needs to become dependable and stable. The Holy Spirit needs to produce in him the fruit of patience, faithfulness, and temperance or discipline. The exact opposite would be true of the melancholy. He needs more love, joy, and peace.

The choleric is a take-charge person. He is very practical and not emotional. But he can also be hot-tempered, impetuous, and cruel. Some people would rather rule hell that serve in heaven. This person has little tolerance and can be very demanding. They can be overbearing, not sensitive. They find it hard to admit they are wrong. They know everything and tend to be domineering. After God saves him, he will still be a choleric, but he must learn to let go of control. He must recognize that God is in control, not him. For him the issue of entire sanctification will center around control issues.

On the other hand the phlegmatic is low-key and easy going; he is easy to get along with and tends to be a good diplomat, but lacks direction, motivation. They always have good intentions, but do not know how to follow through. He is indecisive. After God saves him, he will still be phlegmatic, but he needs more resolve and determination. God will deal with him about issues of responsibility.

Thus, in each instance the Holy Spirit brings balance. One temperament needs to be more serious, while the opposite personality type needs to lighten up and trust God. While the one temperament needs to release control, growing in patience, kindness, and gentleness, the opposite temperament needs more faithfulness and self-control.

In each case, the Holy Spirit brings balance to life. Without changing who we are, God will help us reach our full potential. The Spirit does not work the same way in each case, but deal with us as individuals. Wesley explained, "God's usual method is one thing, but his sovereign pleasure is another. He has wise reasons both for hastening and retarding his work. Sometimes he comes suddenly and unexpected; and sometimes, not till we have looked for him."[1565] In his sermon, "The Imperfection of Human Knowledge," Wesley declared

> There is likewise great variety in the manner and time of God's bestowing his *sanctifying grace*, whereby he enables his children to give him their whole heart, which we can in no wise account for. We know not why he bestows this on some even before they ask for it (some unquestionable instances of which we have seen); on some after they have sought it but a few days; and yet

[1565]Wesley, *Works*, 11:407.

> permits other believers to wait for it perhaps twenty, thirty, or forty years; nay, and others till a few hours or even minutes before their spirits return to him. . . . God undoubtedly has reasons; but those reasons are generally hid from the children of men.[1566]

Too much emphasis has been put on how to get sanctified in three or four easy steps. Sanctification is messy. The emphasis has been upon a formula instead of conformity to Christ. The Holy Spirit does not use a cookie-cutter approach, however, which result in everyone acting alike. Yet in each instance, we are becoming more Christlike.

Brent Peterson wrote that it is not helpful to teach the entire sanctification guarantees sinless perfection, a static state of grace, or that it is a one-size-fits-all experience. He argued that Wesley did not demand that everyone's journey look the same.[1567]

Early in the ministry of D. L. Moody, Henry Varley said to him, "It remains to be seen what God will do with a man who gives himself up wholly to Him." Moody said in reply, "Well, I will be that man."[1568] But it does not remain to be seen what God can do with a person wholly devoted to God, for there are hundreds of thousands of individuals who have wholly given themselves over to God. However, they do not all have the same gifts and abilities. It is falsely implied that if we did what Moody did, God would give us the evangelistic success he gave Moody. It does not follow that God wants to make all who are entirely sanctified like Moody. Part of the seeking after a pure heart may involve dying to the desire to be as successful as was Moody. I must determine to serve God wholly, whether or not I become a great evangelist.

Samuel Chadwick warned, "God does not make every Spirit-filled man a Moody."[1569] All who are entirely sanctified will not look like Moody, but the world has repeatedly seen individuals who were wholly given up to God and his kingdom. Yet, according to John Wesley, such people may exhibit a thousand nameless defects. They are not absolutely perfect, yet they love God with their

---

1566Wesley, Sermon #69, 3.5.

1567Peterson, "Holiness in the Twenty-First Century," 67. While I have expressed some general reservations with the thrust of *Postmodern and Wesleyan?* I do not take exception to what Peterson wrote in this chapter [Reasoner, "Review,"18-19].

1568Torrey, *Why God Used Moody*, 13.

1569Chadwick, *Way to Pentecost*, 106.

whole heart and their neighbor as themselves. Henry Venn also argued that every man will not necessarily emulate the devotion of John Fletcher. Not all barn-yard fowl can be expected to mount up as an eagle.[1570]

Julie Ackerman Link explained that loving God with all my heart answers the question "Where did I come from? I came from God, and all my needs and desire are ultimately met and satisfied in Him alone." Loving God with all my soul answers the question "Who am I? I am a one-of-a-kind person made in God's image with unique talents and abilities, passions and motives, opportunities and experiences, that are best used to glorify God and further His kingdom." Loving God with my mind answers the question"Why am I here? I am here to know God, to enjoy His company and the beauty of His creation, and to participate with Him in the most important work of all — redemption." Loving God with all my strength answers the question "Where am I going? I am going where God leads. I may not know ahead of time where that will be, but I know He will not lead me along the path of least resistance, for He wants me to become strong so that when I am called into action I will be ready to carry the light of His truth, goodness, and love into dark places."

> When I love God with all my heart, my desires match His. I want what He wants and what He says is good. I feel the way He feels about good and evil. . . . By losing herself in God, Mary found her true identity as the mother of God's Son, the world's Savior. In so doing, she gave us another gift: a timeless example of what it means to love God with all our souls. . . . When I love God with my mind, I agree with Him about what is good. I reconcile my thought to His until I think what He thinks. I agree with Him about the way things are, the way things should be, and what He wants me to do about it. . . . Loving God with our strength . . . means daily doing right in the little things that are difficult so that when a "big" opportunity comes along we won't have to waste time figuring out what right is. Loving God with my strength means having the courage to risk my "self" for the sake of what I know is true and right and good.[1571]

In leading us on to perfection, the Holy Spirit will make an issue of some

---

[1570]Venn, *Letters of Henry Venn*, 581-583.

[1571]Link, *Art of Loving God*, 24-55.

point, but it will be a different issue depending on where we are out of balance. All temperaments are naturally self-centered, but that may manifest itself in different ways. Our besetting sin may be anger or laziness, it may be worry or irresponsibility. The root issue may be control, discipline, faith, or responsibility. J. I. Packer wrote,

> I am not to become (or remain) a victim of my temperament. Each temperament has its own strengths and also its weaknesses. Sanguine people tend to live thoughtlessly and at random. Phlegmatic people tend to be remote and unfeeling, sluggish and unsympathetic. Choleric people tend to be quarrelsome, bad-tempered, and poor team players. Melancholic people tend to see everything as bad and wrong and to deny that anything is ever really good and right. Yielding to my temperamental weaknesses is, of course, the most natural thing for me to do, and is therefore the hardest sort of sin for me to deal with and detect. But holy humanity, as I see it in Jesus Christ, combines in itself the strengths of all four temperaments without any of the weaknesses. Therefore, I must try to be like him in this, and not indulge the particular behavioral flaws to which my temperament tempts me.
>
> Holiness for a person of sanguine temperament, then, will involve learning to look before one leaps, to think things through responsibly, and to speak wisely rather than wildly. (These were among the lessons Peter learned with the Spirit's help after Pentecost.) Holiness for a person of phlegmatic temperament will involve a willingness to be open with people, to feel with them and for them, to be forthcoming in relationships, and to become vulnerable, in the sense of risking being hurt. Holiness for a choleric person will involve practicing patience and self-control. It will mean redirecting one's anger and hostility toward Satan and sin, rather than toward fellow human beings who are obstructing what one regards as the way forward. (These were among the lessons Paul learned from the Lord after his conversion.) Finally, holiness for a melancholic person will involve learning to rejoice in God, to give up self-pity and proud pessimism.[1572]

[1572]Packer, *Rediscovering Holiness* (1992), 25-26.

R. S. Foster wrote that two men, equally holy, may under certain circumstances appear to be quite dissimilar. One man is of a highly nervous temperament, another is as decidedly imperturbable. One is sanguine, another distrustful. One is impulsive, another dispassionate. The influence of sanctifying grace will not change their temperament. It will not remove the constitutional difference between them, but only control and regulate them.[1573]

Keith Drury concluded that entire sanctification does not destroy our natural temperament. As we grow in the sanctified life, God continues to mold our personality strengths. He also brings us strengths not inherent to our own basic personality. However, perfect Christlikeness is found within the body of Christ, the Church. In this corporate holiness one believer demonstrates one area of strength, while another believer exemplifies a different strength.[1574]

Different temperaments will naturally gravitate toward specific emphases on holiness. Richard Foster wrote of six streams of spiritual life: the contemplative tradition, the holiness tradition, the charismatic tradition, the social justice tradition, the evangelical tradition, the Incarnational tradition.[1575] Gary L. Thomas identified nine sacred pathways followed by those of various spiritual temperaments.[1576] Don Thorsen wrote of the academic, the activist, the charismatic, the contemplative, the ecumenical, the evangelical, the holiness, and the sacramental emphases of Christian spirituality.[1577] From a biblical perspective, Derek Tidball summarizes the pathways to holiness as

- The Spirit of God
- The Word of God
- The discipline of God
- Union with Christ
- Conflict with the enemy
- Separation from the world[1578]

However, we cannot pick and choose one emphasis. We must maintain

[1573]Foster, *Christian Purity*, 88.

[1574]Drury, *Holiness for Ordinary People*, 99-104.

[1575]Foster, *Streams of Living Water.*

[1576]Thomas, *Sacred Pathways.*

[1577]Thorsen, "Integrated Streams of Holiness," 87.

[1578]Tidball, *Message of Holiness*, 203-276.

a balance between:

- the universality of preliminary grace and the limited actuality of sanctifying grace
- sovereign grace and co-operant grace
- free grace through the Holy Spirit and co-operant grace producing good works
- grace as favor and grace as empowerment
- grace as receiving and grace as responding
- crisis and process
- subjective experience and objective truth
- justification and sanctification
- law and love
- the birth of new life and the death of the old life and nature
- the perseverance of new life and the mortification of the old life
- the finished work of Christ and the ongoing mortification of our flesh
- imputed righteousness and imparted righteousness
- suffering and joy
- purity and power
- brokenness and wholeness or inner healing
- separation from the world and incarnational ministry to our neighbor
- contemplation and social responsibility
- purity of intention and imperfect performance
- the work of self discipline and the quiet rest of faith
- death to self-centeredness and the abundant life
- passive submission to the will of God and active seeking after God
- oneness with God and awareness of humanity
- Christlikeness and the indwelling dynamic of the Spirit
- the struggle against sin and the victory over sin
- hunger after more of God and happiness in the Lord
- the repentance of believers and the beauty of God reflected
- direct and indirect assurance
- personal holiness and corporate holiness
- the already and the not yet — realized and future personal eschatology[1579]

[1579]In the document "Fresh Eyes on Holiness: Living Out the Holiness Manifesto," there is a discussion of seven contrasting dimensions of holiness: individual/corporate; Christ-centered/Holy Spirit-centered; development/end; crisis/process; blessings/suffering; separation/incarnation; forms/essence [Mannoia and

His love conquers our sinfulness. The expression of our holiness is that we love others through forgiveness and love God by obedience to his commandments. Love turns friendship into fellowship. It turns marriage from sexual gratification to a concern for our partner's needs. It calls us to give up our cravings for the goods of the world in order to serve the crying needs of our neighbor.[1580] It purifies self love into concern for others and a desire to please God. "He must increase, but I must decrease" (John 3:30).

David Seamands wrote that self-surrender is the ultimate crisis. It begins with the conviction of our sins, the agony of struggling with guilt, and the realization that we are completely dependent upon grace. Becoming a new creation is followed by growth in grace. We learn to put away childish things and grow more and more mature. Yet everything up to this point has been a minor skirmish in comparison to the ultimate battle to which we are being led. The real issue is the surrender of self to the lordship of Jesus Christ. We are brought to a spot we recognize. It is at the cross that the crucifixion of the self-centeredness of our ego takes place. And this is the greatest battle of every life.[1581] Dennis Kinlaw explained that the self needs to be liberated from the "tyranny of self-interest."[1582]

According to Romans 13:1, God has ordained all authority. The word "ordain" describes an arrangement ordered by God. Everyone must submit to authority which is over them. The word "submit" as used in vv 1 and 5 adds a prefix to that word ordain and means that we are to come under the arrangement made by God.[1583] God ordained three institutions: the family, the church, and the state.

What does all this have to do with holy living? We are to be models of

---

Thorsen, *Holiness Manifesto*, 22-23].

[1580]Bloesch, *God the Almighty*, 149-150.

[1581]Seamands, *Putting Away Childish Things*, 10, 13, 17, 49, 127

[1582]Kinlaw, *Preaching in the Spirit*, 105-106; 108-109.

[1583]The word "ordain"in Rom 13:1 is τάσσω (*tasso*). It describes an arrangement ordered by God. The word "submit" in Rom 13:1, 5 is ὑποτάσσω (*hupotasso*). The prefix ὑπο (*hupo*) means "under." Thus, "submit" means to come under authority. A third related word, to rebel or resist, in Rom 13:2 is ἀντίτασσω. The prefix ἀντί (*anti*) means "against." Everyone is either under God's authority or resisting God's authority.

submission to biblical authority. The opposition of submission is rebellion. In Greek it is the same word for "ordain" with the prefix "anti." The carnal mind will not, nor can it, submit to God (Rom 8:7). The mind controlled by the Spirit has victory over sin (Rom 6:13-14). We must submit to God's Word. We must submit to God-ordained authority in the home, in the church, in the state. According to 1 Corinthians 7:14 there is a positional sanctification whereby the unbeliever is exposed to salvation and experiences the potential of personal salvation by his or her association with a believing spouse. While the personal salvation of their offspring is not guaranteed, they are covenantally holy, sharing in the covenant with the believing parent and protected from spiritual harm.[1584]

Across history we have seen how the gnostic and monastic views of perfection included the renunciation of marriage. Virginity was equated with purity and perfection. Among Roman Catholics marriage was a sacrament for the masses, but for the perfect Christians celibacy was required. Among Protestants purity was to be maintained *after* marriage through sexual abstinence. And there was a holiness teaching that we should not love our family too much lest they become idols to us. While it is true that God must be first, the parents are the first window through which children see God. Thus parents must reflect God's love to their children. At times it may be more spiritual to spend time with family than to attend another church function.

John Wesley struggled to overcome his own warped view of marriage. Across history, those who have denied their own sexuality have often fallen into the temptation of promiscuity or perversion. Among charismatic groups there was occasionally an emphasis on disregarding marriage vows or the teaching of communal or plural marriage. Sometimes it was insisted that God would only sanction the marriage of "Spirit-filled" believers.

The holy life is most transparent at home. It is significant that there have been so many warped ideas concerning human sexuality and marriage which have been connected with sanctification. This may be part of the lasting legacy of Augustine. However, Ephesians 5 addresses the sanctification of the man and the woman in a redemptive marriage context. Here Paul teaches what it means to be a man or a woman in Christ as God reverses the effects of the fall within the context of the marriage relationship. Man was created to be the leader and initiator in his world, but he is now vulnerable to failure because the world he was called to lead is fallen. His tendency, therefore, is to fight back in an attempt to

---

[1584]Whedon connected this passage with Rom 11:16, which also describes a holy influence. While all children are eligible for baptism, the child of Christian parents is more likely to receive it [*Commentary*, 4:49].

prove his strength and the appearance of competency. Thus, his focus becomes concerned with himself and not with those he is to lead.

The woman was created to be the responder and completer of her man, but now she is vulnerable in the area of safety. The man to which she responds may fail her. Rather than respond with an unfailing trust in her God and be the helpmeet she was called to be, she has a tendency to protect herself and become focused on herself rather than upon her husband.

Yet their relationship is to reflect the relationship between Christ and the church, according to Ephesians 5:22. The husband is to lead and nourish as Christ loves the church. The wife is to submit as the church submits to Christ. The call is for husbands and wives to "push back" the effects of the fall and live as redeemed men and women. The process of sanctification for the man is to put to death the fallen natural tendency to put his need for competency ahead of his wife's need for security. The woman must put submission to her husband above her own desire for security. She must learn to trust a man who can fail and uphold his honor. Thus both experience the process of sanctification as they fulfill their roles within the marriage and the marriage itself becomes a redemptive institution in which we are transformed.[1585]

Peter tells us that God's will for us is holiness (1 Peter 1:15-16). Newborn babes are exhorted to lay aside the tendencies of the sinful nature (2:1) such as guile, hypocrisy, envy, and evil speaking. Then Peter connects this with submission to God-ordained authority. After a section which runs twenty verses on submission, there is a description of Christian holiness, which is our calling (3:8-9). An unsubmissive attitude is a major tendency of the sinful nature.

Just as Jesus prayed, "Not my will, but Yours be done," so every Christian must present himself to God and must submit to God ordained authority. No one can be sanctified who is in rebellion against God's creation order.

The first call of Jesus is "Come unto me." And yet the call to "come *after* me" (Luke 14:27) is a far deeper call to commitment and surrender. The cross teaches the brokenness of self denial. The imperative to "hate" in v 26 (Deut 21:15; Matt 6:24; 10:37; Luke 9:23; 16:13) means to love less. Jesus teaches that we must love him more than our reputation, than any relationship, than any possession, than any goal. He must be the center of our life. The real sin is the unsurrenderedness of the ego. This sin is the root of all other sins. Self-surrender is both a definite crisis and a never-ending process since we can only surrender

---

[1585]Talley, "Gender and Sanctification," 6-16. See also Hunt, *Letters on Sanctification*, Letter 18 on family religion where he dealt with the duty of the husband to love, the wife to submit, and the children to obey parental authority.

that of which we are aware. And self-surrender is the ultimate crisis because it is the answer to life. This self dies in order to truly live.[1586] Theodore Monod described this process:

O the bitter shame and sorrow,
That a time could ever be,
When I let the Savior's pity,
Plead in vain, and proudly answered:
"All of self, and none of Thee!

Yet He found me: I beheld Him
Bleeding on the accursed tree,
Heard Him pray, "Forgive them, Father!"
And my wistful heart said faintly:
"Some of self, and some of Thee!"

Day by day, His tender mercy,
Healing, helping, full and free,
Sweet and strong, and ah! so patient,
Brought me lower, while I whispered:
"Less of self, and more of Thee!"

Higher than the highest heaven,
Deeper than the deepest sea,
Lord, Thy love at last hath conquered;
Grant me now my supplication:
"None of self, and all of Thee!"[1587]

While most people are contented to live and die in awakened state, one of the characteristics of those who are truly born again is a desire to be holy. Each person consecrates or yields to the level of light received. There may be many crisis moments, but there is an initial crisis moment when we first are convicted for our transgressions and another initial crisis moment when we are born again. However, when it comes to sanctification or perfection, we can always be more

[1586]Seamands, *Putting Away Childish Things*, 122-132.

[1587]Monod, "The Altered Motto," © 1885, by R. E. Hudson, quoted by Steele, *Mile-stone Papers*, 79. Steele said, "The gradual growth toward perfect purity of love is beautifully expressed in Monod's hymn" ["Sanctification," 4:2686].

Christlike. If the balance has shifted from all crisis to all process, is it important to recover the balance between crisis and process? Wesley taught that a man may be dying for some time, yet there came a moment in which the person was dead[1588] — even if the exact moment of that death is not dramatic or memorable.

Is there any virtue in understanding the salvation process as encompassing two works of grace if there could be many crisis moments? From beginning to end, salvation is all of grace and it is not helpful to divide grace into two works. However, the results of saving grace are two-fold. There is deliverance from the practice and the nature of sin. Thus, the secondness of entire sanctification is based upon the dual nature of sin and a deeper need remaining in the regenerate. Murphree explained,

> The notion of a "second experience" does not describe God's arbitrary formula as much as it describes human personality. It is *descriptive* rather than *prescriptive.* The need for a deeper working of God's grace does not indicate inadequacy of God's initial grace. It simply reflects the inability of the human personality to entertain an adequate love motive for Christ until His fellowship has been consistently shared.[1589]

Evangelicals hold to the one crisis of the new birth and without some understanding of a secondness, we are left with no distinctive doctrine of entire sanctification. Entire sanctification must be entire in the same sense that total depravity is total. It must be more than the new birth or subsequent growth. There must be a balance between crisis and process; between the dramatic and the ordinary

Murphree explained that another "work of grace" referred to something which was equal in significance to salvation. However, he wondered whether salvation was reduced to being rescued from hell. Actually, everything God does to move us away from sin, selfishness, and hell and toward goodness, sanctity, and heaven is a product of grace.[1590]

If we understand entire sanctification to be a pure love which loves God and man with our whole heart to the exclusion of everything contrary to that pure love, there is also an initial crisis moment when we first see our inner depravity,

---

[1588]Wesley, *Works*, 11:402.

[1589]Murphree, *Love Motive*, 24.

[1590]Murphree, *Love Motive*, 53-54.

although the process of deliverance from it may necessitate many subsequent revelations and cleansings. There can also be an initial crisis moment when this love first displaces all sin. However, the believer who loves perfectly can still find areas in which he can be more completely conformed to the image of Christ.

Wesley said, "There is no perfection which does not admit of a continual increase."[1591] The perfect love of the believer is imputed to him for Christian perfection. Thus, instead of Wiley's concept that the Christian life is a series of crisis experiences (two to be exact), the Christian life is a process in which there are several crisis moments: awakening, justification, deliverance, awakening to a deeper level of sin, death to self-centeredness, perfection of love.

Christian perfection is a derived perfection. It is a relative (not absolute) perfection. It is an imputed perfection. W. B. Pope explained, "As faith is reckoned for righteousness, so faith working by love is reckoned for perfection."[1592]

This perfection is a maintained condition, not a permanent state. According to 1 John 4:18 the love of God casts out or expels fear. Miley asked,

> But how does love cast out fear? Certainly not by an eradication of the capacity of fear, but by a suppression of its activity. This is the only mode in which love can cast out fear, or one affection expel another. Every possible affection must have its capacity in our nature. Hence, if in sanctification there is not only a suppression of all disordered affections, but also an eradication of all capacity for them, there can be no possible lapse from that state.[1593]

This verb in 1 John 4:18 is in the present tense indicating an ongoing process. As we trust Christ each moment we are cleansed by his blood and filled with his Spirit. The holy life is a moment-by-moment condition which is maintained by a moment-by-moment obedient faith. This obedience of faith produces good works. These works are the result of God's grace at work within us (Phil 2:13). They are not the basis of our salvation, but the result.

This is to be our lifelong pursuit. We never cease to seek for more because our holiness is derived from God, like the light of the moon. "None feel

---

1591 Wesley, "Christian Perfection," Sermon #40, 1.9.

1592 Pope, *Compendium*, 3:96-97.

1593 Miley, *Systematic Theology*, 2:365.

their need of Christ" like those who have experienced the greatest deliverance from sin. We should always be seeking more love, more grace, more holiness.

Randy Maddox concluded that Wesley's most fundamental concern was a gradual growth in holiness. While affirming the possibility of entire sanctification may have been a *distinctive* of Wesley, the concept of sanctification as a progressive journey, in responsive co-operation with God's empowering grace, was most *characteristic* of Wesley. Wesley surrounded the gracious possibility of Christian perfection with the theme of responsible growth. A sincere conviction of this possibility will nurture growth in grace, whether or not believers ever attain it. Those who are acutely aware that they do not yet enjoy the full deliverance from inward sin that is available are admonished to grow in grace today. A conviction of the possibilities of God's grace must be joined with a recognition of our continuing need for growth. And those who attain are warned not to rest there but to continue to grow in grace. Wesley qualified the type of Christian perfection which he believed could be attained and also insured that it was a perfection which would always leave more to be attained.[1594]

Those who have been perfected in love can grow through freedom from evil thoughts and dispositions. They can grow in grace and in the knowledge of Christ. They can grow in their knowledge and obedience to God's law. They can make fewer mistakes and grow in their love of God. They can also grow in the image of God, growing in the likeness they share with God.[1595]

Thus, entire sanctification is a complete surrender to God, a deeper cleansing of our heart, a maturity of our character, and a perfect love toward our neighbor. Entire sanctification is purity, maturity, and consistency. It is discipline, stability, and character. It is holy love. It is Christlikeness. It is a heart cleansed from all unrighteousness, a death to self-centeredness, a perfection of motive.

God's grace can enable us to love him with our whole heart and to love our neighbor as ourselves. But this condition, which by definition displaces everything contrary to the love of God, must be maintained by appropriating all the means of grace. Wesley advised those who were entirely sanctified to watch and pray continually against pride and fanaticism, to be zealous of good works and to avoid the thinking that because I am filled with love, I need not pray always and I need not set aside time for self-examination. Beware of desiring anything but God, beware of division. Be an example in all things.

[1594]Maddox, *Responsible Grace*, 189-190.

[1595]Schlimm, "Puzzle of Perfection," 124-142.

None of this comes automatically. We must constantly pursue holiness, but not in the sense that it is illusive and unobtainable. We pursue it in the sense that it is not permanent but must be maintained. My great concern is that people thought that when they received a certain experience, the removal of the sin nature, we would live holy without any effort.

The Holy Spirit develops Christian character and maturity within those who are consistently led by the Spirit. Those who walk closest are the most conscious of their imperfections. Yet they can be cleansed at least from all conscious sin. The fruit of the Spirit can be increased in quality and quantity. They can have a greater delight in God's law and a greater consistency in keeping it. They may enjoy a greater sense of God's favor and blessing. They can develop a greater sensitivity and compassion for their neighbor.

The history of revivals reveals that every great move of the Spirit has begun with a revelation of the depth of sin and the holiness of God, a rediscovery of what it meant to be born again and a hunger for holiness. May God raise up such a movement again in our day. In a paper given to the Wesleyan Church, Chris Bounds took the position that "the Wesleyan doctrine of sanctification ought to believe in a personal redemption from inward and outward sin in the present life."[1596]

Our primary commitment must be to truth. We must "buy the truth and do not sell it" (Prov 23:23). We must be committed to seek truth wherever that search leads us. We must speak the truth in love (Eph 4:15). Because we care we may state our convictions in strong terms, but we must never become harsh. Paul warned Timothy, "Don't have anything to do with foolish and stupid arguments, because you know they produce quarrels and the Lord's servant must not quarrel; instead he must be kind to everyone, able to teach, not resentful" (1 Tim 2:23-24). The Holy Spirit can be at work in the lives of people who do not necessarily accept our definitions or exegesis.

Pastors should minister with the confidence that "he who began a good work in you will carry it on to completion until the day of Christ Jesus" (Phil 1:6).[1597] The Holy Spirit is working within the life of every believer to conform him to the image of Christ (Rom 8:29). It is counterproductive to persuade these Christians they should seek a spectacular experience which will produce instant maturity. Instead, they should be urged to cooperate with the indwelling Spirit and keep in step with the Spirit.

[1596]Online: Bounds, "Spiritual Transformation," 9.

[1597]The word "completion" is ἐπιτελέω (*eipteleo*). This is the usual word for perfection with a prefix of intensification.

It is the will of the Father that all believers be conformed to the image of Christ. While all Christians are holy, that holiness may be perfected. While all Christians are sanctified, that sanctification can be entire. While the believer is progressively sanctified, being conformed more and more into Christlikeness, he may be brought by the Spirit to a point of deeper revelation of himself, led by the Spirit to a deeper and more intelligent surrender of himself, and to a confession of need. He is then cleansed to the level of that consciousness. This grace is received and maintained by a moment-by-moment faith. It is not a static state, but is capable of either improvement or loss. Gibson wrote that entire sanctification is not the end of spiritual growth, but an acceleration of it.[1598]

Christian perfection, then, is a relative perfection in which we love God with our total being. That perfect love displaces everything contrary to it. This cleansing from all unrighteousness is provided for and maintained through the blood of Christ. This condition enlarges our capacity for more of the Spirit.

The perfecting grace of God cleanses our attitudes and motives, produces spiritual health, a balance of human temperament, and a maturity of character. It results in a greater consciousness of God and a full assurance of faith. It produces an increase in quality and quantity of the fruit of the Spirit. It is an ethical holiness, producing a greater consistency in keeping God's law, as well as a greater sensitivity and compassion toward our neighbor. Those who walk closest to God are the most conscious of their imperfections. Yet when love is the ruling motive of our life, God imputes perfection to us.

Holy living begins with the baptism of the Holy Spirit in regeneration. Christian Perfection is a relative perfection in which the babe in Christ reaches his full stature, being conformed to the image of Christ. The sanctifying grace of the Holy Spirit imparted to us can so fill us with the love of God that while we are thus filled, everything contrary to that love is displaced. When we love God with our whole being, God imputes perfection to us, meaning that we are fulfilling his purpose for us.

[1598]Gibson, *Sincerity of God*, 6.

BIBLIOGRAPHY

BOOKS

Abbey, C. J. and J. H. Overton. *The English Church in the Eighteenth Century.* 2 vols. London: Longmans, Green, 1878.

Abbott, Hollis F. "Christian Maturity."*The Word and the Doctrine*. Kenneth Geiger, ed. Kansas City: Beacon Hill, 1965.

Agnew, Milton S. "Pneumatology" in *A Contemporary Wesleyan Theology*. 2 vols. Charles W. Carter, ed. Grand Rapids: Francis Asbury, 1983

Albin, Thomas R. "An Empirical Study of Early Methodist Spirituality." *Wesleyan Theology Today.* Theodore Runyon, ed. Nashville: Kingswood, 1985.

Aldrich, Roy. *The Transition Problem in Acts*. Detroit: Detroit Bible Institute, 197-.

Alexander, Estrelda . *Black Fire: One Hundred Years of African American Pentecostalism*. Downers Grove, IL: InterVarsity, 2011.

__________. "G. T. Haywood and the Emergence of Oneness Pentecostalism." *From Aldersgate to Azusa Street*. Henry H. Knight III, ed. Eugene, OR: Wipf and Stock, 2010.

Ambrosiaster. *Ancient Christian Texts: Commentaries on Galatians-Philemon*. Gerald L. Bray, ed. Downers Grove, IL: InterVarsity, 2009.

Anderson, Gary. *Sin: A History*. New Haven, CT: Yale University, 2009.

Anderson, Neil D. *A Definitive Study of Evidence concerning John Wesley's Appropriation of the Thought of Clement of Alexandria*. Lewiston, NY: Edwin Mellon Press, 2004.

Anderson, Neil T. and Rich Miller, *Freedom From Fear*. Eugene, OR: Harvest House, 1999.

Anderson, Neil T. and Robert L. Saucy. *The Common Made Holy*. Eugene, OR: Harvest House, 1997.

Anderson, Robert Maples. *Vision of the Disinherited*. New York: Oxford University, 1979.

Aquinas, Thomas. *Summa Theologica*. 1265-1274. 5 vols. Reprint, Notre Dame: Christian Classics, 1981.

Arminius, James. *The Works of James Arminius: The London Edition*. 3 vols.

translated by James and William Nichols. 1825-1875. Reprint, Grand Rapids: Baker, 1996.
Arndt, William F. and F. Wilbur Gingrich. *A Greek-English Lexicon of the New Testament*. 2nd ed. Chicago: University of Chicago: 1979.
Arnett, William. "The Wesleyan Arminian Teaching on Sin." in *Insights into Holiness*, Kenneth Geiger, ed. 1962. Reprint, Salem, OH: Schmul, 1989.
Aron, Raymond. *The Opium of the Intellectuals.* New York: Norton, 1957.
Arthur, William. *Proceedings of the Second Ecumenical Methodist Conference held in the Metropolitan Methodist Episcopal Church, October,1891, Washington, D. C.* New York: Hunt & Eaton, 1982.
__________. *The Tongue of Fire*. London: Kelly, 1856.
Asbury, Francis. *The Journal and Letters of Francis Asbury*. 3 vols. Elmer T. Clark, ed. Nashville: Abingdon, 1958.
Ashby, Stephen M. "A Reformed Arminian View." *Four Views on Eternal Security*. J. Matthew Pinson, ed. Grand Rapids: Zondervan, 2002.
Atkinson, J. Baines. *The Beauty of Holiness*. London: Epworth, 1953.
Augustine, Aurelius. *A Treatise Concerning Man's Perfection in Righteousness*. A. D. 415. *Nicene and Post-Nicene Fathers*. First Series. Philip Schaff, ed. 1887. Reprint, Grand Rapids: Eerdmans, 1971. Vol. 5.
_______. *Homilies on the First Epistle of John.* A. D. 416 or later. Vol. 7.
Aulén, Gustaf. *The Faith of the Christian Church*. translated by Eric H. Wahlstrom. 5th ed. Philadelphia: Muhlenberg, 1960.
Baab, Otto J. *Theology of the Old Testament*. New York: Abingdon, 1949.
Bach, Jeff. *Voices of the Turtledoves: The Sacred World of Ephrata*. University Park, PA: Pennsylvania State University Press, 2003.
Baer, David A. and Robert P. Gordon, חסד. *The New International Dictionary of Old Testament Theology and Exegesis*, 5 vols. Willem A. VanGemeren, ed. Grand Rapids: Zondervan, 1997.
Baldwin, Harmon A. *Lessons for Seekers of Holiness*. 1907. Reprint, Titusville, PA: Allegheny, 1972.
__________. *The Carnal Mind.* 1926. Reprint, Titusville, PA: Allegheny, 1972.
Bangs, Carl. *Arminius: A Study in the Dutch Reformation*. 1971. Reprint, Grand Rapids: Francis Asbury, 1985.
Bangs, Nathan. *The Necessity, Nature, and Fruits, of Sanctification: in a Series of Letters to a Friend*. 1851. Reprint, Salem, OH: Allegheny, 2006.
__________. *The Present State, Prospects, and Responsibilities of the Methodist Episcopal Church. With an Appendix of Ecclesiastical Statistics*. New York: Lane & Scott, 1850.
Bahnsen, Greg. *Theonomy in Christian Ethics*. Nutley, NJ: Craig, 1979.
Baker, Frank, ed. *The Heart of True Spirituality*. 2 vols. Grand Rapids: Francis Asbury, 1985.
__________. *From Wesley to Asbury*. Durham, NC: Duke University, 1976.

Banks, John S. *A Manual of Christian Doctrine*. 1897. Reprint, Nashville: Publishing House of the M. E. Church, South, 1924.

Barbour, Hugh and Arthur O. Roberts, eds. *Early Quaker Writings 1650-1700*. Grand Rapids: Eerdmans, 1973.

Barclay, Robert. *An Apology for the True Christian Divinity: Being an Explanation and Vindication of the Principles and Doctrines of the People called Quakers*. 1678. Reprint, Glenside, PA: Quaker Heritage Press, 2002.

Barclay, William. *New Testament Words*. Philadelphia: Westminster, 1964.

Barker, John H. J. *This Is the Will of God: A Study in the Doctrine of Entire Sanctification as a Definite Experience*. 1956. Reprint, Salem, OH: Schmul, 1984.

Barna, George. *State of the Church 2002*. Ventura, CA: Issachar Resources, 2002.

Barrett, D. B. And T. M. Johnson. "Global Statistics."*The New International Dictionary of Pentecostal and Charismatic Movements*, Stanley M. Burgess, ed, revised and expanded ed. Grand Rapids: Zondervan, 2002.

Barrett, David, George T. Kurian, and Todd M. Johnson. *World Christian Encyclopedia*. 2 vols. New York: Oxford, 2001.

Barron, Bruce. *The Health and Wealth Gospel*. Downers Grove, IL: InterVarsity, 1987.

Barth, Karl. *Church Dogmatics*. 14 vols. G. W. Bromiley and T. F. Torrance, eds. Edinburgh: T. and T. Clark, 1936-1969.

__________. *The Christian Life*. London: Student Movement Press, 1930.

Bartlet, James. "Sanctification." *A Dictionary of the Bible*. 5 vols. James Hastings, ed. Edinburgh: T. & T. Clark, 1902.

Bartleman, Frank. *How Pentecost Came to Los Angeles: As It Was in the Beginning*. 3rd ed. Los Angles: the Author, 1925.

__________. *Azusa Street*. Plainfield, NJ: Logos, 1980.

Barton, John. "Approaches to Ethics in the Old Testament." *Beginning Old Testament Study*. John Rogerson, ed. Philadelphia: Westminster, 1982.

Bassett, Paul M. *The Historical Development*. Vol. 2 of *Exploring Christian Holiness*. Kansas City: Beacon Hill, 1985.

__________. *Holiness Teaching — The New Testament Times to Wesley*. Vol. 1 of *Great Holiness Classics*. Kansas City: Beacon Hill, 1997.

__________. "The Theological Identity of the North American Holiness Movement" in *The Variety of American Evangelicalism*. Donald W. Dayton and Robert K. Johnson, eds. Downers Grove, IL: InterVarsity, 1991.

Bavinck, Herman. *Our Reasonable Faith*. Grand Rapids: Eerdmans, 1956.

Baxter, J. Sidlow. *A New Call to Holiness*. Grand Rapids: Zondervan, 1967.

__________. *His Deeper Work in Us*. Grand Rapids: Zondervan, 1967.

__________. *Our High Calling*. Grand Rapids: Zondervan, 1967.

Beale, David O. *In Pursuit of Purity*. Greenville, SC: Unusual Publications, 1986.

Bebbington, David. *Holiness in Nineteenth-Century England.* Carlisle, Cumbria, U. K: Paternoster, 2000.

__________. *The Dominance of Evangelicalism.* Downers Grove, IL: InterVarsity, 2005.

Beeke, Joel R. *The Quest for Full Assurance.* Edinburgh: Banner of Truth, 1999.

Beet, J. Agar. *Holiness As Understood by Writers of the Bible.* 1880. Reprint, Salem, OH: Schmul, 1985.

__________. *A Commentary on St. Paul's Epistles to the Ephesians, Philippians, Colossians, and to Philemon.* 1890. Reprint, Salem, OH: Schmul, n. d.

__________. *Manual of Theology.* London: Hodder & Stoughton, 1906.

__________. *Shorter Manual of Theology.* London: Hodder & Stoughton, 1908.

Behm, Johannes. γλῶσσα. *Theological Dictionary of the New Testament.* 10 vols. Gerhard Kittel and Gerhard Friedrich, eds. translated by Geoffrey W. Bromiley. Grand Rapids: Eerdmans, 1964. 1:722-724

Bennett, Dennis. *How to Pray for the Release of the Holy Spirit.* South Plainfield, NJ: Logos, 1985.

__________. "The Gifts of the Holy Spirit" in *The Charismatic Movement.* Michael P. Hamilton, ed. Grand Rapids: Eerdmans, 1975.

Benson, Joseph. *The Holy Bible, with Notes, All the Marginal Readings, Summaries, and the Date of Every Transaction.* 2nd ed. 5 vols. 1811-1818. Reprint, New York: Carlton & Phillips, 1856.

__________. *Sermons on Various Occasions, and Most of Them on the Principal Subjects of Genuine Christianity.* London: G. Whitefield, 1802.

__________. *Sermons, and Plans of Sermons, of Many of the Most Important Texts of Holy Scripture.* Jabez Bunting, ed. 7 vols. Baltimore: Armstrong & Plaskitt, 1827.

__________. *Two Sermons on Sanctification.* Birmingham: E. Jones, 1791.

__________. *The Glory of the House of God.* Salem, OH: Schmul, 2002. Reprint of abridged edition of *Sermons on Various Occasions* (1817).

__________. *The Life of John Fletcher.* 2nd ed. Reprint, Salem, OH: Allegheny, 1984.

__________. *The Life of the Rev. John W. de la Fléchère.* 11th ed. London: J. Mason, 1838.

Berkhof, Louis. *Systematic Theology.* 4th ed. Grand Rapids: Eerdmans, 1941.

Bible Readings for the Home Circle. Mountain View, CA: Pacific Press, 1916.

Binney, Amos and Daniel Steele. *The People's Commentary.* New York: Eaton & Mains, 1878.

Billheimer, Paul E. *Don't Waste Your Sorrows.* Ft. Washington, PA: Christian Literature Crusade, 1977.

Black, Brian. *The Holiness Heritage.* Salem, OH: Allegheny, 2003.

Blackstone, W. E. *Jesus is Coming.* Chicago: Fleming H. Revell, 1908.

Blackwelder, Boyce. *Light from the Greek New Testament.* 1958. Reprint, Grand

Rapids: Baker, 1976.

__________. *Toward Understanding Romans.* Anderson, IN: Warner, 1962.

Blake, William. *The Marriage of Heaven and Hell.* 1790-1793. *Blake: Complete Writings*. Geoffrey Keynes, ed. Buernsey: Oxford, 1966.

Bloesch, Donald G. *God the Almighty* in *Christian Foundations*. Downers Grove, IL: InterVarsity, 1995.

__________. *The Holy Spirit: Works and Gifts*. in *Christian Foundations*. Downers Grove, IL: InterVarsity, 2000.

__________. *Jesus Christ: Savior and Lord* in *Christian Foundations*. Downers Grove, IL: InterVarsity, 1997.

__________. *A Theology of Word and Spirit* in *Christian Foundations*. Downers Grove, IL: InterVarsity, 1992.

Bloomfield, Samuel Thomas. *The Greek Testament, with English Notes, Critical, Philological, and Exegetical*. Philadelphia: Clark & Hesser, 1854.

Blum, Edwin A. "1-2 Peter." *The Expositor's Bible Commentary*. 12 vols. Frank E. Gaebelein, ed. Grand Rapids: Zondervan, 1981.

Blumhofer, Edith L. "Purity and Preparation." *Reaching Beyond*. Stanley M. Burgess, ed. Peabody, MA: Hendrickson, 1986.

Bird, Michael F. *The Saving Righteousness of God*. Colorado Springs: Paternoster, 2006.

Boardman, William E. *The Higher Christian Life*. Boston: Henry Hoyt, 1858.

__________. *Work for Jesus*. Boston: Willard Tract Repository, 1875.

Bobgan, Martin and Deidre. *Four Temperaments, Astrology and Personality Testing*. Santa Barbara, CA: EastGate, 1992.

Bogatzky, Karl Heinrich von. *Golden Treasury*. London: 1773.

Boland, Jeremiah M. *The Problem of Methodism: Being a Review of the Residue Theory of Regeneration and the Second Change Theory of Sanctification; and the Philosophy of Christian Perfection*. Nashville: Publishing House of the Methodist Episcopal Church, South, 1888.

Bonar, Andrew A. *Memoirs and Remains of the Rev. Robert Murray McCheyne*. Philadelphia: Presbyterian Board of Publication, 1844.

Bonar, Horatius. *God's Way of Holiness*. New York: Robert Carter & Brothers, 1873.

Borgen, Ole. *John Wesley on the Sacraments*. Nashville: Abingdon, 1972.

Boswell, Thomas L. "Salvation and Its Individual Relations." *The Methodist Pulpit South*. William T. Smithson, ed. Washington, DC: William T. Smithson, 1859.

Bowne, Borden Parker. *Studies in Christianity*. Boston: Houghton Mifflin, 1909.

__________. *The Christian Life, A Study*. Cincinnati: Curts & Jennings, 1899.

Braaten, Carl E. And Robert W. Jenson, eds. *Union with Christ: The New Finnish Interpretation of Luther*. Grand Rapids: Eerdmans, 1998.

Bradburn, Samuel. *Sketch of Mr. Wesley's Character*. 1791. Located in *Select*

Letters, Chiefly on Personal Religion, by the Rev. John Wesley, A. M. Thomas Jackson, ed. New York: Mason & Lane, 1838.

Brasher, J. Lawrence. *The Sanctified South: John Lakin Brasher and the Holiness Movement*. Chicago: University of Illinois Press, 1994.

Braun. Herbert. *Gesammelte Studien zum Neuen Testament und seiner Umwelt.* Tübingen: J.C.B. Mohr [Paul Siebeck], 1962.

Bray, Gerald Lewis. *Holiness and the Will of God: Perspectives on the Theology of Tertullian*. London: Marshall, Morgan & Scott, 1979.

__________. *Romans: Ancient Christian Commentary on Scripture.* Downers Grove, IL: InterVarsity,1998.

Bready, J. Wesley. *England: Before and After Wesley*. London: Hodder and Stoughton, 1938.

Bretall, Robert, ed. *A Kierkegaard Anthology*. Princeton, NJ: Princeton University Press, 1946.

Bridges, Jerry. *The Pursuit of Holiness*. Colorado Springs: Navpress, 1978.

Brightman, Edgar S. "Personalism." *A History of Philosophical Systems*. Vergilius Ferm, ed. New York: Philosophical Library, 1950.

Brockett, Henry. *Scriptural Freedom from Sin*. Kansas City: Beacon Hill, 1941.

Bromley, Thomas. *The Way to the Sabbath of Rest or, The Soul's Progress in the Work of the New-Birth*. 1759. Reprint, Philadelphia: George W. McCalla, 1905.

Brooks, John P. *The Divine Church*. 1891. Reprint, El Dorado Springs, MO: Witt, 1960.

__________. "What are the Chief Hindrances to the Progress of the Work of Sanctification Among Believers?" *Proceedings of Holiness Conferences held at Cincinnati, November 26th, 1877 and New York, December 17th, 1877*. 1878. Reprint, New York: Garland Publishing, 1985.

Brown, A. B. *A Modified Arminian Theology*. Wendell, NC: published by the author, 2001.

Brown, Charles Ewing. *The Meaning of Sanctification*. 1945. Reprint, Salem, OH: Schmul, 1980.

Brown, Dale W. *Understanding Pietism*. rev. ed. Nappanee, IN: Evangel Publishing House, 1996.

Brown, Francis, S. R. Driver, and Charles A. Briggs. *Hebrew and English Lexicon of the Old Testament*. Oxford: Claredon, 1907.

Brown, Harold O. J. "The Conservative Option." *Tensions in Contemporary Theology*. Stanley N. Gundry and Alan F. Johnson, eds. Chicago: Moody, 1976.

Brown, John. *Expository Discourses on 1 Peter*. 3 vols. 1848. Reprint, Edinburgh: Banner of Truth, 1975.

Brown, Kenneth and P. Lewis Brevard. *History of the Churches of Christ in Christian Union*. Circleville, OH: Circle Press, 1980.

Bruce, F. F. *Tyndale New Testament Commentaries: Romans.* Grand Rapids: Eerdmans, 1963.

__________. *The New International Commentary on the New Testament: The Epistles to the Colossians, to Philemon, and to the Ephesians.* Grand Rapids: Eerdmans, 1984.

__________. *Commentary on the Book of Acts* in *The New International Commentary on the New Testament.* rev. ed. Grand Rapids: Eerdmans, 1988.

__________. *The Gospel of John.* Grand Rapids: Eerdmans, 1983.

Bruner, Fredrick. *A Theology of the Holy Spirit.* Grand Rapids: Eerdmans, 1970.

Brunner, Emil. *The Christian Doctrine of God.* Vol. 1 of *Dogmatics.* translated by Olive Wyon, London: Lutterworth, 1949.

__________. *The Divine Imperative.* translated by Olive Wyon. Philadelphia: Westminster, 1947.

__________. *The Letter to the Romans: A Commentary.* H. A. Kennedy, transl. Philadelphia: Westminster, 1959.

__________. *Truth as Encounter.* Philadelphia: Westminster, 1964.

Brush, Robert L. and Vic Reasoner, eds. *The Wesley Workbook.* Evansville: IN: Fundamental Wesleyan, 1996.

Bryant, T. J. *"A Survey of the Field," and Strictures Thereon by J. P. Brooks.* Harristown, IL: n. p, 1882.

__________. *Plain Things to Holiness People, also Popular errors concerning Holiness Teaching.* Nevada, IA: Highway Press, 1880, Reprint, Oklahoma City: Charles Edwin Jones, 2002.

__________. *A Protest and Criticism of the Western Union Holiness Convention.* Bloomington, IL, 1881 Reprint, Oklahoma City: Charles Edwin Jones, 2001.

Buber, Martin. *I and Thou.* Ronald Gregor Smith, trans. New York: Charles Scribner's Sons, 1958.

__________. *Between Man and Man.* Ronald Gregor Smith, trans. Boston: Beacon Press, 1955.

Buchsel, Hermann Martin Friedrich. ἀναγεννάω. *Theological Dictionary of the New Testament.* 10 vols. Gerhard Kittel and Gerhard Friedrich, eds. translated by Geoffrey W. Bromiley. Grand Rapids: Eerdmans, 1964. 1:673-675.

Burdick, Donald W. *Tongues: To Speak or Not to Speak.* Chicago: Moody, 1969.

Burgess, Stanley M. "Medieval Models of Perfectionism." *Reaching Beyond.* Stanley M. Burgess, ed. Peabody, MA: Hendrickson, 1986.

__________. "The Ancient and Eastern Churches" and "The Medieval and Modern Western Churches" *Initial Evidence.* Gary B. McGee, ed. Peabody, MA: Hendrickson, 1991.

Burnett, Daniel L. *In the Shadow of Aldersgate.* Eugene, OR: Wipf & Stock, 2006.

Burns, William Henry. *Crisis in Methodism.* Chicago: Christian Witness, 1909.

Bunting, Jabez. *Bunting's Sermons.* 2 vols. New York: Carleton & Porter, 1863.

Burwash, Nathaniel. *Manual of Christian Theology on the Inductive Method.* London: Horace Marshall & Son, 1900.

__________. *A Handbook of the Epistle of St. Paul to the Romans.* 2nd ed. Toronto: William Briggs, 1900.

Byrum, Russell R. *Christian Theology.* 1925. Reprint, Anderson, IN: Warner, 1982.

Caldwell, Merritt. *The Philosophy of Christian Perfection.* Philadelphia: Sorin and Ball, 1848.

Callahan, Virginia Woods, transl. *Saint Gregory of Nyssa: Ascetical Works.* Vol 58 in *The Fathers of the Church: A New Translation.* Washington, DC: Catholic University of America, 1967.

Callen, Barry. "The Context: Past and Present." *The Holiness Manifesto.* Kevin W. Mannoia and Don Thorsen, eds. Grand Rapids: Eerdmans, 2008.

__________ and James North. *Coming Together in Christ.* Joplin, MO: College Press, 1997.

Calvin, John. *Institutes of the Christian Religion.* 2 vols. 1559. translated by Henry Beveridge in 1845. Reprint, Grand Rapids: Eerdmans, 1995.

__________. *The Acts of the Apostles 1-13.* David W. And Thomas F. Torrence, eds. 1560. Reprint, Grand Rapids, Eerdmans, 1966.

__________. *Calvin's Commentaries: The Epistles of Paul the Apostle to the Romans and to the Thessalonians.* David W. And Thomas F. Torrance, eds. (Grand Rapids: Eerdmans, 1960.

__________. *Treatises Against the Anabaptists and Against the Libertines.* Benjamin Wirt Farley, ed. Grand Rapids: Baker, 1982.

Campbell, Donald. "Galatians." *The Bible Knowledge Commentary, New Testament.* John F. Walvoord and Roy B. Zuck, eds. Wheaton, IL: Victory, 1983.

Campbell, J. Y. "Perfection." *The Interpreter's Dictionary of the Bible.* 4 vols. George A. Buttrick, ed. New York: Abingdon,1951.

Campbell, Ted. *John Wesley and Christian Antiquity.* Nashville: Kingswood, 1991.

Camus, Albert. *The Rebel.* New York: Knopf, 1956.

Canfield, S. B. *An Exposition of the Peculiarities, Difficulties and Tendencies of Oberlin Perfectionism. Prepared by a Committee of the Presbytery of Cleveland, and by the Presbytery Ordered to be Published under the Direction of Said Committee, October 8th, 1840.* Cleveland: T. H. Smead, 1841.

Catanzaro, C. J. de, translator. *Symeon the New Theologian: Catechetical Discourses.* New York: Paulist Press, 1980.

Caussade, Jean-Pierre de. *Self-Abandonment to Divine Providence.* translated by Algar Thorolds. 1861. Reprint, London: Burns, Oates, and Washbourne,1935.

Chan, Francis. *Crazy Love*. Colorado Springs: David C. Cook, 2008.

__________. *Forgotten God*. Colorado Springs: David C. Cook, 2009.

Chardin, Teilhard de. *The Phenomenon of Man*. New York: Harper & Row, 1959.

Cargill, A. L. *How God Communicates with Man or the Tongues Error*. Florence, CO: Wells of Baca, 1975.

Carnell, Edward. *Philosophy of the Christian Religion*. Grand Rapids: Eerdmans, 1952.

Carradine, Beverly. *The Better Way*. Cincinnati: God's Revivalist, 1896.

Carter, Charles W. *The Person and Work of the Holy Spirit: A Wesleyan Perspective*. Grand Rapids: Baker, 1974.

__________. ed. *The Wesleyan Bible Commentary*. 6 vols. Grand Rapids: Eerdmans and Baker, 1966-1969.

__________. "Baptism with the Holy Spirit." *Beacon Dictionary of Theology*. Kansas City: Beacon Hill, 1983.

Carter, Charles W. and Ralph Earle. *The Evangelical Commentary: The Acts of the Apostles*. Grand Rapids: Zondervan, 1959.

Cartwright, Peter. *Autobiography of Peter Cartwright*. 1856. Reprint, Nashville: Abingdon, 1984.

Cary, Clement C. "Perfect Love." Sermon #8 in *Twentieth Century Holiness Sermons*. Louisville: Pentecostal Publishing, 191-.

__________. "Did Mr. Wesley Change His Views on Sanctification?" in *Entire Sanctification from 1739-1900*, S. L. C. Coward, ed. Louisville: Pentecostal Publishing, 1904.

Catechism of the Catholic Church: Second Edition. New York: Doubleday, 1994.

Cattell, Everett L. "Appraisal of the Keswick and Wesleyan Contemporary Positions," *Insights into Holiness*. Kenneth Geiger, ed. 1962. Reprint, Salem, OH: Schmul, 1989.

Cell, George Croft. *The Rediscovery of John Wesley*. New York: Henry Holt, 1935.

Chadwick, Samuel. *The Way to Pentecost*. 1932. Reprint, Kansas City: Beacon Hill, n. d.

Chafer, Lewis Sperry. *Systematic Theology*. 8 vols. Dallas: Dallas Seminary Press, 1948.

__________. *Salvation*. Philadelphia: Sunday School Times, 1917.

__________. *He That Is Spiritual*. 1918. Reprint, Philadelphia: Sunday School Times, 1924.

__________. *Grace*. Philadelphia: Sunday School Times, 1922.

__________. *Major Bible Themes*. Chicago: Moody, 1926.

Chalfant, E. O. *Forty Years on the Firing Line* (*E.O. Chalfant Tells His Life's Story*). Kansas City: Beacon Hill, 1951.

Charnock, Stephen. *The Existence and Attributes of God*. 2 vols. 1853. Reprint, Grand Rapids: Baker, 1996.

Chiles, Robert E. *Theological Transitions in American Methodism: 1790-1935*. New

York: Abingdon, 1965.
Church, John R. *Why Baptize By Sprinkling*. Louisville, KY: Herald Press, 1950.
__________. *The One Baptism That Jesus Offers*. Wilmore, KY: Seminary Press, n. d.
Chrysostom. *Nicene and Post-Nicene Fathers*. First Series. Philip Schaff, ed. 1887. Reprint, Grand Rapids: Eerdmans, 1978. Vol. 14.
Christ's Sanctified Holy Church. Perry, GA: Christ's Sanctified Holy Church, 1984.
Clapp, Rodney. "Tacit Holiness: The Importance of Bodies & Habits in Doing Church." *Embodied Holiness: Toward a Corporate Theology of Spiritual Growth*. Samuel M. Powell and Michael E. Lodahl, eds. Downers Grove, IL: InterVarsity, 1999.
Clark, Davis W, ed. *The Methodism Episcopal Pulpit*. New York: Lane & Scott, 1850.
Clark, Elmer. *What Happened at Aldersgate?* Nashville: Methodist Publishing House, 1938.
__________. *The Small Sects in America*. Nashville: Abingdon, 1949.
Clark, Gordon H. *Sanctification*. Jefferson, MD: Trinity Foundation, 1992.
Clark, J. O. A, ed. *Wesley Memorial Volume*. New York: Phillips & Hunt, 1880.
Clark, Robert D. *The Life of Matthew Simpson*. New York: Macmillan, 1956.
Clarke, Adam. *The Miscellaneous Works of Adam Clarke*. 13 vols. James Everett, ed. London: T. Tegg, 1836-1837.
__________. *The Holy Bible, Containing the Old and New Testaments: The Text Carefully Printed from the Most Correct Copies of the Present Authorized Translations, Including the Marginal reading and Parallel Texts; with a Commentary and Critical Notes, Designed as a help to a Better Understanding of the Sacred Writings*. 6 vols. 1811-1825. Reprint, Nashville, Abingdon, n. d.
__________. *Christian Theology*. Samuel Dunn, ed. 1835. Reprint, Salem, OH: Schmul, 1967.
__________. *Memoirs of the Wesley Family*. New York: Emory & Waugh, 1832.
__________. *Selected Sermons from the Works of Adam Clarke*. n. d. Reprint, Salem, OH: Allegheny, 2005.
Clouse, Bonnidell and Robert G. Clouse, eds. *Women in Ministry: Four Views*. Downers Grove, IL: InterVarsity, 1989.
Coats, R. H. "Holiness." *Encyclopedia of Religion and Ethics*. 12 vols. James Hastings, ed. Edinburgh: T. & T. Clark, 1908-1927.
Cobb, John B. Jr. *Grace and Responsibility: A Wesleyan Theology for Today*. Nashville: Abingdon, 1995.
__________. *Christ in a Pluralistic Society*. Philadelphia: Westminster, 1975.
__________. "Human Responsibility and the Primacy of Grace." *Thy Nature and Thy Name is Love*. Bryan P. Stone and Thomas Jay Oord, eds. Nashville: Kingswood, 2001.

__________. and David Ray Griffin. *Process Theology*. Philadelphia: Westminster, 1976.

Cohen, Gary G. *Biblical Separation Defended*. Philadelphia: Presbyterian and Reformed, 1966.

Cohn, Norman. *The Pursuit of the Millennium*. New York: Oxford University Press, 1977.

Coke, Thomas. *A Commentary on the Holy Bible*. 6 vols. London: G. Whitfield, 1801-1803.

Cole, R. Alan. *Exodus* in *Tyndale Old Testament Commentaries*. D. J. Wiseman, ed. Downers Grove, IL: InterVarsity, 1973.

Coleman, Robert E. *Nothing to Do but to Save Souls*. Grand Rapids: Francis Asbury, 1990.

Colledge, Edmund and James Walsh, eds. *Julian of Norwich: Showings* in the series *Classics of Western Spirituality*. New York: Paulist Press, 1978.

Collins, Harry J, Jr. and Floyd L. Hagan, Sr. *History of Christ's Sanctified Holy Church*. Zebulon, NC: Christ's Sanctified Holy Church, 2005.

Collins, Kenneth J. *The Theology of John Wesley*. Nashville: Abingdon, 2007.

__________. *Wesley on Salvation*. Grand Rapids: Francis Asbury, 1989.

__________. *The Scripture Way of Salvation*. Nashville: Abingdon, 1997.

__________. *A Real Christian*. Nashville: Abingdon, 1999.

__________. ed. *Exploring Christian Spirituality*. Grand Rapids: Baker, 2000.

__________. *John Wesley: A Theological Journey*. Nashville: Abingdon, 2003.

__________. *A Faithful Witness: John Wesley's Homiletical Theology*. Wilmore, KY: Wesley Heritage, 1993.

Comfort, Ray and Kirk Cameron. *The School Of Biblical Evangelism*. Gainsville, FL: Bridge-Logos, 2004.

Conn, Charles W. *Like a Mighty Army*. Cleveland, TN: Church of God, 1955.

Cook, Thomas. *New Testament Holiness*. 1902. Reprint, Salem, OH: Schmul, 1978.

Cooke, William. *William Cooke on Entire Sanctification*. Herbert McGonigle, ed. Kansas City: Beacon Hill, 1978. Extracted from Cooke, *Christian Theology* (1845).

Coppedge, Allan. *Portraits of God*. Downers Grove, IL: InterVarsity, 2001.

__________. *John Wesley in Theological Debate*. Wilmore, KY: Wesley Heritage, 1987.

Corner, Daniel D. *The Believer's Conditional Security*. Washington, PA: Evangelical Outreach, 1997.

Cotton, John. "Hypocrites and Saints." *The Puritans: A Sourcebook of their Writings*. 2 vols. Perry Miller and Thomas A. Johnson, eds. New York: Harper, 1938.

Cowen, C. E. *A History of the Church of God (Holiness)*. Overland Park, KS: Herald and Banner, 1949.

Cox, Leo. *John Wesley's Concept of Sin*. 1957. Reprint, Salem, OH: Schmul, 2002.
__________. *John Wesley's Concept of Perfection*. Kansas City: Beacon Hill, 1964.
Crabb, Larry. *The Safest Place on Earth*. Nashville: Thomas Nelson, 1999.
Crane, Jonathan Townley. *Holiness: The Birthright of All God's Children*. New York: Nelson & Phillips, 1874.
Cremer, Hermann. *Biblico-Theological Lexicon of New Testament Greek*. 1878. Reprint, Edinburgh: T & T Clark, 1954.
Crooks, George B. *Life and Letters of the Rev. John McClintock, D. D. LL. D., Late President of Drew Theological Seminary*. Cincinnati: Hitchcock & Welden, 1876.
Cropper, Margaret. *Life of Evelyn Underhill*. New York: Harper & Brothers, 1958.
Crowder, Colin. "Rudolf Otto's *The Idea of the Holy* Revisited." *Holiness Past and Present*. Stephen C. Barton, ed. New York: T. &. T. Clark, 2003.
Cullmann, Oscar. *Christology of the New Testament*. Philadelphia: Westminster, 1959.
__________. *Baptism in the New Testament*. Philadelphia: Westminster, 1950.
Cummings, Violet M. *Noah's Ark: Fable or Fact?* Old Tappan, NJ: Revell, 1976.
Curtis, Olin. *The Christian Faith*. 1905. Reprint, Grand Rapids: Kregel, 1978.
Cyril of Jerusalem. *A Select Library of Nicene and Post-Nicene Fathers* [*NPNF*]. Second Series. Philip Schaff and Henry Wace, eds. 1893. Reprint, Grand Rapids: Eerdmans, 1978. Vol. 7.
Dallimore, Arnold A. *George Whitefield*. 2 vols. Westchester, IL: Cornerstone, 1979.
__________. *Forerunner of the Charismatic Movement: The Life of Edward Irving*. Chicago: Moody, 1983.
Dana, H. E. and Julius R. Mantey. *A Manual Grammar of the Greek New Testament*. New York: Macmillan, 1927.
Darwin, Charles. *The Origin of Species by Means of Natural Selection, or the Preservation of Favoured Races in the Struggle for Life*. 1859. Reprint, New York: Penguin, 1985.
Davies, William R. *Spirit Baptism and Spiritual Gifts in Early Methodism*. Jacksonville, FL: Cross Fires Ministries, 1973.
Davidson, C. T. *Upon This Rock*. Cleveland, TN: White Wing, 1973.
Dayton, Donald W. *Theological Roots of Pentecostalism*. Grand Rapids: Francis Asbury, 1987.
__________. "American Methodist Churches." *The New International Dictionary of the Christian Church*. J. D. Douglas, ed. Grand Rapids: Zondervan, 1978.
__________. "Pentecostalism." *Evangelical Dictionary of Theology*. Walter A. Elwell, ed. Grand Rapids: Baker, 1996.
__________. *Discovering An Evangelical Heritage*. New York: Harper and Row, 1976.

Dayton, Wilbur T. "Entire Sanctification," in *A Contemporary Wesleyan Theology*. 2 vols. Charles W. Carter, ed. Grand Rapids: Francis Asbury, 1983.

Demarest, Bruce. "The Process Reduction of Jesus and the Trinity." *Process Theology*, Ronald Nash, ed. Grand Rapids: Baker, 1987.

DeNeff, Steve. *Whatever Became of Holiness?* Indianapolis: Wesleyan Publishing House, 1996.

Deere, Jack. *Surprised by the Power of the Spirit*. Grand Rapids: Zondervan, 1993.

Delling, Gerhard. τέλειος. *Theological Dictionary of the New Testament*. 10 vols. Gerhard Kittel and Gerhard Friedrich, eds. translated by Geoffrey W. Bromiley. Grand Rapids: Eerdmans, 1972. 8:67-78.

Deschner, John. *Wesley's Christology: An Interpretation*. Dallas: Southern Methodist University, 1985.

Dieter, Melvin E. *The Holiness Revival of the Nineteenth Century*. 2nd ed. Lanham, MD: Scarecrow, 1996.

__________. "The Concept of the Church in the Nineteenth Century Holiness Revival." in *The Church*. Vol. 4 of *Wesleyan Theological Perspectives*. Melvin E. Dieter and Daniel N. Berg, eds. Anderson, IN: Warner, 1984.

__________. "Wesleyan-Holiness Aspects of Pentecostal Origins: As Mediated Through the Nineteenth-Century Holiness Revival." in *Aspects of Pentecostal-Charismatic Origins*. Vinson Synan, ed. Plainfield, NJ: Logos, 1975.

__________. *The 19th-Century Holiness Movement*. Vol 4 of *Great Holiness Classics*. Kansas City: Beacon Hill, 1998.

__________, et al. *Five Views on Sanctification*. Grand Rapids: Zondervan, 1987.

Ditzler, Jacob. *Baptism*. Nashville: Southern Methodist Publishing House, 1886.

Dixon, Patrick. "An Altered Christian Consciousness." *"Toronto" in Perspective: Papers on the New Charismatic Wave of the mid-1900s*. David Hilborn, ed. Carlisle, Cumbria, Great Britain: Paternoster, 2001.

Dorsett, Lyle. *Billy Sunday*. Grand Rapids: Eerdmans, 1991.

Doty, Thomas K. *Lessons in Holiness*. 1881. Reprint, Salem, OH: Schmul, n. d.

Drury, Keith. "Response 1," in *Counterpoint*. D. Curtis Hale, ed. Salem, OH: Schmul, 2005.

__________. *Holiness for Ordinary People*. Marion, IN: Wesley Press, 1983.

Dyrness, William. *Themes in Old Testament Theology*. Downers Grove, IL: InterVarsity, 1979.

Duncan, Watson Boone. *Studies in Methodist Literature*. Nashville: Publishing House of the M. E. Church, South, 1914.

Dunn, James D. G. *Romans 1-8* in *Word Biblical Commentary*. Vol. 38A. Dallas: Word, 1988.

__________. *Baptism in the Holy Spirit*. Philadelphia: Westminster, 1970.

Dunn, Lewis R. *A Manual of Holiness and Review of Dr. James B. Mudge*. Cincinnati: Cranston & Curts, 1895.

Dunning, H. Ray. *Grace, Faith, and Holiness.* Kansas City: Beacon Hill, 1988.

__________. *A Layman's Guide to Sanctification.* Kansas City: Beacon Hill, 1991.

__________. *Reflecting the Divine Image.* Downers Grove, IL: InterVarsity, 1998.

__________. "A Wesleyan Perspective on Spirit Baptism." in *Perspectives on Spirit Baptism.* Chad Owen Brand, ed. Nashville: Broadman & Holman, 2004.

Durham, William H. *Articles Written by Pastor W. H. Durham Taken From Pentecostal Testimony and Printed in Booklet Form.* n. p, n. d.

Dyer, Wayne W. *The Power of Intention.* Carlsbad, CA: Hay House, 2004.

Earle, Ralph. *Word Meanings in the New Testament.* 6 vols. Kansas City: Beacon Hill, 1980.

__________. *Acts* in *Beacon Bible Commentary.* Kansas City: Beacon Hill, 1965.

__________. *The Gospel According to Mark.* Grand Rapids: Zondervan, 1957.

Edersheim, Alfred. *Bible History: Old Testament.* 2 vols. 1876-1887. Reprint, Grand Rapids: Eerdmans, 1949.

__________. *The Life and Times of Jesus the Messiah.* 2 vols. 1883. Reprint, Grand Rapids: Eerdmans, 1971.

Edman, V. Raymond. *They Found the Secret.* Grand Rapids: Zondervan, 1968.

Edwards, Jonathan. *The Works of Jonathan Edwards.* 2 vols. Edinburgh: Banner of Truth, 1976.

Eichrodt, Walter. *Theology of the Old Testament.* 2 vols. translated by J. A. Baker. Philadelphia: Westminster, 1961.

Elliott, Charles. *The Life of the Rev. Robert R. Roberts.* New York: G. Lane & C. B. Tippett, 1846.

Elowsky, Joel C, ed. *Ancient Christian Commentary on Scripture: John 11-21.* Thomas C. Oden, ed. Downers Grove, IL: InterVarsity, 2007.

__________. *We Believe in the Holy Spirit.* Vol. 4 of *Ancient Christian Doctrine.* Thomas C. Oden, ed. Downers Grove, IL: InterVarsity, 2009.

English, John C. "John Wesley and the English Enlightenment: an 'Appeal to Men of Reason and Religion.'" *Studies on Voltaire and the Eighteenth Century.* Oxford: Voltaire Foundation, 1990.

Enns, Paul. *The Moody Handbook of Theology.* Chicago: Moody Press, 1989.

Episcopius, Simon. *The Confession or Declaration of the Ministers or Pastors, Which in the United Provinces are called Remonstrants, Concerning the chief Points of Christian Religion.* London: Francis Smith, 1676.

Erickson, Millard. *Christian Theology.* 3 vols. Grand Rapids: Baker, 1983-1985.

__________. *Christian Theology.* 2nd ed. Grand Rapids: Baker Books, 2002.

Ervin, Howard. *Spirit-Baptism: A Biblical Investigation.* Peabody, MA: Hendrickson, 1987.

__________. *Conversion-Initiation and the Baptism in the Holy Spirit.* Peabody, MA: Hendrickson, 1984.

__________. *These are not Drunken as ye Suppose.* Plainfield, NJ : Logos

International, 1968.
Etheridge, J. W. *The Life of the Rev. Adam Clarke, LL. D.* Nashville: Southern Methodist Publishing House, 1859.
Eusebius, *Ecclesiastical History*. A. D. 325. Reprint, Peabody, MA: Hendrickson, 1998.
Evans, G. R, ed. *Bernard of Clairvaux* in the series *Classics of Western Spirituality*. New York: Paulist, 1987.
Failing, George E. "Developments in Holiness Theology After Wesley." *Insights into Holiness*, Kenneth Geiger, ed. Kansas City: Beacon Hill, 1962.
Faulkner, John Alfred. *Modernism and the Christian Faith*. New York: Methodist Book Concern, 1921.
Faupel, D. William. *The Everlasting Gospel: The Significance of Eschatology in the Development of Pentecostal Thought*. Journal of Pentecostal Theology Supplement Series #10. Sheffield, England: Sheffield Academic Press, 1996.
__________, ed. *Six Tracts by W. B. Godbey*. New York: Garland, 1985.
Fee, Gordon D. *God's Empowering Presence: The Holy Spirit in the Letters of Paul*. Peabody, MA: Hendrickson, 1994.
__________. *The First Epistle to the Corinthians* in *The New International Commentary on the New Testament*. Grand Rapids: Eerdmans, 1987.
Fee, Gordon D. and Douglas Stuart. *How to Read the Bible for All Its Worth*. Grand Rapids: Zondervan, 1981.
Ferguson, Sinclair. *The Holy Spirit* in *Contours of Christian Theology*. Gerald Bray, ed. Downers Grove, IL: InterVarsity, 1996.
__________. *Christian Spirituality*. Donald L. Alexander, ed. Downers Grove, IL: InterVarsity, 1988.
Feinburg, Charles L. *Jeremiah* in *The Expositor's Bible Commentary*. Vol. 6. Frank E. Gaebelein, ed. Grand Rapids: Zondervan, 1986.
Feinburg, John. "God Ordains All Things." in *Predestination and Free Will: Four Views of Divine Sovereignty and Human Freedom*. David and Randall Basinger, eds. Downers Grove, IL: InterVarsity, 1986.
Fénelon, Francis. *Christian Perfection*. Charles F. Whiston, ed. translated by Mildred Whitney Stillman. New York: Harper & Brothers, 1947.
Field, Benjamin. *The Student's Handbook of Christian Theology*. New York: Methodist Book Concern, 1887.
Findlay, George G. *Studies in John's Epistles: Fellowship in the Life Eternal*. 1909. Reprint, Grand Rapids: Kregel, 1989.
Finlayson, R. A. *The Holiness of God*. Glasgow: Pickering & Inglis, 1955.
Finney, Charles G. *Lectures to Professing Christians*. New York: Fleming H. Revell, 1878.
__________. *Finney's Systematic Theology*. J. H. Fairchild, ed. 1846. Reprint, Minneapolis: Bethany, 1976.

__________. *Sermons on Important Subjects.* New York: John S. Taylor, 1836.
__________. *Power from on High.* Ft. Washington, PA: Christian Literature Crusade, 1944.
Fisher, G. Richard and M. Kurt Goedelman. *The Confusing World of Benny Hinn.* St. Louis: Personal Freedom Outreach, 1999.
Fisk, Wilbur. *Calvinistic Controversy.* New York: Mason & Lane, 1837.
Fletcher, John. *The Works of the Reverend John Fletcher.* 1833. Reprint, Salem, OH: Schmul, 1974.
__________. *Letters of John Fletcher.* Edward Cook, ed. Yanceyville, NC: Harvey, 1999.
Flew, R. Newton. *The Idea of Perfection in Christian Theology.* London: Oxford University, 1934.
Forde, Gerhard. *Christian Spirituality.* Donald L. Alexander, ed. Downers Grove, IL: InterVarsity, 1988.
Forsaith, Peter. *"Unexampled Labours"; Letters of the Revd John Fletcher to leaders in the Evangelical Revival.* Peterborough, Great Britain: Epworth, 2008.
Forsyth, P. T. *The Cruciality of the Cross.* London: Independent Press, 1909.
__________. *Christian Perfection.* London: Hodder & Stoughton, 1899.
Foster, Philip. "Suggestibility, hysteria and hypnosis." *The Signs and Wonders Movement - Exposed.* Peter Glover, ed. Bromley, England: Day One, 1997.
Foster, Randolf S. *Studies in Theology* 6 vols. New York: Eaton & Mains, 1899-1899.
__________. *Christian Purity; or, The Heritage of Faith.* 1869. Reprint, Salem, OH: Allegheny, 1984.
__________. *Philosophy of Christian Experience.* New York: Hunt & Eaton, 1890.
Foster, Richard. *Streams of Living Water: Celebrating the Great Traditions of Christian Faith.* New York: HarperSanFrancisco, 1998.
Fowler, James W. *Becoming Adult, Becoming Christian.* New York: Harper-Collins, 1984.
Fox, George. *The Journal of George Fox.* 2 vols. Norman Penney, ed. London: Cambridge University Press,1911.
__________. *George Fox, An Autobiography.* Rufus M. Jones, ed. Philadelphia: Ferris & Leach, 1904.
Frame, John. *The Doctrine of God.* Phillipsburg, NJ: Presbyterian & Reformed, 2002.
__________. *Salvation Belongs to the Lord.* Phillipsburg, NJ: P&R Publishing, 2006.
Frank, Douglas. *Less Than Conquerors.* Grand Rapids: Eerdmans, 1986.
Franklin, Samuel. *A Critical Review of Wesleyan Perfection.* Cincinnati: Methodist

Book Concern, 1866.
Frolines, Leroy. *The Quest for Truth.* Nashville: Randall House, 2001.
Fuerst, Julius. *A Hebrew and Chaldee Lexicon to the Old Testament.* London: Williams and Orgate, 1871.
Fuller, Daniel P. *Gospel and Law: Contrast or Continuum?* Grand Rapids: Eerdmans, 1980.
Fung, Ronald. "The Impotence of the Law: Toward a Fresh Understanding of Romans 7:14-25." *Scripture, Tradition, and Interpretation.* Gasque and LaSor, eds. Grand Rapids: Eerdmans, 1978.
Gaebelein, Arno C. *The Gospel of Matthew.* Reprint, Neptune, NJ: Loizeaux Brothers, 1961.
Gale, William D. and Kathryn Dunn. *Miss Winnie Crouch: A Heroine of the Faith.* Mitchell, SC: Faith Bible School,197?.
Gamertsfelder, S. J. *Systematic Theology.* Harrisburg, PA: Evangelical Publishing House, 1913.
Gammie, John G. *Holiness in Israel.* Minneapolis: Fortress, 1989.
Garrison, S. Olin. *Forty Witnesses Covering the Whole Range of Christian Experience.* New York: Eaton & Mains, 1888.
Gee, Donald. *The Pentecostal Movement.* London: Elim, 1949.
__________. *Speaking in Tongues: The Initial Evidence of the Baptism in the Holy Spirit.* Toronto: Full Gospel Publishing House, n. d. 11 pages. Also printed by Gospel Publishing House in Springfield, MO as Tract # 951 and listed in their catalog as early as 1929-1930. Apparently this tract was also printed in Great Britain. See also *The Initial Evidence of the Baptism in the Holy Spirit.* Springfield, MO: Gospel Publishing House Tract #34-4677. 15 pages. This tract was later reprinted without Gee's name, perhaps in the 1980s. These tracts originated with his article "Speaking in Tongues, The Initial Evidence of the Baptism in the Holy Spirit." *Pentecostal Evangel* (12 December 1925) 6.
__________. *Concerning Spiritual Gifts.* Springfield, MO: Gospel, 1972.
Gell, Robert. *An Essay toward the Amendment of the Last English-Translation of the Bible.* London: R. Norton, 1659.
Geisler, Norman. *Systematic Theology.* 4 vols. Minneapolis: Bethany House, 2002-2005.
Gibson, Stephen. *The Sincerity of God.* Salem, OH: Allegheny, 2008.
__________. *Held by Conviction.* Salem, OH: Allegheny, 2008.
Gifford, Edwin Hamilton. Introduction to Cyril of Jerusalem. *A Select Library of Nicene and Post-Nicene Fathers* [*NPNF*]. Second Series. Philip Schaff and Henry Wace, eds. 1893. Reprint, Grand Rapids: Eerdmans, 1978. Vol. 7.
Ginsberg, Allen. *Howel and Other Poems.* 1956. Reprint, San Francisco: City Light, 1996.
Girdlestone, Robert B. *Synonyms of the Old Testament.* 1897. Reprint, Grand

Rapids: Eerdmans, 1976.
Godbey, W. B. *Commentary on the New Testament.* 7 vols. Cincinnati: Revivalist, 1896-1900.
__________. *Spiritualism, Devil-worship and the Tongues.* Cincinnati: God's Revivalist, 190-.
__________. *Sanctification.* Louisville: Pentecostal Publishing, 1884.
__________. *Christian Perfection.* Louisville: Pentecostal Publishing, 1886.
__________. *Autobiography of Rev. W. B. Godbey, A. M.* Cincinnati: Revivalist, 1909.
__________. *Holiness or Hell?* Atlanta: Foote & Davies, 1893.
__________. *Church-Bride-Kingdom.* Cincinnati: Revivalist, 1905.
__________. *Tongues Movement, Satanic.* Zarephath, NJ: Pillar of Fire, 1918.
__________. *Current Heresies.* Cincinnati: God's Revivalist, 1908
__________. *Try the Spirits.* Greensboro, NC: Apostolic Messenger Office, n. d.
Godet, Frederick. *Commentary on the Epistle to the Romans.* 1883. Reprint, Grand Rapids: Zondervan, 1956.
Goff, James M, Jr. *Fields White Unto Harvest: Charles F. Parham and the Missionary Origins of Pentecostalism.* Fayetteville, AR: University of Arkansas, 1988.
Goodman, Felicitas D. *Speaking in Tongues: A Cross-Cultural Study of Glossolalia.* Chicago: University of Chicago, 1972.
Goodwin, John. *A Being Filled With the Spirit.* 1670. Reprint, Edinburgh: James Nichol, 1867.
Goss, Ethel E. *The Winds of God: The Story of the Early Pentecostal Movement (1901-1914) in the Life of Howard A. Goss.* rev. ed. Hazelwood, MO: Word Aflame, 1977.
Graham, James R. "Are There Carnal Christians?" Reprinted as Appendix B in A. J. Smith, *Bible Holiness.* Evansville, IN: Fundamental Wesleyan, 1997.
Granbery, J. C. *Entire Sanctification: The Second Blessing.* Nashville: Publishing House Methodist Episcopal Church, South, 1896.
Greathouse, William M. *Wholeness in Christ.* Kansas City: Beacon Hill, 1998.
__________. *The Historical Development.* Vol. 2 of *Exploring Christian Holiness.* Kansas City: Beacon Hill, 1985.
__________. *The Fullness of the Spirit.* Kansas City: Beacon Hill, 1958.
__________. *From the Apostles to Wesley.* Kansas City: Beacon Hill, 1979.
__________. *Romans* in *Beacon Bible Commentary.* Vol. 8. Kansas City: Beacon Hill, 1968.
Green, Joel B. *Body, Soul, and Human Life: The Nature of Humanity in the Bible.* Grand Rapids: Baker, 2008.
Green, Joel B. and Stuart L. Palmer, eds, *In Search of the Soul.* Downers Grove, IL: InterVarsity, 2005.
Green, Michael. *I Believe in the Holy Spirit.* Grand Rapids: Eerdmans, 1975.

__________. *Entire Sanctification: The Distinctive Doctrine of Wesleyanism.* Kansas City: Beacon Hill, 1980.

Gregory, Benjamin. *Perfect in Christ Jesus.* 190-. Reprint, Salem, OH: Schmul, 1994.

Grenz, Stanley J. and Roger E. Olson, *Twentieth Century Theology.* Downers Grove, IL: InterVarsity, 1992.

Gresham, John L, Jr. *Charles G. Finney's Doctrine of the Baptism of the Holy Spirit.* Peabody, MA: Hendrickson, 1987.

Grider, J. Kenneth. *Entire Sanctification: The Distinctive Doctrine of Wesleyanism.* Kansas City: Beacon Hill, 1980.

__________. *A Wesleyan-Holiness Theology.* Kansas City: Beacon Hill, 1994.

Gromacki, Robert. *The Holy Spirit.* Nashville: Word, 1999.

Groves, Martin. "Charles Wesley's Spirituality." in *Charles Wesley: Life, Literature and Legacy.* Kenneth G. C. Newport and Ted A. Campbell, eds. Peterborough, Great Britain: Epworth, 2007.

Grudem, Wayne. *Systematic Theology.* Nottingham, England: Inter-Varsity, 1994.

__________. *Power an Truth: A Response to* Power Religion. Vineyard Position Pater #4. Anaheim, CA: Association of Vineyard Churches, 1993.

Gruenler, Royce. "Reflections on a Journey in Process," *Process Theology.* Ronald Nash, ed. Grand Rapids: Baker, 1987.

Grundmann, Walter. μομφή in *Theological Dictionary of the New Testament.* Gerhard Kittel and Gerhard Friedrich, eds. translated by Geoffrey W. Bromiley. Grand Rapids: Eerdmans, 1967. 4:571-574.

Guelich, R. A. *The Sermon on the Mount.* Waco, TX: Word, 1982.

Guelzo, Allen. Oberlin Perfectionism and Its Edwardsean Origins, 1835-1870." in *Jonathan Edward's Writings: Text, Context and Interpretation.* Stephen J. Stein, ed. Indiana University Press, 1996.

Gundry, Robert. "The Nonimputation of Christ's Righteousness." in *"Justification": What's at Stake in the Current Debates?* M. A. Husbands and D. J. Treier, eds. Downers Grove, IL: InterVarsity, 2004.

Gunter, W. Stephen. *The Limits of "Love Divine."* Nashville: Kingswood, 1989.

__________. "Aldersgate, the Holiness Movement, and Experiential Religion." in *Aldersgate Reconsidered.* Randy Maddox, ed. Nashville: Kingswood, 1990.

Gurnall, William. *The Christian in Complete Armour.* 3 vols. 1665. Reprint, Edinburgh: Banner of Truth, 1974.

Guthrie, Donald. *New Testament Theology.* Downers Grove, IL: InterVarsity, 1981.

Guyon, Madame. *Experiencing Union with God through Inner Prayer.* Harold J. Chadwick, ed. Gainesville, FL: Bridge Logos, 2001.

Haggard, Emma L. *The Intrepid Builder.* Glendora, CA: Thaddeus Foundation, 1983.

Haldane, Richard. *Exposition of the Epistle to the Romans.* 1847. Reprint,

London: Banner of Truth, 1958.
Hall, Bert H. and Armor D. Peisker. "The Work of the Holy Spirit in Salvation." in *The Word and the Doctrine*. Kenneth Geiger, ed. Kansas City: Beacon Hill, 1965.
Hall, Douglas John. *Imaging God*. Grand Rapids: Eerdmans, 1983.
Hall, J. L. "A Oneness Pentecostal Looks at Initial Evidence." *Initial Evidence*. Gary B. McGee, ed. Peabody, MA: Hendrickson, 1991.
Hambrick-Stowe, Charles. *The Practice of Piety: Puritan Devotional Disciplines in Seventeenth-Century New England*. Chapel Hill: University of North Carolina Press, 1982.
Hamilton, Barry. *William Baxter Godbey — Itinerant Apostle of the Holiness Movement*. Lewiston, NY: Edwin Mellen Press, 2000.
Hanegraaff, Hank. *Christianity and Crisis*. Eugene, OR: Harvest House, 1993.
__________. *Counterfeit Revival*. Waco, TX: Word, 1997.
Haney, M. L. *The Inheritance Restored*. 4th ed. Chicago: Christian Witness, 1897.
Harakas, Stanley. *Toward Transfigured Life: The Theoria of Eastern Orthodox Ethics*. Minneapolis: Light and Life, 1983.
Hardman, Keith J. *Charles Grandison Finney, 1792-1875*. Syracuse, NY: Syracuse University, 1987.
Hare, Edward. *A letter to the Rev. Melville Horne: occasioned by his investigation of the doctrines imputed by him to certain Methodist preachers*. Sheffield: J. Montgomery, 1809.
Harnack, Adolf. *Monasticism*. London: Williams & Norgate, 1913.
__________. *History of Dogma*. 7 vols. translated from 3rd German edition by Neil Buchanan. Boston: Little, Brown & Co, 1901.
Harper, Albert F, ed. *The Wesley Study Bible*. Nashville: Thomas Nelson, 1990.
__________, ed. *Holiness Teaching Today*. Vol. 6 of *Great Holiness Classics*. Kansas City: Beacon Hill, 1987.
__________. "Personalism." *Beacon Dictionary of Theology*. Richard S. Taylor, ed. Kansas City, Beacon Hill, 1983.
Harper, J. Steven. "A Wesleyan Arminian View." in *Four Views on Eternal Security*. J. Matthew Pinson, ed. Grand Rapids: Zondervan, 2002.
__________. *Devotional Life in the Wesleyan Tradition*. Nashville: Upper Room, 1983.
Harris, John L. *Tears and Triumphs*. Louisville: Pentecostal Publishing, 1948.
Harris, Merne A. and Richard S. Taylor. "The Dual Nature of Sin." in *The Word and the Doctrine*. Kenneth E. Geiger, ed. 1965. Reprint, Salem, OH: Schmul, 1989.
Harris, M. J. "Appendix." *The New International Dictionary of New Testament Theology*. 3 vols. Colin Brown, ed. Grand Rapids: Zondervan, 1976.
Harrison, A. W. *Arminianism*. London: Duckworth, 1937.
Harrison, R. H. *Jeremiah and Lamentations* in *Tyndale Old Testament*

Commentaries. Downers Grove, IL: InterVarsity, 1973.
Harrison, W. P. *The Wesleyan Standards: Sermons by the Rev. John Wesley*. 2 vols. Nashville: Smith and Lamar, 1886.
Hart, Larry. "A Charismatic Perspective." in *Perspectives on Spirit Baptism*. Chad Owen Brand, ed. Broadman & Holman, 2004.
Hartley, John E. *The Book of Job: New International Commentary on the Old Testament*. Grand Rapids: Eerdmans, 1988.
Hatch, Nathan O, Mark A. Noll, John D. Woodbridge. *The Gospel in America*. Gand Rapids: Zondervan, 1979.
Hatfield, John T. *Thirty-three Years a Live Wire*. 1913? Reprint, Noblesville, IN: Newby, 1971.
Hauerwas, Stanley. "The Sanctified Body."in *Embodied Holiness: Toward a Corporate Theology of Spiritual Growth*. Samuel M. Powell and Michael E. Lodahl, eds. Downers Grove, IL: InterVarsity, 1999.
Hayes, Doremus A. *The Gift of Tongues*. New York: Methodist Book Concern, 1913.
Hayes, George H. *The Problem Solved, Or the Second Adam and His work; Being a Review of the Second Blessing Theory of Sanctification*. Nashville: Publishing House of the M. E. Church, South, 1892.
Hayford, Jack. *The Beauty of Spiritual Language*. Dallas: Word, 1992.
Headley, Anthony. *Family Crucible: The Influence of Family Dynamics in the Life and Ministry of John Wesley*. Eugene, OR: Wipf and Stock, 2010.
Heath, Elaine A. *Naked Faith: The Mystical Theology of Phoebe Palmer*. Cambridge, UK: James Clarke, 2009.
Heitzenrater, Richard P. *The Elusive Mr. Wesley*. 2 vols. Nashville: Abingdon, 1984.
__________. "John Wesley's Reading of and References to the Early Church Fathers." *Orthodoxy and Wesleyan Spirituality*. S. T. Kimbrough, Jr, ed. Crestwood, NY: St. Vladimir's Seminary Press, 2002.
Helm, Loran W. and Jon L Cullum. *A Voice in the Wilderness*. Parker, IN.: Evangel Voice Publications, 1973.
Henderson, D. Michael. *John Wesley's Class Meeting*. Nappanee, IN: Francis Asbury, 1997.
Hendriksen, William. *New Testament Commentary: John*. 2 vols. Grand Rapids: Baker, 1954.
Hendrix, E. R. *The Perfecting of the Saints*. Nashville: Publishing House Methodist Episcopal Church, South, 1896.
Heard, Gerald. *Is God Evident?* New York: Harper, 1950.
Henry, Carl F. H. "The Stunted God of Process Theology," in *Process Theology*, Ronald Nash, ed. Grand Rapids: Baker, 1987.
__________. *God, Revelation, and Authority*. 6 vols. Waco, TX: Word, 1976-1983.

Henry, G. W. *Shouting, Genuine and Spurious, in all Ages of the church, from the Birth of Creation, when the Sons of God shouted for Joy, until the Shout of the Archangel; with numerous Extracts from the Old and New Testament, and from the Works of Wesley, Edward, Abbott, Cartwright, and Finley, giving a History of the Outward Demonstrations of the Spirit, such as Laughing, Screaming, Shouting, Leaping, Jerking, and Falling under the Power, etc. With extensive Comments, numerous Anecdotes, and Illustrations*. Oneida, NY: Published by the author, 1859.

Henry, Marie. *The Secret Life of Hannah Whitall Smith*. Grand Rapids: Chosen Books, 1984.

Heschel, Abraham. *God in Search of Man: A Philosophy of Judaism*. New York: Farrar, Straus, and Giroux, 1955.

Hilborn, David. "Introduction" and "A Chronicle of the Toronto Blessing." *"Toronto" in Perspective: Papers on the New Charismatic Wave of the mid-1900s*. David Hilborn, ed. Carlisle, Cumbria, Great Britain: Paternoster, 2001.

Hills, A. M. *Holiness and Power*. 1897. Reprint, Noblesville, IN: Newby, n. d.

__________. *The Life of Charles G. Finney*. 1902. Reprint, Salem, OH: Schmul, 1991.

__________. *Fundamental Christian Theology*. 2 vols. 1931. Reprint, Salem, OH: Schmul, 1980.

__________. *Scriptural Holiness and Keswick Teaching Compared*. 1910. Reprint, Salem, OH: Schmul, n. d.

__________. *The Tongues Movement*. Manchester: Ancoats, 1910?

Hinn, Benny. *The Anointing*. Nashville: Thomas Nelson, 1992.

Hinson, E. Glenn. "The Contemplative View." *Christian Spirituality: Five Views of Sanctification*. Donald L. Alexander, ed. Downers Grove, IL: InterVarsity, 1988.

Hodge, Charles. *Systematic Theology*. 3 vols. 1871-1872. Reprint, Grand Rapids: Eerdmans, 1940.

Hodgson Francis. *An Examination of the System of New Divinity; or New School Theology*. New York: Lane, 1840.

Hoekema, Anthony A. "The Reformed Perspective." *Five Views on Sanctification*. Grand Rapids: Zondervan, 1987.

Hofius, Otfried. "Father." *The New International Dictionary of New Testament Theology*. 3 vols. Colin Brown, ed. Grand Rapids: Zondervan, 1976.

Hogue, Wilson T. *The Holy Spirit: A Study*. 1916. Reprint, Winona Lake, IN: Free Methodist, 1950.

__________. "Hymns That Are Immortal." *Living Hymns of Charles Wesley*. Marion, IN: Wesleyan Methodist, 1957.

__________. "Fallen Ministers." *Heart Talks to Ministers and Christian Workers*. E. E. Shelhamer, ed. 192? Reprint, Salem, OH: Schmul, 1968.

Hollenweger, Walter J. *The Pentecostals*. Minneapolis: Augsburg, 1972.
Holloman, Henry. *The Forgotten Blessing*. Nashville: Word, 1999.
Hooker, Richard. *The Works of that Learned and Judicious Divine Mr. Richard Hooker*. 3 vols. London: William Baynes & Son, 1822.
Horner, Ralph C. *Notes on Boland; or, Mr. Wesley and the Second Work of Grace*. Toronto: William Briggs, 1893.
__________. *Pentecost*. 1891. Reprint, New York: Garland, 1984.
Horton, Stanley M. "Spirit Baptism: A Pentecostal Perspective." in *Perspectives on Spirit Baptism*. Chad Owen Brand, ed. Broadman & Holman, 2004.
__________. "The Pentecostal Perspective." in *Five Views on Sanctification*. Grand Rapids: Zondervan, 1987.
House, Wayne. "Apostasia in 2 Thessalonians 2:3 Apostasy or Rapture?" *When the Trumpet Sounds*. Tommy Ice and Timothy Demy, eds. Eugene, OR: Harvest House, 1995.
Howard, Richard E. *Newness of Life*. Kansas City: Nazarene Publishing House, 1975.
Hudson, Oscar. *Gospel Dynamite*. Kansas City: Nazarene Publishing House, 1925.
Hughes, George. *Days of Power in the Forest Temple*. 1873. Reprint, Salem, OH: Allegheny, 1975.
__________. *Fragrant Memories of the Tuesday Meeting and The Guide to Holiness, and their Fifty Years' Work for Jesus*. 1886. Reprint, Salem, OH: Schmul, 1988.
__________. *The Beloved Physician: Walter C. Palmer*. New York: Palmer & Hughes 1884.
Hughes, Philip Edgcumbe. *Paul's Second Epistle to the Corinthians* in *The New International Commentary on the New Testament*. F. F. Bruce, ed. Grand Rapids: Eerdmans, 1962.
Hughes, Richard. "Christian Primitivism as Perfection." in *Reaching Beyond*. Stanley M. Burgess, ed. Peabody, MA: Hendrickson, 1986.
Hughey, G. W. *The Scriptural Mode of Christian Baptism*. Kansas City: Hudson Press, 1907.
Hummel, Charles E. *Fire in the Fireplace: Contemporary Charismatic Renewal*. Downers Grove, IL: InterVarsity, 1978.
Hunt, John. *Letters on Entire Sanctification*. 1849. Reprint, Salem, OH: Schmul, 1984 as *Letters on Sanctification*.
Hunter, H. D. "Ambrose Jessup Tomlinson." *Dictionary of Pentecostal and Charismatic Movements*. Stanley M. Burgess and Gary B. McGee, eds Grand Rapids: Zondervan, 1988.
Huntington, DeWitt Clinton. *Sin and Holiness or What It Is To Be Holy*. Cincinnati: Curts & Jennings, 1898.
Huntzinger, Jon. "Goodness and Worship: A Perspective on Old Testament Holiness." *The Holiness Manifesto*. Kevin W. Mannoia and Don Thorsen,

eds. Grand Rapids: Eerdmans, 2008.
Hurtado, Larry. "Normal, but Not a Norm: Initial Evidence and the New Testament." *Initial Evidence*. Gary B. McGee, ed. Peabody, MA: Hendrickson, 1991.
Hurst, John Fletcher. *The History of Methodism*. 7 vols. New York: Eaton & Mains, 1902-1904.
Hynson, Leon O. "They Confessed Themselves Pilgrims, 1897-1930." *Reformers and Revivalists: The History of the Wesleyan Church*. Wayne E. Caldwell, ed. Indianapolis: Wesley Press, 1992.
Inskip, John S, ed. *Holiness Miscellany.* Philadelphia: National Publishing Association for the Promotion of Holiness, 1882.
Irenaeus, *Ante-Nicene Fathers* [*ANF*], Alexander Roberts and James Donaldson, eds. 1867. Reprint, Grand Rapids: Eerdmans, 1978-1979. Vol. 1.
Ironside, H. A. *Holiness, the False and the True*. New York: Loizeaux Brothers, 1912.
Jackson, George. *The Evangelical Revival and Other Sermons*. London: Hodder & Stoughton, 1880.
Jackson, Thomas. *Memoirs of the Life and Writings of the Rev. Richard Watson*. 1834. Reprint, New York: Mason and Lane, 1836.
__________. *Centenary of Wesleyan Methodism*. New York: Mason & Lane, 1839.
__________. *Life of Charles Wesley*. 2 vols. London: John Mason, 1841.
__________. *The Lives of Early Methodist Preachers Chiefly Written by Themselves*. 3 vols. London: John Mason, 1837-1838.
Jacob, Edmund. *Theology of the Old Testament*. New York: Harper & Row, 1958.
Jacobs, Alan. *Original Sin: A Cultural History*. New York: HarperOne, 2008.
Jacobs, Simon P. *The Real Christian*. Battle Creek, MI: S. P. Jacobs, 1899.
James, Nancy C. *The Pure Love of Madame Guyon*. Lanham, MD: University Press of America, 2007.
James, William. *The Varieties of Religious Experience*. 1902. Reprint, New York: Penguin, 1982.
Jamieson, Robert, A. R. Fausset, and David Brown. *A Commentary on the Old and New Testaments*. 6 vols. 1863. Reprint, Peabody, MA: Hendrickson, 1974.
Janes, Edmund Storer. *Perfect love or, The speeches of Rev. E.L. Janes, Rev. H. Mattison, D.D., Rev. D. Curry, D.D., Rev. J.M. Buckley, and Rev. S.D. Brown : in the New York Preachers' meeting, in March and April, 1867: upon the subject of santification : also, Bishop Janes' sermon, on sin and salvation, at the Newark conference camp-meeting, Morristown, Aug. 18, 1867*. New York: Tibbals, 1868. Charles Edwin Jones reprinted this book in 2001.
Jarratt, Devereaux. *The Life of the Reverend Devereaux Jarratt, Rector of Bath Parish, Dinwiddie County, Virginia written by himself in a series of letters addressed to the Rev. John Coleman*. Baltimore: Warner & Hanna, 1806.

Jeffrey, David L, ed. *Toward A Perfect Love: The Spiritual Counsel of Walter Hilton*. Portland, OR: Multnomah, 1985.
Jenkins, Philip. *The Next Christendom*. New York: Oxford, 2002.
Jennings, Daniel R. *The Supernatural Occurrences of John Wesley*. Oklahoma City: Sean Multimedia, 2005.
Jennings, John. *Two Discourses*. translation, David Jennings. Boston: J. Draper for J. Edward and H. Foster, 1740.
Jensen, Jerry, ed. *The Methodists and the Baptism of the Holy Spirit*. Los Angeles: Full Gospel Businessmen's Fellowship International, 1963.
Jepson, J. W. *Don't Blame It all On Adam*. Minneapolis: Bethany, 1984.
Jeremias, Joachim. *The Prayers of Jesus*. London: SCM, 1967.
Jernigan, C. B. *Entire Sanctification*. 194-. Reprint, Salem, OH: Schmul, n. d.
__________. *Pioneer Days of the Holiness Movement in the Southwest*. 1919. Reprint, Salem, OH: Allegheny, 2008.
Johnston, William. *Arise My Love: Mysticism for a New Era*. Maryknoll: Orbis, 2000.
Jones, Charles Edwin. *Perfectionist Persuasion: The Holiness Movement and American Methodism, 1867-1936*. Metuchen, NJ: Scarecrow, 1974.
__________. "Irwin, B(enjamin) H(ardin)" in *Dictionary of Christianity in America*. Robert D. Linder, Daniel G. Reid, Bruce L. Shelley, and Harry S. Stout, eds. Downers Grove, IL: InterVarsity, 1990.
__________. Charles Edwin Jones, *A Guide to the Study of the Pentecostal Movement*. 2 vols. Metuchen, NJ: Scarecrow, 1983.
__________. *The Wesleyan Holiness Movement*. 2 vols. Lanham, MD: Scarecrow, 2005.
Jones, E. Stanley. *The Christ of the Mount*. Nashville: Abingdon, 1931.
__________. *The Christ of Every Road*. New York: Grosset & Dunlap, 1930.
__________. *A Song of Ascents*. Nashville: Abingdon, 1968.
__________. *Victorious Living*. Nashville: Abingdon, 1936.
__________. *The Way to Power and Poise*. New York: Abingdon-Cokesbury, 1949.
Jones, Rufus M. *Later Periods of Quakerism*. London: Macmillan, 1921.
__________. Introduction" in William C. Braithwaite, *The Second Period of Quakerism*. London: Macmillan, 1921.
Jordan, James B. *Pig Out?* Niceville, FL: Tranfiguration Press, 1992.
Journals of the General Conference of the Methodist Episcopal Church, 1848-1856. New York: Carlton & Porter, 1856.
Journal General Conference, M. E. Church, South, 1894. Nashville: Southern Methodist Publishing House, 1894.
The Journal of the General Conference of the Methodist Episcopal Church, 1896.
Joy, Donald M. "Toward Christian Holiness: John Wesley's Faith Pilgrimage." *Moral Development Foundations*. Donald M. Joy, ed. Nashville: Abingdon, 1983.

__________. "Kohlberg Revisited: A Supra-Naturalist Speaks His Mind." *Moral Development Foundations.*

Kaiser, Walter C, Jr. "Leviticus" in *The New Interpreter's Bible.* 12 vols. Leander E. Keck, ed. Nashville: Abingdon, 1994.

__________. "The Baptism in the Holy Spirit as the Promise of the Father: A Reformed Perspective." in *Perspectives on Spirit Baptism: Five Views.* Chad Owen Brand, ed. Nashville: Broadman & Holman, 2004.

Kant, Immanuel. *Religion Within the Limits of Reason Alone.* translated by T. H. Greene and H. H. Hunson. 1793. Reprint, LaSalle, IL: Open Court Publishing, 1960.

Kärkkäinen, Veli-Matti. *Pneumatology*. Grand Rapids: Baker, 2002.

Kaufman, Paul L. *"Logical" Luther Lee and the Methodist War Against Slavery.* Lanham, MD: Scarecrow, 2000.

Keil, C. F. and Franz Delitzsch. *Commentary on the Old Testament.* 25 vols. 1866. Reprint, Grand Rapids: Eerdmans, 1950.

Kendall, David. "Jesus and a Gospel of Holiness." in *The Holiness Manifesto.* Kevin W. Mannoia and Don Thorsen, eds. Grand Rapids: Eerdmans, 2008.

Keen, S. A. *Salvation Papers.* Cincinnati: M. W. Knapp, 1896.

Kent, John. "The Wesleyan Methodist to 1849." *A History of the Methodist Church in Great Britain.* 4 vols. Rupert Davies, A. R. George, E. G. Rupp, eds. London: Epworth, 1965-1988.

Kerwin, Jim. *The Rejected Blessing.* Coon Rapids, MN: OTC Publishers, 2003.

Kiergan, A. M. *Historical Sketches of the Revival of True Holiness and Local Church Polity from 1865-1916.* Ft. Scott, KS: Board of Publication of the Church Advocate and Good Way, 1971.

King, Paul L. *A Believer with Authority.* Camp Hill, PA: Christian Publications, 2001.

Kinlaw, Dennis. *Lectures in Old Testament Theology.* Wilmore, KY: Francis Asbury Society, 2010.

__________. *Let's Start with Jesus.* Grand Rapids: Zondervan, 2003.

__________. "Sin in Believers: The Biblical Evidence." *The Word and the Doctrine.* Kenneth E. Geiger, ed. 1965. Reprint, Salem, OH: Schmul, 1989.

__________. *Preaching in the Spirit.* Grand Rapids: Francis Asbury Press, 1985.

Kinnear, Angus I. *Against the Tide: The Story of Watchman Nee.* Fort Washington, PA: Christian Literature Crusade, 1973.

Klein, Ernest. *A Comprehensive Etymological Dictionary of the Hebrew Language for Readers of English.* New York: MacMillan, 1987.

Knapp, Martin Wells. *Back to the Bible: or, Pentecostal Training.* Cincinnati: M. W. Knapp, 1900.

__________. *Out of Egypt into Canaan; Or, Lessons in Spiritual Geography.* Albion, MI: Revivalist Publishing, 1887.

Knight, John Allan. *In His Likeness*. Kansas City: Beacon Hill, 1976.
__________. *The Holiness Pilgrimage*. Kansas City: Beacon Hill 1986.
Knowling, R. J. *Acts* in *The Expositor's Greek Testament*. W. Robertson Nicoll, ed. 1903. Reprint, Grand Rapids: Eerdmans, 1983.
Knudson, Albert C. *Systematic Theology*. New York: Eaton & Mains, 1894.
__________. *Principles of Christian Ethics*. New York: Abingdon-Cokesbury, 1943.
__________. *The Philosophy of Personalism*. New York: Abingdon, 1927.
Köberle, Adolf. *The Quest for Holiness*. Minneapolis: Augsburg, 1936.
Koch, Kurt. *The Strife of Tongues*. Grand Rapids: Kregel, 1971.
__________. *Occult ABC*. Grand Rapids: Kregel, 1986.
Koehler, Ludwig and Walter Baumgartner. *Lexicon In Veteris Testament Lubros*. Grand Rapids: Eerdmans, 1951.
Kornfeld, Walter. קדש in *Theological Dictionary of the Old Testament*. 15 vols. G. Johannes Botterweck and Helmer Ringgren, eds. translated by Geoffrey W. Bromiley et al. Grand Rapids: Eerdmans, 1974-2006.
Köstenberger, Andreas J. *John* in *Baker Exegetical Commentary on the New Testament*. Robert Yarbrough and Robert H. Stein, eds. Grand Rapids: Baker, 2004.
Kuhn, Harold B. *God: His Names and Nature*. Washington, DC: Christianity Today, 195-.
Kuyper, Abraham. *The Work of the Holy Spirit*. Grand Rapids: Eerdmans, 1946.
Lacy, John. *The General Delusion of Christians Touching the Ways of God's Revealing Himself to and by the Prophets, Evidenced from Scripture and Primitive Antiquity*. London: Seeley & Burnside, 1713. This was reprinted as *The Spirit of Prophecy Defended*. J. Ramsey Michaels, ed. Boston: Brill Academic, 2003.
Ladd, George Eldon. "The Greek Versus the Hebrew View of Man." *The Pattern of New Testament Truth*. Grand Rapids: Eerdmans, 1968.
__________. *A Theology of the New Testament*. Revised Ed. Grand Rapids: Eerdmans, 1993.
LaHaye, Tim. *Spirit-Controlled Temperament*. Wheaton, IL: Tyndale House, 1966.
LaHaye, Tim and John D. Morris. *The Ark on Ararat*. Nashville: Thomas Nelson, 1976.
Lampe, G. W. H. *The Seal of the Spirit*. 1951. Reprint, London: Longmans, Green, 1956.
Lane, William. *The New International Commentary on the New Testament: The Gospel According to Mark*. Grand Rapids: Eerdmans, 1974.
Langford, Thomas. *Practical Divinity*. Nashville: Abingdon, 1983.
__________. *Wesleyan Theology*. Durham, NC: Labyrinth Press, 1984.
Larkin, William, J, Jr. *Acts* in *The IVP New Testament Commentaries*. Downers Grove, IL: InterVarsity, 1995.

LaRondelle, H. K. *Perfection and Perfectionism.* Berrien Springs, MI: Andrews University Press, 1971.
Larsson, John. *Spiritual Breakthrough: The Holy Spirit and Ourselves.* London: Salvation Army, 1983.
Leclerc, Diane K. *Discovering Christian Holiness.* Kansas City: Beacon Hill, 2010.
__________. *Singleness of Heart: Gender, Sin and Holiness in Historical Perspective.* Lanham, MD: Scarecrow, 2001.
__________. "Holiness: Sin's Anticipated Cure," in *The Holiness Manifesto.* Kevin W. Mannoia and Don Thorsen, eds. Grand Rapids: Eerdmans, 2008.
__________. "Mildred Bangs Wynkoop: Bridging the Credibility Gap." *From Aldersgate to Azusa Street.* Henry H. Knight III, ed. Eugene, OR: Wipf and Stock, 2010.
Lee, Luther. *Elements of Theology or an Exposition of the Divine Origin, Doctrines, Morals and Institutions of Christianity.* 10th ed. Syracuse, NY: Wesleyan Methodist Publishing, 1888.
Lee, Umphrey. *John Wesley and Modern Religion.* Nashville: Abingdon-Cokesbury, 1936.
Léger, J. Augustin. *L'Angleterre religieuse et les Origins du Methodisme au xviiie Siecle.* Paris: Hatchette, 1910.
__________. *Wesley's Last Love.* London: J. M. Dent & Sons, 1910.
Lehman, F. M. *The Man in Black.* 1913. Reprint, Salem, OH: Allegheny, n. d.
Lenski, R. C. H. *The Interpretation of St. John's Gospel.* 1943. Reprint, Peabody, MA: Hendrickson, 1998.
__________. *The Interpretation of St. Matthew's Gospel.* Columbus, OH : Lutheran Book Concern, 1932.
__________. *The Interpretation of the Acts of the Apostles.* Minneapolis: Aubsburg, 1934.
Lessmann, Thomas. *Rolle und Bedeutung des Heiligen Geistes in der Theologie John Wesleys.* Stuttgart: Christliches Verlagshaus, 1987.
Lewis, C. S. *The Problem of Pain.* New York: Macmillan, 1962.
__________. *Out of the Silent Planet.* 1938. Reprint, New York:Macmillan, 1965.
__________. *Mere Christianity.* New York: MacMillian, 1960.
Liardon, Roberts. *God's Generals.* Tulsa, OK: Albury, 1996.
Limborch, Philipp van. *Institutiones Theologiae Christianae, ad praxin pietatis et promotionem pacis, christianae unice directae.* Amsterdam, 1686
Lindström, Harald. *Wesley and Sanctification.* Grand Rapids: Zondervan, 1980.
Link, Julie Ackerman. *The Art of Loving God.* Grand Rapids: Discovery House, 2003.
Lloyd-Jones, Martyn. *The Law: Its Functions and Limits, an Exposition of Romans 7:1-8:4.* Grand Rapids: Zondervan, 1973.
__________. *Joy Unspeakable.* Wheaton, IL: Harold Shaw, 1984.
__________. *The New Man, an Exposition of Romans 6.* Grand Rapids:

Zondervan, 1972.
__________. *Life in the Spirit: Ephesians 5:18-6:9*. Grand Rapids: Baker, 1973.
__________. *Christian Conduct: Romans 12*. Edinburgh: Banner of Truth, 2000.
__________. *The Sons of God: An Exposition of Romans 8:5-17*. Grand Rapids: Zondervan, 1974.
Lodahl, Michael. *The Story of God*. Kansas City: Beacon Hill, 1994.
Long, Gene. *Beverly Carradine: Prince of Holiness Writers*. Salem, OH: Allegheny, 2003.
Long, Stephen D. *John Wesley's Moral Theology: The Quest for God and Goodness*. Nashville: Kingswood, 2005.
Longenecker, Richard N. *Acts* in *The Expositor's Bible Commentary*. Frank E. Gaebelein, ed. Grand Rapids: Zondervan, 1981.
Lovelace, Richard. *Dynamics of Spiritual Life: An Evangelical Theology of Renewal*. Downers Grove, IL: InterVarsity, 1979.
Lovell, Ora. "The Holiness of God." *The Word and the Doctrine*, Kenneth E. Geiger, ed. 1965. Reprint, Salem, OH: Schmul, 1989.
Lowrey, Asbury. *Possibilities of Grace*. 1884. Reprint, Salem, OH: Allegheny, 1977.
Lowery, Kevin Twain. *Salvaging Wesley's Agenda*. Eugene, OR: Pickwick, 2008.
Luther, Martin. *Commentary on the Epistle to the Romans*. translated by J. Theodore Mueller. 1515-1516. Reprint, Grand Rapids: Zondervan, 1954.
__________. *Commentary on St. Paul's Epistle to the Galatians*. Reprint, Grand Rapids: Eerdmans, 1930.
__________. *Table Talk*. Thomas S. Kepler, ed. 1566. Reprint, Grand Rapids: Baker, 1979.
__________. *Saemmtliche Schriften*. 25 vols. Johannes Georg Walch, ed. St. Louis: Concordia, 1880-1910.
__________. *Luther's Works*. American Edition. 55 vols. Pelikan, Javoslav and Helmut T. Lehmann, eds. St. Louis: Concordia, 1955-1986.
__________. *Werke: Weimar Ausgabe*. 120 vols. Weimar: Hermann Böhlan, 1883-2009.
Lyons, George. "The Spirit in the Gospels." *The Spirit and the New Age*. Vol. 5 of *Wesleyan Theological Perspectives*. R. Larry Shelton and Alex R. G. Deasley, eds. Anderson, IN: Warner, 1986.
Mackie, Alexander. *The Gift of Tongues*. New York: George H. Doran, 1921.
Mannoia, Kevin W. "Introduction: A Guiding Vision for the Future." *The Holiness Manifesto*. Kevin W. Mannoia and Don Thorsen, eds. Grand Rapids: Eerdmans, 2008.
MacArthur, John F, Jr. *The MacArthur Bible Commentary*. Nashville: Thomas Nelson, 2005.
__________. *Slave: The Hidden Truth About Your Identity in Christ*. Nashville: Thomas Nelson, 2010.
__________. *The Gospel According to Jesus*. Grand Rapids: Zondervan, 1988.

__________. *Charismatic Chaos*. Grand Rapids: Zondervan, 1992.
__________. *The Charismatics: A Doctrinal Perspective*. Grand Rapids: Zondervan, 1978.
MacDonald, James A. *Wesley's Revision of the Shorter Catechism*. Edinburgh: George A. Morton, 1906.
MacDonald, James. *Memoirs of the Rev. Joseph Benson*. New York: N. Bangs & T. Mason, 1823.
MacMillan, John. *The Authority of the Believer*. Camp Hill, PA: Christian Publications, 1997.
Macmurray, John. *Persons in Relation*. London: Faber and Faber, 1961.
__________. *The Self as Agent*. London: Faber and Faber, 1966.
Madden, Edward H. And James E. Hamilton. *Freedom and Grace: The Life of Asa Mahan*. Metuchen, NJ: Scarecrow, 1982.
Maddox, Randy. *Responsible Grace*. Nashville: Abingdon, 1994.
__________, ed. *Aldersgate Reconsidered*. Nashville: Kingswood, 1990.
__________. "Seeking a Response—able God." *Thy Nature and Thy Name is Love*. Bryan P. Stone and Thomas Jay Oord, eds. Nashville: Kingswood, 2001.
Mahan, Asa. *Christian Perfection*. 1874. Reprint, Salem, OH: Schmul, 1975.
__________. *Autobiography, Intellectual, Moral, and Spiritual*. London: T. Woolmer, 1881.
Maharaj, Rabindranth R. *Escape into the Light*. Eugene, OR: Harvest House, 1984.
Maloney, H. Newton and A. Adam Lovekin. *Glossolalia: Behavioral Science Perspectives on Speaking in Tongues*. New York: Oxford, 1985.
Mantey, Julius R. *The Evangelical Commentary: The Gospel According to John*. Grand Rapids: Eerdmans, 1964.
Mantle, J. Gregory. *Beyond Humiliation*. Minneapolis: Bethany Fellowship, 1975.
Maquarrie, John. *In Search of Humanity*. New York: Crossroad, 1983.
Marsden, George. *Fundamentalism and American Culture*. New York: Oxford, 1980.
Martin, Larry E. *The Life and Ministry of William J. Seymour*. Joplin, MO: Christian Life, 1999.
__________, ed. *Azusa Street Sermons by William J. Seymour*. Joplin, MO: Christian Life, 1999.
__________, ed. *Skeptics and Scoffers*. Pensacola: Christian Life, 2004.
Martin, Walter. *The Kingdom of the Cults*. Minneapolis: Bethany House, 1985.
Marsh, E. G. *The Old Man*. Cincinnati: Revivalist, 1931.
Marshall, I. Howard. *Aspects of the Atonement*. Colorado Springs: Paternoster, 2007.
__________. *New International Commentary on the New Testament: The Epistles of John*. Grand Rapids: Eerdmans, 1978.
__________. *The Acts of the Apostles* in *The Tyndale New Testament Commentaries*, R. V. G. Tasker, ed. Grand Rapids: Eerdmans, 1980.

Martin, Francis, ed. Acts in *Ancient Christian Commentary Series*. Downers Grover, IL: InterVarsity, 2006.

Marston, Leslie R. "Christian Holiness: Its Psychological Frame of Reference." *Further Insights into Holiness*. Kenneth E. Geiger, ed. 1963. Reprint, Salem, OH: Schmul, 1990.

__________. *From Chaos to Character: A Study in the Stewardship of Personality*. 1935. Reprint, Winona Lake, IN: Light & Life, 1948.

McCain, Danny. *Lord Lift Me Up!* Kuru, Nigeria: Reconnex Books, 2003.

McClintock, John and James Strong, eds. *Cyclopedia of Biblical, Theological, and Ecclesiastical Literature*. 12 vols. 1867-1887. Reprint, Grand Rapids: Baker, 1981.

McComiskey, Thomas E. קדשׁ. *Theological Wordbook of the Old Testament*. 2 vols. R. Laird Harris, ed. Chicago: Moody, 1980.

McConkey, James. *The Three-Fold Secret of the Holy Spirit*. 1897. Reprint, Pittsburgh: Silver Publishing, 1920.

McConnell, D. R. *A Different Gospel*. Peabody, MA: Hendrickson, 1988.

McConnell, Francis J. *Borden Parker Bowne*. Nashville: Cokesbury, 1929.

McCown, Wayne. "The Spirit in the Book of Acts." *The Spirit and the New Age*. Vol. 5 of *Wesleyan Theological Perspectives*. R. Larry Shelton and Alex R. G. Deasley, eds. Anderson, IN: Warner, 1986.

McDonald, William. *John Wesley and His Doctrine*. 1893. Reprint, Titusville, PA: Allegheny, 1974.

McDougle, Leonidas. *Salvation; Or, The Conditions of Regeneration and Sanctification, with an Epitome of the Churches' Creed and the Christians Chart of Life*. Wilmington, Delaware: published by the author, 1906.

McGiffert, Arthur Cushman. *A History of Christian Thought*. 2 vols. 1931. Reprint, London: Charles Scribner's Sons, 1953.

McGonigle, Herbert. *Sufficient Saving Grace: John Wesley's Evangelical Arminianism*. Carlisle, Cumbria: Paternoster, 2001.

McGrath, Alister E. *Reformation Thought*. 2nd ed. Oxford: Blackwell, 1993.

McIntire, C. T. "Charles Grandison Finney." *Evangelical Dictionary of Theology*. Walter A. Elwell, ed. Grand Rapids: Baker, 1984.

McIntyre, Patrick. *The Graham Formula*. Mammoth Spring, AR: White Harvest, 2006.

McKenna, David. *What a Time to be Wesleyan!* Kansas City: Beacon Hill, 1999.

McKnight, Scot. "Apostasy." *Evangelical Dictionary of Biblical Theology*. Walter A. Elwell, ed. Grand Rapids: Baker, 1996.

__________. *The Letter of James: The New International Commentary on the New Testament*. Gordon D. Fee, ed. Grand Rapids: Eerdmans, 2011.

McLaughlin, George A. *Commentary on the Acts of the Apostles*. 1915. Reprint, Salem, OH: Schmul, 1974.

McQuilkin, J. Robertson. "The Keswick Perspective." *Five Views on Sanctification*.

Grand Rapids: Zondervan, 1987.
McWherter, Leroy. *The Godbey-Maupin Debate*. Cincinnati: God's Revivalist, 190?.
Melton, J. Gordon. *The Encyclopedia of American Religions*. 3rd ed. Detroit: Gale Research, 1989.
Menzies, Robert P. *The Development of Early Christian Pneumatology with Special Reference to Luke-Acts*. Sheffield, England: JSOT, 1991.
Menzies, William W. and Robert P. Menzies. *Spirit and Power: Foundations of Pentecostal Experience*. Grand Rapids: Zondervan, 2000.
Mezies, William W. *Anointed to Serve: The Story of the Assemblies of God* Springfield, MO: Gospel, 1971.
Merrill, Stephen M. *Doctrinal Aspects of Christian Experience*. Cincinnati: Curts & Jennings, 1882.
__________. *Christian Baptism*. Cincinnati: Cranston and Curts, 1876.
Merritt, Timothy. *Address to Christians and Ministers on Christian Perfection, Especially Such as Deny That State to Be Attainable*. New York: N. Bangs & T. Mason, 1821.
__________. *The Christian Manual*. 1825.
Merton, Thomas. *Elected Silence*. London: Hollis & Carter, 1954.
__________. *Life and Holiness*. New York: Herder and Herder, 1963.
Metz, Donald. *Studies in Biblical Holiness*. Kansas City: Beacon Hill, 1971.
__________. *Some Crucial Issues in the Church of the Nazarene*. Olathe, KS: Pioneer, 1993.
Miley, John. *Systematic Theology*. 2 vols. 1893. Reprint, Peabody, MA: Hendrickson,1989.
Migne, Jacques Paul. *Patrologia Latina*. 1844-1845. 217 vols. Reprint, Alexandria, VA: Chadwyck-Healey, 1995.
Mitchell, T. Crichton, ed. *The Wesley Century*, Vol. 2 of *Great Holiness Classics*. Kansas City: Beacon Hill, 1984.
Mitton, J. Leslie. *A Clue to Wesley's Sermons*. London: Epworth Press, 1951.
Moberly, R. C. *Atonement and Personality*. New York: Longmans, Green & Co, 1905.
Monk, Robert. *John Wesley: His Puritan Heritage*. Nashville: Abingdon, 1966.
Moody, Dale. *Apostasy*. Greenville, SC: Smyth & Helwys, 1991.
Moore, Henry. *The Life of Mrs. Mary Fletcher*. 1830. Reprint, Salem, OH: Schmul, 1997.
Moore, Mary Elizabeth Mullino. "Compassion and Hope: Theology Born of Action." *Thy Nature and Thy Name is Love*. Bryan P. Stone and Thomas Jay Oord, eds. Nashville: Kingswood, 2001.
Moreland, J. P. and Scott B. Rae, *Body and Soul: Human Nature and the Crisis in Ethics*. Downers Grove, IL: InterVarsity, 2000.
Morinis, Alan. *Everyday Holiness*. Boston: Trumpeter Books, 2007.

Moritz, Fred. *"Be Ye Holy": The Call to Christian Separation.* Greenville, SC: Bob Jones University, 1994.
Morris, Leon. *The Apostolic Preaching of the Cross.* Grand Rapids: Eerdmans, 1955.
__________. *The Gospel According to John.* Rev. ed. *New International Commentary on the New Testament.* Grand Rapids: Eerdmans, 1995.
__________. *The Atonement.* Downers Grove, IL: InterVarsity, 1983.
Morrison, H. C. *Baptism with the Holy Ghost.* 1900. Reprint, Salem, OH: Allegheny, 1978.
Moss, R. W. *The Rev. W. B. Pope, D. D: Theologian and Saint.* London: Robert Culley, 1903.
Moule, H. C. G. *Veni Creator.* London: Hodder & Stoughton, 1890.
Mother Teresa. *Come Be My Light.* Brian Kolodiejchuk, ed. New York: Doubleday, 2007.
Mouzon, Edwin D. *Fundamentals of Methodism.* Nashville: Lamar & Barton,1923.
Mudge, James. *Growth in Holiness toward Perfection.* New York: Eaton and Mains, 1895.
__________. *The Perfect Life in Experience and Doctrine.* Cincinnati: Jennings and Graham, 1911.
Murphree, Jon Tal. *Divine Paradoxes.* Camp Hill, PA: Christian Publications, 1998.
__________. *The Love Motive.* Camp Hill, PA: Christian Publications, 1990.
Murray, Iain H. *Revival and Revivalism.* Edinburgh: Banner of Truth, 1994.
__________. *Pentecost-Today?* Edinburgh: Banner of Truth, 1998.
__________. *Evangelicalism Divided.* Edinburgh: Banner of Truth, 2000.
__________. *David Martyn Lloyd-Jones.* 2 vols. Edinburgh: Banner of Truth, 1982.
Murray, John. *The Epistle to the Romans* in *The New International Commentary on the New Testament.* F. F. Bruce, ed. Grand Rapids: Eerdmans, 1959.
__________. *Principles of Conduct.* Grand Rapids: Eerdmans, 1957.
Naudé, Jackie A. קדשׁ. *The New International Dictionary of Old Testament Theology and Exegesis*, 5 vols. Willem A. VanGemeren, ed. Grand Rapids: Zondervan, 1997.
Nee, Watchman. *The Normal Christian Life.* Ft. Washington, PA: Christian Literature Crusade, 1963.
Needham, David. *Birthright*: *Christian Do You Know Who You Are?* Portland, OR: Multnomah Press, 1979.
Neill, Stephen. *Christian Holiness.* Guildford, England: Lutterworth, 1960.
Newport, John."Understanding, Evaluating and Learning from the Contemporary Glossalalia Movement." *Tongues.* Luther B. Dyer, ed. Jefferson City, MO: Le Roi Publishers, 1971.
Newport, Kenneth G. C, ed. *The Sermons of Charles Wesley.* New York: Oxford

University Press, 2001.
Niebuhr, Reinhold. *The Nature and Destiny of Man: Human Destiny*. 2 vols. New York: Charles Scribner's Sons, 1943.
Nienkirchen, Charles W. *A. B. Simpson and the Pentecostal Movement*. Peabody, MS: Hendrickson, 1992.
Nixon, R. E. "Pentecost." *The New International Dictionary of the Christian Church*. J. D. Douglas, ed. Grand Rapids: Zondervan, 1978.
Noll, John Francis. *Father Smith Instructs Jackson*. Lester J. Fallon, ed. Huntington, IN: Our Sunday Visitor Press, 1947.
Noll, Mark, ed. *Eerdmans' Handbook to Christianity in America*. Grand Rapids: Eerdmans, 1983.
North, Gary. *Marx Religion of Revolution*. Tyler, TX: Institute for Christian Economics, 1989.
Norwood, Frederick A, ed. *Sourcebook of American Methodism*. Nashville: Abingdon, 1982.
Nygren, Anders. *Agape and Eros*. 1932-1939. Reprint, Philadelphia: Westminster, 1953.
Oblinger, Carl D. "Religious Mimesis: Social Bases for the Holiness Schism in Late Nineteenth-Century Methodism: The Illinois Case: 1869-1885." Monograph Studies, 1; Evanston: Institute for the Study of American Religion, 1973.
Oden, Thomas C. *The Living God: Systematic Theology: Volume One*. San Francisco: Harper & Row, 1987.
__________. *The Word of Life: Systematic Theology: Volume Two*. San Francisco: Harper & Row, 1992.
__________. *Life in the Spirit, Systematic Theology: Volume Three*. San Francisco: HarperCollins, 1992.
__________. *John Wesley's Scriptural Christianity*. Grand Rapids: Zondervan, 1994.
__________. *The Transforming Power of Grace*. Nashville: Abingdon, 1993.
__________, ed. *Phoebe Palmer: Selected Writings*. New York: Paulist, 1988.
Oder, Slawomir. *Why He Is a Saint: The True John Paul II Explained by the Postulator of the Cause of Beatification*. Rome: Rizzoli, 2010.
Oehler, Gustav. *Theology of the Old Testament*. 2 vols. Edinburgh: T. & T. Clark, 1875.
Ogden, Schubert. "Process Theology and the Wesleyan Witness." *Thy Nature and Thy Name is Love*. Bryan P. Stone and Thomas Jay Oord, eds. Nashville: Kingswood, 2001.
Olson, Roger. *Arminian Theology*. Downers Grove, IL: InterVarsity, 2006.
Oord, Thomas Jay."Wesleyan Theology, Boston Personalism, and Process Thought." *Thy Nature and Thy Name is Love*. Bryan P. Stone and Thomas Jay Oord, eds. Nashville: Kingswood, 2001.

Oord, Thomas Jay and Michael Lodahl. *Relational Holiness*. Kansas City: Beacon Hill, 2005.

Oropeza, W. J. *A Time to Laugh: The Holy Laughter Phenomenon Examined — Guidelines for Distinguishing Genuine Renewal from Human-Induced Phenomena*. Peabody, MA: Hendrickson, 1995.

Orr, J. Edwin. *Full Surrender*. London: Marshall, Morgan & Scott, 1951.

Osborn, George, ed. *The Poetical Works of John and Charles Wesley*. 13 vols. London: Wesleyan-Methodist Conference Office, 1868-1872.

Osborne, Grant R. "A Classical Arminian View." *Four Views on the Warning Passages in Hebrews*. Herbert W. Bateman IV, ed. Grand Rapids: Kregel, 2007.

Oss. Douglas. "A Pentecostal/Charismatic View." *Are Miraculous Gifts for Today?* Wayne A. Grudem, ed. Grand Rapids: Zondervan, 1996.

Otto, Rudolf. *The Idea of the Holy*, translated by John W. Harvey. 1923; New York: Oxford, 1958.

Oswalt, John. *Called to Be Holy*. Nappanee, IN: Evangel Publishing House, 1999.

Outler, Albert C. *Theology in the Wesleyan Spirit*. Nashville: Tidings, 1975.

__________. *Evangelism and Theology in the Wesleyan Spirit*. Nashville: Discipleship Resources, 1996.

__________. *John Wesley*. New York: Oxford University, 1964.

__________. "John Wesley's Interests in the Early Fathers of the Church." *The Wesleyan Theological Heritage*. Thomas C. Oden and Leicester R. Longden, eds. Grand Rapids: Zondervan, 1991.

__________. "John Wesley: Folk Theologian." in *The Wesleyan Theological Heritage*.

__________. "Preface." in *John and Charles Wesley: Selected Writings and Hymns*. Frank Whaling, ed. *The Classics of Western Spirituality*. New York: Paulist Press, 1981.

Owen, John. *The Works of John Owen*. William H. Goold, ed. 1850-1853. Reprint, Edinburgh: Banner of Truth, 1967.

Packer, J. I. "God Is." *Eerdmans' Handbook to Christian Belief*, Robin Keeley, ed. Grand Rapids: Eerdmans, 1982.

__________. *A Quest for Godliness*. Wheaton, IL: Crossway, 1999.

__________. *Keep in Step with the Spirit*. Old Tappan, NJ: Revell, 1984.

__________. *Rediscovering Holiness*. Ann Arbor, MI: Vine, 1992.

__________. *Rediscovering Holiness*. 2nd ed. Ventura, CA: Regal, 2009.

Padgett, Alan. "Putting Reason in Its Place: Wesleyan Theology or Ontotheology?" *Thy Nature and Thy Name is Love: Process and Wesleyan Theologies in Dialogue*. Nashville: Kingswood, 2001.

Page, I. E, ed. *John Brash: Memorials and Correspondence*. London: Charles Kelley, 1912.

Palmer, Edwin H. *The Person and Ministry of the Holy Spirit: The Traditional*

Calvinistic Perspective. Grand Rapids: Baker, 1974.
Palmer, Phoebe. *The Way of Holiness, with Notes by the Way*. 1843. Reprint, Salem, OH: Schmul, 1988.
__________. *Faith and Its Effects: Fragments from my Portfolio*. 1848. Reprint, Salem, OH: Schmul, 1999.
Parham, Charles F. *The Sermons of Charles F. Parham: A Voice Crying in the Wilderness*. 1911. *The Everlasting Gospel*. 1944. Reprint, New York: Garland, 1985.
Parham, Sarah E. *The Life of Charles F. Parham: Founder of the Apostolic Faith Movement*. 1930. Reprint, New York: Garland, 1985.
Parks, W. J. *A Short Essay on Apostasy*. Nashville: Publishing House of the M. E. Church, South, 1890.
Parsons, Elmer L. *Living the Holy Life Today*. Indianapolis: Light and Life, 1990.
Pascal, Blaise. *Penśees*. translated by A. J. Krailsheimer. New York: Penguin, 1995.
Pawson, David. "A Mixed Blessing." *"Toronto" in Perspective: Papers on the New Charismatic Wave of the mid-1900s*. David Hilborn, ed. Carlisle, Cumbria, Great Britain: Paternoster, 2001.
Paxon, Ruth. *Called Unto Holiness*. Chicago: Moody, n. d.
Payne, J. Barton. "אבא." *Theological Wordbook of the Old Testament*. 2 vols. R. Laird Harris, ed. Chicago: Moody, 1980.
Peck, George O. *The Scripture Doctrine of Christian Perfection*. 2 vols. 1842. Reprint, Salem, OH: Schmul, 1990-1991.
__________, ed. *Sketches and incidents from the Saddlebag of an Itinerant*. 1843. Reprint, Salem, OH: Schmul, 1988.
__________. *The Life and Times of George Peck, D. D., written by Himself*. New York: Nelson & Phillips, 1874.
Peck, Jesse. *The Central Idea of Christianity*. 1856. Reprint, Salem, OH: Schmul, 1999.
__________. "Bishop Peck's Address." *Minutes of the Twenty-sixth Session of the Southern Illinois Conference of the Methodist Episcopal Church, September 20-24, 1877, held at Mt. Vernon, Illinois*. St. Louis: Chancy Barns, 1877.
Peliken, Jaroslav and Valerie Hotchkiss, *Creeds and Confessions of Faith in the Christian Tradition*. 3 vols. New Haven: Yale University Press, 2003.
Percy, Martyn. *Words, Wonders and Power*. London: SPCK, 1996.
Peters, John L. *Christian Perfection and American Methodism*. Nashville: Abingdon, 1956.
Pentecost, J. Dwight. *The Words and Works of Jesus Christ*. Grand Rapids: Zondervan, 1981.
__________. *Design for Discipleship*. Grand Rapids: Zondervan, 1971.
Perkins, Harold William. *The Doctrine of Christian or Evangelical Perfection*.

London: Epworth Press, 1927.
Perronet, Vincent. *Some Reflections, by way of Dialogue, on the Nature of Original Sin, Baptismal Regeneration, Repentance, the New Birth, Faith, Justification, Christian Perfection, or Universal Holiness, and the Inspiration of the Spirit of God.* London: J. Roberts, 1747.
Peterson, Brent D. "Holiness in the Twenty-First Century." *Postmodern and Wesleyan?* Jay Richard Akkerman, Thomas Jay Oord, and Brent D. Peterson, eds. Kansas City: Beacon Hill, 2009.
Peterson, David. *Possessed by God.* Downers Grove, IL: InterVarsity, 1995.
Pettit, Benjamin. *The Great Privilege of All Believers.* Vol. 1 in *The Wesleyan Doctrine of No Sin.* no location: no publisher, 2009.
Phillips, J. B. *The New Testament in Modern English.* New York: Macmillan, 1958.
Picirilli, Robert E. *Grace, Faith, Free Will.* Nashville: Randall House, 2002.
Pierard, R. V. "American Holiness Movement." *Evangelical Dictionary of Theology.* Walter A. Elwell, ed. Grand Rapids: Baker, 1996.
Pickett, L. L. *The Pickett-Smith Debate on Entire Sanctification.* Louisville: Pickett Publishing, 1897.
Pilmore, Joseph. *The Journal of Joseph Pilmore, Methodist Itinerant, for the Years August 1, 1769 to January 2, 1774.* Frederick E. Maser and Howard T. Maag, eds Philadelphia: Message Publishing, 1969.
Pink, A. W. *An Exposition of the Gospel of John.* Grand Rapids: Zondervan, 1968.
__________. *Gleanings from the Scriptures: Man's Total Depravity.* Chicago: Moody, 1969.
Pinnock, Clark. "A Theological Evaluation and Critique."in *Tongues.* Luther B. Dyer, ed. Jefferson City, MO: LeRoi, 1971.
__________. *An Evangelical Theology of the Charismatic Renewal.* Vancouver, B.C.: Clark H. Pinnock, 1975. Nine pages, apparently an address given at Regent College in Vancouver, May 1975. Reprinted in *Theological Renewal* (October-November 1977) 28-35.
__________. *Flame of Love.* Downers Grove, IL: InterVarsity, 1996.
__________. "Between Classical and Process Theism." *Process Theology.* Ronald Nash, ed. Grand Rapids: Baker, 1987.
Piper, John. *The Future of Justification.* Wheaton, IL: Crossway, 2007.
Pitzer, D. E. "John Humphry Noyes." *The New International Dictionary of the Christian Church.* J. D. Douglas, ed. Grand Rapids: Zondervan, 1978.
Plantinga, Cornelius. *Not the Way It's Supposed to Be.* Grand Rapids: Eerdmans, 1995.
Platt, Frederic. "Perfection (Christian)." *Encyclopedia of Religion and Ethics.* 12 vols. James Hastings, ed. Edinburgh: T. & T. Clark, 1908-1927.
Poloma, Margaret M. "A Reconfiguration of Pentecostalism." *"Toronto" in Perspective: Papers on the New Charismatic Wave of the mid-1900s.* David Hilborn, ed. Carlisle, Cumbria, Great Britain: Paternoster, 2001.

__________. *Main Street Mystics: The Toronto Blessing and Reviving Pentecostalism*. Lanham, MD: Rowman & Littlefield, 2003.
Pollock, J. C. *The Keswick Story*. Chicago: Moody, 1964.
Poole, W. H. *Ripe Grapes: The Fruit of the Spirit*. 1881. Reprint, Salem, OH: Schmul, 1999.
Pope, William Burt. *A Compendium of Christian Theology*. 3 vols. London: Wesleyan-Methodist Book Room, 1880.
__________. *A Higher Catechism of Theology*. London: Woolmer, 1885.
__________. *Sermons, Addresses, and Charges*. London: Wesleyan Conference Office, 1878.
__________. *The Inward Witness and other Discourses*. London: T. Woolmer, 1885.
__________. *The Prayers of St. Paul*. 2nd ed. London: Charles H. Kelley, 1896.
Powell, Samuel M. *Discovering our Christian Faith*. Kansas City: Beacon Hill, 2008.
__________. *Holiness in the 21st Century*. San Diego: Point Loma Nazarene University, 2004.
__________. "Introduction." in *Embodied Holiness*. Samuel M. Powell and Michael E. Lodahl, eds. Downers Grove, IL: InterVarsity, 1999.
__________. "A Contribution to a Wesleyan Understanding of Holiness & Community." *Embodied Holiness.*
__________. "A Trinitarian Alternative to Process Theism." *Thy Nature and Thy Name is Love: Process and Wesleyan Theologies in Dialogue*. Nashville: Kingswood, 2001.
__________ and Michael Lodahl, eds, *Embodied Holiness: Toward a Corporate Theology of Spiritual Growth*. Downers Grove, IL: InterVarsity, 1999.
Prior, Kenneth. *The Way of Holiness*. Ross-shire, Scotland: Christian Focus, 1994.
Procksch, Otto. "ἅγιος."*Theological Dictionary of the New Testament*. Gerhard Kittel and Gerhard Friedrich, eds. translated by Geoffrey W. Bromiley. Grand Rapids: Eerdmans, 1964. 1:100-115.
Provan, Charles D. *The Church is Israel Now*. Vallecito, CA: Ross House, 1987.
Purkiser, W. T. ed. *Exploring Our Christian Faith*. Kansas City: Beacon Hill, 1978.
__________. *God, Man, and Salvation*. Kansas City: Beacon Hill, 1977.
__________. *The Biblical Foundation*. Vol 1 of *Exploring Christian Holiness*. Kansas City: Beacon Hill, 1983.
__________. *Conflicting Concepts of Holiness*. Kansas City: Beacon Hill, 1953.
__________. *Called Unto Holiness: The Second Twenty-five Years, 1933-58*. Kansas City: Nazarene Publishing House, 1983.
Quanstrom, Mark. *A Century of Holiness Theology*. Kansas City: Beacon Hill, 2004.
Quebedeaux, Richard. *The New Charismatics*. Garden City, NY: Doubleday, 1976.
Rack, Henry D. "Charles Wesley and Early Methodism." in *Charles Wesley: Life,*

Literature and Legacy. Kenneth G. C. Newport and Ted A. Campbell, eds. Peterborough, Great Britain: Epworth, 2007.

Ralston, Thomas. *Elements of Divinity*. 1871. Reprint, Salem, OH: Schmul, 1971.

Raser, Harold E. *Phoebe Palmer: Her Life and Thought*. Lewiston, NY: Edwin Mellen Press, 1987.

Rawlinson, George. *Job: The Pulpit Commentary*. H. D. M. Spence and Joseph S. Exell, eds. 1913. Reprint, Grand Rapids: Eerdmans, 1983.

Raymond, Jonathan. "Social Holiness: Journey, Exposures, Encounters" in *The Holiness Manifesto*. Kevin W. Mannoia and Don Thorsen, eds. Grand Rapids: Eerdmans, 2008.

Raymond, Miner. *Systematic Theology*. 3 vols. Cincinnati: Cranston & Stowe, 1877-1879.

Reasoner, Vic. *The Hole in the Holiness Movement*. Evansville, IN: Fundamental Wesleyan, 1991.

__________. *A Fundamental Wesleyan Commentary on Romans*. Evansville, IN: Fundamental Wesleyan, 2002.

__________. *A Fundamental Wesleyan Commentary on Revelation*. Evansville: IN: Fundamental Wesleyan, 2005.

__________. *The Hope of the Gospel*. Evansville, IN: Fundamental Wesleyan, 1999.

Rees, Seth C. *The Ideal Pentecostal Church*. Cincinnati: Revivalist, 1897.

Reeves, Kevin. *The Other Side of the River*. Silverton, OR: Lighthouse Trails, 2007.

Rhys Davids, C. A. F. "Perfection (Buddist)." *Encyclopedia of Religion and Ethics*. James Hastings, ed. Edinburgh: T. & T. Clark, 1908-1927.

Rice, Richard, John Sanders, and Clark H. Pinnock, *The Openness of God*. Downers Grove, IL: InterVarsity, 1994.

Richards, Lawrence O. *A Practical Theology of Spirituality*. Grand Rapids: Zondervan, 1987.

Richards, Anne. *The Toronto Experience: An Exploration of the Issues*. The Church of England Board of Mission Occasional Paper #7. London: Church House Publishing, 1997.

Richardson, Don. *Eternity in Their Hearts*. Ventura, CA: Regal, 1981.

Ridout, George W. *The Deadly Fallacy of Fanaticism*. Louisville: Pentecostal Publishing, 192-.

Ries, Claude A. "The Holy Spirit and the Converted Man." in *Insights into Holiness*. Kenneth Geiger, ed. Kansas City: Beacon Hill, 1963.

Ridgaway, Henry B. *The Life of the Rev. Alfred Cookman*. New York: Nelson & Phillips, 1873.

Ridgway, James H. "Psychology: Theology of the Human Psyche." *A Contemporary Wesleyan Theology*. 2 vols. Charles W. Carter, ed. Grand Rapids: Francis Asbury, 1983.

Riesenfeld, Harald. τηρέωin *Theological Dictionary of the New Testament*. 10 vols.

Gerhard Kittel and Gerhard Friedrich, eds. translated by Geoffrey W. Bromiley. Grand Rapids: Eerdmans, 1972. 8:140-151.

Rice, Richard. "Biblical Support for a New Perspective," in *The Openness of God: A Biblical Challenge to the Traditional Understanding of God.* Clark Pinnock, et al. Downers Grove, IL: InterVarsity, 1994.

Ridout, George. *The Beauty of Holiness.* Louisville, KY: Pentecostal, 192-.

Riggs, Ralph M. *The Spirit Himself.* Springfield, MO: Gospel Publishing House, 1949.

Roberts, Dana. *Understanding Watchman Nee.* Plainfield, NJ: Logos, 1980.

Robertson, A. T. *Word Pictures in the New Testament.* 6 vols. Nashville: Broadman, 1930.

Robinson, John. *The Works of John Robinson.* 3 vols. Robert Ashton, ed. Boston: Doctrinal Tract and Book Society, 1851.

Robeck, Cecil M, Jr. *The Azusa Street Mission and Revival.* Nashville: Thomas Nelson, 2006.

__________. "William J. Seymour and 'the Bible Evidence.'" *Initial Evidence.* Gary B. McGee, ed. Peabody, MA: Hendrickson, 1991.

Roberts, Oral. *The Baptism with the Holy Spirit and the Value of Speaking in Tongues Today.* Tulsa, OK: published by the author, 1964.

Robinson, Wayne A. *Oral: The Warm, Intimate, Unauthorized Portrait of a Man of God.* Los Angeles: Action House, 1976.

Rogers, Hester Ann. *A Short Account of the Experience of Mrs. Hester Ann Rogers, Written by Herself.* 1811. Reprint, Salem, OH: Schmul Publishing, 2003.

Rose, Delbert. "The Wesleyan Understanding of Sin." *The Distinctive Emphases of Asbury Theology Seminary.* 1963. Reprint, Salem, OH: Schmul, 1976.

__________. *Vital Holiness: A Theology of Christian Experience.* Minneapolis: Bethany, 1975.

Rosell, Garth M. and Richard A. G. Dupuis, eds. *Memoirs of Charles G. Finney: The Complete Restored Text.* Grand Rapids: Zondervan, 1989.

Rosser, Leonidas. *A Reply to the "Problem of Methodism."* Nashville: printed for the author, 1889.

Runyon, Theodore. "Holiness as the Renewal of the Image of God in the Individual & Society." *Embodied Holiness: Toward a Corporate Theology of Spiritual Growth.* Samuel M. Powell and Michael E. Lodahl, eds. Downers Grove, IL: InterVarsity, 1999.

__________. *The New Creation: John Wesley's Theology Today.* Nashville: Abingdon, 1998.

Rupp, Gordon. *The Righteousness of God: Luther Studies.* London: Hodder and Stoughton, 1953.

__________. *Principalities and Powers.* Nashville: Abingdon, 1952.

Rushdoony, Rousas John. *The Institutes of Biblical Law.* Phillipsburg, NJ: Presbyterian and Reformed, 1973.

__________. *Law and Society*. Vol. 2 of *The Institutes of Biblical Law*. Vallecito, CA: Ross House, 1982.
__________. *The Roots of Reconstruction*. Vallecito, CA: Ross House, 1991.
__________. *Systematic Theology*. 2 vols. Vallecito, CA: Ross House, 1994.
__________. *Noble Savages*. Vallecito, CA: Ross House, 2005.
__________. *To Be as God*. Vallecito, CA: Ross House, 2003.
Ruth, Lester. *A Little Heaven Below*. Nashville: Abingdon, 2000.
Ryle, John Charles. *Holiness*. 1877. Reprint, Welwyn: Evangelical Press, 1979.
Ryrie, Charles C. *The Holy Spirit*. Chicago: Moody Press, 1965.
Salter, Darius. *America's Bishop*. Nappanee, IN: Francis Asbury 2003.
__________. *Spirit and Intellect: Thomas Upham's Holiness Theology*. Metuchen, NJ: Scarecrow, 1986.
Samarin, William J. *Tongues of Men and Angels: The Religious Language of Pentecostalism*. New York: Macmillan, 1972.
__________. "Glossolalia as a Vocal Phenomenon" in *Speaking in Tongues: Let's Talk About It*. Watson E. Mills, ed. Waco, TX: Word, 1973.
Sanders, Rufus G. W. *William Joseph Seymour: Black Father of the 20th Century Pentecostal/Charismatic Movement*. Sandusky, OH: Alexandria, 2001.
Sangster, W. E. *The Path to Perfection*. London: Hodder and Stoughton, 1943.
__________. *The Pure in Heart*. 1954. Reprint, Salem, OH: Schmul, 1984.
Sartre, Jean-Paul. *Saint Genet*. New York: Pantheon, 1963.
Schaeffer, Francis. *The Complete Works of Francis A. Schaeffer*. 5 vols. Westchester, IL: Crossway Books, 1982.
Schaff, Philip. *The Creeds of Christendom*. 3 vols. 1877. Reprint, Grand Rapids: Baker, 1983.
__________. *History of the Christian Church*. 8 vols. 1910. Reprint, Grand Rapids: Eerdmans, 1980.
Schleiermacher, Fredrich. *The Christian Faith*. 2nd ed. H. R. Mackintosh and J. S. Stewart, eds. Edinburgh: T & T Clark, 1928.
Schmaus, Michael. *Dogma 6: Justification and the Last Things*. London: Sheed and Ward, 1977.
Schmemann, Alexander. *For the Life of the World*. New York: National Student Christian Federation, 1963.
Schmidt, Martin. *John Wesley: A Theological Biography*. 2 vols. translated by Norman P. Goldhawk. Nashville: Abingdon, 1962-1973.
Schmul, H. E. and Ella Fruin. *Profile of the I. H. Convention*. Salem, OH: IHC, 1992.
Sheldon, H. C. *System of Christian Doctrine*. Cincinnati: Jennings & Graham, 1903.
Sholes, Jerry. *Give Me That Prime-Time Religion*. New York: Hawthorn, 1979.
Schreiner, Thomas R. *Paul, Apostle of God's Glory in Christ: A Pauline Theology*. Downers Grove, IL: InterVarsity, 2001.
__________. *Baker Exegetical Commentary on the New Testament: Romans*.

Grand Rapids: Baker, 1998.
Scofield, C. I, ed.. *The New Scofield Reference Bible*. New York: Oxford, 1967.
__________. *Rightly Dividing the Word of Truth*. Grand Rapids: Zondervan, n. d.
Scott, Otto. *The Great Christian Revolution*. Winsor, NY: The Reformer Library, 1994.
Seamands, David. *Healing Grace*. Wheaton, IL: Victor Books, 1988.
__________. *Putting Away Childish Things*. Wheaton, IL: Victor Books, 1982.
__________. *Healing of Memories*. Wheaton, IL: Victor, 1985.
Seamands, Stephen. *Holiness of Heart and Life*. Nashville: Abingdon, 1990.
Seebass, Horst. "Holy." *The New International Dictionary of New Testament Theology*. 3 vols. Colin Brown, ed. Grand Rapids: Zondervan, 1976.
Selman, Martin J. *2 Chronicles: Tyndale Old Testament Commentaries*. Downers Grove, IL: InterVarsity, 1994.
Seymour, W. J. *The Doctrines and Disciplines of the Azusa Street Apostolic Faith Mission of Los Angeles, California*. Los Angeles: W. J. Seymour, 1915.
Shank, Robert. *Life in the Son*. Springfield, MO: Westcott, 1961.
Shaw, Mark. *Global Awakening*. Downers Grove, IL: InterVarsity, 2010.
Shaw, George. *The Spirit in Redemption*. 1910. Reprint, Hobe Sound, FL: Paul W. Finch, 1965.
Shelhamer, E. E. *Popular and Radical Holiness Contrasted*. Atlanta: Shelhamer, 1906.
__________. *Bible Holiness*. rpt. Salem, OH: Schmul, 196?.
__________, ed. *The Life and Labors of Auntie Coon*. 1922. Reprint, Salem, OH: Schmul, 1964.
Shelly, Bruce L. "Charles G(randison) Finney." *The New International Dictionary of the Christian Church*. J. D. Douglas, ed. Grand Rapids: Zondervan, 1978.
Shephard, W. E. *Bible Lessons*. 1934. Reprint, Salem, OH: Allegheny, 1989.
Sidwell, Mark. *The Dividing Line*. Greenville, SC: Bob Jones University, 1998.
Simmons, Dale H. *E. W. Kenyon and the Postbellum Pursuit of Peace, Power, and Plenty*. Lanham, MD: Scarecrow, 1997.
Smith, A. J. *Bible Holiness and the Modern, Popular, Spurious*. Greensboro, NC: n. p., 1953. Revised Edition. *Bible Holiness*. Revised Edition. Evansville, IN: Fundamental Wesleyan, 1997.
__________. *Jesus Lifting Chinese*. 1929. Reprint, Salem, OH: Allegheny, 2007.
Smith, David L. *With Willful Intent: A Theology of Sin*. Wheaton, IL: BridgePoint, 1994.
Smith, Edward M. *Healing Life's Hurts Through Theophostic Prayer*. Campbellsville, KY: New Creation, 2005.
Smith, George. *Elements of Divinity*. Nashville: Southern Methodist Publishing House, 1860.
Smith, John W. V. *The Quest for Holiness and Unity*. Anderson, IN: Warner, 1980.
Smith, Joseph. *History of the Church of Jesus Christ of Latter-Day Saints*. 6th ed. 7

vols. Salt Lake City: Deseret, 1960.
Smith, Joseph H. *Pauline Perfection*. 1913. Reprint, Salem, OH: Schmul, 1975.
__________. *Things Behind and Things Before in the Holiness Movement*. Chicago: Evangelistic Institute Press, 1916.
Smith, Logan Pearsall. *Unforgotten Years*. Boston: Little, Brown and Company, 1939.
Smith, Timothy L. *Called Unto Holiness*. Kansas City: Beacon Hill, 1962.
__________. *Revivalism and Social Reform*. Baltimore: Johns Hopkins, 1980.
__________. *Nazarenes and the Wesleyan Mission*. Kansas City: Beacon Hill, 1979.
__________. "The Holy Spirit in the Hymns of the Wesleys." *A Contemporary Wesleyan Theology*. 2 vols. Charles W. Carter, ed. Grand Rapids: Francis Asbury, 1983
__________, ed. *The Pentecost Hymns of John and Charles Wesley*. Kansas City: Beacon Hill, 1980.
__________. *Whitefield and Wesley on the New Birth*. Grand Rapids: Zondervan, 1986.
__________, ed. *Charles G. Finney on Christian Holiness: The Promise of the Spirit*. Minneapolis: Bethany Fellowship, 1980.
Smith, William M. *The Backslider and His Recovery*. Westfield, IN: Union Bible Seminary, 1955.
Snyder, Howard A. "Holiness and the Five Calls of God: Holiness in Postmodernity." in *The Holiness Manifesto*. Kevin W. Mannoia and Don Thorsen, eds. Grand Rapids: Eerdmans, 2008.
__________ and Daniel V. Runyan. *The Divided Flame: Wesleyans and the Charismatic Renewal*. Grand Rapids: Francis Asbury, 1986.
Spencer, Herbert. *Social Statics*. 1851. Reprint, New York: Robert Schalkenbach Foundation, 1954.
Spinoza, Baruch. *Ethics*. 1677. Reprint, New York: Peguin, 2005.
Sproul, R. C. *The Holiness of God*. Wheaton, IL: Tyndale House, 1985.
__________. *The Gospel of God*. 1994. Reprint, Ross-shire, Scotland: Christian Focus, 1999.
__________. *Pleasing God*. Wheaton, IL: Tyndale, 1988.
Stackpole, Everett S. *The Evidence of Salvation*. 1894. Reprint, Evansville, IN: Fundamental Wesleyan, 1994.
Stafford, Gilbert W. "Frontiers in Contemporary Theology." *A Contemporary Wesleyan Theology*. 2 Vols. Charles W. Carter, ed. Grand Rapids: Zondervan, 1983.
Stagg, Frank, E. Glenn Hinson, and Wayne E. Oates. *Glossolalia*. Nashville: Abingdon, 1967.
Stählin, Gustav. ὀργή in *Theological Dictionary of the New Testament*. 10 vols. Gerhard Kittel and Gerhard Friedrich, eds. translated by Geoffrey W.

Bromiley. Grand Rapids: Eerdmans, 1967. 5:382-447.
Stamps, Donald C, ed. *The Full Life Study Bible*. Grand Rapids: Zondervan, 1992.
Stanley, Charles. *Eternal Security: Can You Be Sure?* Nashville: Oliver-Nelson, 1990.
Staples, Rob L. *Outward Sign and Inward Grace*. Kansas City: Beacon Hill, 1991.
__________. "Wesleyan Perspectives on the Doctrine of the Holy Spirit." in *The Spirit and the New Age*. Vol. 5 of *Wesleyan Theological Perspectives*. R. Larry Shelton and Alex R. G. Deasley, eds. Anderson, IN: Warner, 1986.
Stark, Rodney. *For the Glory of God*. Princeton, NJ: Princeton University, 2003.
Steele, Daniel. *Leviticus* in *Commentary on the Old Testament*. 9 vols. D. D. Whedon, ed. 1891. Reprint, Salem, OH: Schmul, 1980.
__________. *A Defense of Christian Perfection or A Criticism of Dr. James Mudge's "Growth in Holiness Toward Perfection."* 1896. Reprint, Salem, OH: Schmul, 1984.
__________. *The Gospel of the Comforter*. 1897. Reprint, Salem, OH: Schmul, 1973.
__________. *Half-Hours with St. Paul and Other Bible Readings*. 1894. Reprint, Rochester, PA: Schmul, 1959.
__________. *Love Enthroned*. 1875. Reprint, Salem, OH: Schmul, 1961.
__________. *A Substitute for Holiness or Antinomianism Revived*. 1887. Reprint, Salem, OH: Schmul, 1980 as *Steele's Answers*.
__________. *Steele's Answers*. Chicago: Christian Witness, 1912.
__________. *Mile-Stone Papers*. 1876. Reprint, Salem, OH: Schmul, 1976.
__________. *Half-Hours with St. John's Epistles*. 1901. Reprint, Salem, OH: Schmul, 1972.
__________. *Jesus Exultant*. 1899. Reprint, Salem, OH: Schmul, 1972.
__________. "Sanctification" in *International Standard Bible Encyclopedia*. 5 vols. James Orr, ed. Grand Rapids: Eerdmans, 1930. 4:2685-2686.
Stevens, Abel. *Life and Times of Nathan Bangs, D. D.* New York: Carlton & Porter, 1863.
Stiles, Jack. *The Gift of the Holy Spirit* (Old Tappan, NJ: Revell, 1971.
Stone, Bryan P. "Process and Sanctification," in *Thy Nature and Thy Name is Love: Process and Wesleyan Theologies in Dialogue*. Nashville: Kingswood, 2001.
__________ and Thomas Jay Oord, "Introduction." *Thy Nature and Thy Name is Love: Process and Wesleyan Theologies in Dialogue*. Nashville: Kingswood, 2001.
Stott, John R. W. *The Message of Romans: God's Good News for the World*. Downers Grove, IL: InterVarsity, 1994.
__________. *Baptism and Fullness*. 2nd ed. Downers Grove, IL: InterVarsity, 1976.
__________. *The Message of Acts: Bible Speaks Today*. Downers Grove, IL:

InterVarsity, 1990.

__________. *Understanding Christ*. Grand Rapids: Zondervan, 1979.

Strachan, Alexander, *Recollections of the Life and Times of the Late Rev. George Lowe*. London: John Mason, 1848.

Strahan, James. *The Maréchale*. 5th ed. New York: Hodder & Stoughton, 1914.

Stanley, Charles. *Eternal Security: Can You Be Sure?* Nashville: Oliver-Nelson, 1990.

Stanley, Susie Cunningham. *Feminist Pillar of Fire*. Cleveland: Pilgram, 1993.

Stephens, Randall J. *The Fire Spreads: Holiness and Pentecostalism in the American South*. Cambridge, MA: Harvard University, 2008.

Stewart, Columba. *Cassian the Monk*. New York: Oxford, 1998.

Streiff, Patrick. *Reluctant Saint?* Peterborough, UK: Epworth, 2001.

Stoeffler, F. Ernest. *The Rise of Evangelicalism*. Leiden: Brill, 1965.

Storms, C. Samuel. "Third Wave." *Are Miraculous Gifts for Today? Four Views*. Wayne A. Grudem, ed. Grand Rapids: Zondervan, 1996.

Strong, Augustus H. *Systematic Theology*. Valley Forge, PA: Judson, 1907.

Stronstad, Roger. *The Charismatic Theology of St. Luke*. Peabody, MA: Hendrickson, 1984.

Stuart, Douglas. *Hosea-Jonah* in *Word Biblical Commentary*. David A. Hubbard, ed. Waco, TX: Word, 1987.

Suchocki, Marjorie Hewitt. "Coming Home: Wesley, Whitehead, and Women." *Thy Nature and Thy Name is Love*. Bryan P. Stone and Thomas Jay Oord, eds. Nashville: Kingswood, 2001.

Sugden, Edward H. ed. *The Works of John Wesley*. 18 vols. 1921. Reprint, Grand Rapids: Francis Asbury, 1986.

Summers, Thomas O. *Holiness: A Treatise on Sanctification, as Set Forth in the New Testament*. 1851. Reprint, Louisville, KY: Pentecostal Publishing, 1897.

__________. *The Epistle of Paul, the Apostle, to the Romans*. Nashville: Southern Methodist Publishing House, 1881.

__________. *Commentary on the Gospels*. 4 vols. Nashville: Methodist Episcopal Church, South, 1869-1872.

__________. *Commentary on the Acts of the Apostles*. Nashville: Methodist Episcopal Church, South. 1875.

__________. *The Way of Salvation*. Nashville: Southern Methodist Publishing House, 1881.

__________. *Systematic Theology*. 2 vols. John Tigert, ed. Nashville: Methodist Episcopal Church, South, 1888.

Sutcliffe, Joseph. *A Commentary on the Old and New Testaments*. 2 vols. London: Holdsworth and Ball, 1834.

Swaggart, Jimmy. *Is Speaking in Tongues Scriptural and Relevant to This Day and Age?* Baton Rouge, LA: Jimmy Swaggart Ministries, 1982.

Schwartz, Hillel. *The French Prophets*. Berkeley: University of California, 1980.
Sweet, William Warren. *Religion on the American Frontier*. Vol 4, *The Methodists, 1783-1840, A Collection of Source Material* Chicago: University of Chicago, 1946.
Swindoll, Charles R. *The Grace Awakening*. Dallas: Word, 1990.
Synan, Vinson. *The Holiness-Pentecostal Tradition: Charismatic Movements in the Twentieth Century*. Grand Rapids: Eerdmans, 1997.
__________. *The Holiness-Pentecostal Movement*. Grand Rapids: Eerdmans, 1971.
__________. *In the Latter Days*. Ann Arbor, MI: Servant, 1984.
__________. "Introduction." to Frank Bartleman. *Azusa Street*. Plainfield, NJ: Logos, 1980.
Taylor, George. *The Spirit and the Bride: A Scriptural Presentation of the Operations, Manifestations, Gifts and Fruit of the Holy Spirit in Relation to His Bride with Special Reference to the Latter Rain Revival*. Dunn, NC: published by the author, 1907.
Taylor, Howard and Geraldine. *Hudson Taylor's Spiritual Secret*. 1932. Reprint, Chicago: Moody, n. d.
Taylor, J. Paul. *Holiness: The Finished Foundation*. 1963. Reprint, Salem, OH: Schmul, 1995.
Taylor, Jeremy. *The Whole Works of the Right Reverend Jeremy Taylor, D. D.* 3 vols. London: Reeves & Turner, 1880.
Taylor, Richard S. *A Right Conception of Sin*. Kansas City: Beacon Hill, 1945.
__________. *A Right Conception of Sin*. 2nd ed. Salem, OH: Schmul, 2002.
__________. "Why the Holiness Movement Died." in *Counterpoint*. D. Curtis Hale, ed. Salem, OH: Schmul, 2005.
__________. *The Theological Formulation*. Vol. 3 of *Exploring Christian Holiness*. Kansas City: Beacon Hill, 1985.
__________. "Geneticism." *Beacon Dictionary of Theology*. Kansas City: Beacon Hill, 1983.
__________. *God, Man, and Salvation*. Kansas City: Beacon Hill, 1977.
__________. *Leading Wesleyan Thinkers*. Vol. 3 of *Great Holiness Classics*. Kansas City: Beacon Hill, 1985.
__________. *The Disciplined Life*. Kansas City: Beacon Hill, 1962.
__________. "New Covenant," in *Beacon Dictionary of Theology*. Kansas City: Beacon Hill, 1983.
__________. *Preaching Holiness Today*. Kansas City: Beacon Hill, 1968.
Telford, John. *The Life of John Wesley*. 1886. Reprint, London: Epworth, 1960.
__________. *Wesley's Veterans*. 7 vols. 1912-1914. Reprint, Salem, OH: Schmul, 1976.
Tennant, F. R. *The Concept of Sin*. London: Cambridge University Press, 1912.
Teresa of Avila. *Interior Castle*. translated by E. Allison Peers. New York: Image Books, 1989.

Tersteegen, Gerhard. *Recluse in Demand: Life and Letters* and *Sermons and Hymns.* 2 vols. Reprint, Hampton, TN: Harvey and Tait, 1990.

Thayer, Joseph Henry. *Greek English Lexicon of the New Testament.* 1885. Reprint, Grand Rapids: Zondervan, 1981.

Thomas, Gary L. *Sacred Pathways: Discovering Your Soul's Path to God.* Grand Rapids: Zondervan: 2000.

Thomas, Robert L. *Revelation 1-7.* Chicago: Moody, 1992.

Thompson, J. A. *The Book of Jeremiah* in *The New International Commentary on the Old Testament.* R. K. Harrison, ed. Grand Rapids: Eerdmans, 1980.

Thomson, Edward, ed. *Sermons on Miscellaneous Subjects.* Cincinnati: Hitchcock & Walden, 1869.

Thornton, Wallace, Jr. "Inter-Church Holiness Convention." *Historical Dictionary of the Holiness Movement.* William C. Kostlevy, ed. Lanham, MD: Scarecrow, 2001.

__________. "Sweet Radical Holiness." *Historical Dictionary.*

__________. *Radical Righteousness.* Salem, OH: Schmul, 1998.

__________. "God's Trustee: Martin Wells Knapp and Radical Holiness." *From Aldersgate to Azusa Street: Wesleyan, Holiness, and Pentecostal Visions of the New Creation.* Henry H. Knight III, ed. Eugene, OR: Wipf and Stock, 2010. Advance copy shared by the author.

Thorsen, Donald A. D. *The Wesleyan Quadrilateral.* Grand Rapids: Francis Asbury, 1990.

__________. "Integrated Streams of Holiness: Christian Holiness and Unity, Ancient and Future." *The Holiness Manifesto.* Kevin W. Mannoia and Don Thorsen, eds. Grand Rapids: Eerdmans, 2008.

Thuston, L. F. "C. H. Mason: Sanctified Reformer." *From Aldersgate to Asuza Street.* Henry H. Knight III, ed. Eugene, OR: Wipf and Stock, 2010.

Tidball, Derek. *The Message of Holiness.* Downers Grove, IL: InterVarsity, 2010.

Tigert, John. "Purity and Peace." In *Entire Sanctification from 1739-1900.* L. C. Doward, ed. Louisville: Pentecostal Publishing, 1904.

Tillett, Wilbur F. *Personal Salvation: Studies in Christian Doctrine pertaining to the Spiritual Life.* Nashville: Publishing House of the M. E. Church, South, 1902.

__________ and Charles S. Nutter. *The Hymns and Hymn Writers of the Church.* Nashville: Smith & Lamar, 1915.

Tillich, Paul. *The Courage to Be.* London: Yale University, 1952.

Tomlinson, A. J. *The Last Great Conflict.* 1913. Reprint, New York: Garland, 1985.

Tomlinson, Homer. *Diary of A. J. Tomlinson.* 3 vols. New York: The Church of God, World Headquarters, 1949-1955.

Toplady, Augustus. *The Complete Works of Augustus M. Toplady.* 1794. Reprint, Harrisonburg, VA: Sprinkle, 1987.

Torrey, R. A. *Why God Used D. L. Moody*. Chicago: Moody, 1923.
Tracy, Wesley. *When Adam Clarke Preached, People Listened.* Kansas City: Beacon Hill, 1981.
Treffry, Richard. *A Treatise on Christian Perfection*. 1888. Reprint, Salem, OH: Schmul, 1992.
Trench, Richard C. *Synonyms of the New Testament*. 1880. Reprint, Grand Rapids: Eerdmans, 1953.
Torrance, Thomas F. *Theological Science*. Oxford: Oxford University Press, 1969.
__________. *The Meditation of Christ*. 2nd ed. Colorado Springs: Helmers & Howard, 1992.
Torrey, R. A. *The Holy Spirit*. Old Tappan, NJ: Revell, 1927.
Townsend, W. J, Herbert B. Workman, George Eayrs, eds. *A New History of Methodism*. 2 vols. London: Hodder & Stoughton, 1909.
Tozer, A. W. *The Knowledge of the Holy*. New York: Harper & Row, 1961.
__________. *The Pursuit of God*. Harrisburg, PA: Christian Publications, 1968.
__________. *Keys to the Deeper Life*. Grand Rapids: Zondervan, 1957.
Truesdale, Albert. "Theism." *A Contemporary Wesleyan Theology*. 2 vols. Charles W. Carter, ed. Grand Rapids: Francis Asbury, 1983.
Turner, George Allen. *The Vision Which Transforms*. Kansas City: Beacon Hill, 1965.
__________. *The More Excellent Way*. Winona Lake, IN: Light & Life, 1952.
__________. *The Evangelical Commentary: The Gospel According to John*. Grand Rapids: Eerdmans, 1964.
__________. "The Doctrine of Sanctification." *The Distinctive Emphases of Asbury Theology Seminary*. 1963. Reprinted as *The Doctrinal Distinctives of Asbury Theological Seminary* Salem, OH: Schmul, 1976.
__________. *Witnesses of the Way*. Kansas City: Beacon Hill, 1981.
Turner, Max. *Power from on High: The Spirit in Israel's Restoration and Witness in Luke-Acts*. Sheffield, England: Sheffield Academic Press, 1996.
Turner, Nigel. *Syntax*. Vol. 3 of *A Grammar of New Testament Greek*. J. H. Moulton, ed. Edinburgh: T & T Clark, 1963.
Tuttle, Robert G. Jr. *Sanctity without Starch*. Anderson, IN: Bristol House, 1992.
__________. *Mysticism in the Wesleyan Tradition*. Grand Rapids: Francis Asbury, 1989.
__________. *John Wesley: His Life and Theology*. Grand Rapids: Zondervan, 1978.
__________. "John Wesley." in *Evangelical Dictionary of Theology*. Walter A. Elwell, ed. Grand Rapids: Baker, 1996.
__________. *Guidelines: The United Methodist Church and the Charismatic Movement*. Nashville: Discipleship Resources, 1976.
Tyerman, Luke. *The Life and Times of the Rev. John Wesley, M. A.* 3 vols. London: Hodder & Stoughton, 1872.

__________. *Wesley's Designated Successor.* 1882. Reprint, Stoke-on-Trent: Tentmaker, 2001.
Tyson, John R. *Charles Wesley on Sanctification*. Grand Rapids: Francis Asbury, 1986.
Upham, Thomas. *Principles of the Interior or Hidden Life, Designed Particularly for the Consideration of Those Who Are Seeking Assurance of Faith and Perfect Love*. New York: Harper and Brothers, 1843.
Urquhart, Colin. *Holy Fire*. London: Hodder & Stoughton, 1984.
Van Baalen, Jan Karel. *The Chaos of Cults*. 4th rev. Grand Rapids: Eerdmans, 1962.
Venn, Henry. *Letters of Henry Venn*. 1835. Reprint, Edinburgh: Banner of Truth, 1993.
Vess, A. L. *Were the Disciples Born Again Before Pentecost?* Whitmire, SC: Revival Herald, 1952.
Villars, Isaiah. *The Theory of the Second Blessing — Is It Either Wesleyan or Scriptural?* Read before the District Conference of Rockford District, Rock River Conference, May 11, 1898: Printed by the author, 1898.
Vine, W. E. *An Expository Dictionary of New Testament Words*. 4 vols. Old Tappan, NJ: Revell, 1940.
Vinck, Jose de, ed. *The Works of Bonaventure: Mystical Works*. Paterson, NJ: St. Anthony Guild, 1960.
Yocum, Dale M. *Conformed to Christ*. Cincinnati: Revivalist Press, 1962.
Young, Carlton Raymond, ed. *The Methodist Hymnal*. Nashville: Methodist Publishing House, 1964.
Wacker, Grant. "The Holiness Movement." *Eerdmans' Handbook to Christianity in America*. Mark A. Noll, ed. Grand Rapids: Eerdmans, 1983.
__________. *Heaven Below: Early Pentecostals and American Culture*. Cambridge, MA: Harvard University Press, 2001.
Wagner, C. Peter. *Acts of the Holy Spirit*. Ventura, CA: Regal, 2000.
Waite, Millie Rooke. *A Goodly Heritage: Christ's Sanctified Holy Church*. Summerville, SC: Millie Rooke Waite, 1999.
Wakefield, Samuel. *Christian Theology*. 1862. Reprint as two vols. Salem, OH: Schmul, 1985.
Wallace, D. B. *Greek Grammar beyond the Basics: An Exegetical Syntax of the New Testament*. Grand Rapids: Zondervan, 1996.
Walsh, Thomas. *Sermons by the late Thomas Walsh*. London: Henry Cock, 1764.
Walvoord, John F. "The Augustinian -Dispensational Perspective." *Five Views on Sanctification*. Grand Rapids: Zondervan, 1987.
__________. *The Holy Spirit: A Comprehensive Study of the Person and Work of the Holy Spirit*. Grand Rapids: Zondervan, 1954.
__________. *Doctrine of the Holy Spirit: A Study in Pneumatology*. 3rd ed. Findlay, OH: Dunham, 1958.

Wanamaker, Charles. *The New International Greek Testament Commentary: The Epistles to the Thessalonians*. Grand Rapids: Eerdmans, 1990.
Ward, Horace S, Jr, "The Anti-Pentecostal Argument." *Aspects of Pentecostal-Charismatic Origins*. Vinson Synan, ed. Plainfield, NJ: Logos, 1975.
Ware, Kallistos. *Pseudo-Macarius: Classics of Western Spirituality*. New York: Paulist Press, 1992.
Warfield, *Studies in Perfectionism*. 2 vols. 1931. Reprint, Grand Rapids: Baker, 1981.
__________. *Studies in Perfectionism*. Abridged edition. Phillipsburg, NJ: Presbyterian and Reformed, 1958.
Warner, Wellman J. *The Wesleyan Movement in the Industrial Revolution*. New York: Russell, 1967.
Warren, Rick. *The Purpose-Driven Life*. Grand Rapids: Zondervan, 2002.
Waters, Kenneth. "Holiness in New Testament Perspective." in *The Holiness Manifesto*. Kevin W. Mannoia and Don Thorsen, eds. Grand Rapids: Eerdmans, 2008.
Watson, David Lowes. *The Early Methodist Class Meeting*. rev. ed. Nashville: Discipleship Resources, 1987.
Watson, George D. *Soul Food*. Cincinnati: Revivalist Office, 1896.
__________. *The Bridehood Saints*. Cincinnati: God's Revivalist, 1913.
Watson, Thomas. *A Body of Divinity*. 1692. Reprint,. London: Banner of Truth, 1970.
Watson, Philip S. *Let God Be God!* Philadelphia: Muhlenberg, 1947.
__________. *The Message of the Wesleys: A Reader of Instruction and Devotion*. 1964. Reprint, Grand Rapids: Zondervan, 1984.
Watson, Richard. *Theological Institutes*. 2 vols. 1823-1829. Reprint, New York: Hunt & Eaton, 1889.
__________. *A Biblical and Theological Dictionary*. New York: Carlton & Porter, 1832.
__________. *Sermons and Sketches of Sermons*. New York: Carlton & Porter, 1851.
__________. *An Exposition of the Gospels of St. Matthew and St. Mark*. London: Wesleyan Conference Office, 1833.
__________. *Conversations for the Young: Designed to Promote the Profitable Reading of the Holy Scriptures*. London: John Mason, 1830.
Weeks, Sherwood. *Mysticism, Antinomianism and the Positive Gospel*. Wauseon, OH: Gilson Press, 1955.
Wells, David. *No Place for Truth*. Grand Rapids: Eerdmans, 1993.
Wenham, Gordon. *Genesis 1-15: Word Biblical Commentary*. Waco, TX: Word, 1987.
Wesley Bicentennial. Middletown, CT: Wesleyan University, 1904.
Wesley, Charles. *A Collection of Hymns for the use of the People called Methodists*.

Franz Hildebrandt and Oliver a. Beckerlegge, eds. Vol 7 of the *Bicentennial Edition of the Works of John Wesley*. Nashville: Abingdon, 1983.

__________. *The Journal of the Rev. Charles Wesley, M. A.* Thomas Jackson, ed. 2 vols. 1849. Reprint, Grand Rapids: Baker, 1980.

__________. *Short Hymns on Select Passages of the Holy Scriptures.* 2 vols. Bristol: Farley, 1762.

__________. *A Collection of Hymns for the Use of the People Called Methodists.* London: Paramore, 1780.

Wesley, John. *The Works of John Wesley*, Thomas Jackson, ed. Third edition, 14 vols. 1872. Reprint, Grand Rapids: Zondervan, 1979.

__________. *The Bicentennial Edition of the Works of John Wesley.* 16 vols. Frank Baker and Richard P. Heitzenrater, eds. Nashville: Abingdon, 1976-2003. [*BE*]

__________. *Explanatory Notes upon the New Testament.* 1754. Reprint, Salem, OH: Schmul, 1976.

__________. *Explanatory Notes upon the Old Testament.* 3 vols. 1765. Reprint, Salem, OH : Schmul, 1975.

__________. *An Order of Worship for Such as Would Enter into or Renew Their Covenant with God* (1780); *Directions for Renewing our Covenant with God.* 2nd ed. London: J. Paramore, 1781.

__________, ed. *A Christian Library: Consisting of Extracts from ad Abridgements of the Choicest Pieces of Practical Divinity which have been Published in the English Language.* 50 vols. Bristol: Felix Farley, 1749-1755.

__________, ed. *A Christian Library: Consisting of Extracts from and Abridgments of the Choicest Pieces of Practical Divinity which have been Published in the English Tongue in Thirty Volumes.* 2nd ed. London: T. Cordeux, 1819-1826.

__________, ed. *The Christian Pattern.* Reprint, Salem, OH: Schmul, 1975.

__________. *Letters of the Reverend John Wesley.* John Telford, ed. 8 vols. 1790. Reprint, London: Epworth, 1931.

West, J. W. *Holiness Groups: A "House of Babel," Unscriptural in Teaching and Practice.* 1942? Reprint, Oklahoma City: Charles Edwin Jones, 2004.

Westcott, B. F. *The Gospel According to St. John.* London: John Murray, 1896.

__________. *The Epistle to the Hebrews.* 2nd ed. 1892. Reprint, Grand Rapids: Eerdmans, 1955.

Whaling, Frank, ed. *John and Charles Wesley: Selected Writings and Hymns.* in *The Classics of Western Spirituality.* New York: Paulist Press, 1981.

Wheatley, Richard. *The Life and Letters of Mrs. Phoebe Palmer.* New York: W. C. Palmer, Jr, 1876.

Whedon, Daniel D. *Statements: Theological and Critical.* New York: Phillips & Hunt, 1887.

__________. *The Freedom of the Will.* 1864. Reprint, John D. Wagner, ed,

Eugene, OR: Wipf & Stock, 2009
__________. *Essays, Reviews, and Discourses.* New York: Phillips & Hunt, 1887.
__________. *Commentary on the New Testament.* 5 vols. 1860-1880. Reprint, Salem, OH: Schmul, 1977-1978.
Whidden, Woodrow W. *Ellen White on Salvation.* Hagarstown, MD: Review and Herald, 1995.
White, Alma. *Demons and Tongues.* Zarephath, NJ: Pillar of Fire, 1936.
__________. *My Heart and My Husband.* Zarephath, NJ: Pillar of Fire, 1923.
White, Charles Edward. *The Beauty of Holiness.* Grand Rapids: Francis Asbury, 1986.
White, Ellen G. *Questions on Doctrine.* Washington, DC: Review and Herald, 1957.
White, Kent. *The Word of God Coming Again: Return of Apostolic Faith and Works Now Due on the Earth: with a Sketch of the Life of Pastor W. Oliver Hutchinson.* Winton, Bournemouth, England: The Apostolic Faith Church, 1919.
White, S. S. *Eradication: Defined, Explained, Authenticated.* Kansas City: Beacon Hill, 1954.
Whitehead, John. *The Life of the Rev. John Wesley, M. A.* 2 vols. London: Stephen Couchman, 1793-1796.
Wilberforce, Robert. *The Doctrine of the Incarnation of Our Lord Jesus Christ in its Relation to Mankind and to the Church.* London: John Murray, 1848.
Wilcox, Leslie D. *Profiles in Wesleyan Theology.* 3 vols. Salem, OH: Schmul, 1984.
__________. *Power from on High.* Salem, OH: Schmul, 1979.
__________. *Be Ye Holy.* Cincinnati: Revivalist, 1965.
__________. "Whedon's Position on the Doctrine of Holiness." in the 1977 Schmul Publishers reprint of D. D. Whedon, *Commentary on the Gospels*, Vol. 1, no pagination.
Wiley, H. Orton. *Christian Theology.* 3 vols. Kansas City: Beacon Hill, 1940-1943.
__________. *The Epistle to the Hebrews.* Kansas City: Beacon Hill, 1959.
Wilkins, Michael J. *Following the Master: Discipleship in the Steps of Jesus.* Grand Rapids: Zondervan, 1992.
Willard, Dallas. *The Divine Conspiracy: Rediscovering Our Hidden Life in God.* San Francisco: HarperCollins, 1998.
Williams, Charles. *The Descent of the Dove: A Short History of the Holy Spirit in the Church.* New York: Oxford, 1939.
Williams, Colin. *John Wesley's Theology Today.* Nashville: Abingdon, 1960.
Williams, David J. *Acts* in New *International Bible Commentary.* W. Ward Glasque, ed. Peabody, MS: Hendrickson, 1990.
Williams, J. Rodman. *Renewal Theology.* 3 vols. Grand Rapids: Zondervan, 1988-1992.

__________. *The Gift of the Holy Spirit Today*. Plainfield, NJ: Logos, 1980.
__________. "Charismatic Movement." *Evangelical Dictionary of Theology*. Walter A. Elwell, ed. Grand Rapids: Baker, 1996.
Williams, Robert R. *A Guide to the Teachings of the Early Church Fathers*. Grand Rapids: Eerdmans, 1960.
Wilson, George W. *Methodist Theology vs. Methodist Theologians*. Cincinnati: Jennings & Pye, 1904.
Wilson, W. C. *Well Glory!* mss; Church of the Nazarene Archives, Kansas City, MO.
Wimber, John. *Power Points*. San Francisco: HarperCollins, 1991.
__________ with Kevin Springer. *Power Evangelism*. San Francisco: Harper and Row, 1986.
Winslow, Edward. *Hypocrisie Unmasked A True Relation of the Proceedings of the Governor and Company of the Massachusetts against Samuel Gorton of Rhode Island*. 1646. Reprint, Providence: Club for Colonial Reprints, 1916.
Wiseman, F. Luke. *Charles Wesley, Evangelist and Poet*. New York: Abingdon, 1932.
Witherington, Ben. *The Acts of the Apostles: A Socio-Rhetorical Commentary*. Grand Rapids: Eerdmans, 1998.
Wood, A. Skevington. *The Burning Heart*. Minneapolis: Bethany House, 1978.
Wood, John Allen. *Perfect Love*. 1880. Reprint, Noblesville, IN: Newby, 1967.
__________. *Autobiography of Rev. J. A. Wood*. 1904. Reprint, Nicholasville, KY: Schmul, 2009.
__________. *Christian Perfection, As Taught by John Wesley*. 1921. Reprint, Salem, OH: Schmul, n. d.
__________. *Purity and Maturity*. 1876. Reprint, Chicago: Christian Witness, 1913.
__________. *Mistakes Respecting Christian Holiness*. Chicago: Christian Witness, 1905.
Wood, Jerry. *Pentecostal Holiness: The Life and Preaching of H. C. Morrison*. Salem, OH: Schmul, 2003.
Wood, Laurence W. *Pentecostal Grace*. Wilmore, KY: Francis Asbury, 1980.
__________. *The Meaning of Pentecost in Early Methodism*. Landham, MD: Scarecrow, 2002.
__________. *Truly Ourselves, Truly the Spirit's*. Grand Rapids: Zondervan, 1989.
__________. *Christian Spirituality*. Donald L. Alexander, ed. Downers Grove, IL: InterVarsity, 1988.
Worley, George. *Jeremy Taylor*. London: Longmans, Green, and Co, 1904.
Wright, N. T. *Justification: God's Plan and Paul's Vision*. Downers Grove: InterVarsity, 2009. Wynkoop, Mildred. *A Theology of Love*. Kansas City: Beacon Hill, 1972.
__________. *Foundations of Wesleyan-Arminian Theology*. Kansas City: Beacon

Hill, 1967.
__________. "An Existential Interpretation of the Doctrine of Holiness" (published chapel address: Western Evangelical Seminary, 3 Nov 1955).
Yamauchi, Edwin. טמא. *Theological Wordbook of the Old Testament*. 2 vols. R. Laird Harris, ed. Chicago: Moody, 1980.
Yates, Arthur S. *The Doctrine of Assurance*. London: Epworth, 1952.
Yocum, Dale M. *Conformed to Christ*. Cincinnati: Revivalist Press, 1962.
__________. *The Holy Way*. rev. ed. Salem, OH: Schmul, 1981.
Young, Henry James. "Spirituality and Social Transformation: Perspectives on Wesleyan and Process Theologies." *Thy Nature and Thy Name is Love*. Bryan P. Stone and Thomas Jay Oord, eds. Nashville: Kingswood, 2001.
Zahn, Theodor. *Introduction to the New Testament*. 2 vols. translated by John Moore Trout, et al. Edinburgh: T & T Clark, 1909.
Zink, M. P. *Review of Dr. Huntington on "Sin and Holiness*." Hillsboro, OH: published by the author, 18–. Huntington's book was published in 1898. While the Drew University Methodist Library Pamphlet Collection assigns this the date of 18–, Zink quotes from Stephen Merrill's book, *Sanctification*, which was published in 1901.
Zythoff, Gerrit J. ten. "The Non-Perfectionism of John Calvin." *Reaching Beyond*. Stanley M. Burgess, ed. Peabody, MA: Hendrickson, 1986.

ARTICLES

Abraham, William J. "The End of Wesleyan Theology." *Wesleyan Theological Journal* 40:1 (Spring 2005) 7-25
Allison, Mary. "Issue Sharply Divides Church of Nazarene." *Kansas City Star* (13 November 1976) 1.
Anderson, Josephus. "The Problem Examined." *The Quarterly Review of the Methodist Episcopal Church, South* 10 (January 1889) 373-393; 414-418.
"Annals of the American Pulpit." *Biblical Repertory and Princeton Review* 33 (July 1861) 507.
Arntt, William. "The Role of the Holy Spirit in Entire Sanctification in the Writings of John Wesley." *Wesleyan Theological Journal* 14:2 (Fall 1979) 15-30.
Auxier, Randall E. "God, Process, and Persons: Charles Hartshorne and Personalism." *Process Studies* 27:3-4 (Fall-Winter 1998) 175-199.
Baker, Frank. "John Wesley's Churchmanship." *London Quarterly and Holborn Review* 185 (October 1960) 210-215; 269-274.
Beisner, E. Calvin. "The False God & Gospel of Moral Government Theology." *Christian Research Journal* 17:2 (Fall 1994) 20-23; 41-44.
Bell, Justine. "The Sanctified Band Controversy." *Pamteco Tracings, Beaufort County Genealogical Society Journal* 10:2 (December 1994) 25-30.
Benson, Joseph. "Thoughts on Perfection." *The Arminian Magazine* 4 (October

1781) 549-553.
Berg, Daniel N. "The Theological Context of American Wesleyanism." *Wesleyan Theological Journal* 20:1 (Spring 1985) 45-60.
Besse, H. T. "Speak With Tongues." *The Wesleyan Methodist* 64:3626 (1 May 1907) 2-3.
Beverley, James A. "Toronto's Mixed Blessing." *Christianity Today* 39:10 (11 September 1995) 22-27.
Bible, Ken. "The Wesleys' Hymns on full Redemption and Pentecost: A Brief Comparison." *Wesleyan Theological Journal* 17:2 (Fall 1982) 79-87.
Biema, David van. "The New Calvinism." *Time* 23 March 2009, 50.
Blaney, Harvey. "St. Paul's Posture on Speaking in Unknown Tongues." *Wesleyan Theological Journal* 8:1 (Spring 1973) 52-60.
Blackwelder, Boyce. "The Glossolalia at Pentecost." *Vital Christianity* 83:10 (10 March 1 963) 6.
Bledsoe, Albert. "Review of Pope's *Compendium of Christian Theology*." *Southern Review* 20 (1876) 253–301.
Boddy, Alexander A. "Germany." *Confidence* 3:10 (Oct 1910) 233.
Boland, Jeremiah M. "A Psychological View of Sin and Holiness." *The Methodist Review* 12 (July 1892) 342-354.
__________. "'The Problem' and Its Critics." *The Methodist Review* 13 (January 1893) 339-353.
Bounds, Christopher T. "The Doctrine of Christian Perfection in the Apostolic Fathers." *Wesleyan Theological Journal* 42:2 (Fall 2007) 7-27.
__________. "Irenaeus and the Doctrine of Christian Perfection." *Wesleyan Theological Journal* 45:2 (Fall 2010) 161-176.
__________. "Augustine's Interpretation of Romans 7;14-25, His *Ordo Salutis* and His Consistent Belief in a Christian's Victory Over Sin." *The Asbury Journal* 64:2 (Fall 2009) 20-35. Also published in *The Continuing Relevance of Wesleyan Theology: Essays in Honor of Laurence W. Wood.* Nathan Crawford, ed. Eugene, OR: Pickwick, 2011, 15-27.
Brandt, R. L. "Tongues Are Good for You." *The Evangelist* 19: 9 (September 1987) 35.
Bresee, Phineas. "The Gift of Tongues." *The Nazarene Messenger* 11:24 (13 December 1906) 6.
Brown, O. E. "A Comparative Study of Methodist Theology." *The Quarterly Review of the Methodist Episcopal Church, South* 15 (May 1895) 193-203.
Bundy, David. "Visions of Sanctification: Themes of Orthodoxy in the Methodist, Holiness, and Pentecostal Traditions." *Wesleyan Theological Journal* 39:1 (Spring 2004) 104-136.
Butcher, Andy. "Roberts Liardon Leaves Ministry." *Charisma* 27:7 (February 2002) 36.
Campbell, P. B. "The Gift of Tongues I-III." *The Wesleyan Methodist*

64:3615/3616/3617 (6/13/20 February 1907) 8; 9; 9.
__________. "The Present Tongue Movement And The Bible I-VI." *The Wesleyan Methodist* 64: 3635-3642 (3/10/17/31 July - 14/21 August 1907) 3; 2; 2; 2; 2; 2.
Campbell, Ted. "Charismata in the Christian Communities of the Second Century." *Wesleyan Theological Journal* 17:2 (Fall 1982) 7-25.
Carter, Charles W. "A Wesleyan View of the Spirit's Gift of Tongues in the Book of Acts." *Wesleyan Theological Journal* 4:1 (Spring 1969) 39-68.
Chandler, Majorie Lee. "Fuller Seminary Cancels Course on Signs and Wonders." *Christianity Today* 30:3 (21 February, 1986). 48-49.
Cho, John Chongnahm. "John Wesley's View on Baptism." *Wesleyan Theological Journal* 7:1 (Spring 1972) 60-73.
Christensen, Michael. "Theosis and Sanctification: John Wesley's Reformulation of a Patristic Doctrine." *Wesleyan Theological Journal* 31:2 (Fall 1996) 71-94.
Clark, J. O. A. "Holiness." *The Methodist Quarterly Review* 59 (July 1877) 505-522.
Clayton, Allen. "The Significance of William H. Durham for Pentecostal Historiography." *Pneuma* 1:2 (Fall 1979) 30-31; 34.
Cobb, John B, Jr. "Can a Christian Be a Buddhist Too?" *Japanese Religions* 10 (1979) 1-20.
Coleman, Monica A. "The World At Its Best: A Process Construction of a Wesleyan Understanding of Sanctification." *Wesleyan Theological Journal* 37:2 (Fall 2002) 130-152.
Collins, Kenneth J. "The State of Wesley Studies in North America: A Theological Journey." *Wesleyan Theological Journal* 44:2 (Fall 2009) 7-38.
__________. "Recent Trends in Wesley Studies and Wesleyan/Holiness Scholarship." *Wesleyan Theological Journal* 35:1 (Spring 2000) 67-74.
__________. "Twentieth-Century Interpretations of John Wesley's Aldersgate Experience: Coherence or Confusion?" *Wesleyan Theological Journal* 24 (1989)18-31.
__________. "Other Thoughts on Aldersgate: Has the Conversionist Paradigm Collapsed? *Methodist History* 30:1 (Oct 1991) 10-25.
__________. "A Reply to Randy Maddox." *Methodist History* 31:1 (Oct 1992) 51-54.
__________. "John Wesley's Critical Appropriation of Tradition in his Practical Theology." *Wesleyan Theological Journal* 35:2 (Fall 2000) 69-90.
__________. "John Wesley's Critical Appropriation of Early German Pietism." *Wesleyan Theological Journal* 27:1-2 (Spring-Fall 1992) 57-92.
__________. "The Motif of Real Christianity in the Writings of John Wesley." *The Asbury Theological Journal* 49:1 (1994) 49-62.
__________. "Real Christianity as Integrating Theme in Wesley's Soteriology: The Critique of a Modern Myth." *The Asbury Theological Journal* 51:2 (1996)

15-45.
__________. "Free!" *Light and Life* (Jan 1986) 6-8.
__________. "Book Notes." *The Asbury Journal* 64:1 (2009) 94-95.
Comfort, Glenn S. "Statement from the President." *The Southern Methodist* 28:11 (Nov 1970): 1, 6.
Coppedge, Allan. "Entire Sanctification in Early American Methodism: 1812-1835." *Wesleyan Theological Journal* 13:1 (Spring 1978) 34-50.
Cottrell, Joseph B. "Problem of Methodism." *The Quarterly Review of the Methodist Episcopal Church, South* 11 (April 1889) 97-107.
Cox, F. W. "Speaking With Other Tongues." *The Wesleyan Methodist* 64:3627 (8 May 1907) 2.
Crane, J. T. "Christian Perfection and the Higher Life." *Methodist Quarterly Review* 30 (Oct 1878) 710-711.
Creighton, James. "An Account of the Experiences of the Rev. James Creighton, B.A. ." *The Arminian Magazine* 8 (August 1785) 398-403.
Crouch, Andy. "The Emergent Mystique." *Christianity Today* 48:11 (November 2004) 38.
Cubie, David. "Perfection in Wesley and Fletcher: Inaugural or Teleological?" *Wesleyan Theological Journal* 11:1 (Spring 1976) 22-37.
__________. "'Entire' Sanctification, the Platonic Doctrine of the Soul, and First Thessalonians 5:23." *Wesleyan Theological Journal* 45:2 (Fall 2010) 136-160.
Culp, John E. "Supernatural and Sanctification: Comparison of Roman Catholic and Wesleyan Views." *Wesleyan Theological Journal* 31:2 (Fall 1996) 147-166.
__________. "A Dialog with the Process Theology of John B. Cobb, Jr." *Wesleyan Theological Journal* 15:2 (Fall 1980) 33-44.
Cunningham, Floyd T. "Book Review: Century of Holiness Theology Church of Nazarene." *Wesleyan Theological Journal* 43:2 (Fall 2008) 230-234.
Curry, Daniel. "Book Notices." *Methodist Review* 67:1 (January 1885) 151-153.
Dayton, Donald W. "Asa Mahan and the Development of American Holiness Theology." *Wesleyan Theological Journal* 9:1 (Spring 1974) 60-69.
__________. "The Doctrine of the Baptism of the Holy Spirit: Its Emergence and Significance."*Wesleyan Theological Journal* 13:1 (Spring 1978) 114-126.
__________. "John Fletcher as John Wesley's Vindicator and Designated Successor? A Response to Laurence W. Wood." *Pneuma* 26:2 (Fall 2004) 355-361.
__________. "Rejoinder to Laurence Wood." *Pneuma* 27:2 (Fall 2005) 367-375.
__________. "A Final Round with Larry Wood." *Pneuma* 28:2 (2006) 265-270.
Deasley, Alex R. G. "Entire Sanctification and the Baptism with the Holy Spirit: Perspective on the Biblical View of the Relationship." *Wesleyan Theological Journal* 14:1 Spring 1979) 27-44.
Dennis, Edwin. "Letter to *Confidence*." *Confidence* 3:8 (Aug 1910)190-192.

__________. "The Mulheim Conference." *Confidence* 3:9 (Sept 1910) 208-211.
Dieter, Melvin E. "The Holiness Revival in Nineteenth-Century Europe." *Wesleyan Theological Journal* 9:1 (Spring 1974) 15-27.
__________. "The Development of Holiness Theology in Nineteenth Century America." *Wesleyan Theological Journal* 20:1 (Spring 1985) 61-77.
Dillmann, Charles N. "Book Reviews." *Wesleyan Theological Journal* 18:2 (Fall 1983) 100-108.
Dobson, James. *Focus on the Family Newsletter* (Oct 1990) 3.
Duin, Julia. "An Evening with Rodney Howard-Browne." *Christian Research Journal* 17:3 (Winter 1995) 5-6; 43-45.
__________. "Praise the Lord and Pass the New Wine." *Charisma* 20:1 (August 1994) 26.
Dunlap, Dale. "Tuesday Meetings, Camp Meetings, and Cabinet Meetings." *Methodist History* 87:2 (April 1975) 85-106.
Dunn, Lewis R. "Entire Sanctification. *Methodist Quarterly Review* 49 (October 1867) 555-572.
Dunning, H. Ray. "Holiness, Technology and Personhood." *Wesleyan Theological Journal* 21:1-2 (Spring-Fall 1986) 177-185.
__________. "Holiness: Experience or Relationship?" *Holiness Today* 3:12 (Dec 2001) 45.
__________. "Christian Perfection: Toward a New Paradigm." *Wesleyan Theological Journal* 33:1 (Spring 1998) 151-163.
__________. "Ethics in a Wesleyan Context." *Wesleyan Theological Journal* 5:1 (Spring 1970) 3-10.
__________. "Holiness: Experience or Relationship." *Holiness Today* (Dec 2001) 44-45.
Durham, William H. "An Open Letter To My Brother Ministers in and out of the Pentecostal Movement. A Strong Appeal." *The Pentecostal Testimony* 2.3 (July 1912) 13-14.
__________. "The Finished Work of Calvary." *The Pentecostal Testimony* 2.1 (January 1912) 1-3.
__________. "The Finished Work of Christ — It Makes Plain the Great Work of Redemption." *The Pentecostal Testimony* 2:2 (May 1912) 1-4.
Eby, Patrick. "Images of Perfection in Charles Wesley's Short Hymns." *Wesleyan Theological Journal* 46:1 (Spring 2011) 183-194.
Edman, V. Raymond. "Divine or Devilish." *Christian Herald* (May 1964) 14-17.
Edwards, John E. "The Problem of Methodism." *The Quarterly Review of the Methodist Episcopal Church, South* 9 (Oct 1888) 25-45.
Family News From James Dobson (Sept, 1999) 9.
Farah, Charles. "Differences Within the Family." *Christianity Today* 31:15 (16 October 1987) 25.
Ferrel, Lowell O. "John Wesley and the Enthusiasts." *Wesleyan Theological Journal*

23:1-2 (Spring-Fall 1988) 180-187.
Feraiuolo, Perucci. "Christian Leaders Admonish Hinn." *Christianity Today* 37:9 (16 August 1993) 38-39.
Frame, Randy. "Best-selling Author Admits Mistakes, Vows Changes."*Christianity Today* 35:12 (28 October 1991) 44-46.
__________. "Same Old Benny Hinn, Critics Say." *Christianity Today* 36:11 (5 October 1992) 52-54.
__________. "Account of Hinn's Healings Challenged," *Christianity Today* 39:12 (23 October 1995) 84.
Farrell, Frank. "Outburst of Tongues: The New Penetration." *Christianity Today* 7:24 (13 Sept 1963) 5.
Frazier, J. Russell. "John Wesley's Covenantal and Dispensational View of Salvation History." *Wesley & Methodist Studies* 1 (2009) 33-54.
Faupel, D. William. "Glossolalia as Foreign Language: Investigation of the Early Twentieth-Century Pentecostal Claim." *Wesleyan Theological Journal* 31:1 (Spring 1996) 95-109.
__________. "The Missionary Strategy of John Alexander Dowie." *Wesleyan Theological Journal* 42:1 (Spring, 2007) 199-214.
__________. "Theological Influences on the Teachings and Practices of John Alexander Dowie." *Pneuma* 29:2 (2007) 226-253.
Felleman, Laura Bartels. "John Wesley and the 'Servant of God.'" *Wesleyan Theological Journal* 41:2 (Fall 2006) 72-86.
Fisher, Richard and Kurt Goedelman, "Welcome, Holy Spirit." *Christian Research Journal* 18:3 (Winter 1996) 49-50.
Fletcher, John. "An Essay on the Doctrine of the New Birth." *The Asbury Theological Journal* 53:1 (Spring 1998) 35-56.
Florian, Robyn. "A Sanctifying Process: Amending a Constitutional Article of Religion." *Light and Life* 140:6 (Nov/Dec 2007) 22.
Ford, Marcia. "Toronto's Church Ousted from Vineyard." *Charisma* 21:7 (Feb 1996) 12.
Foster, Richard. "Spiritual Formation Agenda." *Christianity Today* 53:1 (January 2009) 31-32.
Franklin, Barnard. "The Blasphemy Against the Holy Spirit." *Bibliotheca Sacra* 93 (April–June 1936) 232–233.
French, G. R. "The Next Great Awakening." *Word & Spirit* 1:1 (1983) 2.
Grady, J. Lee. "Pentecostals Renounce Racism." *Christianity Today* 38:14 (12 December 1994) 58.
__________. "Memories of Azusa." *Charisma* 21:11 (June 1996): 8
Gallup, George H, Jr. and Timothy Jones. "Uncovering America's Hidden Saints." *Christianity Today* 36:9 (17 Aug, 1992) 26.
Garr, Alfred G. "A letter from Bro. Garr." *Confidence* 2 (May 1908): 21-22.
Gathercole, Simon. "What Did Paul Really Mean?" *Christianity Today* 51:8

(August 2007) 22-28.
Ghiringhelli, Paul Steven. "Kansas City Church Enters Revival Season." *Charisma* 34:7 (Feb 2009) 18-19.
Gill, Kenneth. "Dividing Over Oneness." *Christian History* 17:2 (Issue 58) 22.
Gleason, Randall. "B. B. Warfield and Lewis S. Chafer on Sanctification." *Journal of the Evangelical Theological Society* 40:2 (June 1997) 241-256.
Greenberg, Brad A. "Identity 'Crisis.'" *Christianity Today* 51:7 (July 2007) 17.
Gomes, Alan W. "The Value of Historical Theology." *Sundoulos* (Fall 2009) 5-6.
Gould, James L. "Ideas About Life." *New York Times* 87 (21), book review, 23 May 1982.
Grady, J. Lee. "Don't Drop the Ark." *Charisma* 31:12 (July 2006) 6.
Granbery, J. C. "Dr. Mudge on Growth in Holiness." *Quarterly Review of the M. E. Church, South* 16 (May-June 1896) 198-210.
Graves, A. S. "Wesley's Variations in Belief, and the Influence of the Same on Methodism." *Methodist Quarterly Review* (March 1887) 192-211.
Greathouse, William M. "Sanctification and the Cristus Victor Motif in Wesleyan Theology." *Wesleyan Theological Journal* 7:1 (Spring 1972) 49-55; rewritten for 38:2 (Fall 2003): 217-229.
Grider, J. Kenneth. "The Meaning of 'Old Man.'" *The Nazarene Preacher* (Feb 1972) 15-16; 46.
__________. "Evaluation of Timothy Smith's Interpretation of Wesley." *Wesleyan Theological Journal* 15:2 (Fall 1980) 64-69.
Guelzo, Allen C. "An Heir or a Rebel? Charles Grandison Finney and the New England Theology." *Journal of the Early Republic* 17:1 (Spring 1997) 61-94.
__________. "The Making of a Revivalist." *Christian History* (Issue #20) 28-30.
Gunter, Stephen. "John Wesley, a Representative of Jacobus Arminius." *Wesleyan Theological Journal* 42:2 (Fall 2007) 65-82.
Hamilton, Barry. "The Corsicana Enthusiasts: A Pre-Pentecostal Millennial Sect." *Wesleyan Theological Journal* 39:1 (Spring 2004) 173-193.
Hamilton, James E. "Nineteenth Century Philosophy and Holiness Theology: A Study in the Thought of Asa Mahan." *Wesleyan Theological Journal* 13:1 (Spring 1978) 51-64.
Hanegraaff, Hank. "The Counterfeit Revival, Part 1: Rodney Howard-Browne and the 'Toronto Blessing,'" *Christian Research Journal* 19:4 (July-August 1997) 8-18; 45-46.
__________. "The Counterfeit Revival, Part 2: Visionary Hoaxes and Revisionary History." *Christian Research Journal* 20:1 (September-October 1997) 10-20; 45-46.
__________. "The Counterfeit Revival, Part 3: Separating Fact from Fabrication on the Pensacola Outpouring." *Christian Research Journal* 20:2 (November-December 1997) 10-20; 42.

__________. "The Indwelling of the Holy Spirit." *Christian Research Journal* 19:4 (July-Aug 1997) 54.

__________. "December 1997 Meetings Between Hank Hanegraaff and Brownsville Revival Leaders," *Christian Research Report* 11:2 (March/April 1998) 4.

Hanford, John T. "The Relationship Between Faith Development of James Fowler and Moral Development of Lawrence Kohlberg: A Theoretical Review." *Journal of Psychology and Christianity* 10:4 (1991) 306-310.

Hansen, Collin. "Young, Restless, Reformed." *Christianity Today* 50:9 (Sept 2006) 32-38.

Harrison, W. P. "Editors Table: Wesley and Christian Perfection." *Quarterly Review of the M. E. Church, South* (Jan 1893) 396-397.

Hartley, John E. "Old Testament Studies in the Wesleyan Mode." *Wesleyan Theological Journal* 17:1 (Spring 1982) 58-76.

Hawkes, R. M. "The Logic of Assurance in English Puritan Theology." *Westminster Theological Journal* 52:2 (Fall 1990) 247-261.

Hayword, Leilani. "News." *Charisma* 32:9 (April 2007) 26.

Headley, Anthony. "Marriage and Ministry: Conjugal and Occupational Conflicts in Wesley's Life and Ministry." *Asbury Journal* 65:1 (Spring 2010) 83-96.

Heath, Elaine A. "The *Via Negativa* in the Life and Writing of Phoebe Palmer." *Wesleyan Theological Journal* 41:2 (Fall 2006) 87-111.

Hegre, T. G. *Message of the Cross* 23 (March-April 1970) 5.

Hendrix, E. R. "Entire Sanctification: The Second Blessing." *Quarterly Review of the M. E. Church, South* 15 (Sept 1895) 54-67.

Henke, Frederick G. "The Gift of Tongues and Related Phenomena at the Present Day." *American Journal of Theology* 13:2 (April 1909).

Hertz, Todd. "God and Gays."*Christianity Today* 53:3 (Sept 2009) 86.

"100-Year Commemorative Edition." Apostolic Faith Church, Portland, OR *Higher Way* 99:3 (July-Sept 2006).

Hill, J. W. "St. Paul on Tongues." *The Wesleyan Methodist* 64:3636 (10 July 1907) 11.

Hollenweger, Walter. "Pentecostalism's Global Language." *Christian History* 17:2 (Issue 58) 42.

Hosmer, W. C. "The Philosophy of Christian Perfection." *Methodist Quarterly Review* 31 (July 1849) 484-491.

Howard, Ivan. "Wesley Versus Phoebe Palmer: An Extended Controversy." *Wesleyan Theological Journal* 6:1 (Spring 1971) 31-40.

Huckabee, B. W. "The Gift of Tongues, Again." *Pentecostal Advocate* (14 March 1907) 8.

Hughes, John. "Five Paths to Holiness." *Christianity Today* 34:6 (9 April 1990) 35.

Hunter, Harold. "Spirit Baptism and the 1896 Revival in Cherokee County, North Carolina." *Pneuma* 5 (Fall 1983) 8-9.

Hynson, Leon O. "Original Sin as Privation." *Wesleyan Theological Journal* 22:2 (Fall 1987) 65-83.
__________. "The Wesleyan Quadrilateral in the American Holiness Tradition." *Wesleyan Theological Journal* 20:1 (Spring 1985) 19-33.
Isbell, Charles. "The Origins of Prophetic Frenzy and Ecstatic Utterance in the Old Testament World." *Wesleyan Theological Journal* 11:1 (Spring 1976) 62-80.
Jackson, Andrew."Forerunner Eschatology." *Christian Research Journal* 32:4 (2009) 20-29.
James, Joseph H. "Doctrine Of Tongues Discussed." *The Wesleyan Methodist* 64:3649 (9 October 1907) 2-3.
Jennings, A. T. "Be Wise as Serpents, Harmless as Doves." *The Wesleyan Methodist* 64:3612 (23 January 1907) 1.
__________. "A Fundamental Principle Applied to Speaking With Tongues." *The Wesleyan Methodist* 64:3630 (29 May 1907) 8.
__________. "But It Improves The Religious Experience So Much." *The Wesleyan Methodist* 64: 3631 (5 June 1907) 8.
__________. "What Would Convince You That We Speak With Tongues?" 64:3632 (12 June 1907) 8.
__________. "Some Things in the Tongues Movement to be Greatly Deplored." *The Wesleyan Methodist* 64:3642 (21 August 1907) 8.
Johnson, Prescott. "Crisis and Con-Sequence: Sanctification and the Greek Tense." *Wesleyan Theological Journal* 37:2 (Fall 2002) 172-193.
Jones, Bob, Jr. "What is 'second-degree separation'"? *Faith for the Family* (Nov 1978) 4.
Jones, Charles Edwin. "Anti-Ordinance: A Proto-Pentecostal Phenomenon?" *Wesleyan Theological Journal* 25:2 (Fall 1990) 7-23.
__________. "The 'Color Line' Washed Away in the Blood? In the Holiness Church at Azusa Street and Afterward." *Wesleyan Theological Journal* 34:2 (Fall 1999) 252-265.
Jones, Jack. "First and Second Blessing Holiness." *Faith in the Future* 19:10 (Oct 1991) 1; (July 1992) 11; (August 1994) 5.
Jones, Marsh. "Letter, 8 October 1998." *The Arminian Magazine* 17:1 (Spring 1999): 4.
Jones, Timothy K. "Tracking America's Soul." *Christianity Today* 33:17 (17 Nov. 1989) 22-25.
Joy, Donald M. "Wesleyan Theology and Developmental Structuralism: An Evaluation." *Wesleyan Theological Journal* 20:2 (Fall 1985) 77-90.
Kalu, Ogbu O. "Historical Perspectives: The Third Response: Pentecostalism and the Reconstruction of Christian Experience in Africa, 1970-1995." *Journal of African Christian Thought* 1:2 (Dec 1998) 7.
Kantzer, Kenneth S. "The Charismatics Among Us." *Christianity Today* 24:4 (22

February 1980) 25.
King, Rob. "Eastern Patristic Spirit-Christology for Contemporary Wesleyan Faith Practice." *Wesleyan Theological Journal* 38:2 (Fall 2003) 103-123.
Kinghorn, Kenneth. "Biblical Concepts of Sin." *Wesleyan Theological Journal* 1:1 (Spring 1966) 21-26.
__________. "Question and Answer." *Asbury Herald* 103:3 (Summer 1992) 9. Reprinted in *The Arminian Magazine* 12:2 (Fall 1994) 5-6.
Kelly, Douglas. "Afraid of Infinitude." *Christianity Today* 39:1 (9 Jan 1995) 32.
Kelley, William V. "Book Notices." *Methodist Quarterly Review* 77 (July 1895) 663-665.
Knapp, Martin Wells. "God Answering by Fire, or the Great Chicago Revival." *God's Revivalist and Bible Advocate* (30 May 1901) 1, 6.
Knight, John A. "Presidential Address: The Supreme Pursuit." *Wesleyan Theological Journal* 15:1 (Spring 1980) 7-18.
__________. "John Fletcher's Influence on the Development of Wesleyan Theology in America." *Wesleyan Theological Journal* 13:1 (Spring 1978) 13-33.
Kok, Arie. "Mulheim Declaration." *Confidence* 2:10 (Oct 1909) 228-230.
Kostlevy, William. "Book Review of *Embodied Holiness: Toward a Corporate Theology of Spiritual Growth*," *Wesleyan Theological Journal* 36:2 (Fall 2001) 271.
Lawrence, Donna McGraw. "I Protest!" *The Wesleyan Advocate* 144:18 (20 October 1986) 12.
Lawson, Steve." Most Students, Members Defend Liardon After Confession." *Charisma* 27:8 (March 2002) 16-18.
__________. "Liardon Preaches First Sermon After Stepping Away From Pulpit." *Charisma* 27:10 (May 2002) 26-27.
Leclerc, Dianne. "Holiness and Power: Toward a Wesleyan Theology of Dis-Ability." *Wesleyan Theological Journal* 44:1 (Spring 2009) 55-69.
Lesta, Kenneth A. "The Nature of Sanctification in the New Testament." *Biblical Viewpoint* 14:2 (Nov 1980) 150-157.
Lewis, B. Scott. "William J. Seymour: Follower of the 'Evening Light.'" *Wesleyan Theological Journal* 39:2 (Fall 2004) 167-183.
Long, Elmer. "Pentecost." *The Arminian Magazine* 1:1 (Spring 1980) 1.
Lowery, Asbury. "Dr. Mudge and His Book." *Methodist Quarterly Review* 77 (Nov 1895) 954-959.
Lowery, Kevin T. "A Fork in the Wesleyan Road: Phoebe Palmer and the Appropriation of Christian Perfection." *Wesleyan Theological Journal* 36:2 (Fall 2001) 187-222.
"Lynch's Sanctified Band." *The New York Times*. 24 Sept 1899.
Lyon, Robert. "Baptism and Spirit-Baptism in the New Testament." *Wesleyan Theological Journal* 14:1 (Spring 1979) 14-26.
__________. "The Baptism of the Spirit — Continued." *Wesleyan Theological*

Journal 15:2 (Fall 1980) 70-79.
__________. "John 20:22, Once More." *The Asbury Theological Journal* 43:1 (Spring 1988) 73-86.
Maddox, Randy L. "Celebrating Wesley — When?" *Methodist History* 29:2 (Jan 1991) 63-75.
__________. "Continuing the Conversation." *Methodist History* 30:4 (July 1992) 235-241.
__________. "The Use of the Aorist Tense in Holiness Exegesis." *Wesleyan Theological Journal* 16:2 (Fall 1981) 106-118.
__________. "Reconnecting the Means to the End." *Wesleyan Theological Journal* 33:2 (Fall 1998) 29-66.
__________. "Wesley's Understanding of Christian Perfection: In What Sense Pentecostal?" *Wesleyan Theological Journal* 34:2 (Fall 1999) 78-110.
__________. "Wesleyan Theology and the Christian Feminist Critique." *Wesleyan Theological Journal* 22:1 (Spring 1987) 100-110.
__________. "Holiness of Heart and Life: Lessons from North American Methodism." *Asbury Theological Journal* 50:2-51:1 (Fall 1995/Spring 1996) 151-172.
Mahon, R. H. "The Nature of Sin and Holiness." *The Quarterly Review of the Methodist Episcopal Church, South* 11 (October 1889) 21-35.
Mannoia, Kevin. "The Wesleyan Holiness Study Project." *Wesleyan Theological Journal* 40:1 (Spring 2005) 265-268.
Manwell, S. A. "Speaking with Tongues I-II." *The Wesleyan Methodist* 64:3615/3616 (13/20 February 1907) 8-9; 8-9.
Marston, Leslie. "The Crisis-Process Issue in Wesleyan Thought." *Wesleyan Theological Journal* 4:1 (Spring 1969: 3-15.
Mattison, Hiram. "Deceived Professors of Sanctification." *New York Christian Advocate and Journal* (2 August 1855) 121.
__________. "Deceived Professors of Sanctification." *New York Christian Advocate and Journal* (20 September 1855) 151.
__________. "Believe that Ye Have It and Ye Have It," *New York Christian Advocate and Journal* (29 November 1855) 189.
__________. "Believe that Ye Have It and Ye Have It," *New York Christian Advocate and Journal* (20 December 1855) 201.
__________. "Dr. Perry and The New Theology." *New York Christian Advocate and Journal* (3 January 1856) 3.
McCain, Danny. "The Baptism of the Holy Spirit." *The Arminian Magazine* 24:1 (Spring 2006) 1-5.
McCall, Bradford. "Emergence Theory and Theology: A Wesleyan-Relational Perspective." *Wesleyan Theological Journal* 44:2 (Fall 2009) 189-208.
McClintock, John. "The Conflict of the Ages." *Methodist Quarterly Review* 36 (1854): 176; 189-190.

McCloughry, Roy. "Basic Stott." *Christianity Today* 40:1 (8 Jan 1996) 25-32.
McCumber, W. E. "A Lively Debate." *Herald of Holiness* 68:9 (1 May 1979) 18.
McDonald, William. "Methodist Quarterly Review." *The Advocate of Christian Holiness* 8:8 (March 1878) 64.
__________. "Book Notices." *The Advocate of Christian Holiness* 2:9 (March 1872) 178-179.
McGonigle, Herbert. "Pneumatological Nomenclature in Early Methodism." *Wesleyan Theological Journal* 8:1 (Spring 1973) 61-72.
McKay, K. L. "Style and Significance in the Language of John 21:15-17." *Novum Testamentum* 27:4 (1985) 319-333.
McMullen, Cary. "Holding Their Tongues."*Christianity Today* 53:10 (October 2009) 16.
McPheeters, J. C. "Snowfields Christmas Eve 1744." *Convention Herald* (Dec 1974) 5.
McPherson, Joseph D. "Review of *The Meaning of Pentecost in Early Methodism*." *The Arminian Magazine* 21:2 (Fall 2003) 9-11.
Merritt, John G. "'Dialogue' Within a Tradition: John Wesley and Gregory of Nyssa Discuss Christian Perfection." *Wesleyan Theological Journal* 22:2 (Fall 1987) 92-116.
Metz, Donald. "Theology in Crisis." *The Evangelists' Perspective* (Fall 2007) 5.
Michel, David. "Revisiting the Methodist Legacy in American Pentecostalism: Nuances in the Early Pentecostal Understanding of 'Sanctification' (1896-1950)." *Methodist History* 41:4 (July 2003) 196-205.
Miley, John. "Pope's Christian Theology." *Methodist Quarterly Review* 59 (July 1877) 401-406.
Miller, Elliot. "Theophostic Prayer Ministry: Christian Prayer, Occult Visualization, or Secular Psychotherapy?" *Christian Research Journal* 29:2 (2006) 12-21.
__________. "Teachings in Transition: Recent Changes and Remaining Concerns with Theophostic Prayer Ministry." *Christian Research Journal* 29:3 (2006) 30-39.
Miller, Kevin E, ed. "The Gallery." *Christian History*, Issue #20 (1988) 14.
__________. "Did You Know?" *Christian History* 7:4 Issue #20 (1988) 4.
Mitchell, T. Crichton. "Response to Dr. Timothy Smith on the Wesleys' Hymns." *Wesleyan Theological Journal* 16:2 (Fall 1981) 48-57.
Mitton, J. Leslie. "Romans vii. Reconsidered — II." *The Expository Times* 65:4 (Jan, 1954) 102
Moll, Rob. "The New Monasticism." *Christianity Today* 49:9 (Sept 2005) 38-46.
Moltmann, Jürgen. "The Spirit Gives Life: Spirituality and Vitality." *Journal of Pentecostal Theology* 4 (1994) 25-33.
Munshaw, Robert. "Keepers of the Flame." *Light & Life* 143:3 (May/June 2010) 8-11.
Nassif, Bradley. "The Poverty of Love." *Christianity Today* 52:5 (May 2008) 34-37.

Noble, T .A. "East and West in the Theology of John Wesley." *Bulletin of the John Rylands University Library of Manchester* 85:2-3 (Summer and Autumn 2003) 359-372

Ogden, Schubert. "Bultmann's Project of Demythologization and the Problem of Theology and Philosophy." *Journal of Religion* 37:2 (April 1957) 156-173.

Olson, Mark K. "Aldersgate II and the Birth of the Servant State." *Wesleyan Theological Journal* 43:2 (Fall 2008) 154-176.

__________. "The Roots of John Wesley's Servant Theology." *Wesleyan Theological Journal* 44:2 (Fall 2009) 120-141.

__________. "Strange Bedfellows: Reappraisal of Mildred Wynkoop's Book, *A Theology of Love*." *Wesleyan Theological Journal* 45:2 (Fall 2010) 196-217.

Olson, Roger."Has God Been Held by Philosophy?" *Christianity Today* 39:1 (9 Jan 1995) 30-34.

Olsen, Ted. "What Really Unites Pentecostals?" *Christianity Today* 50:12 (Dec 2006) 18.

O'Malley, J. Steven. "Pietistic Influence on John Wesley: Wesley and Gerhard Tersteegen." *Wesleyan Theological Journal* 31:2 (Fall 1996) 48-70.

"On the Motto of a Seal." *The Arminian Magazine* 4 (August 1781) 439-442.

Oord, Thomas Jay. "Boston Personalism's Affinities and Disparities with Wesleyan Theology and Process Philosophy." *Wesleyan Theological Journal* 37:2 (Fall 2002) 114-129.

__________. "Types of Wesleyan Philosophy: General Landscape and Personal Research Agenda." *Wesleyan Theological Journal* 39:1 (Spring 2004) 154-162.

Orr, Benjamin F. "The 'Problem Solved.'"*The Methodist Review* 12 (October 1892) 91-106.

Ostling, Richard N. "The Search for the Historical Adam." *Christianity Today* 55:6 (June 2011) 23-27.

Outler, Albert. "Beyond Pietism: Aldersgate in Context." *Motive* 23:8 (May 1963) 12-16.

Ozman, Agnes. "When the Latter Rain First Fell: The First One to Speak in Tongues." *The Latter Rain Evangel* 1:4 (Jan 1919) 2.

Packer, J. I. "Charismatic Renewal: Pointing to a Person and a Power." *Christianity Today* 24:5 (7 March 1980) 16-17.

__________. "Piety on Fire." *Christianity Today* 33:8 (12 May 1989) 22-23.

Parham, Charles F. "A Critical Analysis of the Tongues Question." *The Apostolic Faith* 25 (Baxter Springs) (June 1925) 2-6.

__________. "Godby." [sic] *The Apostolic Faith* (Baxter Springs) (Nov

1913) 7.
Patrick, Randy. "Methodist pastor; counselor admits 'moral failure.'" *Jessamine Journal*, 4 August 2005 A1, A5.
Patterson, Ben. "Cause for Concern." *Christianity Today* 30:11 (8 August 1986) 20.
Peck, George O. "Christian Perfection." *Methodist Quarterly Review* 23:2 (April 1841) 308.
__________. "Christian Perfection." *Methodist Quarterly Review* 23:1 (January 1841) 151.
Payton, James R. Jr. "Keeping the End in View." *Christianity Today* 52:10 (October 2008) 66-68.
Peterson, Michael L. "Orthodox Christianity, Wesleyanism, and Process Theology." *Wesleyan Theological Journal* 15:2 (Fall 1980) 45-58.
Phillips, Wade H. "Baptist Rejection of Holiness Revives the Church of God." *Church of God History & Heritage* 4:1-2 (Summer/Fall 2002) 9.
Pinnock, Clark H. "Opening the Church to the Charismatic Dimension." *Christianity Today* 25:11 (12 June 1981) 16.
__________. "A Revolutionary Promise." *Christianity Today* 30:11 (8 August 1986) 19.
__________. "A Pilgrim on the Way." *Christianity Today* 42:2 (9 Feb, 1998) 43.
__________ and Grant R. Osborne. "A Truce Proposal for the Tongues Controversy." *Christianity Today* 15 16:1 (8 October 1971) 6-9.
__________. "The New Pentecostalism: Reflections by a Well-Wisher." *Christianity Today* 17:24 (14 September 1973) 6-10.
Piper, John. "Gutsy Guilt." *Christianity Today* 51:10 (October 2007) 74.
Plantinga, Cornelius, Jr. "Dr. Willard's Diagnosis." *Christianity Today* 50:9 (Sept 2006) 49-51.
Powell, Samuel M. "The Theological Significance of the Holiness Movement." *Quarterly Review* 25:2 (Summer 2005) 126-140.
__________. "Answering the Call to the Relationship of Holiness." *Holiness Today* 6:8 (Nov-Dec 2004) 22-23.
__________. "What is Consecration?" *Holiness Today* 7:2 (March-April 2005) 18-21.
__________. "Faithful Obedience." *Holiness Today* 7:4 (July-Aug 2005) 19-21.
Price, James Matthew. "The Influence of Personalism on the Theology and Education of H. Orton Wiley." *Wesleyan Theological Journal* 41:2 (Fall 2006) 142-160.
Pumphrey, Charles P. "The Gift of Tongues." *The Methodist Review* 68 (September 1908) 757-764.

"A Queer Faith." *Topeka Daily Capital* (6 January 1901): 2.
Rabey, Steve. "Pensacola Outpouring Keeps Gushing." *Christianity Today* 41:3 (3 March 1997) 54-57.
Raser, Harold E. "Phoebe Palmer: Ambassador of Holiness." *The Preachers Magazine* 59:1 (Sept-Nov 1983) 20-23.
Reasoner, Victor Paul. "The American Holiness Movement's Paradigm Shift Concerning Pentecost," *Wesleyan Theological Journal* 31:2 (Fall 1996) 132-146.
__________. "Knowing Christ." *The Holiness Digest* 14:3 (2002) 8-9.
__________. "Holiness Propaganda." *The Arminian Magazine* 16:1 (Spring 1998) 2-3.
__________. "Plugging the Holes." *The Arminian Magazine* 11:2 (Fall 1993) 2-4.
__________. "Wesley: The Undefined Banner." *The Arminian Magazine* 26:1 (Spring 2008) 9.
__________. "Joseph Benson Describes John Fletcher." *The Arminian Magazine* 17:1 (Spring 1999) 5-7.
__________. "Assurance or Presumption? Early Attempts to Reconstruct Methodist Doctrine: 1803-1809."*Wesleyan Theological Journal* 44:2 (Fall 2009) 103-119.
__________. "How to Be a Pharisee." *The Arminian* 12:1 (Spring 1994) 1-3.
__________. "Indulgences," *The Church Herald and Holiness Banner* 101:15 (10 April 1980) 4-5.
__________. " Review of *Postmodern and* Wesleyan?" *The Arminian Magazine* 27:2 (Fall 2009)18-19.
Reed, Gerard. "Thomas Merton's Concept of Sanctification." *Wesleyan Theological Journal* 18:2 (Fall 1983) 90-99.
Rightmire, R. David. "Samuel Brengle and the Development of the Pneumatology of the Salvation Army." *Wesleyan Theological Journal* 27:1-2 (Spring-Fall 1992) 104-131.
Rishell, Charles W. "The Doctrine of Sanctification Psychologically Developed." *Methodist Quarterly Review* 74:8 (1892) 513-529.
Robb, Edmund W, Jr. "American Methodism at 200: The Case for Hope." *Christianity Today* 28:16 (9 November 1984) 20-23.
Rose, Delbert R. "Distinguishing the Things That Differ." *Wesleyan Theological Journal* 9:1 (Spring 1974) 8-12.
Rushdoony, Rousas John. "Perfection versus Maturity." Chalcedon Report # 176 (April 1980).
__________. "Holiness Versus Perfectionism." Position Paper #61. Vallecito: CA: Chalcedon, 1985.
Salter, Darius. "Mysticism in American Wesleyanism: Thomas Upham."

Wesleyan Theological Journal 20:1 (Spring 1985) 94-107.
"'Sanctified Ones' Go to Jail." *New York Times*. 6 Nov 1984.
Sangster, W. E. "The Church's One Privation." *Religion in Life* 18:4 (1949) 493-507.
Scaer, David P. "Sanctification in Lutheran Theology." *Concordia Theological Quarterly* 49:2-3 (April-July 1985) 181-195.
Schlimm, Matthew R. "The Puzzle of Perfection: Growth in John Wesley's Doctrine of Perfection." *Wesleyan Theological Journal* 38:2 (Fall 2003) 124-142.
Schwartz, Karen. "And Your . . . Daughters Will Prophesy." *The Preachers Magazine* 59:1 (September-November 1983) 32X-32AA.
Seamands, David. "Unclogging the Wells."*The Alumni Advance* [Asbury Theological Seminary] (Spring 1991) 12-13.
Sheldon, Henry C. "Changes in Theology Among American Methodists." *American Journal of Theology* 10:1 (January 1906) 38-39.
Shontz, William H. "Anglican Influence on John Wesley's Soteriology." *Wesleyan Theological Journal* 32:1 (Spring 1997) 33-52.
Sill, Sterling W. *Deseret News*, Church Section (31 July 1965) 7.
Smith, Timothy L. "How John Fletcher Became the Theologian of Wesleyan Perfectionism, 1770-1776." *Wesleyan Theological Journal* 15:1 (Spring 1980) 68-87.
__________. "The Doctrine of the Sanctifying Spirit: Charles G. Finney's Synthesis of Wesleyan and Covenant Grace." *Wesleyan Theological Journal* 13:1 (Spring 1978) 92-113.
__________. "John Wesley and the Second Blessing." *Wesleyan Theological Journal* 21:1-2 (Spring-Fall 1986) 137-159.
__________. "The Cross Demands, The Spirit Enables." *Christianity Today* 23:10 (16 Feb 1979) 23.
__________. "The Blessing of Abraham," *Christian History*. Issue #20, 26.
Snyder, Howard A. "John Wesley and Macarius the Egyptian." *Asbury Theological Journal* 45:2 (Fall 1990) 55-60.
__________. "The Church as Holy and Charismatic." *Wesleyan Theological Journal* 15:2 (Fall 1980) 7-32.
Spittler, Russell. "The Pentecostal Tradition, Part IV." *Agora* 2:3 (Spring 1979) 4.
Spross, Daniel B. "The Doctrine of Sanctification in Karl Barth." *Wesleyan Theological Journal* 20:2 (Fall 1985) 54-76.
Stafford, Tim. "Finding God in Small Groups." *Christianity Today* 47:8 (August 2003) 42-44.
__________. "The Pentecostal Gold Standard." *Christianity Today* 49:7 (July 2005) 28.
__________. "Testing the Wine from John Wimber's Vineyard."

Christianity Today 30:11 (8 August 1986) 17-22.
__________ and James Beverley. "God's Wonder Worker." *Christianity Today* 41:8 (14 July 1997) 47.
__________. "Evangelism Plus." *Christianity Today* 50:10 (October 2006) 99.
Staples, Rob L. "John Wesley's Doctrine of the Holy Spirit." *Wesleyan Theological Journal* 21:1-2 (Spring-Fall 1986) 91-115.
__________. "Sanctification and Selfhood: A Phenomenological Analysis of the Wesleyan Message." *Wesleyan Theological Journal* 7:1 (Spring 1972) 13-16.
__________. "Sanctification: A Dangerous Doctrine?" *Holiness Today* 3:11 (November 2001) 36.
__________. "A Rose is a Rose is (Not Always) a Rose." *Holiness Today* 1:10 (October 1999) 25.
__________. "Book Review: Relational Holiness." *Wesleyan Theological Journal* 41:1 (Spring 2006) 248-249.
__________. "The Present Frontiers of Wesleyan Theology." *Wesleyan Theological Journal* 12:1 (Spring 1977) 5-15.
Steele, Daniel. "Personal Pentecosts." *Advocate of Christian Holiness* 5:3 (Sept 1874) 49-51.
__________. "Baptism in the Spirit." *Guide to Holiness* 20 (Feb 1874) 37-38.
Stephens, John. "Mr. Stephen's Sermon, preached before the Sheffield Conference, on the Truth, Importance, and Design of Revelation." *The Methodist Magazine* 35 (March/April 1812) 168-177; 248-256.
Stiles, Jack. "Letter." *Christianity Today* 8:3 (8 November 1963) 17.
Strege, Merle D. "Quilting a Church: The Church of God (Anderson) in 1900." *Wesleyan Theological Journal* 36:2 (Fall 2001) 133-143.
__________. "God's Ways Are Not Our Ways." *Vital Christianity* 107:44 (1 November 1987) 4.
Suchocki, Marjorie Hewett. "Coming Home: Wesley, Whitehead, and Women." *The Drew Gateway* 57 (Fall 1987) 36.
Summers, Thomas O. "Osiandrianism and Zinzendorfianism."*Quarterly Review of the Methodist Episcopal Church, South* 3:1 (Jan 1881) 83-89.
Swaggart, Jimmy. "Pentecostals and Charismatics." *The Evangelist* 19:7 (July 1987) 4-9.
Talley, David Lee. "Gender and Sanctification: From Creation to Transformation." *Journal for Biblical Manhood and Womanhood* 8:1 (Spring 2003) 6-16.
Taylor, Richard S. "The Question of 'Sins of Ignorance' in Relation to Wesley's Definition." *Wesleyan Theological Journal* 22:1 (Spring

1987) 71-77.
__________. "Some Recent Trends in Wesleyan-Arminian Thought." *Wesleyan Theological Journal* 6:1 (Spring 1971) 10-12.
Thompson, Ralph. "An Appraisal of the Keswick and Wesleyan Contemporary Positions." *Wesleyan Theological Journal* 1:1 (Spring 1966) 11-20.
Thorsen, Don. "The Holiness Manifesto: An Ecumenical Document." *Wesleyan Theological Journal* 42:2 (Fall 2007) 209-224.
__________. "Holiness in Postmodern Culture." *Wesleyan Theological Journal* 43:2 (Fall 2008) 123-135.
Thornton, Wallace, Jr. "The Revivalist Movement and the Development of a Holiness/Pentecostal Philosophy of Missions." *Wesleyan Theological Journal* 38:1 (Spring 2003) 160-186.
__________. "Embourgeoisement and the Formation of the Conservative Holiness Movement." *Wesleyan Theological Journal* 33:2 (Fall 1998) 172-197.
Tigert, John James. "Colossians 3:1-16: An Exposition." *The Methodist Review* 14 (November 1894) 274-277.
__________. "Editorial Departments." *Quarterly Review of the M. E. Church, South* 15 (Sept 1895) 120.
__________. "Brief Reviews." *Quarterly Review of the M. E. Church, South* 16 (July-Aug 1896) 456.
__________. "Bishops on Christian Perfection." *Quarterly Review of the M. E. Church, South* 40 (Nov-Dec 1894) 283-284.
Todd, S. C. "Some Sad Failures of Tongues in Mission Fields." *Baptist Argus* 12:4 (Louisville, KY), (23 January 1908) 1-2.
__________. "An Open Letter: Being a calm review of the Speaking in Tongues in South China." Macao, China: Bible Missionary Society, 1908.
Tompkins, John S. "Our Kindest City." *Reader's Digest* (July 1994) 53-56.
Torrance, Thomas F. "The Doctrine of Grace in the Old Testament," *Scottish Journal of Theology* 1:1 (1948) 55-65.
Tracy, Wesley. "Entire Sanctification and Uncertain Trumpets." *Herald of Holiness* 79:10 (October 1990) 6-7.
Trouten, Edsel. "Holes in The Hole of the Holiness Movement." *Convention Herald* (Jan/Feb 1993) 4-5.
Truesdale, Al. "Reification of the Experience of Entire Sanctification in the American Holiness Movement." *Wesleyan Theological Journal* 31:2 (Fall 1996) 95-119.
Turley, Briane. "A Wheel Within a Wheel: Southern Methodism and the Georgia Holiness Association." *Georgia Historical Quarterly* 75 (Summer 1991) 295-320.

Turner, George Allen. "An Evaluation of John R. W. Stott's and Fredrick D. Bruner's Interpretations of the Baptism and Fullness of the Holy Spirit." *Wesleyan Theological Journal* 8:1 (Spring 1973) 45-51.

__________. "The Baptism of the Holy Spirit in the Wesleyan Tradition." *Wesleyan Theological Journal* 14:1 (Spring 1979) 71.

Tyson, John R. "John Wesley and William Law: A Reappraisal." *Wesleyan Theological Journal* 17:2 (Fall 1982) 63-73.

__________. "This One Thing Needful": Charles Wesley on Sanctification." *Wesleyan Theological Journal* 45:2 (Fall 2010) 177-195 .

Wacker, Grant. "America's Pentecostals: Who They Are." *Christianity Today* 31:15 (16 October, 1987) 16.

Waddell, H. C. "Revival And The Gift Of Tongues." *The Wesleyan Methodist* 64:3633 (19 June 1907) 11.

Wagner, C. Peter. "MC510: Signs, Wonders and Church Growth." *Christian Life* 44:6 (October 1982) 42-49.

Wainwright, S. H. "Dr. Boland on the Ninth Article." *The Quarterly Review of the Methodist Episcopal Church, South* 14 (April 1894) 36-40.

Wall, Robert. "Purity and Power According to the Acts of the Apostles." *Wesleyan Theological Journal* 34:1 (Spring 1999) 64-82.

Warfield, B. B. "Review of *He That Is Spiritual*." *Princeton Theological Review* 17 (April 1919) 322-327.

Watson, Kevin. "Form and Power of Godliness: Wesleyan Communal Discipline as Voluntary Suffering." *Wesleyan Theological Journal* 43:1 (Spring 2008) 165-183.

Wax, Trevin. "The Justification Debate: A Primer." *Christianity Today* 53:6 (June 2009) 36.

Wesley, John. "An Account of Baron Swedenborg." *The Arminian Magazine* 4 (January 1781) 46-49.

__________. "Thoughts Upon Jacob Behmen." *The Arminian Magazine* 4 (May 1781) 268-274.

Wesleyan Holiness Charismatic Fellowship Newsletter (1990) 1.

Whedon, Daniel D. "Doctrines of Methodism." *Bibliotheca Sacra* 19 (1862) 241- 273.

__________. "Quarterly Book Table."[sic] *Methodist Quarterly Review* 56 (July 1874) 490-493.

__________. "Quarterly Book-Table." *Methodist Quarterly Review* 56 (Oct 1874): 662-681.

__________. "Quarterly Book-Table." *Methodist Quarterly Review* 56 (Oct 1874) 172-177.

__________. "Quarterly Book-Table." *Methodist Quarterly Review* 60 (Jan

1878) 177-179.
__________. "Quarterly Book-Table." *Methodist Quarterly Review* 41 (October 1859) 666-667.
Whidden, Woodrow W. "Adventist Soteriology: Wesleyan Connection." *Wesleyan Theological Journal* 30:1 (Spring 1995) 173-186.
White, Charles Edwin. "What the Holy Spirit Can and Cannot Do: The Ambiguities of Phoebe Palmer's Theology of Experience." *Wesleyan Theological Journal* 20:1 (Spring 1985) 108-121.
__________. "Phoebe Palmer and the Development of Pentecostal Pneumatology." *Wesleyan Theological Journal* 23:1-2 (Spring-Fall 1988) 198-208.
Williams, D. H. "Reveling in the Mystery." *Christianity Today* 53:9 (Sept 2009) 48-49.
Wilson, John."The Evolution of Sin." *Christianity Today* 54:3 (March 2010) 30-33.
Wilson-Hartgrove, Jonathan. "A Curious Saint." *Christianity Today* 54:8 (Aug 2010) 51-53.
__________. "Joining the Eternal Song." *Christianity Today* 55:5 (May 2011) 42-44.
Withers, H. R. "Problem of Methodism," "Problem Solved," "Friendly Talks." *The Quarterly Review of the Methodist Episcopal Church, South* 14 (July 1894) 338-360.
Wood, Laurence W. "Third Wave of the Spirit, Pentecostalization of American Christianity: A Wesleyan Critique." *Wesleyan Theological Journal* 31:1 (Spring 1996) 110-140.
__________. "Exegetical-Theological Reflections on the Baptism with the Holy Spirit." *Wesleyan Theological Journal* 14:2 (Fall 1979) 51-63.
__________. The Need for a Contextual Interpretation of John Wesley's Sermons." *Wesleyan Theological Journal* 45:1 (Spring 2010) 259-267.
__________. "John Fletcher and the Rediscovery of Pentecost in Methodism." *The Asbury Theological Journal* 53:1 (Spring 1998) 7-34.
__________. "The Origin, Development, and Consistency of John Wesley's Theology of Holiness." *Wesleyan Theological Journal* 43:2 (Fall 2008) 45-51.
__________. "The Biblical Sources of John Fletcher's Pentecostal Theology." *Wesleyan Theological Journal* 42:2 (Fall 2007) 98-113.
__________. "Appreciative Reply to Donald W. Dayton's 'Review Essay.'" *Pneuma* 27:1 (Spring 2005) 163-172.
__________. "Can Pentecostals Be Wesleyans? My Reply to Don Dayton's

Rejoinder," *Pneuma* 28:1 (2006) 120-130.

Woods, Daniel. "Our American Holiness Heritage." *Church of God Evangel* 92:5 (May 2002) 12-13.

Woodward, Kenneth, Jeanne Gordon, Carol Hill, and Barry Brown. "The Giggles Are for God." *Newsweek* (20 February 1995) 54.

Wynkoop, Mildred. "Theological Roots of the Wesleyan Understanding of the Holy Spirit." *Wesleyan Theological Journal* 14:1 (Spring 1979) 77-98.

__________. "Sanctification is Existential," *The Preacher's Magazine* 33:7(July 1958) 1-5.

__________. "Love is Existential" *The Preacher's Magazine* 33:8 (Aug 1958) 16-20.

__________. "Practical Norm of Love." *The Preacher's Magazine* 33:9 (Sept1958) 29-31.

__________. "Life Spiritualized by Love." *The Preacher's Magazine* 33:10 (Oct 1958) 12-13.

__________. "Wesleyan Theology and Christian Development." *The Asbury Seminarian* 31 (April 1976) 36-41.

THESES/DISSERTATIONS

Bangs, Carl. "Arminius and Reformed Theology." PhD diss, University of Chicago, 1958.

Ballard, Richard. "Acts: Interpretation of the Biblical Narrative Vis-à-Vis the Wesleyan-Holiness Tradition." Masters thesis, Anderson University School of Theology, 2004.

Bence, Clarence L. "John Wesley's Teleological Hermeneutic." PhD diss, Emory University, 1981.

Bounds, Christopher Todd. *The Doctrine of Christian Perfection in the Ante-Nicene Fathers*. PhD diss, Drew University, 1997.

Callahan, Leslie Dawn. "Fleshly Manifestations: Charles Fox Parham's Quest for the Sanctified Body." PhD diss: Princeton University, 2002.

Clark, Robert Burton. "The History of the Doctrine of Christian Perfection in the Methodist Episcopal Church in American up to 1845." ThD diss, Temple University, 1946.

Cooley, Stephen D. *The Possibilities of Grace: Poetic Discourse and Reflection in Methodist/Holiness Revivalism*. PhD diss, University of Chicago, 1991.

Cowan, Raymond. "The Arminian Alternative: The Rise of the Methodist Episcopal Church, 1765-1850." PhD diss, Georgia State University, 1991.

Dunlap, Dale. "Methodist Theology in Great Britain in the Nineteenth Century."PhD diss, Yale University, 1956.

Pheobus, Samuel J. "The Fire Baptized Holiness Church: Its History and Practices." thesis, The Biblical Seminary in New York, 1949.

Forsaith, Peter Stuart. *The Correspondence of the Revd. John W. Fletcher: Letters to the Revd. Charles Wesley, Considered in the Context of the Evangelical Revival.* PhD diss, Oxford, 2003.

Fraser, Robert M. *Strains in the Understandings of Christian Perfection in Early British Methodism.* PhD diss, Vanderbilt University, 1988.

Gaddis, Merrill E. *Christian Perfection in America.* PhD diss, University of Chicago, 1929.

Hertel, Alice Phyllis. "Missing Links Between Phoebe Palmer and the Earliest Leaders of the Earliest Conventions of the Keswick Higher Life Movement." M. A. thesis, Wheaton College Graduate School, 1986.

Hollon, David L. "Love as Holiness: An Examination of Charles G. Finney's Theology of Sanctification, 1830-1860." PhD diss, Southern Baptist Theological Seminary, 1984.

Hudson, Greg. "A Wesleyan Minister's Guide to John Wesley and Christian Perfection." Masters thesis, Indiana Wesleyan University, 2006.

Jones, Curtis K. *Personalism as Christian Philosophy.* PhD diss, Union Theological Seminary, 1944.

Jones, Marsh. *Pulpit, Periodical, and the Pen: Joseph Benson and Methodist Influence in the Victorian Prelude.* PhD diss, University of Illinois, 1995.

Kim, Stephen S. "An Evaluation of the Doctrine of Spirit Baptism as a 'Second-Blessing.'" M. Th. thesis: Dallas Theological Seminary, 1993.

Kostlevy, William C. "Nor Silver, Nor Gold: The Burning Bush Movement and the Communitarian Holiness Vision." PhD diss, Notre Dame, 1996.

Lewis, Stephen. "William H. Durham and the 'Finished Work of Calvary' Theory of Sanctification Within Early Pentecostalism." M. Th. thesis, Dallas Theological Seminary, 1986.

McCormick, K. Steve. "John Wesley's Use of John Chrysostom on the Christian Life: Faith Filled with the Energy of Love." PhD diss, Drew University, 1983.

Mueller, Mark Allen. "A Biblical Examination of the Relation of Christian Maturity to Entire Sanctification in the Wesleyan Tradition." Masters thesis, Wesley Biblical Seminary, 1998.

Nelson, Douglas J. "For Such a Time as This: The Story of Bishop William

J. Seymour and the Azusa Street Revival: A Search for Pentecostal/Charasmatic Roots." PhD diss, University of Birmingham, 1981.

Quanstrom, Mark R. "The Doctrine of Entire Sanctification in the Church of the Nazarene: From the Conquest of Sin to an New Theological Realism, 1905-1997." PhD diss, Saint Louis University, 2000.

Rader, Paul A. "A Study of the Doctrine of Sanctification in the Life and Thought of Charles G. Finney." B. D. thesis, Asbury Theological Seminary, 1959.

Reasoner, Victor Paul. "The Spirit and Sanctification: The Changing Emphasis within American Wesleyanism." MDiv thesis, Talbot School of Theology, Biola University, 1987.

__________. "The Spirit and Sanctification: Changes within American Wesleyanism." DMin diss, Asbury Theological Seminary, 1994.

Riss, Richard Michael. "The Latter Rain Movement of 1948 and the Mid-Twentieth Century Evangelical Awakening." Master of Christian Studies thesis, Regent College, 1979.

Scott, Leland. "Methodist Theology in America in the Nineteenth Century." PhD diss: Yale University, 1954.

Shumway, Charles William. "A Study of 'The Gift of Tongues.'" A. B. thesis, University of Southern California, 1914.

__________. "A Critical History of Glossolalia." PhD diss, Boston University, 1919.

Snyder, Howard. "Pietism, Moravianism, and Methodism as Renewal Movements: A Comparative and Thematic Study." PhD diss, University of Notre Dame, 1983.

Thompson, Claude. "The Witness of American Methodism to the Historical Doctrine of Christian Perfection." PhD diss, Drew University, 1949.

Wynkoop, Mildred. *An Existential Interpretation of the Doctrine of Holiness*. PhD diss, Northwestern Baptist Seminary, 1958.

ONLINE SOURCES

Barna, George. "State of the Church 2006." Barna Research Group, Ventura, CA. Online report 27 March 2006. http://www.barna.org/barna-update/article/5-barna-update/157-barna-survey-reveals-significant-growth-in-born-again-population.

__________. "The Concept of Holiness Baffles Most Americans." Ventura, CA: The Barna Group, Ltd, February 20, 2006. http://www.barna.org/barna-update/article/5-barna-update/162-the-concept-of-holiness-baffles-most-americans

"The Berlin Declaration."

http://www.immanuel.at/Immanuel/MessageE.htm#_.
"Biography of Nathan Bangs." Christian Classics Ethereal Library. http://www.ccel.org/b/bangs
Bounds, Chris. "John Wesley's Doctrine of Salvation, Part 4." http://cbounds.blogspot.com/2006/08/john-wesleys-doctrine-of-salvation_18.html
__________. "Spiritual Transformation: What is the Range of Current Teaching on Sanctification and What Ought a Wesleyan to Believe on this Doctrine?" A Doctrinal Symposium Sponsored by the Wesleyan Church, 20-21 May 2005. http://www.wesleyan.org/Media/MarketingManager/chris%20bounds%20document.pdf
__________. "Legitimate and Illegitimate Definitions of Entire Sanctification." Out of Bounds Blog on 10 May 2006. http://cbounds.blogspot.com/2006_05_01_archive.html
__________. "What is Entire Sanctification?" "Out of Bounds" blog for 5 May 2006. http://cbounds.blogspot.com/2006/05/what-is-entire-sanctification.html
Cain, Paul. "Letter of Confession." Posted online March 2005. Later taken down. http://web.archive.org/web/20050305180223/http://paulcain.org/news.html
The Center for Process Studies. http://www.ctr4process.org/
Cobb, John B, Jr. "Process Theology." http://www.religion-online.org/showarticle.asp?title=1489
__________. "Wesley the Process Theologian," Feb 2000 lecture at Point Loma Nazarene University, San Diego http://www.religion-online.org/showarticle.asp?title=1097
"Faith Expressed as Doctrine." http://nwfriends.org/what-friends-believe/faith-expressed-as-doctrine
Goodwin, John. "Testing the Fruit of the Vineyard." http://www.biblebelievers.net/Charismatic/kjcviney.htm
Johnson, John. "Divine Intervention or Historical Accident? A Social Science Perspective on the Conservative Holiness Movement." http://www.geocities.com/Athens/Olympus/1802/submissions/jjohnson.htm.
Mercer, Brad. "Sin and Holiness." http://www.crivoice.org/sinholiness.htm
Metcalfe, Russell F, Jr. "Life Begins With Thanksgiving." http://russellmetcalfesermons.nazarene.nl/SermonTexts/dad.life_begins_with_thanksgiving
Oord, Thomas Jay. "Revisioning Article X: Fifteen Changes in the Church of the Nazarene's Article on Entire Sanctification."

http://wesley.nnu.edu/wesley_conferences/2007/Oord%20Revisioning%20Article%20X%20Paper.pdf>
__________. "Eleven Suggestions for a Reformulated Article X." http://wesley.nnu.edu/wesleyan_theology/Eleven%20Suggestions%20for%20a%20Reformulated%20Article%20X.doc
__________. "Changing Sanctification." http://thomasjayoord.com/index.php/blog/archives/test_entry11/
__________. "The Emergence of Open Theology." http://thomasjayoord.com/index.php/blog/archives/the_emergence_of_open_theology
__________. "Relational Holiness: An Integrative Paradigm for Our Time." crivoice.org/relational.html
Price, J. Matthew. *We Teach Holiness: The Life and Work of H. Orton Wiley*, Chapter 3, "Molded by Personalism," 51-68. http://wesley.nnu.edu/wesleyctr/books/2601-2700/HDM2607.pdf
Schenck, Kenneth. "The Church and the Holy Spirit," 2007 Doctrinal Symposium on Ecclesiology. "A Wesleyan View of the Church." 2 June 2007. http://www.wesleyan.org/bgs/assets/downloads/doctrinal%20symposium/down.php?dfile=The Church and The Holy Spirit.pdf
Staples, Rob. "Things Shakeable and Things Unshakeable in Holiness Theology," Conference on Revisioning Holiness, 9 February, 2007. http://wesley.nnu.edu/wesley_conferences/2007/Staples%20-%20Revisioning%20Holiness%20address%20at%20NNU.pdf
Strege, Merle D. "'The Union Heaven Gave Us:' The Doctrinal Practice of Unity in the Church of God." Online: http://www.anderson.edu/sot/ccl/Strege.pdf Given at North American Convention of the Church of God, June 2006.
"Theology of Martin Luther." http://en.wikipedia.org/wiki/Theology_of_Martin_Luther
Truth in Heart: The John Wesley Library. http://truthinheart.com/WesleySeries.html

PERSONAL CORRESPONDENCE

Black, Warren. Telephone interview with Vic Reasoner. 20 April 1989.
Carpenter, L. A. Open Letter. 31 December 1951.
Collins, Harry. Telephone conversation with Vic Reasoner. 3 December 1995
Collins, Kenneth, email to Vic Reasoner. 25 May 2010.
Dunning, Ray. Letter to Donald Metz. 2 February 1994.
Earle, Ralph. Letter to Robert Shank. 9 January 1960

Gale, William D. Telephone interview with Vic Reasoner. 2 December 2009.
Greathouse, William. Letter to Donald Metz. 31 January 1994.
Oord, Thomas Jay. email to Vic Reasoner. 13 December 2007.
Page, Don. Telephone interview with Vic Reasoner. 6 February 2009.
Ravenhill, David. Interview with Vic Reasoner. Lexington, KY. 13 July 2006.
Ries, Claude A. Letter to A. J. Smith. 19 November 1956.
Seevers. O. C. Open Letter. no date, but refers to recent events on May 28, 1952.
Schmul, H. E. Letters to Vic Reasoner. 17 March 1988; 8 January 1992; 13 January 1993.
Taylor, Richard S. Letter to Ray Pollard. 23 September 1981.

UNPUBLISHED MANUSCRIPTS

Agreement of the Association of Churches Under the Name Christ's Sanctified Holy Church, 1983.
Beckham, Richard. The Conservative and Truth.
Maxey, Gary. Lecture notes. Kansas City College & Bible School, 1976.
__________. "The Wesleyan-Holiness Roots of Classical Pentecostalism," *Papers for the School of the Prophets*, 1973-1975. 2 vols.
__________. "Gifts, Signs, and Miracles." TH 121, West Africa Theological Seminary, 1990.
"Minutes of the Board-Panel Meeting Held at Intercession City, Florida (1951) During Which Charges Preferred Against Dr. A. J. Smith, President of Southern Wesleyan Bible College, by the Students of 'Christian Perfection Class' Were Discussed." 16 pages.
Oblinger, Carl D. "John P. Brooks: Separatist Tendencies in the Holiness Movement: 1869-1882." Northern Illinois University, January 1968.
Staples, Rob. "The Current Debate on the Baptism with the Holy Spirit." March 1979.

RECORDINGS

Copeland, Kenneth. "Inner Image of the Covenant." Ft. Worth, Kenneth Copeland Ministries, 1985 audio tape #01-4406.
Crabb, Larry. "Spiritual Formation or Relational Holiness." AACC National Conference in Branson, MO, Fall 2010.

SERMONS

DeNeff, Steve. Asbury College chapel. 14 September 2005.

POETRY

Bishop, C. “Such Love.” Kansas City: Lillenas Publishing, 1929.
Monod, Theodore. “The Altered Motto.” © 1885 R. E. Hudson.

SCRIPTURE INDEX

Psalms

Proverbs

Isaiah

Acts

Romans

1 Corinthians

2 Corinthians

Galatians

Ephesians

Philippians

Colossians

1 Thessalonians

2 Thessalonians

1 Timothy

2 Timothy

Titus

Hebrews

Jude

Revelation